THE COMPLETE PRACTICAL GUIDE TO
DIGITAL AND CLASSIC
PHOTOGRAPHY

THE EXPERT'S MANUAL ON TAKING GREAT PHOTOGRAPHS

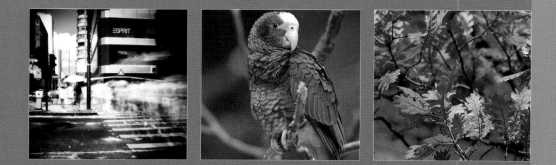

STEVE LUCK AND JOHN FREEMAN

CONSULTANT EDITOR: MARC WILSON

southwater

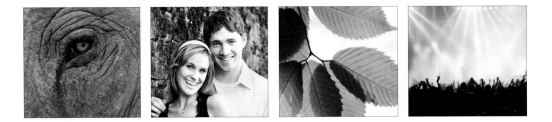

This edition is published by Southwater,
an imprint of Anness Publishing Ltd,
108 Great Russell Street,
London WC1B 3NA;
info@anness.com

www.southwaterbooks.com; www.annesspublishing.com; twitter: @Anness_Books

Anness Publishing has a new picture agency outlet
for images for publishing, promotions or advertising.
Please visit our website www.practicalpictures.com
for more information.

A CIP catalogue record for this book
is available from the British Library.

Publisher: Joanna Lorenz
Senior Editor: Felicity Forster
Consultant Editor: Marc Wilson
Designer: Nigel Partridge
Production Controller: Ben Worley

PUBLISHER'S NOTE
Although the advice and information in this book are believed to be accurate
and true at the time of going to press, neither the authors nor the publisher can
accept any legal responsibility or liability for any errors or omissions that may
have been made nor for any inaccuracies nor for any loss, harm or injury that
comes about from following instructions or advice in this book.

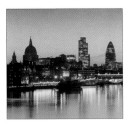
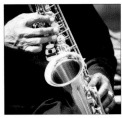
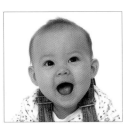
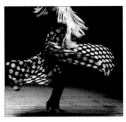

Contents

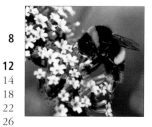
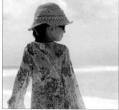

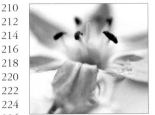
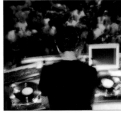

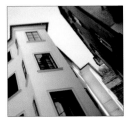
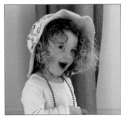
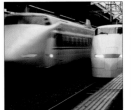
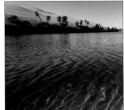

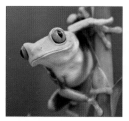
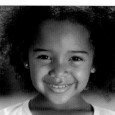

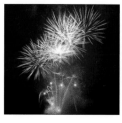
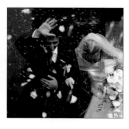
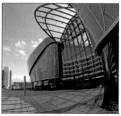
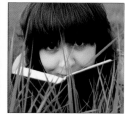

Introduction

The word 'photography' comes from the Greek for 'drawing with light'. It is a technology with a long path of development that seems destined to continue as new possibilities for capturing images are discovered.

As early as the 5th century, Chinese philosopher Mo Ti wrote about camera obscura and pinhole cameras. Various advances in chemistry, such as the discovery of silver nitrate and silver chloride and the photochemical effect – where light darkens some chemicals – led to the development of the first photograph in 1825 by Nicéphore Niépce. Louis Daguerre went on to take the first photograph of a person in 1839, when someone stopped for a shoeshine long enough to be in the exposure Daguerre was taking of a Paris street. By 1840, William Fox Talbot had refined Daguerre's process so that he could produce large volumes of photographic material, making the art more available to the general population. Many advances were made in the next few

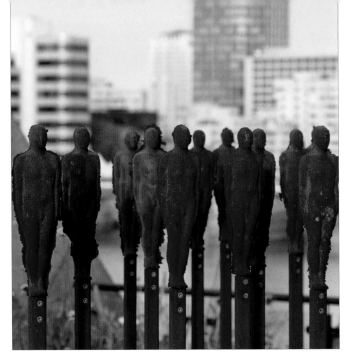

years, and it was George Eastman who developed film technology to take over from photographic plates in 1884. The advances continued so that, less than a century later, cameras were cheap and the general population was used to using colour and black and white film, and seeing photographic images all around them.

Working with film

Today, hardly anyone thinking of buying a general 'all-purpose' camera would even consider buying a conventional film camera – things have moved on apace and most people now

prefer digital photography for the sheer convenience. The film versus digital image-quality debate seems a thing of the distant past – the general consensus seems to be that neither one is 'better' than the other, they simply have a different look. There are many people who still like to work with film because they prefer the end result. There is also a trend for 'lomography' that is a positive kick against the predictability and control

▼ **BELOW** Learning to take great photographs involves seeing in a different way. We are all surrounded by picture possibilities, but the art of the photographer is to use these well.

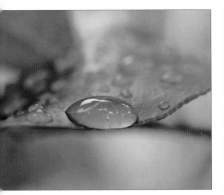

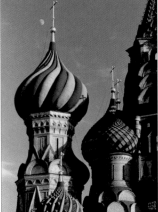

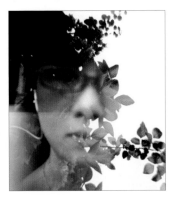

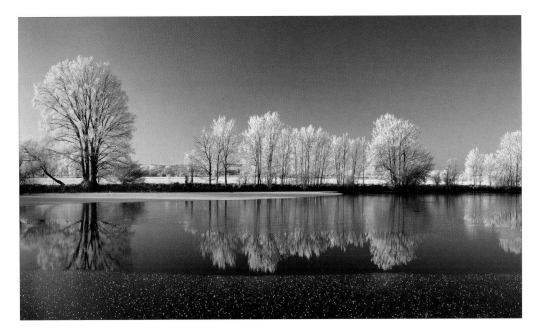

ABOVE If you carry your camera around with you, you will be able to capture stunning shots if an opportunity arises.

of digital photography. If you are working with film you can be experimental with your shots, and even do your own processing and printing, to come up with some very interesting results. The first chapter of this book looks at working with film.

BELOW In wildlife photography, you will need to learn how to get close enough for a good shot without disturbing the animals or putting yourself in danger. This requires the right kit.

A digital world

Digital photography has come a long way in a short amount of time. The digital camera, which was heralded by many in the industry as little more than an overpriced gimmick that had no real value in the world of photography, has been through some staggering changes.

To keep sales of their cameras bouyant, camera manufacturers – many of whom are worried about the inexorable rise of the camera-phone – are developing cameras that make it increasingly easy for us to take well-exposed, sharply focused images.

Sophisticated metering and auto-focusing systems, together with face detection and anti-shake technologies, mean that technically incompetent shots are becoming a thing of the past. But we need to be wary of an over-reliance on such technology – as innovative and exciting as it is – if we are to improve as photographers and to really enjoy what can be an extremely satisfying and rewarding pastime.

Being able to take as many photographs as we like, pretty much with financial impunity, can be seen as a double-edged sword. On the one hand, it encourages experimentation – and

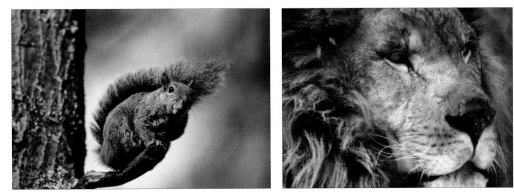

you only have to look at a website such as Flickr (www.flickr.com) to see some of the hugely creative things people achieve with their digital cameras, which are unlikely to have come about without the digital revolution. On the other hand, it also encourages an almost 'scattergun' approach to photography – keep firing and sooner or later you're bound to come up with some interesting images. Although there's nothing inherently wrong with such an approach, it does in many ways negate the need or desire to learn. We must slow down and look at our images in a more considered way – why does one shot 'work' when another from the same sequence fails? Why doesn't the image appear so full of movement? Why are the vibrant colours less intense? If we reassess each shot, we're going to increase our success rate, and by analysing what exactly it is about some images that makes them stand out, we can mix the visual components a little to see what else works, and in that way our experimentation has some reason and method to it.

Capturing great shots

In this book the technical has been mixed with the creative. To be a good photographer it helps if you have a

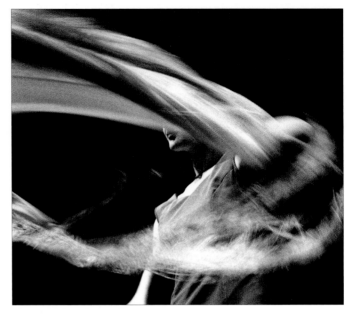

basic knowledge of how a digital image is created – learning the 'vocabulary' of the photographic process will make your learning curve smoother and quicker; more important, however, is to have a thorough understanding of your equipment, particularly if you're either new to cameras or have 'upgraded' from a simple point-and-shoot to a more complex model. To the uninitiated, the often mind-boggling settings and options might seem surplus to requirements, but all are there for a very good reason and it pays to spend some time learning how they work and what they do.

▲ **ABOVE** Colourful subjects can lend themselves surprisingly well to black and white photography, as in this striking action shot.

However, any amount of technical knowledge and skill would come to nothing without you having some idea about what makes a good subject to point the lens at. If you're reading this, then it's fairly safe to assume that you have an appreciation for images and sights that you've seen and a desire to capture them in a way that most accurately reflects both how they appeared to you and what they particularly meant to you.

▼ **BELOW** An eye for colour, texture and form are all important. Plan your shots and take the right equipment with you to capture each subject at its best.

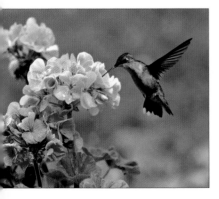

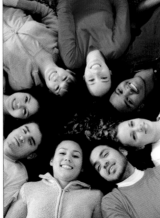

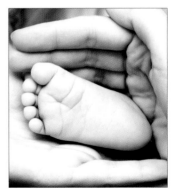

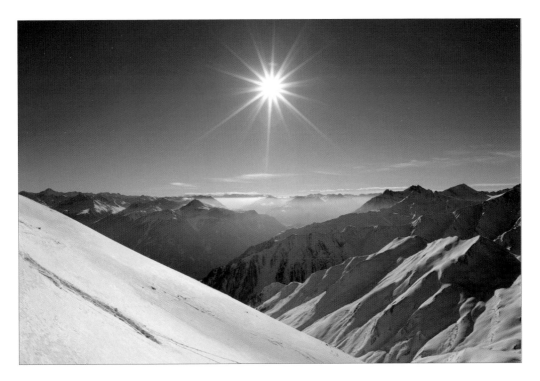

▲ **ABOVE** When on holiday ensure that you have lightweight, well protected kit in case the opportunity for a great shot comes up.

The aim of the first six chapters is to provide you with a good technical knowledge of what your equipment is capable of producing. They offer hints on how best to creatively translate the scene in front of you into a distilled, two-dimensional replica that elicits the sense of time and place. Interspersed along the way are exercises that help you to put the theory into practice.

Post production

As you gain proficiency and confidence with your photography it's very likely that you'll want to assume greater control over your images once you've captured them. Even basic editing techniques such as cropping can vastly improve an image. The book discusses a range of the image-editing techniques for film and digital photographers, and explains the basic concepts of how image-editing soft-

ware works. This is by no means exhaustive, but should provide you with enough information to start experimenting and to see what these powerful applications can do.

There is a brief rundown of how to go about sharing your photographs – whether in print or online, before the

final chapter discusses ways in which you can sell your work. Whether you want to get noticed in competitions or become a full time photographer for weddings and other events, it is possible for you to turn your passion into cash if you have the desire and, more importantly, the commitment.

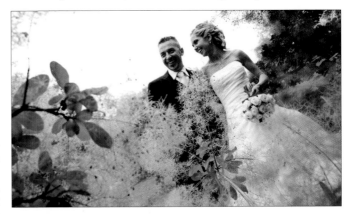

▲ **ABOVE** Events such as weddings are a great way for photographers to start making money from their art. However, it is a very competitive industry. You will need to take unusual shots for your portfolio that show you can really capture the atmosphere of the day and the personalities of the couple.

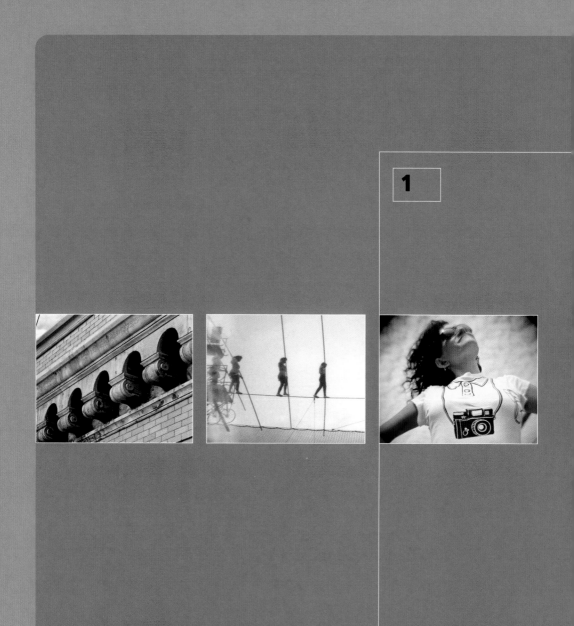

1

Working with Film

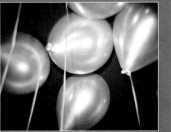 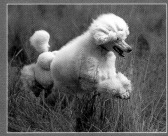 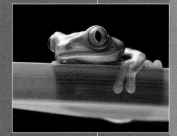

Film is not outmoded – many photographers still prefer it. Using film makes you slow down and think more about what you are shooting. It adds the element of anticipation to your shoot, as of course you must wait to see your processed negatives and prints. These you can process yourself, and produce handmade prints in a darkroom. There are also 'lomos' that allow an unstructured photographic style and a sense of pure fun. Large format cameras offer a simply incredible quality of image as yet unseen in the digital realm. These allow you to share the pioneering spirit of the earliest and most famous photographers.

Film Cameras

Whether shooting with film or digitally, the question that professional photographers are probably asked most frequently is, 'What is the best camera I can buy?' Unfortunately there is no simple answer. Even though many people consider the Rolls-Royce to be the best motor car in the world, it is not suited to all uses: it would be at a distinct disadvantage in a Formula One race, for example. In the same way, there are some cameras that some photographers consider the 'Rolls-Royce' of their kind yet it does not always follow that these are the best choice for all shooting situations. Undoubtedly the camera that historically has proved most popular for film users is the 35mm SLR.

The important aspects to consider when choosing a camera are application, variety of accessories and cost.

▼ **BELOW** Kit such as this Nikon 35mm SLR may look dated and even retro today, but it still works well and is much loved by many photographers. Many used-equipment stockists will let you 'test drive' models.

The range of cameras available is still wide, yet each type is very distinct in its uses. Photographers should examine the different models and decide which might be the most suitable for their requirements. Ultimately, however, whichever camera is used, the elements that go to make up the final image will be those that the photographer brings to the camera, rather than the number of dials, buttons, functions or modes it has. Even a disposable camera can produce a good picture in the hands of an attentive and enthusiastic photographer who takes care with composition, gives thought to foreground and background, and notes the prevailing lighting conditions.

Great shots can be achieved with even the most modest budget and a little technical knowledge. The more money the photographer is prepared to spend, generally the more sophisticated the camera can be; usually the higher rated models will include auto focus, motor drives, an extensive menu system with different functions and a more sophisticated metering system to measure the light and help you choose, or select itself, the correct exposure. This is not always the case though, and some of the more expensive cameras available are in fact the simplest, giving incredible strength, reliability and user-friendliness. The more expensive models obviously expand the creative possibilities of the 35mm camera, although even the basic models are reliable and will produce effective shots.

The 35mm camera

Before the arrival of inexpensive portable digital cameras and camera phones, the compact 35mm camera (so-called because it uses 35mm film) was the camera of choice for those who wanted, with the push of a button, snap shots of holidays, birthdays and other similar events. Although this type of camera is no longer in production, the used market is plentiful, and most of these cameras, especially the

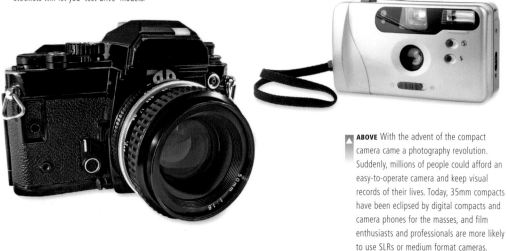

▲ **ABOVE** With the advent of the compact camera came a photography revolution. Suddenly, millions of people could afford an easy-to-operate camera and keep visual records of their lives. Today, 35mm compacts have been eclipsed by digital compacts and camera phones for the masses, and film enthusiasts and professionals are more likely to use SLRs or medium format cameras.

better ones, will still work just as well today as they ever did. The simplest and cheapest will be a 'point-and-shoot' version without a built-in exposure meter or flash, where the film is loaded and advanced manually. The more complicated will normally have the automation of the simple model, but also contain more features such as manual exposure, manual focus, spot metering and the like. However, with pre-owned film SLRs (see below) now readily available at really affordable prices, if you're looking to explore what film has to offer as an alternative to digital, then this type of camera will provide you with much greater flexibility and versatility when compared with a 35mm compact camera, together with much better image quality thanks primarily to higher quality lenses.

The single reflex (SLR) camera

This camera is portable and extremely adaptable. Since its introduction in the 1940s, the SLR (single lens reflex) has proved to be one of the most popular cameras available. The original design evolved into a multiplicity of models, the majority of which have quite a formidable array of lenses, filters and other accessories.

When you look through the viewfinder of an SLR camera what you see is what the lens 'sees'. This is because there is a mirror behind the lens that reflects the image up to a device called a pentaprism. This turns the image the right way up and the correct way round, and is situated on the top of the camera in front of the viewfinder. In normal conditions, when the shutter release button is pressed several functions operate in a fraction of a second. First the mirror flips up 45 degrees so that light can pass through the lens on to the film. The aperture you have chosen stops down. The focal plane shutter opens for the amount of time you have chosen on the shutter speed dial and then

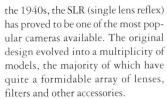

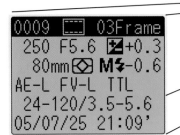

LEFT When shooting with a rangefinder camera, such as this 1970s model, you look through a viewfinder rather than through the lens. You line up the images seen through the viewfinder and the lens to get a sharp image, then shoot.

closes, then the aperture opens up to its full extent and the mirror comes back down so that you can view the scene again.

Using available 35mm film, the basic SLR model can be adapted by the addition of all sorts of equipment, including telephoto or zoom lenses, motor drive and flash units. This means that it is the ideal 'system' camera; it can be adapted as quickly or as slowly as budget allows.

Today, although very few 35mm SLRs are available new, the cost to buy a top-quality second-hand camera, containing the specification that you choose, is low, and certainly less expensive than many comparative digital versions. Modern and older models from companies such as Nikon, Canon, Pentax and Olympus are great value today if you choose to shoot with film.

The rangefinder camera

This is another model of camera that proved very popular with professional photographers over the years. The most famous brand of rangefinder is the Leica, although models by Zeiss and Voightlander

BELOW Nikon's F6 began production in 2004, and it is still produced today. It introduced many new technologies to the film format. For example, the engineers have reduced the vibrations associated with film operation.

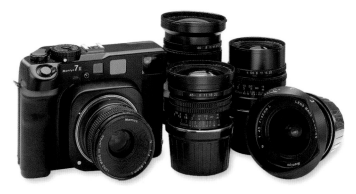

ABOVE AND BELOW RIGHT Mamiya produced a range of film-back medium format cameras that were used widely by professional photographers. If you are looking for a film camera, don't rule out second-hand models, as they still create great images. Above is the 7ii rangefinder camera, a lightweight medium format rangefinder camera that was popular with travel photographers. Below is the 645 afdII autofocus SLR medium format camera.

cameras are in general made up of three main parts, the lens, the body, and the back. The back contains the 120 (or less commonly 220) roll film, or can be swapped for a digital back where wanted. They are bulkier than 35mm SLR cameras.

Although they are often used on a tripod, SLR medium format cameras are also extensively used hand-held by fashion and portrait photographers. Today, although some manufacturers of medium format cameras are no longer in existence – such as Bronica and Contax, for example – other companies including Hasselblad and Mamiya Leaf are still thriving. And as with the 35mm film camera, many second-hand models of medium format SLRs will work today as well as ever, with many older versions of the Hasselblad, Contax or Mamiya camera system being widely available from your local stockist.

are also available second-hand. The French photojournalist Henri Cartier-Bresson shot nearly all his most memorable pictures using one.

In contrast to the SLR camera, the rangefinder allows the subject to be seen through a separate viewfinder rather than through the lens. In the centre of the viewfinder are two images. When the lens is focused on the subject these two images become aligned with one another and the picture will then be sharp. This method of working is preferred by some photographers who find that the camera is quieter to operate and is less prone to being affected by vibration as there is no mirror to flip up. Although the rangefinder does not have quite as wide a range of accessories as the SLR, it is a sturdy and reliable camera with extremely high-quality lenses. The rangefinder is available in 35mm or medium format models.

The digital revolution has been slower to affect rangefinder cameras and there are far fewer digital rangefinders available than digital SLRs. Over a decade after Nikon introduced the D1, the first truly professional digital SLR, there are still only a handful of digital rangefinders available, all made by Leica. For years

professional photographers, including those shooting for the world famous picture agency Magnum, used film-based rangefinders, as they provided exactly what was needed: reliability and speed, with very few electronic components. In fact, early Leica models, originally made in the 1960s, are still very popular today.

The most popular medium format film rangefinder camera, the Mamiya 7 was an updated version of the Mamiya 6 and was favoured by many travel photographers, as it combined the essential qualities of size, weight, fantastic lenses and the superior image quality of the larger medium format film.

The SLR medium format camera

These cameras come between the 35mm and the large format cameras in size and application. They take pictures in a variety of formats including 6 × 4.5cm, 6 × 6cm and 6 × 7cm. These cameras have extensive ranges of lenses and accessories and are still much favoured by professional photographers, shooting both film and digital – many of these cameras have the ability to take both a film back and a digital back. These

The 5 x 4 camera

This is a large format, tripod mounted camera which takes photographs where the transparencies or negatives are 5 × 4in (13 × 10cm). The film can be loaded into double dark slides, each one holding just two sheets. Film known as quickload or readyload was also available, where each sheet came in an individual package and a

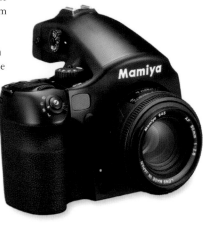

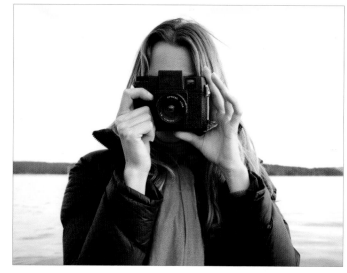

special quickload, or readyload holder was used instead of a double dark-slide. There is no viewfinder in the conventional sense: the image is seen upside-down and back-to-front on a ground glass screen. In order to see the image and keep out any stray light, the photographer covers the camera and his head with a dark cloth. Despite the rather old-fashioned appearance of the camera, many models are extremely sophisticated and can be expensive.

The range of applications of the 5 × 4 camera is very varied both in the studio and on location. It produces pictures with excellent clarity and sharpness of detail. However, it would not be the best choice for spontaneous and fast action shots where a more portable camera with quick shooting capability might be more suitable. These cameras are also available in 10 × 8in (26 × 20cm) and even up to 24 × 20in (60 × 52cm), with other sizes in between.

BELOW The Kowa 66mm SLR takes 120 or 220mm medium format film. Late 1960s models are still being used.

Instant and 'lo-fi' cameras

Although not as popular now as they were in the days of Polaroid cameras, instant cameras are still available, notably Fujifilm's Instax range and those made by LOMO. These cameras offer another dimension to picture-taking. After the picture is taken, the film is impregnated with the chemicals required for processing the image and the picture begins to appear just seconds after the shutter is pressed; development is complete within minutes. As well as providing an imme-

diate image of the subject, these cameras also offer as many possibilities for creative photography as their conventional counterparts.

LOMO, along with the Hong Kong company Holga, have grown an enthusiastic following for their so-called 'lo-fi' cameras. Little more than toy cameras, they are cheap to produce, often have plastic lenses, and light can leak to the film. The results are often magical and surreal, offering creative possibilities in a pleasingly hit or miss fashion.

RIGHT Hasselblad's iconic 503CW medium format SLR. The film can be hand cranked or moved on by remote control. It is ergonomically designed to be hand-held in comfort. Hasselblad lenses are made by Carl Zeiss, a world-leader in optics manufacture, and give great results.

Lenses

Just as there is no one camera that is ideal for every shooting situation, the same is true of lenses. Some lenses in certain situations have distinct advantages over others. An extra element of challenge can be added to photography by experimentation with different lenses, perhaps applying a certain lens to a situation in which it is not normally used.

Lens mounts

All SLR cameras have interchangeable lenses, attached to the camera by means of a mount. There are several different sorts of mount, the most popular being the bayonet mount. This is operated by depressing or sliding a small button positioned on the camera body near the lens. The lens can then be turned 45 degrees in a clockwise direction and pulled gently forward from the camera body, and another lens inserted using the reverse procedure.

Choice of lenses

Interchangeability of lenses opens up a vast array of options and is probably the biggest single factor in improving photographic creativity. Lenses for 35mm cameras come as either a prime lens or a zoom lens. The prime lens

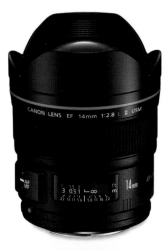
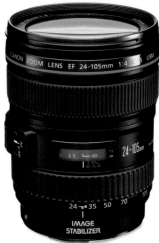
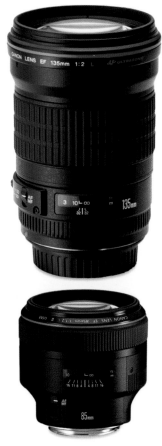
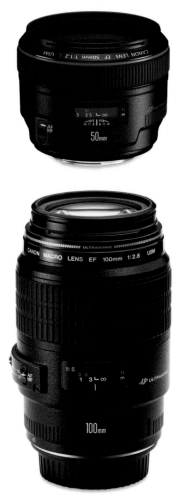

BELOW A selection of Canon lenses. Your stockist can advise which types you need for your particular photography.

has a fixed focal length, such as 28mm, or 50mm, or 135mm; and a zoom lens has variable focal length in one lens such as a 17–40mm lens or a 24–105mm lens.

The benefits of a prime lens are the highest possible image quality; often a larger maximum aperture (known as a faster lens) which means better low light shooting and a shallower depth of field which can be very useful in portraiture especially; and they are fairly small and discreet. Usually though you will want to carry at least three prime lenses with you to cover the range of focal lengths. Most new prime lenses made today are autofocus, but still offer the option to focus manually, but there are also some very high quality manual focus prime lenses being made today and many older lenses will also still produce outstanding results.

A zoom is very practical in that one lens will often cover the focal length of three prime lenses. They are, however, generally larger in size and in many cases the pure image quality

is not as high as a prime, and the distortion may be greater. On the other hand, some of the latest zoom lenses do offer an image quality equal to that of a prime lens at certain focal lengths. All zoom lenses being made today are autofocus, but will also still offer the option to focus manually.

Wide-angle lenses

A wide-angle lens (14mm to 35mm) gives a wider angle of view, so more of the area in front of the camera will appear in the shot. Like any piece of equipment there are disadvantages as well as benefits; the most common in the case of the wide-angle lens occurs with landscape photography where the foreground may lack interest so the eye is not naturally led to the central point of the picture.

On the other hand, using a wide-angle lens does allow subjects to be photographed much closer to the lens than usual, while at the same time keeping the background in focus. In some cases this effect can greatly enhance a composition.

RIGHT, LEFT AND BELOW Wide-angle and medium telephoto lenses by Canon. Start out with a medium telephoto lens and get used to using it before splashing out on a set of more specialist lenses that you may not really need.

Standard lens (50mm)

This focal length will give an angle of view roughly equivalent to what we see with our own eyes. Standard lenses are generally small in size with a large maximum aperture of 2.8, 1.8 or 1.4.

Telephoto lenses (70mm to 800mm)

A medium telephoto lens has many advantages. As well as bringing distant objects closer, it is a superb lens for portraits. It has definite advantages over a wide-angle lens in this situation as, when used straight on to someone's face, a wide-angle lens will

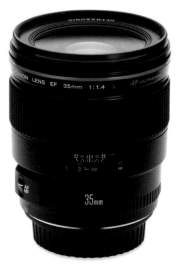

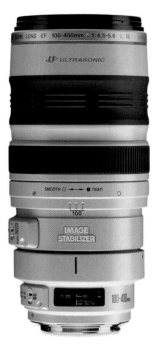

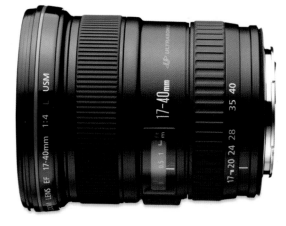

add an unflattering, albeit at times amusing quality. A telephoto lens in the region of 100 mm enables the photographer to stand some distance away, making the subject more relaxed and allowing an unblocked light source. The lens will very slightly compress the image, making for a far more pleasing portrait. The depth of field will be less, so the background can be put out of focus and a part of the subject's face, such as the eyes, can be highlighted. Very long telephoto lenses from 200mm and above will allow you to get even closer to the action and are invaluable in sports and wildlife photography.

Fisheye lenses

These lenses can be used to dramatic effect, but as an everyday piece of equipment it has limited applications and its novelty value can soon wear off.

A macro lens

The macro lens allows the photographer to get very close to the subject without the need for special close-up attachments on the camera. Depending on the lens used, small objects can be magnified to produce a final print that shows them life-size. Many of the lenses in the 28–300 mm range have this facility built in and it is often worth considering paying a bit extra at the outset if macro photography is of interest. Certainly, if you are thinking of nature or abstract photography, you should be interested in macro effects.

Shift/tilt lens

The shift or perspective control lens allows photography of a subject that is very tall, without the problem of converging verticals; this occurs when the sides of the subject taper toward the top of the picture. The conventional rule for preventing this from happening is to ensure that the film plane is parallel to the vertical plane of the subject and then all vertical lines will remain

straight in the final shot. However, with a fixed lens the top of a very tall subject is usually cut off, but with a shift lens the axis can be altered, allowing the camera to remain straight while the lens is moved upwards: the top of the building will then come into view.

Some shift lenses also allow you to tilt the lens which means you can alter the plane of focus for very creative possibilities, such as creating cityscapes that look like toys, portraits where only very small sections of the face are in focus at seemingly impossible angles, or as in the case of product and macro photography, getting all the product in focus even when using very close focus with the camera and lens at an angle to the subject matter.

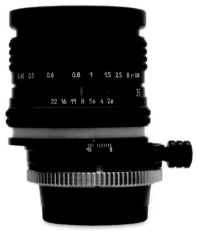

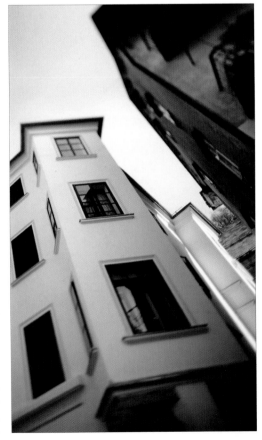

▲ **ABOVE** Using a shift lens enables you to keep the vertical sides of a building parallel, while keeping the whole of the building in the shot. See page 249 to see how this works.

◀ **LEFT** When you photograph a tall building, it can sometimes be necessary to point the camera upwards to get all the building in the frame. This will cause converging verticals, which means the vertical sides of the building will appear to taper in towards the top.

▶ **RIGHT** A fisheye lens has produced this shot, where the trees look as if they are bending protectively over the path.

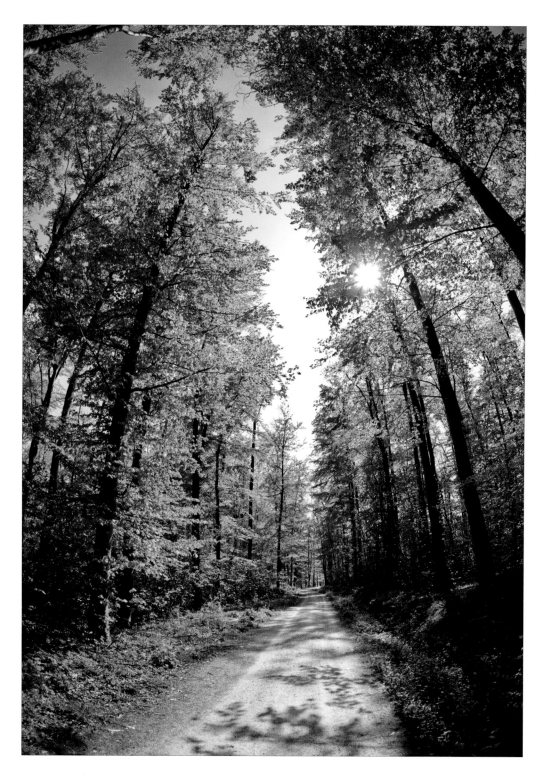

Accessories

There are many accessories that can be added to a basic camera unit when building up a tailor-made, comprehensive 'system'. It is important to bear in mind that no accessory on its own is going to provide a magic formula for improving your photographic skills. Accessories do lend technical help, yet it is the photographer's eye for seeing a good picture that is the essence of photography.

Accessories are important, as they can take your photographs to that next step in terms of technical expertise. You will find that your equipment allows you to create photographs that match your vision. With only basic or amateur kit, you will not be able to attain this. Your local camera stockist should be able to talk to you about the kind of kit you need, and help you make some wise investments according to your needs.

A UV filter

Having decided on and purchased the camera and lenses, the next thing to buy is a UV filter. This can be kept on the lens at all times, whether you are using colour or black and white film.

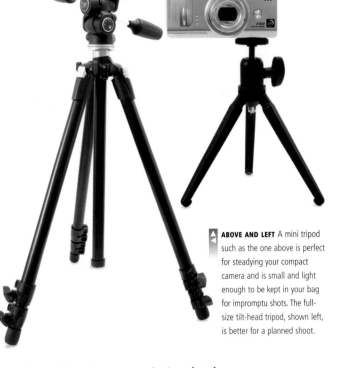

ABOVE AND LEFT A mini tripod such as the one above is perfect for steadying your compact camera and is small and light enough to be kept in your bag for impromptu shots. The full-size tilt-head tripod, shown left, is better for a planned shoot.

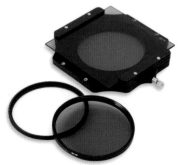

BELOW Filters can be round screw-ins or squares that drop into a filter holder on the front of the camera lens.

As well as reducing the amount of ultraviolet light passing through the lens (cutting down haze and minimizing the risk of a blue cast appearing on the film), it will also protect the lens itself. It is much cheaper to replace even a good quality glass filter if it gets scratched than a scratched lens. Consider buying a UV filter for each lens.

A polarising filter is also invaluable, as this will allow you to reduce any unwanted reflections in water or windows. As well as the UV and polarizing filter, there is a whole selection of special filters and holders available. These range from colour correction and colour-balancing filters to special effect filters and masks.

Lens hood

This should be bought at the same time as any lens. Look at any picture of professional photographers at work and they will all be using lens hoods. The hood prevents most stray light from entering the lens. This stray light causes flare, and can ruin the picture. It may be caused by sunlight falling directly into the lens or being reflected off a building or shiny surface. If you are in any doubt as to the necessity of a lens hood, next time you are walking or driving into the sun, notice how you need to shield your eyes from the light with a hand or the sun visor in the car. A lens hood works in exactly the same way for the camera lens.

Tripod

A tripod keeps the camera steady during shooting at long exposures. To be effective the tripod must be rigid. Some tripods are very flimsy when fully extended so it is often well worth paying a little extra money for a truly sturdy model. Tripods are available in many sizes from the smallest, which are about 15cm (6in) high, to much larger, heavy-duty models which can extend to well over 3m (10ft).

Some tripods come complete with all attachments; others need a head, the part that fixes the camera to the tripod. Heads can vary and it is important to look at several before making a final choice. The most common type is the 'pan and tilt' head, which allows the camera to be moved smoothly through 360 degrees – the 'pan' movement. At the same time it can be adjusted vertically; this is usually in the range of 90 degrees forwards and 45 degrees backwards – this is the 'tilt' movement. (If an angle of 45 degrees is not sufficient, turn the camera round and use the head back-to-front.)

Another useful tripod head is the 'ball and socket' version. Normally this has two knobs that allow the camera to be moved when fixed to the tripod in much the same direction as the pan and tilt head.

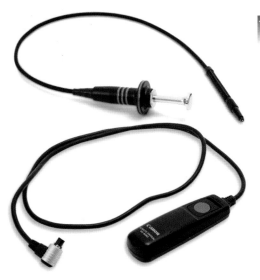

Monopod

Since many tripods are often bulky, some places such as buildings of historical interest, churches and museums do not allow their use without a permit. Sometimes a tripod can slow you down and trip you up, such as at a sporting event where you are trying to follow the action from a crowded sideline. One solution to this may be to use a monopod. As its name suggests, it consists of a single leg which can be adjusted to different heights. Obviously, a monopod will not stand unaided but it can be used to help brace the camera. Professional photographers at most sports events, for example, nearly always use a monopod, as it gives support with added flexibility of quick movement due to its small size and weight.

Cable release

A cable release (also known as shutter release cable) can be attached to any camera which allows it to be screwed into the shutter release button; when the plunger on the end of the cable is depressed it fires the shutter without the need for any direct manual contact. It is often used in conjunction with a tripod when shooting at slow speeds to reduce the vibration that often occurs when the shutter is released manually.

Cable releases are now available for SLR cameras that work so that when the cable is depressed half-way the mirror-up mechanism is activated. Any vibration that occurs when the mirror goes up is then eliminated by this intermediate stage in the shutter release process. When the cable plunger is depressed fully the shutter is fired and the camera remains steady. You can also activate the mirror up facility yourself and use the cable release as normal.

LEFT The ball head gives you easy control of a camera mounted on a tripod.

BELOW A monopod is perfect for sports events, as it allows you to follow the action but keeps your camera steady enough for great shots.

Extension rings or bellows

These are used in conjunction with SLR cameras and allow for close-up photography of detail in stunning clarity. Close-up macro lenses can be used for the same purpose but extension rings give a far better result.

The rings or bellows are attached to the body of the camera on the lens mounting; the lens is then attached to the front of these. The rings offer a single magnification whereas with the bellows the magnification is variable.

Camera bag or case

A padded bag or case to carry your camera, lenses and all the accessories is convenient and also provides extra protection for equipment. The most effective cases have hard outer shells, and compartments moulded from foam rubber to hold the individual accessories. However, more popular are the softer-style camera bag, that come in many different styles such as rucksack, shoulder bag, and sling bag. While they do not provide the protection of a hard case they do offer great flexibility and some are made with a high level of added interior padding, allowing you to take your delicate equipment to places you may have not thought safe, such as ski slopes or on mountain walks.

Many camera bags are obviously meant for carrying cameras. This attracts thieves, so do lock them out of sight if you leave them in a car. Insuring expensive photographic equipment is becoming increasingly costly; if you think that you may have to leave equipment in a locked car, make sure that the insurance policy covers theft from vehicles.

Flash attachments

Most film-based SLR cameras do not have built-in flash so it is certainly worth purchasing a flash unit to attach to the 'hot shoe' or accessory shoe on the camera. Some are quite compact but are nevertheless sophisticated and powerful.

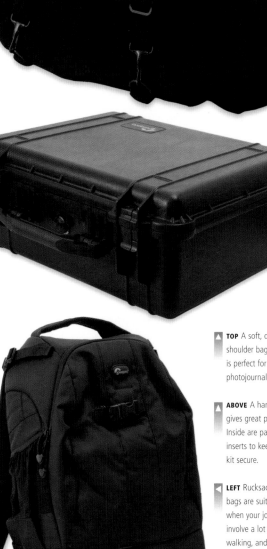

TOP A soft, discreet shoulder bag, top, is perfect for photojournalist work.

ABOVE A hard case gives great protection. Inside are padded inserts to keep all your kit secure.

LEFT Rucksack-style bags are suitable when your job will involve a lot of walking, and speed of access is not of paramount importance.

Some of the more powerful flash units are mounted on a bracket that is screwed into the base plate of the camera. This is linked to the flash synchronization socket on the camera by means of a cable. When the shutter is activated a signal is sent to fire the flash.

Exposure Meters

Although many cameras have some sort of built-in mechanism for evaluating exposure, a separate hand-held exposure meter is very useful. Older photoelectric meters need no batteries and register the amount of light available. Although reliable, they are not as powerful nor as sensitive as the battery-powered meters; many of these can be used as flash meters as well as for reading ambient light. In ambient light mode, they can be used to take incident light readings as well as reflected light readings. An incident light reading is taken when the meter is placed on or near the subject and pointed towards the light source to take a reading. A reflected light reading is taken when the meter is directed at the subject from the camera position.

It will take a little practice to be able to evaluate the various benefits of the different types of reading.

▼ BELOW Extension rings/tubes for macro photography.

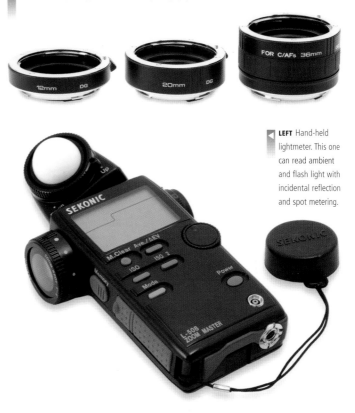

◄ LEFT Hand-held lightmeter. This one can read ambient and flash light with incidental reflection and spot metering.

▼ BELOW Photography kit has changed in its appearance and capabilities over the years, as these old cameras and flashes illustrate. 'Old' kit may not necessarily be outdated, however, and it is worth looking at the used section of kit in your camera stockist.

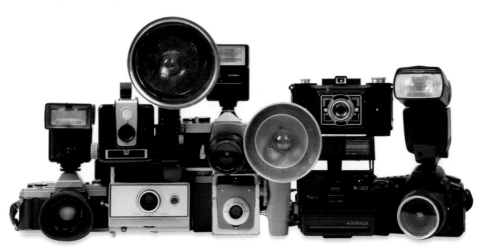

Travel Prepared

Before travelling away from home, especially for a long trip or holiday, collect together all the photographic equipment needed to record the journey. Do not try to take every piece of equipment and all additional lenses, lighting and accessories: just take enough to cover most situations.

Holiday checklist

• How long have the batteries been in the camera? Do they need replacing? Make sure spares are packed; it is still difficult to find certain types of battery in some countries. If the camera uses rechargeable batteries, be sure to pack the charger, together with an international plug converter.

• Take one or two zoom lenses; these will cover most of the focal lengths required and will save on the weight and space that a number of prime lenses would take up.

• Two camera bodies will mean faster work as the time taken to change lenses will be reduced; one camera could be fitted with a 28–80mm lens and the other with a 100–300mm lens.

• Consider having black and white film in one camera and colour in the other; alternatively try loading one body with fast film and the other with slow.

• Try to purchase all film likely to be needed from a reputable supplier before leaving. The film will be fresh and probably cheaper. In some countries it is difficult to obtain very fresh film, and in hot climates it may have been on a shelf in bright sunshine. If you are concerned about it passing through the X-ray security machine at an airport there are protective bags available from specialist stores.

• Think about taking one or two filters; an 81A will help add a little warmth to the pictures, while a polarizing filter will enhance the quality of the sky and sea while also cutting down on or eliminating unwanted reflections. A graduated neutral density filter will help balance the areas of the picture that require different exposures, for instance a bright sky above a dark landscape. A yellow filter when used with black and white film will help retain the clarity of clouds.

• A flash gun is useful in cases where the light is low as well as in bright sun as a fill-in light. As with the camera, make sure the batteries are fresh and that a spare supply is packed.

• A small portable reflector is an asset, especially for portraits.

• It is worth taking a tripod, together with a cable release. If the tripod is too bulky, consider a monopod.

• Lens cleaning tissue and a blower brush are essential, especially in sandy or dusty locations. Wrap and secure the camera in a plastic bag to protect it from dust or sand particles, and as a general measure against the effects of the environment and extreme weather conditions.

• A camera case to hold all this equipment is extremely useful; when travelling by air and not keeping the case as hand luggage, it is best to have a hard case for maximum protection. Don't stint on protecting your gear, as baggage handlers are not known for their sensitivity.

ABOVE Take everything you are likely to need for a trip. This camera case contains the essential items for travel photography: a compact but sturdy tripod, a variety of film for colour as well as black and white shots, a camera body and lenses, and filters and flash equipment. Always check everything thoroughly before setting off on your travels, and remember to pack spare batteries!

Care of Equipment

Cameras and lenses are delicate and expensive instruments that need to be treated with care. Water, dust, dirt and grit are the worst enemies, although leaving a camera in bright sunlight or in the glove compartment of a car will not do it any good either, and so any strong heat should be avoided. Wrapping the camera in aluminium foil is one solution. If the camera is taken to a sandy beach, keep it wrapped in a plastic bag when not in use. Even on the calmest days sand seems to get into every crack; extra care needs to be taken as sand can easily ruin expensive equipment. It is possible to buy a waterproof cover that attaches to the bottom of the lens and allows you to operate the camera through the material. This would be useful for protecting your camera if you are taking it to a beach or some other potentially wet or dusty environment for a shoot.

When a camera is not in use it should be kept in its case or together with the other pieces of equipment in a proper camera bag away from any source of heat such as a radiator. If the camera is not going to be used for some time the batteries should be removed; if left in the camera the acid may corrode the contacts and cause irreparable damage. If you use film, keep it cool – even refrigerated– if possible to retain its quality.

Lenses and filters

Always keep a skylight UV filter on the lenses. This will keep out UV light and will help protect the lenses themselves. This filter can be kept on the lenses permanently, with either colour or black and white film. A scratched filter is cheaper to replace than a damaged lens. If the filter or lens becomes dirty first blow away the dust and any other particles of dirt. The most efficient way of doing this is to use a pressurized can of air. Alternatively, use a soft brush with a blower attached to it. If neither of these pieces of equipment is available, simply blow gently on to the surface. The next stage is to remove any grease by gently wiping the lens or filter with a soft tissue or lens cloth. You may or may not need cleaning solution. Do not use regular house-

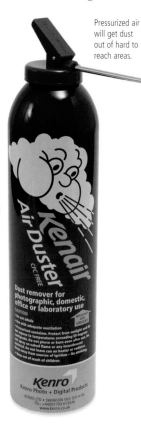

Pressurized air will get dust out of hard to reach areas.

RIGHT Always use products specifically designed for cleaning cameras, and follow the instructions. Photographic equipment is sensitive so needs care.

An air blower brush is useful for blowing dust off the lens and cleaning film before processing it.

Use specialist camera cleaning fluid for your equipment.

Soft cloths and cotton wool buds are ideal for the careful cleaning of lenses. Never touch the camera sensor.

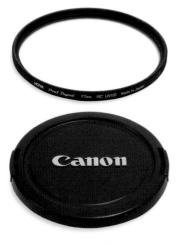

hold cleaning products or any unspecialized cleaning equipment on your camera. It is not worth the risk.

Broken equipment

If something jams in or on the camera and the fault is not apparent never force the piece, as more serious damage could be caused. If the lens or camera develops a serious fault send it to a reputable camera repair shop. If it is under guarantee, return it to the dealer or direct to the manufacturer. Is is certainly unwise to fiddle with the camera sensor in any way.

Anything beyond day to day maintenance should be left in the hands of experts. If you are not sure about maintenance and repair issues, staff in your local camera stockist will be able to advise you on the best course of action.

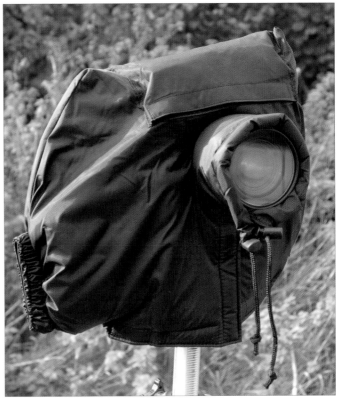

▲ **ABOVE** Some covers are available that are insulated as well as waterproof, which may be particularly useful in the winter. Holes at the sides allow you to slip your hands in and operate the controls, and perspex or clear plastic windows at the back allow you to see the screen, if using a digital SLR.

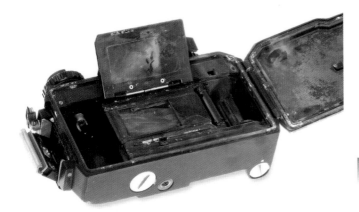

◀ **LEFT** This underwater camera has been damaged by water leaking in through faulty seals. In cases like this, cleaning will not help, and the camera must be thrown away.

Understanding Your Autofocus 35mm Camera

Many compact cameras have an auto focus facility built in; this allows for even more spontaneity in instant, 'point and click' shots. The autofocus camera emits an invisible infrared beam which bounces back off the subject to the camera in much the same way that radar works. The camera can then work out how far the subject is, and sets the focus to the correct distance by means of a small electric motor. This is ideal for anyone who is not keen on technicalities.

It sounds simple and it is, but there are a still few points to remember before shooting the picture. On the most simple autofocus cameras the area analysed by the autofocus mechanism will be in the centre of the frame; it will be this part that the camera focuses on even if the main subject is to one side and therefore out of the autofocus range. It is very simple to learn how to alter the focus by manually overriding this mechanism, when necessary.

Some of the more sophisticated cameras have a larger area of focus than that of the central spot found in the more simple models. These cameras send out three separate beams and make a 'judgement', either from one of these or from a combination. Many of the single lens reflex cameras that take interchangeable lenses are now of the autofocusing type. Most of these have a manual override but in the autofocus mode the same alterations may be required.

Autofocus windows – these send out an infrared beam to judge the focusing requirements of a picture.

Multifunction LCD and mode controls – a display panel and controls to measure and adjust additional flash requirements and the selftimer.

Auto exposure metering window – a light measuring device which judges the amount of light and any flash requirements; some models have a 'spot' reading mechanism.

Self-timer indicator lamp – a blinking light that speeds up as the shutter is about to be released.

Shutter release button – this may also include a pre-set focus control to allow overriding of the autofocus mechanism.

Viewfinder – this gives an accurate visual image of the photograph about to be taken.

Lens – this can contain both an autofocus and a zoom facility, allowing for variety in depth of the image.

Flash – this charges up almost instantly and may include a blinking anti-red-eye device.

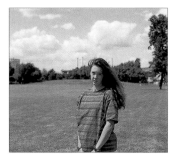

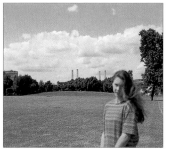

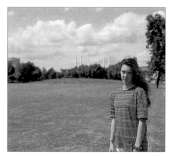

▲ **ABOVE** In this shot the person is in the centre of the frame and is perfectly sharp. The background is out of focus as the automatic focusing mechanism has 'fixed' on to the subject in the foreground. Perhaps the subject needs to be moved to one side in order to reveal or conceal part of the background.

▲ **ABOVE** By repositioning the camera so that the person is at one side of the picture the background comes into sharp focus but the girl is now blurred.

▲ **ABOVE** To eliminate the problem, point the camera at them and gently depress the shutter release button to half-way. This will fix the autofocus mechanism on the subject. Keeping the shutter release button depressed, move the camera to the desired position so that the picture is composed well. Now depress the shutter release button fully. The shot now has the person in focus.

Why choose automatic?

• Automatic focusing allows spontaneous pictures to be captured instantly without time-consuming dial adjustments. You can just point and press. This applies to digital and film-back cameras equally.
• The built-in flash provides quick, on-the-spot lighting for every occasion. It won't provide the perfect results you can if you manually adjust, but it will be good enough for most purposes.
• Light exposure is metered automatically, saving on adjustment and measuring time.
• Hands-free pictures can be taken using the self-timer; even the photographer can appear in the shot. Great for family occasions or proving you have been somewhere!
• The small, compact shape makes the camera easily portable in all situations. Minute digital cameras are now available, too.

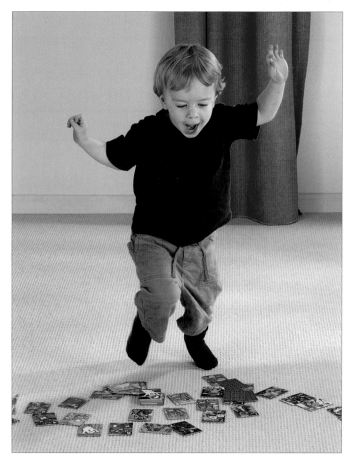

▶ **RIGHT** Autofocus is excellent for capturing instant and spontaneous shots that retain the essence of a particular moment.

Lomography and Large Format Photography

Most of us who have used a film camera will have used either a 35mm SLR or a compact camera. Other types, however, are alive and well. At either end of the film photography spectrum are the fun, spontaneous and unpredictable world of the mainly plastic lomo cameras and the painstaking, deliberate and very slow world of large format photography with cameras using sheets of film up to 24 × 20in (60 × 50cm).

Lomography

This is the term that has now become synonymous with photography that uses small, often plastic, cameras of a certain style. Depending on what camera you use, they may shoot with 35mm or medium format film, both colour and black and white, and may have a normal lens, or a fisheye, an array of one to eight lenses, or produce panoramic images.

Some of these cameras are reissues of classics such as the Diana, the twin lens Lubitel or the Fed from the former Soviet Union in traditional

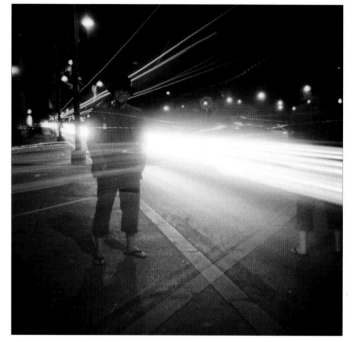

ABOVE Experimentation is key to the art of lomography. Here we can see the effects of a long exposure.

BELOW Double exposures are simple with a lomo camera, and lead to some really interesting shots.

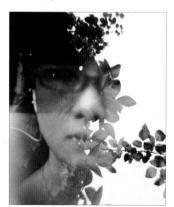

BELOW The classic 'Diana' camera with flash attached has a truly retro look.

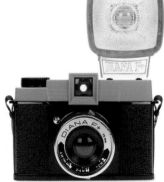

black, but many others are brand new designs, available in funky colours to suit their informal image.

No rules

The very nature of these 'lomo' cameras means that there are no hard and fast technical rules. You can choose to follow the traditional rules of composition or break them altogether. Get your exposures spot on as you normally do, or overexpose wildly and see some interesting results. Do all you can to get your pictures pin sharp, or deliberately focus to create blur and movement instead.

Communities

While lomo cameras are very much rooted in film, they do embrace modern technology in terms of how the pictures taken with them are shared.

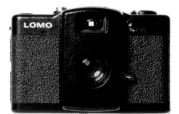

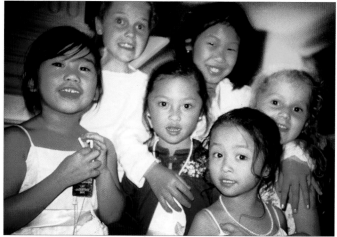

▲ **ABOVE** A typical lomo camera. These are becoming more and more popular – perhaps as a backlash to digital photography.

▶ **RIGHT** Lomo photography does not take itself seriously, and the shots you get with this type of camera tend to be fun and quirky.

Many websites dedicated to lomography can be found on the internet, and all over Flickr and other online picture-sharing facilities, examples of this style of photography can be found and discussed. This type of photography has a real following and quite a community has built up. The Lomographic Society International has 10 rules for using the cameras which range from 'Take your camera everywhere you go' to 'Shoot from the hip' to 'Don't think' and of course to rule number 10... 'Don't worry about any rules'. The main focus with this type of photography and with using these cameras is on having fun, while taking your pictures.

▶ **RIGHT** The cameras are cheap and easy to carry – perfect when you want shots where the camera may be splashed or scuffed.

▼ **BELOW** This Holga flash camera uses medium-format film.

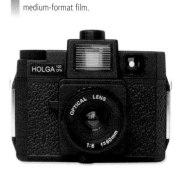

Special lenses

As well as having fun with the cameras, special lenses are widely available now, which are fairly cheap and accessible, yet provide incredible creative possibilities for those who want to get more from their camera. Called lens babies, these lenses will fit on to your film (and digital) SLR camera and allow you to manipulate the image to almost any form you wish. In doing so, they provide some of the tilt available by using a very specialized and expensive shift/tilt lens or large format camera but in an affordable, very easy to use, experimental and fun package.

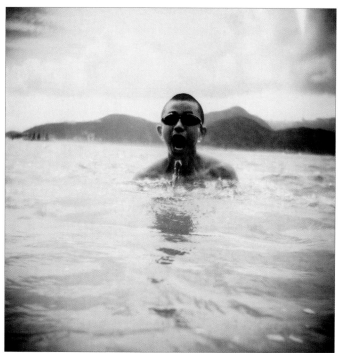

Large format photography

At the complete opposite end of the photographic spectrum to lomo cameras, and the fun, point and click style, is large format photography. This style of photography, and camera, can be traced back to the early pioneers of photography such as Niepce, Daguerre and Fox-Talbot.

Cameras

These large format cameras range in size from the most popular 5 × 4in (13 × 10cm) and 10 × 8in (26 × 20cm) models to a quite staggering to 20 × 24in (50 × 60cm) with many variations in between. They consist of a front standard that holds the lens, and a rear standard that holds the focusing screen and film, and a bellows in between for focusing.

The image is composed on the rear 'ground glass screen' and focus is achieved by moving both the front and rear standards back and forwards with the bellows until the image appears in focus. The image appears on the screen upside down and you really need to view it hidden under a dark cloth to shade it from the light. It is not a small and tiny image in a dark viewfinder but a detailed image the size of the camera… the experience is like watching a movie unfold in front of you.

The film is produced in sheets that are held in a sheet film holder, usually double sided, that is then inserted in front of the ground glass screen and the exposure, always using a shutter release cable, is then made. This is a slow and meticulous process; the cameras are heavy and need to be mounted on a tripod and sometimes you will take just two pictures in a whole day.

There is no autofocus, no eight frames per second, no zoom lenses and you can't carry them in your pocket for snapshot photography. To compose and focus you have to manually open up the lens to its largest aperture and then close it down to the working

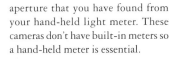

aperture that you have found from your hand-held light meter. These cameras don't have built-in meters so a hand-held meter is essential.

Why use large format?

Firstly the process itself, by slowing you down, can often lead to stunning images because you have spent so much time in composition, waiting for the light and the right moment.

Secondly, the physical size of the film used means that prints of quite sensational clarity, sharpness, and power can be achieved. While you can print any image, either film or digital, as large as you want, once you start to make large prints you will see either film grain or digital pixels and artefacts. Images shot on 5 × 4 film can be printed at over a meter wide and show stunning detail, images shot on 10 × 8 film even more so, and so on. Even the contact print you get from

a large format image is quite astounding. Images depicting portraiture, landscape or architectural subjects can be quite outstanding when shot with a large format camera

Camera movements

One of the features of large format cameras is their ability to perform camera movements. These are the movements of the front and rear standards to aid in keeping lines straight in architectural photography or altering the plane of focus to either keep everything sharp from the very near foreground to the far background or creating wonderful and visually appealing effects in portraits or other styles of photography.

These tilt and shift movements are already discussed in the chapters on tilt/shift lenses as limited versions of these movements are available on 35mm camera tilt/shift lenses.

On large format cameras, however, not only are these movements much greater, but as they happen with the camera, not the lens, all large format lenses are in effect tilt/shift lenses.

So while there is nothing fast or spontaneous about large format photography, it is perhaps the most rewarding type of photography there is in terms of both the process itself and the images produced, and there is very good reason that commercial and fine art photographers such as Ansel Adams, Edward Weston, Sally Mann, Joel Meyorwitz and Andreas Gursky have, and in some cases continue to use them for their work.

If you don't mind their cumbersome size, it need not cost a fortune to put together a basic large format kit of a camera and two or three lenses.

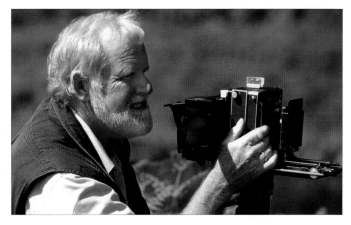

ABOVE A photographer in the field with his large format camera. Carrying the kit to a location takes some effort, so have a good idea of the shot you want first, then make a list of the exact kit you will need.

BELOW A portable large-format field camera set up ready for action on a tripod. The camera operator may take a long time setting up the perfect shot, but the result will be well worth the effort.

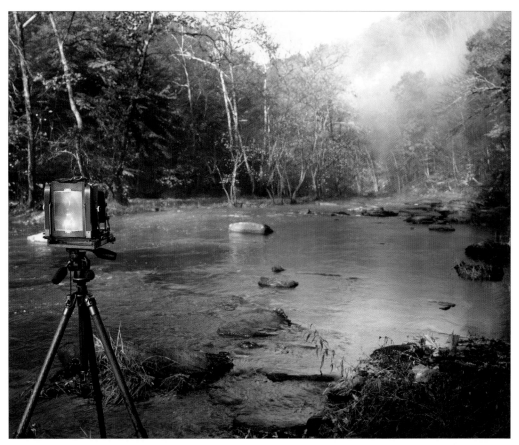

Focus on Film

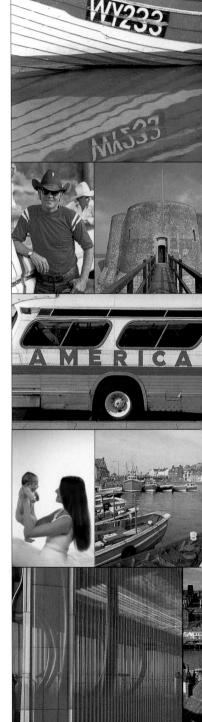

Using photographic film, both colour and black and white, is a wonderfully tactile and emotive experience. That very act of loading your film into the camera leads to expectation of the events and places you are about to capture forever.

You will have chosen each roll of film due to its own specifications or characteristics. Colour or black and white, slow fine grained film or fast high grain follow light shooting. Quick and easy to use 35mm for your compact ot SLR camera or slow and contemplative sheets of large format film where you may shoot just two or three sheets in a day.

We see the world in colour, so it is hardly surprising that most people tend to load their cameras with colour film. Even before the invention of colour film, black and white prints were toned or sometimes hand coloured to add 'realism'.

Modern colour films make it possible for everyone to get a reasonably exposed photograph. But exposure is not the only element of a successful colour image. In the same way as a painter controls the colours on his palette, the way we combine colours in photographs, and juxtapose different and complementary hues, plays a vital role in achieving a successful photographic image.

What we see and what the camera sees are not always the same. The colours we see are reflected off the objects we look at. The light that falls on these objects constantly changes, and with it their colours. Daylight is warmer – that is, redder – at the beginning and end of the day than at midday. Weather also changes the quality of daylight. On an overcast day we see colour as cooler – bluer – than in bright sunshine. Hazy sunlight gives muted colours. However, the most important element in colour vision is not the eye but the brain. If we know that a jacket is a particular shade of red we will see that shade of red at any time of day, in any weather, and even indoors under artificial light – ordinary tungsten bulbs throw out a light strongly biased towards the orange and red end of the spectrum, and give colours markedly different from those produced by natural sunlight.

Film reacts differently. When we move indoors from daylight our vision adjusts to the change in light quality. But if we load a camera with a film made for use in daylight, and use it to photograph the red jacket first out of doors then indoors under tungsten light, the first shot will look about right but the second shot will have a strong orange cast to it. If we use film balanced for tungsten light, the indoor shot will look fine but the outdoor one will be skewed towards the other end of the spectrum, with a blue-violet cast.

It is important to understand how our eyes record colour, and how colour film does it, and to experiment with these effects, in order to create successful colour photographs.

▶ **RIGHT** The juxtaposition of varied coloured images produces a startlingly vibrant collage of contrasting and complementary shades and tones.

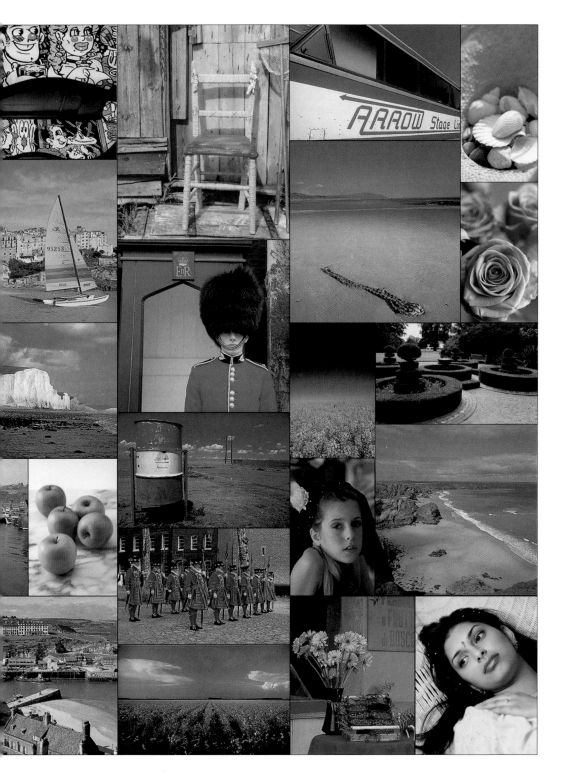

Choosing Your Film

At first, when confronted with the mysterious numbers and words on film canisters, it can be confusing. It won't be long before you know what you need, however. There are two main types of colour film used.

• Colour reversal film produces transparencies that can be mounted as slides and projected or viewed with a slide viewer or on a light box. Transparencies can also be made into prints, either directly, or from what is called an internegative, which involves photographing the transparency on to the other kind of film, colour negative film. Of course transparencies can also be scanned and digitally printed.

• Colour negative film is the type used to make prints. Colour negative is simple to use as it is easy to get processed and have prints made.

Both types of film come in a full range of sizes, from 35mm to 10 × 8in (26 × 20cm) sheet film. They also come in various speeds. These are given as an ISO (International Standards Organization) number from about 25 for the slowest up to 1600 and beyond for the fastest. The slower the film, the finer the grain and sharpness, and the greater the colour saturation and contrast. 1600 ISO film can be uprated to 3200 ISO and more for work in low light but the result will be very grainy – an effect which may be sought out.

Uprating film and DX coding

Uprating, also called speed readjustment, means using film as if it had a higher ISO rating than it actually does, and so shortening exposure

time. Uprated film needs a longer development time, and if you uprate any film you must let the laboratory know that you have done this so that they can 'push', or extend, development. Some laboratories charge extra for handling uprated film.

Many 35mm film are now DX coded: this means that the film cassette has a bar code on it. Many of the most recent film cameras have sensors that read the code and automatically change the camera's ISO setting to the appropriate speed. Using your camera's exposure compensating dial, you can adjust this to uprate the film.

Lighting

There are two types of colour film: one for daylight and electronic flash, the other for tungsten light (ordinary lamps). If daylight film is used in tungsten light the shots will come out very warm, with an orange and red glow to them. If tungsten-balanced film is used in daylight the pictures will have a blue cast. Although both these films are made for the specified lighting conditions there is no reason why they should not be used in different lighting to create a special effect.

▶ **RIGHT** From 35mm to large format, there is an extensive variety of colour film available. Even film that is no longer in production can often be found with a quick search on the internet.

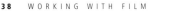

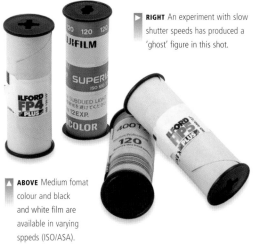

ABOVE Medium fomat colour and black and white film are available in varying sppeds (ISO/ASA).

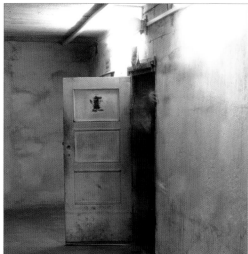

RIGHT An experiment with slow shutter speeds has produced a 'ghost' figure in this shot.

Either of them can also be used with a light-balancing filter. Using an 85B filter, which looks orange, on a camera allows tungsten film to be used in daylight or with electronic flash to get a normal colour balance. An 80B filter, which is bluish, allows daylight film to be used in tungsten film with normal results.

Accurate exposure

Exposure needs to be far more accurate for colour reversal film than for colour negative because the transparency is the final result. With colour negative film any inaccuracies in the negative can be corrected at the print stage. It is a great help to make a test with an instant film so that any adjustments necessary can be made on the spot.

Infrared film

You might also like to experiment with infrared film. This gives unusual though unpredictable results, quite different from the colours we normally see. For example, foliage becomes magenta and pale skin tones green.

Black and white

Although shooting in colour has become the norm in photography, many amateurs and professionals still like to shoot in black and white. Some of the best known photographers, such as Steven Miesels, Herb Ritts, Ansel Adams and Robert Mapplethorpe, are famous for their work in black and white, and exhibitions and books of their work consist almost entirely of beautiful black and white prints.

Undoubtedly most people relate immediately to a colour photograph, which is hardly surprising as we see the world in colour. Therefore any colour image is relatively acceptable, while an image in black and white has to be spot on for it to get the attention it deserves. One reason for the decline of black and white film among most amateur photographers is that it is generally more expensive to process and get true black and white prints from than with colour. It also takes longer to process. However, there is a type of black and white film, known as C41-compatible film, that allows you to process the film in the same

BELOW Black and white and colour 35mm films are still easy to obtain, even if the world seems to have gone digital.

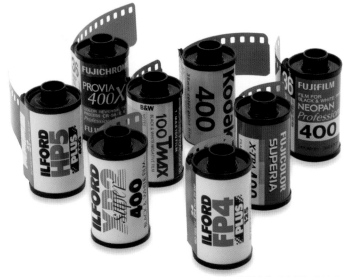

chemicals as colour negatives. You can then also get prints made as if from colour negatives on to the colour printing paper. While these prints will not have the same tonal qualities of a 'true' black and print, they are very close and the ability to get your black and white film processed and printed like colour film and at the same cost, is a real boon.

Unlike colour film, which has negative and reversal types, black and white film is almost always negative. There is no need to worry about colour balance, as black and white film can be used under any lighting conditions. It comes in speeds from very slow, such as 25 ISO, to ultra-fast at 3200 ISO – and even this can be 'push processed' to increase the

speed still further. Slow film gives very fine grain and good shadow detail, and pictures can be enlarged with little loss of quality. In contrast, the faster films are generally very grainy and the shadow detail inferior. Traditionally, when you had a black and white film processed you asked for a contact sheet. For instance, a 36 exposure roll of film was cut into six strips of six negatives. These were placed on a $10 \times 8in$ ($26 \times 20cm$) sheet of printing paper to make a positive print. On this contact sheet you selected and marked the negatives you wanted to have made into enlarged prints. In making this selection you could ask for unwanted parts of the negative to be cropped out by drawing around the area you wanted to

▶ **RIGHT** Stunningly simple images are possible with black and white film. Often a colourful subject such as a flamenco dancer actually works best in black and white.

appear on the contact sheet as a guide. Some laboratories still provide this service, but it is more common for the film to be developed before the images are scanned and burned on to a CD. That way you can either make prints from the CD or copy the images on to a computer and crop and edit the photos using digital imaging software.

Specialist laboratories can provide prints in different finishes, from matt to glossy. Paper types include resin-coated, which has a plastic surface that gives faster development, needs less washing and dries faster than the traditional type. The older fibre-based paper, which gives a more subtle effect, is favoured by photographers for exhibitions and portfolios. On both these papers you can have toned prints. Sepia is the best known, but there are others.

▶ **RIGHT** Once you have first negotiated your way through the maze of photographic films, you will get to know the types you prefer to work in. Ask a stockist for advice.

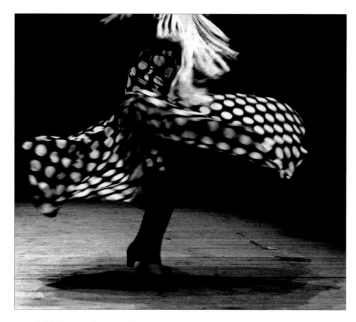

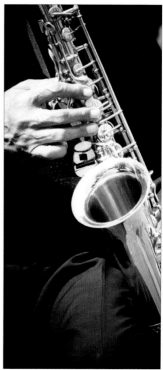

Special black and white film

Today there are far fewer special black and white films available, although one that has endured is infrared black and white film. When used in conjunction with an infrared (IR) filter, infrared black and white film gives unusual results: pictures taken in daylight look like night scenes. This film should be tested before you use it, to avoid mistakes.

Filters for black and white

Although you do not need to use light balancing filters for black and white film, some coloured filters can add dramatic interest to your images. For example, using a yellow filter will darken a blue sky and make the clouds stand out sharply.

A red filter will exaggerate the effect: even a blue sky with white clouds will look positively stormy.

ABOVE This shot in sepia matches the smoky, classic image of a jazz saxaphone. In black and white, the image would not have been so atmospheric.

LEFT Film for large format film-back cameras comes in boxes of sheets, both in colour and black and white.

Processing Your Film

Once you have taken your photographs, you will want to see the results as soon as possible. Although fewer high-street chemists now offer one-hour film processing turnaround, the service is still available in some areas. Check with your local stores to see what they can offer. Similarly, although specialist photographic shops are also thinner on the ground today, you may have one relatively nearby that can help you with film processing. Most are unlikely to be able to offer a one-hour service, but 24 hours may be possible. Alternatively, a quick search on the internet will provide you with a number of online film processing labs. Of course you'll have to send your film over to them in the post and wait for them to send the processed film back, but many offer a free postal service. Finally, you may find it useful to ask around at your local camera club to see if they have any recommendations. Camera clubs usually have a few members who shoot with film, and they'll know of local film processing.

The professional way

A professional photographer has a close relationship with the technicians at his laboratory. The laboratory will maintain the highest standards, because if it does not, photographers will not use it any more.

A professional laboratory can clip test film: before the technicians process the whole film. This means that they will cut off the first few frames and process them. You can then check these and ask for adjustments to the rest of the batch. The processing can be adjusted in increments of as little as $\frac{1}{8}$ of a stop (one stop is equivalent to the difference between f/8 and f/11, or between exposure times of $\frac{1}{60}$ and $\frac{1}{125}$ sec).

Which laboratory?

A simple way to choose your processing lab is to pay them a visit. Are they accredited by Kodak or Fuji? Can you see the processing facilities, and if so do they look very clean and well organized? If there is someone at work are they working in cotton gloves and a clean lab coat or similar? Have a chat to them, asking them about the kind of processing they do, whether they can push and pull your film, can they perform clip tests and make selective enlargements from your negatives and make certain areas lighter or darker. By asking these questions you will be able to gauge the quality and knowledge of the lab and feel confident in leaving them your precious films.

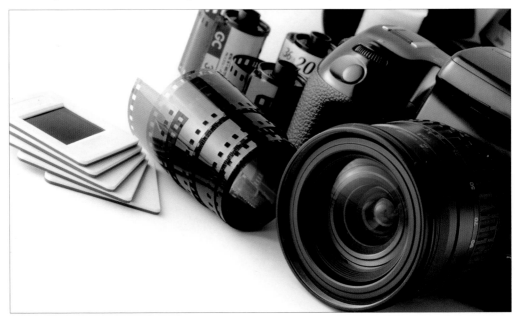

Of course, for this to be worthwhile the film must be consistently exposed, and where the film is cut one or two frames will be lost. There is also a small extra charge for the clip test on top of the cost of processing the rest of the film.

Pushing and pulling

If a film is underexposed, for instance if it is uprated, it needs to be given a longer than normal development time. This is called 'pushing'. Overexposed film is 'pulled' by being developed for a shorter time than normal. These techniques are common, but use them with care as both of them cause a certain loss of picture quality: the harder a film has been pushed or pulled, the greater the loss. More modern films, especially colour negative, are flexible enough to allow a bit of pushing or pulling. And in fact some films are sold on that very concept. Black and white film especially has the ability to be pushed or pulled as it easier to then bring the image 'back' in the print. But there really is no substitute for getting your exposures spot on.

Enlarged prints

Again, a professional laboratory will give you substantially better enlarged prints. You will be able to discuss how you want your picture cropped and positioned on the masking frame of the enlarger. If a transparency that is to be printed has a colour cast you can ask for this to be corrected. If you wanted to darken or brighten an image you can have specific areas of a negative or transparency shaded or printed up. This can be important if there is a quite large discrepancy between the tones in highlighted areas and shadows.

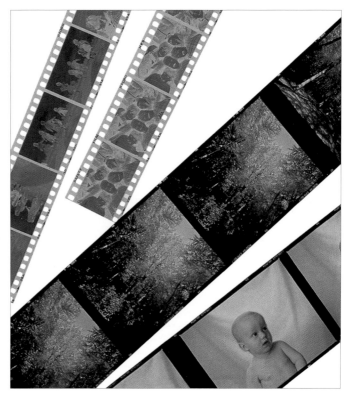

ABOVE Colour or black and white, transparency or negative – before you commit yourself to having a whole reel processed, why not ask for a clip test to check the processing quality.

BELOW You can check through old negatives using a light box to check if you have some photographs worth making into prints, transparencies or slides among them. Be selective, as it can become expensive.

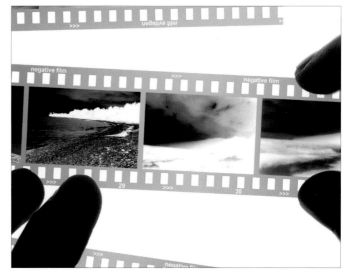

◀ **LEFT** Regardless of the type of film or camera you have used, or whether you want slides, transparencies or prints, you can have some control over the processing. Quality processing can make a good shot excellent.

Processing and Printing Black and White Film

One of the great things with shooting with black and white film is that it allows you to process your own film and make your own black and white prints.

You can let a laboratory do either or both of these things but they are really fun to do yourself, very satisfying and often cheaper. You really will never forget that first time you see your white bit of printing paper turning into a wonderful black and white photograph before your eyes in the developer.

Either of the processes explained over the next four pages can be done at home with the right equipment, but you may find it easier or preferable to go to one of the many black and white darkrooms that are available to hire, for example, at art colleges and universities.

If you choose to process and print your own black and white negatives at home you will need a changing bag (or dark room) and an area with a sink and running water to process, wash and dry the films. Printing requires a larger space and one which you can make completely light proof, but you can set up a temporary darkroom in your bathroom, or convert a room into a permanent darkroom.

If you are intending to convert a room at home choose a small room with an electric light and power, and cover any windows with blackout material. Make sure that no cracks of light are visible around the door – rig up a blackout curtain if necessary. Ensure that you are not interrupted at a crucial moment in your processing by putting a sign outside the door while you are working.

PROCESSING

To process a black and white film, once you have all the equipment together you first go into a completely dark room to load the film into the developing tank.

Instead of a dark room you could use a changing bag. This is a large black cotton bag, into which you place your developing tank, film and scissors in at one zipped end, and then insert your arms in through light-tight holes at the other. This allows you to load your film into the developing tank, as shown in step 1, without going into a darkened room.

Required equipment:
Developing tank with spiral
Chemicals (film developer, stop bath, fixer, wetting agent)
Film retriever or film cap remover
Graduated measuring cylinders
Large measuring jug
Funnel
Thermometer
Timer/clock
Scissors
Film clips (two for each film)
Negative storage bag
Film squeegee

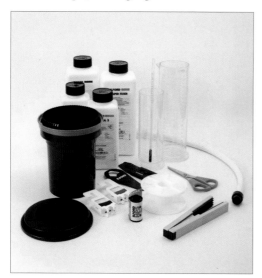

Using a film retriever

A film retriever will normally have instructions on it. Insert the two 'tongues' into the film canister and then withdraw just the lower 'tongue'. Now rewind the film until you hear a faint click, insert the lower 'tongue' again and then withdraw both tongues together, bringing the film leader back out. (You can practise this as many times as you want on an unwanted roll of film.) This process ensures that light does not get to the film.

If you do not have a film retriever you can, with the light switched off, open the canister with a film cap remover and then slide the film leader out of the opening. If you use this method the next step must also be done in the dark.

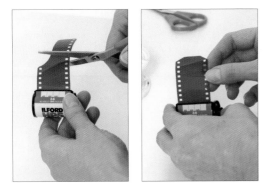
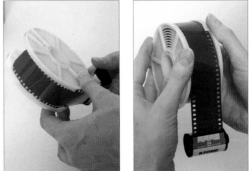

1 Work with the light switched on for steps 1 and 2. The film leader (the end of the film) should be sticking out of the film canister. If it is not, simply use a film retriever to pull it out. See box on opposite page.

2 Using clean scissors, cut the end of the film leader to remove the curved shape and gain a blunt point as in the picture above.

3 Now, in the dark room or changing bag, load the film on to the spiral. Small projecting pieces on either side guide you as to where to load the film. Move the film up and beyond the small ball bearings about 5 or 6cm (2in) along. You may find that practicing this in the light, with an unwanted roll of film that you do not wish to process, helps.

4 With the film in place, pull about 30cm (12in) of film out of the canister and rotate each side of the spiral backwards and forwards between your hands to wind the film on to the spiral. Do not touch the film.

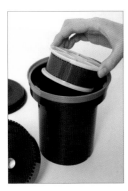
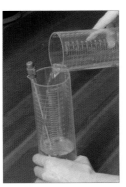
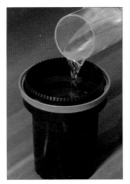
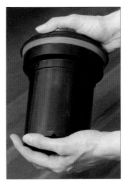

5 When you reach the end of the film cut the film from the cassette, then, giving a few extra turns of the spiral, ensure the film is loaded correctly. Now place the spiral into the developing tank and screw on the light-tight cover.

6 Mix the chemicals according to the instructions on the bottles, aiming to get the developer and other solutions to 21°C. (This is very important when using the developer but less so with the stop and fixer). Pour out the developer that you need, measure its temperature, then mix in water to make the temperature up to 21°C. So if the developer is 19°C, then the water should be 23°C, and so on.

7 Now all your chemicals are mixed you can start developing the film. The time it takes to develope will depend on the combination of film and developer that you are using, so be sure to check your film or developer packaging. (If you have lost your packaging it is very easy to find the information online.) Set your clock, then pour the developing solution into the developing tank and start timing.

8 Hold the lid firmly and agitate the tank for the first 10 seconds, and then again for 10 seconds at the start of every minute of developing time. To do this, hold the top and bottom of the developing tank in your palms and smoothly turn it upside down then the right way up. After each agitation period tap the base of the tank to release any air bubbles.

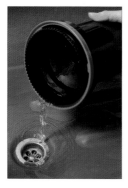 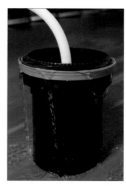 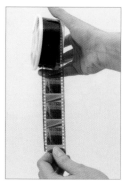

9 When the development time is almost up, pour the developer out of the tank (either into the sink or back into the bottle depending on the developer you are using) so that the time is up just as you empty it. Immediately pour in the stop bath, agitating for about 5 seconds. Leave for another 10 seconds.

10 Now pour the stop back into the bottle, reset the timer, pour in the fixer, then start timing again and agitate as for the developer. The time for the fixer will depend on the type you are using, so read the bottle instructions carefully, but it is generally between 3 and 5 minutes.

11 Now wash the film. If you have a force film washer attach it to the taps, remove the developer tank lid, insert the tube end into the developing tank and turn on the taps. Wash the fill for about 10 minutes at 20°C. Colder water will take a little longer to wash the film.

Another way to wash the film is to fill the tank up with water, replace the lid and invert 5 times. Then repeat this process, inverting 10 times, and then again inverting 20 times. Now pour away the water.

12 Use a wetting agent to help the water run off the film and avoid drying spots or streaks. Fill up the developing tank with water again, drop in a tiny amount of wetting agent, again reading the instructions for the correct amount. Lift the spiral out and then back into the water. Now remove the spiral from the tank. Pull the end of the film out of the spiral and slowly unwind it completely from the spiral.

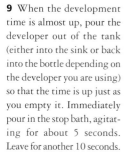

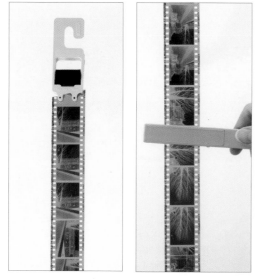

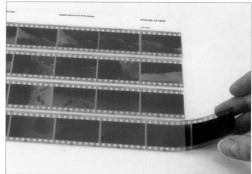

13 Attach a drying clip to one end of the film and hang it up. Run the film squeegee down the film to remove any water, and attach the weighted film clip to the base of the strip. Your film can now dry, preferably in a drying cabinet or over a tray to catch any drips.

14 Once your film is dry, cut it into strips of six frames with a clean pair of scissors and insert each strip into a negative storage bag. This last stage is really important to keep your precious negatives clean and safe for the next stage: making your own prints.

MAKING A BLACK AND WHITE PRINT

Once you have made your contact sheet (see page 49) and selected the image you want, you are ready to produce a black and white print.

Many different types of printing paper are available, both resin coated (RC) or fibre based, multigrade and individually graded, neutral or warm toned, and are available in a variety of sizes ranging from 3.5 × 5in (10 × 15cm) to 16 × 20in (40 × 50cm) and above. The simplest paper to start with is RC multigrade.

Although preparations can be done in the light, before you remove your printing paper from its package you must be under safelight conditions. This means using a red safelight that all darkrooms will have installed. This light allows you to see what you are doing but does not affect photographic paper. You will also need to be under these conditions when you check the size and focus of your image, as described on page 48.

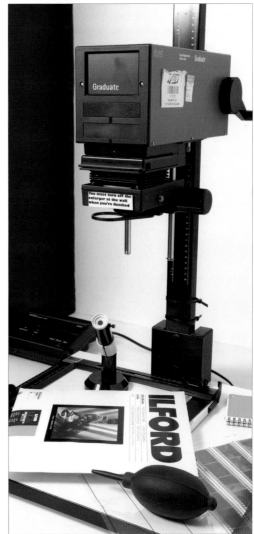

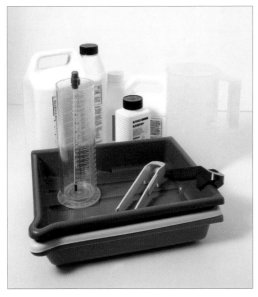

Wet equipment required:
Chemicals (print developer, stop bath, fixer)
Developing trays
Tongs
Graduated measuring cylinders
Large measuring jug (pitcher)
Funnel
Thermometer
Timer/clock
Washing tray with running water
Drying rack or clips on a line

Dry equipment required:
Enlarger with lens
Enlarging easel
Photographic paper
Multigrade filters
Timer
Negatives
Blower brush
Focus finder

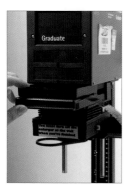 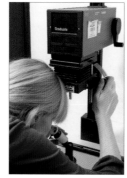 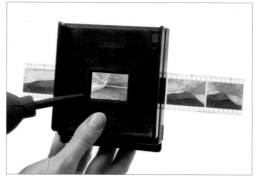 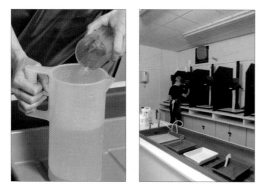 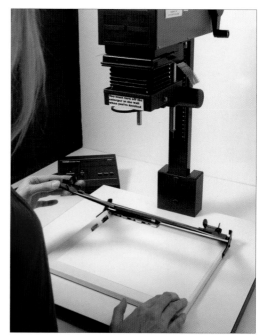

1 First set up the wetside, with the developer, stop, and fixer prepared according to the instructions given on the bottles. Pour the mixed chemical into the three processing trays. Always make sure you order them with developer first, then stop, and then fix. The washing tray/washing area should be after the fixing tray.

2 Set up the easel on the enlarger baseboard. Take the strip of film that contains the frame you would like to print, and place this into the negative carrier, shiny side up and back to front, with the frame to print in the window. Holding it firmly, use a blower brush to blow any dust off the negative.

3 Place the negative carrier into the enlarger, open up the enlarger lens fully (smallest number) and switch it on. Set the timer tfocus.

4 Under safelight conditions check the negative image projected on the easel. Raise and lower the enlarger head to get the image to the correct size on the easel. Raise and lower the lens to get sharp focus. Now set the enlarging lens back to a 'middle' aperture such as f/8, which will allow you to choose a usable amount of exposure time (not too short and not too long) and turn the timer focus button off.

NB You can check sharp focus by using a focusing finder, a small device that allows you to check the exact focus of the projected image.

Timer and focus

The timer will have both a focus and time button or switch. Setting the timer will keep the enlarger light on. This is used when you check focus, but must be turned off when you place photographic paper under the enlarger.

5 Set the timer to the time you selected from your test strip (see box) and make sure you have the correct multigrade filter in the filter draw (see box). Now that the enlarger is set up, and the timer set, with the focus button off, place a piece of printing paper on to the easel.

6 Turn on the timer and the negative image will be projected on to the printing paper for as long as you set the timer to. It will then turn itself off.

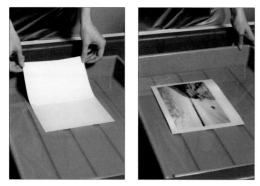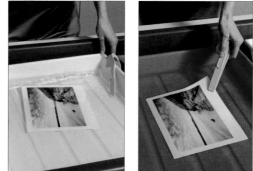

7 Lift up the easel blades and, watching your clock, gently slip the now exposed printing paper into the developer tray. Most prints need between 1.5 and 2 minutes in the developer but this may vary according to the instructions on the developer and printing paper packaging.

Immediately rock the print in the developer tray, then repeat a few times intermittently in the time allowed.

After a short time the magic begins as a faint positive image begins to appear on your blank paper, quickly getting darker until the full image appears.

8 Once the correct development time is up, using tongs, carefully lift the paper at the edge (not touching the image), and transfer the paper into the stop bath and agitate with the gentle rocking movement as before. After between 10 and 30 seconds, depending on the printing paper used, transfer the print into the fix tray using the tongs. Gently rock the tray a couple of times and then leave it for between 2 and 5 minutes (again, the chemical and paper manufacturer instructions will guide you). The image should now be fully developed and clear.

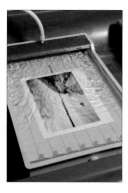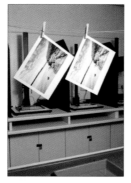

9 Now transfer the fixed print into the wash. Keep the paper washing for the time recommended by the paper manufacture, then take it out to dry. Generally, paper must be washed for a minimum of 5 minutes, but 20 minutes is better as this will make sure every trace of chemicals is washed away.

10 You can now dry your print by hanging them on a rack or on a line. Once dry your print is ready to mount, frame, put in your portfolio or simply gaze at.

Test strips

A test strip is used to work out how long the timer needs to be set to make the perfect print for any one negative. Follow the process laid out on these pages, but instead of placing a whole sheet of paper on the enlarging easel you place a strip. Cut a piece of paper into a few 'strips' for just this use. Then set the timer to 3 seconds. Covering up all of the test strip with a piece of card held just above, but not touching, the paper, except for one area, expose the paper for the 3 seconds. Then move the card along a bit and expose again for 3 seconds, and so on to create about 5 strips. You will end up with the whole test strip being exposed in strips of 3, 6, 9, 12 and 15 seconds. Then process the strip as described, look at it in the light once fixed – don't worry about washing it – and choose which exposure time has worked best. You can then use this time to make the whole print.

Contact prints

A contact print is one sheet of paper usually 10 × 8in (26 × 20cm) that shows a small print of all of your negatives in one film. From this contact print you can then decide which images you want to make a larger print, or perhaps show your selection of shots to someone. The chemical process is the same as described on these pages, but instead of putting a single strip of negatives into the negative carrier, you simply place all of your negatives on to a whole sheet of paper on the enlarger baseboard, cover with a sheet of glass to keep them flat, and turn on the enlarger for a given amount of time as discovered by doing a test strip.

Editing Your Pictures

Once you have got your pictures back from the processing laboratory the next step is to edit them. How often you must have visited friends and been subjected to all their holiday snaps, with comments like, 'You can just see part of that church we told you about in the background,' or, 'This is a bit blurred but you can recognize John.' Not all their pictures may be like that, but they have not given enough thought to weeding out the unsuccessful or uninteresting ones. Even good pictures will make little impact if they are submerged in a flood of bad shots.

Look at any magazine and consider the pictures that have been used. In a photo spread the few pictures that have been printed will have been chosen from several rolls of film. In a newspaper or magazine, pictures of an event may have been chosen not just

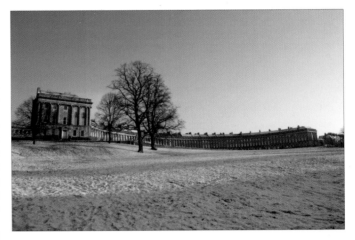

from many rolls but from the work of several photographers.

When looking through your prints, discard those that are badly exposed. Next, look at subjects of which you have taken more than one picture.

ABOVE A classic view taking in the whole breadth of the architecture, but the frame is shot with a shift lens to prevent the vertical lines from converging.

BELOW This shot contains no unwanted cars, people or other elements. The lines are straight and uncluttered. Compare this to the shot on the right.

BELOW Here, there are cars just at the edge of the shot and a person has wandered into the picture but is too distant to be of any interest – they just add distraction.

BELOW A well known subject such as Bath Abbey can be more interesting if shot in an unusual manner, as in this silouhette.

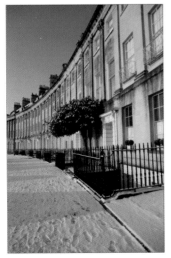

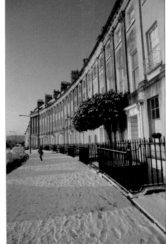

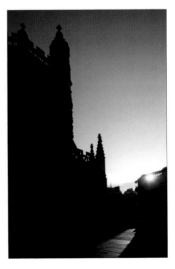

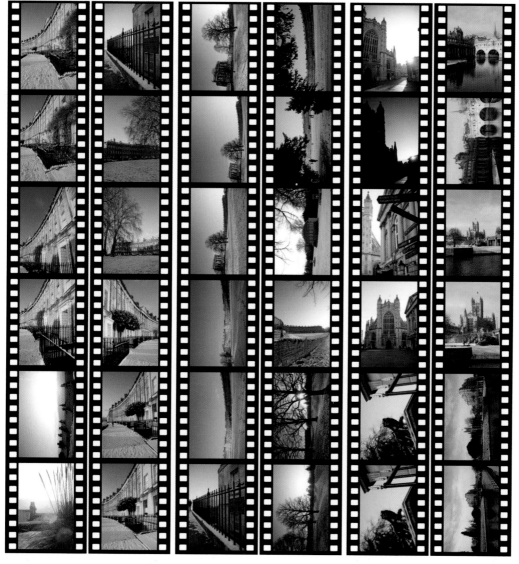

ABOVE A reel of film may give you many good shots, or sometimes, particularly when you are just starting out in photography, mainly bad shots. It is important to be selective about the ones you keep and have printed. Some pictures will not work and are better discarded.

Select one or two pictures that give a good overall view. If there are others where you have gone in close, choose the ones that give the most interesting details. After this initial editing, decide whether any pictures would be improved by being cropped or differently framed when reprinted.

It is quite easy to select the best of a series of holiday pictures, but greater care is needed for a series of portraits or other studio pictures. These will have been taken in controlled conditions and will probably all be technically sound. Here you must look for the frames that show the model or subjects in the most flattering and engaging way.

It may seem wasteful to discard so many pictures, but the results will be that people actually look forward to seeing your pictures, and the people you have photographed will be pleased with being seen at their best.

Taking Care of Negatives and Transparencies

Negatives and transparencies form an archive of images, preserving memories and moments forever. Traditionalists will defend them even today when most people are storing their images on a computer hard drive. If your computer malfunctions, your images could be lost, and of course this does not apply to a drawer full of slides! Perhaps the best thing to do, if you work in film, is store your negatives and transparencies as well as scanning your prints to keep an electronic record.

With film, as with digital photography, a visual diary of children can be built up from birth. These children may well have children of their own, and even grandchildren. What better way of seeing a family's devel-opment, a history of its background, even the country it has come from, than in a series of photographs? Perhaps your photographs will become an extension of your grand-parents' collection, forming a set with a long time span. If all the negatives have been kept in good condition, then future generations can assemble a fascinating visual family tree down through the ages.

It is only too easy to mislay colour negatives and transparencies. This can be a great pity; if prints are destroyed, or friends or relatives would like copies of pictures, others can always be produced from the negatives. While it is possible to reproduce an image from an existing print the qual-ity will not be as good.

Storage of negatives

When negatives are printed at a lab they are usually returned with prints in a wallet. If they are catalogued and dated properly these provide a per-fectly adequate storage system. The wallets can be filed in a drawer with a simple log of what they are. Alternatively, special negative storage filing systems are available; these con-sist of double-thickness plastic or paper sheets with pockets or channels for holding the negatives. The sheets are then stored in binders, archival boxes or hung from metal rods in fil-ing cabinet drawers. It is quick and

▼ **BELOW** Ring binders are cheap to buy and will keep your slides and transparencies neat, accessible and well protected.

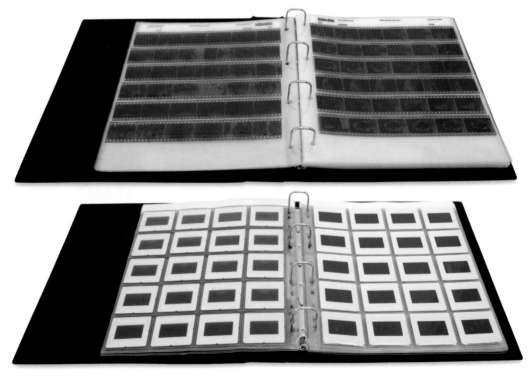

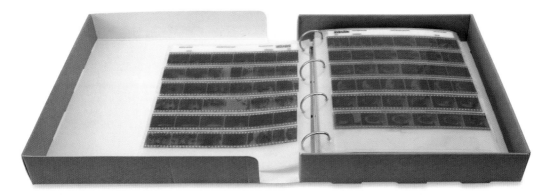

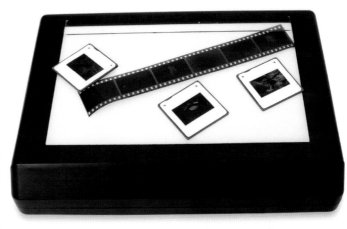

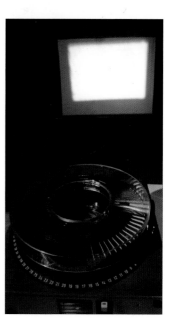

ABOVE A box file such as this one is easy to store flat or stacked and keeps your transparencies in mint condition, ready for you to have developed at some point in the future if you want to.

RIGHT A lightbox is handy for viewing your slides and negatives. You can purchase equipment such as this second hand at very little cost.

simple, if you have a neat and simple filing system, to find the series of photographs you want, pull the sheets out and scan through the pictures by holding them against the light from a window or using a light box. You can then get any new prints made.

Storage of transparencies

If they are mounted as slides, transparencies can be stored in the same way as negatives above, or in slide boxes, grooved to take a mounted slide, with an index for cataloguing the pictures. If the slides are for projection, they can be kept in a slide projector magazine or tray. These have dust covers and can be clearly indexed as before.

It is a good idea to edit your collection of slides and transparencies from time to time. Be ruthless. There may be some photographs that do not work and have no particular value either aesthetically or by being the only visual record of a person or a place that you have. Try to resist the temptation to keep every photograph you have ever taken, and remember

RIGHT Slides can be loaded into a viewer and projected on to a screen or clean white wall in a darkened room. This is a pleasant and simple, if rather old fashioned, way to view your photographs or show them to friends.

that there is nothing more boring than a poor quality, endless slide show of somebody else's family event or holiday. If you sit down and enjoy going through your collection you can edit it down and discard the less interesting shots. In this way you can keep any subsequent shows short and interesting for viewers. Of course, the great side effect of a clear out is that it will make more room for new shots in your binders and files. It's also interesting to see how your work and interests have developed over the years – often your photography has improved far more than you give yourself credit for.

Multiple Exposures

A camera with a facility for multiple exposures – that is, taking more than one picture on the same piece of film – allows unusual images, and in the right hands can give stunning effects. As figures or other elements move across the frame, the camera will record them, so you can end up show-

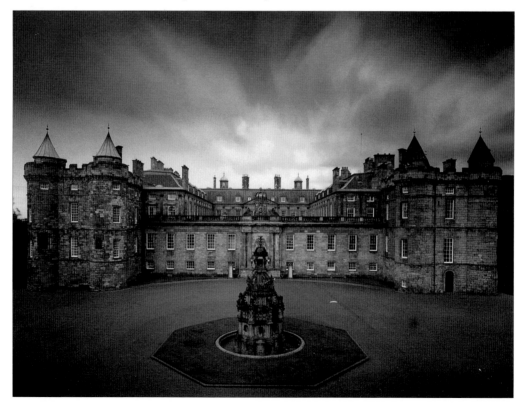

BELOW At first glance this picture of the Palace of Holyroodhouse in Scotland may not look like a multiple image. But look at the sky. It is in fact a sequence of ten separate exposures taken at 30 second intervals. Each time the clouds were in a different position. By the final exposure they had moved a considerable way, giving the effect of a celestial explosion.

ing the same figure or clouds in different positions on the same, apparently single-exposure, photograph.

When you are planning to take a multiple image shot it is important to remember that light subjects will show up on dark areas. Try to frame the subjects so that a dark area is placed where a subsequent image will have a light subject, or vice versa. Images with large amounts of light areas are not suitable for multiple exposures. For instance, a great expanse of light sky in one image will more or less obliterate anything else that appears in that part of the picture. As with any new technique, practice is necessary.

Viewfinder screens

A range of screens is available for many SLR cameras. A grid screen is best for multiple image shots. As its name suggests, it is marked with a grid of vertical and horizontal lines which allows exact positioning of each image.

The screen fits under the pentaprism on top of the camera. Release this, take out the existing screen, drop in the new one and put back the prism. Try to avoid touching anything other than the very edge with your fingers.

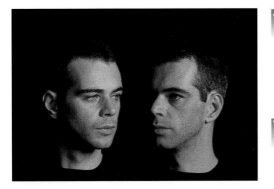

LEFT This multiple exposure shot was taken indoors against a black background and lit by flash. First, the model was positioned at the left side of the frame, looking to the right. Then he was positioned looking the other way, and the camera was moved so that he was at the right of the frame. The result is a striking shot of both sides of his face in a single image.

BELOW The same technique was used in this picture, except that the first image was taken much closer in than the next two. This has made the central image much more dominant than the others. With such a technique care must be taken that the close-up image does not come out distorted.

Multiple exposures

This can be done on many film SLR cameras, but it needs some practice. To take three pictures on one frame, take the first picture in the normal way. Turn the film rewind crank as though rewinding the film back into the cassette, but *do not* press the rewind button. When the slack in the film has been taken up, then press the rewind button. Turn the rewind crank 1½ turns and release the rewind button. Take the next picture and repeat the process. Take the third picture and advance the film in the normal way.

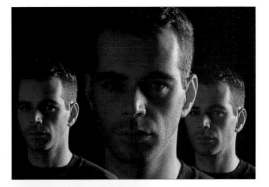

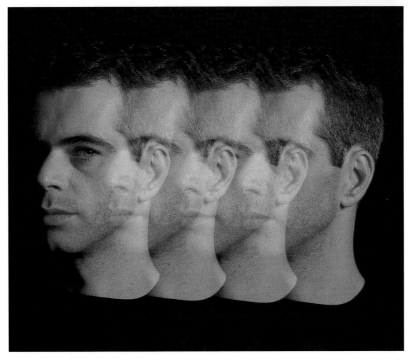

LEFT In this sequence of four exposures the camera was moved slightly sideways after each exposure. It is important to avoid making multiple exposure shots simply confusing.

Special Filters

If you are printing from film, you won't have all the post-shot manipulation opportunities that are available with digital photography. Filters are simple attachments for the front of the lens – or sometimes the rear – that can radically alter the effect of a picture. There are many types to choose from. As with any camera accessory, you must pay attention to a few points in order to get a satisfying result.

Some filters cut down the amount of light entering the lens to such an extent that a longer exposure is needed. If your camera has TTL metering this will not be a problem, but with other cameras you will have to adjust exposure manually. Manufacturers of filters generally state the necessary amount of exposure adjustment: this is called the filter factor.

With a wide angle lens, vignetting may occur when a filter is put in front of the lens. This means that the corners of the frame are cut off, because the angle of view of the lens is so great that it takes in the filter holder ring. This usually happens with lenses of 21mm or wider.

It is possible to use more than one filter at a time, but do this only if it will enhance the image.

Some special effect filters, such as multiple image types, are fun but

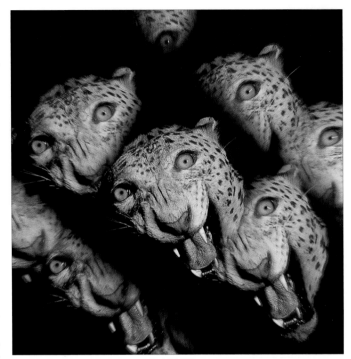

their use is strictly limited. Imagine looking at your holiday photographs and seeing them all as if through a kaleidoscope. You would quickly get bored. Even a graduated tobacco filter, which can help to lift a dull sky, would be tedious if all your pictures had this coloured sky.

ABOVE A multiple image filter makes several heads appear. These filters come in different types, such as 2, 4 or 6 images. They can be used creatively but not too often.

BELOW In the left image, no filter has been used. Whereas in the right, a soft focus filter has been added to diffuse the image.

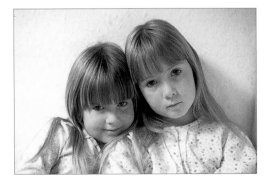

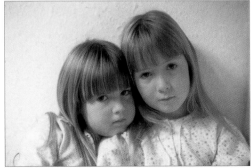

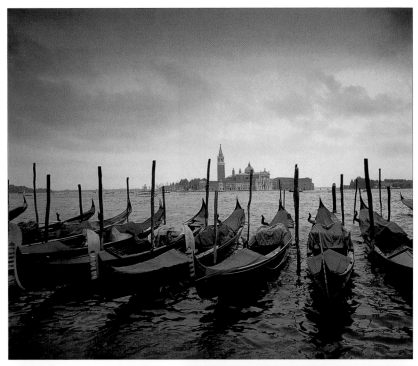

LEFT When this shot of Venice was taken the sky was rather grey and flat. A graduated tobacco filter has changed the colour of the sky, but the rest of the picture is unaffected. This is an effective filter but use it sparingly, or all your shots will look too alike.

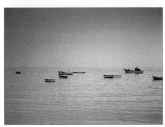

ABOVE An alternative to the tobacco filter is this pink graduated filter. Although this shot was taken at midday the filter, carefully used, makes it look like dawn.

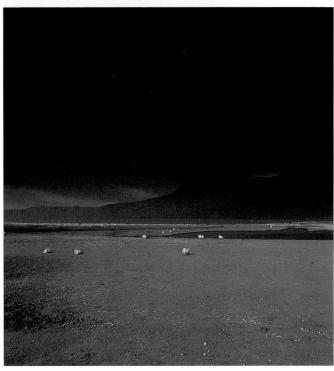

RIGHT A graduated neutral density filter will darken a sky without changing the colour. In this shot of Loch Torridon it has altered an already moody sky to take on a virtually night-time hue.

Special Film Techniques

As on the previous spread, film users need not feel too limited compared to their digitized peers when it comes to creative effects. Special films can be used for their normal purpose as well as to enlarge a photographer's creative scope.

For example, tungsten-balanced film used in daylight gives pictures a predominantly blue cast. In some cases this can give a night-time look to a picture, or, if the film is slightly overexposed, a hard, slightly bleached look – this can often be seen in high fashion photography. Using daylight-balanced colour film in tungsten light gives results with a predominantly orange cast. This can be exploited creatively, especially when the film is slightly overexposed. In either case, be imaginative and prepared to experiment with new effects.

Infrared film gives strangely coloured pictures. Black and white infrared film gives a night effect even on pictures taken in daylight. The results can be unpredictable, and some trial and error is needed to get good results – though there is always the possibility of getting a striking effect by accident. Processing infrared film can be a problem, since the chemical process required is the type known as E4. All ordinary laboratories now use a process called E6. It can be difficult to track down a laboratory with facilities for the older process. One of the main uses of infrared film is in medical photography, and the photographic laboratory of a large hospital may be able to advise you.

Very fast film can also be used to give special effects. It gives very grainy, high-contrast pictures, and if it is uprated the effect is exaggerated. 1600 ISO black and white film can be uprated to 3400 or even higher.

LEFT Here 64 ISO daylight-balanced film was used. A meter reading was obtained, and the aperture was deliberately closed three stops from that setting. This has made the surroundings look as if it was night-time, though in fact the picture was taken at noon in full daylight. The girl dressed for Hallowe'en was then lit with flash, so that only she is correctly exposed.

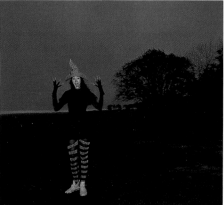

LEFT The same idea is carried a stage further. This picture was also taken in full daylight; 50 ISO tungsten-balanced film was used, underexposed by two stops, which has made the sky deep blue. To both expose and light the girl correctly, a flash unit was used with an 85B filter placed over it instead of over the lens.

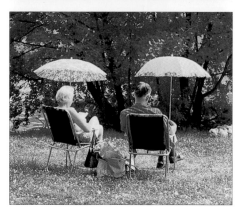

LEFT Infrared film can produce unexpected results, and a certain amount of experimentation is required. The leaves of the trees and the grass appear magenta. At a different time of day or with a different light source the results would have been quite different.

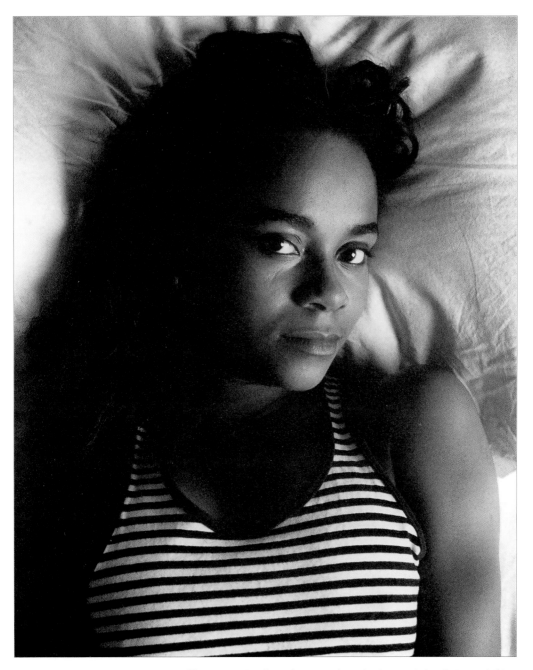

ABOVE Using 1600 film rated at 3400 ISO has produced a very grainy but effective portrait. This shot was taken with available light from a window. Of course, if a film is uprated it is necessary to tell the processing laboratory that this has been done and what the increase is, so that the lab can adjust the processing time accordingly.

Common Problems with Film Cameras

Even when you think you have taken every possible care with your film photography, things can still go disappointingly wrong. Often these errors are caused by a momentary lapse of concentration, but in extreme cases the fault can be traced to a malfunction in the camera or other equipment. With practice, spotting how your errors have occurred will become second nature.

Do not be discouraged by faults in your photography; problems are usually easy to fix and rectify. Look at the examples of 'shots gone wrong' shown here and compare your own pictures to diagnose and correct the fault.

Probably the most common fault that shows up during processing is fogging of the film. This occurs when the camera back is opened before the film has been completely rewound into the cassette, or because light is leaking into the camera, if this is the case, take the camera to a repairer.

If the film is blank when it comes back from the processors, the most likely fault is that the film has not been advancing. When you load the camera with film, always check to make sure the rewind crank turns when you advance the film; if it does not, the film will stay in the cassette.

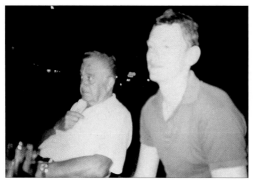

▲ **ABOVE** Flash overexposure. Cause: the sensor that determines the power of the flash was covered by part of a hand. To correct: always leave the sensor clear.

▼ **BELOW** Flare and marks on the film. Cause: after loading, the film has not been wound on two or three frames before shooting begins. The laboratory's processing marks and number are visible over the image. To correct: always be sure to wind on the film for at least a couple of frames before beginning photography.

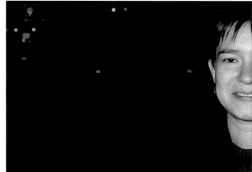

▲ **ABOVE** Incorrect framing. Cause: parallax error. When shooting with a compact camera the viewfinder does not see exactly what the lens sees. To correct: refer to the manufacturer's parallax adjustment guide.

▼ **BELOW** Out of focus. Cause: going too close or incorrect use of an autofocus mechanism so that the middle distance is measured, in this case the plants behind the subject have been focussed on so the kitten is blurry. To correct: semi-depress the shutter on the main foreground subject before framing the shot.

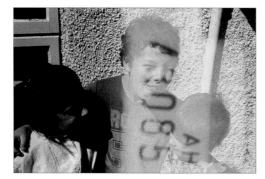

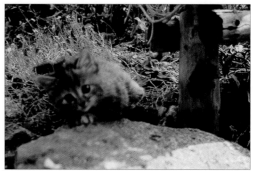

Consistent overexposure of film may be caused by a defective meter. However, it may also occur if the wrong speed is set or the metering system is set to the wrong ISO speed. Alternatively, this may take place if the aperture on the lens is not stopping down when the shot is taken; this means that the lens needs repairing. Again, once you have made an informed diagnosis, speak to a camera repairer and get a quote. Is the fault worth fixing or do you need to think about investing in new equipment?

Blurred shots are usually caused by camera shake. This will occur if you are using a slow shutter speed without securing the camera to a tripod. If the camera has aperture priority mode and you are shooting in dull light, the camera will select a slow shutter speed if you choose a small aperture. This is simply a case of using your tripod or a beanbag to steady your camera and practising until you find you are consistently taking good shots.

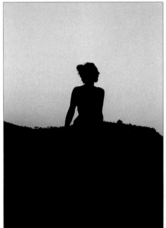

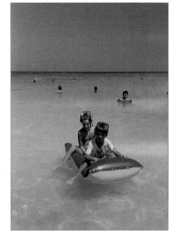

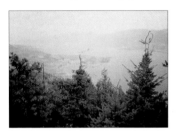

▲ **ABOVE** Overexposed background. Cause: the auto-exposure meter in the camera has taken a reading for the trees in the foreground and overexposed for the background. To correct: ensure the readings are taken from the main area of interest.

▼ **BELOW** 'Red eye'. Cause: the flash is too close to the lens. To correct: move the flash to one side if possible, or activate the anti-red-eye flash mechanism if one is fitted.

▲ **ABOVE** Underexposure. Cause: the auto-exposure meter has read from the sky rather than from the person. To correct: be sure to take a reading from the main subject.

▼ **BELOW** Underexposure. Cause: the flash is not powerful enough to light the subject, the batteries are weak or a finger is over the flash. To correct: ensure the flash is not obscured, the batteries are fresh and you are positioned within the flash exposure range.

▲ **ABOVE** Marks on prints. Cause: the camera back was opened before the film was wound back into the cassette. To correct: ensure the cassette is fully rewound before opening the camera back.

▼ **BELOW** Murky print. Cause: the camera case or a hand is often obscuring part of the lens. To correct: ensure the lens is never obstructed.

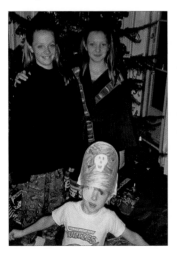

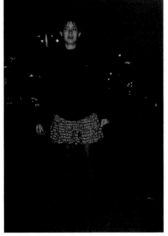

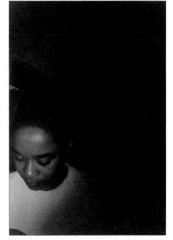

Seeing in Black and White

Taking photographs in black and white is a most rewarding exercise. It is sad that most people today would not dream of putting anything other than colour film in their cameras. Undoubtedly this is because they want their photographs to record the way they remember a particular scene. Yet the absence of colour in a black and white photograph can make a far more striking interpretation of that scene. And since black and white imagery is an interpretation rather than a mere record, the onus is on the photographer to create a picture through the use of texture and tone; these are important considerations in colour photography, but in black and white they are paramount.

If you have two cameras, try loading one with black and white and the other with colour. When you compare your prints you might be surprised at the power of the black and white images compared to the colour.

Tonal range

The tonal range from black through various shades of grey to white is known as the grey scale. Professional photographic stores sell charts of these scales called step wedges, which can be used to analyse a photograph. A black and white print where most of the tones are from the extremes of the scale – without any mid-tones – is referred to as a high-contrast print. If these tones are mostly towards the white end it is called a high-key picture. A picture where most of the tones are near the black end is a low-key print. One that uses the full range of tones is called a full-tone print.

One of the great exponents of black and white photography was the American Ansel Adams. His landscapes combine stunning composition with a powerful grasp of tonal range.

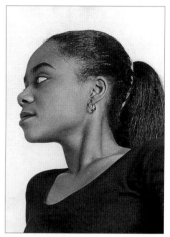

ABOVE This picture emphasizes the girl's soft, velvety skin. She is lit using a single studio flash unit fitted with a large diffuser or soft box. This gives a very soft and even light. The picture was shot on 100 ISO film, as was used for the older man, opposite.

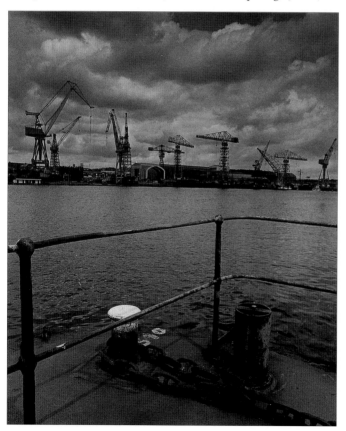

LEFT By shooting this ship-building dock threatened with closure in black and white, the dark mood is emphasized. The print was deliberately made darker to reinforce this image of despair.

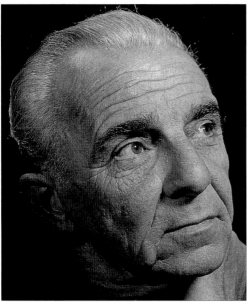

LEFT This studio picture shows a good tonal range. The black at the extreme end of the scale is rich and even, and the mid-tones show a well-defined gradation. The lines and wrinkles of the man's skin are enhanced by the use of black and white. One main light was used to the right with a fill-in light on the other side. A light above the head was used to illuminate the hair. The shot was taken on 100 ISO film.

BELOW If you are in doubt as to whether a shot should be in colour or black and white and you have two cameras, shoot both as here. The black and white print was deliberately printed on a hard paper to bring out the contrast in the grass. Both shots were taken with the same wide angle lens within minutes of each other.

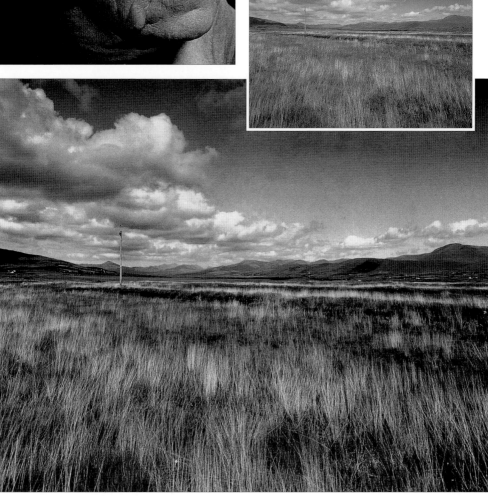

Processing Tricks

Many areas of photography lend themselves to manipulation. Often such treatment goes completely against what is accepted as normal procedure; it might even be seen as a 'mistake'. Yet the results can be so exciting and dynamic that such mistreatment becomes a valid technique in its own right. Many of these techniques do not require any special equipment or even a darkroom: just a camera and film.

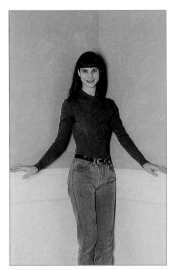

▲ **ABOVE** Here 100 ISO colour negative film was rated at 25 ISO and given the E6 process normally used for colour reversal film. The skin tones are quite bleached out, and the effect is much less vibrant.

▶ **RIGHT** This picture was taken on 64 ISO colour reversal film rated at 12 ISO and push processed half a stop in the C41 chemicals designed for use on colour negative film. This has increased the contrast and intensified the colour, especially on the floor and the yellow wall. A different type of film would have produced a totally different effect. Only trial and error will perfect the technique.

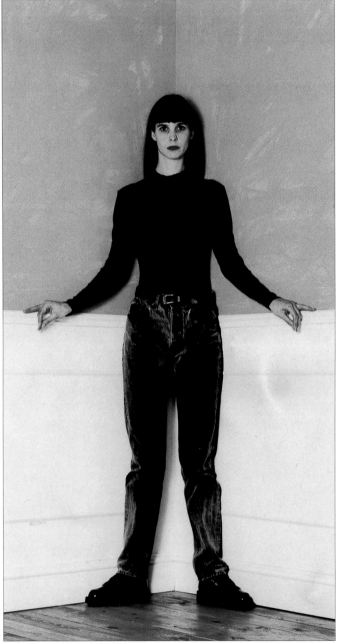

For example, colour reversal film, which produces colour transparencies, is processed using a chemical solution known as E6. Colour negative film, which produces prints, is processed using C41. What happens if reversal film is processed using C41 or negative film is processed using E6? The colours go crazy in a completely unexpected way. Some films turn magenta, others bluish green. Start with one type of film and see what happens. Study carefully what has happened to each colour. This may give a pointer to further interesting results. Does the film need more exposure – for example, should 400 ISO film be rated at 100 ISO? Should it also be 'push processed' – given more development time than usual? Only persistence and careful evaluation of the results will give the answer. In any case, the technique will give wild results and these might include some great shots.

Another 'deliberate mistake' is to have black and white negatives printed on a colour printing machine. When a colour negative is printed the light passes through three filters: cyan, magenta and yellow. Asking the printer to print with only one of these filters will give a positive print in that colour. Try each filter in turn, or try two of them – for example, magenta and yellow combine to make red. Of course, to do this you need to establish a good relationship with your processing lab. Most labs pride themselves on trying to get the processing 'right' so you will need to make it clear that you intend to be experimental with your processing.

BELOW This shot was taken on black and white film and printed in the normal way.

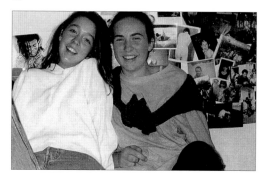

RIGHT The black and white negative was printed on a colour processing machine, using only the yellow filter (top), then the cyan (middle), then the magenta (bottom). Experimenting like this, if you have a sympathetic processing lab, can sometimes throw up a surprisingly successful image.

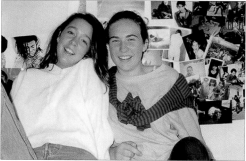

BELOW There are endless variations to experiment with. This picture was printed through all three colour filters.

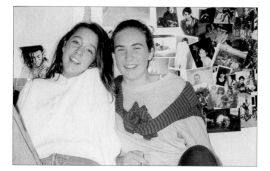

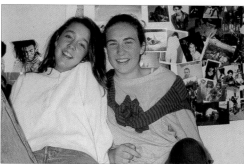

Photocopying Prints

One of the simplest yet most effective ways of producing prints from transparencies or photographic prints is a photocopying machine that will produce same-size copies, enlargements or reductions. The prints can be selectively enlarged and the colours manipulated. Sections of prints can be cut up and rearranged.

As well as making prints on to paper, photocopied images can be transferred on to fabric; many stores offer a T-shirt printing service, for example, and liquid transfer kits make it easy to decorate fabric using colour photocopies.

Some photocopies produce prints directly from 35mm transparencies by means of a projector. Positive prints can be produced from negatives, and vice versa. Colours can also be manipulated and images can be created by 'dragging'; this is where the original image is moved while the machine is in the process of scanning. Pictures can be repeated and built up into a mosaic. Details such as jewellery or a hand, for instance, can be

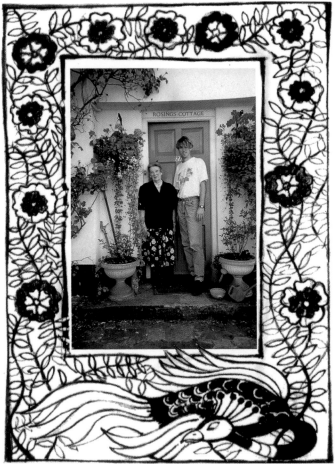

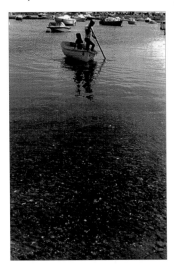

ABOVE In a method used by scrapbookers, the addition of a hand-drawn border around a photograph gives an extra quality to the image. This border was photocopied and then cut out. Slightly overlaying the border on to the photograph before re-photocopying it gives the effect of a single image.

LEFT The original black and white photograph was selectively hand-coloured using fluorescent inks. This was then photocopied; the result is a brightly coloured boat sailing on a monochromatic sea.

scanned and used as images on their own or overlaid with other details. By making a copy of a copy, the original image can be broken down to create an abstract graphic picture.

The obvious attraction of using a photocopier to produce a collage is that the effect can be seen immediately and adjustments made without having to wait for the film to be developed. Photocopying is an economical way to print your favourites as postcards or greetings cards.

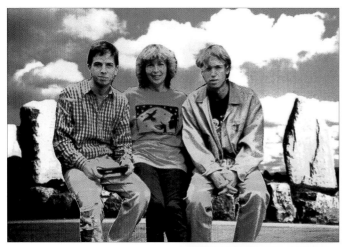

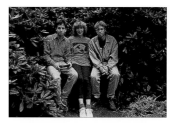

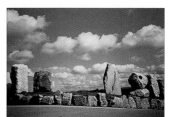

ABOVE By photocopying two different photographs, interesting collages can be made. The people from one picture were cut out and pasted on to a photocopy of another image. This in turn was re-photocopied. This simple technique means that family and friends can be transported to a totally different environment or country.

RIGHT Surreal results can be achieved by photocopying your holiday snaps. These two photographs, above, are not particularly interesting by themselves, but when placed together and photocopied the effect is visually intriguing. There appear to be two viewpoints: one of the swimmers under the water, and another from a higher viewpoint.

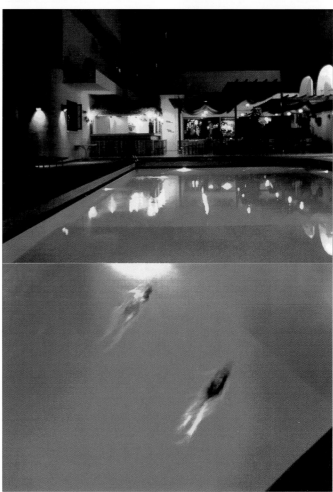

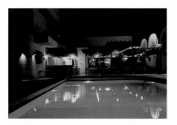

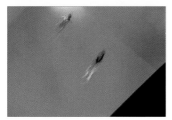

Joiner Pictures

Joiner pictures were made famous by the artist David Hockney. They consist of a cluster of images joined together by literally sticking them to a board. Almost any subject lends itself to this treatment. All that is needed is imagination and a good eye for composition. This is an artform that really exploits the nature of film photography – once your shots are taken they are set and cannot be hugely manipulated, unlike digital images. Your film photographs are true recordings of a moment in time.

When making a joiner picture, it is important to remember that the aim is to create an imperfect match between the images. They may be of different sizes or taken through different lenses. It is not even necessary for all the images to have been taken at the same session. A joiner could be made of shots taken outdoors of parts of the same scene over a period of hours. This would show different lighting and shadows as the sun moved across the sky.

Have the film processed at a laboratory which does borderless prints. Lay the prints out loosely at first and experiment with juxtaposing different elements to find the most effective layout. Discard any prints that do not enhance the overall final effect. When the design has crystallized in your mind's eye, stick the prints down on a mounting board, bearing in mind that the picture will have irregular edges around which the board will be visible. A board that picks out one of the colours in the pictures might give the best effect.

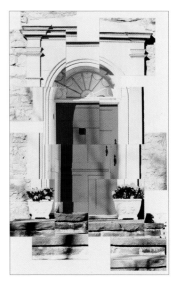

ABOVE What would be an image of an ordinary, albeit quite attractive, front door becomes an abstract work of art when the image is made up from different photographic prints. The door looks as if it is fragmenting, or even pixelating and the shadow looks wrong.

BELOW This joiner picture of the New York skyline, including the twin towers of the World Trade Center, is particularly interesting because some of the shots were taken at sunset, where the sun was throwing a golden light on to the buildings, and some where taken in the daytime. The sun and its different effects on the city thus becomes a statement in this work of art.

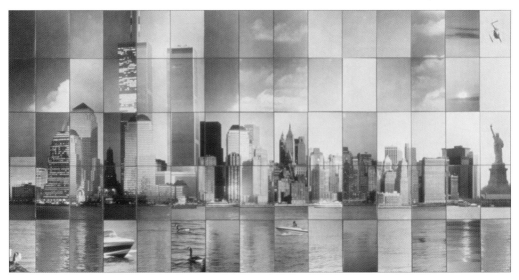

Gradually changing light is only one of the time effects that can be exploited in a joiner. For example, a city scene might show the changing traffic – the difference between the look of a street at rush hour and in the middle of the day might be quite dramatic, for example. Or, of course, you could opt to include people, either the odd jogger in a park or dog walker in a rural landscape, or a thronging crowd of shoppers in a bustling town centre. The final image should show the viewer the complete scene as a series of different glances, much in the same way as it is seen by the eye in real life. This is the huge appeal of joiners.

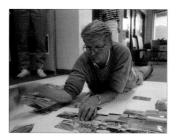

ABOVE David Hockney's photomontage used between 5 and 150 prints or polaroids of the same subject, arranged in a grid layout. Either the subject or the camera would move around during the photography session, so that the resultant montage showed the subject from different viewpoints.

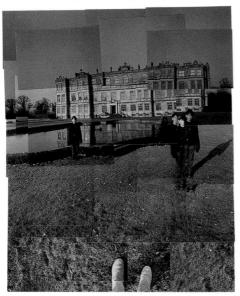

LEFT Building up joiner pictures enables the photographer to include the same person in different positions. In this picture the boy appears on both sides of the shot and the photographer's feet can be seen in the bottom of the frame.

BELOW Taking lots of shots of a building at different times of day and then joining together the images is good fun and can result in an interesting view of a familiar landmark, such as this flower store.

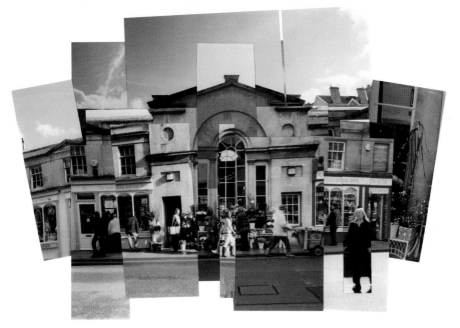

Sandwiching Transparencies

Montages can be made not only with prints, but also by sandwiching together transparencies made with colour reversal film. A reasonable-sized collection of transparencies will probably yield quite a few pictures that would make succesful images by being combined.

Pictures discarded for being slightly overexposed are likely to be just the right ones for this technique; so are correctly exposed pictures with plenty of highlights or a prevailing light tone. Do not try to put two dark subjects together: they will absorb most of the light and the result is likely to be a muddy image.

Skies, tree bark, water, leaves, even mud, can be used as an overlay for a more defined image such as a portrait, which should preferably be one taken against a white or pale background.

Try the combinations on a light box. When a good one is found, fix the two transparencies together with a narrow strip of clear tape wrapped around the blank edge of the film and put them in a plastic slide mount for projection or viewing. A really good image made by this method is worth having copied, though good copies of transparencies are quite expensive.

With some experience of sandwiching transparencies, it should be possible to see opportunities for shots which may not be too interesting on their own but will be ideal as part of a sandwich. These can be made into a collection for use when a suitable pair presents itself.

While the aesthetic qualities of the transparencies will obviously be your first consideration, keep in mind that the resultant image will have a 'message'. Someone looking at the picture will try to find meaning in it – they may wonder, for example, if you have sandwiched a portrait of a woman with a shot of dried mud because you are making some comment about her. It is an image with fairly negative connotations. The image of the woman with the leaves opposite is more positive, in contrast, and suggests she is a person who is in close contact with nature. There is are elements of fantasy about them. The photographs of the wheel and woman with the mushroom macro may seem more abstract and experimental.

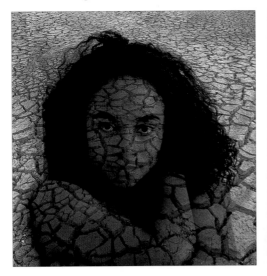

▲ **ABOVE** This girl was photographed against a white background. This image is combined with one of a dry river bed. Combining two images makes a statement and adds meaning to a picture.

▶ **RIGHT** The wheel of an army trunk and a tree trunk are the two photographs sandwiched together here. You can experiment endlessly to produce great abstract images.

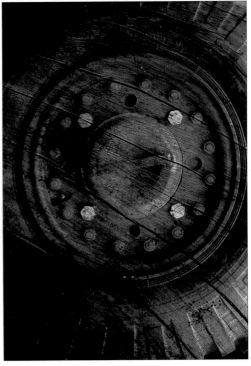

RIGHT Superimposing a portrait of a girl against a shot of a hedgerow has formed some interesting patterns.

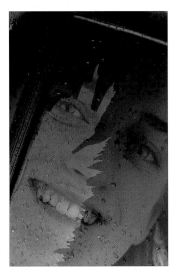

ABOVE A combination of a girl's face photographed against a white background and part of a car window covered in raindrops produces this stylish image.

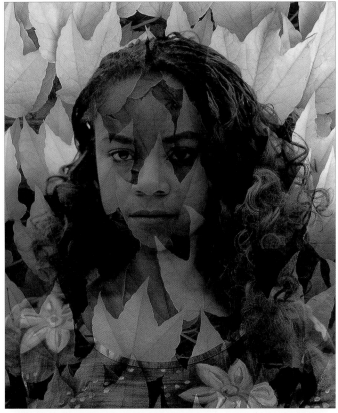

RIGHT One transparency was of a group of logs on end. The other was a section of a dry stone wall.

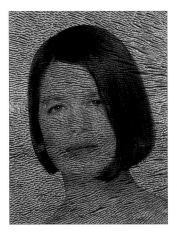

ABOVE A girl's face is used against a photograph of a mushroom taken with a macro lens.

Manipulating Polaroids

Today, Polaroid cameras still have their place, even though digital cameras and camera phones provide very stiff competition. Polaroids can be great fun and can still provide you with an instant print to keep, unlike digital cameras.

Instant photographs from Polaroid cameras have the obvious advantage over other film cameras that the picture can be seen within seconds. But Polaroid film also lends itself to a wide variety of manipulations. Many of these need no more than the camera, the film, and a blunt-ended instrument such as a pen.

With Polaroid image film, available from Impossible, as soon the picture is ejected from the camera the dyes inside the picture 'sandwich' can be squeezed around before they set. This

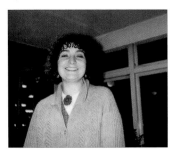

ABOVE This Polaroid camera picture was allowed to develop in the conventional way. The image is attractive but the background is rather boring. As it is, it is not a picture the subject would want to keep.

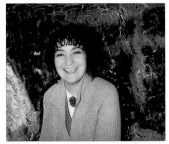

ABOVE Careful manipulation with a blunt pen of the dyes around the girl while the print was developing has created a much more interesting, almost abstract background.

will create bizarre patterns which can be precisely controlled. The finished results can be amazing.

Polaroid backs (which can still be found second-hand) fitted to a conventional camera offer another technique, which is known as image transfer. Once the film has been exposed, it is pulled through a pair of rollers built into the back. These squeeze and spread the chemicals that develop the film. Development of a conventional print usually takes 90 seconds. But as soon as the film emerges it can be peeled off its backing sheet and this sheet is pressed face downward on to a piece of paper that is thoroughly dampened with water. It is then left for the remainder of the development time. This process transfers the image to the paper, after which the original print material is discarded. The result has none of the smoothness of a conventional Polaroid print. The effect is raw and blurred, but often very eye-catching.

Apart from Polaroid cameras and backs there is also the Polaroid transparency printer, which makes instant prints from conventional film slides. These can be manipulated in the same way as those from a Polaroid back, described above.

These are only some of the techniques available for Polaroid users. There are many others, including immersing the film in boiling water and scratching the emulsion.

BELOW A variation of the same technique: here only the faces of the three girls have been allowed to develop normally.

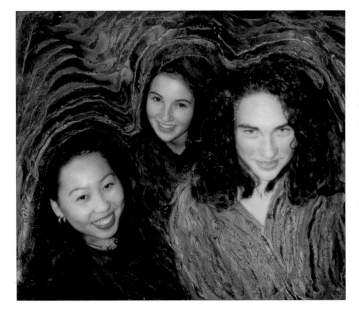

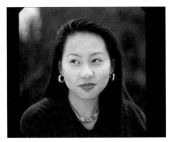

ABOVE A conventional print from a Polaroid camera back.

RIGHT Before the print could develop, the backing sheet was separated and laid on wet paper. It was pressed into the paper with a rubber roller and left to develop. Peeling away the backing left this striking image.

BELOW This still life was created in the same way, but a different textured paper was used.

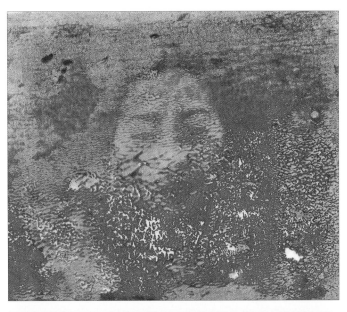

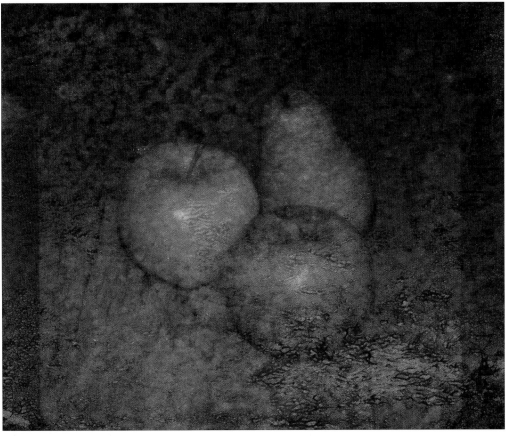

Making Collages with Photographic Prints

There are endless ways of making a photographic collage out of your processed film or prints. The simplest can be made from a single image, which can be either a negative or a transparency. Alternatively, a highly complex design can be made from a large number of images.

To take the simplest case first, two prints could be made of a single image. Then the negative or transparency might be flipped over and another two prints made as a mirror image. The four prints could then be fitted together with a normal one the right way up at the top left, a mirror-image one the right way up at the top right, the other mirror image turned upside-down at bottom left, and the

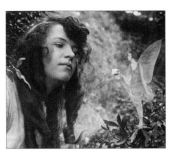

ABOVE An early 20th century montage made with a Kodak Box Brownie camera of fairies at the bottom of the garden caused a furore at the time, as the girls who took the photographs managed to convince many people that the fairies were real. This is now an iconic picture that captures the spirit of the nation at the time.

remaining normal one upside-down at bottom right. This will make a design with fourfold symmetry for a kaleidoscope effect. There are in fact four symmetrical ways of arranging these prints, and all could be tried to see which looks best. Such a collage could be enlarged endlessly by adding more prints to the outside, using the same image or a different one.

A more complicated design could be produced by cutting up the prints diagonally and fitting them together to make a radiating design. Again, more pieces of the same image or different one could be added in rings around the central circle. Naturally there is no need to stick to a symmetrical design. A free-form collage

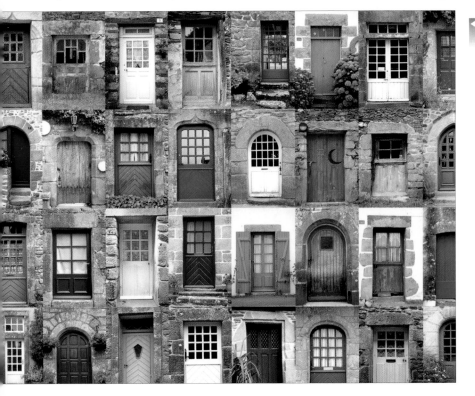

LEFT A collage made up of many images of different versions of the same subject. The different colours and styles of door in this picture make it an effective composition.

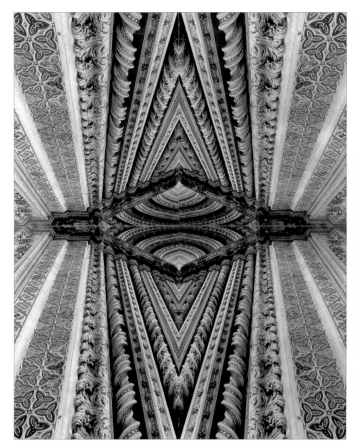

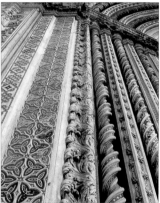

ABOVE AND BELOW Often the best kaleidoscopic collages are made with normal and reversed prints of a single image. This works particularly well with a landscape where there is strong detail on one side of the picture.

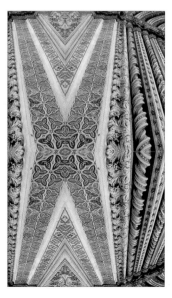

can also give a stunning result. Experiment to find which layout seems to give meaning or drama to your overall collage image.

You can also take a series of individual photographs of a similar subject, and place then next to each other to form one large collage.

A photo-montage, a technique used as early as 1858, is created where different images are put together and then re-photographed to give one final image. This can include adding to an image with paint or other media or objects, to form either a new image with obviously overlain stages, or something more subtle where the viewer is led to believe the montage is actually a truthful single image. A famous example is the Cottingley fairies photographs (see opposite).

Again, experimentation and research into artists who have used the technique will be helpful as you explore this skill.

A three-dimensional construction can be formed out of a mixture of elements and then this can be shot to look like a single image.

Different images can be joined and retouched to form a seamless look, and this can then be re-photographed to produce a new image.

Montage has famously been used in the past for both political purposes, including the Stalinist propaganda machine in the early 1900s.

In both collage and montage, the most important factor is experimentation. Have a good idea of what you are setting out to achieve, but do not worry if it alters along the way.

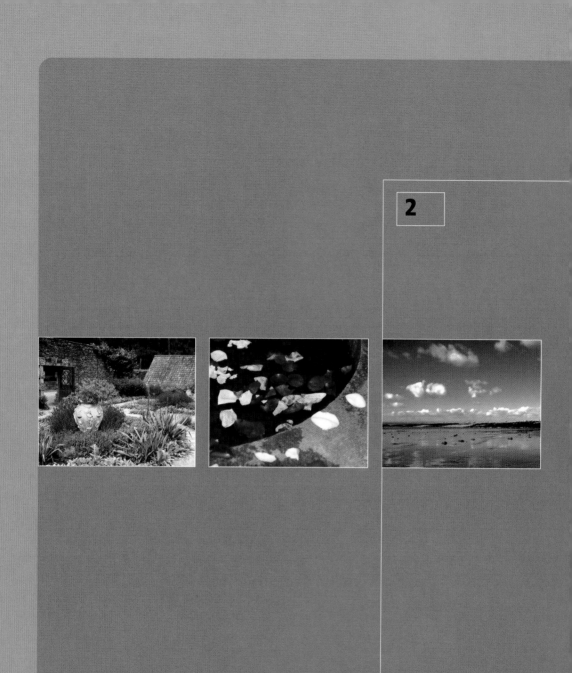

2

The Digital Environment

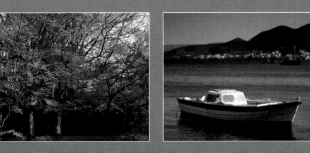
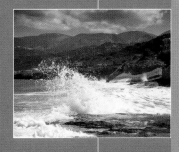

The 'language' of digital photography can sometimes seem at best baffling and, at worst, impenetrable. Is it really necessary to know all the technical jargon? While not essential, a grasp of the language of digital imaging will help you to navigate around the digital environment more smoothly, and to understand the technical requirements for a good-looking image. In this chapter, we'll look at the physical make-up of a digital image, and how it is captured and stored, and finish with a rundown of the most popular digital cameras and various lenses available to today's photographers.

Pixels and Resolution

All digital images are composed of minute blocks known as 'pixels', which is short for 'picture elements'. An individual pixel carries information that governs its colour, the strength of that colour, and how light the pixel is displayed or printed – three aspects that are usually referred to as the pixel's Hue, Saturation and Brightness (HSB) values. Because most digital images are made up of millions of pixels they are not usually visible to the naked eye, so when we look at a digital image we see the gradual and subtle changes in light and shade, and tone and colour as smooth transitions, or 'continuous tones'.

The number of pixels that an image has dictates the image's resolution (how much detail it contains) and the more pixels, the higher the resolution. The number of pixels also relates to the maximum print size, as more pixels mean you can achieve a larger print size. It is for this reason that resolution is one of the key factors governing the quality of digital images, but as we shall see later, the number of pixels in the image is by no means the only factor.

Print resolution

The resolution of a digital image is measured in pixels per inch (ppi), and the standard resolution to achieve photo-quality prints is 300ppi. So, if you know how many megapixels (millions of pixels) a digital camera has, it's simple to work out the optimum print size the camera is capable of producing. For example, let's assume a 12 megapixel (12MP) camera has a sensor with 4,288 pixels across by 2,848 pixels down (12 million pixels in total). To work out the optimum print size the camera is capable of, simply divide 4,288 and 2,848 pixels by 300ppi. This gives you 14½ and 9½. Therefore, a 12MP camera is capable of producing a print measuring 14½ × 9½in (37 × 24cm).

It's important to remember, however, that 300ppi is considered to be the optimum industry-standard resolution. Depending on the image, the camera, the printer and the intended size of the print (larger prints tend to be viewed from farther away), you may find that a resolution of 200ppi (or lower) can produce perfectly acceptable results.

Screen resolution

Because a computer's monitor has a standard resolution of either 72ppi (Windows) or 96ppi (Macintosh), images from a digital camera that are to be viewed on screen can be set to the same 72ppi or 96ppi resolution (which are extremely low in terms of print) and will still appear as continuous-tone images when viewed on screen.

In terms of image size, it follows that with a monitor resolution that is set to 1024 × 768 pixels, the image from the camera only needs to be 1024 × 768 pixels for the image to fill the screen completely.

Digital colour

Almost all the colours in a digital image are made by combining the three additive primary colours – red, green and blue – often referred to as the RGB colour model. For the vast majority of digital images, each of these three colours has 256 different shades ranging from 0 to 255.

Digitally, each of these colours is known as a channel, and a typical digital image that can display up to 16.7 million colours is often described

▶ **RIGHT** The more pixels that are used to make up an image, the more detail is visible and the smoother the image appears. In this sequence of images, the number of pixels in the image has been halved each time, but the image's physical size has remained the same. As the number of pixels decreases so detail is lost and the pixels become increasingly visible – so that by the final image, it's possible to see the individual pixels that make up the image.

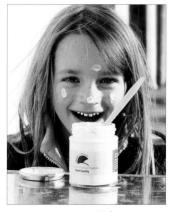

320 x 320 pixels

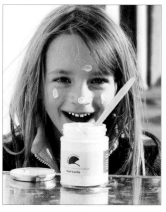

160 x 160 pixels

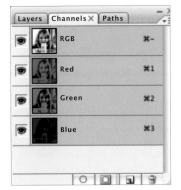

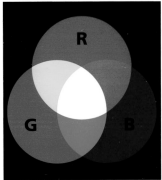

as having 8 bits per channel or 24-bit colour (the total of each of the three channels having 8 bits of colour). The term 'bit' stands for 'binary digit', the basic unit of computing.

Bits utilize the binary counting system in which '0' equals 'off' and '1' represents 'on'. A true 1-bit image would only be made of either '0' (off or black) or '1' (on or white), while a 2-bit image would be made up of '00' (black), '11' (white) and '01' (grey) or '10' (a different grey). By the time we get up to 8 bits, there are 254 additional greys in between black and white. Substitute the white, black and greys for one of the red, green and blue channels and you have a combination of different colours made up of 256 (red) multiplied by 256 (green) multiplied by 256 (blue), or 16.7 million colours in total.

ABOVE This screen shot taken from an image-editing program shows the image used in the sequence below broken into its three red, green and blue channels. All colour digital images use the 'RGB colour model' to show more or less all the colours the human eye can see.

ABOVE The additive primary colours – red, green and blue – are the colours of natural light, and can be used to make up just about all the colours our eyes are able to differentiate. This is why the RGB model is used in digital imaging to represent most of the colours of the visible spectrum.

MEGAPIXELS VERSUS PRINT SIZE

Camera	Pixels	Approximate print size at 300ppi	Approximate print size at 200ppi
7MP	3,072 x 2,304	10 x 7½in (25 x 19cm)	15½ x 11½in (39 x 29cm)
8MP	3,264 x 2,448	11 x 8in (28 x 20cm)	16½ x 12in (42x 30cm)
10MP	3,888 x 2,592	13 x 8½in (33 x 22cm)	19½ x 13in (49 x 33cm)
12MP	4,288 x 2,848	14½ x 9½in (37 x 24cm)	21½ x 14in (55 x 36cm)
13MP	4,160 x 3,120	13½ x 10½in (35 x 26cm)	20½ x 15½in (52 x 39cm)
16MP	4,608 x 3,072	15½ x 10½in (39 x 26cm)	23 x 15½in (58 x 39cm)
24MP	5,472 x 3,648	18 x 12in (40 x 40cm)	27½ x 18in (70 x 46cm)
51MP	8,688 x 5,792	29 x 19½in (74 x 50cm)	43 x 29in (109 x 74cm)

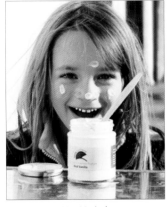

80 x 80 pixels

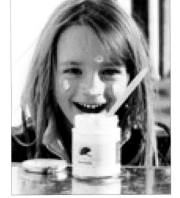

40 x 40 pixels

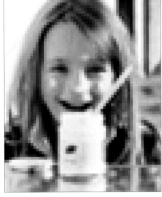

20 x 20 pixels

Camera Sensors

A digital camera's sensor takes on the same function as film does in a conventional camera. The sensor is where the camera's lens focuses the subject or scene and it is where the image is initially 'captured' before being converted to digital data and relayed to the camera's memory card for longer-term storage.

Anatomy of the sensor

The surface of the sensor is covered with a grid of millions of microscopic, light-recording devices called 'photosites'. Each photosite represents one pixel of the captured image. When manufacturers refer to a 16MP camera, the camera's sensor has approximately 16 million photosites.

One of the key components of a photosite is the photodiode, which converts light into an electrical charge – the stronger the light, the greater the charge. The array of photosites records the various light levels and converts them to cor--responding, electrical charges. These electrical charges are then amplified and sent to an analogue to digital (A/D) converter, where the charge is converted into digital data.

Seeing red, green and blue

Photosites record light intensity, but cannot differentiate between light of different wavelengths, and cannot, therefore, record colour. To generate a colour image, a thin filter is placed over the layer of photodiodes. Known as a colour filter array (CFA), the filter is a mosaic of red, green and blue squares, with each square sitting directly above a photodiode. With a CFA in place, each photosite is able to record varying intensities of red, green or blue light. To make up an almost full spectrum of colours, the camera's processor analyses the colour and intensity of each photosite, then compares it with the colour and intensity of its direct neighbours. In this way, the processor interpolates, or 'estimates', a much more accurate colour for each pixel. This complex and sophisticated interpolation process is known as 'demosaicing' and is how each pixel in the image can display one of millions of colours.

Processing and formatting

Once the demosaicing interpolation process is complete, the image undergoes further processing, which may, for example, enhance colours, adjust brightness and contrast, or even sharpen the image depending on the camera's settings. Once these adjustments have been applied, the data is then formatted and fed to the camera's memory card for storage.

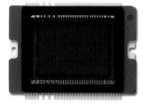

ABOVE A CCD sensor from a digital SLR. The image area measures 1 x ⅔in (2.54 x 1.67cm) but contains 16 million individual photosites, or pixels.

BELOW Millions of photodiodes cover a digital sensor. A coloured filter enables it to record colour, while the microlens optimizes the light from the camera lens.

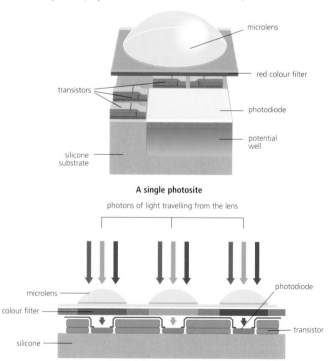

microlens

red colour filter

transistors

photodiode

potential well

silicone substrate

A single photosite

photons of light travelling from the lens

microlens

colour filter

silicone

photodiode

transistor

Three colour-filtered photosites

SENSOR TYPES

Almost all digital cameras use one of two types of sensor – a complementary metal oxide semiconductor (CMOS), or a charge-coupled device (CCD). Both capture an image as described on these pages. The principal difference between the two is how the information from each photosite is processed.

In a CCD, each row of photosites is connected or 'coupled'. After an image is taken, the accumulated charge value from each photosite is passed down row-by-row and read at one corner of the array before being deleted. The values are then fed to another chip for the analogue to digital (A/D) conversion to take place.

In a CMOS chip, each photosite is equipped with its own amplifiers and circuitry so that the charge value can be read directly from each individual photosite before passing directly to the A/D converter. Each type of sensor has its own benefits and drawbacks. Historically, CCDs, which are the more common of the two types, were more efficient at gathering light and tended to produce higher-quality images, while CMOS sensors were cheaper to manufacture and were more energy efficient.

Manufacturers of both systems have worked hard to improve them and it is now difficult to say that one works significantly better than the other.

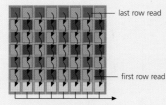

A 'coupled' CCD sensor array

A CMOS has individual amplifiers

THE COLOUR FILTER ARRAY (CFA)

As an image sensor's photodiodes can only recognize shades of grey, a colour filter array (CFA) is placed over the sensor so the photodiodes record red, green or blue light. There are twice as many green squares as either of the other colours, because the human eye is much more sensitive to green light. The most commonly used pattern in today's CFAs is called the Bayer pattern, after the Kodak technician who invented it.

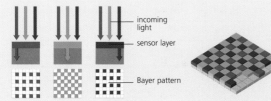

Filters enable a photodiode to 'see' colour — incoming light — sensor layer — Bayer pattern

Bayer pattern filter array

SENSOR SIZE

It's important to know that sensor sizes vary enormously from camera to camera and this can impact on the quality of digital images. For example, there are a number of digital cameras on the market featuring 12MP sensors, but this doesn't mean that the sensors are the same size. This is quite significant because the physical size of the sensor determines the size of its individual photosites. To fit 12 million photosites on a smaller sensor they have to be much smaller. Smaller photosites are less sensitive to light, less able to capture very dark or very light areas of a scene accurately, and can result in increased levels of 'noise' (see pages 82–83). The images show the relative size of the common sensors used in today's digital cameras. Some advanced dSLRs have 'full-frame' sensors, which are the same size as a frame of 35mm film.

Designated sensor type	Sensor's dimensions

1/2.5in sensor = 5.8 x 4.3mm

1/1.8in sensor = 7.2 x 5.3mm

2/3in sensor = 8.8 x 6.6mm

Typical dSLR sensor = 23.5 x 15.7mm

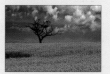

Full-frame dSLR = 36 x 24mm

ISO, Sensitivity and Noise

Those who are familiar with film photography will know that different films have different ISO (or ASA) ratings. The ISO (International Standards Organization) rating determines how sensitive the film is to light – the higher the rating, the more sensitive the film. Similarly, the sensor in a digital camera can also be adjusted to be more or less sensitive to light, and helpfully this is given as an equivalent ISO rating or setting. A compact camera, for example, may have ISO settings of 125, 200, 400, 800 and 1600, while a digital SLR will often feature incremental settings of 100, 200, 400, 800, 1600, 3200, 6400, 12800 and 25600. As with ISO ratings for film, the higher the digital camera's ISO setting, the more sensitive the sensor is to light, but in reality this means the signal created by light striking the sensor is amplified to a greater degree.

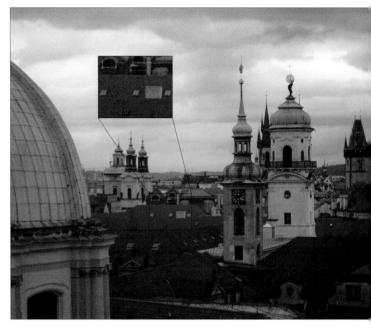

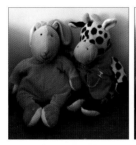

dSLR at ISO 100

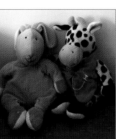

dSLR at ISO 200

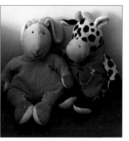

dSLR at ISO 400

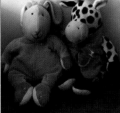

dSLR at ISO 800

dSLR at ISO 1600

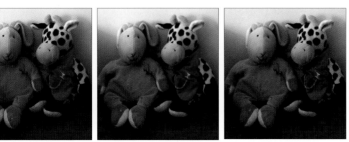

dSLR at ISO 3200

ABOVE This shot of rooftops over Prague was taken in late afternoon, low-light conditions. A high ISO setting of 800 was used to ensure a shutter speed of $\frac{1}{60}$ sec could be used to avoid camera shake. The result, however, is a 'noisy' image, characterized by an unpleasant speckled effect that is more noticeable in the darker areas of the red roof tiles, clearly shown in the inset image.

LEFT This series of images shows how 'noise' increases with higher ISO settings. These images were taken from a dSLR. Those on the opposite page were shot with a high-specification compact camera. At a low ISO and small print size there's little difference between the two.

Low light

The benefit of being able to increase a camera's ISO setting is apparent in low-light situations, such as indoors or outdoors in dark or very overcast conditions. In such circumstances (and where using flash or a tripod is not an option), if the camera is set with a low ISO setting of 50 or 100, the camera would have to have a slow shutter speed of, for example, $^1/_8$ or $^1/_{15}$ of a second (sec), or an increased lens aperture size (see pages 158–159). At these slow shutter speeds you run the real risk of the camera moving slightly as you take the picture, which results in a blurry image. This usually undesirable effect is commonly referred to as 'camera shake'. Alternatively, your subject may move during the exposure, again resulting in a blurred image.

High ISO

There is a direct correlation between shutter speed and ISO setting. By increasing the ISO setting, the shutter speed increases proportionately, so that, for example, from $^1/_{15}$ sec at ISO 50, the shutter speed increases to $^1/_{30}$ sec at ISO 100, $^1/_{60}$ sec at ISO 200, $^1/_{125}$ sec at ISO 400 and $^1/_{250}$ sec at ISO 800. At these later speeds, you'll avoid camera shake and 'freeze' most human movement. You can adjust the ISO between shots to suit the shooting conditions.

Noise

Unfortunately, there is a drawback to using high ISO settings and comparisons can be drawn with

conventional film photography. Photographers who use 'fast' film (film with a high ISO rating), will end up with speckled or 'grainy' prints. Likewise, in digital photography, increasing the ISO setting amplifies the electronic signal from the sensor, but will also amplify the background electronic 'noise' that is present in the camera's circuitry and result in interference – think of it as 'visible hissing'. This distorts the image signal and creates a speckled or 'noisy' image, which, unlike certain film 'graininess', is rarely pleasant to look at.

Low ISO

It's sensible to use the lowest ISO setting that will still allow a fast enough shutter speed to avoid camera shake and resulting blurred images. Alternatively, use a tripod, as you'll be able to use a lower ISO setting and slower shutter speed than is possible when holding the camera. If you're using slow shutter speeds use the camera's 'Noise Reduction' facility if it has one.

Noise and sensor size

Larger sensors, such as those found on digital SLRs (dSLRs), are less prone to 'noise'. This is because the larger photosites found on such sensors collect light more effectively and thus don't need as much amplification (high ISO) to capture a poorly lit scene as a small sensor. In addition, because photosites are set farther apart on larger sensors, increasing the ISO setting will cause less overall interference, and so create less noise. Therefore, you can obtain acceptable results from a dSLR when the ISO is set at 800 or 1600 – settings that are unavailable on many compacts.

Auto ISO

Most cameras will have an automatic ISO option. When selected, the camera will monitor the shutter speed and if the speed drops below the point at which camera shake may occur (usually around $^1/_{30}$ sec), it will automatically increase the ISO setting. This can help you avoid taking blurred images, but it can also introduce noise. On some cameras the automatic ISO range is limited, so the camera avoids using very high ISO settings. Remember, manually set the lowest possible ISO if you're using a tripod as there's no danger of camera shake and you'll get noise-free images.

▼ **BELOW** At higher ISO settings (or larger print sizes), the differences between a digital compact camera's small sensor and the larger sensor of a dSLR become much more obvious. The compact camera suffers from far more 'noise', resulting in coloured speckles appearing in images.

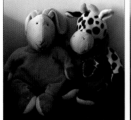
Compact at ISO 100

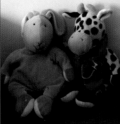
Compact at ISO 200

Compact at ISO 800

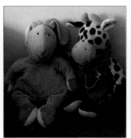
Compact at ISO 3200

File Formats

As the light from a captured image passes through a digital camera it is turned into digital information. For this to be safely stored and retrieved, it must be digitally organized, or formatted. For those new to digital photography, the file formats and associated quality and size settings available in a camera's menu can be bewildering – not helped by the use of technical-looking abbreviations such as .JPG or .TIF – but in reality they are quite straightforward.

JPEG

Pronounced 'jay-peg', the JPEG format (.JPG/.jpg being the file extension) is the most widely used image format due to its versatility. JPEG stands for Joint Photographic Experts Group after the committee that developed the format. JPEGs are able to 'compress' the image files and so reduce their size. This allows you to fit more images on to the memory card. Most digital cameras use the

JPEG format and allow you to select the amount of compression applied to the image. This is often expressed as 'High/ Medium/Low' or 'Fine/Normal'. However described, it should be clear which setting will apply the most compression, as the more the image is compressed the greater the amount of picture information that is lost.

Sophisticated interpolation algorithms, known as 'lossy' compression, assess which pixel information can be discarded without overly degrading the image. The trade-off for having more images on a memory card is reduced image quality, but depending on how the images are going to be viewed, the level of detail lost may be negligible. You'll need to

experiment with the settings to find the most appropriate level of compression suitable for your needs. If storage space is an issue, you'll want a high level of compression, but if image quality is the overriding factor, you should opt for a low level.

Resolution

Don't confuse the compression setting with the resolution setting (in other words the physical dimensions of the image). The menus for both are often combined into one setting 'Large/ Medium', or 'Small/Fine'. The first refers to the image size (in pixels) and the second refers to the amount of compression applied. More compression means smaller files, but lower quality.

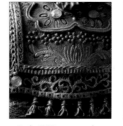 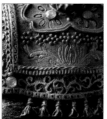 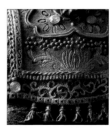

▶ **RIGHT** Basic JPEG files produce the smallest files. Fine compression gives the best JPEG image. Normal files are a good compromise.

| **Basic JPEG compression** | **Fine JPEG compression** | **Normal JPEG compression** |

IMAGE-RECORDING QUALITY

This table shows image settings, resultant file and print sizes (at 240ppi) and the number of images that can be stored on a 500MB card for a typical 8MP camera.

Image-recording quality	File format	File size in pixels and MB	Print size	No. of shots
Large/Fine	JPEG	3,504 x 2,336 (3.6MB)	A3 or larger	132
Large/Normal	JPEG	3,504 x 2,336 (1.8MB)	A3 or larger	266
Medium/Fine	JPEG	2,544 x 1,696 (2.2MB)	A5 > A4	224
Medium/Normal	JPEG	2,544 x 1,696 (1.1MB)	A5 > A4	442
Small/Fine	JPEG	1,728 x 1,152 (1.2MB)	A5 or smaller	390
Small/Normal	JPEG	1,728 x 1,152 (0.6MB)	A5 or smaller	760
RAW	RAW	3,504 x 2,336 (8.7MB)	A3 or larger	54

RAW + JPEG

Some cameras, particularly the higher-end models, provide a RAW and JPEG setting, usually called 'RAW + JPEG'. When using this setting, the camera will produce two files for every image captured – a RAW file, which is the unprocessed data recorded by the camera's sensor, and which can be saved on to a computer for further editing, and also a JPEG image that can be sent directly to a printer.

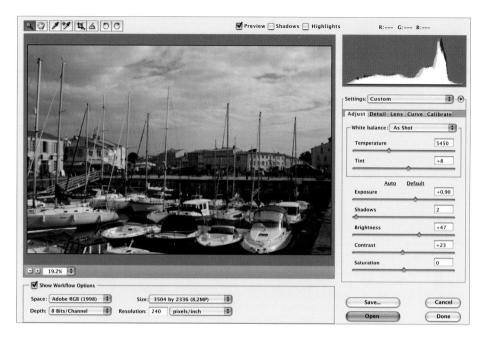

Processing

When images are saved as JPEGs, they will usually be adjusted by the camera's internal processors before being saved to the memory card. The specific processes and the level at which they're applied will depend on the camera and the settings you choose, but colours may be boosted, contrast and brightness levels adjusted, and the image may be sharpened. The idea behind these internal processes is that they help to ensure that any images stored on the memory card can be printed without further digital editing work on a computer. Most cameras will allow you to adjust the level of processing, but it's important to try out the various settings.

TIFF

The TIFF format (.TIF/.tif) is rarely available on digital cameras, but it's an important format as it is the industry standard. Most photographs that are published in books and magazines are saved as TIFF files, and almost all image-editing software allows you to save files as TIFFs. The reason TIFF is an important format is that no information is lost when the image is saved (unlike JPEGs). In other words, it is a 'lossless' file format. As a result, TIFFs are capable of producing higher-quality prints, but file sizes tend to remain large and so use up more storage space.

RAW

The third commonly used format is RAW; the file extension differs depending on the manufacturer. Canon use the file extension '.CR2'; other manufacturers will have their own extension names. RAW files comprise the unprocessed data exactly as recorded by the camera's sensor at the time of shooting. The benefit of RAW is that it can record up to 14-bit colour (compared with JPEG's 8-bit), which translates into billions of colours (compared with JPEG's 16.7 million). Having all this additional information gives you far greater control over adjustments to colour, contrast, brightness, tone and so on when you edit your images using image-editing software. Furthermore, the fact that RAW images are not compressed in-camera like JPEGs means that you can use your computer's powerful processor to make adjustments rather than relying on the camera's smaller processor. The drawback is that RAW images cannot be printed directly from the camera or card.

Memory cards

All cameras have memory cards. These come in a variety of shapes and sizes depending on the make and model, but all have storage space measured in gigabytes (GB). If you're buying a digital camera for the first time, it's probably wise to invest in a memory card that is capable of storing more images than the one that will have been provided with the camera, so you're less likely to run out of storage space before having to download the images.

Camera Phones and Compact Cameras

Imaging sensors have come a long way in the last few years. At around the year 2000, few digital cameras boasted sensors with more than a million pixels, whereas in the space of 10–15 years, mobile phones with 10MP cameras became commonplace, and many of today's compact cameras feature 14MP sensors or more.

Camera phones

From a purely photographic point of view, camera phones have some major disadvantages. The lenses are usually wide angle and fixed-focus, so they're designed to capture a broad view and ensure as much of the scene as possible is in focus. Although this helps you get sharp images, there's very little creative control. Although with the more recent phones it's possible to 'zoom' in to frame images, this generally means enlarging the image (known as 'digital' zoom) rather than employing a true optical zoom. In addition, the sensors in a camera phone have to be very small, leading to 'noisy' images.

Setting these disadvantages to one side, however, a camera phone's portability, ease of use, and the fact that many people carry a camera phone with them at all times, encourages the taking of pictures. And as technology advances yet further – there are camera phones with 41MP sensors and 3x optical zooms – increasingly impressive photographic results will become attainable.

Compact cameras

A step further up the photographic ladder from camera phones is the plethora of compact digital cameras currently on the market. These vary from the inexpensive, 'entry-level' models to the feature-packed, high-specification and relatively expensive 'super' compacts. Basic compacts usually have a simple 3x optical zoom and are unlikely to have a separate viewfinder or a manual focus setting. They provide a few standard shooting modes, such

as 'sport', 'landscape' and 'portrait'. However, even in the hands of someone with little photographic experience, most basic 'point-and-shoot' cameras can produce good-quality holiday snaps up to large postcard size.

At the other end of the spectrum, there are compacts that feature large 20MP sensors, 15x optical zoom, a vast array of shooting modes, manual override, continuous shooting, image stabilization, and so on. In the right hands, and with favourable conditions, these super compacts are capable of producing photographs that are comparable to those of many digital SLRs.

Noise, dynamic range and response time

There are, however, some definite drawbacks to most compact cameras. The first is the perennial problem of noise. There's no getting away from the fact that, in many conditions and particularly when light is low, noise will be more apparent in images created by small sensors with small photosites, as found on the great majority of compact cameras.

The second issue with smaller sensors is their narrow dynamic range – their ability to record detail in areas of shadow or highlight. Compared with larger sensors, small sensors will tend to make more shadow areas black, and more highlight areas white.

The final drawback can be most noticeable to photographers moving from film to digital compacts. The first thing many people notice is the time it takes for the digital compact camera to actually take the picture once the shutter button has been pressed. Known as 'shutter lag', the delay is caused by the camera focusing, setting the correct exposure,

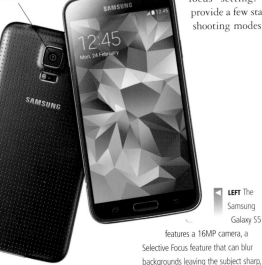

camera lens

LEFT The Samsung Galaxy S5 features a 16MP camera, a Selective Focus feature that can blur backgrounds leaving the subject sharp, and responsive phase detection autofocus.

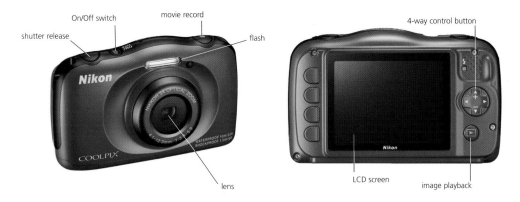

On/Off switch

movie record

shutter release

flash

4-way control button

Nikon

WATERPROOF 10M/33ft
SHOCKPROOF 1.5m/5ft

COOLPIX

lens

LCD screen

image playback

▲ **ABOVE** An entry-level compact, Nikon's S33 is a 13MP waterproof and shockproof camera ideal for family holidays.

and then 'charging' the sensor in preparation for capturing the image. In some entry-level compacts this can take up to 0.5 seconds – often long enough to miss a great shot, especially if it is a person's expression or pose.

Convenience

On the other hand, many of the more advanced compacts exhibit very little lag, produce good-quality A4 or even larger prints and provide the more experienced photographer with

▼ **BELOW** The Fujifilm XQ2, despite its compact size, features a large CMOS sensor similar to those found in many dSLRs. It's an ideal 'walkaround' camera for enthusiasts.

sufficient manual control for more creative images. In addition, many compact cameras are able to shoot bursts of relatively high-quality video with sound. These features, combined with their relatively low cost and the fact that most people want to pop a camera in their pocket rather than carry a bagful of equipment, are the

reasons why more compacts are sold than any other type of digital camera.

Before choosing a model, think about your photographic needs. A digital SLR is overkill for fun, quick holiday snaps and may attract unwanted attention; an entry-level compact, on the other hand, is unlikely to provide stunning A3 landscapes.

Zoom lenses

A compact camera's zoom lens is usually described as being 3x, 5x or 10x. For a 5x zoom, this means an object will appear five times larger when the lens is set at its maximum setting than when it appears at its widest setting. Digital SLR zoom lenses are described using focal length – from a wide-angle setting (e.g. 35mm) to a telephoto setting (e.g. 105mm). You may also see an impressive-looking 'digital zoom' figure, but since the zoom is artificially created by the camera's software, it's best to ignore this as, in general, the more digital zoom you use, the more you degrade the final image.

shooting mode dial

shutter release

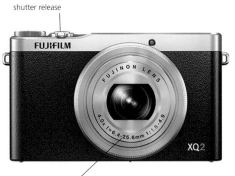

FUJIFILM

FUJINON LENS

4.0x f=6.4-25.6mm 1:1.8-4.9

XQ2

focal length

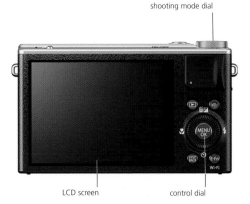

MENU OK

Wi-Fi

LCD screen

control dial

Bridge, Digital SLR and Mirrorless Cameras

Bridge cameras

Bridge, hybrid or 'prosumer' cameras, as they are also known, resemble dSLRs in several respects. So called because they 'bridge' the wide gap between compacts and dSLRs, bridge cameras are much larger than compacts and, in terms of shape, they can easily be mistaken for a dSLR.

Fixed lens

One of the key differences between bridge cameras and dSLRs is that the lens on a bridge camera is fixed, and so is not interchangeable. For this reason, most bridge cameras have powerful zoom lenses ranging from 10x (25–250mm equivalent) to 60x (24–1440mm) so that most shooting opportunities are catered for, from wide-angle landscapes to close-up sport or nature photography.

Manual control

Like dSLRs bridge cameras offer a good level of manual control, from manual focusing to complete manual exposure. This provides greater creativity and encourages experimentation. In addition, bridge cameras

▼ **BELOW** Nikon's P610 'megazoom' has an incredible 60x optical zoom lens ranging from 24–1440mm.

respond almost as quickly as dSLRs and behave very much like them when in use.

Electronic viewfinders

Unlike dSLRs, all bridge cameras have electronic viewfinders (EVFs). These relay exactly what the camera's lens is focusing on and framing – in fact, EVFs display exactly the same view as that shown by the camera's rear liquid crystal display (LCD). In this way, EVFs behave more like a dSLR's viewfinder, except that there is a slight delay as the image is digitized and relayed to the viewfinder.

In terms of sensor size, bridge cameras are usually fitted with similar-sized sensors to those found in the higher spec compacts, so are capable of producing good-quality images in most bright conditions, but will struggle in low light.

Digital Single Lens Reflex

The key differences between dSLRs and other types of digital camera are the ability to change lenses, bright, 'instant' viewfinders, large sensors and negligible shutter lag.

Lenses

Being able to use lenses of different focal lengths, such as 10–20mm wide-angle zooms, 100–300mm telephoto zooms or even fixed length lenses such as a 60mm macro lens, allows you to use the same camera body for extreme wide-angle landscape or interior shots, and for close-up action sports or nature photography. Lenses vary enormously in quality and price, and owning a dSLR body allows you to build up a selection of good-quality lenses that will resolve more detail than the 'mega-zoom' lenses that are trying to cover both wide angle and telephoto.

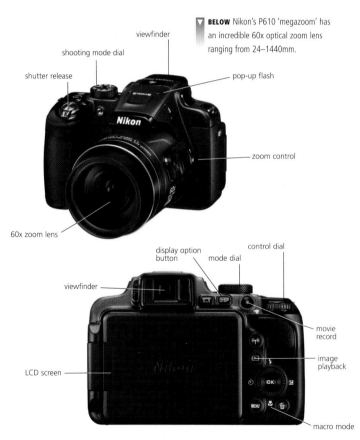

viewfinder
shooting mode dial
shutter release
pop-up flash
zoom control
60x zoom lens
display option button
control dial
mode dial
viewfinder
movie record
image playback
LCD screen
macro mode

Instant viewfinders

All dSLRs have instant and bright viewfinders. This is because the light from the scene passes through the lens via a mirror set at 45° and then through a prism and out through the viewfinder. Thanks to this configuration of mirrors and prisms, the viewer is seeing exactly what the sensor will be exposed to when the mirror flaps up as the shutter release button is depressed to take the photo. This allows for more accurate framing and easier composition, particularly in poor light, when electronic viewfinders have trouble relaying a dark scene and also suffer from a slight lag.

Sensor size and shutter lag

At the risk of labouring the point, the large sensors used in all dSLRs provide almost noise-free images up to ISO settings of 800 or even 1600. Even at ultra-high ISO settings such as 25000, when viewed at normal viewing distances, noise is often difficult to detect. Having the option to use a much wider range of ISO settings allows the photographer to try a greater variety of exposure settings and experiment with depth of field (see pages 168–175) and other creative techniques. Also, dSLRs do not suffer from noticeable shutter lag, making it easier to catch fast-moving action.

The combination of high-quality (albeit expensive) lenses with large sensors results in extremely high-quality images. If you want the best possible images and intend to photograph a variety of subjects in various shooting conditions, a dSLR with a selection of lenses is far and away the best option.

REFLEX VIEW

The term 'SLR' stands for 'single lens reflex' and refers to the camera's viewfinder system of a mirror and prism that allows you to look through the lens to compose your photographs. Essentially, this means that what you see in the viewfinder is what you get in the final picture.

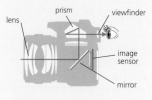

Light (red) passing through a dSLR

Mirrorless

Mirrorless interchangeable lens cameras (MILCs) are the most recent class of digital camera to hit the market. As their name suggests, these cameras lack the reflex mirror of a standard dSLR and are therefore much lighter and smaller. However, despite their compact size, mirrorless cameras can be fitted with different compatible lenses, from wide-angle to telephoto, offering almost the same versatility of a dSLR.

One distinct advantage of mirrorless cameras over most bridge and compact models is that they feature larger sensors, thereby gaining all the benefits in image quality associated with big sensors. In fact, most mirrorless cameras feature sensors of comparable size to many dSLRs. The larger the sensor, the more expensive the camera. It's this winning combination of portability, versatility and excellent image quality that have made mirrorless cameras the largest growing camera class. However, one draw back to mirrorless cameras is that they lack the bright optical viewfinder found in all dSLRs, instead relying on an EVF or just a rear LCD screen with which to compose images.

RIGHT AND BELOW With its large sensor and interchangeable lenses, a dSLR is the best option if you want to take high-quality photographs of a wide range of subjects in a wide range of conditions.

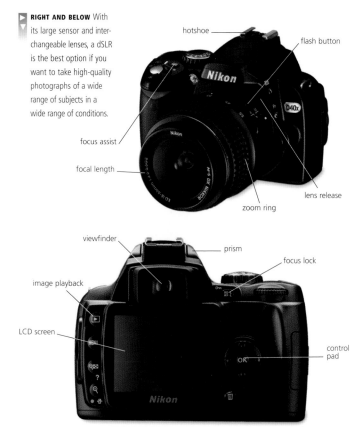

Camera Lenses and Digital Cameras

Since the advent of digital cameras, manufacturers – and to a certain degree, camera magazines and websites – have been preoccupied with the performance of the cameras' internal components, especially the sensors and pixel count. Anyone new to digital photography could be forgiven for thinking that picture quality was ultimately down to the number of pixels crammed on to the imaging chip. In many ways this is unsurprising given the relative novelty of the technology and the amount of money spent on research and development in that specific area of digital imaging.

However, more experienced photographers are aware that the obsession with pixel count is something of a red herring. While sensors are a big piece of a camera's jigsaw puzzle – they are the part of the camera that records the image, and it's vital that they can record as wide a dynamic range as smoothly as possible – many would argue that the lens that gathers the light information in the first place is equally as important, if not more so.

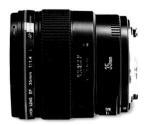

ABOVE This fixed 35mm lens would be a wide-angle lens in a 35mm film camera or 'full frame sensor' dSLR. However, because sensors are smaller in most dSLRs the effective focal length is around 50mm.

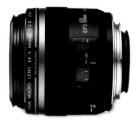

ABOVE Macro lenses have the ability to focus extremely close to objects and so provide a greatly magnified image. True macro lenses have a ratio of 1:1 (1:1 will be printed on the lens barrel).

Lens technology

Although it would be difficult to argue that lenses have undergone a similar revolution to camera bodies, huge amounts of money have been spent on developing lens technology. At the turn of the century, if you said you could produce a lens that covered a zoom range of 28–300mm, weighed less than 1.1lb (500g), produced acceptable results throughout its focal length range and had the ability to

focus within 1.6ft (0.5m) to boot, no one would have taken you seriously – yet such lenses now exist.

Modern lenses are lighter, sharper, focus faster and are less prone to flare than ever before. Throw in the fact that many now have image stabilization (or vibration reduction) systems that allow you to hand hold a camera using shutter speeds as low as $^1/15$ sec and still obtain sharp images, and it would be fair to say

Aperture range

A lens's maximum aperture is usually printed either on the barrel or the front of the lens. For example, a lens with a maximum aperture of f/2.8 will feature the figures 1:2.8. For zoom lenses, an aperture range is often provided, such as 1:4–5.6. This indicates that at the shorter focal length, such as 70mm for example, the aperture will open up to f/4, while at the longer focal length of the zoom, such as 300mm, the maximum aperture is reduced to f/5.6. These figures are important as they

indicate how 'fast' the lens is – the wider the possible aperture, the faster the lens. In other words, given the same lighting conditions a lens with a maximum aperture of f/2.8 will allow faster shutter speeds to be used, while still obtaining a correct exposure, than a 'slower' f/4 lens. The faster the lens the greater the creative control the photographer has, as it allows for a greater number of shutter/aperture exposure combinations, in turn resulting in greater control over depth of field and the shutter speed (see pages 158–159).

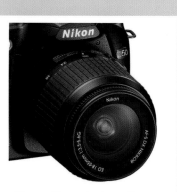

ABOVE This zoom lens has a wide aperture setting ranging from f/3.5 to f/6.5.

that photographers have never had it so good. Inevitably however, such technology does come at a price. There are lenses on the market today that cost the combined equivalent of a decent compact camera, printer, computer and all the software that is needed to edit images.

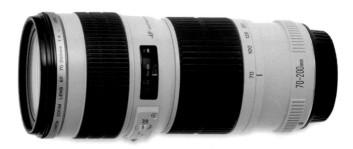

▶ **RIGHT** There are numerous types of zoom lens available for dSLRs. This 70–200mm zoom lens from Canon has the ability to zoom 3x.

OPTICAL LENS ELEMENTS

All lenses, whether interchangeable SLR lenses or those fixed to compact or hybrid cameras, are made up of a series of individual lenses known as 'elements'. Elements are one of either two types – diverging or converging. Both types of element exploit the fact that as light passes through glass (or clear plastic) with non-parallel sides, it will change direction. In a converging lens, the light will bend more at the thinner (top and bottom) parts of the lens than it does toward the thicker centre. This way the image converges to a point (known as the focal point) at some distance from the lens, and, if left, will continue to form an upside down image on any surface, such as an imaging sensor.

However, because of the optical aberrations that result from a single converging lens, a camera's lens employs a series of diverging and converging elements to try and correct these aberrations as far as possible. Other elements are also used to alter the focal length of a lens.

The number and exact shape of the elements in a camera lens, together with the space between each element and the type of glass or plastic used in their manufacture, are determined by the lens designer, who will use a computer to ensure that all the measurements are as precise as possible. The glass components are ground and polished and any plastic elements moulded to

extremely fine tolerances before being coated with anti-reflective materials. They are then assembled in the lens barrel together with the iris diaphragm (which controls the aperture), all of which are then optically aligned.

The overall construction must allow the optical elements to move in a controlled way so that the lens can focus accurately and consistently and, if necessary, allow a change in focal length in the case of zoom lenses. When you consider the fine tolerances and precise engineering used to create a lens and take into account that it must be strong enough to withstand minor knocks, it's not surprising that it can cost a great deal of money.

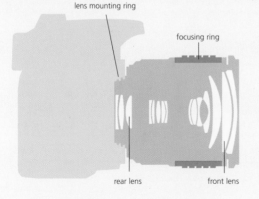

Typical lens array for a standard SLR lens

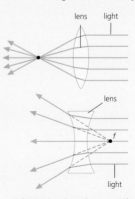

Light passing through a convex lens (top) and concave lens (bottom)

Choosing Lenses

The quality of any camera's lens will ultimately affect the overall image quality, yet all too often we overlook one of the most important elements of a camera system.

Compact and hybrid cameras

If you're looking to buy a compact or bridge camera, or intending to upgrade your existing one, make sure you find out as much as you can about the quality of the lens. Many such cameras come fitted with 'superzooms', offering as much as 60x magnification (equivalent focal length 20–1200mm). This is a big zoom, and the lens is unlikely to perform equally as well throughout the range. If you can, find out at what focal lengths the lens performs best, and see if that fits in with your photographic interests. If sports photography is your passion and you need to get close to the action, make sure the lens performs well at longer focal lengths. By contrast, if you're more interested in landscapes, you should ensure that the shorter focal length settings are its strong point.

▼ **BELOW** A diagram to show how moving the position of the same three lens elements can modify the path of light through a zoom lens.

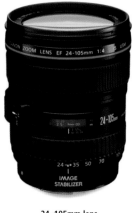

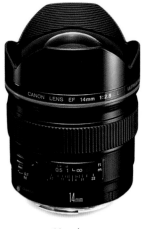

24–105mm lens

14mm lens

Alternatively, consider whether you need such a long zoom in the first place. Tempting as the figures are, a 3x (28–85mm) or 5x (28–140mm) lens may be perfectly adequate for your needs, in which case you may find a camera that, although featuring a lens with a smaller range, has superior quality glass and performance. As always, before spending large amounts of money on camera equipment, do as much research as you can. There are plenty of excellent magazines and websites that exist offering unbiased advice.

dSLRs

For those of you who have made the leap to a dSLR, the issue of lenses is much more complicated – and, unfortunately, more expensive. One of the great advantages of a dSLR is that the lenses are interchangeable and usually provide excellent image quality. On the one hand, this is a good thing, as it allows access to a vast variety of lenses, with focal lengths ranging from around 10mm to 500mm (even 1200mm lenses are available). The downside is that the choice (and prices) can be bewildering.

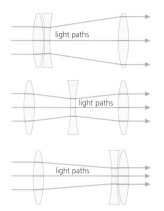

Zoom: digital versus optical

Some digital cameras boast an optical as well as a digital zoom, and the figures are often combined to make the camera's overall zoom capability sound very impressive. However, be cautious, as there is a distinct difference between an optical and digital zoom. When you use the optical zoom, the lens actually magnifies the image that is captured by the sensor;

so as long as the lens performs well the image will be well defined. Digital zoom works by zooming in on the actual pixels already captured by the camera. So, although you're still magnifying the image, the camera is only magnifying the size of the pixels, which will usually lead to a fuzzy, degraded image. Avoid using digital zoom if you can.

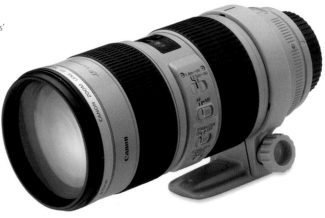

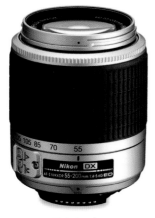

55–200mm lens

Zoom versus prime

One of the big questions for SLR owners used to be whether to buy zoom or 'prime' lenses (lenses with a fixed focal length). While zooms offered much greater flexibility, primes were far superior in terms of image quality. However, the general improvement in lens technology, construction and components in recent years has seen a great leap in the image quality offered by zoom lenses, to the point where their convenience outweighs issues of quality.

The one area in which primes do still outclass zooms is their speed. Prime lenses are typically much faster (have a wider maximum aperture) than zooms, and so offer greater creative control. On the whole, however, improved high ISO performance and image stabilization do mean that you get better value for your money with zooms than a series of primes. With two good-quality zoom lenses covering, say, 24–70mm and 70mm–300mm equivalent focal lengths (efl), you'll have most photographic situations covered from wide-angle landscapes to telephoto sports.

Upgrading

With camera technology seeming to move so fast these days, it's tempting to save up and upgrade your camera as soon as the latest version becomes available. But before doing so, take a long look at the supposed benefits. They may be an additional megapixel or two (which doesn't translate to much), or more program settings (which you may never use), in which case, consider investing the money in a new lens instead. Perhaps you could increase the focal range of your system by buying a really wide-angle

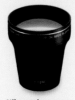

ABOVE The professional quality lens features image stabilization to help reduce camera shake. Tiny gyros in the lens are able to sense movement and move one of the lens elements to counter it.

lens. A wide-angle lens (such as efl 15–20mm) opens up all sorts of new compositional opportunities.

Alternatively, if you're happy with your range of focal lengths, trade in an existing lens and buy a higher-quality version – you'll notice a bigger improvement in image quality than with a slightly modified camera.

TELECONVERTERS

One way to add focal length to an existing lens is to fit a teleconverter. These effectively increase the focal length of the lens to which they're attached. Teleconverters are available for some makes of compact camera and screw on to the end of the lens, while others are designed for interchangeable lenses and sit between the dSLR body and the lens. The amount of magnification provided by a teleconverter depends on the specific type, but generally they provide a magnification of between 1.4x and 3x. These optical devices can be a less expensive way of increasing focal length, but can slow down the camera's autofocus system and reduce the maximum aperture setting of the lens.

Canon teleconverter

Nikon teleconverter

Shooting Video with a Digital SLR

Today, shooting HD video with a dSLR is now widspread. Entire TV shows are now recorded using dSLRs. When coupled with good-quality, fast lenses, these cameras, thanks primarily to their large sensors, provide video comparable to much more expensive, bulkier, dedicated professional video cameras.

Settings

In many respects shooting video on your dSLR is as simple as selecting the video mode and pressing the start button. However, depending on your particular make and model of camera, there are a few things to consider that will improve the quality of your movie footage.

PAL vs NTSC

You may find lurking in your menus the option of choosing between PAL and NTSC. These are alternative television transmission standards. PAL (625 vertical lines) is the standard used in Europe and Asia, while NTSC (525 lines) is used in the Americas. Modern computer monitors will display both perfectly happily and you're unlikely to tell the difference, but if you're intending to eventually burn your movie to DVD to watch on TV, choose the appropriate standard.

Frame rate

Depending on which standard you use, and also what options are available to you with your specific camera, you may be given a choice of frame rates (measured in frames per second) – usually 25fps/50fps for PAL, and 30fps/60fps for NTSC. You may also see a 24fps option. In Europe the 25fps setting is the best all-round setting. Use 50fps (60fps in NTSC) for fast-moving action or if you want to create a slow-motion

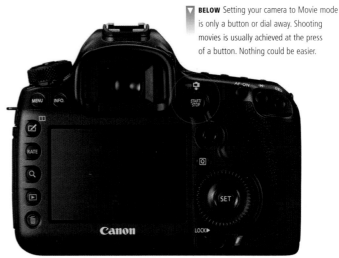

BELOW Setting your camera to Movie mode is only a button or dial away. Shooting movies is usually achieved at the press of a button. Nothing could be easier.

sequence. The 24fps setting is inended to replicate the frame rate of cinema cameras for a 'filmic' look. It's barely perceptible, but try it for yourself. You may find that action shots looks 'choppy' with this rate.

Resolution

It's likely that you'll have a choice of resolution in Movie mode, as you do in normal shooting. The common options are 1080, 720 and VGA. When shooting normal video, it's best to shoot at the highest resolution as you can always downsize later, but you can't interpolate up. However, if you want to shoot at a faster frame rate to capture fast-moving action or for slow motion, you may have to shoot at the lower 720 resolution.

Shutter speed

You may not have the option of adjusting your shutter speed when in Movie mode. If so, your camera will probably automatically set the shutter speed so that the reciprocal is twice the frame rate – in other words with a frame rate of 24fps or 25fps the camera will set a shutter speed of

Movie rec. size
1920x1080   30fps   60:00
Low comp (ALL–I)

1920 30 ALL-I   1280 60 ALL-I
1920 30 IPB   1280 60 IPB
1920 24 ALL-I   640 30 IPB
1920 24 IPB

LEFT Your dSLR will have various video settings to choose from. Familiarize yourself with these settings so that you know how to get the optimum movie quality for your needs.

1/50th sec. This will always provide the best results, so if you do have the option to adjust the shutter speed, try not to stray too far from this rule of thumb. If you do, you'll probably find your video has a strange stroboscopic look to it. The exception to the rule comes when you want to shoot a sequence for slow motion. Use the fastest available frame rate and experiment with shutter speeds of around 1/2,000th sec.

Exposure

As with shutter speed, you may find that your camera will automatically adjust exposure as the lighting conditions change. This makes life easier because you don't have to think about making any manual adjustments. However, some cameras do offer manual control, in which case adjusting the aperture, changing ISO, and using exposure compensation will all affect the brightness of the image.

Shooting tips

When it comes to shooting your video, it's simply a case of selecting Movie mode and pushing the Start/Stop button. Few dSLRs will use continuous autofocus when in Movie mode, so a good tip is to prefocus on your subject before shooting, and avoid using the autofocus mode when filming as the sound of the lens focusing will be picked up by the camera's

▶ **RIGHT** Once you start taking your movie-making seriously, you can buy all manner of accessories for your camera. This device is called a Steadicam and is made in England by SmoothShot. It features weights at the bottom to counterbalance the camera, thus keeping your movements as smooth as possible.

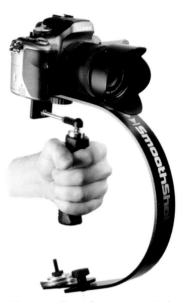

microphone. Additionally, the focus may jump unexpectedly.

When you set the camera in Movie mode, the viewfinder will go black and the LCD screen will become active (as in LiveView mode). You will need to use the LCD screen to shoot all your video.

Controlling depth of field

One of the best things about shooting movies with a dSLR is that you can film with a narrow depth of field. Controlling depth of field when shooting a video is exactly the same as when photographing stills, and it creates the cinematic look that is so popular. Use a tripod to keep the camera steady and set up your shot so that your subject sits in front of a pleasingly out-of-focus background. You can even try adjusting the focus so that the subject becomes blurred and the background comes into focus, but you need to be careful not to jar the camera.

Stability

Keeping the camera as still as possible is the first rule of movie making.

Viewers will quickly grow tired of shuddering images as the camera moves about. As you hone your skills, by all means start experimenting with moving the camera, and there are a number of handheld devices on the market that will help you to keep camera movements smooth.

Sound

Finally, a quick word about sound. Don't expect to be able to capture high-quality sound recordings with your camera's built-in microphone. Even professional film-makers add a sound track seperately to the moving images. If you won't take your movie-making to the next level, invest in a dedicated external mircophone that will cancel background noise and provide a cleaner sound track. These can be attached to the camera using the hotshoe connection, with the sound being recorded via a cable that plugs into a socket on the side of the camera.

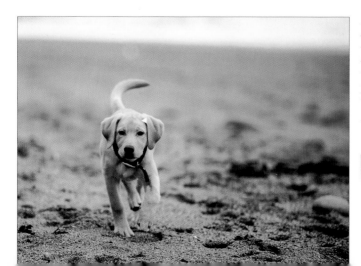

◀ **LEFT** Shooting video with a wide aperture, f/2.8 or f/4, creates a narrow depth of field just as in still photography. This gives your movie a professional cinematic look, but can make it difficult to keep subjects in focus.

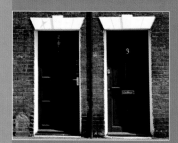

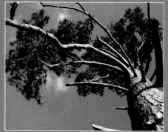

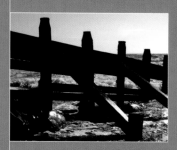

3

Basic Shooting and Composition

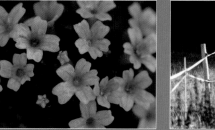 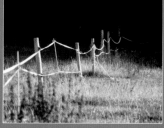 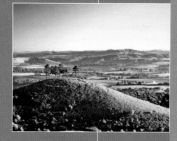

Having learned about the anatomy of an image, and the location of the main controls on your camera, it really pays to gain a good understanding of what these controls do to make the most of your photographic equipment. It may be tempting to leave the camera on fully automatic, but if you spend some time experimenting with the settings, you'll quickly see an improvement in the quality of your images. In this chapter, you'll find some basic tips and hints on composition – these are intended to act as pointers to help you start to think in visual terms and to find your own unique style.

Holding a Camera

Whether you own a small compact or are shooting with an SLR fitted with a long telephoto lens, holding and supporting the camera properly will help to prevent camera shake.

Ultra compacts

Many 'ultra' compact-style digital cameras offer an LCD screen on the back of the camera to help you compose pictures. However, to use the screen, the camera has to be held away from the body, which can contribute to camera shake. In addition, many 'ultra' compacts are often smaller than the palm of your hand. People with larger hands sometimes hold the camera with the very tips of their fingers to avoid covering the lens. Although understandable, this can lead to camera shake as well.

Compacts

For compacts with a viewfinder, it's recommended that you use the viewfinder wherever possible. This will conserve power, help you keep the camera steady, and, in bright, sunny conditions, you will have a better chance of seeing the subject. The only time you really need to use the screen to compose a shot is when taking a close-up, as the offset viewfinder shows a somewhat different view to the one the lens is actually 'seeing'. This can lead to the subject being photographed slightly off-centre.

SLR and bridge cameras

For those not used to an SLR, its size and weight may come as a surprise. However, it's these aspects of dSLRs that make them stable and easier to hold steadily.

Many bridge cameras have a similar layout, with a long lens centred in the camera body, so much of the advice for holding a dSLR applies to bridge cameras. However, many such cameras are slightly smaller and lighter than a true dSLR.

Shutter release

Whatever type of camera you're using, avoid 'stabbing' the shutter release button. Instead, gently squeeze the shutter release button until the camera takes the photo.

Tripods

For all those times when you need some form of camera support but have no tripod with you there are many products available that are small enough to keep in your camera bag or car that will still do a good job of providing steady support. Miniature tripods are strong and portable, and will sit on a table or chair. A bean bag support is mouldable so can hold your camera steady on a non-flat surface. Bean bags work well as they can take even a heavy camera and lens combination with minimal balancing.

Just before you capture the image, it also helps if you breathe in slightly and hold your breath. This will stop your chest moving up and down, which can potentially cause the camera to move or shake just as you're taking the shot. Even this kind of slight movement can result in a blurred or out-of-focus photograph.

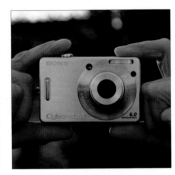

▲ **ABOVE** Some ultra compact cameras don't have viewfinders and are very narrow and small. The best way to support such cameras is with both thumbs resting on the base of the camera, and both index fingers on the top.

▲ **ABOVE** To keep the camera steady, use most of both fingers and thumbs, not just the tips. Also note how the remaining fingers are folded into the palms to avoid getting in the way of the camera's lens or flash unit.

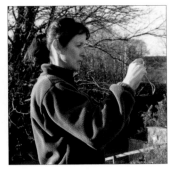

▲ **ABOVE** If you're using a compact without a viewfinder, avoid holding the camera with both arms outstretched, as this increases the risk of camera shake. For a more stable position, tuck your elbows into your body.

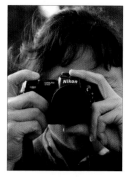

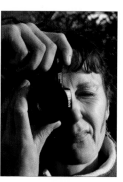

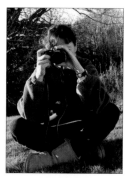

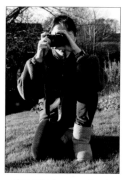

| Landscape grip | Portrait grip | Lower-angle grip | Alternative lower-angle grip |

▲ **ABOVE** Viewfinder compacts are bulkier than ultra compacts, allowing you to grip the camera with all the fingers of the right hand. Keep the fingers of the left hand clear to avoid them wandering in front of the lens.

▲ **ABOVE** When turning the camera 90° to take a portrait shot, grip the top of the camera with the right hand, which will also be used to press the shutter release button. Support the bottom of the camera with the left hand.

▲ **ABOVE** When taking a shot from a lower angle, don't just crouch down, or you'll run a high risk of camera shake. If the ground is dry, sit down cross-legged and rest the part of your arm just above the elbows on your knees.

▲ **ABOVE** If the ground is too wet to sit on, kneel on one knee and rest your arm on your knee. Don't rest your elbow directly on your knee as you'll end up with bone contacting bone which is likely to cause camera shake.

Digital SLR lenses

The lens of a dSLR plays a key role in how you handle the camera. The left-hand base of the camera should rest against the fleshy part of the left palm beneath the thumb. Wrap one, two or three fingers of the left hand around the barrel of the lens, depending on its length and how comfortable you feel, to support the camera/lens, manipulate the focus and, if using a zoom lens, the zoom ring. In this way you can frame, compose and focus the shot without taking your eye away from the view-finder, while your left hand makes adjustments to the camera settings.

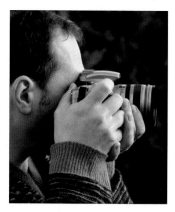

HANDLING A TELEPHOTO LENS

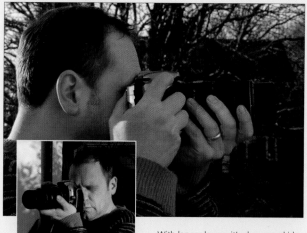

With a long telephoto zoom lens attached, the position of the hands is much the same as when using a shorter focal length. However, depending on the length of the lens, the camera may feel more balanced and stable if the entire left hand is used to support the lens, with only the right hand supporting the camera body.

With longer lenses, it's also a good idea to support yourself against a wall, or try kneeling or even lying on the ground to give yourself a little extra stability. This is especially important when using long focal length lenses. As well as holding the camera safely and steadily, it's also important to ensure that you use an appropriate shutter speed for the focal length of the lens, as this will also help you avoid camera shake.

Using a Tripod

A tripod should be an essential part of your equipment. It will enable you to be far more creative than you can be with hand-held shots.

There are many different types of tripod, ranging from very small to very large and heavy studio tripods, and many in between, some fairly cheap and some made out of incredible materials that give a very light yet strong piece of kit.

On top of the tripod is the head where the camera is attached. Again, there are many different types of heads for various uses, including pan and tilt, ball and geared, those with a quick release mount that allow you to attach and detach your camera quickly, and those without.

A tripod can be used in many situations. With the legs extended and steady, and the camera mounted on to the head, it allows you to have the camera in the landscape (horizontal) position and also the portrait (vertical) position, and anything in between. With a tripod, the camera can be very low to the ground or very high, and at all times completely steady. For best results use a shutter release cable and, if your camera lets you, the mirror lock up.

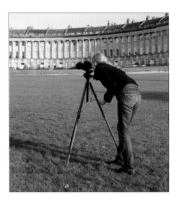

ABOVE With the camera on a tripod you can now concentrate on getting the perfect composition for your shot.

Long exposures

With your camera on the tripod your exposures (shutter speeds) can be as long as you desire, because the tripod will hold the camera completely steady. This is important for many types of shot.

When shooting a landscape, a long exposure allows you to have a very small aperture (small apertures often mean long shutter speeds) and so a very large depth of field to get everything, from the foreground to the far background, in focus.

If you are shooting in low light, perhaps at dusk, you may well need a long shutter speed to get correct exposure while still using a slow film or ISO setting.

You can shoot at night with long shutter speeds and get trails from the car lights, or even from the stars.

If you are taking a picture in a crowded scene, you can use your long shutter speed to make the figures blur or even completely disappear – a tripod is essential for this kind of work. With the camera on the tripod you can really experiment with different shutter speed settings to get the exact effects you want.

Perfect framing

When photographing buildings, landscapes, street scenes and portraits, you may want to be quite exact about the framing of your picture. With the camera on the tripod, you can make large and then very small adjustments so that the framing of the picture is exactly as you want it to be with nothing in the edges of the picture that you don't want there. Tiny adjustments like this also allow you to get the horizon exactly right and compose with the rule of thirds if you want to.

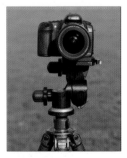

ABOVE The camera is shown level, in the horizontal position, ready for a shot.

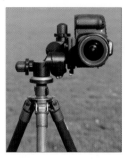

ABOVE Here the camera is rotated on the tripod head to a vertical position.

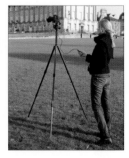

ABOVE The tripod allows the camera to be positioned high but remain stable.

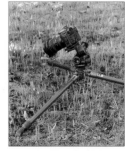

ABOVE Most tripods also allow the camera to be set steady very close to the ground.

RIGHT AND BELOW To create a simple three-frame panoramic picture you can rotate the camera on the tripod to take three separate shots, then make up the panorama as below.

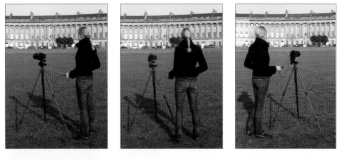

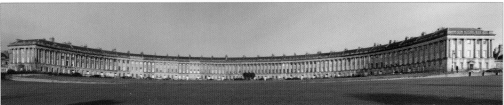

Long lenses

If you are using a long telephoto lens, or the zoom lens fully extended, or even one of the modern heavier wide-angle zoom lenses, it's sometimes quite hard to keep the camera completely steady. So to avoid a blurred picture when you are shooting with a shutter speed of even as fast as $1/125$ of a second, having the camera firmly attached to your tripod will mean getting a sharp shot every time.

BELOW When shooting close up, the tripod keeps the camera completely still. The added bonus is that you won't have to lie down on the ground to get sharply detailed shots such as this one.

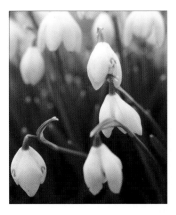

This is especially important when using a shallow depth of field in close-up photography.

Panoramas

With so much software available now offering the ability to 'stitch' together shots to make panoramas, with the camera on the tripod you can take a series of images, either horizontal or vertical, and then merge them together to create a panoramic image as wide as you want.

Simply set up the tripod and camera so that you are framing to the far side of the panorama you want to capture, take a shot, and then move the camera across to the other side in stages taking a shot each time, making sure you are overlapping the edges of each frame. Having the camera mounted on your tripod will mean that the horizon stays level in all of your shots.

Self-portraits

If you want to get yourself in the shot, with a tripod it's simple. Frame the shots as you like, set the cameras self-timer, press the shutter and then get into position in front of the camera and wait for the shutter to go off. Great for recording your travels.

You could get really creative here and mix this with a long exposure to get yourself in the shot, but moving. You could even take a series of images with yourself in different positions but the camera always steady, and then merge them together.

Whatever tripod you choose to buy, remember it needs to keep the camera steady in all situations and be portable, so choose the right combination of weight and stability.

BELOW With the camera on the tripod and the self timer set, you can take a self portrait. This might be useful for getting a sense of scale into pictures of landscape or architecture, or having a record of a trip.

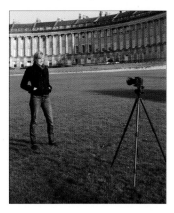

Automatic Shooting Modes

Most cameras, from an entry-level point-and-shoot compact to a professional dSLR, have a variety of auto or preset shooting modes. These modes, such as 'Portrait', 'Landscape' or 'Sports', indicate the type of image or the conditions in which the photograph is being taken and allow the camera to decide on the most appropriate settings. These differ from the semi-automatic or manual modes, which determine how much and the type of manual control the photographer has over the camera.

Common preset modes

The number and specific type of preset or automatic modes that a camera has vary depending on the make and model, but just about all will feature the modes listed below. The icons indicating the modes will also vary, so if you're unsure about which icon represents which mode, look in the camera's manual.

Auto

As the name suggests, in Auto mode everything is automatic, with the camera taking complete control of all the settings. It will set the ISO, white balance and focusing mode, then focus the lens, assess light

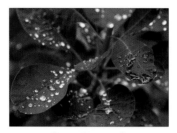

Close-up/Macro mode

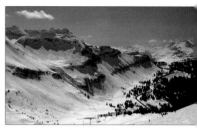

Beach/Snow mode

levels and set an appropriate exposure, plus fire the flash if necessary. This mode is often used by beginners or those unfamiliar with a new camera as it almost guarantees a correctly exposed and sharp image.

Close-up/Macro

The Close-up or Macro mode is used to take close-up pictures of small subjects such as flowers or insects. How close you can get to the subject depends on the camera and lens, but with most compacts it will be between $2/3$ –6in (2–15cm). The depth of field at this small distance is very narrow (see pages 172–173), making it difficult to keep everything in focus. This can often result in effective, creative shots where only the centre part of a flower is in focus, for example. However, if you want the entire subject to be in focus,

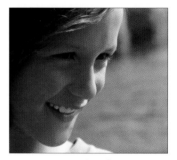

Portrait mode

you should shoot from directly above (or directly below) the subject so as much of the subject as possible is at the same distance from the lens.

Portrait

In this mode, the camera will set the largest possible aperture (smallest number) to create a narrow

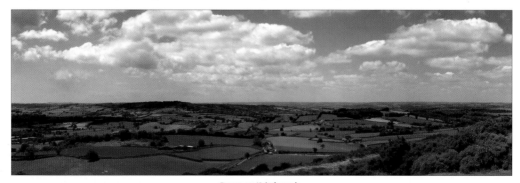

Panorama/Stitch mode

depth of field. This throws the background out of focus so that more emphasis is placed on the subject's face.

Landscape
This mode works in the opposite way to Portrait. The camera will set the smallest possible aperture (highest number) to create the widest possible depth of field. This ensures that as much of the scene – and ideally from foreground to background – is in focus.

Sports/Action
When photographing any fast-moving sport or action scene – such as football or motor racing – select the Sports (or Action) mode. In this mode, the camera will automatically select the fastest possible shutter speed (depending on the available light) in order to 'freeze' the action. You'll usually have better success if you follow, or pan, the subject through the lens for a few seconds before taking the shot. If the camera has a variety of focusing modes then it will usually select 'continuous focus' and also 'continuous shooting' if that's another option.

Night Portrait
The Night Portrait mode is designed for taking photographs of people outside during the evening or at night. The camera will set a relatively long shutter speed to ensure that the dark background is captured, while firing the flash to light and 'freeze' the subject. This is known as 'slow sync'. You should always make sure that your subject remains still – even after the flash has fired – as the camera may still be recording, albeit only for a fraction of a second.

Movie
Most recent compacts and bridge cameras have the ability to record video with sound. Although the quality of image and sound won't be as good as a dedicated video camera,

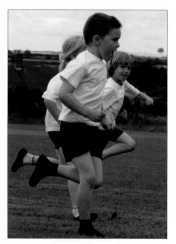
Sports/Action mode

for many people the option to record short video clips is important. Be aware, however, that recording video will use up a great deal of space on the memory card.

Other preset modes
Other common modes that appear on many digital cameras include:

Beach/Snow
Both these modes will ensure the camera accurately exposes images in conditions where you are faced with bright ambient light.

Panorama/Stitch
In this mode, after the first image of a prospective panorama is taken, the exposure and white balance

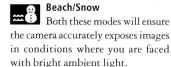
Fireworks mode

are 'locked' so that all subsequent images have the same coloration, tone and contrast. You then pan the camera to the next section of the panorama and align the next image with the previous one, of which about a third appears semi-transparent on the LCD screen.

Fireworks
Using Fireworks mode the camera will deliberately select a slow shutter speed so that the trails from fireworks are captured.

Black and White

Numerous cameras, including some dSLRs, feature a Black and White mode, which allows you to shoot black and white or sepia-toned images. You can often achieve better results using image-editing software, but if you print directly from the memory card and want black and white images this mode is essential.

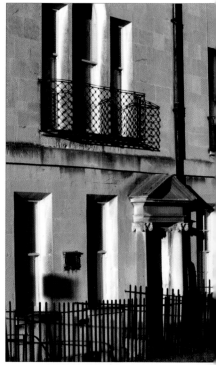
Black and White mode

Semi-automatic Shooting Modes

In addition to the main automatic shooting modes found on almost all compact cameras and most dSLRs, many other compacts and just about all dSLRs also feature a number of semi-automatic modes. These are usually Program (P), Shutter priority (S), which is also known as Time value (Tv), and Aperture priority (A), which is also known as Aperture value (Av). These modes offer lots of creativity in that you have greater control over aperture and shutter speed selection. At the same time they help you to achieve an appropriate exposure. If your camera has these modes, it will also have a Manual (M) option, which we will look at later (see Understanding Exposure on pages 158–159).

Program (P)

Depending on the make and model of your camera, the Program (P) mode will usually behave in a similar way to the full Auto mode, in that the camera selects a suitable combination of aperture and shutter speed to achieve the correct exposure. However, selecting P will also allow you to change the ISO setting, image size and quality, the metering mode and a number of other settings that are set automatically when the camera is in Auto mode. In other words, while Program allows you to tailor certain settings, you'll generally produce correctly exposed pictures.

Program shift/Flexible program

Another way in which Program differs to Auto in most cameras is that while Program mode will automatically set an initial aperture/shutter speed combination, it will also allow you to change that combination. If, for example, you want a fast shutter

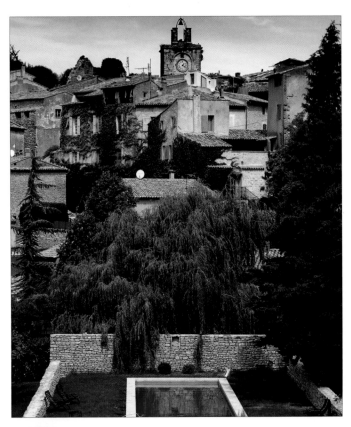

LEFT Most digital cameras, including dSLRs, support modes that are selectable either by a dial or a menu.

ABOVE With the camera in Program (P) mode, it will set an aperture/shutter speed combination that is appropriate for the amount of light available.

speed to freeze action, you can select a faster shutter speed using a control dial and the camera will automatically increase the size of the aperture (select a smaller number) so that you will still obtain a correct exposure. This is usually known as 'Program shift' or 'Flexible program'.

In a similar way, if you want to reduce the size of the aperture (select a higher number) in order to ensure that as much of the scene as possible is in focus, the camera will select a slower shutter speed to make sure that the image is still correctly exposed. With most cameras, if you select a aperture/shutter combination that will produce an under- or overexposed image, the camera is likely to provide either a visual or audible warning. Altering the ISO setting so that a correct combination of aperture and setting is made available can often be the solution to this.

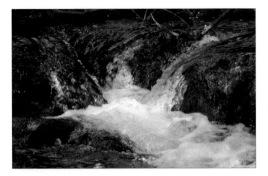

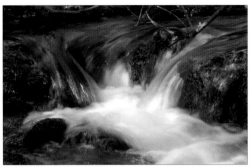

▲ **ABOVE** This image was taken in Shutter priority/Time value mode, with a fast shutter speed ($^1/_{250}$ sec) selected manually to 'freeze' the movement of the water. The camera then automatically set an appropriate aperture (f/4.5) to ensure accurate exposure.

▲ **ABOVE** This image was also taken in Shutter priority/Time value mode, with a slow shutter speed ($^1/_{6}$ sec) deliberately chosen in order to capture the blurred movement of the flowing water. Again, the camera automatically set the aperture (f/22).

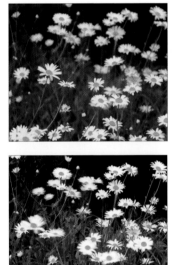

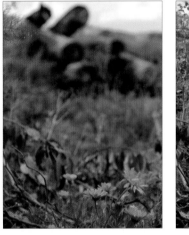

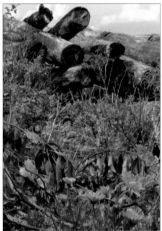

▲ **ABOVE** Both images were taken in Aperture priority/Aperture value mode. On the left, a wide aperture (f/4.0) gives a narrow depth of field and the camera automatically sets the shutter speed ($^1/_{1000}$ sec). On the right, a narrow aperture (f/22) is chosen resulting in a wide depth of field – the camera automatically set the shutter speed ($^1/_{50}$ sec).

▲ **ABOVE** Using the Program shift or Flexible program modes is a good way to begin experimenting with aperture and shutter speed combinations. In the top image, a fast shutter speed/wide aperture combination has 'frozen' the flowers, but because of the wide aperture (low number) some of the flowers are out of focus. In the lower image, the slow shutter speed/narrow aperture combination has resulted in an image that is sharply focused front to back, but the slow shutter speed has resulted in some blurry flowers as they were blown in the wind.

Shutter priority (S)/Time value (Tv)

In this mode you can set a specific shutter speed – fast to freeze action, or slow to deliberately blur people or objects. The camera will set an appropriate aperture depending on the available light. If the shutter speed is set too fast or too slow, the camera will either blink or beep to warn that the image will be incorrectly exposed, but the shutter will still fire in case the 'incorrect' exposure is deliberate. Or, you could alter the ISO to see if that produces an acceptable exposure.

Aperture priority (A)/Aperture value (Av)

This mode works in a similar way to the S/Tv mode, but the opposite way around. You can set a large aperture (small number) to throw a background out of focus, or set a small aperture (large number) to increase the depth of field (to ensure a landscape is in focus from foreground to background). The camera will automatically select an appropriate shutter speed to ensure a 'correct' exposure or warn you of an 'incorrect' exposure.

Autofocusing Modes

To make life easier for us, today's digital cameras have sophisticated autofocusing (AF) systems that help ensure our images are in focus while we can concentrate on composition or predicting someone's expression. Most AF systems in today's digital cameras are known as 'passive' autofocus and work in one of two ways.

Contrast measurement

This is the least complex AF system, which is used in entry-level compact cameras. It uses a simple sensor (as opposed to the camera's main image sensor) to detect at which point the lens produces an image with the highest level of contrasting pixels. This indicates the lens is sharply focused – an in-focus black and white stripe will have higher contrasting pixels than an out-of-focus stripe, which will appear more grey.

Phase detection

This more complex AF system is used on sophisticated compacts and most dSLRs. Known as 'phase detection', light from the scene is split into two from different parts of the lens. These parts are compared by the AF sensor, which will then direct the AF servos (tiny electrical motors) to make adjustments to the lens, depending on the similarity in light patterns between the two images.

Under most conditions both systems work well and can provide fast, accurate focus. However, if the light is poor, or the scene exhibits little contrast (such as a blue sky or a repetitive pattern), you'll hear the camera's AF system 'hunting' as it tries to find the point of focus.

To combat the first situation, the camera will automatically 'fire' a rapid succession of light beams from an

'AF assist lamp' so that the AF system can 'see'. If there is no AF assist lamp, most cameras will fire the flash. Where the scene is too uniform in tone and colour for the camera to accurately

▼ **BELOW** Many cameras feature a continuous AF system, which tracks the subject and keeps it constantly in focus. As soon as the shutter release is depressed, focus is locked and the picture taken.

▼ **BELOW** Occasionally, even continuous AF cannot keep up with the pace. Here, due to shutter lag, by the time the camera actually fired, the subject had moved too close to the camera to remain in focus.

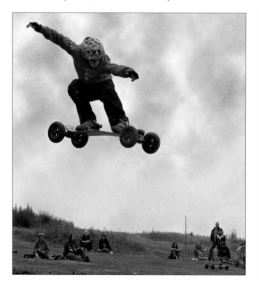

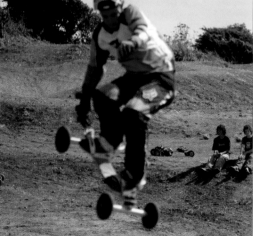

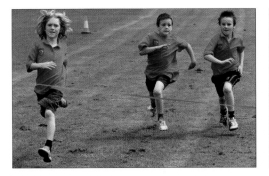

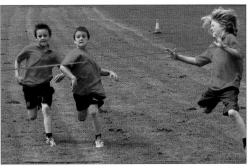

▲ **ABOVE** Advanced autofocus systems can track moving elements and predict where they will be at the exact moment the shutter fires. With 'predictive' or Artificial Intelligence focus, these racers are pin sharp.

▲ **ABOVE** Less than a second later, predictive autofocus has accurately estimated the runners' positions, counteracting the slight delay between pushing the shutter release and the camera firing.

differentiate pixels, the quickest way to resolve this is to find something the camera can focus on that is the same distance away. Otherwise, if the camera has the option to switch to manual focus you can focus the lens yourself.

Single AF versus continuous AF

Many cameras have two AF settings – single AF and continuous AF. Single AF (also known as 'one-Shot'/'single-Shot') should be used when the subject is relatively still, such as landscapes or portraits. Pressing the shutter release halfway will set the focus, and the camera will go on to take a picture if it focuses and the shutter release is fully

pressed. In continuous AF mode the camera focuses continuously, and only 'locks' on to the subject when the shutter release is pressed halfway. This makes a continuous AF mode useful for taking photos of moving subjects. The idea is to follow the subject through the viewfinder or on the rear LCD screen and the camera will try to keep it in focus until you want to take the photo. This mode is not without its problems. There is often a delay between pressing the shutter release and the camera taking the picture – and subjects in motion, by their very nature are moving – often resulting in images that will be out of focus.

Predictive AF

To combat such situations, some cameras (mostly dSLRs) incorporate a 'predictive' AF system. This mode works best when the subject is either moving toward or retreating from the camera at a constant rate. The camera's AF system will track the subject as it moves into the frame and attempt to predict where it will be at the precise moment the shutter fires. In effect, the camera is estimating the time it takes for the shutter release to be pressed and for a picture to be taken. In this way it helps to ensure the subject will remain in focus at the precise moment the exposure is made.

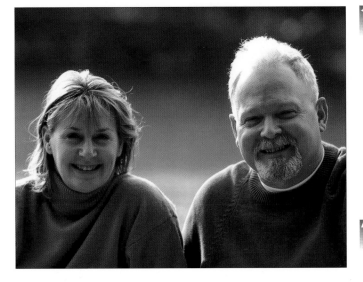

◄ **LEFT** For stationary subjects, 'single' autofocus is recommended. Depressing the shutter release halfway will lock the focus.

▲ **ABOVE** These diagrams illustrate how some cameras rely on contrast to achieve focus. The in-focus lines (left) have greater contrast than the out-of-focus lines (right).

Metering Modes

In order to produce an image that is not too bright (overexposed) or too dark (underexposed), every type of camera needs a way to assess how much light is present. Some photographers still use hand-held meters to measure the amount of light falling on to the subject. There are two main ways of taking a light reading with a hand-held meter:

• For a reflected light reading, point the meter at the subject and take a reading of the light reflected from it. (Some meters have a spot metering function that allows the reading to be taken off a very precise area.)

• For an incident light reading, place a small white disc, or invercone, over the meter cell. Some meters have a white blind which can be slid down over the cell. Hold the light meter against the subject and point it back towards the camera. This gives a more accurate reading of how much light is falling on the subject.

For most of us this is not often practical, so all modern cameras have built-in light meters that measure the light reflected from the subject or from the scene as a whole. However, because light levels can vary drastically – even within the same scene – many cameras provide a number of different ways to measure light to help you achieve the correct exposure. These are known as metering modes. There are three common metering modes, and all digital cameras will have at least one.

Centre-weighted metering

This is the most commonly used metering system in digital cameras. In this mode, the metering is biased or weighted to the centre of the viewfinder and then averaged for the entire scene. The idea is that for most shots the subject of the image will be in the centre of the frame and therefore accurately exposed, while the rest of the scene is averaged out. If there is a big difference between the lightest and darkest parts of the image (such as land and sky), then the camera will attempt to find the most appropriate setting to ensure that most of the photograph is exposed accurately.

This mode is very useful when taking portrait shots, particularly if the subject is standing in front of a light background (backlit). However, if the subject of the picture is off centre, or the background or foreground is extremely light or dark, they may well be incorrectly exposed.

Spot/partial metering

As its name suggests, spot or partial metering takes a reading only from the centre spot of the viewfinder and sets an accurate exposure for that part of the image only – no readings are taken from any other part of the scene. True spot metering measures the central 1–2 per cent of the viewfinder

RIGHT When set to centre-weighted, the camera sets an exposure that puts most emphasis on the central part of the image, but takes into account the rest of the scene. Here, the flower is slightly overexposed because of the dark leaves around it. The schematic diagram (far right) shows how centre-weighted metering assesses the scene.

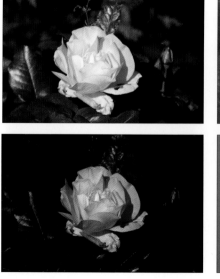

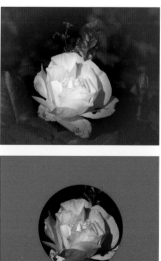

RIGHT When set to spot or partial, the camera sets an exposure appropriate only for the central part of the scene. Here, the flower is accurately exposed and the surround underexposed. The diagram (far right) shows how the metering assesses the scene.

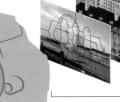

1. Individual light measurement is made in every segment of the scene to be shot.

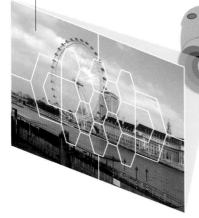

2. The camera searches a database with light measurements from 50,000 characteristic subject situations.

3. After analysis, the optimal exposure values are calculated.

LEFT Put simply, in evaluative or matrix mode, the camera assesses the scene to be photographed and compares it with a database of many thousands of 'comparative' shots to work out the optimum exposure.

area, whereas partial metering will measure around 9–10 per cent of the area. This metering mode should be used when the subject must be correctly exposed, no matter how much light is falling on the surroundings, or during close-ups. If the area used to take the light reading from does not provide the best average, the subject will be over or underexposed. For this reason, spot or partial metering is often not available on point-and-shoot cameras.

Evaluative/matrix metering

This is the most sophisticated of all the metering systems, and is the 'default' mode for most cameras that offer metering options. It works by taking multiple readings from various points in the scene, while also assessing the position of the main subject, foreground and background, overall brightness, any front- or back-lighting, and colour. The camera then compares these readings with a database of tens of thousands of 'typical'

photographic scenes and selects the exposure that most closely resembles one in its database. In other words, the camera guesses what type of picture is being taken, whether it's a landscape with a bright sky and dark land or a portrait at dusk. Most of the time, evaluative or matrix metering does a surprisingly good job at selecting the most appropriate exposure for any given scene, but it's by no means foolproof as it employs a certain amount of 'guesswork'. More experienced photographers often complain that they lose a certain amount of control when using evaluative metering.

Which mode is best?

If there are no marked differences between highlights and shadows, then evaluative or matrix metering is more likely to get the exposure right. If, however, there are distinct differences between the light and dark areas, or if the subject is backlit, or if you need to expose for a specific area of a scene, you will probably discover that using either spot/partial or centre-weighted metering will serve you better.

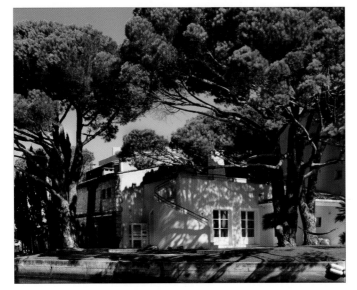

LEFT The camera's matrix metering has accurately captured this scene, which contains bright highlights and dark shadows.

Histograms

Working digitally has a number of benefits, one of the most important being that the colour, brightness and tonal values of the individual pixels that make up the image are recorded as soon as the image is taken.

These values can be reviewed in two ways on the camera's LCD screen – firstly, as the image itself or secondly, as a graphic tonal representation which is known as a histogram.

Being able to interpret histograms will help you to assess whether or not your image has the acceptable tonal values that make for a well-exposed shot, particularly in bright sunlight when it's difficult to see clearly a review of the image on the camera's LCD screen.

Interpreting a histogram

A histogram can normally be called up on the LCD screen on the back of your camera when shooting or playing back images. It is a form of graph where the x- (horizontal) axis represents the entire digital tonal range from black to white (0–255), while the y- (vertical) axis represents the number of pixels with a specific tonal value.

It can be helpful to try to mentally divide the x-axis into three sections – shadows to the left, midtones in the middle and highlights to the right. An ideally exposed image would generate a symmetrical, humped-shape histogram that smoothes gently out to the black and white points at either end of the histogram. For less well-exposed examples, a histogram that features the majority of the pixels in the left part of the histogram would indicate an underexposed, or dark (low-key), image, while one in which most of the pixels were grouped to the right would suggest an over-exposed, very light (high-key) image.

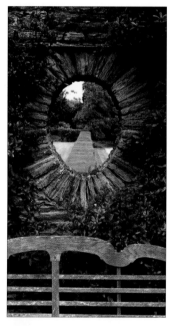

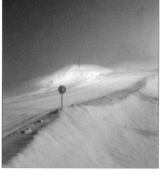

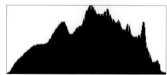

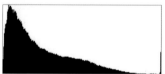

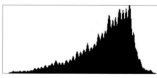

▲ **ABOVE** A snowy scene will produce a histogram that has a large number of pixels grouped to the highlight (right) end of the histogram. However, both ends of the histogram curve uniformly to both the black point (left) and the white point (right). This indicates a good range of tones from black to white.

▲ **ABOVE** Although exhibiting a number of individual peaks that represent specific regions of the image, such as buildings and mountain shadows, this image has produced an even histogram overall. Both ends drop gradually to the black and white points – indicative of a well-exposed image with a full tonal range.

▲ **ABOVE** This dark, reflective shot of a garden wall showing the garden beyond has resulted in a histogram with a grouping of pixels to the shadow (left) end of the histogram. But again, because the graph drops down to the base of the black point (albeit sharply) most of the shadow detail is discernible.

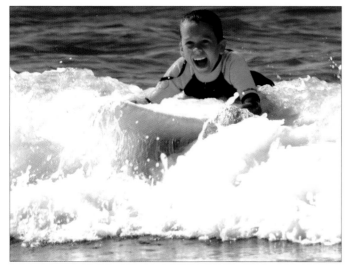

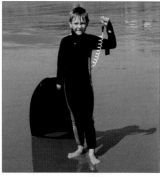

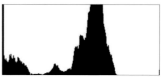

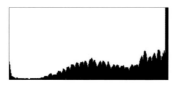

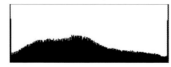

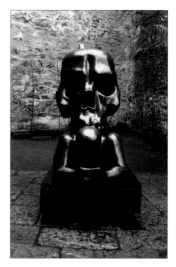

ABOVE AND RIGHT The dark water in the background and the relatively dark subject have fooled the camera into overexposing the surf in this image. This is shown by the spike of pixels against the right-hand end of the histogram.

ABOVE The boy's dark wetsuit has been underexposed in this image despite the relative lack of bright highlights. The spike of pixels at the black point of the histogram shows this and indicates that some shadow detail has been lost.

Clipped highlights/shadows

One of the most useful aspects of reviewing an image's histogram is that it will quickly alert you to any clipped highlights or shadows. Either of these can occur in a scene that exhibits a very wide tonal range – that is, an image that contains large areas of dark shadows and equally large areas of bright highlights. Depending on your specific camera and how its metering system works, in such a difficult lighting situation it's likely that the dark shadows will be underexposed and become entirely black with no discernible detail (clipped shadows) or the highlight areas will be overexposed and rendered entirely white (clipped highlights), or both. Bright areas of an image that are overexposed to the point at which they appear as pure white are often referred to as 'blown highlights'.

Both clipped shadows and clipped highlights are quickly detected on a histogram in the form of a large group

or distinct 'spike' of pixels stacked against either end of the histogram. If, when reviewing a histogram, you see that groups of pixels are pushed to either end of the histogram try recomposing the shot so that fewer bright areas or less shadows are visible in the frame.

Blown highlights are extremely intrusive and are usually impossible to remedy in photo-editing software as there's no information to start with. Detail can be far more easily extracted from dark shadows in editing software. For this reason, it's often better to ensure you get a more accurate

ABOVE AND RIGHT Unsurprisingly, this grey black and white image produces a fairly uniform histogram, apart from the peaks at either end created by dark shadows and bright highlights.

exposure for the lighter areas than for the darker ones, especially if you are using a compact camera. There are various techniques you can use to help you get the best possible results in difficult light situations and we'll cover these in the Manual Exposure section on pages 164–165.

Colour Temperature and White Balance

While watching a glorious sunrise, enjoying a spectacular view at midday, or walking down an artificially lit street at night, our eyes and brain make adjustments so that in most circumstances we compensate for the possible variation in the colour of the light – to us a white sheet of paper looks white no matter where or when we look at it. However, this is misleading, and in order to get accurate colours from your camera, it's important to understand a little about how light can vary in colour.

Natural light

Colour, or light, temperature can be accurately measured using the Kelvin (°K) temperature scale. During the course of a day (depending on where you live and the time of year), the light temperature will vary and this affects the colour of the light. For example, at sunrise, the light will often take on a reddish hue and has a temperature of around 2,500°K.

As the sun rises higher in the sky the light becomes increasingly white, until around midday when the light reaches a temperature of around 5,500°K. At this temperature there is no noticeable colour bias, which is why flash units also use this neutral colour temperature.

As the sun begins to set, the colour temperature drops again, and the light will often return to the red colours apparent at sunrise.

Cloud cover (or a lack of it) can also affect the colour of light. For example, while a cloudy day has relatively neutral light of between 6,000°K and 7,000°K, a bright blue sky has a temperature of around 10,000°K. This will cast a noticeably blue light, which can make your pictures appear cool.

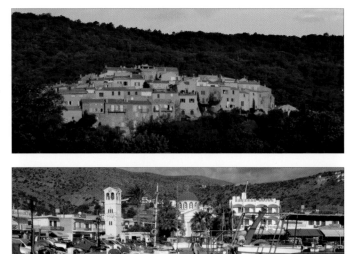

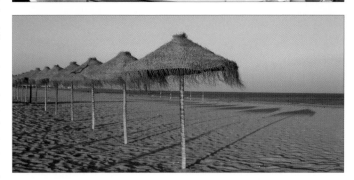

Artificial light

It's not just natural light that exhibits varying colour temperatures. Various types of artificial light also have different temperatures, and usually these are much more apparent than natural colour temperature shifts. For example, a standard 60-watt incandescent (tungsten) light bulb, the type used in a great many table lamps, will generate a colour temperature of around 3,000°K,

▲ **ABOVE** These three shots were taken at different times of the day – sunrise, midday and sunset. The top image was taken at around 5:30am and the sunrise was uninterrupted by cloud. The red quality to the light is typical of a colour temperature of around 3,000°K. By comparison, the second image appears much more neutral in colour. However, by sunset (bottom image), the colour temperature returns to around 3,000°K, reintroducing the red glow that accompanied sunrise.

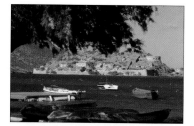

Auto white balance

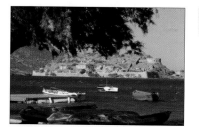

Daylight

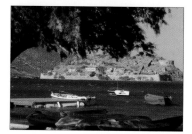

Cloudy

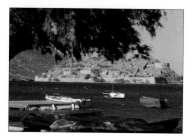

Shade

creating a warm, reddish light, while some fluorescent lights have relatively high temperatures of around 7,000°K, creating a cold, green-blue colour cast.

White balance

Traditionally, photographers used to use a variety of coloured filters attached to the camera's lens to counteract the effect of colour casts. If the light was too blue, they would use a red-coloured filter to 'warm-up' the image, and vice versa. While using filters on a digital camera that accepts them is certainly one way of correcting colour casts, many compacts won't take filters. However, all digital cameras have a white balance (WB) setting that does the same job.

Auto white balance (AWB)

All digital cameras have an auto white balance (AWB) setting. In simple terms, this works by making the brightest element in the image white and then, using that as a point of reference, adjusting all the other hues to create true-to-life colour. However, if there's no 'white' reference point, or the scene is dominated by one particular colour, the camera's AWB

setting can be tricked into making the wrong decision. To counteract this, your digital camera is likely to feature a number of preset white balance modes, including incandescent (tungsten), fluorescent, daylight, flash, cloudy and shade. These modes use a fixed temperature setting common to those specific lighting conditions and will usually produce more accurate colours than the AWB setting.

In addition, more feature-packed compacts and many dSLRs also feature a custom white balance setting. With this setting you shoot a white card under the lighting conditions in which you're working. The camera will record this as white and use that setting for all subsequent shots. Some cameras will also allow you to input the exact Kelvin setting if you know the colour temperature of the light source being used.

Quick correction

If your images appear too warm or red, selecting a higher temperature setting ('daylight' to 'cloudy' for example) and retaking the photo should give you more accurate colours.

Similarly, if the image appears too cool or blue, selecting a lower temperature setting will warm the image. Finally, although we usually strive to get an accurate white balance, correcting a wonderful sunset shot so that pinkish walls are accurately rendered as white would detract from the picture. This is an obvious case where we might want to retain the colour cast, as it adds atmosphere to the picture. Similarly, the sickly green of certain street lighting may be exactly what you're after to portray an urban environment so, for creative effect, try using the 'wrong' white balance and see what results you get.

Colour temperature

The average colour temperature in Kelvin for a variety of typical light sources:

Candle light	1,500°
Incandescent/tungsten	2,500°
Sunrise/sunset	3,000°
Midday sun/flash	5,500°
Overcast sky	6,500°
Hazy sky	8,000°
Blue sky	10,000°+

The Difference a Filter Makes

Any camera accessory used while taking a photograph can enhance the final image; however, care must always be taken to ensure the images produced are effective and give you the results that you want and predict. One of the least expensive and yet most important of accessories you can buy is a filter. Certain filters improve the colour saturation of the image or enhance the sky or quality of water. Before deciding on which filter you are going to use for a shot, or indeed before selecting any accessory, test it in similar situations before using it for a specific, planned shot.

Colour correction filters

If you use a film-back camera, you will find that some manufacturers' film has a natural bias towards results that are too blue or green, giving an unwanted coldness to the photographs. On the other hand, the film may be too warm and the results will then tend towards red or yellow. To correct these tendencies there is a huge range of CC (colour correction) filters; for most photographers one or two colourbalancing filters will prove more than adequate to have in their stock of kit.

Polarizing filters

A polarizing filter is a useful accessory for outdoor photography of all kinds; it will enhance the quality of the blueness of a sky, making any clouds stand out with greater clarity, and it can be used to cut out unwanted reflections, such as those in shop windows or on shiny tabletops. Taking pictures of a lake or sea may give some interesting results. You can also take a photograph through a window without a reflection of yourself interfering with your shot.

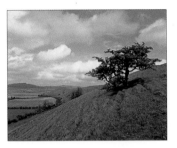

ABOVE In this picture no filter was used. Although the image is correctly exposed it has a slightly blue cast which makes it look rather cold. The sky lacks definition and appears flat.

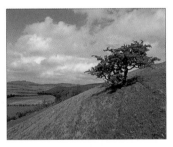

ABOVE In this picture an 81EF filter was used to eradicate the blueness of the overall picture. The grass and tree are well defined and the clouds and sky have body.

Exposure compensation

Since many filters cut the amount of light that passes through the lens, compensation in exposure must needs to be made. With cameras that have TTL meters this will be done automatically, but for manually operated cameras this must be taken into account before the final exposure is made. This is quite easy as each filter comes with a number known as a filter factor which indicates the amount of compensation required for each exposure. For instance a filter factor of 1 requires one stop increase in exposure.

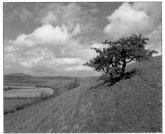

ABOVE By adding an 81A filter the blue cast has been reduced, the picture appears warmer and the contrast between the different tones is increased.

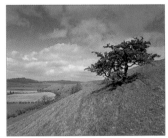

ABOVE As well as using an 81EF filter, a neutral density graduated filter has been added. This filter allows two differing areas of brightness to be brought into line with one another. In this case the hill and background required an exposure of $^1/_{125}$ second at f8, but the sky only needed an exposure of $^1/_{125}$ at f11. The graduated filter brings both areas into line so that the sky is well defined yet the land area is not underexposed.

RIGHT Here a polarizing filter has been used. This has made the blue sky darker and the wispy white clouds stand out with great clarity. If this filter is used with an SLR camera the effect can be seen in the viewfinder as the filter is rotated.

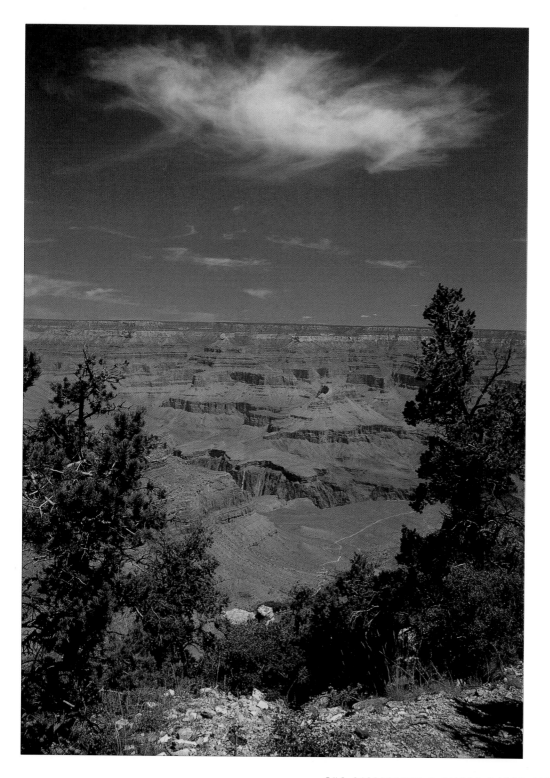

When the Light Is Low

Low light, whether due to the time of day or prevailing weather conditions, does not mean that good photographs cannot be taken. It is sometimes even possible to obtain more dramatic shots in low light than in brilliant sunshine. If the weather is misty or foggy, moody pictures can be taken. If the sun is low, at the beginning or end of the day, for instance, the colour of the light will be much warmer, and can be used to dramatic advantage,

emphasizing the sky and clouds. Even indoors, light filtering through a window is often perfectly adequate to light a subject without using flash.

A tripod is an asset in many low light conditions where slow shutter speeds are necessary. An alternative is to use a fast film or ISO, although the results will be grainier. Graininess can be used to creative effect but often it will detract from the final image if not used carefully.

BELOW Even adverse weather conditions can be used to the photographer's advantage. This picture of Bodiam Castle in Great Britain was taken early on a misty morning. The mist rose and fell, sometimes completely obscuring the castle. By waiting for the right moment it was possible to take a shot in which the light had an ethereal quality. The mirror image reflected in the still waters of the moat adds to the general composition. As with many great shots, the key is to wait patiently for the right moment.

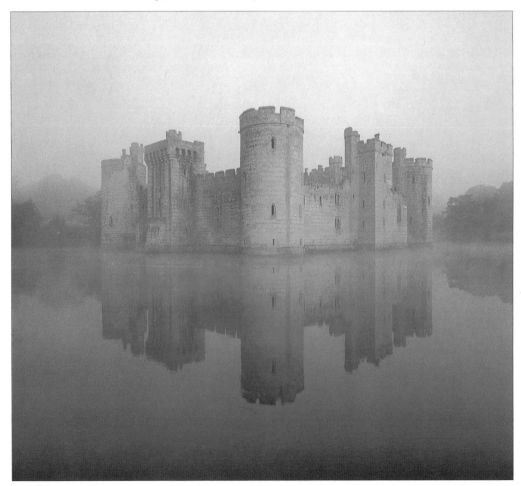

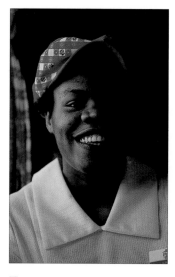

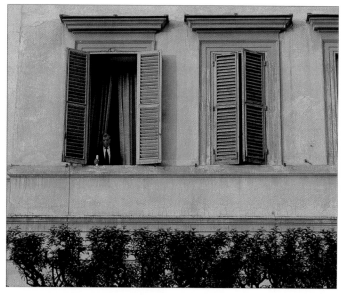

▲ **ABOVE** This shot was taken using only available light coming in from a window. The shutter speed required was ¹/₁₅ sec; this was too slow to allow the camera to be held by hand so a column in the restaurant was used as a support. It is virtually impossible to hold a camera steady at ¹/₃₀ sec or less without suffering camera shake; with a little ingenuity it is usually possible to find something to support the camera.

▲ **ABOVE** The late evening light bathes this building in a wonderful reddish glow. The anonymous figure at the window lends an air of mystery to the overall composition. Always be on the look-out for the unexpected, especially when the light is low and hopes of a good shot are fading.

For film work

Instead of using fast film, ordinary film can be uprated. If the film in the camera is 100 ISO, for instance, then the speed dial on the camera can be altered to 200 or 400 ISO. Remember, however, to tell the laboratory that you have done this when the film is sent in for processing, so that it can be developed accordingly. The disadvantage of this method is that the whole film has to be rated at the same ISO and any increase in development will result in loss of shadow detail, increase in contrast and a grainier texture.

▶ **RIGHT** Here the setting sun has painted the sky completely red and the clouds lend it extra depth. No tripod was available here so the camera was braced on the barrier wall of the river.

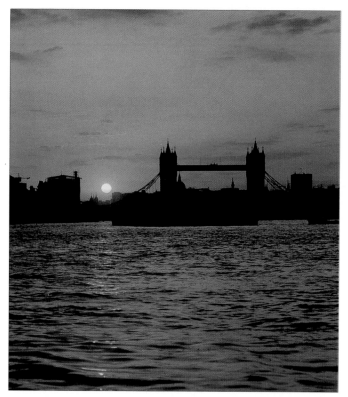

Composition Basics

Having covered basic automatic and semi-automatic shooting, metering and focusing modes, it's time to look at some basic composition principles. Learning about the added creativity these can bring to the photographer will not only help you visualize how your pictures will turn out, but give them greater impact, too.

Good composition

Various techniques have been employed by artists and photographers over many years to improve composition. But what are the key elements for a good composition?

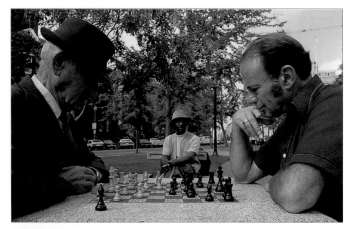

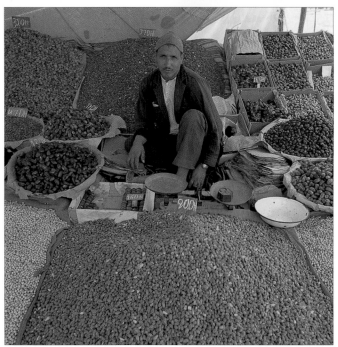

ABOVE This nut-seller is the centre of interest and as such occupies the middle position in the shot. Do not be afraid of placing the subject in a prominent position within the frame of the picture. Here the subject sits among a display of his wares; this helps draw the eye towards him yet also around him as more and more items become apparent. Always retain an even balance between the subject and their surroundings.

ABOVE Even when a photographic opportunity occurs by chance, it pays to take time to consider the general composition. Here the chessboard fills the centre of the foreground and the two subjects are positioned on either side, creating a perfect balance. The scene captures a particular image of society, especially with the inclusion of the third man in the background; although not deliberately arranged, the three people and the juxtaposed chessboard have become key elements in the photograph.

BELOW This shot has all the ingredients of a good composition. The foreground is uncluttered, and the pathway leads from the foreground directly to the centre of interest, the house. The backdrop of hills provides a contrast and add interest by breaking up the uniform stretch of blue sky.

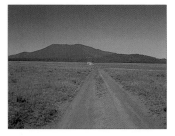

On one level, good composition is all about 'arranging' the elements in the viewfinder or on the LCD screen so that their shape, form, colour and tone interact with one another in a way that looks visually appealing. Of course this is very subjective – an image that resonates with one viewer may quite easily leave another cold. Employing certain compositional techniques, however, is usually a good place to start.

Capture the moment

For many new photographers, one of the hardest skills to learn is how to capture the complete essence of a moment or scene, just as we experienced it when taking the image. For example, if we're at the beach we have the added benefit of experiencing the smell and the sound of the seagulls squawking, the fine texture of sand and the heat of the sun – all of which formulate that very specific sense of time and place. Yet when we come to view our images on screen or in print we often find that

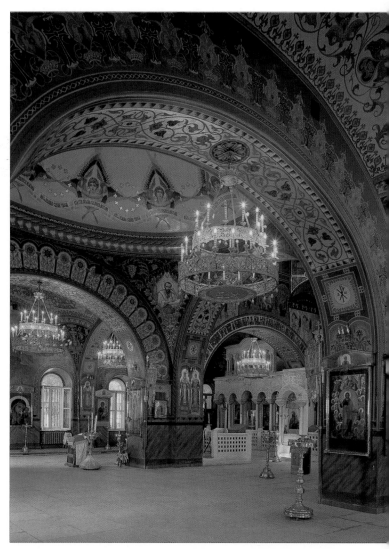

RIGHT The arch in the foreground provides a natural frame for this scene in a church in Moscow. This arch is complemented by a series of other arches that can be seen in the background as the eye travels from one to the other in a smooth sequence. There are no unsightly intrusions in either the foreground or background. This is a strong composition which may well have been weaker if taken from a different viewpoint.

Three key areas to be considered in composition:

1 The centre of interest – having decided what the central subject of the photograph is to be, ascertain where the photograph is to be shot from to achieve the most effective background.

2 Possible distractions or intrusions – examine the subject, background and foreground very carefully to ensure that

the picture will not be spoiled by an unwanted element. It is only too easy to mar a beautiful building with a traffic sign in the foreground, which you may not even have noticed, or to produce a portrait of some friends complete with a telegraph pole emerging from the top of one of their heads. Usually an intruding object can be removed from the

composition simply by moving slightly to one side. It is worth waiting for any moving vehicles to pass by.

3 Enhancing the foreground – it is important to decide if there is anything that might add to the foreground without detracting from or obscuring the centre of interest.

they don't necessarily recreate the original sense of time and place that we felt when taking the shot.

Good composition is a way of using techniques that will help you create images that are visually pleasing and successfully conjure up the emotions and memories of a specific location or event. We're now going to examine a number of the first rules of composition. However, it's important not to become preoccupied by these 'rules' as this can stifle creativity and hinder spontaneity, so consider these rules more as guidelines; something to help rather than struggle to adhere to.

▶ **RIGHT** Look for details and interesting juxtapositions rather than always shooting straight on. Curves contrasting with straight lines, and curves lined up to the frame of your shot, can be very interesting.

▼ **BELOW** Getting in close to the subject of an image is a good way of emphasizing the subject and also helps to eradicate distracting backgrounds.

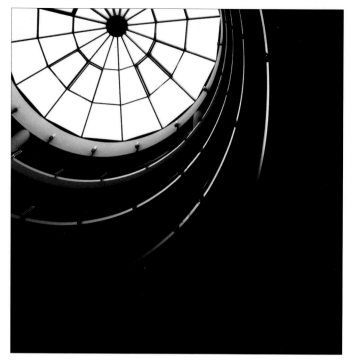

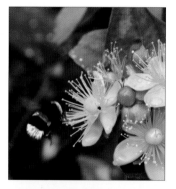

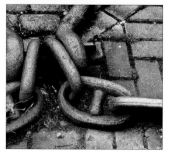

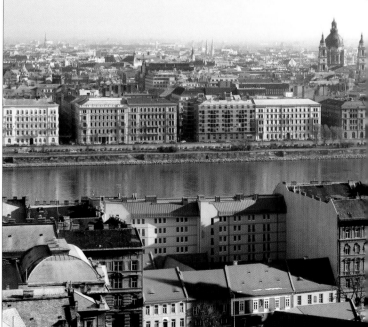

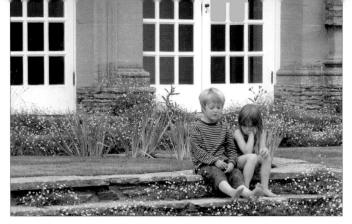

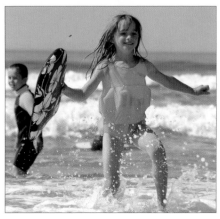

ABOVE The children in this picture aren't in the middle of the frame and there's a lot of background around them, but there is still no doubt that they are the focus of the photograph.

BELOW The landscape form of this city shot captures the sweeping river front of Budapest, with its uniform rows of windows.

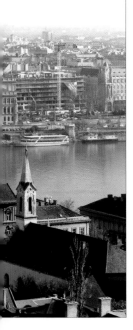

ABOVE By using a fast shutter speed, the girl in this image has been frozen, making it possible to clearly see her expression and capture the moment.

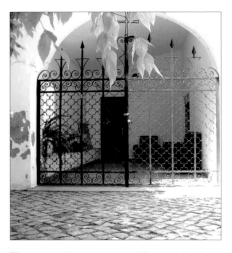

ABOVE Here the photographer has deliberately included some leaves in the top of the image. This is a form of 'framing' that adds depth to an image.

BELOW When faced with a seascape or landscape, most photographers will naturally use their camera in a horizontal, or 'landscape', orientation. But there is no rule that says you can't shoot an 'upright' image if the scene warrants it.

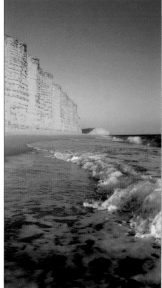

Finding inspiration

There will certainly be times when, as a photographer, you feel uninspired. Prolonged periods of poor weather or a sense that you have little in the way of subject matter will often bring on these periods. Joining a camera club is a good way of helping you through such moments. You'll meet like-minded people, be given specific photographic challenges and learn and share techniques that will improve your images.

Alternatively, join an online photographic community, such as Flickr (www.flickr.com). Most are free to join, have innumerable forums, and specific areas for certain subjects and styles of photography. They're also a good way of getting feedback on your own images.

Fill the Frame

Of all the compositional rules and tips, perhaps the most effective (and straightforward to understand) is to 'fill the frame'. It's amazing how many photographs – especially portraits – are taken either from too far away or do not use the camera's zoom facility to its full potential.

Part of the reason for this is because our brains are excellent at 'filtering' out the sights and sounds that we're not specifically concentrating on. When we focus on something, it is that object that fills our 'mental frame' and has our undivided attention. In our mind's eye it appears to fill the frame even though we might physically be some distance away. This will almost certainly result in images that render the subject small and insignificant in the frame.

Optical proximity

Robert Capa, who was one of the greatest war photographers and one of the founders of *Life* magazine – once famously remarked that, "If your photos aren't good enough, you're not close enough". This is precisely what filling the frame is all about. Although at the time he said it, Capa was undoubtedly implying physical 'closeness' – and, of course, getting physically closer to your subject will certainly help fill the frame – with today's more sophisticated and superior lens technology, we can also get closer optically. Later on in the book, we'll be looking in more detail and focal lengths, and the impact a long focal length (or telephoto) lens has on an image, but for now, use your camera's zoom facility to get in close to your subject – you'll be amazed at the impact this can bring.

By filling the frame, you will not only reduce the risk of inadvertently including any distracting background or foreground clutter, but viewers will be left in no doubt about the subject of the photograph.

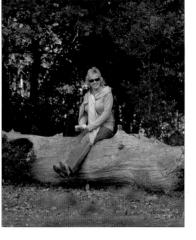

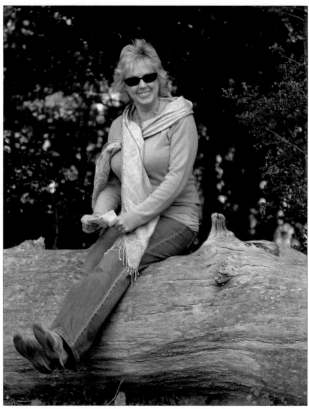

ABOVE AND RIGHT Our mind can play strange tricks on us when we're behind the camera. Because we're so 'focused' on the subject of a photograph, we're not always aware of the extraneous parts of the scene surrounding the subject. One good tip is to compose the image, then close your eyes and visualize the scene that you have just composed. When you open your eyes again you may be surprised to discover how different the reality is from the image you thought you were about to take in your 'mind's eye'. Always try to fill the frame with your chosen subject.

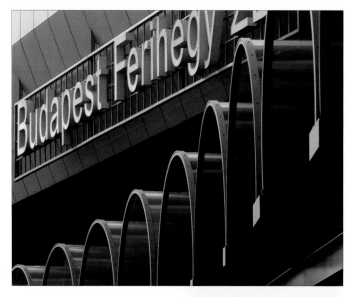

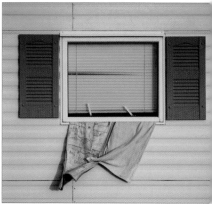

ABOVE Even something as mundane as a trailer window with two dish cloths can create an interesting, symmetrical composition if used to 'fill the frame' under favourable lighting conditions.

ABOVE Budapest's airport has some interesting geometrical shapes, patterns and lines that are difficult to capture in their entirety. After a while, the photographer stopped trying to capture the whole frontage and instead focused on the name and the structural elements that had first caught his attention.

RIGHT Here the photographer wanted to capture the wonderful purple of a species of flower growing on cliff tops. With the first image, the colour and quantity of the flowers is adequately captured, but including the beach and sea distracts the viewer from the subject – it's just not clear what exactly we're meant to be looking at. By filling the frame, the colour and abundance of the flowers are enhanced as they are the only subject in the frame with no added distractions.

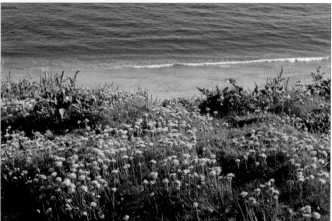

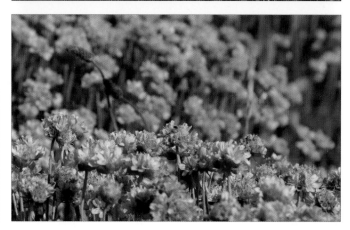

Get in close

There are two ways of filling the frame for maximum impact and eradicating unwanted backgrounds:
• Move closer to the subject.
• Zoom in or use a longer focal length lens.

Keep It Simple

This next compositional tip is a logical extension of filling the frame. Almost all keen, novice photographers are guilty of trying capture too much – whether it's a landscape, portrait, architecture or still-life picture. It's difficult to know quite why this is – perhaps we're trying to provide the viewer with a more 'complete picture' of the scene in the hope that this will convey more powerfully what we want the viewer to see? But things work in exactly the opposite way – the less visually cluttered an image, the more powerful it becomes.

Pick your subject

One way of keeping your images simple is to pick a specific subject from the scene you're photographing. Say, for example, you're enjoying a holiday in a stunning tropical location and want to capture the sun, sea and sand. If you simply stand up and point your camera along the length of the beach and take a shot that includes just about everything you can see, you're likely to capture all the other sunbathers and swimmers, people walking down the beach, hotels and bars in the distance, and so on. When you show the image to friends and family back home,

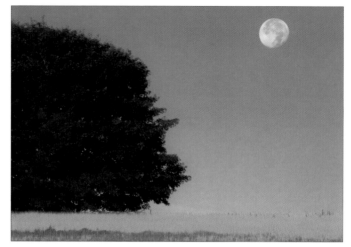

ABOVE In this image, the tree, the moon and the foreground form three simple yet discrete elements, with the uniform blue sky adding to the image's simplicity.

they'll have a good idea of your physical environment, but not why your holiday was so special. However, pick a specific viewpoint, such as a trail of footprints in the wet sand or a colourful towel and beach umbrella and your shots will evoke a much greater response and the images will have a much greater visual impact.

BELOW These two images, which were taken at the same location, show the significant advantage of keeping your images simple. The photographer aimed to highlight the colourful house fronts juxtaposed against the yachts and dinghies. In the first image on the left, there is too much going on in the picture and no easily identifiable subject. By moving farther along the harbour wall, the photographer found a better position that not only provided an excellent view across to the houses, but also still captured the contrasting spirit of modernity in the modern sailing dinghies.

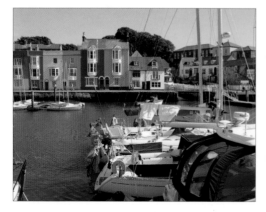

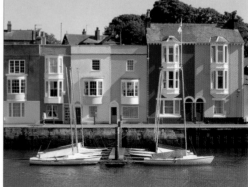

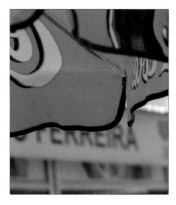

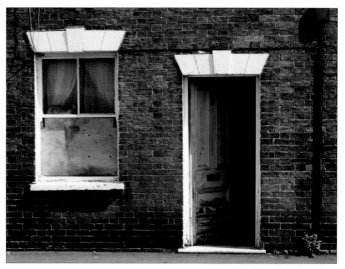

ABOVE A photograph of this parasol in its entirety would have meant including people and more of the building in the shot, which would reduce its impact.

ABOVE RIGHT The three main elements of this image, the window, door and drainpipe, provide a simple arrangement to the brick backdrop.

BELOW These simple footsteps in the sand are emotive, while also creating a graphic image. The surf and its recession have sorted the sand grains into clear patterns.

RIGHT We don't need to see the whole of this building to know that it was taken in an exotic location – the blue sky, terracotta walls, vibrant flowers and pristine white shutters suffice.

BELOW RIGHT A solitary figure placed in an urban setting can often create a powerful composition.

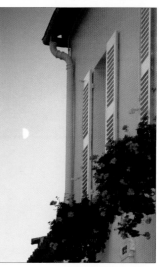

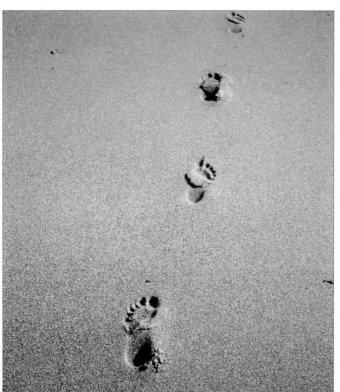

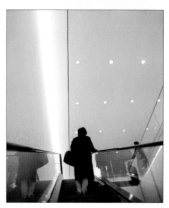

Rule of Thirds

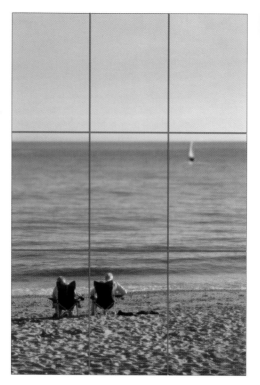

One of the most popular and widely used compositional tools is the rule of thirds. The 'rule' was developed in the mid-19th century, primarily as a guide for landscape artists, but was quickly adopted by photographers who spotted its value, first in landscape photography, then in other genres.

Grid

When employing the rule of thirds the photographer mentally imposes a grid over a potential scene. The grid is comprised of two vertical and two horizontal lines that divide the scene into thirds, both vertically and horizontally, or into nine squares (see example on the right). The rule works on the basis that any continuous horizontal line running the width of the image, such as the horizon or a row of distant trees, has greater dynamism and interest if placed on one of the horizontal grid lines than if it were placed in the centre of the image. Similarly, any strong vertical objects in the scene would be best placed on one of the two vertical lines.

Points of interest

In addition to using horizontal and vertical lines as guides, it is also important to consider the four points at which the dividing lines cross – these are known as the points of interest or the points of power. When composing a shot, try to ensure that principal elements in the scene are placed over one or more of these points of interest. Doing so will ensure that focal points in your image are kept away from the centre of the picture and add interest to the image. You don't have to slavishly ensure that key objects sit directly over points of interest – they are intended as guidelines only.

LEFT The idea behind the rule of thirds is that it prevents you from placing the subject of a picture right in the middle of the frame, where there's a danger it will draw in viewers, and stop them from visually exploring the rest of the image. The image is divided into nine equal rectangles. Where the horizontal and vertical lines cross (the points of interest) is roughly where important elements of an image should be placed. This image is further balanced by the placement of the boat in the distance.

Portraits

Although the rule of thirds was devised primarily for landscape artists and photographers, it can also be used with other forms of photography. In portrait photography, for example, it is best to avoid having the subject's eyes run through the centre of the photograph if shooting a close-up of someone's head and shoulders. Instead place them along the top horizontal line. Similarly, if the portrait is a full-length shot, don't place the subject in the centre of the frame. Instead, try placing him or her along one of the two vertical lines.

In fact, the rule of thirds can apply to all styles or genres of photography – architecture and still life, as well as landscape and portraiture. It is worth bearing in mind, as mentioned earlier, rules are there to be learned, practised

RIGHT Portraits will often benefit if the subject's eyes are placed in line with the top horizontal rule.

Grid guidelines

The rule of thirds is a simple yet effective way of focusing the viewer's attention. Remember to:
- Mentally put horizontal or vertical lines in your image on thirds lines.
- Place key elements in your image on the four points of interest.

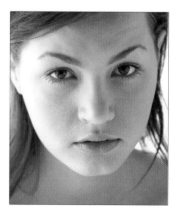

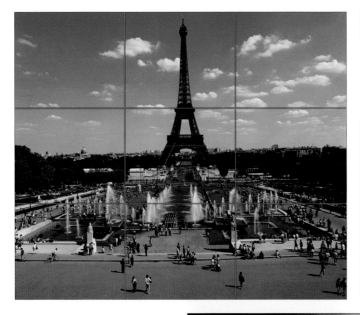

LEFT Like all composition 'rules', the rule of thirds is only a guide; there will be many times when placing the subject in the centre of the frame just feels right.

Viewfinder grid

On many of today's digital cameras, it is possible to electronically 'super-impose' a rule of thirds grid on to the viewfinder as you compose your image. As well as helping you to place the important elements of the scene on a point of interest, it can also help to remind you to hold the camera straight, so horizons or buildings don't slope off to one side.

and then broken. Once you try the rule of thirds for yourself, you'll likely find that many of your images become more balanced and dynamic. However, there are bound to be times when a piece of architecture or a tree just feels right when placed centrally, or when equal weight should be given to the land and the sky. In those instances, you should follow your gut instinct.

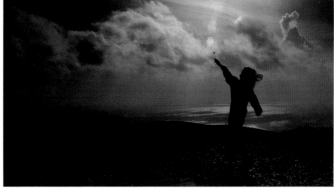

RIGHT In this silhouette shot of a boy throwing a stone, the figure has been deliberately placed in the right third of the shot. The composition is stronger and the stone consequently has 'space' into which it can be thrown.

BELOW Interestingly, research seems to show that compositions with one principal focal point are more successful if that element is positioned on the right-hand point of interest, rather than on the left, as we tend to look at images from left to right. It's thought that when the element is on the left, the viewer's eye stops travelling through the image as soon as it encounters its point of interest.

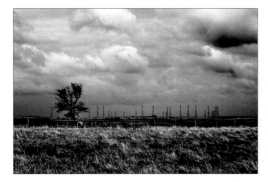

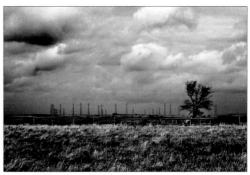

Frame Within a Frame

Like the rule of thirds, a 'frame within a frame' is a technique first used by landscape artists and subsequently by photographers. There is a number of ways the technique can be used to create very different results.

Landscape

One of the most popular frame-with-in-a-frame techniques is used in landscape photography, where trees or other foreground subjects are used to frame a distant view. Although the technique has been widely used (to the point where many consider it somewhat hackneyed), it can still be very effective and usually helps add depth to the composition, as well as enhancing the significance of the

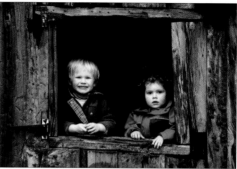

subject of the image. Also, the person viewing the image will often get a sense of the photographer's point of view, helping to create a shared experience of the scene and making the viewing all the more intimate.

Focus

To create the perception of depth, this technique usually works best if both the foreground 'border' and subject are in sharp focus, but it does pay to experiment. Walk farther back from the elements that you're intending to use as the border, use

your camera's zoom to close in on the distant subject and ensure that the camera doesn't focus on any of the foreground elements. If necessary, temporarily recompose the shot so that the foreground is out of the picture, then recompose the scene so that the foreground elements are once again in the frame, only now they should be out of focus. Take the picture and compare the effect of having a foreground that is either in or out of focus. Some photographs work far better with one technique than the other.

BELOW Using the branches of a tree is a classic way of framing a landscape image or a view of a historic building. Use this technique sparingly – it has been widely applied and is somewhat clichéd.

BELOW RIGHT A more creative interpretation of the 'frame-within-a-frame' concept.

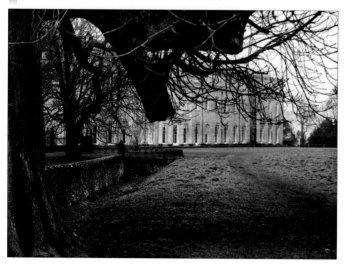

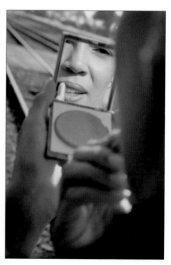

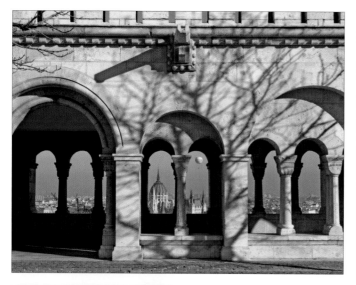

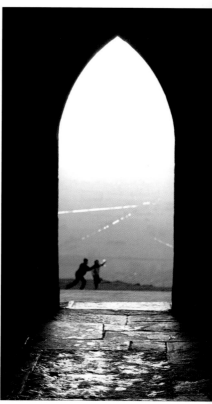

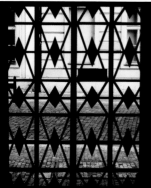

Portraits

This technique works in a slightly different way in portrait photography, as the subject is often within the object that is acting as the frame. Since the frame and subject are the same distance from the camera, you won't get the same perception of depth. Instead, the frame acts like a border, visually containing the subject and enhancing his or her significance. At the same time it will also contextualize the shot by putting the subject in a specific place or situation.

ABOVE When using a frame within your frame, experiment with the point of focus. Here, the doorway that acts as a frame is sharp, but the children in the background are out of focus.

TOP This image is about using frames within frames, although it has been taken further with the columns in the foreground and the smaller arched openings acting as frames.

ABOVE Sometimes the frames themselves can become the subject of the image. Here, the geometrical shape of the frame acts as the subject, making the viewer peer through to see the street.

RIGHT In this image the low-growing olive trees provide a frame or border for the bottom of the picture, while the bay is further framed by the rocky promontory near the top of the shot.

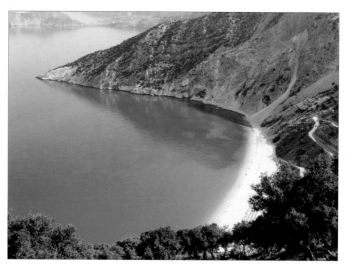

Choosing A Viewpoint

There are many situations when taking a photograph where a simple alteration of viewpoint can make all the difference between the resulting shot being very good or mediocre. Viewpoint can be defined as the position from which a photograph is taken. The photographer takes into account the background and foreground, and any interesting angles that will lead the eye naturally towards the emphasis of the image. By using different viewpoints the photographer can dramatically alter the impact of a picture.

Often people will say to a professional photographer something along the lines of, 'But you've got all the equipment!' In fact, all that it takes to achieve a better view is a little thought of where one should stand and how the foreground can be utilized to the greatest effect. On many occasions it may be possible to utilize detail in the foreground by either tilting the camera downward or simply by moving slightly to one side. These small shifts of position or angle, that may seem insignificant at the time, can produce the difference between a dramatic shot and a dull one.

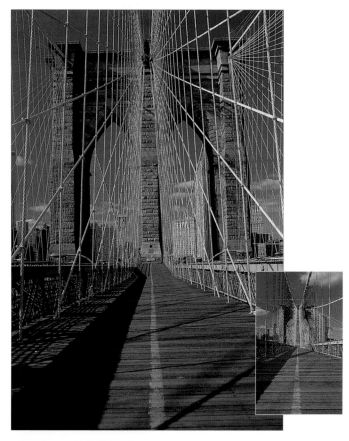

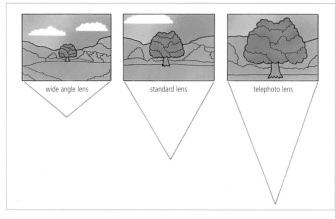

wide angle lens   standard lens   telephoto lens

LEFT The choice of lens is important for the composition of a picture. When you can't get closer to a subject, use a longer lens. This also compresses the image. A shift lens can be used to alter the composition of the shot without you having to move.

Easy Estimating

To help judge your choice of viewpoint, simply form a rectangle between the thumbs and forefingers of both hands, and look through to judge your chosen image.

To tighten the 'frame', slide the right hand closer to the left, keeping the rectangle steady. In order to create a 'zoom' effect, extend your arms so that the background is removed and the subject of the picture appears larger in relation to the rectangle. You can then set your camera and tripod up and perfect the viewpoint before shooting. If you are working

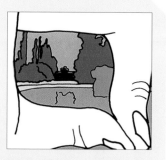

with a large format camera this is a particularly useful technique, and one that involves hauling no extra kit around with you.

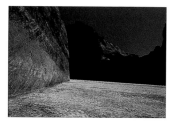

ABOVE Standing close to one element of a photograph can add extra emphasis. The viewpoint for this picture was created by standing close to the canyon wall that appears on the left. The dramatic sweep of the wall and its horizontal strata lead the eye straight into the picture. If taken from a different position or angle the effect would have been weaker.

OPPOSITE Viewed individually there may seem little to choose between these two pictures of Brooklyn Bridge. The shots were taken within 46m (150ft) of one another and within a short space of time. The inset picture was taken from further away than the larger one; much of its impact is lost by the inclusion of too much sky at the top of the frame, and the cloud is an added distraction.

The larger picture was taken from much nearer to the bridge using a slightly lower viewpoint. This means that the verticals have converged to a greater degree than they would have done had the shot been taken from a higher position, and the tension cables fill the frame, fanning out in all directions to draw the eye into the shot. The cloud has been cropped out which extends the symmetry of the shot; with fewer distractions the graphic qualities of the composition are enhanced.

RIGHT By tilting the camera slightly downward the lilies on the water are brought into the picture. This provides extra interest in the foreground without detracting from the mountains and sky. If the camera had been horizontal or tilted upward slightly, without including the lilies, the result would have been a rather dull stretch of water and reflected cloud in the foreground.

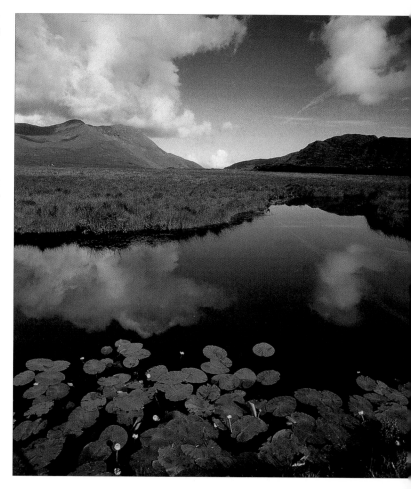

When looking through a series of images, one of the biggest clues that gives away the novice photographer is that all the images have been taken from a standing eye-level view. There's absolutely nothing wrong with this point of view (POV) – some of the most striking images have been shot from it – but by altering the camera height and angle every so often, you're not only more likely to create images with a fresh and exciting perspective, you'll also train your mind's eye to visualize scenes differently.

People

Of all the many different genres, it is with portrait photography that changing your point of view can have the most dramatic impact in your pictures. This is most likely down to the psychological responses we experience when communicating with other people. Generally we become aware in a very short space of time if we converse with someone at a radically different eye level. Somehow it just feels uncomfortable – reinforced by the expressions 'looking down on' or 'looking up to' someone. It's quite possible to recreate similar tensions by photographing people from above or below. However, be wary of overusing the technique. Just as we

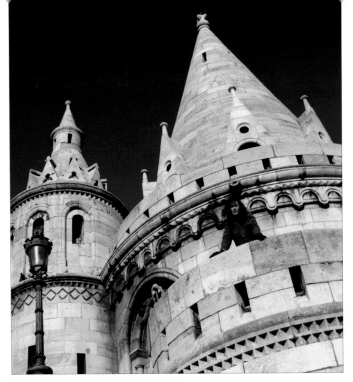

feel most comfortable talking to someone at the same level, so too do we feel most comfortable viewing portraits that have been taken at the same eye level. This is often most important when photographing children and with close-up, head-and-shoulder portraits – it definitely pays to kneel down so that the camera is at the child's eye level.

ABOVE The low viewpoint allowed the photographer to get the top of the turrets in the shot, and it has also emphasized the angles of the building for added drama. If the photograph had been taken standing on the same level as the subject herself, it would have lost the sense of scale.

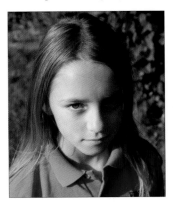

ABOVE When photographing a person sitting down, or a child, avoid pointing the camera down at the subject as this can create tension as he or she looks up into the camera.

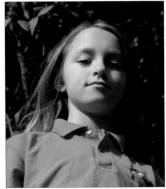

ABOVE Similarly, avoid photographing people from below unless you're trying to make them appear more powerful and authoritative or you are making a deliberate photographic point.

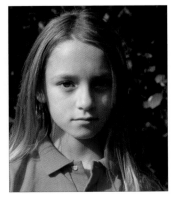

ABOVE By getting down to the same level as the subject, they can look directly into the camera, so avoiding any tension in their face from looking up or down at the camera.

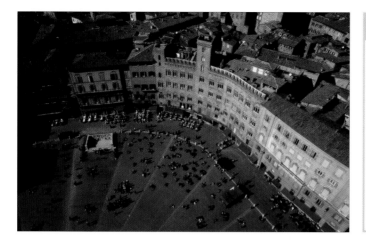

Camera angle

Just as shooting the same scene from different heights can provide new perspectives so, too, can trying out alternative angles. Generally we react most positively to accurately aligned horizons, but occasionally, with an appropriate subject matter, a skewed horizon or misaligned vertical can create a sense of unease and add drama to an image. Experiment with all sorts of varying angles to see what results you can achieve.

General photography

If you come across an interesting scene worthy of photographing, try experimenting with shots from different heights. Kneeling or lying down will provide new perspectives, as will finding something to stand on or finding a much higher viewpoint from which to shoot.

In addition, there's no rule that states that the camera must be held either vertically or horizontally straight. Try taking a few shots with the camera at an angle as this, too, may add a fresh perspective on a common scene. Any unusual viewpoint is likely to create an image that will attract and hold the viewer's attention.

ABOVE Shooting from a great height can sometimes provide a new perspective on a familiar scene, with shape, form and line being made more apparent.

RIGHT The unusual viewpoint of a copy of Michelangelo's David, which stands outside the Palazzo Vecchio in Florence, helps to maintain our attention.

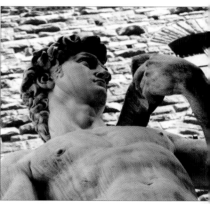

BELOW Taken from eye level, these mushrooms would have become lost against the field. By getting down low and using a wide aperture to give a shallow depth of field, they've become the focus of this photograph and have been put in the context of their surroundings.

BELOW Photographing buildings, and specifically skyscrapers, from below helps to reinforce their size.

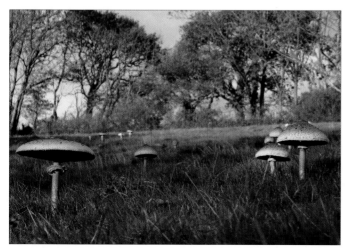

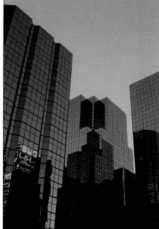

Using Foreground

Foregrounds can play an important part in the general composition of photographs. A point of interest in the foreground close to the camera can be used either as a framing device or as a tool to lead the eye into the picture. This type of added interest can make all the difference between the exciting and the mediocre.

Using foreground as a disguise

Foregrounds can also be used to hide untidy objects or unwanted intrusions in the middle or background of the picture. However, it is important to make sure that the foreground does not dominate the picture as then it will detract from the main subject of the photograph, becoming as much of an intrusion as the detail it is attempting to disguise.

Objects in the foreground

Although objects in the foreground of a picture can often add interest, it is all too easy to let them appear with monotonous regularity. This is a danger with a series of pictures taken from similar viewpoints, yet can be easily avoided with a little fore-thought. Take time to evaluate what is in front of the camera before you start to shoot; then use all the components to their best advantage in the final picture.

When objects are included in the foreground care must be taken with the exposure. Check to see if the objects are in shadow compared to the central portion of the shot and background as this may produce an ugly dark shape with no detail visible. If the shadow is unavoidable try correcting it using a reflector or fill-in flash.

Also check to see if the camera needs to be higher than the object in the foreground. If not, ensure the object is not filling too much of the frame.

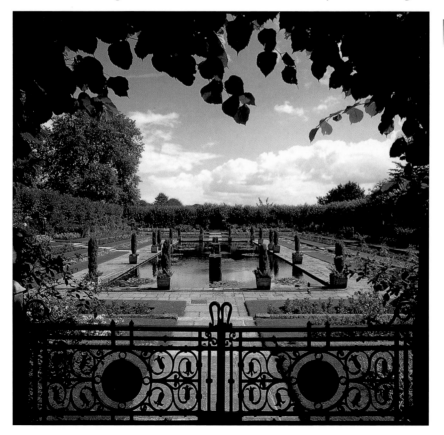

LEFT This picture of a formal garden has been enhanced by the use of the foliage of the outer trees as a framing device. The gates at the bottom of the frame complete the foreground interest. The result gives the impression of peering into a 'secret' garden. If the camera had been positioned farther forward and the foreground lost, the picture would have looked entirely different.

Use of perspective to create foreground interest

Additional foreground interest can be created by the use of perspective, for example the long, straight furrows in a ploughed field stretching out into the distance. In this case, a low viewpoint might be most effective. When taking a landscape shot the sky can often be a dominating factor so that the landscape scene itself is undermined. If this happens, perhaps the inclusion of a tree with overhanging branches within the shot could frame the top of your picture and diminish the overpowering impact of the sky. Of course, sometimes you will want to maximize the effect of huge sky in a shot, particularly if the landscape is bleak or wide open, but plan for the approach that will work best for the photograph you want.

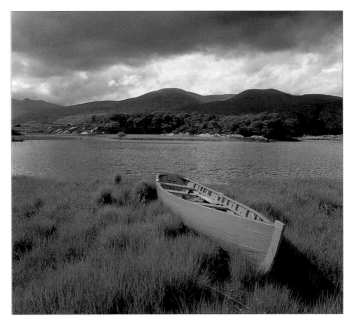

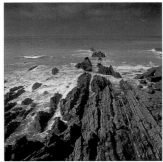

▲ **ABOVE** Foreground objects do not always need to be placed dead centre. Here the boat is in the corner of the frame and creates an added foreground interest. The colour of the boat complements the colour of the grass without providing too harsh a contrast. If a picture of this sort is to be part of a series, try to vary the position of the object in the foreground so that it does not become a dull motif, detracting from the shots themselves.

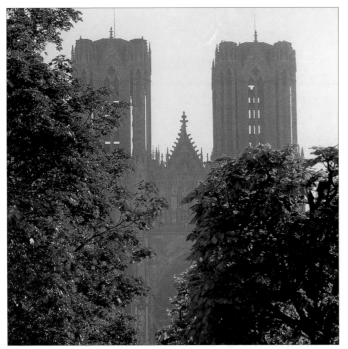

▲ **ABOVE** Historical buildings are not always at their best – as here in Reims, France, where the cathedral was covered in scaffolding. Added to this, the morning sun rose behind the cathedral, and as there was no time to wait for the sun to move, a viewpoint was found some distance from the front of the building. A telephoto lens, 200mm, was used and by having the trees as a framing device the untidy scaffolding was concealed and the direct sunlight was blocked.

▲ **ABOVE** The strong lines of the strata shoot out from the foreground and pierce the sea, leading the eye straight into the picture and creating a powerful composition. If the photograph had been taken from a position at the end of the rocks, the foreground would have been merely a stretch of sea.

Using Background

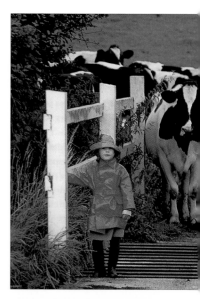

The background of a picture can enhance the overall composition of an image as much as the foreground. As a general rule, backgrounds should not dominate the photograph, and obscure the main subject. This jars the eye and gives an overall impression of a cluttered photograph. Similarly, a flat, dull background can influence the whole picture so that all interest is lost. A telephoto lens can produce a compressed image by reducing the depth between the middle-and the foreground.

The weather can create dramatic 'background' effects; if dark clouds are hanging in the sky watch out for isolated bursts of sunlight that can spotlight areas of the foreground, underexposing and making the dark areas even darker.

When taking a shot of a tranquil landscape, check to see if there are any roads running through. If there are, wait until traffic has dispersed and shoot from an angle that reduces their intrusion, as an unsightly track can ruin an otherwise beautiful scene.

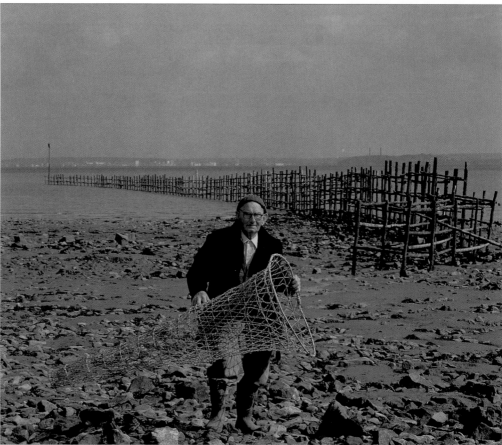

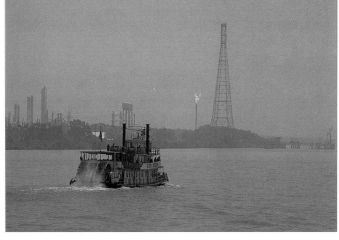

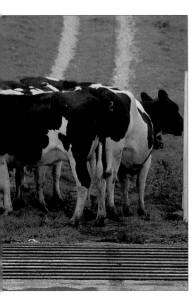

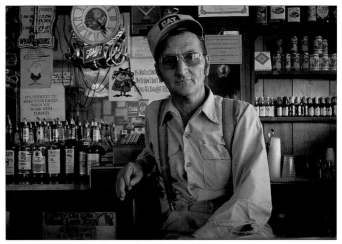

ABOVE The ever-burning flame of this oil refinery on the banks of the Mississippi at New Orleans relieves an otherwise dull background. It also provides a powerful contrast with the more traditional technology of the old paddle steamer in the foreground. It always pays to be alert to pictures where the back- and foregrounds provide not only a visual contrast but can also make a wider abstract statement in visual terms.

ABOVE The cows form an almost monochromatic background to this picture. The track that comes down to the gate balances the picture and enhances the general composition, yet nothing detracts from the young girl. Her bright raincoat and hat are set off by the black and white cows, and the juxtaposition of her diminutive size alongside the cows adds a subtle touch of humour to the shot.

RIGHT This picture was taken using only the available light coming in through a small window and with an exposure of $^1/_8$sec, bracing the camera against the bar. It is a clear example of how the background can provide information about the subject while at the same time adding extra interest.

LEFT This salmon fisherman is holding a putcher, a funnel-shaped basket used to catch salmon as they swim out to sea. The stakes stretching out behind echo the mood of the putcher, and convey a greater sense of the man and his work.

Key points to note about backgrounds

1 Is the background overpowering? Will it overshadow the subject of the picture? On the other hand, does it have enough interest to prevent it from being dull?
2 Does the background behind a human subject represent anything about the person's work or environment?
3 Are the background colours harmonious or unusual in some way? A telephoto lens can push the background out of focus, throwing up some interesting shapes and muted colours.
4 Does the sky appear in the background? If there are any clouds, try to retain their clarity and detail, perhaps by using a graduated neutral density filter or polarizing filter, or a yellow filter with black and white film.

Shape and Form

The visual building blocks that make up our images can be thought of as shape and form. Often it is their proportion and relationship to the space they sit in that make the difference between a good image and a great one. For many photographers – and, in particular, those who have had little art education – it can sometimes be difficult to differentiate between shape and form. So, let's look in more detail at these two elements and see how they fit into the overall composition of an image.

Shape

The simplest way to visualize the difference between shape and form is to think of shape as two dimensional and form as three dimensional. Our concept of shape develops at a very early age, and is something that we encourage our children to learn. Our almost instantaneous and positive reaction to shapes can be successfully exploited in photography, so try to make a habit of looking out for both natural and man-made objects that have clearly defined shapes. Start by looking out for simple outlines such as circles, squares and triangles and progress to shooting more complex shapes, such as flowers, architectural details, the crook of an elbow or the curve of a back.

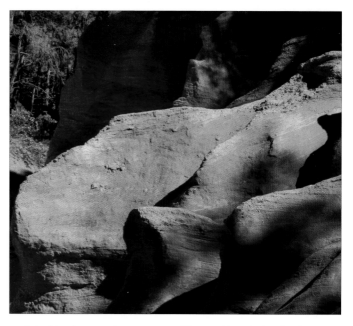

ABOVE Light coming from the side casts shadows that are the best tool for helping to describe a subject's form.

Silhouette

As another type of shape, silhouettes are an effective way of exploiting the outlines and shapes made by specific objects, especially if photographed against a strong light, such as the sun or a full moon. Alternatively, for a portrait photograph, place a table light behind the person's head and ask him or her to turn their head 90 degrees to the camera for the shot.

Form

Although silhouettes exploit our recognition and understanding of shape, they can appear very two-dimensional and lack 'body'. This is where form comes into play. To appreciate the three-dimensional aspect of an object, we need to see its form, and for us to fully appreciate the form, we need light and shade. Look for smooth, rounded objects and photograph them in soft, even lighting. The relationship between the light and dark areas provides us with the visual information we need to recognize the object's form.

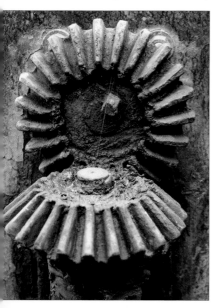

LEFT Although the lighting is soft in this eye-catching photograph of decaying gears, the shadows between the teeth give them a three-dimensional form.

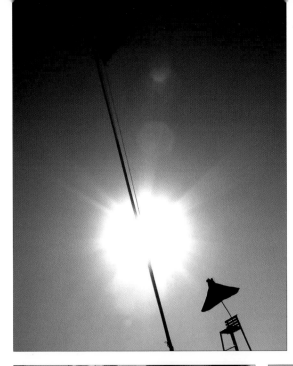

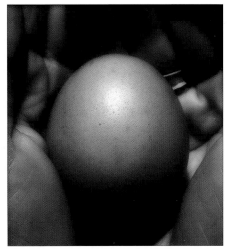

ABOVE In black and white photography, the relationship between the tones in an image is essential in describing the subject – without colour, it is only the interplay of light and dark that tells viewers what they are looking at.

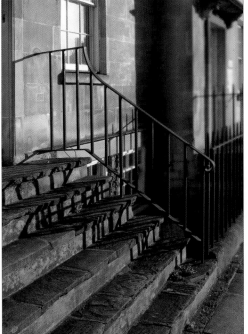

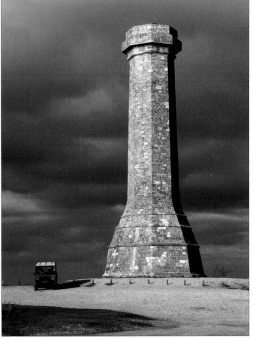

TOP It's not always necessary to see every last detail to recognize what something is or evoke a response. Here we can almost feel the heat from the sun, while the silhouetted flag and chair suggest a beach setting.

ABOVE Even objects as simple as the stone steps and iron railings to the entrance of this building can provide pleasing shape and form, here reinforced by the shadows thrown on to the steps.

ABOVE Contrast plays a key part in describing form in a subject. Here, there is contrast between the lit and shaded sides of the monument, as well as between the light stone and brooding sky.

Pattern and Texture

Two other compositional tools to consider in photography are pattern and texture. Of the two, pattern is probably the visual element that you're less likely to think of as a strong compositional tool. When we think of patterns, many of us might initially consider the repetitive shapes and colours found in wallpaper or curtains, whose function is sometimes to create a visually relaxing backdrop that doesn't overly stimulate our senses or attract attention.

Lateral thinking

So how can you use a pattern to provide a visually stimulating image? As a photographer, your aim should be to provide a view of the world that others have not considered before. Spotting patterns in everyday objects and scenes will provide a fresh and new perspective on the world. More

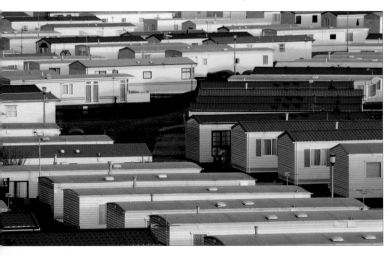

BELOW Interesting patterns are all around us – we just don't tend to notice them. If you look a little harder, you will find potential subjects everywhere, such as these neatly aligned mobile homes.

obvious examples include a row of flowers of a similar shape, the uniform ripples in an area of sand, a tiled floor, a brick wall or a flight of stairs. But what about a row of identical cars on a production line or hundreds of stacked cargo containers? These all have the repetitive elements of pattern, and if shot sensitively – in the right light and following some of the other rules of composition discussed already – they

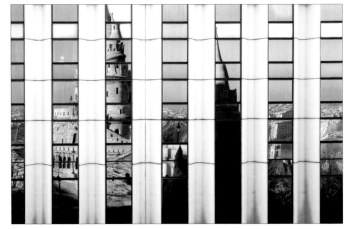

ABOVE There's a good contrast in this image between the regular pattern of the windows themselves and the irregularity of the old buildings reflected in the glass.

can create a striking image and, depending on the subject matter, may also convey a message.

Remember to look out for elements that break the pattern, as this will help to create an even stronger composition. Supposing in the sea of red cars or containers one or two were blue or silver – both would break the pattern and add drama. Once you've spotted a pattern, don't simply record it and move on. Consider other angles that might reveal other patterns that you had not seen initially.

Proximity and light

Unlike pattern, texture seems to have a much more immediate relevance and resonance as a compositional tool. Our sense of touch is highly developed and at times seems to have a direct link to our sense of sight – we only have to look at an object and in most cases we know instantly how it will feel to touch it. Teasing out the texture in the

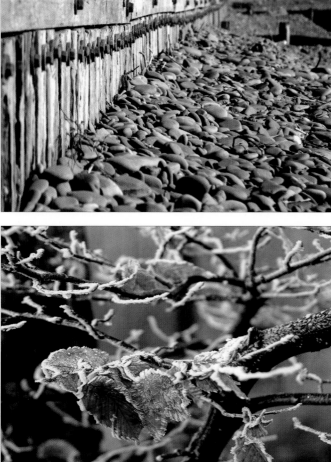

LEFT This image exhibits contrasting pairs of textures and patterns between the retaining wooden posts and the pebbles on the beach, creating an interesting photograph from what at first appears uninspiring surroundings.

BELOW Soft lighting, combined with the water has created bright reflections and deep shadows that help to bring out the texture of the stone.

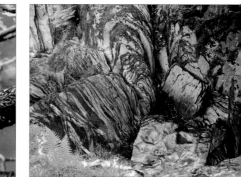

LEFT The thin ice enhances the subtle textures within this classic shot of leaves enveloped by frost.

BELOW By photographing a group of one species of flower, we become instantly aware of nature's natural patterns. This in turn places more emphasis on the bee.

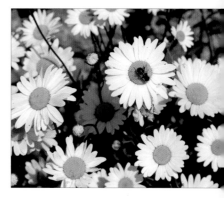

objects we photograph will, therefore, elicit a strong response from viewers, even though they know it is simply a two-dimensional image of the object.

To really appreciate the texture of individual objects, you'll often need to focus as close as you can to the object you're photographing. Light needs to meet the object's surface at 45 degrees or less so that the object casts shadows, which emphasize the texture itself. To ensure the texture is as pronounced as possible, the object is best lit from one side, as this will create the strongest shadows. So, if you're shooting outdoors and you want to capture the texture of peeling paint on an old wall (at 90 degrees vertical), shoot when the sun is high in the sky (at around midday). However, if the object is flat on the ground, shoot early in the morning or late in the afternoon when the sun is lower.

Although we usually get in close to isolate an object's texture, this isn't a hard and fast rule. Texture can also be appreciated on a much larger scale, particularly if it helps to convey an emotion or message. For a texture-filled landscape, for example, set your lens to its widest angle and get low on the ground to ensure you focus as close as you can to what's beneath you. Point the camera up slightly so that the distant view is also visible and then make a couple of exposures.

Composing with Lines: Horizontals

In photographic composition, lines, no matter how they are formed, whether artificial or natural, are a key element – from the horizontal horizon of a serene landscape, through the powerful, towering verticals of a cityscape, to the diagonal lines that can lead a viewer's eye through a photograph.

On the next few pages, we will look at how lines can add structure to a composition, and how – if badly managed – they can spoil an otherwise good composition.

Landscapes

Horizontal lines in the composition of an image are likely to be most apparent in landscape photography, where a horizontal format best suits the subject matter. Horizontal lines tend to imbue an image with a feeling of calm and stability, and even timelessness and permanency.

▼ **BELOW** The unbroken horizon works well with the much smaller broken horizontals of these hay bales.

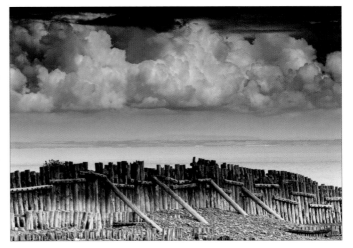

Horizons

The most commonly occurring horizontal line is the horizon of a landscape or seascape, which will often be the basis from which the rest of the image emanates. An unbroken horizon can sometimes make an image appear flat and lifeless, so try to punctuate it with other elements, such as trees, hills or buildings, unless

▲ **ABOVE** This image mixes horizontals and verticals. The groynes, clouds and the sea form strong horizontals, but the groynes themselves are also vertical, contrasting with the clouds.

▼ **BELOW** The repetitive horizontal lines of the bridges running off into the distance create a sense of tranquillity in this late afternoon photograph of Prague.

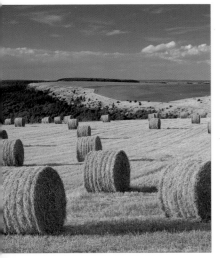

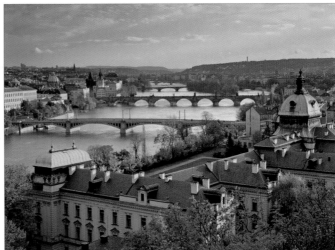

you're trying to convey a specific message or visual impact. Additionally, concentrate on ensuring that the horizon is as straight as possible.

Rule of thirds

When deciding where the horizon should be positioned in your image, remember the rule of thirds (see pages 126–127). As a general rule, images tend to work better if the horizon is either a third up or down the image – but this is only a guideline and there are plenty of successful images that feature horizons in the centre of the frame. Horizontals also help to add depth to photographs by providing visual breaks. Think of a view down a city river that features a number of bridges or a landscape image that shows fields of different crops running off into the distance.

Portrait format

If there are a number of strong horizontals in the scene, try turning your camera through 90 degrees and taking a portrait-format photograph. Too many horizontals can cause the eye to tire, but as a portrait-format shot, the eye will tend to look down and register the depth of the image.

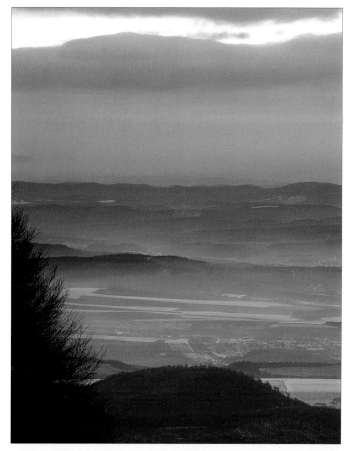

▲ **ABOVE RIGHT** When an image displays so many horizontals that the image, if shot in landscape format, would tire the eye. In these instances, it's better to shoot portrait.

▶ **RIGHT** The numerous broken horizontals of the roofs of the houses add to the chaotic atmosphere of this image.

Straight horizontals

If horizontals are a significant element of an image's composition, it's essential that they are straight. If you don't intend to edit your images on computer, use a tripod with built-in levels to ensure horizontals are exactly straight.

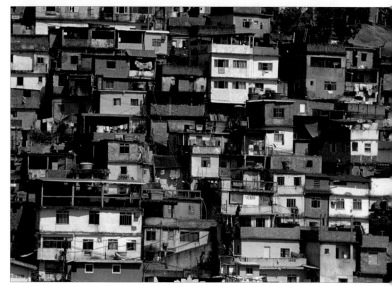

Composing with Lines: Verticals

Like horizontals, vertical lines can also convey strong emotions. Power, grandeur and strength are all words that are associated with images that feature numerous vertical lines.

Many of the rules that apply to horizontals also apply to verticals, not least trying to keep them parallel to the edge of the image. This can be quite difficult, as they often feature in images in which the camera has been pointed upward in order to capture the entire scene. This can create the problem of 'converging verticals', where a building or other tall object seems to grow increasingly narrow the higher up you look. It's the same as the vanishing point effect in which railway lines appear to reach a single point as they stretch out into the distance – only with converging verticals you're looking 'up' rather than 'along'.

If you have a single, vertical object in the image, use the rule of thirds and don't place it in the middle of the frame, unless the resulting symmetry adds to the composition.

Landscape format

Most photographs that contain strong verticals are usually shot with the camera held vertically, not only to better accommodate the image, but also to accentuate the height of the vertical lines. As with horizontals, however, it doesn't always have to be this way. Experiment by shooting the odd frame in landscape format. Numerous vertical lines all in a row can accentuate the width of the scene or form a pattern. In addition, try to remember that your images will be reproduced in two dimensions and visualize this when you are out taking photographs. For example, lines that are painted on a flat road

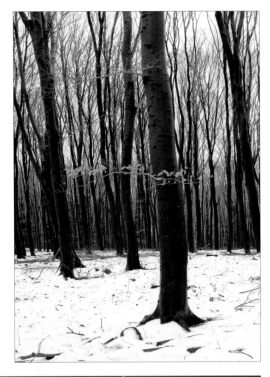

RIGHT The strong vertical lines of the trees are exaggerated and emphasized by choosing a portrait-format shape for this photograph.

BELOW The verticality of many modern cities makes for very dramatic images and conveys a sense of scale.

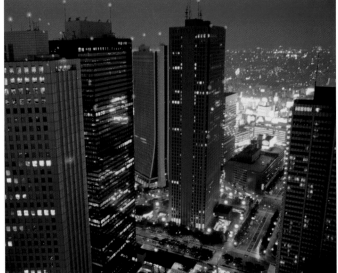

leading off into the distance will translate as converging verticals in your two-dimensional image, not only adding a sense of depth to the image but also leading the eye.

RIGHT Look out for the pattern that occurs in repeating vertical structures.

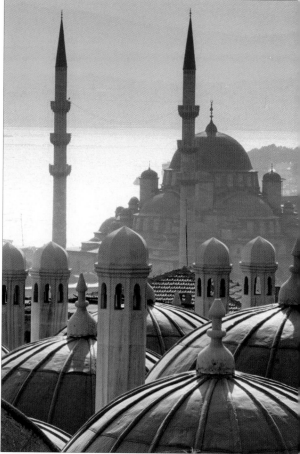

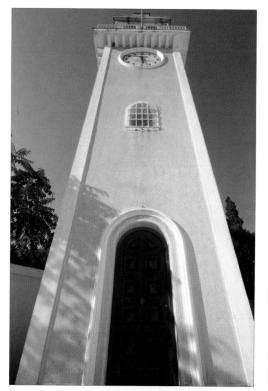

ABOVE The height of this imposing bell tower has been exaggerated by using a wide-angle lens placed at the base of the tower and pointed upward.

RIGHT The mix of vertical lines in the field and the horizontal row of trees in the distance work in either a portrait or landscape format, with the horizon remaining central in the frame.

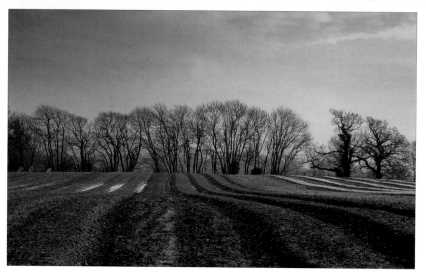

Composing with Lines: Diagonals

While strong vertical and horizontal lines provide structure to an image and create visual boundaries, they can at times 'ground' an image, making it solid yet static. If you want to add a sense of movement to an image, look for strong diagonal lines instead. These tend to produce the most dynamic results and lead the viewer's eye through an image, especially when they lead to the subject of the photograph.

Symmetry

It's unlikely that it would happen, but avoid recording a line that runs directly from one corner of the image to another. Diagonals work better when they appear from one-third/two-thirds up or one-third/two-thirds along the frame – and usually from bottom left if they are to serve as a leading line.

Of course, if you're trying to show how different two areas of a specific scene are, then dividing them exactly in half with a diagonal that runs corner to corner may well provide a striking image.

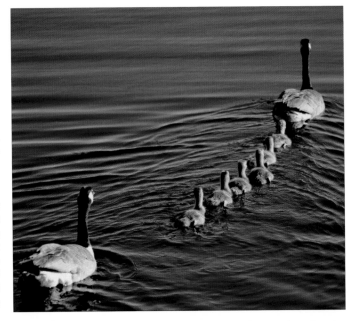

ABOVE The diagonal representation of this common wildlife scene helps to make the image a little more dynamic.

BELOW The breaking waves form a diagonal, leading the viewer to San Francisco's famous Golden Gate Bridge – the subject of the image.

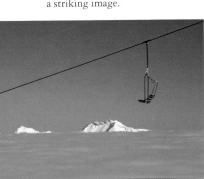

ABOVE Diagonal lines work best when they don't run from corner to corner, but instead enter the frame one-third or two-thirds up or across the image, as in this shot of a lone ski lift chair.

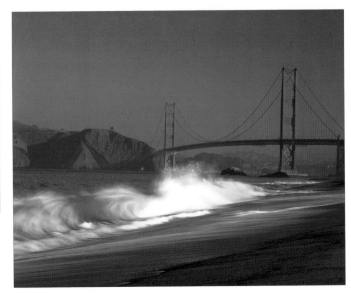

Most of the time, one diagonal line will be enough to add dynamic effect and to lead the viewer's eye into the frame, but look out also for clashing diagonals as these can add tension to an image and create a sense of chaos (which may or may not be a good thing).

Vanishing point

One of the most powerful ways in which diagonals are used is when they converge to create a vanishing point. When we first think of vanishing points, we usually think of the somewhat clichéd railway tracks or roads, but vanishing points occur naturally as well, it's just that they're usually less well-defined in form, tone or colour. For example, you may find you can create a vanishing point by using a diagonal line of clouds converging on a hedge that runs from you into the distance.

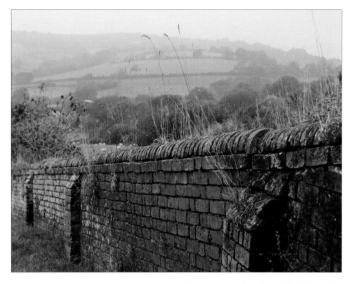

ABOVE The wall in this image runs diagonally, but it isn't that successful as it runs across the frame in the wrong direction – from left to right and out of the frame.

BELOW The raking diagonal highlights add to the sense of movement and purpose in this shot, and create a contrast with the pattern of the tiled floor.

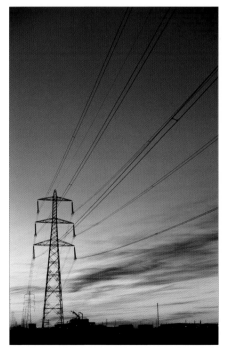

ABOVE The converging diagonals of the power lines take the viewer into the shot and out the other side.

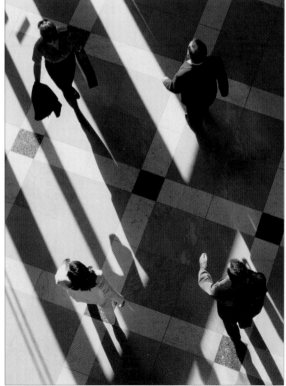

Composing with Curves

We have seen that straight lines can help to add structure, inject movement and elicit specific emotional responses from a composition. But what do curves do for an image? Curves, like diagonals, tend to add dynamism and movement to an image and help to lead the viewer's eye through the picture. Furthermore, several conflicting curves can add tension and chaos to a composition.

S-curve

The most powerful compositional curve is the S-shaped curve, or S-curve. This not only provides motion to an image, but it also adds balance and grace. Look out for S-curves both in nature, such as a meandering river or the edge of a stand of trees, or ones that have been made artificially, such as a winding path. The latter provide a visual way through the image and suggest to the viewer both a literal and metaphorical journey.

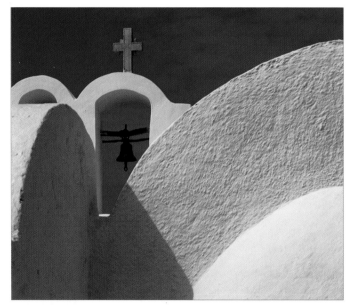

ABOVE The curves of this Greek Orthodox church contrast against the vertical and horizontal lines of the cross.

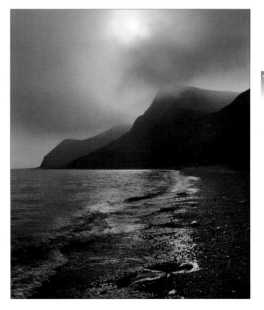

LEFT Most of the compositional curves that appear in photographs are likely to be made up of something solid and fairly permanent – such as hedgerows, roads or river courses – but remember you're freezing an instant in time, during which anything can form a curve for a short time.

Leading lines

During our discussion of diagonal lines and curves, there has been a number of references to 'leading lines' and 'leading the eye'. As their names suggest, leading lines lead the viewer into the image, and should ideally lead the viewer's gaze to the subject of the image.

Leading lines tend to work best when they start from the bottom left of the frame, as it's more natural for the eye to 'read' from left to right. An important tip to consider, however, is that while it's good practice and recommended that the line can lead in from an edge, in most cases it's unwise to have it running out of the frame at the other side. The reasoning behind this is that while you want to encourage viewers into the frame with a leading line, you don't want them then to follow the line out of the frame, without stopping and considering the image for a while.

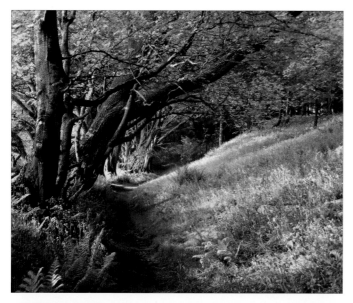

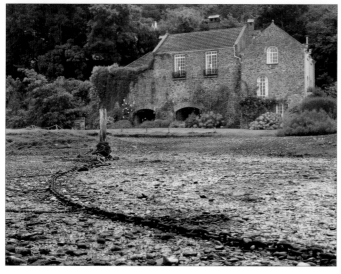

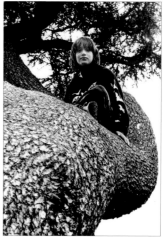

▼ **BELOW** The slight S-shape to the remains of the sea at low tide adds movement to this image, as well as drawing our attention to the boat.

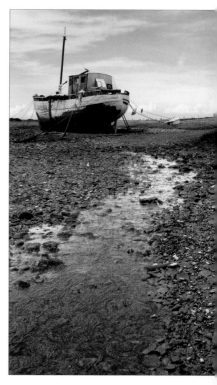

Using curves

When walking around looking for potential landscape images, remember that not all landscapes are shot with a wide-angle lens or zoom setting. Telephoto lenses or settings can reveal compositional elements that were not immediately visible with wide-angle lenses.

▲ **TOP** Curves, like diagonals, can act as leading lines, taking or guiding the viewer through an image. The most successful are leading lines or curves that lead the viewer from the edge of the frame into the body of the image where the subject can be found.

▲ **ABOVE** Here, a rusty old mooring chain revealed only at low tide acts as a leading line curve to the house beyond.

Landscape versus Portrait

A clue to the novice photographer's picture collection is that it's likely to contain images shot solely in the horizontal or landscape shape or format. Convention used to dictate that landscapes were shot horizontally and portraits vertically, but it doesn't have to be that way, and nor should it be.

Fresh perspective

There are plenty of examples when turning the camera through 90° will provide you with a much better shape for your landscape image. Trees obviously spring to mind, especially if you've had to retire some distance to fit your subject into the landscape format. By photographing a golden, autumnal tree in the vertical format, not only are you more likely to be able to get closer, you'll also avoid having unwanted elements to the left and right of the tree in the frame.

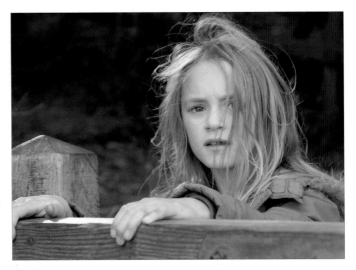

ABOVE Not all portraits have to be taken in an upright, portrait format – the rules can be broken. The lines of the gate and the gatepost contain this image, while the subject is perfectly placed using the rule of thirds.

There are many examples where shooting landscapes vertically will offer a much more complementary framing shape – mountains, valleys and rivers may all benefit from this treatment. Try to get into the habit of framing a potential landscape in the vertical format, even if you've successfully captured the scene in the more conventional horizontal landscape format. After a while, you'll look at landscapes in different ways and when you come to show your images to other people, particularly when putting a small portfolio or exhibition together, you'll be grateful for the variety of images in both shapes.

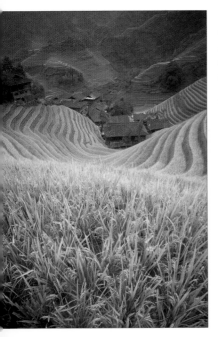

LEFT Using a portrait format has emphasized the shape of the terracing of these paddy fields and helped to add depth to the fields in the distance.

Architecture

Buildings and cityscapes offer more opportunities to experiment with both horizontal- and vertical-format photographs. Once you've become used to turning your camera, you'll start to see how certain elements make for an attractive landscape format image, while changing your angle or point of view slightly may bring other background elements into play that would make for a more pleasing portrait-format shot.

In context

While full-length portraits lend themselves to the vertical format, not all portraits need to be shot this way. A landscape format may be the better option, depending on the position of your subject's arms – especially if outstretched – or whether you want to include contextualizing background. Also, don't forget the rule of thirds. Even if the portrait is just a head-and-shoulders shot, you may want to position the subject to one side to avoid it being in the centre of the frame.

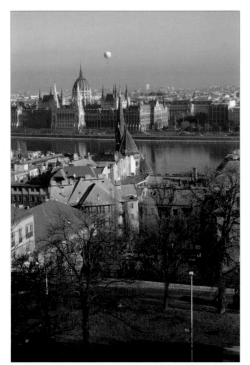

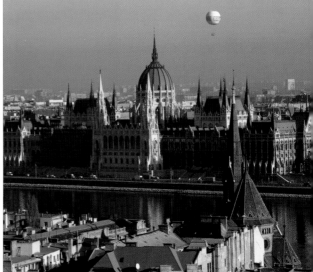

LEFT AND BELOW Both of these images are of the same scene taken from an identical viewpoint, but they both look very different. In the first image (left), a wide-angle lens and portrait format show us much more of the scene, while in the second image (below), a long focal length lens and a landscape format create a tightly cropped picture.

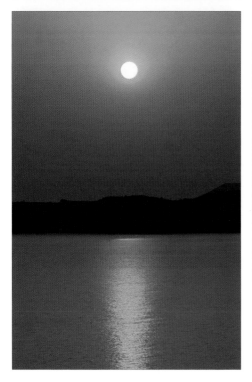

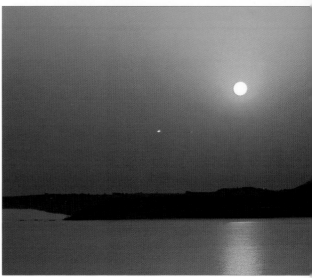

LEFT It pays to experiment with a landscape or portrait format. Here the photographer has used a portrait format to emphasize the long reflection of the sun on the sea.

ABOVE In this landscape version, the sun's reflection plays a less important role, but the wider format includes more of the delicately coloured sky and the calming horizontal of the land.

Compositional Balance

When you look at certain images, particularly those that feature two or more key elements, you may often get a sense that things aren't quite right, although the reason for this is not immediately apparent. If so, it may be that the image is unbalanced in terms of its composition.

Vertical axis

Balance in composition is mostly determined by how well the primary elements of the image are divided by the vertical axis that runs more or less down the centre of the image.

Balance can also be achieved through the horizontal axis, such as the reflection of a tree in a pond.

Symmetrical balance

The easiest and most straight-forward compositional balance is often referred to as 'symmetrical' balance. As its name suggests, symmetrical balance is achieved when two objects of equal 'weight' are positioned on either side of the central vertical dividing line, so that one object on one side of the image balances out the other object on the other side.

Symmetrical balance creates a sense of stability, order and tranquillity in an image, and it is used successfully in architectural photography, formal group portraits and for any number of 'artificial' landscapes, such as an avenue of trees or a formal garden.

Asymmetrical balance

While symmetrical compositions certainly provide visual balance and bring a sense of order and calm to an image, viewing a succession of symmetrically balanced images would ultimately be a rather dull and boring affair. Of much greater visual interest are asymmetrically balanced images. These can provide a sense of depth to an image and are much more dynamic, but you do need to think harder about how balance is achieved.

Asymmetrical balance works on the basis that objects in an image each have their own visual 'mass' – whether it's their physical size, how colourful they are, how bright they are, whether or not the object is in focus and so on. A well-balanced image will have the various components arranged in such a way

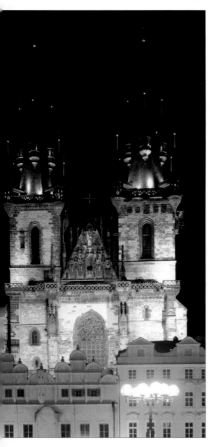

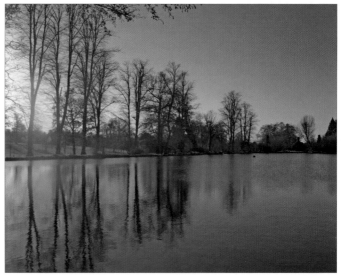

LEFT This picture is a strong example of a symmetrically balanced composition, where the two towers in the background balance each other perfectly.

ABOVE This scene also relies heavily on a symmetrical composition to balance the image – in this case with the row of trees and their reflections in the water.

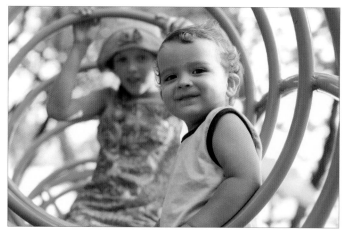

that their various 'weights' are balanced. For example, objects with greater contrast have more weight than low-contrasting elements, therefore to achieve balance the low-contrasting element needs to be bigger than the high-contrasting one.

There's no quick way to master asymmetrical balance, and rather than stifling your creativity by

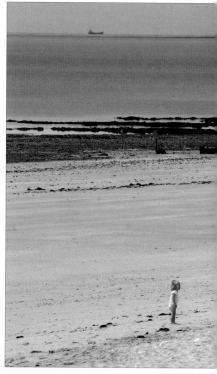

ABOVE Colourful subjects and larger subjects may carry more weight in a composition, but this is balanced here by the figure in the foreground being in sharp focus.

rigidly sticking to the 'rules', it's better to keep shooting and simply be aware of how objects of a different size, colour, contrast and visual appeal interact with each other.

ABOVE This asymmetrical composition is well balanced thanks to the colours of the sea and the sand, their relative sizes and the isolated subjects at the bottom and top.

Asymmetry in action

It is important to be aware of the weight that the different components in the composition can carry. The basic ideas are:

- An object at the edge of the frame has more weight than a centred one.
- Irregular shapes have more weight than regular ones.
- Colourful elements carry more weight than less colourful ones.
- Isolated objects carry more weight than those that are surrounded by other objects.
- More interesting objects attract greater attention than less interesting ones. For example, people's faces have greater weight than buildings or landmarks.
- Objects in focus take precedence over out-of-focus objects.
- Objects being looked at by people in an image gain emphasis.

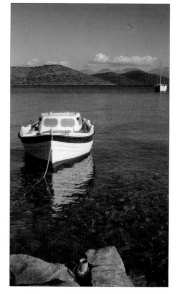

ABOVE While our attention is initially grabbed by the larger boat in the foreground, the image is balanced thanks to the smaller boat in the background and to the right.

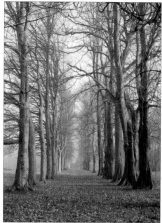

ABOVE Symmetrical balance is easily achieved in this image of an avenue of trees in a misty parkland setting. The trees also create a pleasing vanishing point.

Basic Composition – Try It Yourself

Now that we've looked at some of the basic compositional tips, it's time to get shooting. Below is a short summary of the compositional 'rules' discussed so far, with some key assignments that will help you to explore them further so you can begin to see for yourself how following some of the rules some of the time can help make your images more dynamic. Remember, it's important not to get too tied up with these rules, particularly if you start to find that you're not taking any photos at all because your scenes don't apparently meet any of the compositional requirements. Often a scene will look inviting, yet you can't quite understand why. Don't stop and try to work out what compositional rules it's fulfilling; simply take the shot and review your image later.

Keep it simple

Take several shots that make it very clear to the viewer what the subject of the picture is. Try to ensure there isn't any marginal clutter or any other distracting objects.

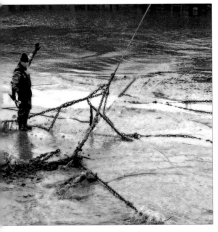

Framing

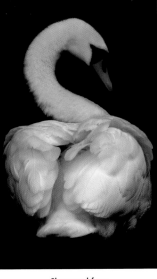

Shape and form

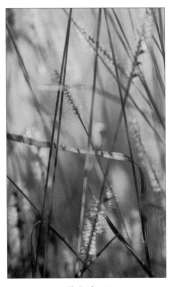

Fill the frame

Fill the frame

Take a few shots of different objects that appeal to you because of their shape, colour or form, or because the light reflecting off them is attractive. Really zoom into the subject to ensure that there is no surrounding clutter.

Rule of thirds

Try to find different scenes that fulfil the 'rule of thirds'. Bear in mind that you don't have to find four key elements to fit all the 'points of interest'. Sometimes just one or two will do to make an effective composition.

Framing

Create some instances where you have the opportunity of putting a frame within a frame. Remember that the key word is 'create', so you can be proactive here and take a picture of someone looking through a window or even take a shot looking out of a window. Bear in mind that the frame should ideally be attractive in its own right and it should also complement the subject of the image in some way.

Camera height and camera angle

Take some shots with a radically altered camera height and others using different camera angles. The objective is to give a fresh perspective to a scene that will make the viewer take a closer look at the image.

Shape and form

Remember that we tend to use two-dimensional shape to recognize objects, while form gives an object a three-dimensional appearance. Take several shots of various objects so that the viewer gets only a sense of its shape, and then use different lighting conditions or a different angle to take some more shots of the same objects that provide the viewer with a sense of the objects' form.

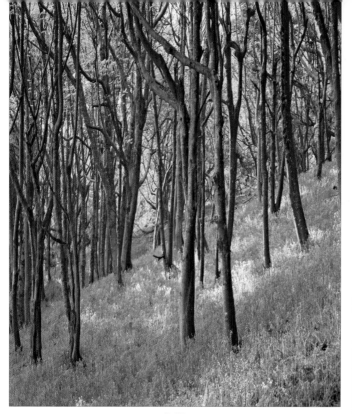

Vertical lines

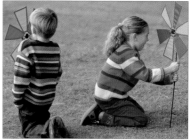

Landscape versus portrait

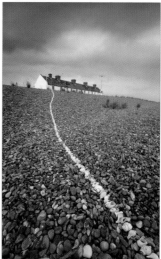

Leading lines

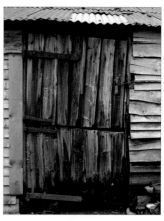

Texture

Pattern and texture

A fun and surprisingly rewarding exercise; simply take several images that exploit an object's pattern or texture. Remember to consider the angle of the light to emphasize texture, and think laterally about what constitutes 'pattern'.

Horizontals and verticals

Shoot a few objects or scenes that evoke a sense of peace and calm due to the presence of horizontal lines and three objects or scenes that use vertical lines.

Working with diagonals

Look out for scenes in which a diagonal line leads the viewer through the image. Ideally it should take the viewer to the subject of the photograph.

Curves and leading lines

S-curves and leading lines help viewers into the image, and ideally take them to the subject of the image.

Look for S-curves and leading lines in both nature and man-made scenes and try to take five images that feature these compositional aids.

Portrait versus landscape

When you find a good subject for a photograph, it's worth considering the benefits of turning the camera through 90° to see if it provides a fresh perspective. Remember that landscapes don't always have to be shot in a landscape format, and nor do portraits always have to be shot in the standard portrait format.

Compositional balance

From now on, try to think about achieving compositional balance in your images. If one of the subjects of your image is large, try to offset it with one that is smaller, but pushed more to the edge of the image area, or is more colourful, brighter, has greater visual appeal and so on.

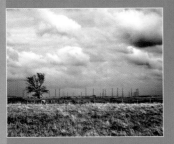
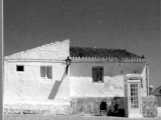
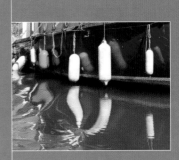

4

Exposure – the basics

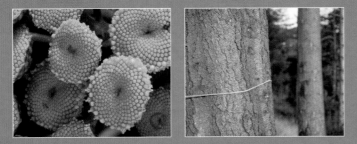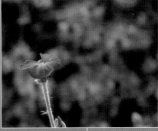

Armed with a sound knowledge of the camera's settings, we put that knowledge to more creative uses in this chapter. The importance of understanding exposure, aperture and taking light readings, depth of field and selective focusing are all covered – and are essential concepts to understand in order to advance your photography. Also explored is the significance of shutter speed and how blur, speed and panning can all be used to creative effect. We take a look at lighting and the pivotal role it plays when taking photographs. Finally, the chapter concludes with exercises to reinforce your familiarity with aperture and shutter controls.

Understanding Exposure

The most fundamental technical aspect of photography is exposure. When it comes to exposure, digital cameras behave almost exactly like film cameras. Exposure governs whether a picture is too bright, too dark or just right – although this is often subjective, of course.

There are three settings that govern exposure – the shutter speed (which determines how long the sensor is exposed to light); the aperture (which determines how much light reaches the sensor); and the ISO setting (which determines the sensitivity of the sensor). Setting the latter on a digital camera is the same as choosing film speed. These three elements combine to provide a specific exposure – if one element is altered, one of the other two settings must also change if the same exposure is to be retained.

Shutter speed and aperture

To provide complete information about a specific exposure you need to know the shutter speed (usually a fraction of a second, but it can be much longer than a second), the aperture (expressed as an 'f'-number) and the ISO setting/film speed; this is why you will often see an exposure setting written as $1/125$ sec at f/5.6 (ISO 200). If these individual settings provided the 'correct' exposure, then altering one setting without altering either of the other two would result in an 'inaccurate' exposure. For example, if the shutter speed was reduced by half to $1/250$ sec, the image would be underexposed. If, however, at the same time the shutter speed was reduced by half the size of the aperture was doubled (from f/5.6 to f/4), or the ISO setting/film speed was increased to 400, then the exposure would remain

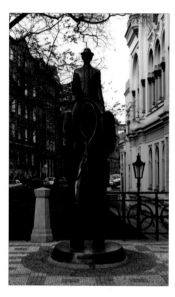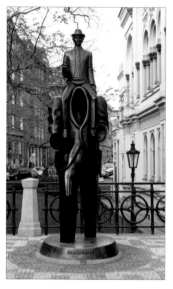

the same – in this way, $1/125$ sec at f/5.6 (ISO 200) provides the same exposure as $1/250$ sec at f/4 (ISO 200), which in turn provides the same exposure as $1/250$ sec at f/5.6 (ISO 400).

ISO settings

Specific to digital photography, ISO settings now play an integral part in governing exposure. Previously, the relationship between shutter speed and aperture primarily governed the exposure, since you couldn't change the film in a camera with every shot. Now that digital ISO can be altered at will, this setting can be used in a proactive way to get the optimum exposure for every shot you take. The lowest ISO setting will always provide the best image quality, so you should aim to use the lowest possible ISO setting at all times (especially if you're using a compact camera), and only increase the sensitivity if, for example, there's a risk of camera shake due to slow shutter speed.

Low ISO

Assuming, that you set the ISO at the lowest possible setting (while still being able to hold the camera without the risk of camera shake), it's the relationship between shutter speed and aperture that will ultimately dictate the exposure.

As we shall see over the following pages, these are the two important elements to control. The aperture setting determines the depth of field (how much of the scene is sharply in focus) while shutter speed determines whether a moving object is blurred or not. Aside from the general composition, these two main photographic controls will govern how your images will turn out.

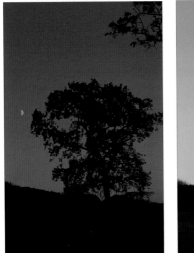 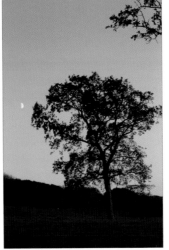 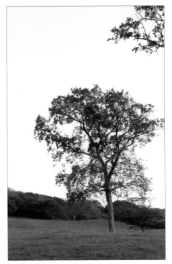

ABOVE These three images were taken at the same time of day, but they appear very different. Using a tripod to ensure the scene was exactly the same, the first shot, the darkest, was given a manual exposure of f/5 at ¹/₃₂₀₀ sec (ISO 200); the second shot was taken using f/5 at ¹/₂₀₀ sec (ISO 200); while the final image, the brightest image, was exposed at f/5 at ¹/₁₆ sec (ISO 200). Manually altering the shutter speed has greatly affected the exposure of each shot.

BELOW This shot demonstrates a well balanced exposure giving detail in the trees but not blowing out highlights in the distance. Being able to manually alter exposure is essential for a shot such as this one.

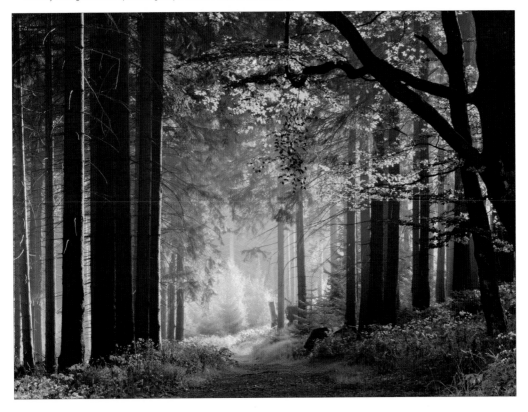

What the Aperture Does

There are different sized apertures on a camera to allow different amounts of light to pass through to the sensor.

When the shutter is released it allows light to pass through the aperture. The aperture controls depth of field as well as contributing to the exposure of an image. The correlation between shutter speed and aperture size is a direct one; the immediate situation or the effect required dictates the necessary combination of shutter speed and size of aperture. If, for instance, an exposure of ¹/₁₅ sec and an aperture of f/22 are needed, the aperture would get wider as the shutter speed increases.

Automatic cameras

Some automatic cameras have a system called aperture priority. When the aperture is set the camera automatically adjusts the shutter speed. Care must be taken in cases where the chosen aperture is quite small, e.g. f/11 or f/16, as the shutter speed selected may be too slow to take an accurate shot without the steadying aid of a tripod or other support. As always, with practice you will get to know the best approach.

▶ **RIGHT** These leaves are in focus while the forest background is completely lost. See pp168–175 for more on depth of field.

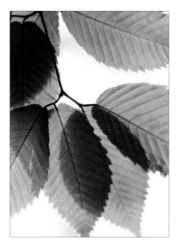

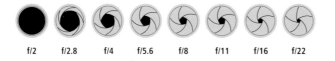

| f/2 | f/2.8 | f/4 | f/5.6 | f/8 | f/11 | f/16 | f/22 |

◀ **LEFT** Not all lenses will have such a wide range of aperture sizes as this; many will only offer from f/4 to f/16, but this shows that the higher the number; the smaller the aperture. This has a direct bearing on depth of field. Changing the aperture from f/5.6 to f/8 halves the amount of light reaching the sensor, or how changing the aperture from f/16 to f/11 doubles the amount of light reaching the sensor.

EXPOSURE ALTERNATIVES

Aperture	f/2	f/2.8	f/4	f/5.6	f/8	f/11	f/16	f/22
Shutter speed	¹/₁₀₀₀	¹/₅₀₀	¹/₂₅₀	¹/₁₂₅	¹/₆₀	¹/₃₀	¹/₁₅	¹/₈
ISO	100	100	100	100	100	100	100	100

ISO ALTERNATIVES (TABLE A)

Aperture	f/2.8	f/4	f/5.6	f/8	f/11	f/16
Shutter speed	¹/₃₀	¹/₃₀	¹/₃₀	¹/₃₀	¹/₃₀	¹/₃₀
ISO	100	200	400	800	1600	3200

◀ **LEFT** If using f/2.8 at ¹/₃₀ sec with ISO 100 provides an accurate exposure, by changing the ISO setting you will also have to change either the aperture (Table A) or the shutter speed (Table B). In Table A, changing the ISO to 800 allows an aperture of f/8 to be used, giving much greater depth of field than f/2.8, so more of the image will be in focus. In Table B, changing the ISO to 800 has enabled a shutter speed of ¹/₅₀₀ sec, which would be good for fast action. Although film speed (ISO) is as important as the ISO setting on a digital camera, once a film is loaded, the only possible alterations of exposure for that roll are based on aperture and shutter speed selection.

ISO ALTERNATIVES (TABLE B)

Aperture	f/2.8	f/2.8	f/2.8	f/2.8	f/2.8	f/2.8
Shutter speed	¹/₃₀	¹/₆₀	¹/₂₅₀	¹/₅₀₀	¹/₁₀₀₀	¹/₂₀₀₀
ISO	100	200	400	800	1600	3200

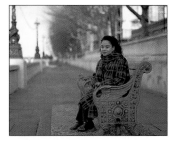

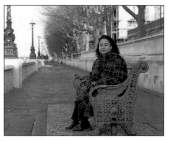

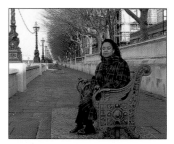

▲ **ABOVE** This picture was taken using a standard lens at an aperture of f/2.8. The girl is in focus and so is the front arm of the seat but everything else is out of focus.

▲ **ABOVE** In this picture an aperture of f/8 was used. More of the seat and background are sharper but the distance is still unclear.

▲ **ABOVE** Here the lens was stopped down to f/22. All the seat is sharp and the far distance is only slightly soft. By reducing the size of the aperture more of the picture is brought into focus, i.e. the depth of field increases.

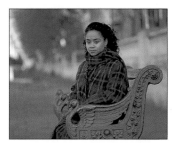

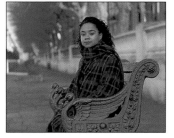

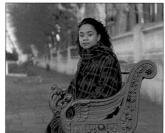

▲ **ABOVE** In this picture a medium telephoto lens was used and focused on the girl. Depth of field is minimal at an aperture of f/4.5.

▲ **ABOVE** Using the same telephoto lens an aperture of f/11 has been used but the background still remains very soft.

▲ **ABOVE** With the lens stopped right down to f/32 much more of the picture is in focus, yet it is not as sharp as in the first picture. Depth of field is greater with wide angle lenses than it is with telephoto lenses.

▶ **RIGHT** Using the aperture to achieve a very shallow depth of field (see pp 168–175 for details) enables you to focus on just one part of an image for a powerful shot.

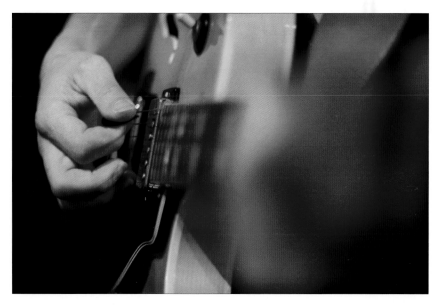

Light Readings

Most cameras today have built-in exposure metering systems. These should enable the photographer to get the correct exposure every time. However, in many situations the metering system can be led astray by the general level of light, so that the subject of the photograph is over-or underexposed. This is because many systems take an average reading of the illumination over the whole frame. If you are photographing a person against a white wall, or if there is a lot of sky in the frame, these big light areas will have the greatest influence on the meter. Unless you compensate for this the person will come out underexposed, in extreme cases reduced to a silhouette. Conversely, if you place a person against a dark

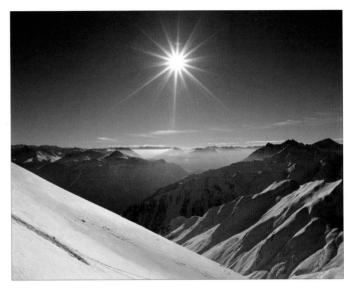

background the metering system will read mainly for this area, and if you do not make an adjustment the person will come out overexposed.

The automatic exposure lock

The overexposure problem described above can usually be resolved by using the camera's automatic exposure lock. This sets itself when the shutter release is lightly pressed, or held halfway down. It maintains the current exposure setting until the release is pressed to fire the shutter, or until the button is released altogether. So

▲ **ABOVE** Bright sun and snow could lead to underexposure if using an autometer, but manual overexposure will fix this, leading to well-balanced exposure in the final shot.

you can go up close to your subject, take an accurate reading from their flesh tones, keep holding the shutter release halfway down and go back to your chosen viewpoint to perfect the composition of the shot. Then, fully depress the shutter release button. If you want to take several shots you will have to follow the same procedure for each one.

▼ **BELOW** Bracketing exposures lets you make slight variations in exposure that may make all the difference to the final picture. In this case the difference was ⅓ of a stop between each one. Here, left, the meter gave a reading that has slightly underexposed the girl, making her eyes look heavy and dark.

With the aperture increased slightly, middle, the skin tones are more natural and the shadowiness of the eyes has been eliminated.

A further increase in the exposure has made the facial features begin to burn out. So the picture on the right would be chosen for the final print.

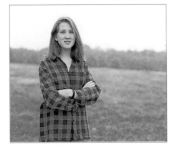

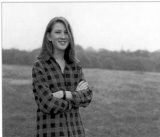

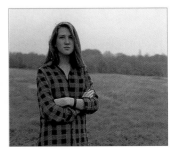

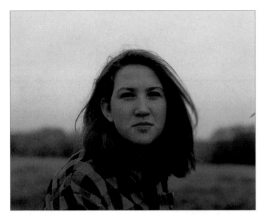

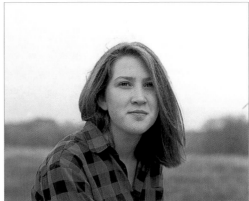

Spot metering

If your camera has a variable metering system, you can use spot metering in such cases. This restricts the meter to measuring the light falling on a small spot in the centre of the viewfinder, so you would just need to have your subject's face at the centre of the composition.

Using a hand-held meter

There are two main ways of taking a reading with a hand-held meter:
• For a reflected light reading, point the meter at the subject and take a reading of the light reflected from it.
• For an incident light reading, place a small white disc, or invercone, over the meter cell. Some meters have a white blind which can be slid down over the cell. Hold the meter against the subject and point it back towards your camera. This gives a much more accurate reading of the light falling on the subject.

Bracketing

Another way of getting the correct exposure if you are using a film-back camera is to bracket, or effectively hedge your bets. Imagine that the metering system is giving a reading of $\frac{1}{125}$ at f/8. If you take one shot at this setting, one slightly over it and one slightly under, when the film is processed you can judge which exposure has worked best and make a print from that negative.

ABOVE The camera meter took an average reading. As there was so much sky, which even on a dull day is bright in comparison to other areas of the picture, the girl has come out underexposed in the left hand picture. On the right, going in close and using the camera's exposure lock has given a truer reading of the flesh tones and a far more flattering exposure.

BELOW Spot metering has given an accurate exposure of the girl. If your camera does not have this feature you will have to use the exposure lock or a hand-held meter.

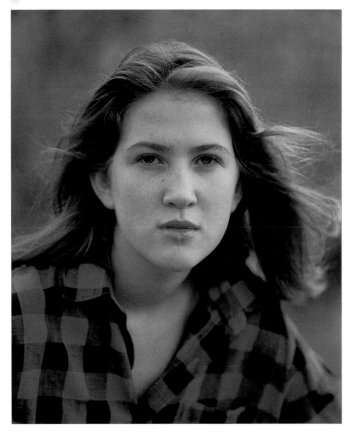

Manual Exposure with a Digital Camera

The modern camera has various preset automatic and semi-automatic settings and modes, which are found on almost all digital cameras. These help us to obtain sharply focused and accurately exposed photographs between 80–90 percent of the time in a variety of popular shooting scenarios. For many people, understanding these modes and settings will provide them with everything they need to get the photographs they want. However, if you want to stretch your creativity, take control and make the most of your camera in more challenging lighting conditions, it's important to understand how to use your camera in its Manual (M) mode. Experimenting with a variety of shutter and aperture settings with the camera in Manual, ensures that you end up with more accurately exposed images – more consistently.

Exposure

Having discussed how the relationship between aperture and shutter speed (and ISO setting) works to determine exposure, we're halfway there to understanding how to use a camera in its Manual mode.

With the camera in Manual you set both the shutter speed and the aperture independently of one another. This can lead to horrendous exposure miscalculations, particularly if you're used to using automatic or semi-automatic modes. You may, for example, set the shutter speed to $^{1}/_{500}$ of a second (sec) to freeze action and an aperture setting of f/11 to get as much of the scene as possible in focus, but unless you're in anything other than an extremely bright lighting situation at the time you press the shutter release, you're going to end up with a very underexposed image.

Alternatively, in the heat of the action, you may simply forget that the aperture is set on f/4 and keep firing away only to find that all your images are overexposed.

Viewfinder scale bar

To help you obtain the correct exposure in Manual mode, look through the viewfinder and there should be a form of scale bar. It will usually have a '0' in the centre and then some marks to both left and right (or above and below), with perhaps the figures '-1' and '-2' to the left (or below) and '(+)1' and '(+)2' to the right (above). The '0' indicates 'correct' exposure, while the minus figures indicate slight underexposure and the positive figures overexposure. Each mark is referred to as a 'stop', so +2 indicates 2 stops overexposed. You'll notice that as you adjust either the aperture or shutter speed settings, the marker will indicate the new exposure on the scale bar.

Aim for 'zero'

While ideally you're trying to 'zero' the exposure, anything within the -2 to +2 range will usually provide a usable image. In fact, this is the whole point of shooting in Manual mode. You may in fact find that when you review your images, the one with a -1 or even -2 setting (slightly underexposed) provides a better overall image than '0', which is theoretically more accurately exposed. This is down to complex lighting situations when the camera's metering system, however sophisticated, is not able to read your mind and know exactly what it is you're exposing for. For example, with the camera set in an automatic mode, in very shadowy conditions, the camera will often

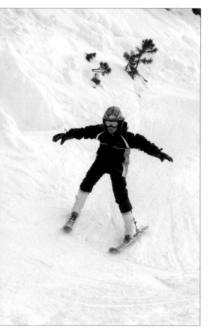

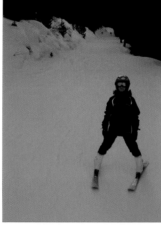

LEFT AND ABOVE Under certain lighting conditions, especially those in which there is a lot of reflected light, the camera's metering system is likely to underexpose the scene (as on the right). In cases such as this, exposure will need to be set manually.

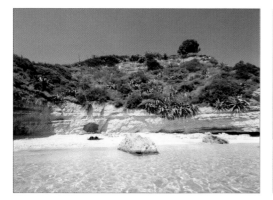

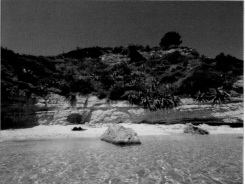

overexpose the subject as the dark ambient light tricks the metering system into thinking it's darker than it really is. Similarly, in very light conditions, such as snow scenes, the opposite will often occur – the bright, reflected light will fool the camera into thinking it's brighter than it really is and underexpose the subject. When ready to shoot, set an appropriate exposure (aiming for close to 'zero'), take a shot and review the results using the histogram and image preview on the LCD. Adjust any settings if necessary and fire the shutter again.

If at any point during your exposure adjustment the pointer reaches the end of the scale bar and flashes, this may well indicate that the image, if taken, will be so over- or under-exposed that it will be unusable.

Creativity

One of the principal reasons for using Manual mode is when you deliberately want an under- or over-exposed image for creative reasons. In any automatic or semi-automatic setting the camera will always aim to achieve a 'correct' exposure. As we'll see later, shooting in Manual mode is also often the only way to capture very low-light or night scenes.

Doubtless you'll find that when you first start shooting in Manual mode you'll work more slowly and make a number of exposure errors, but stick with it and you'll soon be reaping the benefits.

ABOVE Cameras with less sophisticated metering systems, such as centre-weighted metering, are more likely to get exposure wrong. Here the camera has exposed for the plants (left) resulting in an overexposed beach. Reducing the exposure by 2 stops (right) resulted in a far better photograph.

RIGHT Many cameras have a 'blown highlight warning' facility. When switched on, any 'blown' highlights in an image, when reviewed on the LCD screen, will flash (here shown in red) to let you know parts of the image are entirely overexposed.

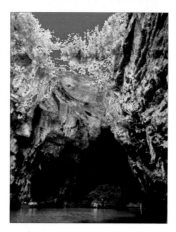

Automatic Bracketing

Most advanced compacts and dSLR cameras have the ability to 'bracket' images. Usually described as 'auto exposure bracketing' (AEB), the camera will fire three shots in quick succession, each with a slightly different exposure compensation setting. The amount of compensation can be pre-selected, but usually it's $1/3$-stop, $1/2$-stop and 1-stop (i.e. the bracketed images would be say '$-1/3$, 0, $+1/3$' or '$-1/2$, 0, $+1/2$'. The images below were bracketed a full stop.

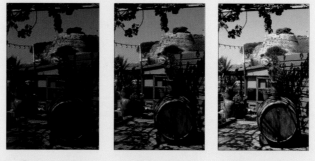

| Exposure -1 stop | Exposure 0 | Exposure +1 stop |

Manual Focus with a Digital Camera

With digital camera manufacturers spending so much money on research and development into increasingly sophisticated autofocus modes, a novice photographer might wonder why we need to focus manually?

While your camera's autofocusing system is likely to provide sharp images the majority of the time, as we've already seen, there are occasions when even the most advanced auto-focus modes can fail to work. These include in low-light conditions when the camera cannot 'see' well enough, or when there is insufficient contrast for the camera to detect the point of focus. Similarly, if there are a number of potential subjects, the camera may not know which one to focus on. While you can often select a specific focus point that the camera will use as its reference point, it can sometimes be quicker to focus manually.

In addition, focusing manually may be necessary when the main subject of an image is behind a distracting foreground, such as a window, iron railings or the bars of a cage. In these instances, the camera's autofocusing system may continually try to focus

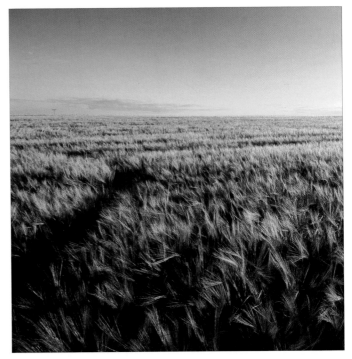

ABOVE In landscape photography, there's little need for a fast autofocusing system. With subjects like this, the camera may not always focus where you want it to.

BELOW This image was taken through an airplane window. The photographer manually focused on the land in case the camera autofocused on the window.

Focus ring

Cameras that are best suited for manual focus are those that feature a focus ring on the camera lens, such as dSLRs or fixed-lens dSLR-like cameras. Although many compacts have a manual focus option, this will often involve the use of buttons, which can be cumbersome to operate, slow to react and use up valuable power. A manual focus ring, on the other hand, is quick, intuitive and uses no power.

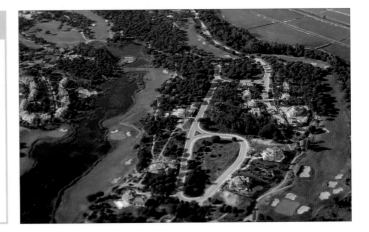

on the foreground object rather than the background – switch to manual and your problems are solved.

Shutter lag

In our earlier discussion of autofocus modes, we covered the issue of shutter lag, which is particularly apparent in sports and action photography. One way to avoid this annoying time lag is to set the focus to manual and prefocus on the area in which the action is about to take place. Half press the shutter release so that the camera makes its other calculations, such as setting the correct exposure and white balance, and as soon as the subject comes into view, fire the shutter. This can work using autofocus as long as the camera has something to focus on that is on the same focal plane as the action, but often the area you'll want to focus on is empty until filled by the action, and the camera may well focus on an object beyond the area of interest. Of course this will only work in those sports, such as motor racing, in which you can predict where the action is going to take place.

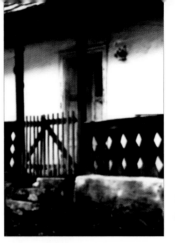

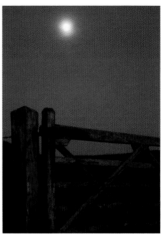

Close-up/macro

In some instances, especially with close-up or macro photography, it becomes almost impossible to use autofocus, as the subject is so close to the lens. As we'll discover, more often than not, it's much easier to set the camera to manual focus and the lens to its shortest focusing distance, and physically move the camera backward and forward, until the specific element you're trying to capture is in focus.

ABOVE LEFT Using manual focus may well be the only way to deliberately shoot a scene out of focus for creative effect.

ABOVE With low light scenes, focusing manually is essential as very few cameras will be able to 'see' to focus in such dark lighting conditions.

BELOW LEFT An increasing number of dSLRs feature 'Live View', in which the LCD screen can be used to focus a shot. This is a more convenient way of focusing macro shots.

BELOW If your camera's autofocus can't keep up with fast-moving subjects, pre-focus on the ground, for example, on which the action will take place and wait for your subject to enter the frame.

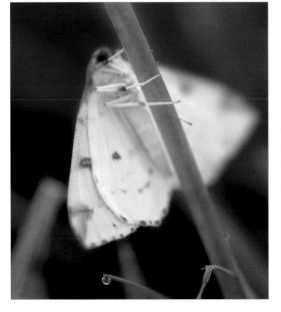

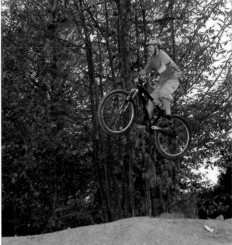

Depth of Field

▶ **RIGHT** These three images show narrow depth of field. Using a wide aperture of f/4, depth of field has been restricted so the photographer can simply focus on different areas in turn to bring them into focus.

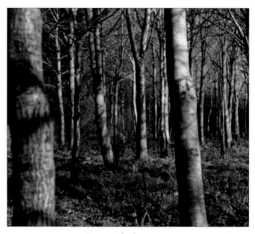

Focus on farthest trees

Although we've yet to cover the topic in detail, the term 'depth of field' has already cropped up in numerous places. That's unavoidable as, after 'exposure', it is the second most fundamental aspect of photography.

Depth of field (DoF) is a technical way of describing how much of an image is in focus – its 'zone of sharpness'. An image with narrow or short depth of field is one that has a small zone of sharpness, while an image with a wide depth of field has a large zone of sharpness.

Point and shoot

If, up until now, you've been using a point-and-shoot camera, you may never have given depth of field a second thought. That's because the lens on a point-and-shoot camera, especially a fixed (non-zoom) lens, is deliberately designed to provide the maximum possible depth of field – the rationale being that for holiday and similar snaps most people will want their images to be sharp all the way from the foreground to the background.

However, with advanced compacts and SLRs, you can control the depth of field so that a selected area of the image, whether foreground,

background or the middle distance, is in focus. Selective focus is a key element in more advanced photography.

Aperture

Let's look in more detail at the factors that control depth of field; there are essentially three.

The first and most obvious factor determining depth of field is the aperture. It's been impossible to avoid any discussion of how the size of a lens's aperture affects depth of field as they are so closely related. But to reinforce the concept here, a large aperture (small number, such as f/2.8) will create a small or narrow depth of field, while a small aperture (large number, such as f/16) will create a large or wide depth of field. Because the amount of available light has a direct impact on the aperture setting (in other words the amount of light that reaches the sensor), it therefore follows that the amount of available light also has some impact on depth of field. For example, in low-light conditions (assuming an ISO setting of 100), the only way to achieve a wide depth of field (using a small aperture of f/11) would be to have a long exposure of, say, 2 sec or longer, in which case you'll certainly need a tripod. The opposite happens in very bright conditions, where the only way to achieve a very

narrow depth of field (using a large aperture of f/2.8) would be to have an extremely fast shutter speed of, say, $^1/_{4000}$ or even $^1/_{8000}$ sec. Many cameras don't have those fast shutter speeds, so the only way to achieve such a shot would be to use dark filters over the lens to restrict the light striking the sensor. Although extreme, these examples illustrate why it's so important to familiarize yourself with your camera's manual controls so that you can achieve the shots you want in the conditions that are available to you.

Focal length

The second factor affecting depth of field is the focal length of the lens. Wide-angle settings on zoom lenses (such as 28mm) provide greater depth of field at the same aperture setting than telephoto lenses or telephoto settings (such as 200mm). We won't go into the optical rules that make this so, but it's important to understand how depth of field is affected by focal length so that you can begin to 'previsualize' the results you can expect from varying focal lengths. Having done so, you will then begin to make considered judgements about how different lenses or zoom settings can achieve different creative results. There's

---

Aperture priority

The safest way to experiment with depth of field is to set the camera to Aperture priority (A/Av). In this semi-automatic mode, you can alter the aperture setting, and thus change the depth of field, knowing that the camera will adjust the shutter speed automatically, and/or the ISO setting (when set to Auto) to ensure you still get an accurately exposed image.

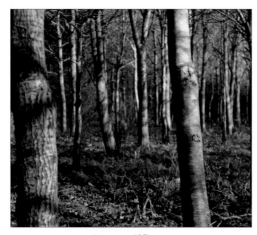

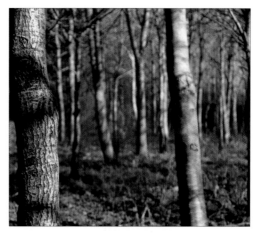

Focus on middle tree

Focus on nearest tree

certainly more to focal length then simply getting 'closer' or 'farther away' from your subject.

Focusing distance

The final factor that determines depth of field is the distance between the subject and the lens. The closer the subject is to the lens the narrower the depth of field. As the subject moves farther away from the lens the depth of field increases, up to a point where – depending on the focal length of the lens and the aperture setting – everything beyond will be in focus. This is often referred to as 'infinity' (∞).

Preview button

Many cameras have a depth of field preview button that helps to show an image's zone of sharpness before taking a photo. Simply press it after setting the aperture. The viewfinder will likely darken as the aperture closes to the chosen setting, but you'll get a preview of what will be in focus.

APERTURE

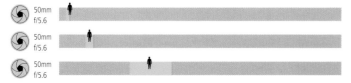

50mm f/1.4

50mm f/5.6

50mm f/16

LEFT Changing the size of the lens aperture radically alters the amount of the scene, from foreground to background, which is captured in focus (represented by the yellow blocks). The wider the aperture (the smaller the number), the less of the scene is in focus.

FOCAL LENGTH

28mm f/5.6

50mm f/5.6

200mm f/5.6

LEFT The second factor affecting depth of field is focal length. As the diagram shows, the longer the focal length (shown in millimetres), the narrower the depth of field. Compare the wide-angle (28mm) lens with the telephoto (200mm) lens.

FOCUSING DISTANCE

50mm f/5.6

50mm f/5.6

50mm f/5.6

LEFT Finally, distance affects depth of field, although compared with the other two factors, the variation is much smaller. With the same focal length lens set at the same aperture, depth of field increases the farther the subject is from the camera.

Wide Depth of Field

Landscape photography springs to mind most readily when we think of wide depth of field, with photographers traditionally aiming to ensure that the zone of sharpness is as great as possible.

Sweeping views

For broad, sweeping, pin-sharp landscape views choose a wide-angle lens or zoom setting (around 28mm is appropriate) and 'close' the aperture down as far as it will go – in other words set the aperture to its smallest opening (highest 'f' number). The most appropriate mode for controlling the aperture setting is, unsurprisingly, the Aperture priority (A/Av) mode. If possible, place the camera on a tripod or a stable surface and select the camera's self-timer; alternatively use a shutter-release cable or remote shutter release.

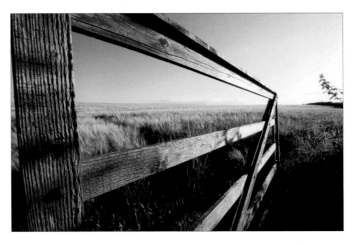

Next, frame the shot, focusing a third of the way into the image (see Hyperfocal distance box), which should provide you with the deepest possible depth of field. Using both a

ABOVE A wide depth of field coupled with a wide-angle view can be used to good effect to show scenes from unusual viewpoints.

tripod and self-timer/remote or cable shutter release will ensure that the camera is as stable as possible when the shutter actually fires. This is particularly important in low-lighting conditions when the shutter speed may be a relatively slow $^1/_{15}$ sec or $^1/_{30}$ sec. Fixing the camera to the tripod and then using your finger to press the shutter release is somewhat self-defeating as you're likely to shake the camera, although only by a tiny fraction, which can soften the image.

Review

Once you've taken the shot, review the principal elements of the image to check that they're sharp. You may want to make adjustments to the point of focus depending on which parts of the image are more significant. If the foreground plays a more important role in the composition than the background for example, you'll want the foreground to be sharper than the background.

Hyperfocal Distance

One technique employed by all professional landscape photographers is hyperfocal focusing. This works on the basis that when you focus on a subject, a third of the scene in front will be in focus, while two-thirds behind will also be in focus – the point of focus is known as the hyperfocal distance. Focusing here will give you the maximum possible depth of field. There exist fairly complex charts (www.dofmaster.com) that will tell you exactly what the hyperfocal distance will be for a given focal length at a specific aperture.

However, an easier, if not absolutely accurate way to find the hyperfocal distance is to focus manually a third of the way into the scene. This will give you maximum depth of field.

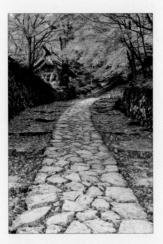

ABOVE By focusing at the hyperfocal distance, everything from foreground to background is sharp in this shot.

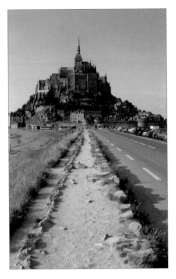

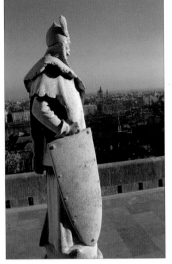

If you don't have a tripod or anything on which to rest the camera when shooting landscapes, check that, having set the aperture, the shutter speed is sufficiently fast to prevent camera shake. You may need to increase either the aperture slightly or the ISO setting to get a suitably fast shutter speed. You'll find yourself increasingly making this sort of compromise the more you take control of the camera. But doing it manually, rather than letting the camera choose the settings, means you're the one making the important decisions; and if you don't get the image you want when you come to preview it, you'll have a better idea about how to improve it.

▲ **ABOVE** Ensuring that the path from the bottom of the image is sharp has helped to reinforce it as a leading line.

▲ **ABOVE** Keeping the view of Budapest in focus in the distance helps to reinforce the relationship between the statue and the city.

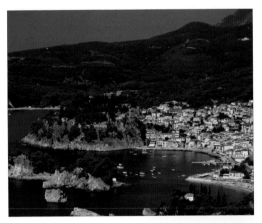

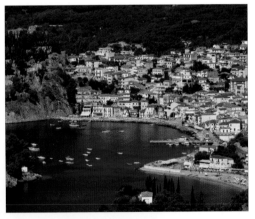

▲ **ABOVE** When using wide depth of field with a wide-angle lens in landscape photography, it's natural to want to include the horizon and sky. But remember, this can lead the viewer's eye out of the image. To contain the viewer in the picture, dispense with the horizon and sky. In the second image (right), by excluding the sky our attention remains much more focused on the bay and the picturesque town.

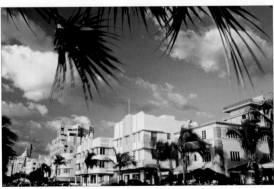

◄ **LEFT** By including some sharply focused foliage in the foreground, the photographer has added a sense of depth and scale to this view of the Art Deco district of Miami.

Narrow Depth of Field

Deliberately throwing regions of an image out of focus might seem counterintuitive, particularly if you're used to a point-and-shoot camera that is designed to keep as much of the scene as possible in focus. However, being able to select which parts of an image are in focus and which are blurred is a fundamental aspect of creative photography and is often referred to as differential focus.

In the discussion on compositional balance in Chapter 3, we learned that an in-focus element attracts our attention much more than one that is out of focus. Photographers can use this to their advantage in a variety of situations by keeping depth of field down to a narrow margin.

Portraits

One genre of photography where restricting depth of field is often critical is portraiture. The ability to throw a potentially distracting background or foreground out of focus is the key to many successful

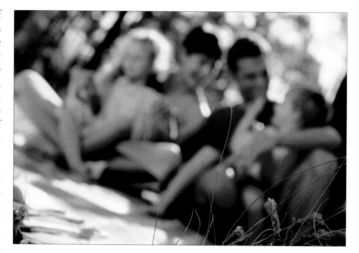

portrait shots, as it concentrates the viewer's attention on the subject of the image. The most effective way to obtain a narrow, or shallow, depth of field – so that only the subject is in focus – is to start with a telephoto lens or zoom setting between 100mm and 300mm. This is because telephoto lenses have a narrower depth of field

than wide-angle lenses, making it easier to throw backgrounds out of focus. Then, in Aperture priority (A/Av) mode, 'open up' the lens by selecting the largest aperture setting (smallest 'f' number). You'll find that this is exactly what the camera does automatically if you select Portrait mode. Having selected the largest aperture, make sure that the shutter speed is sufficiently fast to prevent camera shake. This is particularly important with longer focal length lenses or zoom settings, as these are more prone to suffering from camera shake because slight movement is exaggerated over distance. Position yourself at an appropriate distance from the subject so that just the head and shoulders are in the frame and fire the

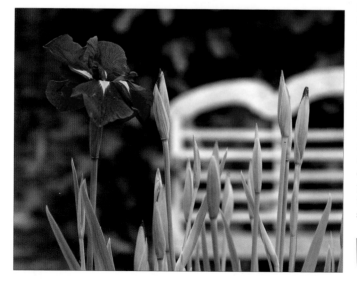

LEFT Using a narrow, or shallow, depth of field can make a background less distracting, so the main subject stands out.

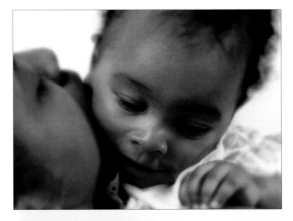

LEFT A narrow, or shallow, depth of field helps the viewer to focus on the main subject of an image – in this case the baby.

BELOW We know what the subject of this picture is, despite most of it being blurred, but this adds to the creative effect.

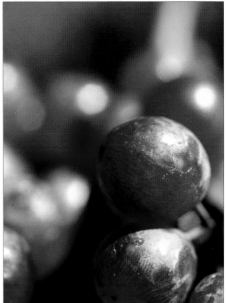

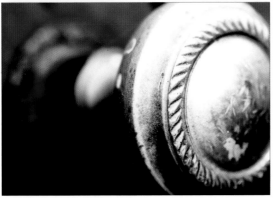

ABOVE As depth of field decreases the closer you are to your subject, there's a very narrow depth of field in macro photography.

shutter. When reviewing the image, you should find that the subject is nice and sharp and that the foreground and/or background is so out of focus that your eye glosses over them.

Evidently, it's not just portraiture photography that can benefit from controlling depth of field. Narrow depth of field has its place in just about all genres of photography, especially when it comes to nature and art photography. Later on in the book we shall be looking in more detail at close-up and macro photography, where a narrow depth of field can be particularly effective with shots of insects and flowers, or any small object photographed close up.

Bokeh

As your skill at controlling depth of field and using differential focus increases, you'll become aware of blurry hexagonal shapes, particularly in highlights. These are created by the shape of the lens's aperture blades as they close down to the aperture setting, and are called 'bokeh', the Japanese word for 'blur'.

Bokeh is a subjective aesthetic quality, but the general consensus is that the smoother and more circular the bokeh, the more pleasing the out-of-focus area. Much relies on the lens quality, and as such is out of your control. However, by adjusting the aperture you can control the amount by which the background is thrown out of focus, thus controlling the size of the bokeh highlights.

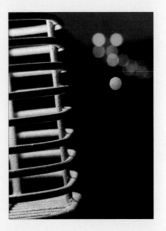

ABOVE 'Bokeh' are the circular, defocused highlights seen in the right of the image.

Depth of Field – Try It Yourself

Having covered the theory of controlling depth of field and armed with a knowledge of how to maximize or minimize the zone of sharpness, it's time to put that knowledge into practice. The exercises below are much easier to carry out, and the results more apparent, if you use a tripod, but it's not essential.

Increasing depth of field

Let's begin by learning how to increase depth of field, or the zone of sharpness. Place three objects about 24in (60cm) apart in a line on a long table. Size is not an issue, but apples and oranges are an appropriate size. Set the camera on the tripod about 3ft (1m) from the front object, but slightly higher and off to one side. Now, adjust the zoom lens so that the front object almost fills the viewfinder and the other two objects are still visible.

Focus on the lead object and select the largest aperture (smallest number) setting your camera lens has (for example, f/2.8). Take a photo and review it. You should find that only the lead object is in focus, while the other two are out of focus, with the rear object more out of focus than the middle one. Now, close the aperture down by about 3 stops (to f/8 in our example) and take another shot. On reviewing the second shot, the first two objects should now be in focus, but the final one still out of focus. Finally, close the lens right down (to f/22, for example). The final shot should feature all of your objects sharply in focus.

▶ **RIGHT** By controlling the depth of field so that both the foreground and background in this image are out of focus, our eyes are immediately drawn to the subject of the shot.

Focal length

As we know, adjusting a lens's focal length also impacts on depth of field. For this next exercise, take the camera off the tripod if you've been using one. Set the aperture to f/4 and set the camera lens to its longest focal length (in other words zoom right into the first object, but make sure the other two objects

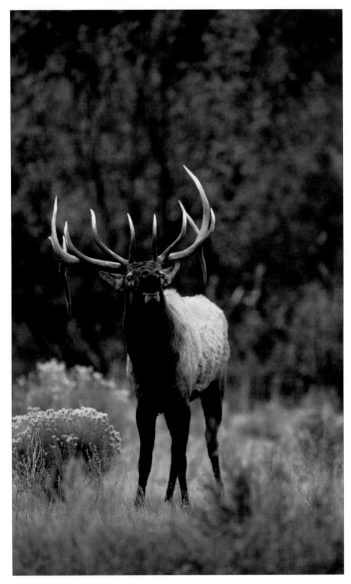

are still visible), and take a picture, but from a slightly higher position than previously. Then set the lens to its shortest focal length (zoom out), but move closer to the objects so that the first one still fills the frame, and take another shot.

When comparing these two images, you should be able to see how the zone of sharpness is greater with the shorter focal length setting. It should also be apparent how the longer focal length has foreshortened the distance between the three objects. When we look at focal length we'll discover how this foreshortening effect can be used to our advantage.

Selective focus

In this next exercise, we're going to selectively focus on one of the three objects. Simply set the aperture to f/4, focus on the first object and take a shot. Next, focus on the centre object and take a shot, and then do the same with the rear object. When you review your shots you should find that each object in turn is sharp while the other two remain blurred. This is an excellent way of placing emphasis on specific elements in a scene.

Real world

Next time you are out and about with a camera, look to repeat the exercises above, but on a larger scale, such as with a line of trees. At larger scales the differential focus should be more apparent, and you should start to get a feel for how controlling depth of field can be used in your real world photography.

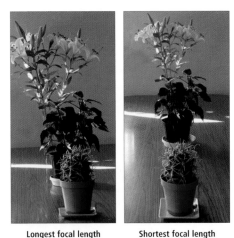

Longest focal length

Shortest focal length

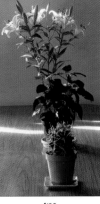

LEFT These two images demonstrate the effect of focal length on depth of field. The first image shows a narrower zone of sharpness compared with the second (compare the walls at the end of the room). But also note how in the first image the three objects appear much closer together than in the second – this is because longer focal lengths foreshorten the distance between objects.

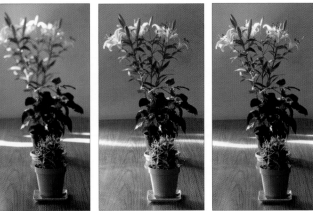

f/2.8   f/8   f/22

▲ **ABOVE RIGHT** This sequence of three images shows how closing down the aperture increases depth of field. Compare the zone of sharpness from f/2.8 with that from f/22.

▶ **RIGHT** These three images demonstrate how effective selective focus can be at drawing the viewer's eye to a particular part or element of a scene.

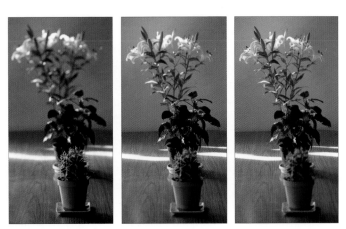

Focus on first object   Focus on centre object   Focus on rear object

Shutter Speed

Along with the aperture setting, shutter speed is the other factor that governs how much light reaches the camera's sensor. The faster the shutter, the less time the sensor is exposed to light. Shutter speeds are usually measured in fractions of a second (sec), although much longer exposures are sometimes used, and historically each setting is either half or double the next. For example, a typical digital camera may have the following shutter speeds: $^1/_{1000}$ sec; $^1/_{500}$ sec; $^1/_{250}$sec; $^1/_{125}$ sec; $^1/_{60}$ sec; $^1/_{30}$ sec; $^1/_{15}$ sec; $^1/_8$ sec; $^1/_4$ sec; $^1/_2$ sec; 1 sec; 2 sec; 4 sec; 8 sec, 15 sec and 30 sec. Sophisticated cameras may have a wider range, featuring faster shutter speeds of $^1/_{2000}$ sec, $^1/_{4000}$ sec and $^1/_{8000}$ sec, or include $^1/_2$-stop or $^1/_3$-stop 'intermediary' speeds such as $^1/_{80}$ sec or $^1/_{100}$ sec.

The opening of the shutter determines the amount of time light is allowed to pass through the lens to the sensor. As well as affecting exposure, the shutter speed can also freeze a moving object as a sharp image on film and reduce camera shake.

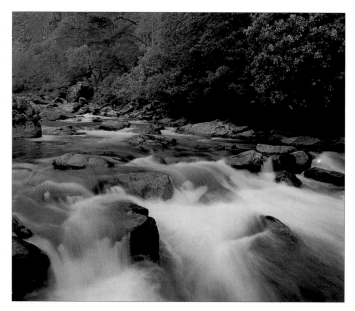

ABOVE In this picture the camera was mounted on a tripod and a slow shutter speed, ¼ second, was used.

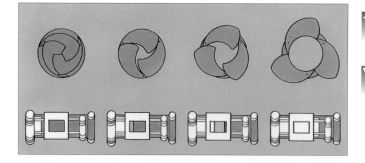

LEFT A leaf shutter (top) and a focal plane shutter (below) are shown, step by step, in the process of opening.

BELOW When using flash with a camera that has a focal plane shutter, set the camera at the manufacturer's designated speed. This could be ¹/₁₂₅ second, or there might be a flash symbol on the shutter speed dial. If you use a speed in excess of this setting, only part of the frame will be exposed.

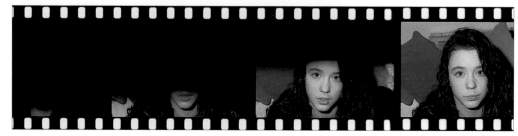

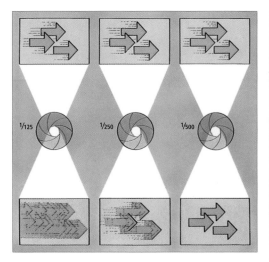

▲ **ABOVE** Faster shutter speeds are needed to produce a shot in which a fast moving subject appears to be frozen – crisp and in focus rather than blurred.

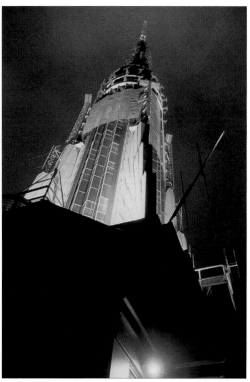

▶ **RIGHT** When a long exposure is required, in this case 20 seconds, the shutter was set to the T setting. This meant that when the shutter was fired it remained open until it was depressed again. If the camera only has a setting on the shutter speed dial marked B, the shutter release has to remain depressed.

Portraying fast-moving objects

Imagine a car or a person passing quickly across a chosen viewpoint. If the shutter speed is set at $1/60$ sec or less, the moving object would appear blurred on the photograph. However, if the shutter speed were $1/250$ sec or more the moving object would be clear, 'frozen' in action.

In the case of a car, it can be difficult to tell whether it is moving or stationary. This static effect may result in a dull picture. A better way to illustrate action is to use a slower shutter speed and 'pan' the camera, following the moving object, in this case, the car, and taking the picture when it is directly in front. This type of photography may take a little practice to perfect but it does produces striking images where the background is blurred and the moving object clear and sharp, illustrating very effectively the speed at which it was travelling.

Camera shake

When you are deciding on the shutter speed to use, particularly with hand-held photography, try to ensure that you select a shutter speed that is fast enough to prevent inevitable 'camera shake'. Camera shake occurs when the camera moves while the shutter is open, resulting in a blurred image. Depending on the focal length of the lens or the zoom setting, different shutter speeds are needed in order to avoid camera shake. For example, with a short (wide-angle) focal length setting of 28mm, a shutter speed of $1/30$ sec will be fast enough to prevent camera shake, but with a very long (telephoto) focal length setting of 200mm, you'll need a shutter speed of $1/250$ sec.

▼ **BELOW** If the camera is moved in line with a moving object and a shutter speed of $1/60$ second is used, the object will remain sharp but the background will be blurred. This technique is called panning.

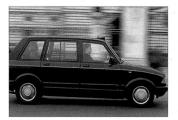

▼ **BELOW** By contrast, a shutter speed of $1/250$ second was used to photograph this bird in flight, and it has 'frozen' virtually all movement. This method is often used for photographing wildlife and sports events.

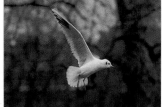

This is because the longer the focal length; the more camera shake becomes apparent.

Minimum shutter speeds

As a rule of thumb, to prevent camera shake the shutter speed should be close to the reciprocal of the focal length of the lens. For example, if the focal length is 60mm the shutter speed should be a minimum of $^1/_{60}$ sec, while a focal length of 125mm requires a shutter speed of at least $^1/_{125}$ sec and a 500mm focal length needs $^1/_{500}$ sec. Remember, however, these are only guidelines and they won't guarantee that you'll get sharp pictures every time. Rules such as these are a very good basis from which you can practise getting the effective photographs you want.

In addition to using the minimum shutter speed as described above, try leaning against a solid support, such as a wall or tree, and gently squeeze the shutter release rather than 'press' it. Some professionals, whenever they're shooting hand held, set their

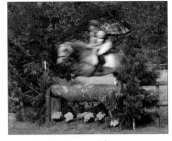

Shutter speed: $^1/_{60}$ sec

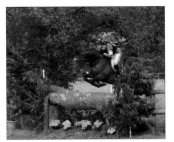

Shutter speed: $^1/_{125}$ sec

camera's drive or shooting mode to 'continuous' and fire off three or four shots so that they can select the sharpest image from the set. Of course, by doing this, you'll use up far more memory, but if it's an important shot and you're worried about potential camera shake, it is certainly an option to consider.

Alternatively, you can increase the ISO sensitivity setting to obtain a faster shutter speed. As we know, the more sensitive the camera's sensor is to light, the less time the sensor needs to be exposed to the light from the scene being photographed. Each incremental ISO setting allows you to halve the shutter speed. So, if you're worried about camera shake at $^1/_{30}$ sec at ISO 100, set the ISO to 200 and you can set the shutter speed to $^1/_{60}$ sec, or use ISO 400 for a shutter speed of $^1/_{125}$ sec.

▲ **ABOVE** This sequence of images clearly shows how increasing shutter speed freezes movement. Compare the slowest shutter speed ($^1/_{60}$ sec) with the fastest ($^1/_{1000}$ sec).

Shutter speed and exposure

The shutter speed you have chosen for a specific shot also plays a role in determining how an image will look – whether, for example, a moving element in the shot is blurred or frozen, or whether the image has a wide or narrow zone of sharpness. This latter is due to the relationship between the shutter speed and aperture setting. For example, the lack of a tripod in low-light conditions may well need a fast shutter speed of $^1/_{125}$ sec. Such a fast shutter speed in low-light situations will need a wide aperture to allow more light to reach the sensor, and the wider the aperture the narrower the depth of field.

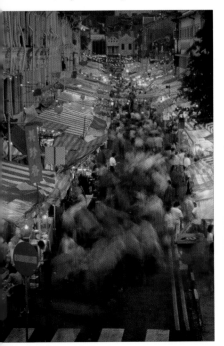

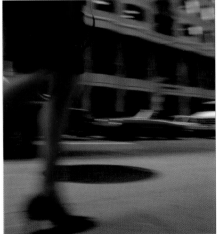

◀ **FAR LEFT** In this shot a tripod was used with an exposure of around 1 sec. This way the buildings and stalls remained sharp but the bustling crowd blurred.

◀ **LEFT** This deliberately blurred shot was hand held with a shutter speed of around $^1/_{15}$ sec. The blurred effect conveys the pace of city life.

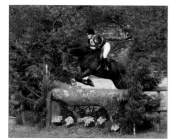

Shutter speed: ¹⁄₂₅₀ sec

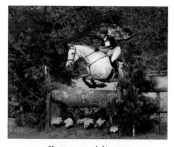

Shutter speed: ¹⁄₅₀₀ sec

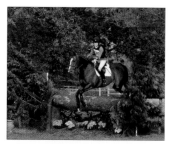

Shutter speed: ¹⁄₁₀₀₀ sec

▶ **RIGHT** Very fast shutter speeds can freeze the wings of a hovering bird. A slow shutter speed here would have produced a blur. The key is to get to know your camera and choose your speed for each picture you take.

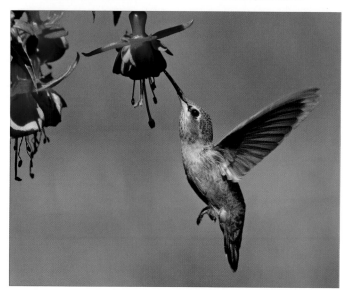

Using flash with SLR cameras

With SLR cameras the shutter speed should be set to the manufacturers' recommended setting when using flash. This is usually ¹⁄₆₀ or ¹⁄₁₂₅ sec. If a faster speed is used, only part of the film will be exposed as the flash will fire before the blinds of the shutter have fully opened. With cameras that have a leaf shutter or a shutter between the lens, the flash can be synchronized to any speed. This is a great advantage in situations where flash has to be balanced with daylight.

B and T settings

On some shutter speed dials there are two settings marked B and T. When the shutter ring is set to B the shutter will remain open for as long as the shutter release button is depressed. If it is set to T, the shutter will remain open even when the shutter release button is released, closing only when the button is depressed again. Both these settings are for use with pictures that require a long exposure.

Automatic shutter speed

Some automatic cameras have metering modes called shutter priority. This simply means that when the shutter speed is adjusted manually the camera then selects the correct aperture automatically.

Image Stabilization

Some cameras and individual lenses for dSLRs have image-stabilization (IS) systems. These work in a variety of ways, but generally they feature gyroscopic motors that detect and counteract any movement in the camera or lens. The systems vary in how successful they are, but generally you can expect to reduce the shutter speed by 2–3 stops and still retain sharp images. For example, if you had selected a shutter speed of ¹⁄₂₅₀ sec without image stabilization, with image stabilization enabled you would be able to shoot with a speed as slow as ¹⁄₆₀ sec (or even ¹⁄₃₀ sec) and still get blur-free results.

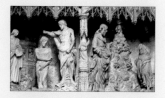

IS off

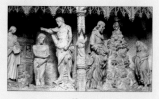

IS on

Fast Shutter Speeds

Shutter speeds of around $^1/_{250}$ sec and shorter are generally considered fast. With the most commonly used focal lengths ranging from around 40mm to 125mm, using fast shutter speeds should certainly prevent camera shake. In fact, speeds of $^1/_{500}$ sec and shorter will freeze fast-moving action beyond the perception of the human eye.

Freezing action

Ever since the 19th-century English photographer, Eadweard Muybridge, shot his famous sequence of a horse galloping, we have been fascinated with the ability to freeze photographs of fast-moving action.

The actual shutter speed required to arrest movement very much depends on the direction the object is moving. A speeding car heading toward the camera, for example, won't require as fast a shutter speed as someone walking across the viewfinder or something moving directly up or down in front of the camera. In addition to the direction of movement, the distance of the object from the camera and the focal length of the lens are also critical factors. The farther the

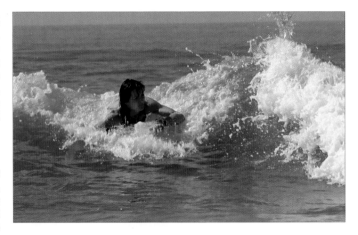

object is from the camera, and the shorter the focal length, the slower the shutter speed can be before action is frozen. Or in other words, the farther away a fast-moving object is, the slower it appears to move.

However, for sports photography, when you're likely to be using the longest focal length setting available on the lens, such as 300mm, in order to get optically as 'close' as you can to the action, speeds of around $^1/_{1000}$ sec are probably necessary to freeze the action. At these shutter speeds it's

ABOVE A shutter speed of $^1/_{400}$ sec has been used to make sure the surfer and the water are 'frozen'.

BELOW LEFT A fast-moving subject that is travelling across the frame requires a fast shutter speed to prevent blur – in this instance $^1/_{620}$ sec.

likely you'll need to use the lens's widest aperture setting to get a correct exposure, and unless the lighting conditions are very bright you may need to increase the ISO.

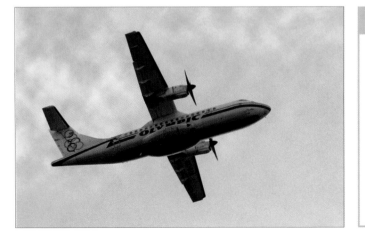

Fast-motion freezing

In order to freeze motion you need to make sure you've set a shutter speed that's fast enough, so follow this guide:
• Subjects moving across the frame need a faster shutter speed than subjects moving toward (or away from) the camera.
• Use the Shutter Priority (S/Tv) mode in order to control the shutter speed, and let the camera select the aperture.

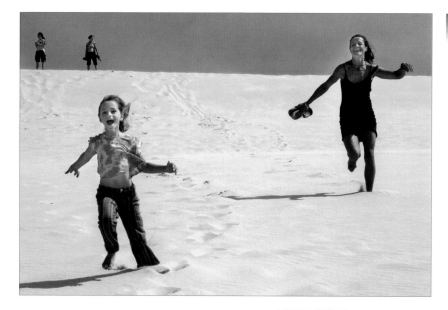

LEFT Fast-moving subjects moving toward the camera don't necessarily need as fast a shutter speed as a subject moving across the frame, but here a shutter speed of $^1/_{500}$ sec was used to freeze the action.

Shutter priority

The best way to experiment with shutter speeds is to select the Shutter Priority setting (S/Tv), choose an appropriate shutter speed, then focus on an area where the action will take place. Check in the viewfinder to see if an underexposure warning is flashing. If it is, you'll either need to increase the ISO setting until an acceptable exposure is available or, if that still doesn't provide the correct exposure, reduce the shutter speed slightly as well.

RIGHT Although the photographer has used a sufficiently fast shutter speed to capture this beautiful shot of a hummingbird hawk moth, its wings are beating so fast that even a very fast shutter speed of $^1/_{1000}$ sec can't freeze their movement.

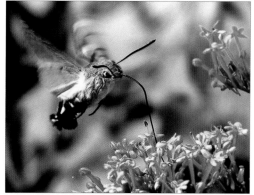

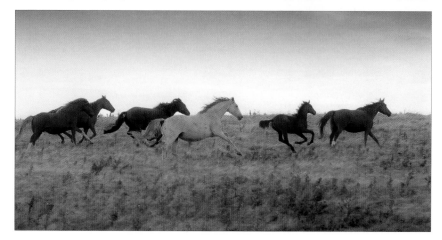

LEFT Although moving across the image, the horses are still relatively small in the frame, allowing $^1/_{320}$ sec to be used for this action shot.

Standard Shutter Speeds

For most hand-held photography, shutter speeds of between $^1/_{30}$ sec and $^1/_{250}$ sec are most commonly used. At these speeds, images that are captured tend to replicate our perception of the world around us, so some parts of a scene will be sharply in focus, while more rapidly moving elements may appear slightly blurred.

The essence of speed

While on one level it's interesting to look at images that freeze time, there are occasions when freezing an object entirely can detract from the sense of action, especially if the background is also frozen. An obvious example is high-speed motor sport, in which a racing car or motorbike, if captured with a fast shutter speed, can look static and lose the sense of speed.

▼ **BELOW** Not all images have to be pin sharp. The slow shutter speed used in this hand-held urban shot provides a sense of movement and adds to the atmosphere of the image.

Deliberate blur

There are two ways to stop action shots appearing static and dull, both of which involve deliberately introducing blur. The first method is to select a slower shutter speed than you would usually use to freeze the action. Begin around 3 stops slower, so set $^1/_{30}$ sec instead of $^1/_{250}$ sec, for example, then prefocus on an area into which you know the subject will enter and take the shot as it enters the frame. If the subject is relatively stationary, for example a golfer, simply take the shot using the slower shutter speed. The result will be a blurred, or partly blurred, subject in front of a sharp background (or foreground). Depending on the amount of blur and the subject matter this may evoke the sense of action you need. The golfer is a good example, as ideally the head, shoulders and legs should remain relatively still and therefore sharp while the arms and club form a blurred arc.

Panning

For many types of action photography, and in particular fast-moving sports photography, the danger with the technique described previously is that the sharp background becomes the focus of attention, while the blurred subject – especially if it's entirely blurred with nothing sharply in focus – will not attract the viewer's eye. To overcome this, try using the well-known technique called 'panning'. Ensure that your feet are well planted and hold the camera to your eye. Frame the subject of the shot and by turning your body from the waist up only, follow the subject through the viewfinder. As the subject passes, take a shot, using your camera's continuous shooting mode if it has one. Continue to turn

▼ **BELOW** For subjects that are moving across the frame, panning is a great way of showing speed. Just follow the subject with the camera as it moves.

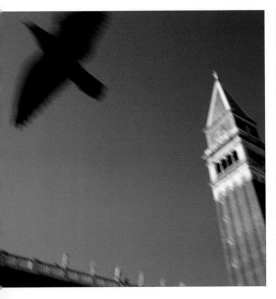

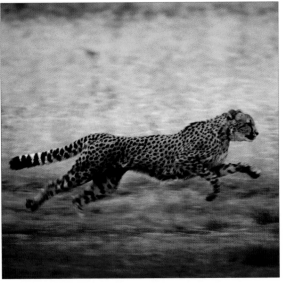

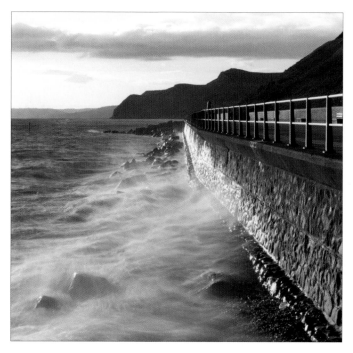

Framing

It takes time to learn how to pan successfully. Don't start by zooming close in to the subject so it fills the frame, as any error will result in part of the subject being cut off. Instead, zoom out a bit to give yourself a better chance and crop away excess background later if required. Also, start by trying to get the subject in the centre of the frame, so you're less likely to cut the front or back off the subject. As you become more proficient, try zooming in with a longer focal length lens or setting to get 'closer' to the subject and framing the shot so that there is more space in front of it than behind. Moving subjects look better if there's space in the frame into which they can move.

your upper torso and track the subject as it moves out of view, while you are making the exposure. You'll find that you can probably only comfortably turn through around 45 degrees, but the result should be a sharp subject in front of a blurred background. This will not only give you a sense of speed, but it will also show a well-focused subject that holds the viewer's attention.

When panning, select the same shutter speed as in the previous technique – that is around 4 stops less than necessary to freeze the action (between $^1/_{30}$ sec and $^1/_{125}$ sec usually works for most sports). If it's possible, also try to position yourself in front of a background that features a lot of light and dark tones, as these will make the blurred effect more apparent.

ABOVE LEFT Slow shutter speeds can be used to add a sense of movement to landscapes. Here the waves have become a 'mist' thanks to the use of a slow shutter speed.

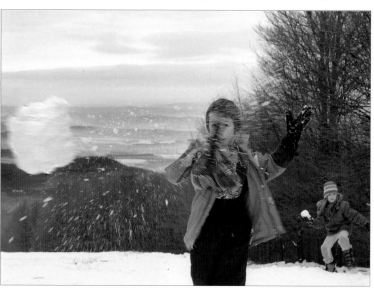

LEFT A wide-angle lens has increased the dramatic perspective here, while a slow shutter speed records the snowball hurtling toward the photographer as a blur.

Long Exposures

Although most photographs are taken using shutter speeds of a fraction of a second, most advanced digital cameras have the facility to shoot much longer exposures – anywhere between 1 and 30 seconds. Some cameras also feature a 'Bulb' (B) setting, which keeps the shutter open for as long as the shutter release is held down (or until the battery runs out). But when would you use such long exposures?

ZOOM BURST

If your camera has a manual zoom control, try creating a 'zoom burst'. With the camera on a tripod, select the smallest aperture and a slow ISO setting to obtain a long shutter speed – anything from around $\frac{1}{4}$ sec to $\frac{1}{2}$ sec or longer is sufficient. Focus on an area that contains a mix of light and dark tones and centre it in the viewfinder. With the lens zoomed in, set the camera's self-timer and press the shutter release. When you hear the shutter fire, gently twist the zoom control so the lens zooms out. The result should be an abstract zoom burst.

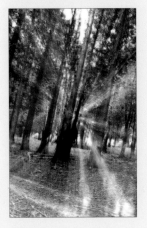

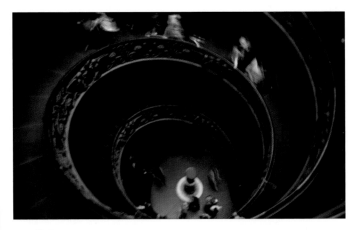

Low light

Normally, exposures of a second or more are used in low light, where you won't be able to hold the camera and still obtain sharp images. To start with, you'll need to use a tripod, or at least rest the camera on a sturdy support, to avoid blurry night-time (or early morning) shots. Also, use either the camera's self-timer, a shutter release cable or a remote control so you don't run the risk of moving the camera with your finger while firing the shutter.

Because the camera is mounted on a stable platform it's not necessary to set a high ISO setting, so set the ISO to the lowest setting available to produce less noisy images. In addition, use the camera's noise-reduction setting.

Some of the most effective extended exposures taken during night-time – especially in towns and cities – show the trails made by the lights of passing cars. Find a vantage point overlooking a busy thoroughfare, set the camera on a tripod, and experiment with a variety of long exposure times.

RIGHT Use a long exposure to record several fireworks in a single frame for eye-catching shots such as this one.

ABOVE Shooting indoors using a slow shutter speed to get an appropriate exposure has resulted in blurred figures, which add to the movement of this photograph.

Trails made by stars can also create effective long-exposure images. For these, you'll probably need to use the camera's Bulb setting as exposures often have to be several minutes long, if not longer, to chart the progress of the stars. For best results, choose a clear night that's free of cloud and other ambient light, and experiment with the length of your exposures.

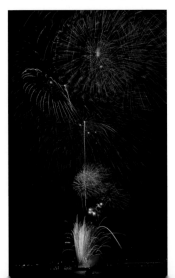

Extended daytime exposures

It's not just at night that you can use long exposures for creative effect. Certain daytime scenes also benefit from extended exposures, especially scenes featuring flowing water, mist or low-lying cloud. The long exposure will smooth out the water or cloud so it appears as a soft, nebulous mass.

Because of the relatively high light levels present during the day, the smallest aperture and lowest ISO settings might not allow you to set a suitably long exposure, so you'll have to reduce the amount of light reaching the sensor some other way. To do this you'll need to use a neutral density (ND) filter. These filters work a bit like sunglasses in that they reduce the amount of light hitting the sensor, but they don't affect the colour of the light – hence 'neutral' density.

White Balance

Because most extended exposures are shot at night, and many are city- or townscapes, you'll instantly become aware of the colour cast created by sodium, tungsten and mercury vapour lights. If there is a sufficient variety of lighting in the shot, it may add to the effect of the image, but a dull overall orange cast simply looks unpleasant, as shown in the image below left.

In such instances, it's likely that the camera's Auto White Balance won't be able to address the problem, and you'll need to resort to fixing the colour cast using image-editing software to bring back the whites, or by setting a manual white balance if your camera has this option available.

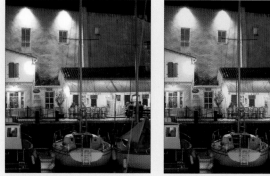
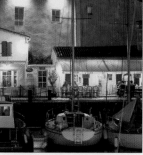

Auto White Balance   **Corrected White Balance**

Creative Exposure

Armed with a better understanding of the concept of exposure, how the various metering systems operate and how to use the camera's manual settings, you should now feel much more confident to experiment with exposure settings. As sophisticated as your camera's matrix or evaluative metering system is, and as tempting as it is to let the camera work out the shutter speed/aperture setting for you, you're really missing out on producing some great shots if you let the camera do all the work. The beauty of shooting digitally is that experimenting with seemingly 'inaccurate' exposures doesn't cost a thing, apart from a bit of battery power. If you don't like an image, simply delete it and start again. There's nothing to lose by experimenting a little, and nothing to be gained if you don't.

Light

Often, the difference between an average shot and one that attracts a little more attention is the quality of light and the relationship between the light and dark areas. You may find that if you leave the decision about the

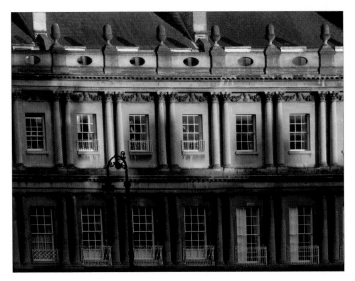

exposure to the camera, it will attempt to set an exposure that ensures detail is visible in both highlight and shadow regions. Of course, in many cases this is absolutely the right course of action, but if the interplay of light and dark areas is the key to the image, rather than specific detail, it's time to override the camera and experiment with different exposures.

▼ **BELOW LEFT** This is a well-exposed floral study enhanced by the backlighting and the lone pink flower in a sea of blue and green.

▼ **BELOW** The same shot as the one on the left, but this time a longer shutter speed has been used, and the camera moved during the exposure. The result is an abstract blur of colour that creates an entirely different effect to the first picture.

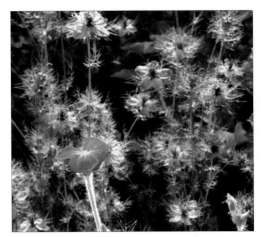

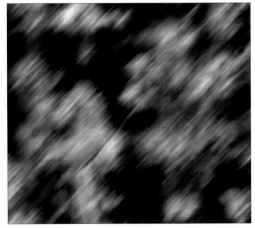

OPPOSITE There's absolutely nothing 'wrong' with the exposure for this building, but the exposure has retained all the shadow areas, and it appears to be lacking contrast.

BELOW Here the exposure has been adjusted slightly, so the scene is a little darker than the first one. Deepening the shadows makes the windows stand out more for a dramatic effect.

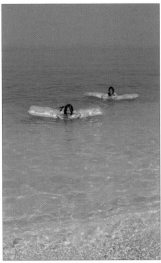

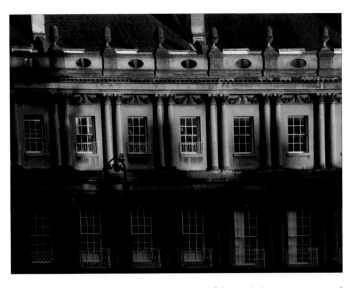

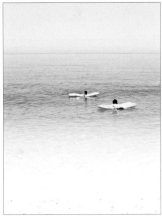

You may find that deliberately underexposing a shot brings richer tone and colour to the highlight areas, and although the shadows may 'fill in' a little, so detail becomes less visible, the viewer is struck more by the contrast between light and shade. Similarly, there may be times when overexposing an image, so that many of the highlight areas are 'blown out', has more impact and evokes a greater impression of heat, light or even space than an accurately exposed image.

Movement

As we've discovered over the last few pages, you can use shutter speeds to bring a creative touch to an image – either fast shutter speeds to freeze fast-moving action or slow shutter speeds to generate a sense of movement in an image. With longer shutter speeds, general wisdom suggests that you use a tripod to avoid camera shake, so ensuring that your images are pin sharp. However, images don't always have to be sharply focused to be

successful. People have experimented by deliberately moving the camera when the shutter is open in all sorts of ways to see what results can be achieved, a process known as 'kinetic photography'. The online photography site Flickr (www.flickr.com) even has a group called 'Camera Toss', which demonstrates the results you can achieve from simply throwing your camera in the air during an exposure of $^{1}/_{2}$ sec or longer.

While going to such extremes with an expensive camera may not be advisable, there's absolutely nothing to stop you from setting a very slow shutter speed and moving or waving your camera around to see the results. Bear in mind that it's best to try such exposures in front of a scene that has contrasting tones or colours, as that way the movement will be more apparent. There are countless ways to experiment with light and movement with a camera, and while a lot of the time the results may not come to much, every now

TOP Using the camera's evaluative/multi-segment metering pattern gives a nice record shot of this scene, and it wouldn't look out of place in a holiday album.

ABOVE By overexposing a similar photograph, we have a shot that's fit for exhibiting. The overexposure has helped to blur the tonal distinction between the foreground sand and the sky in the background. This focuses our attention on the middle of the frame – the strip of blue water in which the subjects of the image can be found.

and again you'll end up creating an image that will be unique, personal and striking.

Exposure – Try It Yourself

You should by now have a better understanding of the relationship between shutter and aperture, and having run through the 'depth of field' exercises, be more confident with your camera's semi-automatic and manual settings.

The exercises here will help to reinforce your familiarity with the camera's aperture and shutter controls, and also get you to think about how adjusting exposure can introduce atmosphere into an image, or create a sense of movement. Unlike the 'depth of field' exercises, which dealt with how the mechanics and optical properties of the camera and its lens can be used specifically to draw

attention to certain elements of an image, these exercises are far more subjective, and the final results will be very personal to you.

Controlling light levels

First, reacquaint yourself with the camera's controls. Having a tripod and a form of remote shutter release will make life easier, but they are not essential. Try this exercise outdoors, using objects and a setting that exhibit good tonal variation – such as a dark object on a light table.

Set your camera to its Manual mode, select a medium aperture (such as f/8), and a focal length of 100mm. Look through the viewfinder, focus on an

object 16ft (5m) away, ensuring that you can see regions in front of and behind the object. Adjust the shutter speed until the exposure level indicator is set to '0', and fire the shutter. Now reduce the shutter speed 2 stops (from say $^1/_{500}$ sec to $^1/_{125}$ sec) and increase the aperture to compensate (from f/8 to f/16). The exposure indicator should still read '0'. Fire another shot and compare the two images. You should see little or no difference in the overall exposure, but the second image should have a wider zone of sharpness – as we would expect having completed the 'depth of field' exercises.

Next, having reduced the shutter speed, don't increase the aperture to compensate. The exposure level indicator should read around '-2' – take a shot. Increase the shutter speed 2 stops (the level should read around '0'), but reduce the aperture by 2 stops to take the reading back down to around '-2' again. These last two shots will be underexposed by 2 stops, but look closely, first at the overall tones of the images. Although the darker areas are likely to be underexposed, the lighter tones may well have become richer and easier to define, and where colour is present these tones may appear more saturated. This is because the lighter an image is, the less saturated the colours. When comparing the zone of sharpness between the two images, the second image should show a wider depth of field.

Carry on experimenting with the exposure settings so that you under-expose by 1 stop and overexpose by 1

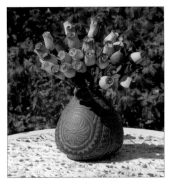

Aperture: f/8

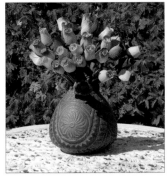

Aperture: f/16

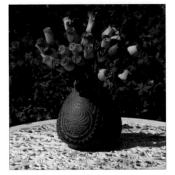

Underexposed by 1 stop

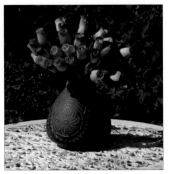

Underexposed by 2 stops

LEFT Different but correct exposure variations result in the same overall exposure, but both images at the top have greater depth of field; the underexposed images have richer colours.

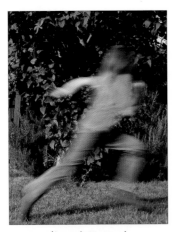

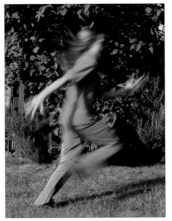

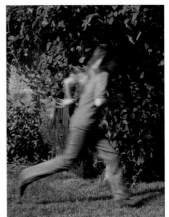

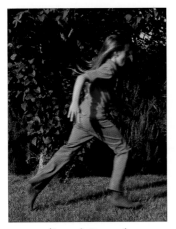

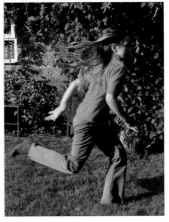

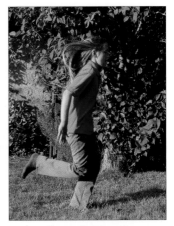

$^1\!/_{30}$ sec shutter speed

$^1\!/_{60}$ sec shutter speed

$^1\!/_{125}$ sec shutter speed

$^1\!/_{250}$ sec shutter speed

$^1\!/_{500}$ sec shutter speed

$^1\!/_{1000}$ sec shutter speed

and 2 stops. Compare the images to see how over- and underexposure affect tones and colours.

Controlling blur

Using a focal length of about 50mm, set the camera to Shutter Priority (S/Tv). Begin with a slow shutter speed ($^1\!/_{30}$ sec) and ask a friend to run in front of the camera at approximately 10ft (3m) from the lens. When your subject appears in the viewfinder take a shot. Repeat the exercise, increasing the shutter speed by 1 stop each time. By around $^1\!/_{500}$ sec most of the movement should be frozen, and by $^{1/}_{1000}$ sec the figure

ABOVE AND RIGHT The simple exercise described here shows you how shutter speed controls sense of movement. Although it's tempting and seems natural to use a fast shutter to freeze fast action, this may result in a static-looking image.

should be entirely sharp. Reduce the shutter speed to $^1\!/_{30}$ sec and focus on your friend as he or she begins to run forward. Start panning and fire the shutter when your friend moves directly in front of you. Continue to pan as the exposure is made and the image should show your subject more or less frozen, but the background should be blurred.

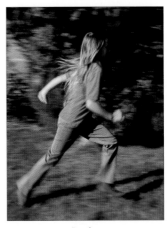

Panning

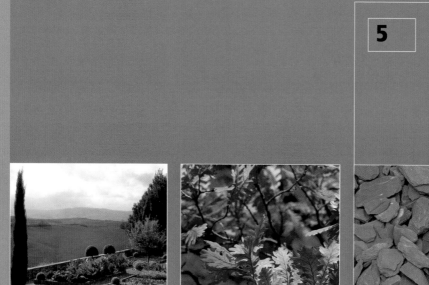

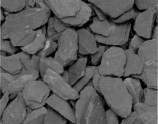

5

Tone, Colour and Light

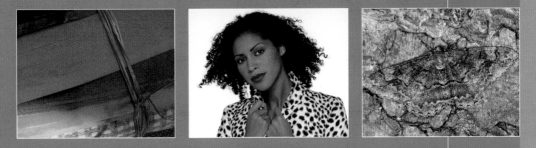

As well as composition and subject matter, the power of a photograph is controlled by the tones and colour it contains. Think of the difference that the light can make between a landscape shot in the misty early morning, compared to a high contrast image of a group of trees silhouetted against the setting sun. Or visualize a bright blue sky above a sandy beach and how the vibrant colours lend a power and almost abstract quality to the picture. With a black and white image you can also consider the wide range of tones available in a print. In this chapter we look at colour, tone and lighting and how you can control their effects.

Tonal Contrast

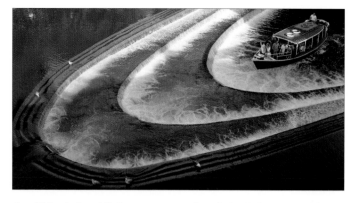

The vast majority of us have an inherent understanding of how a high-contrast image and a low-contrast one differ. However, it's important to understand what factors make an image exhibit a high or low degree of contrast, so that you can quickly spot high- or low-contrast situations in order to make the most of them.

High contrast
Essentially, images that are comprised of very dark and light tones, with little in between, are referred to as high-contrast images. In fact, many of us still most closely associate high-contrast images with black and white photography. However, the juxtaposition of the tones can also influence our perception of how much contrast there is in an image. If, for example, dark and light tones sit next to one another, then the image appears to have higher contrast

than if the dark and light tones are separated by more neutral tones, even though the overall tonal content is similar. In this respect, it's the subject that determines the contrast of the photograph.

Lighting
A second factor that contributes to contrast is lighting. If you fold a piece of paper continually back and forth to make a zigzag shape, then lay it on the surface of the table and light the paper from above, it appears almost continuous in tone with very little contrast. But shine a light from the

side and the shadows created by the ridges of the paper make the surface appear almost black and white.

Silhouettes
By their very nature, silhouettes are the most extreme form of high-contrast shots. Placing the subject against a light background and then exposing for the background will ensure that all detail within the subject is severely underexposed, leaving just the outline.

Silhouettes have passed out of fashion slightly for being somewhat clichéd, but they can still create

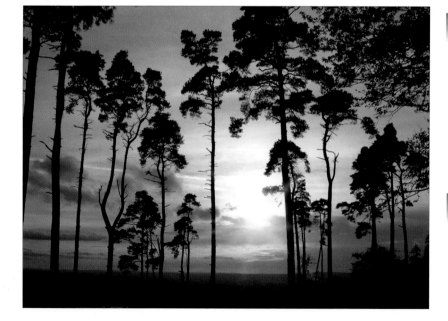

ABOVE The contrast in this shot doesn't come from the lighting, but from the subject – in this case the light and dark curves of the water.

LEFT Silhouettes work best when the background is much lighter than the subject. Here the sun acts as the background, turning the trees black.

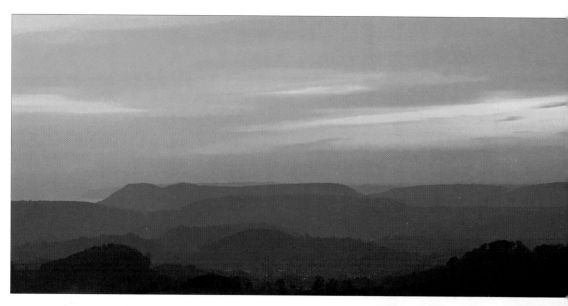

some powerful, atmospheric images. Remember to pick your subject carefully for its shape, rather than its form. Always bear in mind that you will not only lose the subject's form but pretty much all of its colour, too.

Low contrast

Shots that are said to be 'low contrast' rely on the image's neutral tones graduating into one another, creating a calm, gentle atmosphere. We tend to associate low-contrast images with hazy distant hills, the soft, shadowless lighting you get before the sun has risen or after it has set, or on a cloudy day – all conditions that the majority of photographers don't like because everything appears dull and flat. But striking images can be found under such circumstances – it's simply a case of finding subjects that emphasize the serene, tranquil and ethereal nature.

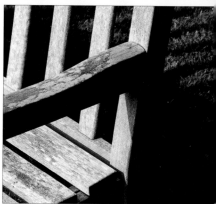

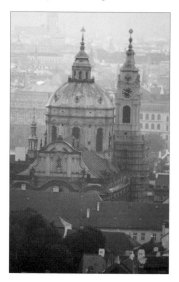

TOP Taken just before sunrise, the light in the sky is diffuse and soft, resulting in a low-contrast image. However, this suits landscape photographs, as does the light at the end of the day.

ABOVE RIGHT Hard lighting that gives a high-contrast result suits strong graphic shapes, such as this detail of a park bench.

LEFT Soft, diffused lighting created by an early misty morning will even out colour variation and create a low-contrast scene.

RIGHT Hard, directional lighting produces bright highlights and deep shadows – perfect for the shiny, silvery scales of these fish. The result is an almost monochrome high-contrast image.

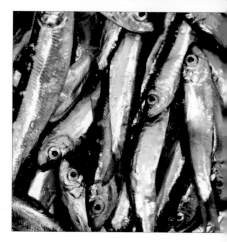

Colour Contrast

Although we usually think of tone as a decisive element that dictates whether an image exhibits high or low contrast, determined by the presence and juxtaposition of light and dark tones, there is another factor that determines our perception of contrast – colour. In the same way that tonal variation can determine the contrast in black and white images, colour variation can have the same effect in colour photography.

High colour contrast

Later we'll look in more detail at the emotions that certain colours can elicit and the effect of colour saturation, but here we're going to concentrate on how colour can be used to augment or reduce contrast, and the impact that it has on the viewer.

When closely juxtaposed, colours that lie opposite one another on the colour wheel, such as cold blues and warm reds, will create a strong high-contrast effect and, as with tonal contrast, this adds dynamism to an image. When using colour in this way, the most important thing is to ensure that the colour in the image is the

Colour wheel

Colours that occupy adjacent areas on the colour wheel create a calming, low-contrast effect, while those that sit opposite each other add high-contrast drama to a picture.

main subject. In many ways it's irrelevant if the subject is unrecognizable, as the response you're aiming to get from the viewer is triggered by the

▼ **BELOW LEFT** These umbrellas provide a high colour-contrasting image, helped by the fact that the orange and blue sit almost opposite one another on the colour wheel.

▼ **BELOW RIGHT** The reds and oranges of these fruits create a strong colour contrast when seen against the green leaves and blue sky beyond.

colour, rather than by the subject. The best way to explore high colour contrast is to look for subjects that feature only two colours, that are ideally situated opposite one another on the colour wheel. The impact will be greater if you zoom in as much as possible to exclude any other potentially distracting objects or colours.

Low colour contrast

Colours that share similar regions of the colour wheel create low colour contrast, and have a soothing or calming effect. The same applies to images that are made up primarily of only one colour (although this can vary depending on the colour).

The principal difference between high and low colour contrast is that with the former it's the colours, or rather the juxtaposition of the colours, that evokes the viewer's response, whereas with low colour contrast, the image needs to feature additional compositional elements in order for it to work successfully. Elements such as texture, form or even subtle tonal differences will all help to reinforce the colour harmony.

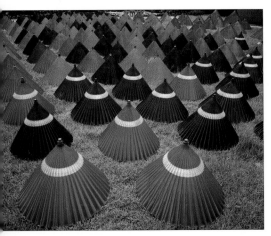

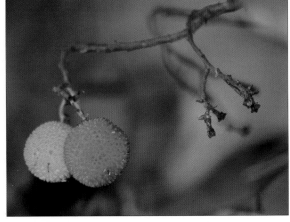

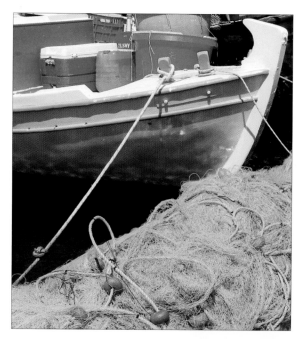

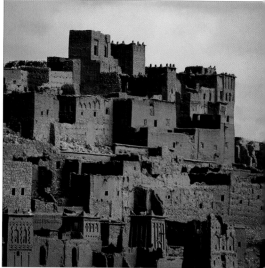

BELOW This image of an old Moroccan town is striking for the uniform brown colour of the buildings, which encourages the viewer to focus on their shape and pattern.

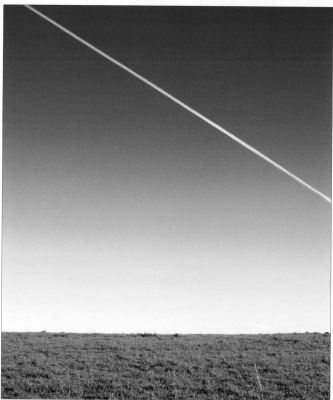

ABOVE The bold colours of the nets and the barrels on the fishing boat appear even stronger as they sit next to the neutral tones of the boat itself and the dark water.

RIGHT An incredibly simple image that would lose all its drama if it wasn't for the highly saturated colours and perfectly placed vapour trail.

BELOW With lots of tones of the same colour, low-contrast colour shots like these abstract petals have a calming and soothing effect.

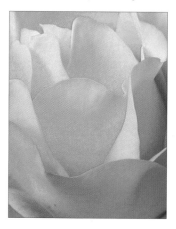

Low-key Photography

Low-key images are those that comprise large areas of dark midtones and shadows. For this reason, such images are often perceived as sombre, moody and even threatening, and indeed most low-key images are exactly that. However, successful low-key images will often feature areas of bright highlights, which, as well as offering a visual balance to the mass of dark tones, can also inject an uplifting note into the image.

Many people when confronted with an overcast, cloudy day or a grey flat interior, will put their camera away and wait for the sun to come out. However, these occasions can often provide just the sort of light required for an effective low-key photograph – and, in fact, conditions just before or just after a storm are often the best time to capture a really dramatic landscape. Look for a break in the clouds, try to establish when the sun is likely to make a brief appearance and position yourself so that you have a suitable backdrop against which you can capture the sun's rays.

Expose for highlights

Remember in such conditions, and in fact in any low-key image where the small highlight areas are very bright, it's essential that you correctly expose for these areas. They are likely to become the focal point of the image, and it's better for the surrounding areas to be underexposed than for the highlights to be overexposed, or 'blown out'. This may be unavoidable if you're actually pointing the camera toward the sun or any other very bright region or object, for example, but such areas should be restricted to

Dynamic range

Often, particularly when shooting landscapes, the camera's sensor is unable to capture detail in both highlight and shadow regions. Use a tripod to overcome this, thus ensuring images have as wide a dynamic range as possible, with highlights and shadows containing visible detail. First expose for the highlights, then adjust the exposure for the shadow areas and take another shot. The two images can later be merged with editing software, resulting in a single image with high dynamic range.

BELOW A classic low-key image; the dark, brooding sky and dark silhouetted landscape are uplifted by the sun's rays.

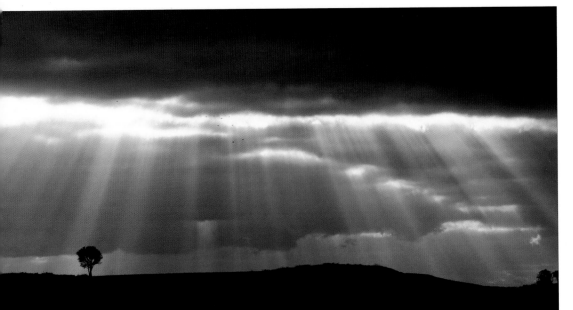

as small an area as possible. Use the LCD preview screen on the back of your camera and also take a look at the histogram (see pages 100–111) after each shot to make sure that the highlights are correctly exposed. Your camera may also feature a 'blown highlights' warning option, which will indicate overexposed areas on the LCD preview image through the use of a flashing colour.

Image editing

Once you have some candidates for potentially striking low-key images that include some interesting highlights, open them on the computer and begin by cropping any excess dark background or foreground areas. You can then experiment with your imaging software's brightness controls to add even greater contrast and impact to the image.

Black and white

Since the vast majority of low-key images comprise expansive areas of dark and shadow tones interspersed with a few areas of bright highlights, such images lend themselves particularly well to black and white photography.

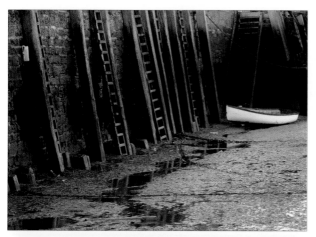

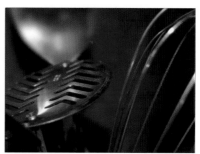

▲ **ABOVE** Even mundane items, such as these kitchen utensils, can make effective low-key subjects.

◄ **LEFT** The dark harbour walls and mud are offset by the white rowing boat in this low-key image.

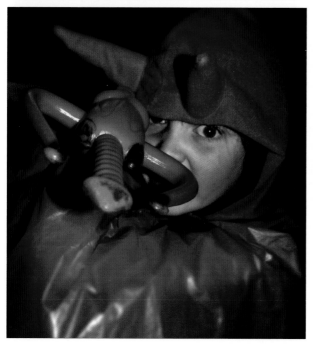

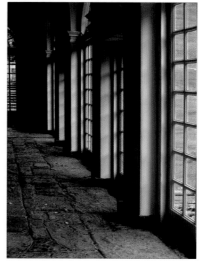

▲ **ABOVE** Here the dark flag stones are nicely juxtaposed with the woodwork and light columns.

◄ **LEFT** Low-key effects can create sombre portraits, but here the Halloween costume sets the scene.

High-key Photography

In the way that successful low-key images rely on large areas of dark midtones and shadows juxtaposed with small areas of bright highlights, successful high-key photographs utilize expansive areas of white and light tones in which are found small regions of dark tones, or even black. Although not essential from a purist's point of view, these regions can often form the focal point of the image, so it's important that exposure is set to ensure that as much detail as possible is captured there.

High-key landscapes need to have a prevailing area of light tones and, for this reason, snowscapes, seascapes and large sand-dunes are ideal subject matter.

In terms of weather conditions, a dark, stormy sky full of forbidding clouds is unlikely to provide you with the ideal lighting conditions for high-key landscapes, but, at the same time, a clear, blue, cloud-free sky isn't entirely necessary either.

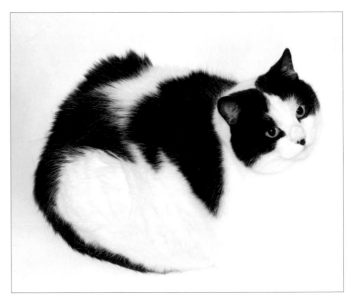

▼ **BELOW** High-key portraits result in a loss of skin texture and will often flatten facial features. Here the girl's face is framed by the darker hair, and the dark eyes make a strong focal point of the image.

▲ **ABOVE** This image was shot against a white background and deliberately overexposed. The white fur of the cat merges into the background, helping to emphasize the cat's markings and body contours.

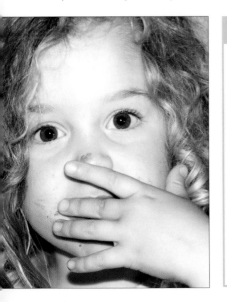

Overexposure

The metering system in most digital cameras will always attempt to expose for a neutral grey. In other words, when faced with a potential high-key scene, the camera will automatically attempt to underexpose, in order to hold detail in the highlight areas.

You can set the camera's exposure compensation (EV) control to +1 or +2 to overcome this. It's quite probable that you'll get a 'blown highlight' warning if you review the image on the camera's LCD screen, but ignore this, as overexposed highlights are part of the artistic effect in high-key images.

Ideally, you'll want either hazy summer skies or misty, thin layers of cloud – as is often found during the late autumn and early winter months in temperate regions.

Expose for dark areas

Just as you should expose for highlights in low-key images, the opposite is true for high-key images. If you expose for the dark, shadowy areas, you'll capture any detail there – which is likely to be the focal point of the image – while it's less important to retain detail in the lighter areas. Most high-key images work best if little or no detail is visible in these lighter areas, as this helps to evoke and reinforce the light, delicate and airy nature of high-key images.

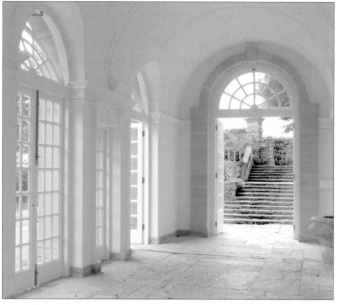

LEFT If you left the camera's metering system to its own devices with an interior shot like this, it would most likely underexpose, so the white walls came out a darker grey.

BELOW LEFT Setting the exposure to 1–2 stops more than the camera suggests (effectively overexposing the image) will help keep highlight areas light.

BELOW RIGHT Shadows that are dark, but not necessarily black, typify high-key images and give this style of photograph a light, airy feel.

BOTTOM An extreme example of a high-key picture, with very little highlight detail, and very few black tones.

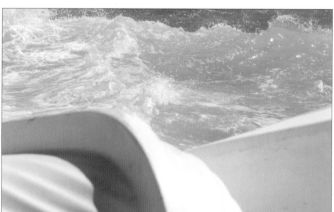

Image editing

As with low-key pictures, once you have some candidates that you think would make great high-key images, open the photographs on your computer and begin experimenting. Start by cropping any excess background or foreground areas. You can then experiment with your imaging software's brightness controls to add even greater contrast and impact to the image.

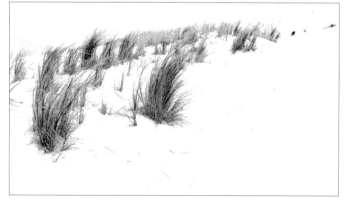

Composing with Colour

Colour is an amazingly emotive and evocative thing. People will react to it whether they're aware of it or not, so for this reason, it must be considered with care in photography. Volumes have been written about how colour affects our emotions, and we can only touch on it briefly here. Much of it we inherently know. We all perceive red to be a passionate, powerful colour, for example, and a warning sign in both nature and the human environment. However, it is also a warm colour, of course – the colour of sunsets.

Red is generally considered the most 'advancing' colour in that it's often perceived as being closer than it really is, and therefore more likely to attract our attention. **Blue** is one of the most 'receding' colours in that it's often perceived as being more distant than it really is. Blue is a cool colour that evokes a sense of calm and peace in an image and it also provides a great contrast with red. **Green** is associated with nature, which is perhaps why it is often used to symbolize renewal and hope. It shares the same neighbourhood on the colour wheel as blue and is another receding colour that contrasts

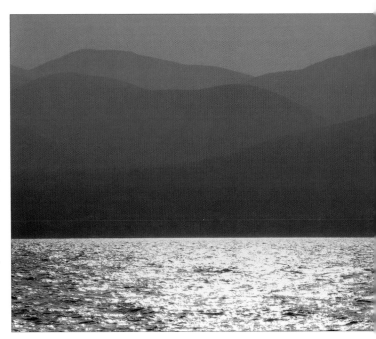

▲ **ABOVE** At sunrise and sunset the colour of light changes toward red, which gives landscape photographs a warm feel. This can be enhanced through the use of coloured filters, as demonstrated here.

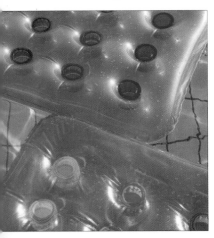

▼ **BELOW** Brightly coloured, man-made objects are often great for bold abstract images, such as this swimming pool shot.

with red. **Yellow** is more akin to red in that it is an advancing colour and one that helps to add warmth; it is the colour associated with the hot midday sun and fire.

These four colours are the most important in the visible spectrum. From these we get not only the additive primary colours (red, green, blue) of television sets, computer screens and digital cameras, but in terms of light, these colours mixed together to provide the secondary colours cyan, magenta and yellow. Also from our initial four colours we get the primary colours of the artist's paint palette (red, blue and yellow), from which we get the secondary colours violet, orange and green.

Saturated versus muted

Surprisingly, while vibrant, saturated colours have an initial impact and are good at attracting our attention – hence their liberal use in advertising, packaging and warning road signs – it's the muted colours that usually leave a longer-lasting impression in art and photography, particularly in landscapes and portraits. Unsaturated colours are more evocative and thought provoking, and the colours won't detract from the subject of the picture. However, if you're using colour to emphasize contrast, then they should be as vibrant as possible. Colours are most saturated in the

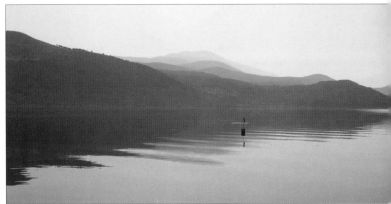

RIGHT Although bright, saturated colours grab our attention initially, it is often muted and gentler colours that have a longer-lasting impact.

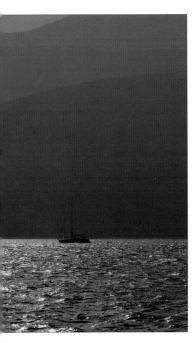

RIGHT Colour is the key to this simple yet striking landscape photograph. The richly saturated greens of the grass and blue of the sky are incredibly eye-catching.

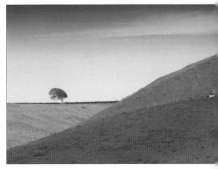

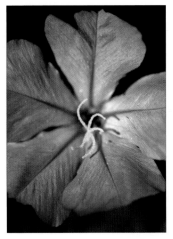

middle of a clear sunny day, when there are fewer shadows to interfere with expanses of colour. However, the cooler colour temperature at the end of the day can make reds, yellows and oranges more vibrant.

LEFT Less saturated colours, such as those found in some flowers, might not jump out of the page, but the effect is less jarring and far more calming.

BELOW The powerful flavour of chillies is successfully evoked by the rich, saturated reds (which contrast well with the green stalks) in this image.

Desaturation

You can desaturate strong colour by using a long focal length under soft lighting conditions, as over long distances the light is more likely to be diffused by particles in the air. However, if you're using a long focal length lens or zoom setting, you may not get the framing that you want. Alternatively, you can also tone down the colour on your computer using your image software's colour controls.

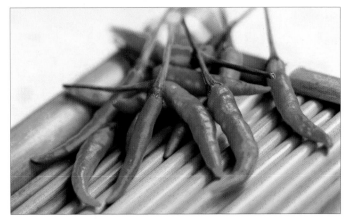

Black and White

Although technological advances have been the catalyst for a transition from black and white to colour in both television and the movies, and similar technological advances have made it possible for us now to capture and print accurate colour photographs, black and white photography is still very much alive and kicking. There are numerous websites, magazines and books devoted to the art of black and white photography and, for many, the black and white image is the pinnacle of art photography.

Colour photography can, in many ways, be seen simply as a way of capturing and conveying an image of the world around us – as beautiful or as shocking as it may be – because most of us see the world in colour. A black and white image, however, is already one step removed from 'reality', and so it immediately becomes less a way of simply conveying a scene, and more about conveying the photographer's interpretation of the scene. The same applies for colour photography, of course, but even more so with black and white photography, which is why it is and will always remain such a popular genre.

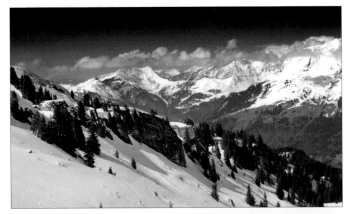

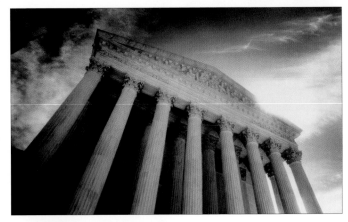

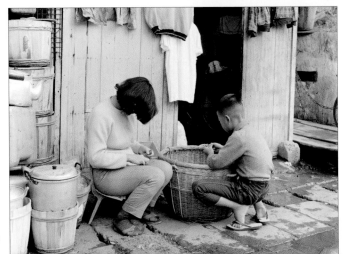

TOP Removing colour often helps us to reveal nature's extraordinary forms and shapes more clearly.

ABOVE Black and white images can often convey a greater sense of gravitas or austerity than colour.

LEFT For many photographers, black and white is the only medium for street photography, immediately giving pictures a 'gritty' newspaper look.

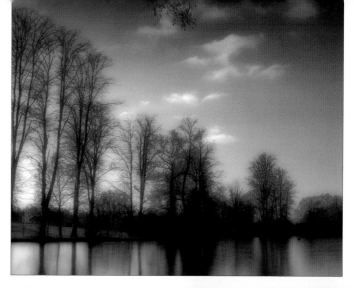

Digital black and white

Traditionally, with film cameras, the photographer has to decide whether to shoot on black and white or colour film, and once the decision has been made, it is impossible to change. With digital imaging you do not need to make that decision. If you want, you can shoot everything in colour and decide at a later stage which images are potential candidates for black and white conversion.

While there's nothing inherently wrong with this approach, it can make for a slightly hit or miss approach to black and white, and it's far better to know in advance what ingredients you need for a good black and white composition. There's no doubting that for most photographers used to working in colour, switching to black and white can come as something of a surprise. Until we start shooting black and white, we are unaware of how reliant we are on colour to make our images work, and that's a very good reason to spend at least some time 'thinking', and if at all possible shooting, specifically in black and white.

Shooting black and white

Most cameras have a black and white mode, and although this isn't the best way of capturing black and white images, using this setting when you're next out with your camera is an excellent exercise as it provides you with an instant black and white preview. To obtain the best black and white results, shoot in RAW if you have the option, as this will retain much more tonal information than shooting JPEG.

However, if you print directly from your camera, you'll have to shoot black and white JPEGs. Although these will provide adequate black and white prints, you won't have the same level of control compared with converting the images on a computer.

Over the next few pages, we'll be looking at ways of learning how to best compose for black and white photography. Not only is this essential if you're to produce attention-grabbing black and white images, but it will also prove enormously helpful whenever you revert to colour photography.

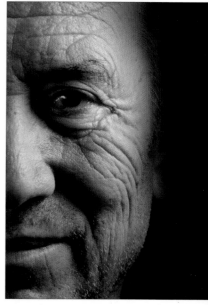

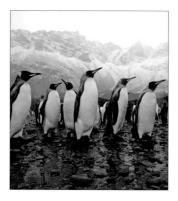

Noise

When shooting in black and white, or for black and white conversion, it's even more important to set the lowest possible ISO than it is when shooting in colour. The reason for this is that noise is more evident in dark tones, such as dark greys and blacks, than in any other colour, particularly in low-light photography.

TOP This gorgeous shot is all about the soft tones in the image, which have been enhanced by a gentle blur and a slow shutter speed smoothing the water.

ABOVE Black and white portraits can often be far more powerful than their colour counterparts.

LEFT Shooting in black and white forces you to concentrate on tone and texture, avoiding the potential distraction of colour.

Black and White Composition

Without colour, it's inevitable that other elements of composition must come to the fore for a black and white image to be successful. This is the beauty and challenge of black and white photography, and the reason why so many people hold it in such high esteem. It forces us to be more aware and to look much more closely at potential subjects.

Tone, shape and texture

Without colour, it's crucial that the subtleties of tone are captured in as much detail as possible, and for this it's doubly important to be aware of the quality of light at different times of the day or year. Morning and late afternoon will usually provide light that best draws out the subtlety of the tones, but that's not to say that strong, midday light is inappropriate for black and white photography. With the sun high in the sky, shape is emphasized and – depending on the angle of light in relation to the

subject – texture can also be clearer. Furthermore, with harsh light, you'll find that you can achieve a greater dynamic range; whites tend to be whiter and blacks darker. Given the right subject matter, the presence of strong blacks and strong whites – with little greyscale in between – can result in a powerful graphic image.

Over time, you'll appreciate how light impacts on black and white imagery in different ways to colour. For example, you'll quickly discover that dull light that may be unsuitable for colour photography because colours are rendered uninteresting and drab, is ideal for black and white as it allows the photographer to explore and emphasize the tones of a scene without fear of harsh,

complicating shadows and blown highlights. Similarly, such light is often best for shooting portraits, as the tones are more flattering and the reduced contrast allows the intricate form of a face to be fully represented.

Pattern

One aspect of composition that does not rely too heavily on the prevailing lighting conditions is pattern. You can seek out appropriate patterns for potential black and white treatment whether the light is harsh or soft. For many photographers, the repetitious nature of pattern is made stronger without the distracting presence of colour, which in many scenes could be the only way that one element is differentiated from another.

▼ **BELOW** Strong lines are even more important in a black and white picture than a colour one as they help hold the viewer's attention.

▶ **RIGHT** The lack of colour in this shot of St Basil's Cathedral, Moscow, encourages the viewer to concentrate not only on the form and texture of the domes, but also on the spaces in between the domes.

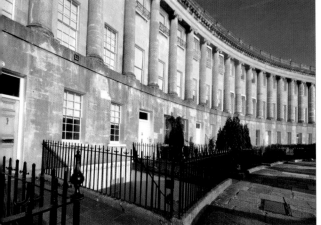

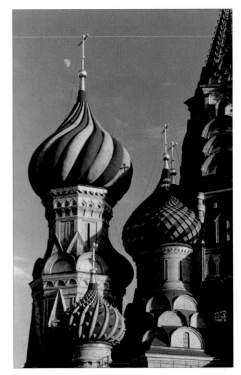

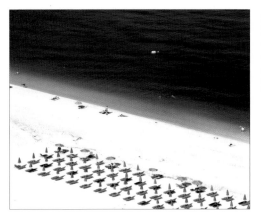

▲ **ABOVE** Without colour, the form, shape and tones of a subject take on a much greater significance if you want the viewer to be able to 'read', or interpret, an image successfully.

▲ **ABOVE** With strong shadows, it's possible to create striking images in black and white pictures that might not have as much impact in colour.

Horizontals, verticals and curves

Without colour, another way of keeping the viewer's attention is to look for strong leading lines to guide the viewer around the image. Although leading lines are important in colour photography, they can be the key to a good black and white image and the stronger they are, the less the image is about representing a recognizable scene, and the more it becomes a visual statement.

Tonal contrast

Perhaps the hardest aspect of 'seeing' in black and white is forcing yourself to differentiate between tonal contrast and colour contrast. For example, reds and blues are on the opposite sides of the colour wheel and therefore contrast strongly, but when they are converted to black and white that contrast may well be diminished, or even lost altogether. When working in black and white, it's important to remember that it's not the hue of a colour that's important, but its brightness value.

While the rules of composition for colour and black and white photography are pretty much identical, you'll find at first that you have to work that little bit harder to get black and white images

that you're happy with. But, after a while, seeing potential black and white scenes should become second nature, while shooting them in colour and converting them on computer will give you the option of having two versions of the same scene. It will also give more control over the black and white conversion process.

▼ **BELOW** Although the subject of a silhouette is always black, silhouettes can often work better as black and white images as they have no distracting background colour.

Composition

Colour in composition can be a help as well as a hindrance. Without colour to fall back on, you will need to work much harder to take black and white photographs that have real impact. Always be on the look-out for strong leading lines, patterns, textures and shapes in a potential image, as well as subtleties of light and shade and tone.

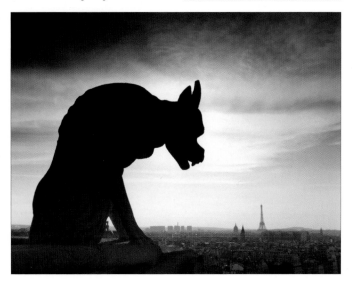

Black and White – Try It Yourself

There are no short cuts to taking successful black and white images; it's a skill that develops over time and with experience. As we've seen, although more or less the same 'rules' of composition apply to black and white photography as well as colour, you really do have to plan a black and white composition more, and ask yourself exactly what it is that you're trying to achieve with the shot.

Comparative shots

The best way to start experimenting with black and white photography is to return to local places where in the past you have taken some successful colour shots. Replicate as closely as possible the shots that worked well and re-photograph them using the camera's black and white mode.

Download the images on to your computer and compare them on screen with prints that you have of the colour images. Alternatively, if you have image-editing software, try converting some of your favourite images into black and white.

Don't worry if the black and white images look nowhere near as good as the colour versions, the purpose of the exercise isn't to go out and take stunning black and white images, the purpose really is to compare the two sets to see how the compositional elements translate into black and white. Look to see how the colours have converted into different shades of grey. Examine the images to see if shape and form are emphasized in the black and white versions. Does the absence of colour change the overall atmosphere of the images?

RIGHT The age and scale of this building in Prague lend themselves to a black and white image, taking us back to a bygone era.

Shoot black and white

Having carried out the comparative test, you should be a little more aware of what makes a good black and white composition. The next time you're out with your camera, make a deliberate point of shooting for black and white only. Aspects that should be at the forefront of your mind are:
• Texture and tone – look out for objects or scenes that have a good gradation of tone, from very dark greys to light whites. Try to shoot under varied lighting to see how it can affect the overall contrast of an image. Return to the same scene but under different lighting conditions to compare the effect of harsh, high-contrasting with soft, low-contrasting light. Look for objects and scenes that feature texture so apparent that you can almost 'feel' it just by sight.
• Pattern and shape – a lack of colour can emphasize rather than detract from pattern. There are numerous artificial as well as natural objects and scenes that reveal pattern often in quite unexpected ways. Also look out for objects with well-defined and interesting shapes – in a similar way to pattern, these can also benefit from being captured in black and white.
• If you're an avid landscape photographer, look out for blue skies with plenty of white clouds. Famous American photographer Ansel Adams is perhaps most famous for his black and white landscapes, many of which featured dark, almost black, skies with broad sweeps of white cloud. Use a polarizing filter to enhance the contrast between the sky and clouds.
• Leading lines and curves are important in colour photography, but they are often even more essential in black and white photography; look out for scenes with strong diagonals, verticals, horizontals and curves. These visual guides can lead the viewer through an image and provide the image with graphic elements.

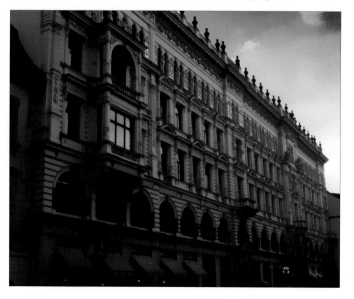

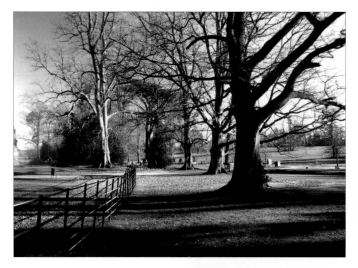

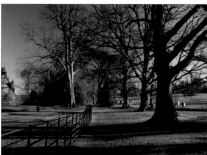

ABOVE AND ABOVE RIGHT Converting some of your images on computer is a good way to begin to learn what works well as a black and white shot. Here, the juxtaposition of the structures of the trees and the fence – one natural, one artificial – is more apparent in the monochrome shot; so, too, are the sweeping shadows.

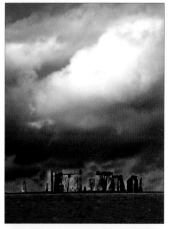

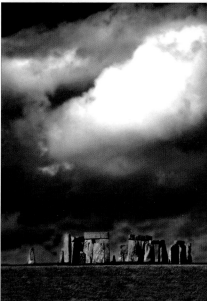

RIGHT AND FAR RIGHT The purpose of these images is to compare the sense of texture between the colour image and the black and white, between both the stones and the clouds above.

LEFT AND BELOW In the black and white version the dappled light is still apparent and the image assumes a more abstract quality.

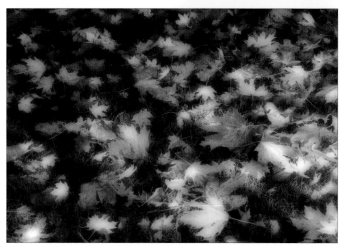

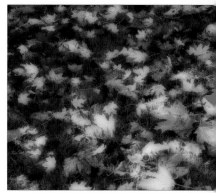

Lighting

The significance of lighting in photography cannot be overestimated – in fact the very word photography is derived from the Greek, literally meaning 'drawing or writing (*graphis*) with light (*photos*)'.

The strength, angle, temperature and quality of light – the last of which is affected by time of day, time of year, location and countless atmospheric conditions – will affect just about every aspect of an image. They will determine how bright the colours will be rendered, how strong and long the shadows will be, how visible distant objects are, and how much detail is obvious in foreground objects.

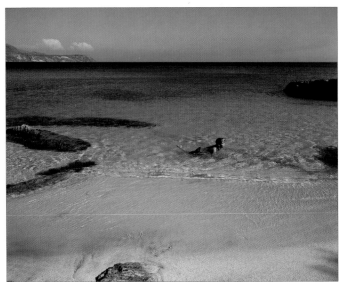

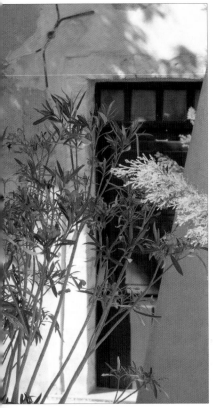

LEFT Despite being shot in the shade, the bright red flowers contrast with the pale-coloured walls and green leaves, while the shadows in the background add to the sense of warmth.

ABOVE AND BELOW These two images show the sea in very different light. The one below is dark and brooding and the lack of sun has created an almost monochromatic image, while the other, shot in strong late-afternoon sun, has saturated colours, strong shadows and a clear sky resulting in clear water.

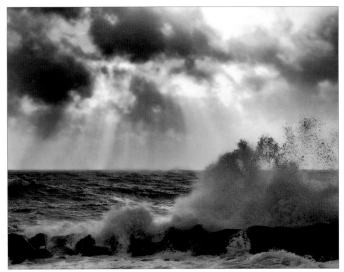

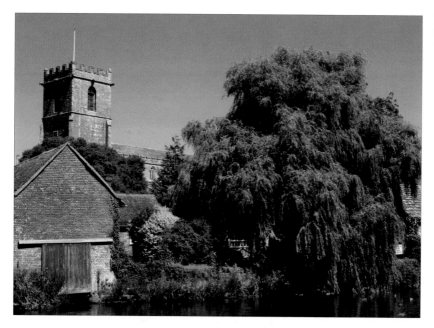

Certain types of lighting can make objects appear flat or uniform in tone, while other lighting can make the same objects appear highly textured, pitted or undulating, and full of contrasting tones. In fact, the only parts of an image in which light does not carry as much significance is the subject, and the juxtaposition of the image's various elements to one another. In many ways, this is the very essence of photography. Setting aside studio photography, as a photographer it's essential that you are aware of the possibilities (and limitations) of different lighting situations.

Almost all of us, when we first become interested in photography, fall into the trap of assuming that you need bright sunny weather to create successful images. While it is true that these conditions do make for glorious photographs, so too can grey, overcast days — they're likely to elicit entirely different emotions in the viewer, but both conditions have the ability to produce striking images. As far as photography goes, there's no such thing as bad light. There may be inappropriate light for

a specific shot, but in photography, 'bad' light should never stop play — you can find ways around it.

Timing

An important traits all photographers should develop is patience. There will be many times when you know that the quality of the light is perfect for the

scene in front of you, but you need some rays of light to highlight a specific element. It pays dividends to wait, as it could be the difference between a good shot and an excellent one.

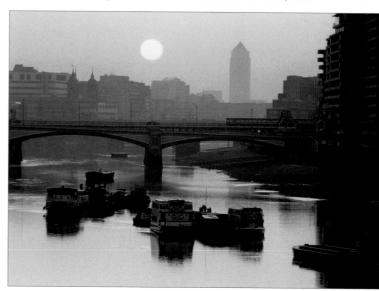

BELOW Early morning light enhances the soft misty atmosphere and brings a rosy glow to this shot of the river Thames, London.

Quality of Light

You will no doubt have heard or read about photographers discussing the 'quality' of light. While on a general level the term is used to describe anything from light temperature (such as the warm, red colour cast of a sunset), through to brightness levels, and the angle at which light is striking objects, more specifically, 'quality of light' strictly refers to how 'hard' or 'soft' it is.

Soft lighting

As its name suggests, soft lighting is a gentle, diffuse illumination and, outdoors, is usually the result of a layer of cloud. The water droplets and particles in the cloud scatter the sun's light rays as they pass through the cloud, sending the light in different directions. The most characteristic aspect of soft lighting is the lack of strong shadows, or sometimes any shadows at all. However, clouds come in an infinite variety of types, and different layers of cloud can often be moving at different speeds in relation to one another. For these reasons, the soft light of cloudy conditions can vary slightly from minute to minute.

In particular, with thick cloud conditions, when even the position of the sun in the sky is not discernible, objects can appear flat and free of texture, and colours somewhat muted. But that does not mean that such light cannot serve a useful photographic purpose. The lack of strong shadows and bright highlights can render complex shapes and scenes in a more intelligible fashion. Portraits are also sometimes more pleasing when there are no shadows to distort and alter peoples' features.

Hard lighting

Lighting is at its hardest when there's no cloud or haze to diffuse it – on clear summer days, for example. In these conditions the visibility tends to be good, making hard light ideal for 'long-view' landscapes. As we know from looking at texture, hard lighting can turn an apparently flat, featureless object into a mass of minute peaks and troughs. This is due to the strong shadows cast by direct, undiffused light. While this is often desirable and can be used to the photographer's advantage to create crisp, high-contrasting and dramatic images, deep shadows also have their drawbacks. They can render a busy scene, such as a shot of a market or street, too complex to view clearly because of the number of shadows, and they rarely help in portraits either.

RIGHT To make your subject stand out from its surroundings, try taking the shot when the light on the background is soft.

BELOW Soft, even lighting has ensured that the colours of the holly and berries are captured accurately, while the lack of strong shadows doesn't create a confusing image.

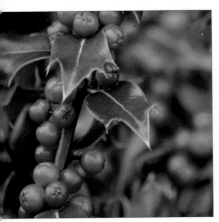

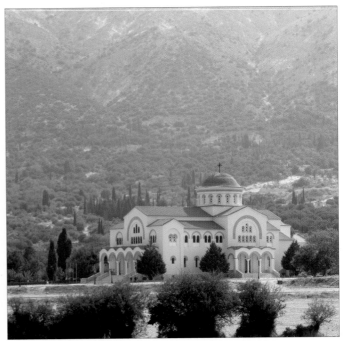

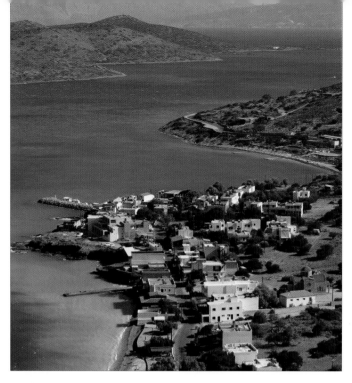

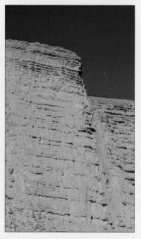

LEFT Hard lighting offers good visibility and crisp, clear photographs with sharply defined shadows.

SOFT AND HARD

Whether you shoot in soft, diffused light or strong, direct light has a significant impact on a photograph's appearance. Hard light will increase the contrast and colour saturation, while diffused light makes colours softer and also reduces the contrast for a more 'natural' appearance.

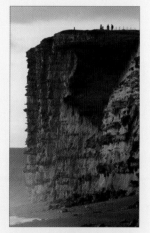

Soft light

Angle of light

One crucial aspect of hard light that must be considered is its angle and direction in relation to the subject or scene. The general characteristics and colours of an object lit from the front can look entirely different if lit from the side or from the back. So, having assessed the generic qualities of hard light, let's now look in more detail at how these qualities can alter the way in which individual objects or indeed entire scenes appear, depending on the direction of the light.

BELOW Strong, direct light is rarely flattering for portraits, but here the hat diffuses the light, so the face is softly lit.

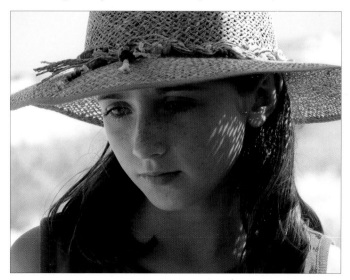

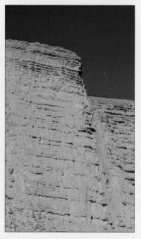

Hard light

Shooting Film in Artificial Light

Daylight and artificial light have different colour temperatures. Daylight tends to be hotter in colour temperature than artificial light, so you should avoid mixing them.

The wide spectrum of artificial lighting produces varying colours. For instance, halogen lighting gives a yellow cast to its subjects; fluorescent lighting gives a greenish pallor in some skin tones; and the light from an incandescent light bulb gives a slight blue tint in pictures.

Daylight colour film, as its name suggests, is for use with daylight-lit subjects or with electronic flash. If daylight film is used indoors where the main source of illumination is provided by tungsten light bulbs, for example, the resulting pictures will have an orange cast to them. This is because what is known as the 'colour temperature' of the light source would be at variance with the colour balance of the film. You will need to plan so that this does not occur.

Warmth and coolness

Colour temperature is usually measured in values of kelvin. To achieve the correct balance when using daylight film in artificial light of 3200 kelvin requires the use of an 80A filter. This is a blue-coloured filter which corrects the orange cast that is otherwise created. However, the blue-coloured filter is quite a dense filter and will cut down the amount of light passing through the lens on to the film; to compensate for this, 64 ISO film must be rated at 16 ISO. Take care when adjusting for these factors as a long exposure is needed.

When you expose daylight-balanced colour film for exposures of longer than approximately 1 sec, the film will suffer from reciprocity failure i.e. where the stated ISO rating no longer applies. An example of this is where a 100 ISO film may only be 25 ISO at an exposure of 10 sec. Owing to the unpredictable nature of the film in these circumstances, the only sure way of getting the right exposure is to test the film in the prevailing light conditions to see what ISO it should be rated at.

When using tungsten-balanced films these problems are solved. There is no need to add a filter to the camera when shooting in situations where the colour temperature is 3200 kelvin, and tungsten-balanced film can be used at far longer exposures than daylight film without suffering from reciprocity failure.

If daylight-balanced colour negative film is used in tungsten light it can always be corrected at printing stage. If daylight-balanced colour reversal film is used in tungsten light without an 80A filter the resulting transparencies would have to be corrected at the printing stage.

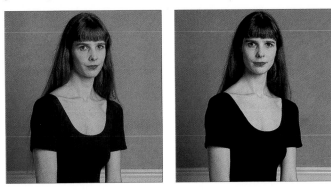

ABOVE If daylight-balanced colour film is used in-artificial light the results will have an orange cast. To correct this imbalance an 80A filter needs to be used, top right. Alternatively, tungsten-balanced film used in artificial light does not require a colour-balanced filter.

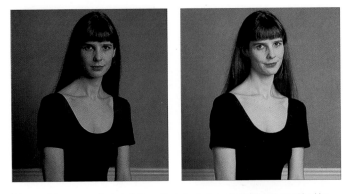

ABOVE Using tungsten film in daylight or with electronic flash will result in pictures with a blue cast. To correct this, use an 85B filter, right. As an alternative, use daylight-balanced film in daylight or with electronic flash as this does not need a colour-balanced filter.

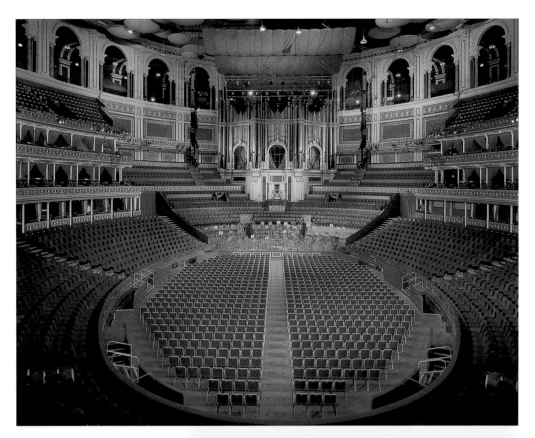

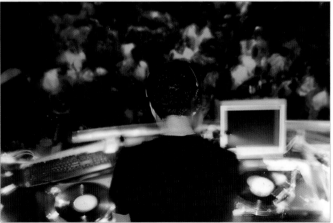

ABOVE When shooting in artificial light it is often necessary to use long exposures. This picture required the shutter to be open for 30 sec. Since the lighting was tungsten, tungsten-balanced colour film was used. Apart from the fact that it rendered the colour correctly, tungsten film suffers far less from reciprocity failure than daylight-balanced film.

RIGHT A long exposure on this shot has led to motion blur, and the movement of the crowd in the UV light contrasts well with the still, darker figure of the DJ in the foreground.

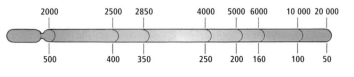

RIGHT Light is measured in values of kelvin. The measurements change according to the type of light, from warm to cool.

average tungsten light			average daylight			
2000	2500	2850	4000	5000 6000	10 000	20 000
500	400	350	250	200 160	100	50

Shooting Film in Mixed Light

Occasionally there are situations, especially indoors, when the light comes from many different sources. These sources may all have different colour temperatures, so using only tungsten-balanced colour film or filtering daylight-balanced film to 3200 kelvin may not be adequate.

Fluorescent light

One of the most difficult lights to balance is fluorescent light. This is because there are many different types of fluorescent light tubes ranging from cool to warm white. When a tube wears out it might be replaced with a tube of a different colour temperature. To the naked eye, all the tubes may look the same yet they are in fact giving off different temperatures of colour which makes choosing the correct filter very difficult.

Daylight and artificial light

Sometimes when using two mixed light sources, such as tungsten light and daylight or fluorescent light and daylight, the practical solution may be to expose for the greater light source. A more elaborate method – when shooting in a room lit by tungsten light with windows that let in daylight – is to place light-balancing material over the windows to convert the daylight to the same balance as the tungsten light.

In situations that combine daylight with tungsten, the warmth of the tungsten light can add a mellow tone. If the situation is one which combines daylight, tungsten and flash, the trick is to balance all of these elements. The best method to achieve this is to work out the exposure for the daylight coming in through the windows.

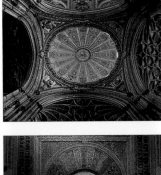

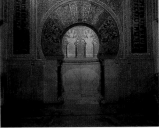

ABOVE In the top shot daylight predominates and the picture works well on daylight film. Underneath, using the same film and pointing the camera down to a small area of lit by tungsten light without the use of an 80A filter has created an orange cast.

For example, it may be 1 second at f/16. If so, adjust the power of the flash to give an exposure of f/16. (Shooting at speeds slower than the flash setting on the camera will not alter the flash exposure; this will only happen if a faster speed is used than is recommended for the camera.) Set the shutter speed to 1 sec and take the shot. At this exposure tungsten light (coming, for example, from a table lamp) will be recorded without causing an unnatural colour cast.

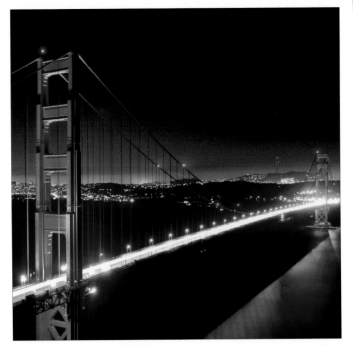

LEFT This picture, taken at dusk, shows several different light sources but due to the expanse of the picture and its varied elements it appears correctly exposed despite the lights having differing colour balances.

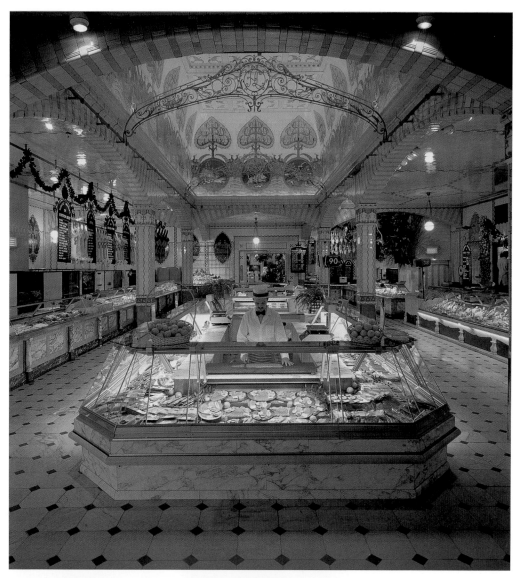

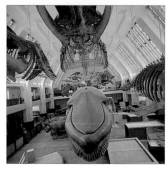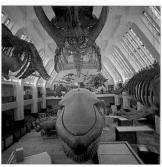

ABOVE In this shot of the Harrods food hall, the ceramic well set into the ceiling is lit by fluorescent lighting yet the rest of the store is lit by tungsten. Since the fluorescent light was on an isolated area, the whole shot was exposed for tungsten.

FAR LEFT This museum room has fluorescent light as the dominant source which has given the left shot a green cast. An FLD (fluorescent daylight) filter on the right shot removes this and adds a natural tone.

Direction of Light: Front and Side Lighting

With heavily diffused light, the position of the light source – which in most cases is likely to be the sun – is of little consequence in relation to the position of the subject. With hard light, however, the direction from which the subject is lit is fundamental to how it will appear in a photograph. How high or low the sun is in the sky also plays a significant role.

Frontal lighting

When the sun is located behind the photographer and falls directly on to the subject, the subject is said to be 'front lit'. This is perhaps the most common way to capture photographs and even those of us not that familiar with photography will probably remember being told that we should always shoot with the sun behind us.

Frontal lighting certainly has its benefits. With the sun directly behind us, shadows are cast away from the camera and, depending on the viewpoint, may well be out of our line of sight. Without strong shadows to cater for, getting an appropriate exposure for both light and dark areas is more straightforward with front-lit scenes due to the lack of contrast (or

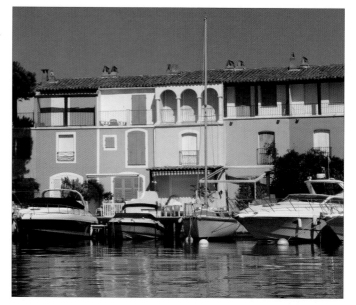

ABOVE Lit from the front, these houses appear almost two-dimensional, so the shot is about their flat colour, rather than form.

BELOW This partially buried wooden fence has been shot with side lighting, creating shadows that make for a pleasing, almost abstract effect. The side lighting also helps to bring out the texture in the sand.

low dynamic range). The photograph's colours also tend to be more evenly illuminated, so subtleties in tone become increasingly apparent.

The drawback of frontal lighting is that the lack of shadows will underplay the visibility of any texture the subject might have, and potentially reduce perspective across the entire scene. For these reasons shots may appear rather flat and lacking in any depth.

For really successful frontally lit images, you should be relying on interesting and strong colour and tonal contrast. Bear in mind, too, that reflective surfaces will throw back most light when front lit. Finally, do be mindful of your own shadow when shooting with the sun behind you. Depending on how low it is in the sky, the sun could cast your shadow a surprisingly long way into the scene you're photographing and potentially ruin a great shot. Some photographers, if confronted with this problem, will

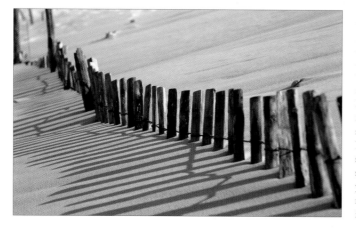

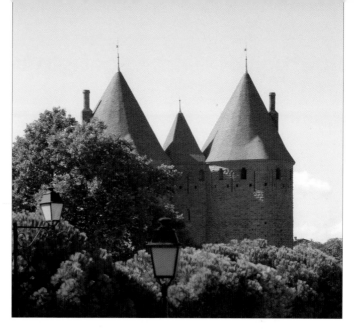

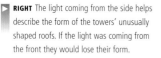

RIGHT The light coming from the side helps describe the form of the towers' unusually shaped roofs. If the light was coming from the front they would lose their form.

try to disguise their body shape so that it resembles less a human figure and more an anonymous shrub, or whatever is appropriate for the scene.

Side lighting

With the sun to one side of both you and the subject, the image is said to be side lit. While front lighting tends to flatten objects, side lighting emphasizes texture and form as shadows are prominent and potentially long, depending on how low the sun is.

Side lighting also adds drama to an image. Parts of a scene may be well lit and the colours saturated, while other parts may be in shadow and their colours muted. In very bright, side-lit situations, the scene may be so heavily contrasting, with bright, white high-

lights and dark, almost black shadows (creating a very high dynamic range), that the camera's sensor won't be able to capture all the detail in the scene. In these situations you must decide to expose either for the shadows or the highlights. The decision will ultimately be down to the subject matter and the emotions you are trying to evoke in the viewer. For these reasons, it's sensible to bracket high-contrast, side-lit scenes, as that way you'll have a greater chance of getting an exposure that works. You can further increase your chances of success by shooting RAW (see page 85).

BELOW Strong side lighting creates bright highlights and deep shadows, which gives a greater idea of the subject's form.

BELOW LEFT Shooting group shots in bright sunshine has many pitfalls. To avoid subjects squinting into the sun and strong shadows running down their faces, try positioning the group so that they're lit from the side.

Front versus side

- Front lighting reduces the texture of a subject, but can help make strong colours appear even bolder.
- Lighting coming from the side will reveal a subject's form, but watch out for confusing shadows.

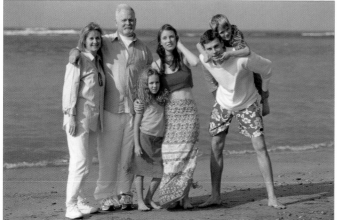

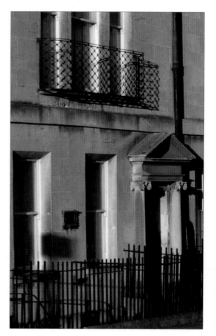

Direction of Light: Back Lighting

Another popular way of working with direct, undiffused light is to place the subject more or less between the sun and the camera. This is known as back lighting a subject, and the technique is sometimes referred to as *contre jour*, French for 'against the day'. Back lighting can create dramatic results due to the high contrast inherent in back-lit scenes.

Silhouettes

The best-known back-lit technique is the silhouette. To shoot a silhouette, simply position the subject directly in front of a large bright area, or indeed the sun itself, and the camera will usually automatically underexpose the subject to create the silhouette. Ensuring that the sun is masked by the subject usually works best, otherwise you run the risk of not being able to capture any information at all due to the brightness of the sun. Unless the subject is translucent you're unlikely to capture any detail, colour or texture. The only clue as to what the subject is will be its outline shape. Silhouettes can, of course, make for very powerful images, but it's important to choose your subject on the merits of its shape alone and to position it so its shape is shown to best advantage. The most striking silhouettes have an almost uniform, light-coloured background to make the subject most obvious.

Buildings (particularly structures with interesting shapes such as bridges or piers), trees, a face in profile – in fact anything, as long as it has an interesting or emotive shape – make excellent subjects for a silhouette.

Translucency

For variation, try shooting a translucent object placed in front of the light source. Depending on the object, fine detail will be visible, such as the veins of a leaf, and colours will be bright and saturated. You do need to be careful, however, not to overexpose the subject.

Rim lighting

As dramatic as silhouettes are, the effect should be used sparingly in any portfolio. There are other back-lighting effects that are just as striking. Rim lighting is a form of back lighting in which the light source is behind, but also slightly off to one side. The resulting shot, depending on the object being photographed and the background, will have brightly lit, almost glowing edges, and can make for a spectacular image.

BELOW Shooting directly into a light source increases the risk of 'lens flare' in your picture. Here, it is shown by the purple and green patches of colour in the corners.

RIGHT Back lighting can be used effectively to throw long shadows toward the camera creating a dramatic result.

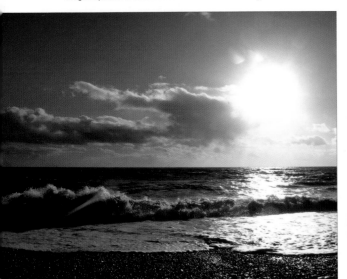

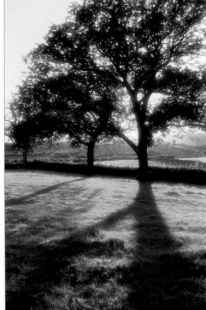

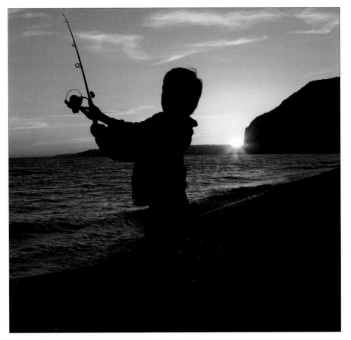

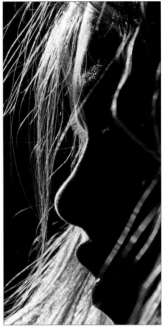

ABOVE The most striking silhouettes are made when you have a subject that is recognizable, even when there is no detail – as in this shot of a boy fishing.

BELOW Rim lighting produces very striking results, with the heavy lighting from behind and to the side of the subjects, creating glowing highlights.

Flare

Lens flare is apparent in silhouettes or other forms of back-lit shots in the form of rows of hexagonal-shaped circles of light emanating from the sun (or any other light source). The shape of the light pools is determined by the shape of the lens' aperture (or diaphragm) when the shot is taken. Although this type of lens flare (which is caused by reflections within the camera's lens) can add atmosphere to a shot, it is better to try to prevent it. This is why you sometimes see a lens fitted with a lens hood, which is a petal- or cup-shaped piece of plastic that fits on the end of the lens and acts as a sunshade for the lens.

Taking back-lit shots

• Silhouettes work best when you can identify the subject only by the shape of its outline.
• Use light from behind and to the side of the subject for intense highlights and added drama.
• Avoid lens flare by shielding the front of the lens from the light by using a lens hood.
• Remember that colour will usually be very muted with most back-lit shots; if colour is an important element of the shot, try front lighting.

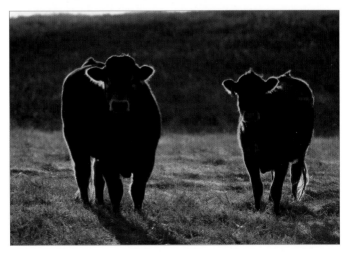

Shooting against the Light

Many people think that you can only take good photographs if the sun is directly behind or to one side of the camera. By taking shots straight into the sun, flare and incorrect exposure may result, although, if dealt with carefully, these can be avoided or used to create dramatic effects. A lens hood should eliminate flare – you should ideally have a lens hood attached to your camera whichever way you are shooting. Flare can result from light indirectly reflecting off a shiny surface as well as directly from the sun.

Judging exposure

You need to take time over calculating exposure as, if your subject is strongly backlit, it could appear as a silhouette. Although this may be the effect you are after, an adjustment to exposure will be necessary if you want your subject to be more than a shape. If you are using a camera with built-in metering that has a choice of exposure modes such as average, centre-weighted or spot metering, then the spot metering mode will give a more accurate reading. If your

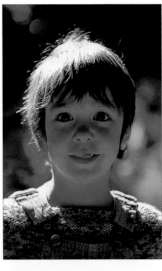

▶ **RIGHT** In this picture the sun is at about 45 degrees behind the young girl. A reflector was used to bounce back a small amount of light into her face. Without this she would have been almost silhouetted against the background. Although a lens hood was used, flare can still be seen in the top left-hand corner of the picture.

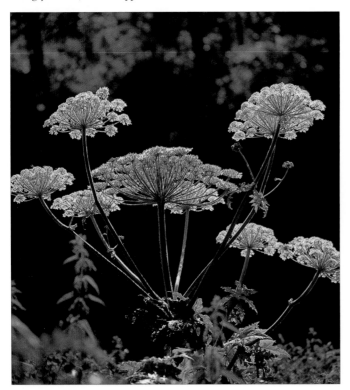

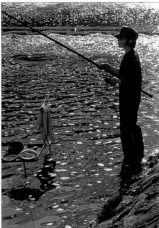

▲ **ABOVE** By exposing for the light reflecting off the water, this boy is shown almost in silhouette. In this case it works well because you can still tell what he is doing.

◀ **LEFT** A combination of a long lens and small aperture have resulted in isolating this plant from its surroundings. The back light has helped to emphasize this effect and the eye is drawn immediately to its delicate blooms.

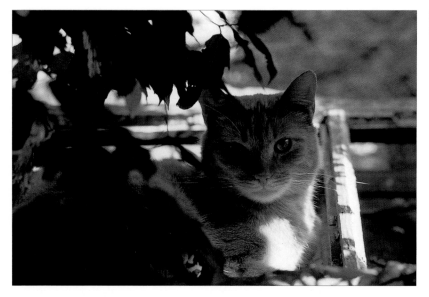

LEFT Often there is no time to use fill-in flash or a reflector to throw light back on to a subject, and this is often the case with animals. By exposing for the shadows enough detail has been retained to record this cat's peaceful posture in the shade.

camera only has metering in the average exposure mode, it will probably underexpose your subject. It is possible to overcome this if you move in close so that the viewfinder is covering only the subject. Take your meter reading at this distance – depress the shutter release button about half-way. If your camera has an auto-exposure lock, keep the shutter release button slightly depressed and return to your original viewpoint. Without taking your finger off the button take your shot. Your subject will be correctly exposed although the background will be overexposed.

Another method is to use the exposure compensation dial – if applicable – on your camera. Set the dial to give two stops more exposure than the reading on the camera meter. If you can operate your camera manually and have a separate exposure meter then you could move in close to take a reading.

Care must be taken not to cast a shadow on your subject, as an incorrect reading and overexposure will result. The best method of taking a reading with a hand-held meter is to use the incident light method. This means attaching an invercone to the exposure meter sensor. The meter is pointed to the camera and a reading taken. This records the amount of light falling on your subject.

Be careful: looking through your lens directly at the sun could cause damage to your eyes!

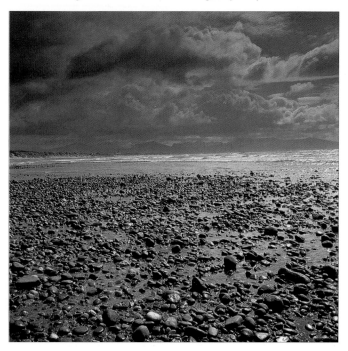

RIGHT By shooting straight into the sun a very dramatic backlit picture has been obtained. A lens hood is essential here, to eliminate flare. Be careful when shooting into the sun that you do not point the camera directly towards it.

Available Light

In photography 'available light' refers to any natural light source used to light a scene, and while this includes daylight for outdoor photography, here we're going to concentrate on daylight (and standard domestic lighting) for indoor photography and certain natural sources for night-time.

Although some keen amateur photographers may own a small lighting set-up, many will not, so all photographers will have to rely on available, or 'existing' light, such as standard tungsten light bulbs, at some point, especially when taking photographs indoors or outdoors during late evening or at night.

Of course just about every camera today has a small flash built into the body of the camera (and later we'll be looking in more detail at what we should expect from built-in flash units), but as useful as they are, such units usually only provide relatively low light levels and often subjects are harshly lit.

Indoors

Using available indoor light, by which we mean daylight from windows shining into a room and normal domestic lighting, can result in very pleasing images. Pictures taken using available light are often much more atmospheric and exhibit a greater sense of realism than those that have been painstakingly lit using a variety of studio lights and accessories.

The most important aspect to bear in mind when taking photographs under such lighting conditions is that, when captured, images will appear to have far more pronounced areas of light and shade than seemed apparent to the naked eye. When we spend time in a room our eyes are constantly and almost instantaneously

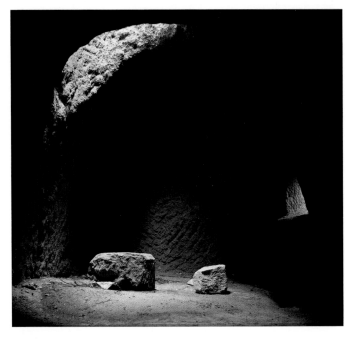

▼ **BELOW** Simple side lighting from a window was used in this pet portrait.

▲ **ABOVE** Using the available light from the two 'windows' in this cave, the rocks on the floor have been picked out and appear to be incredibly three dimensional.

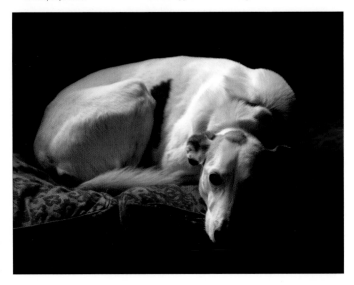

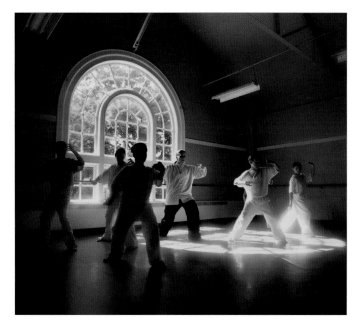

Using natural light

- Ambient light will allow you to retain more of the atmosphere of a scene than flash will.
- Use slow shutter speeds, wide apertures or high ISO settings in low-light conditions.
- Remember, however, that high ISO settings will introduce digital noise.

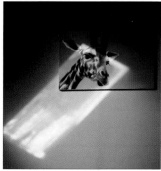

▲ **ABOVE** Here the light from a window not only illuminates the image on the wall, it also becomes part of the picture.

▼ **BELOW** Using the light from the fire has kept all the atmosphere of this scene. Flash would have ruined the shot in an instant.

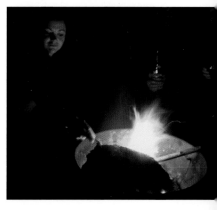

adjusting for the well-lit and dimly lit areas as we look around, which create the appearance of a fairly evenly lit room. However, the camera is only capturing one specific part of the room at one specific moment, so resulting images will appear to have greater contrast. Use this to your advantage to place emphasis on certain elements or people – for example, sit someone in a chair that has been positioned in a brighter area of a room and you'll notice that the darker regions of the room will recede, placing greater emphasis on the sitter.

Setting exposure

If you're including a window in the shot, the comparative brightness of the window in relation to the rest of the room needs to be accounted for when setting exposure. Take a reading from a bright region near to the window, press the exposure lock button, recompose the shot and take the picture. Depending on the strength of the light coming through the window, you should be able to hold most of the detail in the room without 'burning out' too much of the window

itself. Try bracketing the exposure if you're uncertain and checking the results on the camera's LCD screen.

Colour cast

Given the relatively low temperature of tungsten light bulbs – the most commonly used bulbs in the home – make sure that the camera's white balance setting is set to Tungsten or Auto to counteract the orange colour cast caused by such lighting. Even then, you may find that images will suffer from a colour cast that you'll have to correct using editing software.

Tripod versus ISO

With low-light conditions there's a risk of camera shake if the shutter speed is insufficiently fast. If you don't have a tripod, increase the ISO setting, but do this in stages as noise from high ISO settings is more apparent in dark scenes (see pages 82–83). If you do have a tripod, then you can shoot at the lowest possible ISO setting without the risk of camera shake. Bear in mind that even relatively slow-moving action may blur at speeds of $^1/15$ sec or longer.

Shadows

Any discussion about the significance of light in photography would not be complete without turning our thoughts to shadows. In many ways, shadows help to reinforce the prevailing lighting conditions and add atmosphere to an image. We recognize the presence of bright sunlight in an image not just by bright highlights or saturated colours, but also by deep black shadows. Equally, the lack of strong shadow will lower the overall contrast of an image and give a softer look to a picture.

Almost all photographs that are taken outdoors during daylight hours will contain shadows, except for those taken under the most diffused lighting conditions. However, shadows are very easy to overlook when composing an image, as we tend to focus our attention on the subject of a shot. Also, because shadows are such a common phenomenon they don't register – until we review the shots and discover that strong shadows have spoiled the composition.

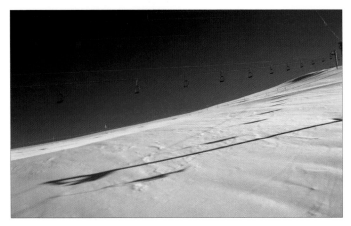

ABOVE Without the shadows in this wintry scene the snow would be a flat, featureless expanse of white.

BELOW The Grand Canyon with the sun low in the sky is modelled by the shadows, which help to reinforce the Canyon's peaks and troughs and add scale and perspective.

Strong light

When taking photographs outdoors, it is worth deliberately looking for the shadows in a potential scene. Check to see if your position in relation to the sun results in any shadows falling across an important compositional element of the photograph. Although altering your position won't change the direction in which the shadows are cast, you may discover that an alternative angle provides a similar shot that makes the shadow invisible, or less of a distraction.

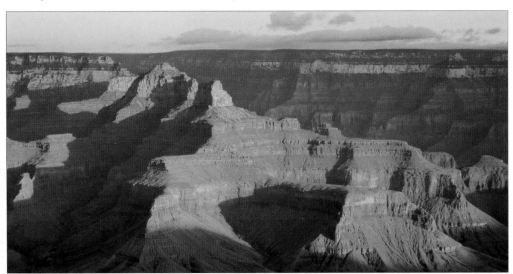

Composition

An alternative to eliminating shadows from an image is to look deliberately for ways in which to include them. Not only can they add to the image by introducing their own unique, obscure shapes, but they can also help to draw the viewer into an image – often a shadow can act as a leading line taking the viewer directly to the subject of the photograph.

Shadows can also provide visual clues about an image – such as the time of day the photograph was taken, how bright (or overcast) the conditions were and even the type of environment in which the image was shot. While it may be obvious from the subject of the picture itself whether the image was taken in a city or in a forest, shadows cast by objects not visible in the scene will help to evoke the atmosphere, whether they're the geometric, blocky shadows of buildings or the organic shapes of branches or leaf fronds.

Form and texture

With light coming in at a low, raking angle, shadows can also help to tease out the texture from objects and to emphasize their form. This modelling attribute can be used in a variety of

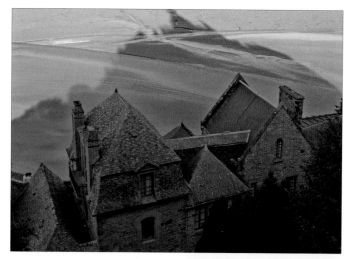

photographic genres – from nudes to landscapes – whenever you want to reveal the texture of your subject.

ABOVE Although taken on a sunny day, the cool shadows contrast pleasantly with the pale yellow sand.

RIGHT Low-angle light casts shadows that help describe a subject's form.

BELOW In this woodland scene, the long shadows add another layer to the image, making it all the more dramatic.

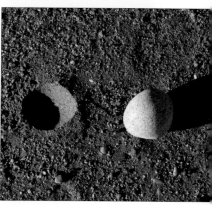

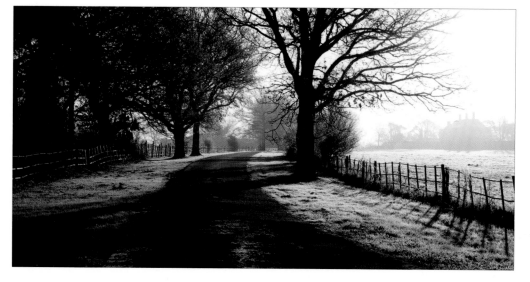

Low-light and Night Photography

If captured well, low-light and night scenes can result in wonderfully strong, atmospheric shots. Quite understandably, people are often put off capturing low-light or night-time shots thinking that the lack of light throws up too many technical difficulties to overcome. However, with a little perseverance and a certain amount of trial and error, the skills of low-light photography can be quickly mastered.

Just about any scene is suitable for low-light treatment – especially cityscapes. With their numerous and variously coloured lights and towering skylines, cityscapes usually provide the most dramatic night images, while rural scenes often work best just after the sun has set rather than late at night. As a rule of thumb, when taking photographs of low-light landscapes, there will still be sufficient light available to capture a photograph that will adequately show the surrounding countryside up to around 30 minutes after the sun has set, or less in the Tropics.

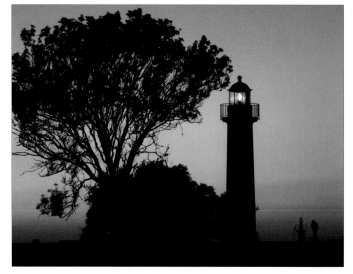

Noise

A recurring issue with low-light photography is digital noise and, depending on your camera, it may well always be present in night shots. However, there are actions you can take to keep noise to a minimum. The most obvious is to use as low an ISO setting

ABOVE A sunset on a clear summer's day is a good time for photographs of silhouettes. Here, the light of the lighthouse is a focal point.

BELOW Cities at 'night' can create colourful and evocative images. The best time to capture city lights is at twilight, about 45 minutes after the sun has set, rather than at night.

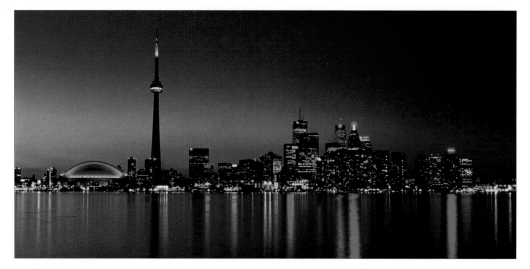

as possible. This means that you'll need a tripod or a makeshift surface on which to rest the camera while taking the shot. If there is a noise-reduction facility available on your camera, try using this. It will double the time it takes for the images to be saved, but may help reduce background noise.

White balance

With long exposures, there is a chance that the auto white balance setting (which neutralizes colour casts created by certain temperatures of light) will be tricked by the various light sources, especially in cityscapes where light sources may include car head-lights, neon signs, streetlamps and so on. The variety of light sources and resulting colour casts can often create a pleasing result.

However, if you want white objects to appear white, you need to manually set the white balance. Most advanced cameras allow you to do this with a 'custom white balance' setting. With the camera set to 'custom white balance' (the setting name may vary depending on the manufacturer), fill the frame and photograph a white object that you wish to be reproduced as white. The camera will automatically allow for the overall colour temperature and white objects will appear white.

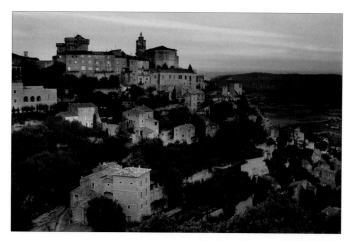

ABOVE At sunrise and sunset the sky can turn from a rich blue to a deep orange-red in an instant, but choosing the right white balance is crucial.

RIGHT This shot almost looks like a toned black-and-white picture, with its matching sky and water. Only the distant yellow light tells you it isn't.

BELOW Towns and cities at night make for good low-light subjects thanks to the mix of colour temperatures in the lighting – from 'white' to orange.

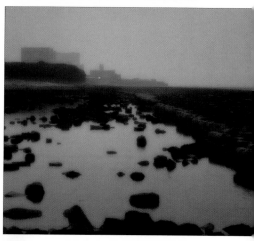

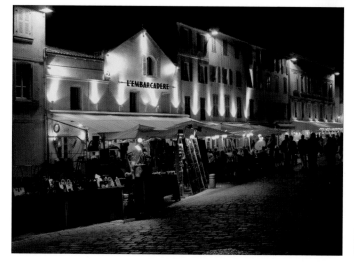

Low-light composition

Stunning results can be achieved in low-light conditions and it certainly pays to experiment with different sources of light, whether it's the warm glow of a sunset or the artificial lighting from office blocks or street lighting.

Look out for reflective surfaces, such as ponds, lakes or even wet pavements. The reflected light will not only give you more illumination to experiment with, but the reflected image can add another dimension to your composition.

Using Flash

At one time or another, all of us need a relatively powerful, if short-lived, light source that enables us to take photographs at night or indoors, using shutter speeds that are fast enough to freeze action. For that reason most cameras, from point and shoot to dSLRs, come equipped with a built-in flash.

Built-in flash

As useful as built-in flash is – and it certainly makes it possible to shoot in some situations where, without it, you may not have any usable images at all – such units do have limitations.

The first drawback is the effective range, as most on-camera flashes are only capable of throwing light a distance of between 5ft (1.5m) and 10ft (3m) from the camera, which won't be powerful enough to light larger groups or scenes.

The other significant problem is 'redeye'. This occurs because the flash unit is so close to the axis of the lens. When the flash fires, it fires directly into the subject's eyes, bounces off the retina in the back of the eye, and

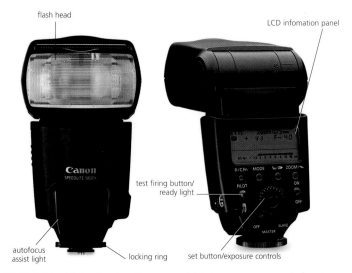

flash head

LCD infomation panel

test firing button/ ready light

autofocus assist light

locking ring

set button/exposure controls

▲ **ABOVE** External flash units, such as this Canon model, provide more powerful lighting and a much greater degree of control than on-camera flash units.

illuminates the eye's blood vessels. The proximity of the flash to the lens can also be a problem with wide-angle lenses on dSLRs, as the flash isn't designed to cover the width of a scene visible through a wide-angle lens. The result is a vignetted image, in

which the corners appear darker than the central part of the image. Finally, perhaps the worst problem of all with built-in flash is simply the quality of light it produces. Built-in flash will often produce stark pictures with harsh shadows. While this can be partly remedied by reducing the strength of the flash using the camera's 'flash exposure compensation' setting (if it has one), you may find that large parts of the image are underexposed.

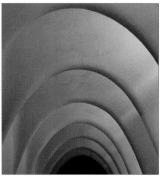

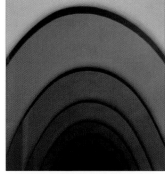

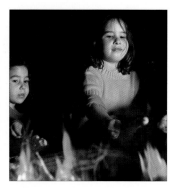

▲ **ABOVE** These two shots of an arched corridor show how flash can only throw light a certain distance. The image on the left was taken using a tripod and long exposure; the daylight entering from the right has provided a more or less evenly lit corridor. The one on the right was taken with flash, and clearly shows the arches becoming progressively darker the farther they are from the flash.

▲ **ABOVE** Flash units are a convenient way of lighting a subject when there is insufficient ambient light available. However, getting natural looking light can be problematic.

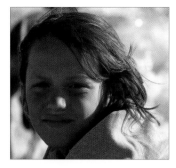

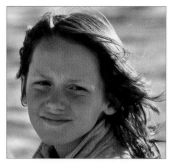

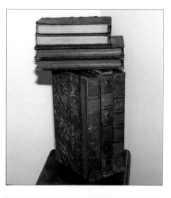

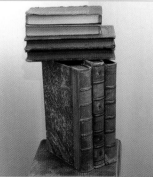

LEFT You don't just need to think of flash as a low-light tool. Here (in the picture on the right), it's been used in strong sunlight to fill-in the shadows on the subject's face.

Fill-in flash

Despite these drawbacks, built-in flash is an excellent tool for 'fill-in' lighting. It may seem strange to use flash during the day, but you'll probably have noticed that whenever you see wedding photographers or photojournalists in action, they'll invariably have a flashgun attached to their cameras, even if the weather is bright and sunny. This is used for fill-in flash.

Fill-in flash throws additional light onto a subject that may be in shadow or underexposed due to strong back lighting. In both cases using flash will improve the quality of the images, adding brightness and colour to an otherwise drab element of the image. Because fill-in flash doesn't need to be particularly powerful, a camera's built-in flash is often ideal for the job.

Flashguns

If you find that you're increasingly relying on the camera's built-in flash and you're not happy with the results, you may want to consider buying a flashgun. These are self-powered flash units that are fixed to the top of the camera via the camera's 'hot shoe' plate. Flashguns vary enormously in price depending on how powerful they are and how sophisticated the metering system, but for a relatively modest outlay you can improve the quality of your flash photography enormously using such a device.

Most of today's flashguns can be set to synchronize automatically with the camera so that the shutter opens at the same time the flash fires, as it does with the built-in flash. Often a 'pre-flash' is fired so that the camera's metering system can set the correct exposure for the subject (known as Through The Lens, or TTL, flash). Sophisticated flashguns will also take information from the camera's focusing system to gauge the distance from camera to subject, and therefore determine more precisely how much light is needed for an accurate exposure.

Power and bounce

The greatest benefit of using a flashgun is that it produces more light than a built-in flash. One obvious advantage of this is that more distant objects can be lit, but there's another, more significant benefit. The most useful flashguns have heads that tilt (and swivel), allowing you to 'bounce' the light off walls, ceilings or other reflective surfaces. Bounced flash produces much softer light, as in effect the light is coming from a much larger surface area, which has the effect of diffusing shadows. You need the increased power from a flashgun to make the most of this bounced flash effect. Additionally, because the light is not coming directly from the camera, but from above (or to the side), the lighting appears more natural. Finally, because the flash unit of a flashgun sits much higher than that of a built-in flash unit, there's a much reduced risk of redeye.

ABOVE When used direct from the camera, a flash creates hard shadows (top). Bouncing it off the ceiling will give a much more natural looking result (bottom).

Diffusers

Another way in which to soften light from a flashgun is to fit a diffuser. Diffusers are moulded pieces of white translucent plastic that fit over the head of the gun and spread the light when the flash fires. By their very nature, diffusers drastically cut down the range of the flashgun – another reason why professionals opt for the most powerful units – but they give a light that looks much softer and far more natural than direct flash.

Slow Sync Flash

Flash used normally will freeze a moving object, and, if the exposure is correct, will evenly illuminate everything within its range. But, as in every aspect of photography, creative rule-breaking can produce stunning results; and this is particularly true of the unorthodox technique of slow sync flash.

Most 35mm SLR cameras have a mark on the shutter speed dial that synchronizes the flash when the picture is taken. Usually this speed is $1/60$ or $1/125$ sec. If a shutter speed faster than this is used the blinds of the focal plane shutter will not have time to open fully, so that part of the picture comes out unexposed. However, it is possible to use a lower speed such as $1/15$ or $1/8$ sec and still synchronize the flash. The flash will not last any longer than usual, which means that it will be illuminating the scene for only part of the time the shutter is open.

If a slow shutter speed is used with flash to photograph a moving object when there is a reasonable amount of ambient light, the subject will be marked by a faint trail looking like 'speed lines' in cartoons. This can look very effective in an action shot such as the picture of a roller skater here.

The important thing is to use a shutter speed compatible with both the ambient light and the desired flash effect. For example, the film is 100 ISO; a meter reading of the ambient light says $1/125$ at f/5.6. To get the slow sync effect a shutter speed of $1/15$ sec is needed. To compensate for the difference the aperture should be reduced to f/16. Set the dial on theflashgun to f/16 or, if it is a manually controlled one, work out the flash-to-subject distance that normally requires an aperture of f/16. The result should be worth the effort.

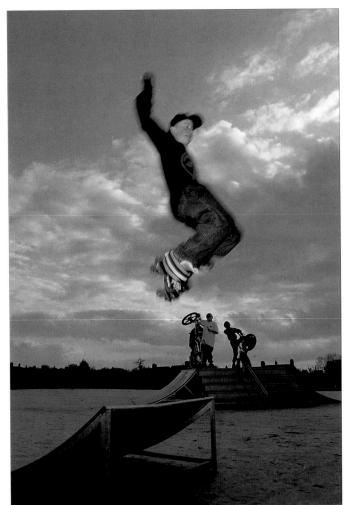

ABOVE The young boy is almost frozen in mid-flight, even though the shutter speed used was only $1/15$ sec. This is because he was lit mostly by the flash, not by ambient light. However, the daylight has had a curious effect on his outline so that it looks as if the sky were directly behind him. The ambient light needed a full stop more, but it was decided to underexpose for this to give the shot more impact.

RIGHT A similar technique was used indoors to photograph the baby. Here a shutter speed of $1/8$ sec was used. The baby turned his head as the shot was taken and the flash fired. There was enough ambient light to let this movement show up. It has created an attractive background which increases the effectiveness of the portrait.

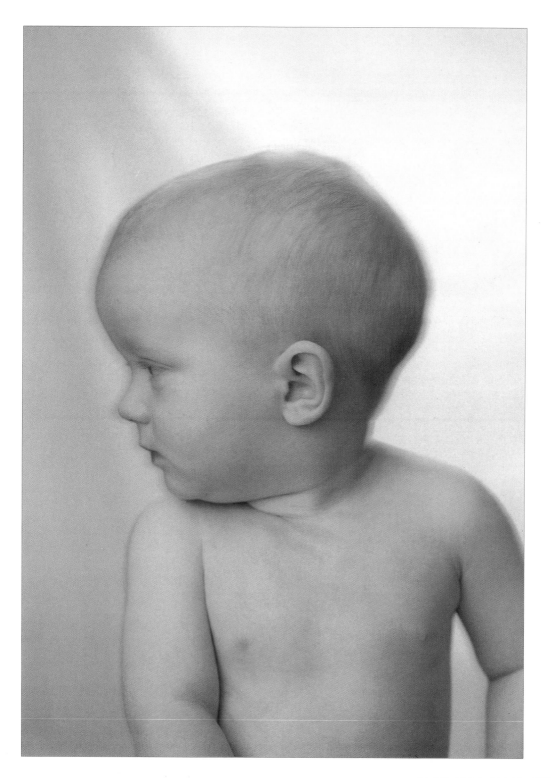

When to Shoot

So many factors govern lighting that to make any hard and fast rules about the best time to take photographs would be meaningless – season, location and local weather conditions all affect the quality, strength, direction and colour of light.

The environment in which you live will offer varying photographic opportunities depending on the prevailing weather conditions. For example, a gentle mist and low-lying cloud may provide the perfect conditions for certain rural landscapes but they would do absolutely nothing for a city shot.

However, it's important to know what sort of results you can expect under certain lighting conditions, so you learn to know what type of photograph works best in the conditions you're shooting under. This, of course, can only come with experience, using your eyes and a certain amount of common sense.

Morning
Sunny mornings, and specifically within a hour of the sun rising above the horizon, will provide a low, raking

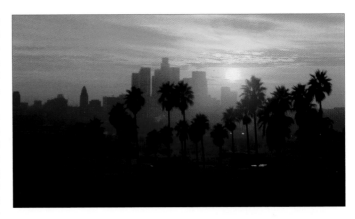

ABOVE Clear, late afternoons in temperate regions can often impart a warm, rosy glow to images. Make sure the camera's Auto white balance doesn't try to 'correct' the red glow resulting in a more neutral white colour.

light that offers the opportunity to shoot all four major variations of lighting – frontal, side, back and rim. This makes early morning one of the most dynamic times to be out with a camera. Depending on the season, you may also have early morning mist in low-lying areas or over standing water, and the sun will reflect strongly off tall buildings. At this time of day, the light temperature will be relatively low, creating a glowing orange cast, while the sun itself can make a spectacular subject.

Mid-morning can provide a good compromise between the first hour or so after sunrise and midday. There's variation in the direction of light, and shadows will be flattering, but the light is more neutral and colours will reproduce more accurately. Look for texture, modelling shadows and subtle, yet distinct, colour.

By midday, with the sun high in the sky, light is at its harshest and you need to turn your attention away from subtle modelling and flattering shadows and look for well-defined, interesting shapes, and bright, saturated colours. The consistent quality of light at this time of day tends to produce sharp, crisp images, but remember that strong shadows may add confusion to certain scenes.

BELOW These two images of the Taj Mahal, although not taken from the same place, still show how the light at different times of the day can radically alter the same scene.

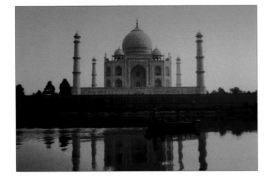

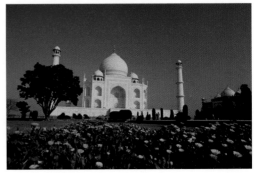

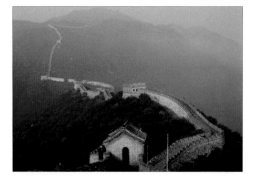

LEFT Although early morning haze reduces visibility and distant detail, it's perfect for atmospheric landscape shots, especially when using a telephoto lens or zoom setting.

Some of the most dramatic shots can be taken just before or just after a storm. At such times it's not unusual to have a backdrop of black, forbidding skies while the foreground is bathed in strong sunlight. Furthermore, sooner or later, as the clouds disperse, the sun's rays will break cover and appear as powerful beams of light.

Hazy days

Haze can bring unique qualities of light to a variety of scenes. As well as diffusing harsh light and helping to soften shadows, haze can add a sense of depth by flattening and desaturating colour. This can result in an evocative layering effect if there are distant ranges of hills. To make the most of this effect, shoot with a telephoto setting or lens.

Mid-afternoon and sunsets

As with mid-morning and dawn, from mid-afternoon until about 30 minutes after the sun has set, the light temperature will decrease and take on an increasingly golden hue. Shadows will lengthen and light levels will gradually decrease. This is a good time to look for potential silhouette subjects, as a glowing red sun can make for a more interesting backdrop to a silhouette than a bright white mass. Even after the sun has set, keep taking shots, as successful low-light images during twilight can be among the most atmospheric, with the sun's afterglow helping to create soft and subtle tonal gradations.

Finally, consider indoor light shots available at this time of day. With the sun low in the sky, you may find that some parts of a room are lit with shafts of strong light, throwing other parts into shadow.

Cloudy days

The quality and strength of light on cloudy days will vary depending on the types of cloud and how numerous they are. Generally, cloud will soften light and help diffuse shadows. On windy, predominantly sunny days, scudding clouds create fluctuating levels of light, which require patience on the part of the photographer as he or she waits for the clouds to pass over and bathe the scene in sunlight. This is often a time when strong light and shade can be captured, adding tonal interest to a composition.

A vast blanket of cloud will have a dulling effect. Shadows will all but disappear, along with the chances of exploiting texture and form. However, such soft, consistent light can often simplify potentially complex scenes such as woods and forests, so use this light to exploit intricate shapes and subtle colour variations.

RIGHT Around 30 to 45 minutes after the sun has set (or less in the Tropics), is the best time to photograph buildings that are artificially lit. The light remains strong enough to show surrounding detail, but the building still appears well lit.

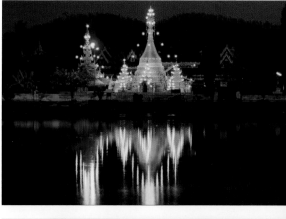

RIGHT Around midday, when the sun is high in the sky, light is at its most neutral colour, and if the sky is clear, this is when images will be at their sharpest.

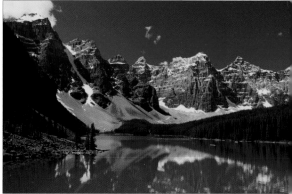

Lighting – Try It Yourself

An effective way to discover the impact of different lighting conditions is to use a 'source' scene and shoot it at different times of the day, and preferably at different times of the year and under varying weather conditions.

For the sake of convenience, select a scene that is within easy reach; the more varied the scene the better. For example, try to find a location that includes natural objects such as fields, trees, rocks and grass, as well as artificial ones, such as buildings, roads or any other man-made structures. That way, you'll hopefully see how the changing quality of light impacts on a wide variety of surfaces, textures, shapes and forms.

Time of day

When the weather looks set to be predominantly sunny, aim to get to your location just before sunrise. Set up the shot with a focal length of around 50mm, using a tripod so you can shoot at the lowest ISO setting. Carefully make a note of the position you've taken up, and at sunrise take a few shots. Return to the same spot every hour, or if that's not possible, at least every two hours, and photograph the same scene. Keep returning to the location until sunset, at which point take your final shots.

Review

Download the photographs on to a computer and review them. The first thing you'll notice is the way in which the scene becomes increasingly well lit as the sun begins to rise. Depending on the scene, long shadows may form and, depending on the weather conditions, time of year and location, you'll see a gradual shift in colour temperature – from red to neutral – as the sun progresses across the sky.

By midday, shadows are more likely to have shortened, but they may well have strengthened, and any colour will appear more saturated. However, most noticeable will be the way in which objects are lit – whether it's side, front or back lighting. As the sun moves in the sky, surfaces will be lit in different ways and this will have the biggest impact on the image.

As noon passes and the sun begins its descent into the west, shadows will gradually start to grow longer, surfaces that were not previously lit may become illuminated, and colours will become more muted.

By late afternoon, the light will cast everything in a rosy glow (depending on time of year, location and the weather conditions), while shadows will lengthen. As the sun sets, elements of the scene may be visible only in silhouette and any clouds will reflect the red glow of the setting sun.

Time of year

Try to repeat this exercise at various times of the year to see what impact the changing seasons have on your environment. Test whether you can tell the difference between the quality and temperature of the light on a sunny summer's day and a sunny winter one. When younger, those of us brought up in a mild temperate climate would often equate a blue sky with warm weather, but in fact it's impossible to tell the temperature from a blue sky alone.

▼ **BELOW LEFT** Each part of the day will bring its own unique quality of light and radically alter how a particular scene photographs.

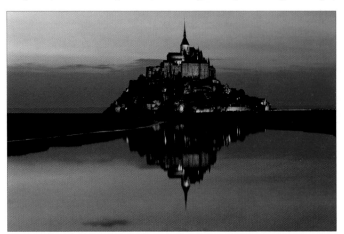

Weather conditions

Deliberately photograph your selected location in a variety of weather conditions. Test out if the old adage that dull weather makes for dull photographs is true in the case of your chosen scene. If so, then what weather conditions are needed to bring a bit of sparkle to the shot? Does it require a sunny day or can subtleties of light, shade and tone be teased out under overcast conditions?

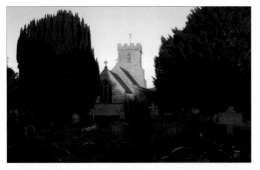

06.30

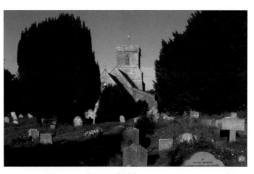

07.30

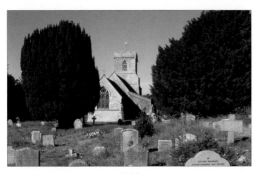

09.30

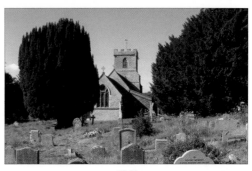

12.00

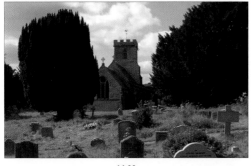

14.00

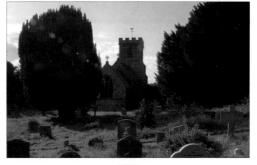

16.00

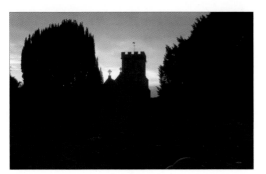

18.00

THIS PAGE To see the effect that different lighting conditions have on a picture, find a suitable location and take a series of pictures throughout the day – from sunrise through to sunset. As morning changes to afternoon and then evening (left), so the shadows change size and direction, while the colour of the light is also constantly shifting from warm to cool colours.

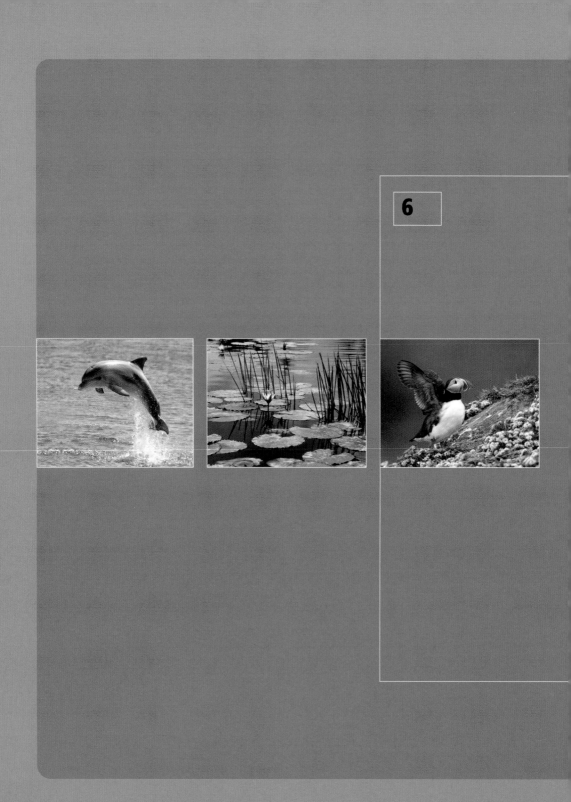

6

Which Lens, Which Viewpoint?

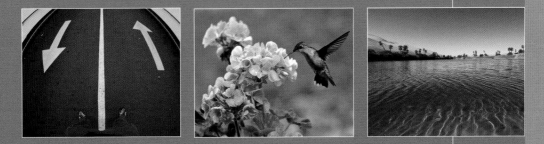

The lens you choose allows you to control what you see in the picture and how it is seen. From fisheye to macro, from wide angle to telephoto and many others in between, it's important to know what's available. If you shoot with a wide angle lens, you will get a lot into the picture but it will look far away. If you shoot with a longer lens you will see less from left to right, but everything will seem closer. A standard lens will give a natural perspective, a fisheye a distorted one. Generally a wide lens is seen as best for landscapes and a longer lens better for portraits. Getting to know what works, when, will give you the creative control you need.

Focal Length

A lens's focal length is the distance between its optical centre (the point at which the light rays begin to converge), and the focal plane (the surface of the image sensor).

Focal length is always measured in millimeters (mm). For 35mm film cameras, understanding a lens's focal length is relatively straightforward. However, digital cameras – or more accurately the varying sensor sizes used in digital cameras – have made the issue of focal length less easy to understand.

Whereas all lenses were once designed to project an image on to the standard 35mm (24 × 36mm) film frame, because of the numerous different sensor sizes available in today's dSLR cameras, a lens of a specific focal length will project a different view of a scene, often increasing the effective focal length.

Equivalent focal length

Let's try to explain this more clearly using numbers. A 35mm film frame, or a 'full-frame' digital sensor, has a diagonal measurement of 43mm. Therefore, to provide an unmagnified,

standard view, a lens would need a focal length of 43mm (historically this has been rounded up to 50mm).

A number of popular compact zoom cameras have much smaller sensors, with a diagonal measurement of 9.5mm (the measurement of a standard 1/1.7in sensor). With a sensor measuring 9.5mm, the lens only needs a focal length of 9.5mm to achieve a x1 magnification.

So, while a theoretical 43mm lens provides a standard view on a full-frame sensor (×1 magnification – 43 divided by 43 = 1), where as on a smaller sensor measuring 9.5mm diagonally, the magnification would be 43 divided by 9.5 = 4.53, or the equivalent focal length (efl) 43 × 4.53 = 195mm, which is quite a powerful telephoto lens.

On many compact zoom cameras you may see the lens labelled along the lines of 9–70mm, which would make no sense in the 35mm format, but when converted to allow for the smaller sensor size this lens provides the equivalent focal lengths (efl) of 9 × 4.53 = 41mm, zooming to 70 × 4.53 = 317mm.

To make sense of these potentially confusing focal lengths, the equivalent focal length is often used in conjunction with real focal lengths in magazines, websites and sales material to give people a point of reference. This is why many hybrid camera lenses are advertised as 38–380mm (or 10x) instead of, or as well as, their true focal lengths.

Angle of view

A lens's focal length determines its angle of view. The longer the focal length, the narrower the angle of view and the greater the degree of subject enlargement. The shorter the focal length, the wider the angle of view and the smaller the same subject appears. With hindsight, if lenses were described by their angle of view we wouldn't have the confusion over focal lengths. The diagram below shows the angles of view for the four main types of lens used by dSLRs – wide-angle, standard, telephoto and extreme telephoto.

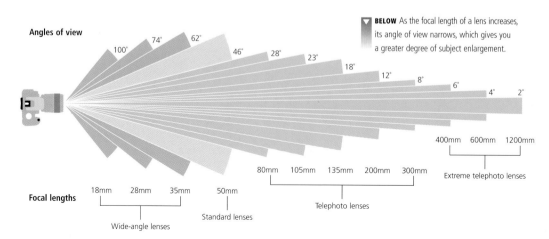

BELOW As the focal length of a lens increases, its angle of view narrows, which gives you a greater degree of subject enlargement.

Angles of view

100° 74° 62° 46° 28° 23° 18° 12° 8° 6° 4° 2°

400mm 600mm 1200mm

Extreme telephoto lenses

80mm 105mm 135mm 200mm 300mm

Telephoto lenses

18mm 28mm 35mm   50mm

Focal lengths

Standard lenses

Wide-angle lenses

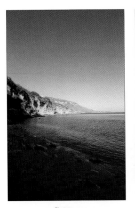
efl 16mm

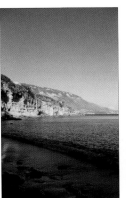
efl 32mm

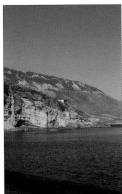
efl 56mm

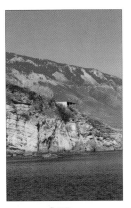
efl 112mm

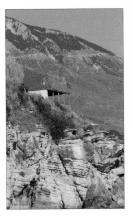
efl 160mm

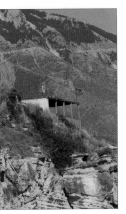
efl 220mm

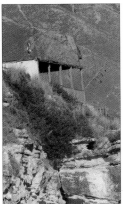
efl 320mm

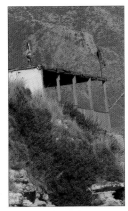
efl 480mm

ABOVE Focal lengths are measured in millimetres (mm) and range from effective wide-angle focal lengths of around 16mm (or less) to equivalent telephoto lengths of 480mm (or more).

APS

The majority of SLRs use APS-sized sensors. APS (Advanced Photo System) was originally a film format developed for point-and-shoot cameras. The system is now almost defunct, but the format has been taken up by the major camera manufacturers as a popular sensor size for dSLRs, because it is less expensive to manufacture, while still providing excellent digital images. To confuse matters slightly more, there are a number of APS sizes, but most are around 22 x 15mm.

CROP FACTOR

APS sensors are smaller than full-frame 35mm sensors. To standardize things, interchangeable lenses for dSLRs are labelled with their actual focal length. dSLR owners need to know the size of the sensor in their camera to find the equivalent focal length. The same calculation (dividing the diagonals) results in the 'crop factor'. For example, Canon's semi-professional dSLR sensors have a diagonal of close to 27mm, giving a crop factor of 1.6.

To find the EFL for a lens attached to the body, you multiply the real focal length by 1.6 – so a 60mm lens has an EFL of 95mm. Nikon, Fuji and Sony

sensors have a crop factor of 1.5, so a 60mm lens has an EFL of 90mm.

Many lenses are made specifically for these new digital cameras with a cropped sensor, so even if they fit on a full frame digital or film camera, they will not provide you with a full image.

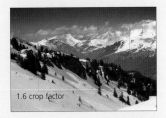
1.6 crop factor

Short Focal Length

Lenses with an equivalent focal length (efl) of between 18mm and 35mm are described as having a short focal length. Offering an angle of view between 100 degrees (efl 18mm) and 62 degrees (efl 35mm), they are also known as wide-angle lenses. They provide an angle of view greater than that seen by the human eye (around 46 degrees).

Capturing such a wide view has a number of benefits and can be used to great compositional effect. One of the most common uses of a wide angle lens is photographing interiors. With such a broad view, these lenses can photograph much more of a room than a standard (efl 35–50mm) lens.

Wide-angle lenses are often used in landscape photography to help emphasize wide-open spaces. As well as having the ability to encompass more of a scene, wide-angle lenses also tend to differentiate more clearly between the various planes within a scene, clearly separating the foreground, middle-distance and background objects from each other.

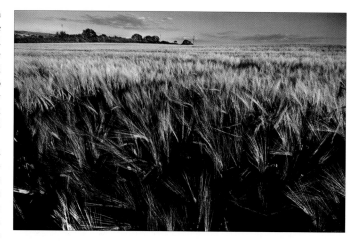

Depth of field

One of the most useful optical properties of wide-angle lenses is their great depth of field, as the shorter the focal length, the greater the depth of field at the same aperture setting. This allows the photographer to ensure that very close foreground objects are in focus, as well as objects in the distance. This can bring an increased illusion of depth to the image, but the disadvantage is that it becomes harder to selectively blur specific elements within a scene.

A wide-angle lens's short focal length is particularly helpful with hand-held photography, as the risk of camera shake is reduced the shorter the focal length of the lens. For example, shooting at ¹/₃₀ sec with a lens setting of between 35–50mm would often result in camera shake or

▼ **BELOW** When you can't move too far back from your subject, use a wide-angle lens to squeeze in as much of the scene as possible.

▲ **ABOVE** Wide-angle lenses let you get a lot of a scene in the frame, and the increased depth of field also lets you get everything sharp.

▼ **BELOW** Short focal-length lenses can introduce a 'barrel distortion' effect, in which vertical lines, such as walls, seem to bulge outwards.

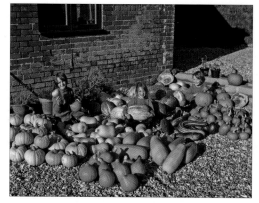

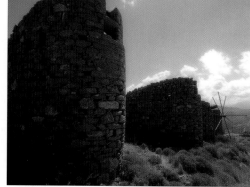

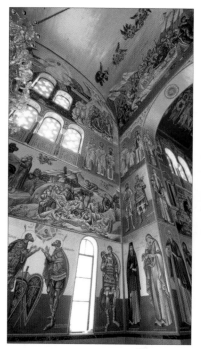

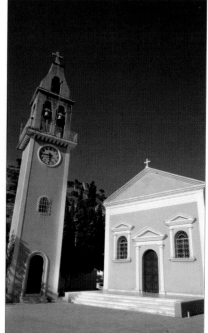

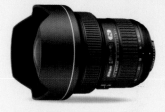

FAR LEFT Using a wide-angle lens indoors will help you get as much of the interior in the frame as possible, but there can be potential problems with distortion.

LEFT 'Converging verticals' can occur because of a wide-angle lens's angle of view.

blur, but with an effective focal length of 18mm camera shake is much less likely to occur.

Distortion

Another key characteristic of wide-angle lenses is distortion – again, the shorter the focal length the greater the distortion. This effect becomes most apparent in photographs that include objects with straight lines, such as tall buildings. One form of distortion, known as 'barrel' distortion, makes vertical and horizontal lines bulge outward, most noticeably at the edges of the frame. Wide-angle and super wide-angle lenses are not appropriate for portraits due to the effect of barrel distortion, unless you're aiming for that particular effect of course.

Another common problematic issue associated with wide-angle lenses is converging verticals – where lines appear to move closer together the higher they rise. This is most noticeable in architectural shots and is a result of the wide-angle lens. Using your tripod can really help you here to get the camera set up as level as possible to reduce any converging verticals wherever possible.

True wide angle

For those owners of dSLR cameras without full-frame sensors and who are considering buying a wide-angle lens, remember that it's important to take into account the crop factor of the sensor (see Crop Factor box, page 239). For example, the crop factor for most Nikon dSLRs is 1.5 – this means that in order to achieve an efl of 18mm, the lens needs to have a real focal length of 12mm (12 x 1.5 = 18mm).

Compact and Hybrid Wide Angle

You don't have to own a dSLR to get a really wide angle of view. As well as the main camera manufacturers, there are several third-party companies that make wide-angle converters, (such as the one pictured) to fit most compact or hybrid cameras, as long as the lens has a thread at the end. You'll need to know the size of the screw mount, and the angle of view the converter will provide will vary, but they typically range from x0.8 to x0.5. A x0.8 converter, for example, will change a 35mm focal length lens to 28mm.

Long Focal Length

Lenses with a focal length of between 80mm and 300mm are generally considered to have long focal lengths – although 400mm, 500mm and even 600mm focal length lenses are quite common. Such lenses are often referred to as telephoto lenses and cover an angle of view of between 28 degrees (80mm) and 6 degrees (400mm). It is a telephoto lens's narrow angle of view that creates the magnifying effect, for which there are numerous uses.

Sports and nature

Telephoto lenses are commonly used for sports and nature photography. The specific focal length needed depends on the type of nature or sports. It's often easier, for example, to get closer to the action when photographing tennis than it is with stadium sports such as football or

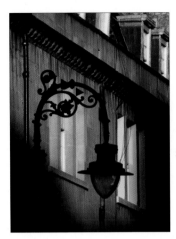

track and field. Similarly, photographing large mammals that are relatively accustomed to humans and to which the photographer can get close requires less telephoto power than photographing small birds.

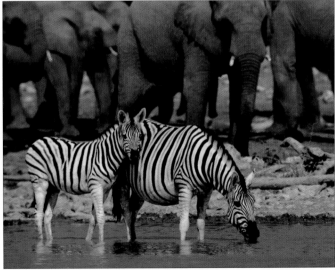

LEFT A long focal length can be used to great effect to record details that might otherwise get lost in a wider picture.

There are a number of zoom compacts offering 10× magnification, (which is roughly the equivalent of efl 30–300mm), and this should provide most keen amateurs with the magnification that they need. For SLR owners, with zoom lenses that are now capable of resolving and capturing almost as much detail as prime lenses, the best option is to opt for a 70–300mm lens, which will provide a useful telephoto range, particularly if the camera's crop factor is taken into account. A 300mm focal length with a 1.6 crop factor provides an efl of 480mm. Even professional sports and nature photographers rarely use lenses longer than 500mm – their enormous size is down to the fact that

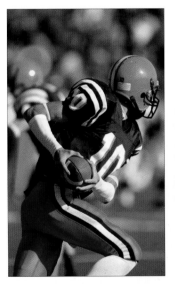

ABOVE Shooting sports often requires the use of a telephoto lens; however, many telephoto lens have a minimum aperture of f/5.6 or even f/8, for example, which means a relatively slow shutter speed will be needed to ensure an accurate exposure.

ABOVE The long telephoto lens is essential equipment for all wildlife photographers, allowing them to get 'close' to the action without disturbing the animals or risking their own safety.

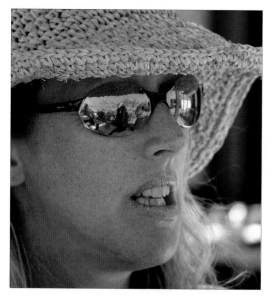

▲ **ABOVE** Using a telephoto lens for portraits allows you to easily throw potentially distracting backgrounds out of focus.

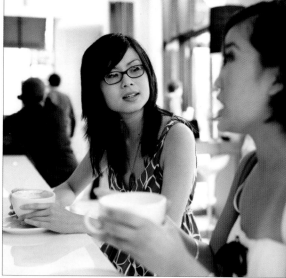

▲ **ABOVE** For candid street photography, a telephoto lens is the perfect choice as it allows you to keep your distance from your subject.

they're extremely fast lenses that are often able to open up to apertures as wide as f/2.8.

Landscapes and candid shots

Surprisingly, a telephoto lens can also be a useful addition to the landscape photographer's kit. One of the key characteristics of long focal lengths is that scenes are foreshortened, so that distant, rolling hills take on a pleasing layered effect. In addition, landscape photographers can isolate and enlarge particularly attractive visual elements of a scene with a telephoto lens. Effectively, this is the case for all genres of photography. Telephotos are excellent at helping the photographer to fill the frame and the great benefit of using a zoom telephoto is that it's possible to frame shots in camera, rather than having to crop them later on the computer.

Another use for a telephoto lens (in this case the more discreet the better), is in candid street photography. You'll have only a very short amount of time to frame and take the shot, but the results can be rewarding as the pho-

tographer will often capture an action or expression that becomes apparent only when reviewing the image.

Portraits

Finally, short telephoto lenses of between efl 80mm and 130mm make excellent portrait lenses. In fact, in the early days of photography, such telephoto lenses were often referred to as 'portrait' lenses. They're good for the job because they not only help to distance the sitter from the photographer (so making the sitter feel less self-conscious), but the longer focal length also has the effect of slightly flattening the subject's features. This results in a more flattering portrait and, when combined with a wide aperture, the narrow depth of field ensures that backgrounds are more easily thrown out of focus.

▼ **BELOW** This 70–300mm 'super zoom' covers a wide range of telephoto focal lengths in a single lens. Vibration-reduction technology helps avoid camera shake.

maximum aperture

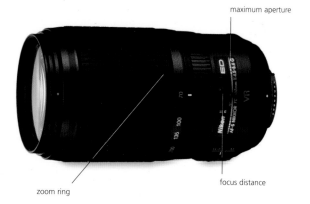

zoom ring

focus distance

Using a Wide-angle Lens

Extra lenses are the accessories that will probably do the most to improve your photography, and a wide-angle lens offers you a completely different perspective on a traditional view. Some modern wide-angle lenses, whether a prime or zoom lens, can have a focal length of just 12mm. Not only will its wider angle of view get more into the picture, but it also has a greater depth of field than a normal or telephoto lens, so that more of the shot will be sharp.

You can have an object relatively close to the lens and still keep the background in focus with a wide-angle lens. If an object is close enough to the lens, it will look disproportionate in size to the other elements in the picture, which can be very effective both for foregrounding a subject or giving an impression of great depth to the picture.

Very wide-angle lenses are invaluable when photographing buildings or interiors, but great care must be taken when composing and levelling your camera so that the straight lines in your image are not at odd angles to each other. Some wide-angle lenses are better than others for these types of photography as they have less distortion. This distortion can also be a problem when you photograph people from too close in, as your picture will give unflattering results. For instance, even a 21mm lens pointed directly at someone's face will make the nose look enormous, the cheeks puffed out, and the ears as if they have moved round towards the back of their head. This might be fun at first, but the novelty will soon wear off and it will be time to turn to more serious applications. Used carefully in the right situations, a wide-angle lens can help you get spectacular results.

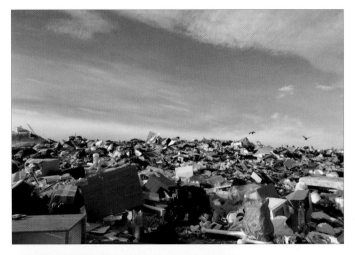

ABOVE The impact of this shot relies on the feeling of the 'big' landscape. The wide field of view gives a feeling of overwhelming space covered in rubbish. The clouds, which get whispier as they are farther away, help with perspective, and give the impression that the garbage goes on endlessly.

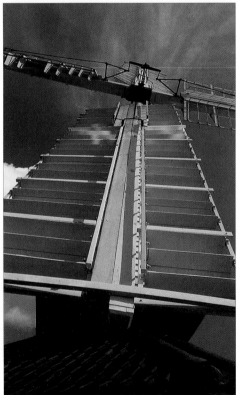

LEFT Using a low viewpoint with a wide-angle lens makes it look as if the windmill sails are soaring into the sky. The great depth of field offered by the lens makes the whole picture sharp even though the bottom of the sail is quite close to the lens.

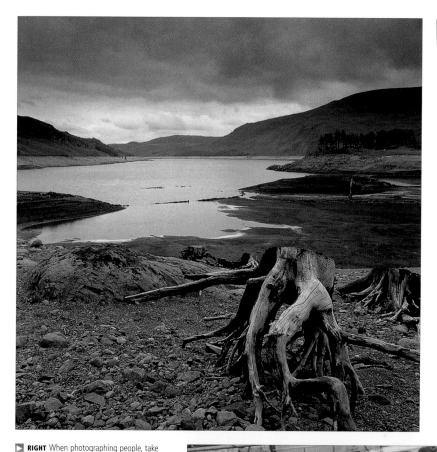

◀ **LEFT** A drought has dried up this lake, exposing an old tree stump. Again, the wide-angle lens keeps the whole picture sharp. Placing the stump at one side of the frame gives it an almost living quality, as if it is walking towards what remains of the lake.

▶ **RIGHT** When photographing people, take great care to avoid unflattering distortion. In this picture, although the hands and arms are distorted this is within tolerable limits and does not unbalance the composition as the viewpoint and angle of the shot have been carefully chosen. Although the arms look long and the hands, which are closest to the lens, enormous, the imbalance is acceptable because the strong hands represent the nature of the fisherman's work. His arms lead the eye straight to his face, which is framed in turn by a backdrop of his working environment. The busy background keeps the eye from dwelling too long on his hands so that, large as they are, they simply appear to be part of the composition.

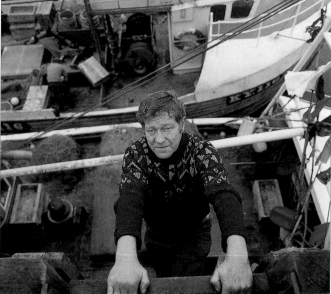

Using a Telephoto Lens

Telephoto lenses do much more than just bring distant objects closer. They can greatly enhance general composition. Their shallow depth of field can blur the background in a portrait to isolate and emphasize the subject. In contrast to wide-angle lenses, going in close to people has a positively flattering effect. This is because a telephoto lens slightly compresses the picture so that prominent features such as the nose and ears stay in proportion. Careful use of a telephoto lens can also help to cut out unwanted foreground clutter, allowing you to get to the heart of the picture.

Exposure and aperture settings

Some compensation has to be made in settings when using a telephoto lens, especially a long one. This is because the magnifying effect of the lens spreads the available light out thinly, and the longer the lens the greater this effect. With cameras that have TTL metering this is no problem, but a manual camera will have to be adjusted.

Whereas telephoto lenses used to suffer from having smaller apertures than normal or wide-angle lenses, so that exposure needed to be longer, many of the latest telephoto lenses have apertures as big as f/2.8, or larger. Certain lenses, such as the 85mm telephoto lens, that are ideal for portraits, have apertures as large as f/1.2, which lead to an incredibly shallow depth of field.

Using a tripod

Due to the size and weight of most telephoto lenses, it is advisable to use a tripod, or monopod, where possible, to avoid camera shake giving you blurred pictures, which will occur even at fairly fast shutter speeds. You may find that your subject is able to relax more over a series of shots if the camera is on a tripod rather than being held by you. In this way, if they are not over-confident in front of a camera, they can try to forget it is there. You can also interact more freely with subjects this way.

Converters

Instead of buying two or three very expensive telephoto lenses, you can use a converter that fits between the camera body and an existing lens. For example, a 2 × converter will increase the focal length of a 250mm lens to 500mm. The price is of these converters is reasonable and the image produced is almost as sharp as that from a long lens. Converters are made by most of the major camera/lens manufacturers.

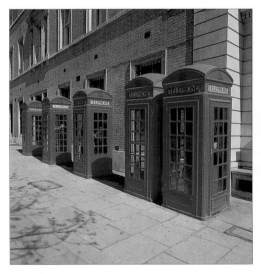

▲ **ABOVE** This was shot with a 28mm wide angle lens. It has stretched the telephone boxes apart and given a very elongated effect.

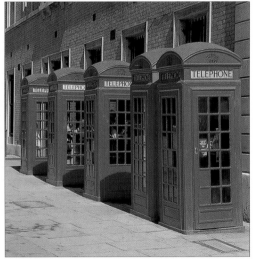

▲ **ABOVE** Here a 135mm telephoto lens has been used. It has compressed the boxes so that they look closer together. The composition is far tighter in this picture than the one to the left, and cuts out much unwanted detail from the frame.

RIGHT The use of a 200mm telephoto lens has cropped a lot of clutter out of the picture. The lens has compressed the picture, reducing the apparent space between buildings. Such a composition emphasizes the contrasts between the various architectural styles, from the Victorian classical façade to the modern skyscrapers in the background.

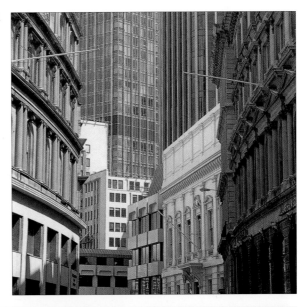

BELOW A 100mm telephoto lens is ideal for portraiture. Its short depth of field, especially at wide apertures, can put the background out of focus and thus allow the viewer to concentrate on the main subject. In such shots it is best to focus on the eyes and expose for the skin tones.

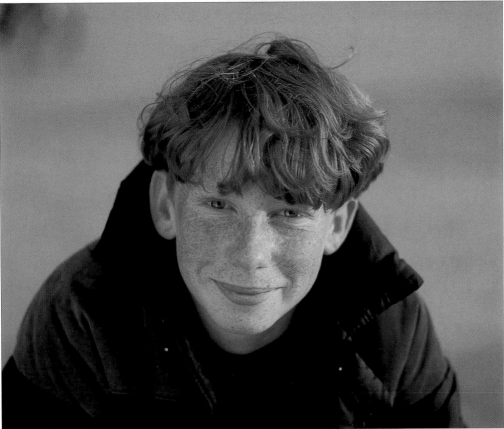

Using Tilt/Shift Lenses

A shift lens or perspective control (PC) lens, is especially useful for architectural photography. With a 5 × 4 camera it is possible to move the front panel, on which the lens is mounted, up and down and from side to side, or to swing it vertically or tilt it horizontally. For 35mm SLR and some medium format cameras there are lenses that can be moved up and down or across, and in the 35mm range these lenses usually have a focal length of between 24 and 90mm. Many of the newer lenses also allow you to tilt the lens (as you can tilt a large format lens panel) to alter the plane of sharp focus and therefore extend the depth of field along the plane of your choice. This is usefull in both portrait and landscape photography, and can also be used as a creative effect to produce images with a very shallow depth of field along a seemingly impossible plane of focus.

When using one of these lenses to photograph a tall building, instead of tilting the camera up to fit in the whole building, the camera can be kept pointing straight ahead and the axis of the lens is shifted relative to the film plane – that is, the lens is moved upward but kept parallel to the film. This movement is known as a shift. The whole building now appears in the picture, but with a difference. With a normal lens and the camera angled up, the vertical lines of the building will converge towards the top of the frame. With a shift lens, as long as the camera is kept horizontal, all verticals in the picture will appear vertical and there will be no convergence, even when the lens is shifted as far as it can go.

Even when photographing things that are less strongly vertical, distortion can still be caused by angling the

camera to cut out features such as an untidy foreground. Here, keeping the camera level and using a shift lens can eliminate areas around the frame without causing distortion.

These very specialist lenses are generally quite expensive so before deciding to buy a shift lens, it is a good idea to hire one from a professional photography store and try out its effects.

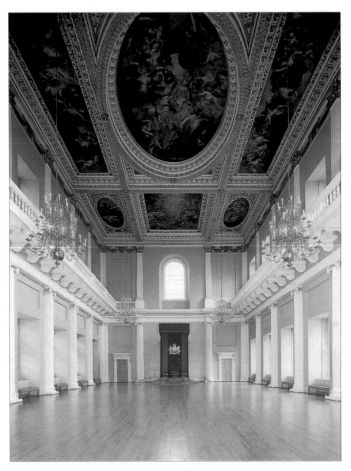

ABOVE To keep all the columns vertical in this shot of the Banqueting House in London, the camera had to be kept level. With a normal lens this would have cut out the wonderful ceiling painted by Rubens, and would have included a lot of the floor. Using the shift lens to its maximum has cut out much of the floor and brought in the ceiling.

RIGHT A problem with shooting objects with shiny reflective surfaces, such as cars, is that the photographer's reflection can appear. The effect can be corrected by standing to one side of the car, but by using the horizontal shift movement of the lens the car can be brought into the centre of the frame without reflection problems.

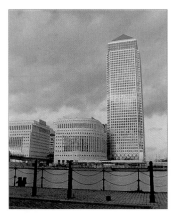

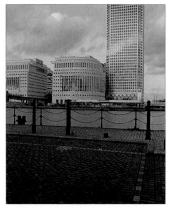

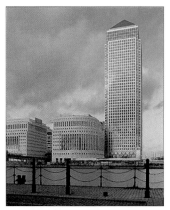

▲ **ABOVE** Using a conventional lens, the camera had to be tilted upward to fit the whole building into the frame. The vertical lines converge so that the building seems to be leaning.

▲ **ABOVE** To keep the verticals straight the film or sensor plane must be parallel to the plane of the front of the building, which means that the camera body must be absolutely level. But here this results in the top of the tallest building being cut off.

▲ **ABOVE** Here the camera is still level, but the shift lens has been moved upward. The whole building is now in view, but its sides are completely vertical. Also, a lot of uninteresting foreground detail has been cropped out of the picture.

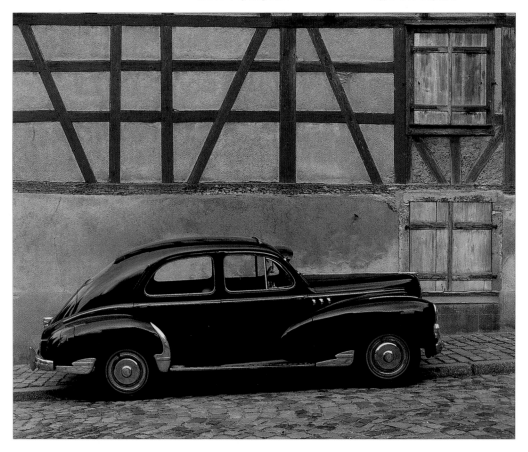

Using a Fisheye Lens

Among all the lenses that are available the fisheye lens is usually low on most people's list of priorities as the uses of this lens are limited. Nevertheless, it can be highly effective in the right situation.

It is sensible to hire a fisheye lens from a professional photographic dealer and try it out before deciding to buy one. If there seems to be many genuinely worthwhile uses for it, then and only then consider a purchase.

Most people looking through an SLR camera with a fisheye lens for the first time find it highly amusing to see the world through a 180 degree angle of vision. Objects appear severely distorted, especially faces, and it is easy to get carried away by gimmicky shots of people or animals up close, but used thoughtfully, a fisheye lens can produce uniquely striking images. The art of exploiting the lens is to make the photograph look as if a fisheye lens has not been used at all. Great care is needed in choosing a viewpoint and in framing the subject to obtain the best effect.

Because of its very wide angle, the fisheye lens needs special filters that are fitted in at the back of the lens, or in some cases attached using a very large filter holder system. Graduated filters cannot be used.

The problem when using flash with a fisheye lens. Even when a flash gun is fitted with a wide-angle attachment, the area that it illuminates is only the field of view of a 28mm lens, and this falls short of what is needed for a fisheye. If flash is needed, at least two flash heads must be deployed.

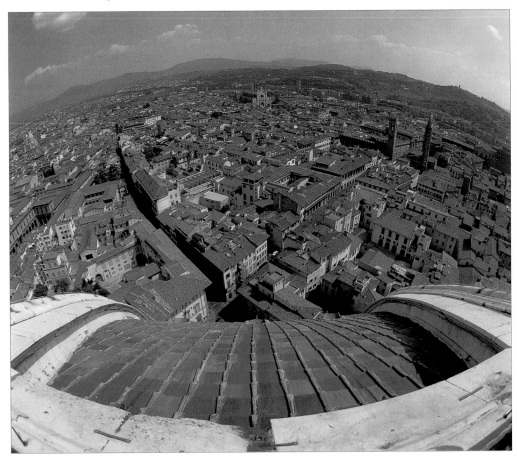

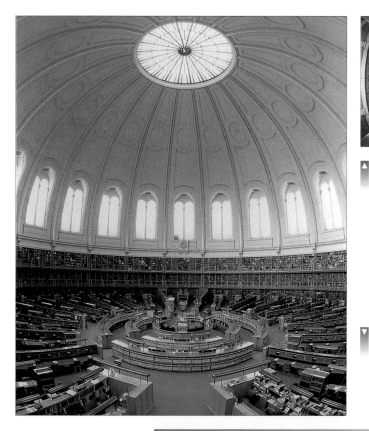

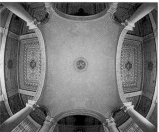

ABOVE This hallway ceiling needed to be lit with flash, and four flash heads were necessary to give the required coverage. The symmetry of the design has created an interesting architectural conundrum.

BELOW An otherwise quite ordinary shot is enhanced by adding the curves as accentuated by a fisheye lens. Shooting off centre has also helped with the varying curves, leading to a strong composition full of visual interest and complementary to the design and architecture of the buildings.

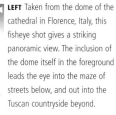

ABOVE A good example of how to use a fisheye lens without the result looking gimmicky. The Reading Room of the British Museum has a domed ceiling and the reading desks radiate out from the centre of the floor. Keeping the camera level allows the dome to be seen in its entirety. The curved lines of the room harmonize with the distortion caused by the lens, so that the shot looks as if it had been taken with a normal wide-angle lens.

LEFT Taken from the dome of the cathedral in Florence, Italy, this fisheye shot gives a striking panoramic view. The inclusion of the dome itself in the foreground leads the eye into the maze of streets below, and out into the Tuscan countryside beyond.

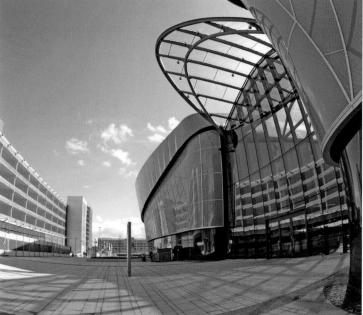

Using a Zoom Lens

Zoom lenses allow the use of a continuous range of focal lengths without having to change lenses. If two zoom lenses are used, it is possible with only one change to go from 16mm wide angle to 300 or 400mm telephoto. In general the image quality is not quite as good as that of a prime lens, but the slight difference will be apparent only to the most critical viewer, and in fact some of the newer zooms do equal their prime lens equivalents in terms of pure image quality but even then there may slight differences in terms of distortion, especially in the wider zoom lenses.

When to zoom

The obvious advantage of a zoom lens is the flexibility it gives. Not only do you have to carry less lenses to cover the focal range you wish to use, but you can use the zoom to compose, and crop an image in camera so that you will not need to crop later on and therefore lose image area. Having one zoom of say 24–105mm means that with the

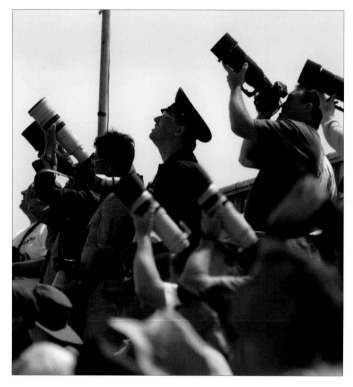

ABOVE RIGHT Photographers are often seen at events, such as this airshow, using long zoom lenses.

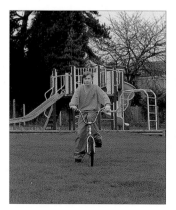

BELOW The left hand picture is a standard view of a boy. Below, the lens has been moved from 80mm to 300mm, so he seems to be moving at speed.

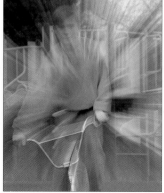

BELOW Here, a shutter speed of ⅛ sec was chosen, and the lens was zoomed half-way through its range of focal length during exposure. This created strong radiating lines.

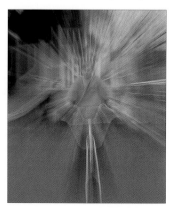

one lens on your camera you can have most general shooting situations covered so there is less likelihood of missing a shot because you are too far away and can not change your prime lens in time, and of course the same with a wide lens. For certain applications, such as sporting events, a zoom lens is invaluable as you may well be stuck in the one position so that means either having a large selection of prime lenses or just the one or two zooms. It is no surprise that when you see the ranks of photographers at football matches or the Olympics you can also see the array of white Canon, or black Nikon, telephoto zoom lenses. They cannot afford to miss a shot that changing a lens could entail.

For wedding photographers, the fast f/2.8 24–70mm zoom lens has for many years been very popular. Great quality, large aperture for natural light photography where flash is not allowed such as during the service, and shallow depth of field to pick out the individuals where necessary, and the flexibility of a zoom covering three or four focal lengths.

There are of course factors that make a prime lens better than a zoom such as generally faster apertures, lighter weight and smaller size, and that extra bit of image quality and in some cases lower distortion. But the flexibility of a zoom lens is very hard to ignore and many professional photographers will work with a mixture of both zoom and prime lenses.

Special effects

As well as taking conventional pictures at any chosen focal length, a zoom lens can also be 'zoomed' during the exposure to create an interesting effect. This should be done during a moderately long exposure,

say $1/8$ sec, to make the movement apparent. There will be a pattern of streaks radiating from the centre of the frame. Zooming from wide angle to telephoto will create a different effect from going the other way. The most effective shots with this technique are those which have strong highlights or colours which will make a distinct and noticeable pattern. This gives a feeling of movement within a

picture, as if the objects are flying straight out of the frame. The slow shutter speed will require the camera to be mounted steadily on a tripod. It may take a little practice to perfect the technique, but passable results should be achieved fairly quickly, and it is fun to experiment. As is the rule with all special effects, zooming should not be over-used in your portfolio – less is definitely more.

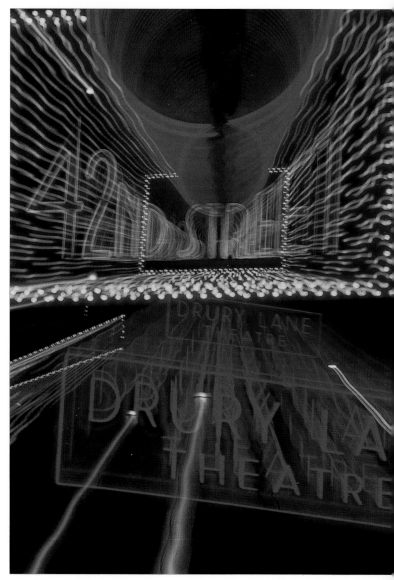

▶ **RIGHT** Neon lights make a good subject for zooming as you can produce striking 'tracers' in different colours.

Close-up and Macro

With the great improvement in lens technology – which is apparent on both fixed-lens compact and hybrid cameras, as well as lenses for all SLRs – an increasing number of people have become fascinated with taking photographs of tiny objects using the macro feature on the camera or lens.

True macro

Before looking at some of the equipment and techniques that will help you capture great close ups, it's important to differentiate between macro and close-up photography. Strictly speaking, macro photography involves being able to project an image on to the sensor the same size as the subject itself, in other words at a scale of 1:1. (Some of the latest high end macro lenses actually have a 1.5:1 magnification.)

Over time, however, this definition has been relaxed somewhat, so that today lenses capable of projecting an image half the size of the original object (1:2) are widely considered macro. Many camera and lens manufacturers have gone even further, and have started to label lenses with only 1:4

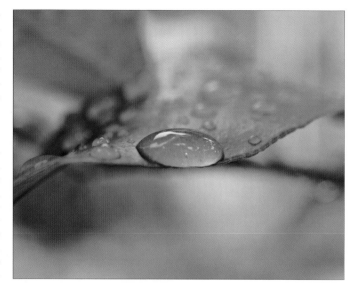

magnification as 'macro', although these lenses aren't strictly macro, they simply have the ability to focus 'close up', enabling the photographer to capture the object in close detail.

At the other end of the scale, there are some very specialized macro lenses available that are almost like scientific

ABOVE High scale macro allow incredible detail, as seen in this shot of a rain drop. Such things are rarely seen so clearly.

BELOW A 'true' macro photograph allows you to image the subject at a ratio of 1:1 on your sensor, but some lenses allow even greater enlargement.

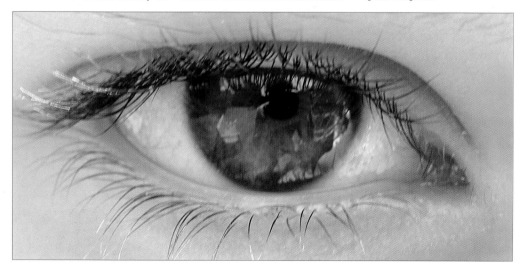

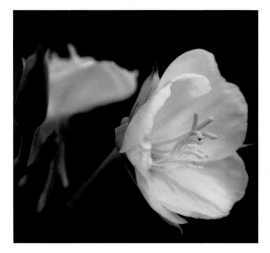

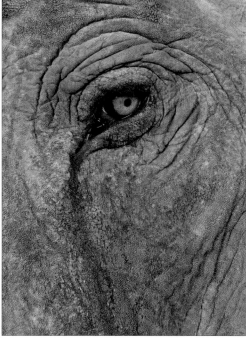

ABOVE Focusing so closely leads to a very shallow depth of field as well as detail, both of which help the main subject to feature very strongly in the composition.

RIGHT Zooming in on details of subjects you usually see in their entirety leads to some quite startling shots. This elephant's eye seems almost miraculous, peeping out of the incredibly thick skin.

instruments, having the ability to capture images at 5:1, or five times larger than the size of the original object.

Equipment

If you're an SLR owner, for the best results and in terms of ease of use, a dedicated macro lens is the best option. Such a lens will retain all the usual functions, such as autofocus, auto metering and complete depth of field control, as well as providing excellent results. Macro lenses are available in focal lengths ranging from around 50mm to 200mm. The longer the focal length, the farther you can be from the subject while still being able to capture true 1:1 macro shots. This has its benefits when shooting insects, for example, which may fly away at the sight of an approaching camera lens. Remember with a digital SLR to take into account the camera's crop factor before deciding on a specific lens – a 60mm focal length on most dSLRs will have an efl of around 90mm, for example. While designed specifically for

macro shots, the majority of macro lenses also make excellent portrait lenses. The efl of 90–100mm (the usual macro focal length) is long enough to create flattering portraits and usually such lenses are quite 'fast', with a maximum aperture of around f/2.8.

Reversing rings

A much less expensive option to a dedicated macro lens is a reversing ring. As its name suggests, this device allows you to attach the front of the lens to the camera body, which has the effect of greatly magnifying the subject. Although good results can be achieved with reversing rings, you may find that you'll have to focus manually and that the aperture closes down as you adjust it, resulting in a dark viewfinder. This makes it much harder both to frame and focus potential shots.

RIGHT Even with modern autofocus systems, macro focusing can still be quite tricky, so try using manual focus.

Extension tubes

More expensive than a reversing ring, but again much cheaper than a dedicated macro lens, are extension tubes. These non-optical devices increase the distance between the lens and the sensor, thus allowing the lens to focus closer to the subject. Extension tubes work with a variety of focal length lenses and can provide good results.

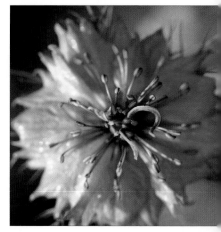

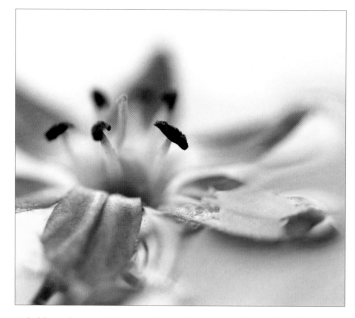

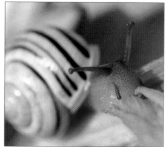

Hybrids and compacts

Some excellent close-up photography can be taken with hybrid and compact cameras. This may surprise you, but the reason for it is that the small image sensor only requires lenses with a very short focal length. This, in turn, means that you can get close to the subject and keep it in focus.

Manual focus

No matter what type of camera you're using, it may be much easier to turn off the camera's autofocus setting and focus manually on the subject when you want to take a close-up shot. Rather than using the focus ring or focus buttons, set the focus close to the point you want to be sharpest, and move your entire upper body nearer to or farther away from the subject, until you achieve the focus you want.

Tripod support

A common problem with macro photography is the extremely narrow depth of field you get. This can be used to the photographer's advantage by adding impact to an image, but it does mean carefully considering the subject before deciding which elements should be sharp and which can be out of focus.

One way of increasing depth of field is to use a small aperture and long exposure. For this you will require a tripod, and the object being photographed must stay still during the exposure.

BELOW The narrow depth of field common to many macro shots is often apparent in advertising images.

Macro tools

For the highest quality results, a dedicated macro lens for your SLR is the best, but most expensive, option. Alternatives include extension rings that fit between your normal lens and the camera to enable close focusing, or a reversing ring that allows you to attach the lens 'back to front'. Although cheaper, both options can mean you have to focus manually and may also mean you have to set the aperture manually as well.

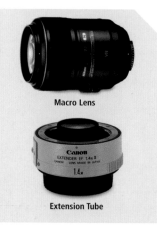

Macro Lens

Extension Tube

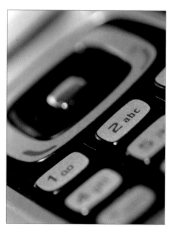

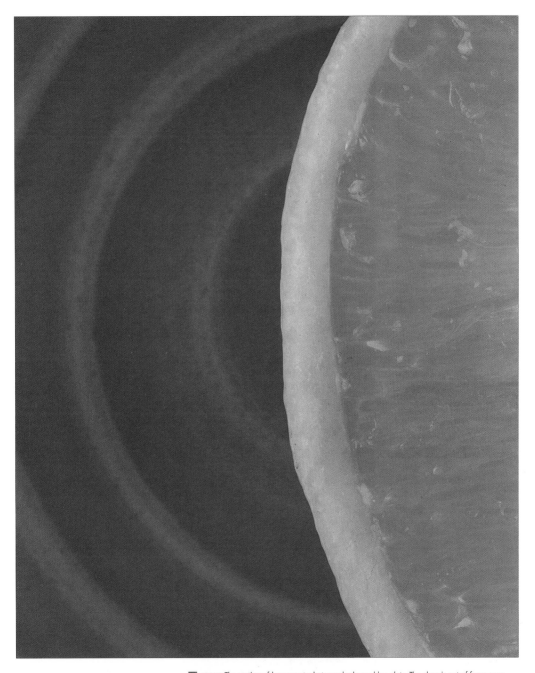

▲ **ABOVE** The section of lemon was photographed on a blue plate. The glaze is out of focus even though a tiny aperture of f/45 was used, because the depth of field is so shallow. The high magnification and small aperture called for a very long exposure. The camera will always need to be mounted on a tripod, and it is advisable to use a cable release. If the camera has a mirror-up facility, operate this before firing the shutter, since even the slightest vibration caused by the mirror may blur the picture. It is also vital to make sure that the subject stays still.

Focal Length and Backgrounds

In the earlier section on depth of field we discussed how, together with the lens's aperture setting and the focusing distance, the third factor governing depth of field was focal length. Now that we've examined focal length in more detail, let's return to the relationship between depth of field and focal length and look more closely at how adjusting focal length can be used to alter backgrounds.

Focal length and depth of field

As we know, a short focal length lens of efl 28mm set at f/5.6, for example, will have a zone of sharpness almost twice as wide as an efl 50mm lens set at the same aperture. This is why it's often advantageous to use a telephoto lens for portraits, as it's easier to throw a potentially distracting background out of focus with a longer focal length lens. You just have to walk farther back from your subject, zoom in so that you achieve the same shot and retake the picture – the longer the focal length the more blurred the background. However, it's not just depth of field that alters with focal length; you can also use varying focal lengths to alter the actual view of the background.

Altering viewpoint

A popular camera trick in the movies – one that's often used to promote a sense of unease or panic – is to show the subject standing still, but the background viewpoint changing from narrow to wide or vice versa. The technique is known as a dolly zoom, and was made famous by Alfred Hitchcock in his movie *Vertigo*. To achieve the shot, the camera tracks back or forward on rails while at the same time zooming in or out. This way, the size and view of the subject remains unchanged, but because the

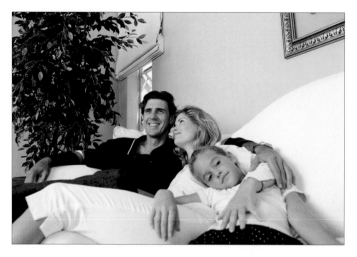

ABOVE By using a wide-angle lens with a narrow aperture, everyone from the girl in the foreground to the man in the background is sharply in focus, creating a feeling of unity.

focal length and, therefore, angle of view are changing as the camera zooms in and out, the background viewpoint and perspective also change. This trick can also be used by stills photographers to great effect.

BELOW Using a long focal length lens or setting makes it easier to throw the foreground and background out of focus, so concentrating the viewer's attention on the subject.

The effect works on the basis that in a photograph, objects closer to the camera appear disproportionately larger than those positioned farther away. So with a short focal length lens and the subject positioned close

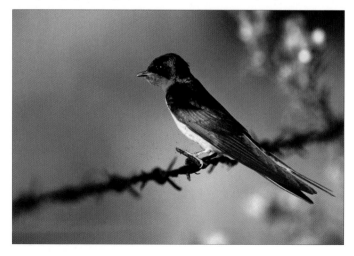

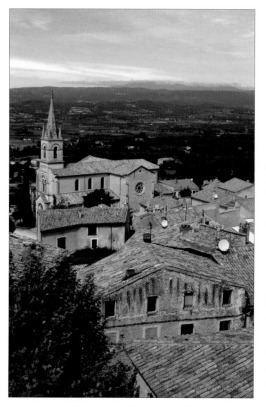
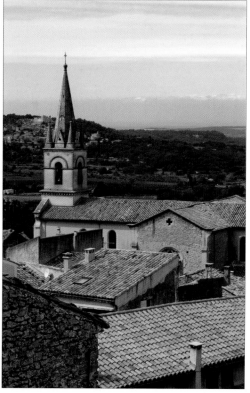

to the camera, the subject will appear exaggerated in size and the background far in the distance – this can often be used to create a sense of isolation. Moving back, using a long focal length and filling the same amount of frame with the subject, the background will appear much closer to the subject and relatively larger in size – in this shot the subject would appear much more part of his or her surroundings. This is partly due to the foreshortening effect of long focal length lenses.

Selecting background

Knowing that focal length alters view-point helps you to exclude or include background elements in a shot while the subject remains the same size. Also, since the angle of view affected is vertical as well as horizontal, a steeper perspective is also provided by a close camera view, which can be used to help isolate detail.

ABOVE AND ABOVE RIGHT By adjusting the viewpoint and zooming in slightly, the photographer has successfully isolated the tower so that it stands out more from the background.

BELOW By getting low to the ground and using a short focal length setting or wide-angle lens pointing upward, the photographer has captured the pigeons silhouetted against the sky, creating a dramatic shot.

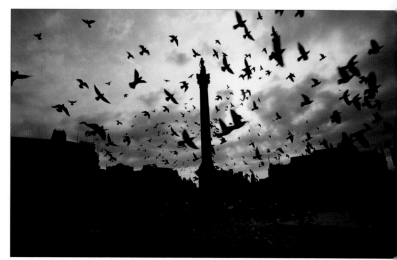

Focal Length – Try It Yourself

These exercises are designed to explore how varying focal length will affect images. The first exercise shows how focal length affects depth of field, while the second will show how focal length can be used to effectively change background viewpoints.

It's helpful if you have the camera on a tripod, as that way it's easier to set up the shots and compare the results, and you don't have to worry about slow shutter speeds if you're shooting in dim lighting conditions.

Depth of field

On a small area of land, set up two objects about 10ft (3m) apart. Place the camera around 13ft (4m) in front of the first object. The distances don't really matter – all that's important is that, with focal lengths ranging from 35mm (efl) and 170mm (efl), you can see both objects clearly. Now, with the

▼ **BELOW** For these three pictures, the lens was zoomed out as the photographer moved closer to the subject to match the framing. Notice how the longer focal length compresses the foreground and background areas.

zoom set to around 170mm, frame the front object so that it fills around half the height of the viewfinder and focus on it (making sure the rear object is still clearly visible). With the camera set to Aperture priority, choose the widest aperture and take a shot. Without moving the camera, zoom out to around 80–100mm and take another shot. Finally, zoom out to around 28–35mm and fire the shutter once more.

To see the shots at their best, you ideally need to download them onto a computer and crop the second and third shots so that they show more or less the same scene as the first – that is, the front object filling half the height of the viewfinder. You'll be cropping right into the third shot, but don't worry about the image quality – all you're assessing is depth of field.

With all three images showing approximately the same scene, the rear object should be entirely out of focus in the 170mm focal length shot, in the 80–100mm picture the rear object should be more sharply defined, while the final shot – taken at 28–35mm – should show both objects in focus.

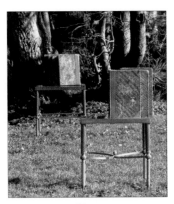

38mm

Changing viewpoint

For the second exercise you'll need a slightly larger area to work in, and the greater the difference between the shortest and longest focal length lens, the more apparent the results. The images shown were shot with a 35–170mm (efl) zoom and show the effect well. Use a tripod if you have one so the camera doesn't move between shots.

Begin by picking an object between 3 and 7ft (1m and 2m) tall – a family member or friend is ideal. Position

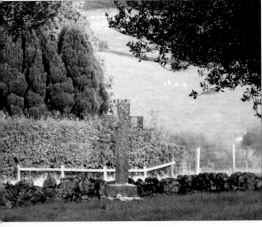

170mm

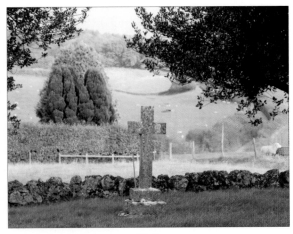

80mm

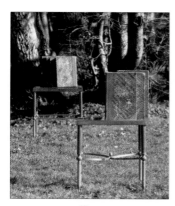

80mm

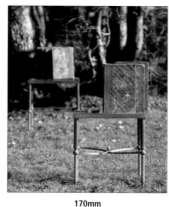

170mm

◀ **LEFT** Taken using 38mm, 80mm and 170mm focal lengths these three images were then cropped to the same size. Notice how by increasing the focal length it reduces the depth of field, making the books that are farther away out of focus.

▼ **BELOW** Increasing the focal length can often be a more practical alternative to getting physically closer to the subject, particularly when taking shots of wild animals. Here a 500mm telephoto lens was used to get close to the doe and her calf.

your subject so there is variety and recognizable depth to the background, such as a tree at one distance, a hedge at another and a fence at a third. As long as you can see the relative distances between the objects it doesn't matter what they are.

Set the zoom to the longest focal length and position yourself so that the object fills the bottom half of the frame before taking a shot. Then, zoom out to half the original focal length, but also walk closer to the subject (trying to stay in line with the background), so that it still fills roughly the bottom half of the viewfinder and take another shot. Finally, repeat the exercise, but zoom out to the shortest focal length (widest angle) that your lens offers. Walk toward the subject, fill half the frame once again, and take a final shot.

Download the images on to a computer and review them carefully. It ought to be apparent how, in the longest focal length shot, the background appears to be compressed and the angle of view narrow. With the second and third shots, although the size of the subject should have remained more or less the same, you will see that the background appears to stretch out away from the subject, and the space between the various background objects should be increasingly well delineated. Notice also, however, how the angle of view is both wider and taller as you zoom out with your lens.

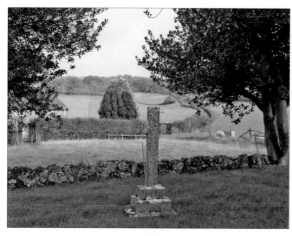

38mm

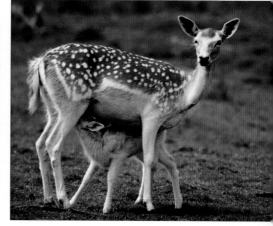

Lens Filters

In recent times, with ever more sophisticated image-editing software on the market, an ever-increasing number of photographers are turning to the digital darkroom to replicate the effects of lens filters. So does this spell the end for lens filters?

Lens filters are made of glass or plastic. They either screw on to the end of the lens, or are part of a kit that features a filter holder and an adapter ring that screws on to the end of the lens, to which the filter holder then clips. The former tend to be circular, while the latter can be square and simply slide into a slot in the filter holder.

All SLR lenses and many hybrid camera lenses can accept lens filters – look for a screw thread on the end of the lens. Screw-in filters come in various diameters, ranging from around 45mm up to 95mm, and filter holder kits usually come in similar sizes. There should be a label on the front of the lens indicating that lens's specific filter size. Some compact cameras may also feature a lens with a screw thread.

Colour filters

Traditionally, when used with film cameras, colour filters are used either to correct a colour cast caused by artificial light or to add an overall colour to an image – neither of which can be easily carried out in the dark-room after the image had been shot.

The use of colour filters to correct colour casts when shooting digitally is certainly still possible, but if you're shooting in RAW, you're likely to achieve a more accurate colour-corrected image by editing it on computer. Similarly, using a colour filter to 'warm up' (make slightly more red) or 'cool' down (make slightly more blue) an image is possible, and

many photographers – even when shooting digitally – will still use this method. However, equally good results are again possible on the computer, and this also provides a much greater level of control in terms of both the specific colour and its strength.

Yet while much can be done in post-production to replicate the effect of certain filters, there are a number of filters that you may still want to consider purchasing.

Ultraviolet (UV) filters

Fitting a UV filter to a lens is worth considering, not so much for its inherent optical properties, but for the protection it affords the lens. The aim of a UV filter is to reduce the amount of ultraviolet light entering the lens, which can cause haziness in certain situations. Because such filters are usually clear they can be left on the lens and won't have any impact on the colour or tone of the image. Many photographers fit such filters to protect the front element of the lens, as it's much cheaper to

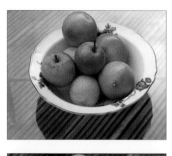

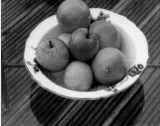

ABOVE These two shots show the effect of a polarizing filter. Without such a filter (top) reflections, which render the glass milky white, are clearly apparent in the glass table top. With a polarizing filter attached to the lens (bottom) the reflections disappear and the glass becomes more transparent.

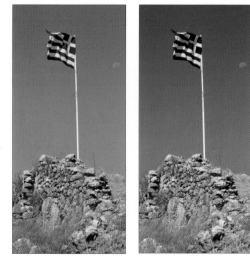

LEFT Polarizing filters should be considered as almost essential for landscape photography. Not only will they cut reflections, but they can also make skies appear bluer.

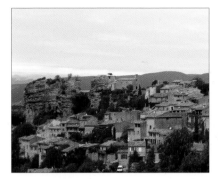

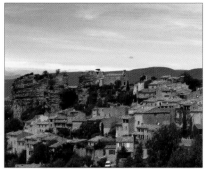

replace a filter than to have a scratch removed from an expensive lens. In addition, frequently wiping a filter is preferable to constantly cleaning the lens, which may damage the lens coating over time.

Polarizing filters

A polarizing filter is one example where the effect of the filter cannot be replicated easily on a computer. Such filters behave in exactly the same way as the polarizing lenses in a pair of sunglasses, in that they cut down on reflected light and reduce glare and haze. While these optical properties are often exploited in photography, polarizing filters can also be used to add contrast to blue, cloudy skies (making the sky bluer and the clouds whiter) and can boost the general colour saturation in an image as well.

Due to the overall darkening effect of polarizing filters, it's important to be aware that exposure can be reduced by one or two stops. In other words, a landscape that needs an exposure of

f/16 at $^1/125$ sec, may need an exposure of f/16 at $^1/60$ sec or $^1/30$ sec, or f/11 or f/8 at $^1/125$ sec when it's taken using a polarizer filter – or you could increase the ISO setting one or two steps.

If you're seriously considering adding a polarizer filter to your kit, ensure that you buy a circular polarizer. There are linear polarizers on the market, but the way in which they filter the light can sometimes stop a camera's metering and autofocusing systems from functioning properly.

Graduated neutral density filters

Another group of filters that all professional landscape photographers carry with them are graduated neutral density filters. These are a neutral grey at the top, graduating to clear at the bottom. Their purpose is to overcome the common issue of exposing for both bright sky and darker land. With such a large dynamic range, often either the sky is overexposed and the land correctly exposed, or the sky correctly exposed

and the land underexposed. By using a graduated neutral density filter, you can expose for the land, while the grey element (the 'neutral density') at the top half of the filter prevents the sky from being overexposed.

Graduated neutral density filters come in a variety of 'strengths', with darker or lighter grey being used depending on the brightness levels of the sky. As well as graduated grey filters, they are also available in a range of colours such as red, blue and yellow.

Plain neutral density filters

You can also get plain neutral density (ND) filters, which are uniformly grey. By reducing the amount of light reaching the sensor (without affecting colour), such filters allow for a longer exposure or narrower depth of field, both of which can be used creatively in certain circumstances. Like the graduated filters, ND filters are available in a variety of 'strengths' – ND2, ND4 and ND8 – that reduce exposure by one, two and three stops.

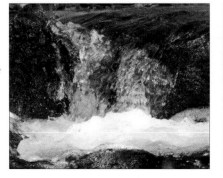

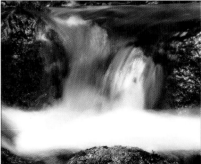

Shooting through Glass

There are many ways of changing the appearance of a subject. One of the easiest is to photograph through glass. This can create a whole range of fascinating images with a minimum of equipment. The technique can also be used to change the appearance of photographs taken previously, by copying them through glass.

Both plain and patterned glass can be used. Many patterns are on sale, and some of them produce interesting distortions or multiple images. Colour can be introduced by adding a 'gel' – a sheet of coloured acetate.

There are a few different techniques for photographing through glass. An object may be placed on glass and backlit, perhaps with a gel under the glass; The object could also be under the glass; a sheet of glass can be sprayed with water to give the effect of rain through a window.

An autofocus camera may not be able to decide whether to focus on the object or the glass. If the camera has

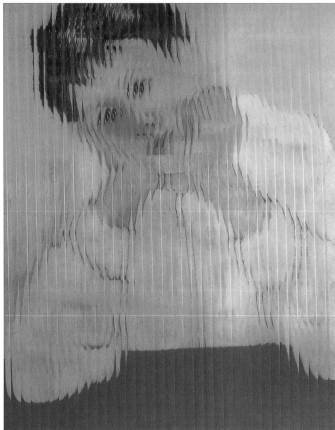

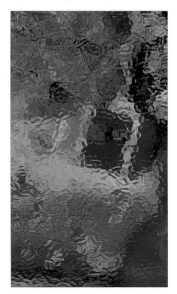

◀ **LEFT** This abstract image resembles a painter's palette and was created by placing various brightly coloured objects under a sheet of distorted glass.

▲ **ABOVE** This painting was photographed through glass and was lit by available light only. The distance of the glass from the subject alters the final effect. The nearer the glass, the more defined the subject; the further away it is, the more obscure the image will seem.

a focus lock, mount it on a tripod, remove the glass, lock the focus on the object and replace the glass.

Such photographs are often taken from close in. A macro lens or extension rings or bellows will allow really close shots, which can be effective.

When backlighting a subject, make sure that the front lighting is weaker, otherwise the backlight may not show up sufficiently and your resulting image may be murky or indistinct, and you will lose effect.

As with any special technique, there is no limit to the effects that may be obtained by using a little imagination and experimenting.

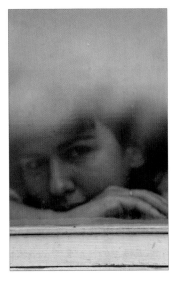

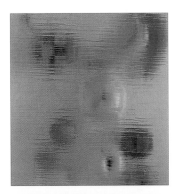

RIGHT Attractive still life images can be produced through glass. Here fruit is lit by available light using a reflector. Many different objects lend themselves to this concept; the effects can be seen immediately and can be altered as required.

BELOW By using a different pattern of glass over a painting another effect is achieved. Here the glass is placed farther from the subject and the degree of obfuscation is greatly increased.

ABOVE Although you have posed your subject, because they are in a separate space, photos taken through glass have a 'candid' quality.

BELOW Including the window frame adds an extra sense of distance and inner and outer space. It allows the viewer to feel they are looking through the window at the exact view the photographer is seeing. This can create a fairly claustrophobic picture, or act as an invitation to look or walk through, depending on the scene outside, your composition, and the frame itself.

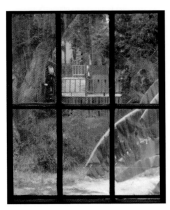

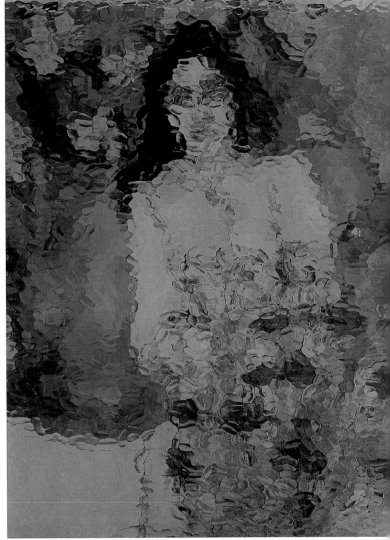

Abstract Views

There are many ways of photographing everyday objects to give them a completely new and unfamiliar look. Sometimes the images may be so transformed that the picture becomes abstract or surreal. To achieve such an effect calls for an eye for composition and an understanding of how the image will appear on film, or however it is to be reproduced or displayed, rather than how it looks to the eye.

One example is a moving object such as a flag fluttering in the breeze. To the eye it simply looks like a moving flag. It is not blurred, nor is it frozen into a particular momentary shape; however, if it is photographed it will appear in one of these ways. If a fairly slow shutter speed is used, and the moment is well judged so that the flag falls subtly into the frame, a strikingly dynamic image will result. A fast shutter speed could freeze the flag into a sharp image, but in comparison this will look stiff and lifeless.

This is only one example of seeing in an abstract way. Other images can be created by selecting part of an object, for example a building, which in isolation forms an abstract shape. Often the most ordinary objects or views can take on an abstract quality when viewed from a new angle.

There are no hard and fast rules as to what makes a good abstract picture. An acute eye will see the photographic potential in any scene. As a photographer, time spent in deliberately trying to see the world from unusual angles is never wasted.

BELOW The American flag was flying near the Washington Monument. The camera was angled upward so that part of the monument could be seen, forming a background and giving the one hard edge in the picture. The flag was moving gently in the wind. A series of pictures was taken at a shutter speed of ⅛ sec. This created a swirling blur in the picture. Although it is abstract it expresses the movement of the flag in a way which a frozen image taken with a faster shutter speed could never have achieved.

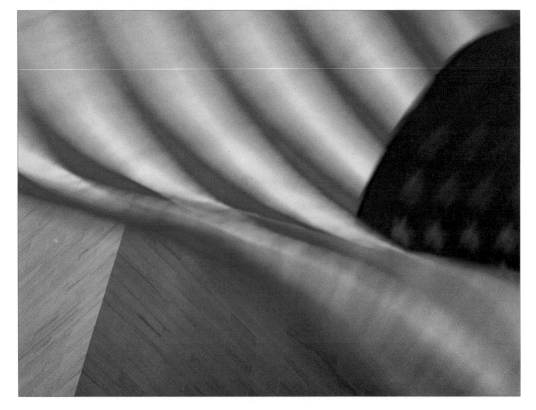

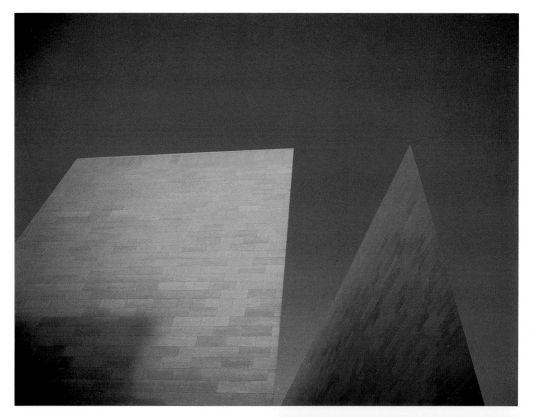

ABOVE AND BELOW Both these pictures are sections of a building taken at slightly different angles and at different times of day. Both form abstract images, but the quality of light in each one has produced quite different results. There is an endless variety of ways of seeing an object. Re-examine familiar sights – there will always be a fresh way of looking at them.

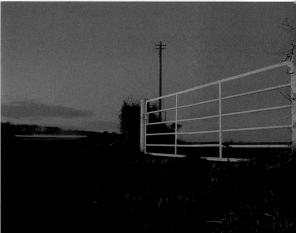

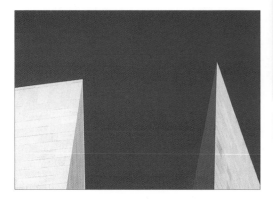

ABOVE Taken at dusk from a low viewpoint, the white gate stands out from its darker surroundings. The angle exaggerates the perspective and gives a strong lead into the picture. The slow shutter speed has allowed the tail-light of a passing car to leave a red streak. This dash of vivid colour adds a curious, almost surreal feel to the picture.

Details

Look at a magazine feature on travel at home or abroad. What strikes you about the photographs? More often than not, as well as the large scenic shots of landscapes and buildings there will be many smaller photographs. These may be used over several pages or individually, or in a block on one page or double-page spread. Individually, any one of these little pictures may not make a great impression, but in their context all these small pictures unite to bring the photo documentary to life. They not only complement the big set pieces, they become important to the narrative as a whole.

The lesson to be learned here is that wherever you are, you should be alert to the chance of getting these small

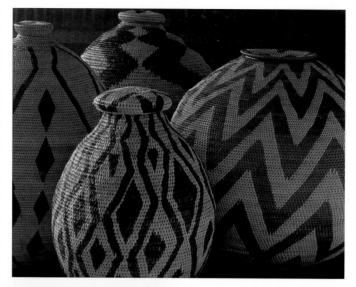

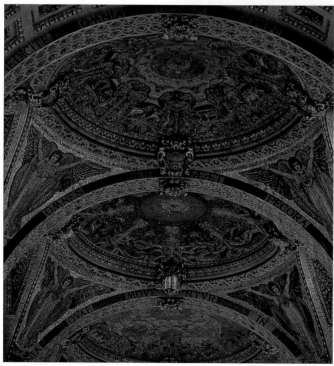

ABOVE The pattern of these woven African pots makes a pleasing picture in itself. Grouping them produces an interesting composition.

LEFT A detail of the ceiling of St Paul's Cathedral in London. In many churches the details of the decoration – mosaics, frescos, mouldings – are the most interesting thing. These can often be lost in one overall view of the interior.

but vital shots that will record how it feels to be somewhere; the textures, colours and shapes. Think of how the shots might fit into an album of your travels. You could mount them as a collection in one frame. When you are taking the great view, the grand palace, look around at the immediate vicinity too. You will be surprised at what you find. All the pictures here were originally such 'secondary' shots, but they have all made it into various publications. One of them even became a magazine cover.

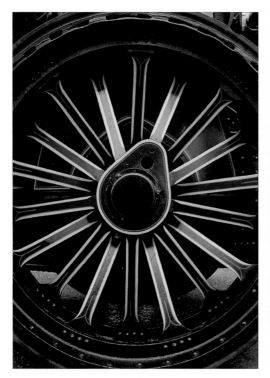

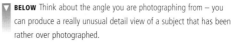
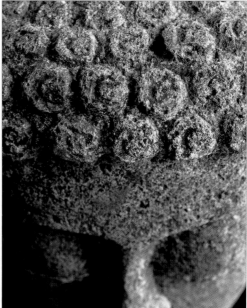

▲ **ABOVE** Going in close to this locomotive wheel gives a strong geometrical pattern. The well-defined paintwork adds to the effect. Imagine this in a group with other details of the engine. It would make an interesting presentation of fine engineering.

▼ **BELOW** This was taken while photographing the town of Sante Fé in New Mexico. It works as a composition because the vivid blue of the pot complements the terracotta wall. Both textures sit well together. As a vignette it would fit well into a mosaic of shots of the town.

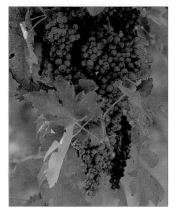

▲ **ABOVE** A sequence taken in a vineyard called not only for shots of the rows of vines but also for details of the grapes. They were shaded by the leaves, so a reflector was used to bounce light back on to them. This has made them glow and look more succulent.

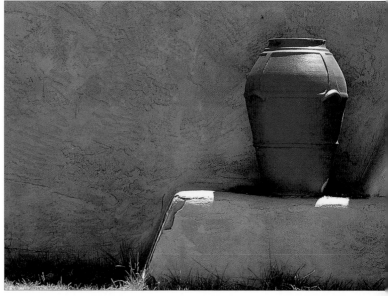

Finding Pictures

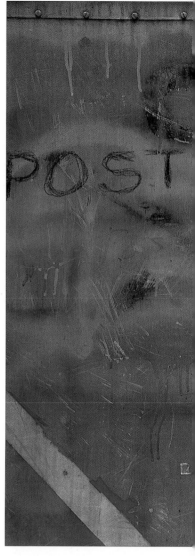

There are many places where good pictures can be found, but it is easy to overlook them. Often they are camouflaged by their surroundings, or they need to be looked at from a different angle. Sometimes the chance of a picture appears suddenly, and if the camera is loaded and ready the opportunity can be seized.

When the picture is of a person, producing a camera may inhibit them and the chance of a great shot may be lost. But sometimes seeing the camera will make them strike a pose, and this may produce an image even better than the scene or posture that first caught your eye.

Simple and apparently uninspiring things can also be the basis of a great picture. It could be a wall, a fence or a door – perhaps the texture of peeling paint or weathered stone, or torn posters or graffiti.

To find these pictures what is chiefly required is constant awareness. There is usually no need for special or expensive equipment. Sometimes a picture is waiting to be taken, but this is not apparent from normal eye level. It may need a high or low viewpoint, or the different field of view given by a wide-angle or telephoto lens to fit the composition into the frame.

Take time to evaluate the surroundings. Look at the things around you selectively. With practice, even the most ordinary places and objects can be made to yield striking images that most people in the area will simply have overlooked. Even if your first attempts largely fail, it is worth persevering. A collection of prints or images that are not particularly interesting in themselves can often make a successful collage or series of pictures on a theme.

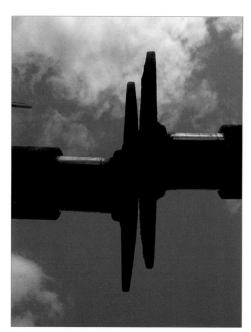

▶ **RIGHT** Looking for different angles can often result in original and unusual pictures. This one was taken while lying on the ground and looking upwards. The train couplings form a strong shape that seems to be a strange mechanical mating ritual. Always try a different viewpoint before giving up an idea as unpromising.

▲ **ABOVE** The picture came into view on a stroll down a street in New York city. The rear of the street vendor's stall is made of aluminium and has been rubbed down several times to remove graffiti. This has formed interesting patterns and shapes. The photograph of the girl is worn but her hopeful expression is still visible. Like the surface it is stuck to, the image is monochromatic, but the remains of another poster add a touch of red and blue. It is satisfying to think that over the months thousands of people have passed this stall, but probably no one else has got this shot.

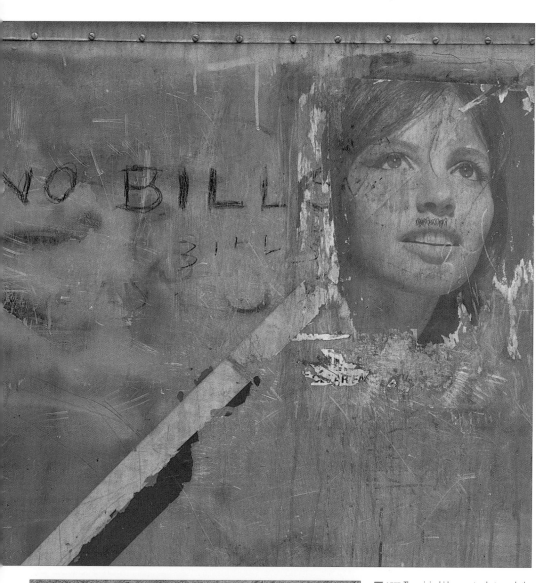

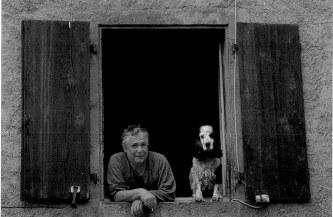

◀ **LEFT** The original idea was to photograph the building, but while this was being done the man leaned out of the window with an enquiring look. He spoke no English, but a little sign language persuaded him to stay put while the lens was changed for a telephoto. He turned out to be a willing subject, and after a few shots suggested including his dog. The dog posed as uninhibitedly as he did. Without these two posturing figures the picture would have been dull, but by seizing a chance opportunity a good picture was obtained.

Photojournalism

Up until now, we've concentrated on learning as much as we can about the intricacies of how digital and film cameras work; how to get the best possible results using manual and semi-manual modes and how to improve photographs through the application of some basic tips and hints on composition. This will help you to take photographs that are optimally exposed and have aesthetic merit in terms of their composition.

However, as well as the beautifully composed shot, always look out for images that will hold the viewer's attention in other ways. This may be through humour or poignancy, or through a specific issue the image raises. Frequently, you may only have a fraction of a second to capture the image – in which case the best policy may be to select Auto and fire away. You may not end up with the most creative exposure, but if you don't have time to consider the scene carefully, Auto should at least provide a reasonably accurate exposure and well-focused shot. And, once you've got a usable image, you can always switch to manual or semi-manual and try to improve on depth of field or exposure, if time allows.

Consider compact

Many professional photographers eschew their pro SLR kit when they are out and about, in favour of a small compact camera. For grabbing quick, candid street shots while on the move, such a camera can certainly come into its own. Recent digital camera models start up and respond relatively quickly, and their size certainly makes them far less conspicuous than a digital or film SLR with a long zoom lens, and this allows you to wander around more or less unnoticed. You might

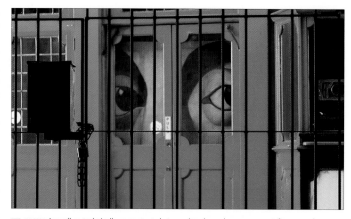

ABOVE As well as technically competent photographs, always keep an eye out for unusual subjects, such as this 'giant' staring out from behind the doors.

not have quite the same creative control as you do with a SLR, but at least you'll be able record what's going on around you well enough.

Many professional photographers, including those working for picture agencies such as Magnum, use a rangefinder camera instead of a SLR camera as they are generally smaller, more discreet and much quieter, but give the same high image quality. They focus manually with very compact lenses and while some do contain aperture priority and light meters, in general the type of photographer using one will know and understand his equipment and shooting environment so well as to not have to rely on any electronics at all. There are a variety of new rangefinder cameras available (although you will find that older rangefinders will work as well today as ever and there are also some options, although often quite expensive, for digital rangefinders).

It's worth getting into the habit of taking a camera with you wherever you go, even if you don't have a specific photographic opportunity in

mind. Just a compact will do, if you have limited space. It's likely that you'll find something worth photographing during the course of each day, and getting into the habit of looking for and assessing potential scenes will help you with just about every aspect of your photography.

BELOW The children in this image are completely unaware of the camera. Candid shots are much easier to obtain if you are using a compact than if you are wielding a bulky, professional-looking SLR.

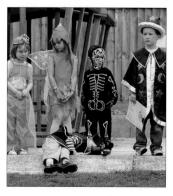

Photographers' rights

What you can and cannot legally photograph varies enormously from country to country and can change from year to year. If you're in any doubt, seek advice or permission from people who you trust – this may well be embassy or consulate staff if you're travelling abroad. If you plan to shoot a specific famous landmark, it pays to contact the owner or the people responsible for the property to ask for their permission first. If you're concerned about simply walking around a city or large town taking photographs, you may find some helpful advice at a tourist information centre.

Historically in the UK, USA and in most of Europe, photography would attract little attention. Photographers could happily walk around large cities taking pictures of major landmarks without fear of attracting the notice of either security staff or the police. Now, due to increased security and awareness, photographers often find themselves being confronted by the local authorities. This is especially the case if you are using a large SLR with a long zoom lens attached as opposed to a more discreet compact camera. Often, using a tripod will bring you to the attention of the security personnel. While legally you're perfectly within your rights to photograph most buildings and people in public places, you'll find that in larger cities you may be asked who you are and what you're doing. You may even find that attempts will be made to seize your equipment. Only a police officer is legally entitled to seize property and then he or she has to be making an arrest; the police cannot seize property without a court order. If you're asked to hand over equipment to security staff, politely but firmly ask for their names and under what authority they're acting. If they refuse to tell you, but persist in demanding the equipment and won't let you simply leave, call the police.

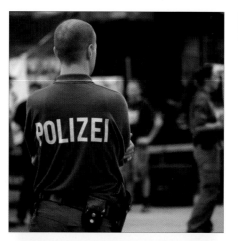

LEFT Political rallies and marches can often provide strong graphic images. In these situations you may find a compact camera attracts less attention than an SLR.

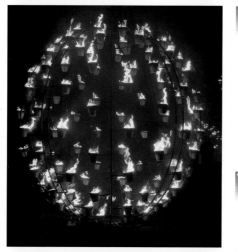

LEFT Many modern compacts are capable of capturing an acceptable image even in the most difficult lighting circumstances, so it pays to have one with you all the time in case you come across unexpected events such as this fire display.

BELOW If you carry a camera with you at all times you'll be in the position to take a picture of anything that interests you, such as this store window display.

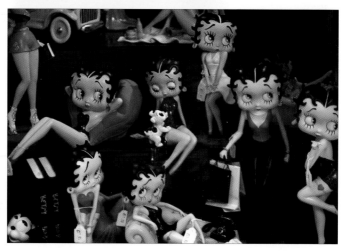

Telling a Story: 1

The ancient Chinese proverb that 'a picture is worth a thousand words' has never been truer than it is today. Even with the rapid growth of on-the-spot television reporting, still images have a key role in conveying the intrinsic nature of a story. In modern history it is the still photograph taken in war, famine or natural disaster that stays in people's memory. On a lighter note, it is very often the photograph on the cover of a magazine that will persuade the consumer to buy it.

Photographs can tell a story in many different ways. The pictures here may not make up what many people would think of as a story, but they tell us quickly what this man is associated with: ancient music

and instruments. On the shoot many pictures were taken of him in his workshop, cutting, chiselling, glueing, polishing, tuning. Further shots showed the craftsman by himself, with his instruments, in his home. And many were taken of the instruments themselves. When it came to editing all these it was decided that a strong portrait with one of his instruments was required. Another decision was to show the detail of many finished instruments, rather than have a story of the making of a single one. Different angles showed the elegant curves of the lutes' bodies. The detail in the frets and roses showed the delicacy of the craftsmanship. Keeping the lighting low

emphasized the featured part of each instrument. Restricting the picture sequence to these shots has let the feeling of precision, sensitivity and sheer art shine through.

When you are planning to photograph a person or their work, or an event, try to see how several shots can be used. You may be photographing a member of your family for the album rather than shooting a sequence for a magazine, but think of how you can create a series of shots that will make an attractive and rewarding layout. It may seem difficult to edit your pictures – even wasteful – but to do justice to your best shots good presentation is vital, and so a wide selection is important.

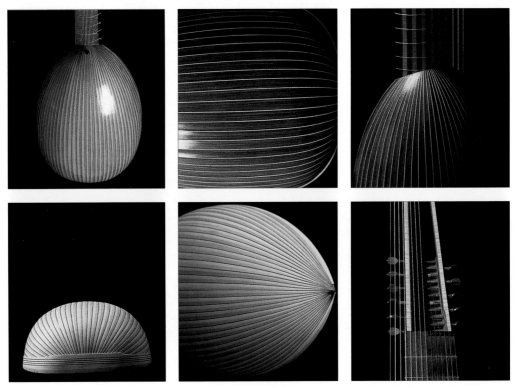

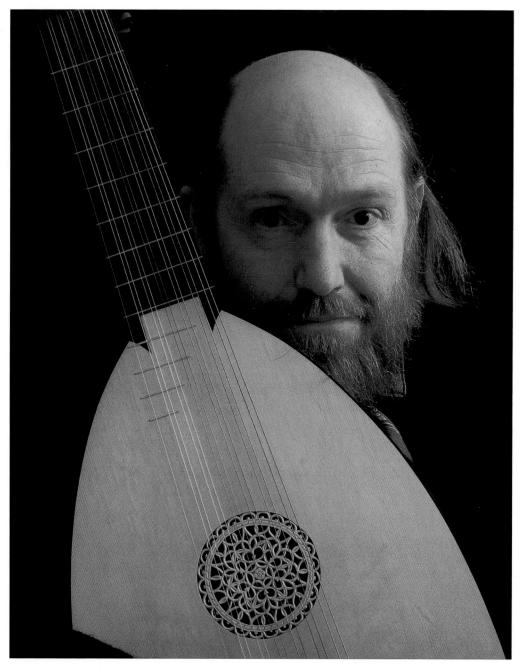

Telling a Story: 2

In a world where colour photography has become the norm people are often surprised at the power of the images produced by black and white. This is particularly the case where a serious subject or a sombre mood has to be portrayed. Black and white can convey squalor and misery in a way that colour can never do. The memorable images of great documentary photographers such as Don McCullin remain in the mind partly because they are shot in stark black and white.

When telling a story in black and white, the basic ingredients are much as they would be for a colour sequence, but the vital things to look for are tone and texture.

Make a plan of the kind of pictures that are needed before starting to shoot. Look at photo features in a news magazine. The number of pictures used in one story is usually quite small, and each one has a purpose. If the geographical location of the story is relevant, there must be a picture that gives the viewer some idea of what the place looks like.

If the story is one based on people, try to get to know them first. Not only will they supply information, they will take more kindly to a photographer who is interested in them and who seems to be including them in his work, rather than snapping them surreptitiously from behind a tree. People in some regions, or in inner cities, may seem intimidating, but it is better to have them on one's side than to treat them as strangers, which only invites hostility.

If you use film, medium speed film, about 400 ISO, is adequate for most situations you will find yourself in. If necessary it can be uprated to a higher speed and also given a longer development time.

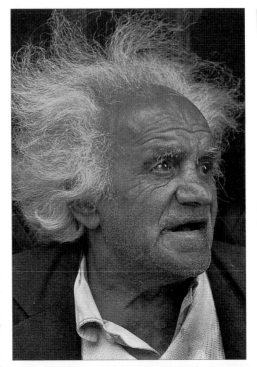

LEFT Only by going in really close could this portrait be made to work. This man's leathery skin and tousled hair show what it means to live rough. He gladly accepted a cigarette and talked ramblingly, but sadly he seemed oblivious to what was going on around him.

BELOW This picture tells us about the location: part of London's East End. The scruffy appearance gives us an indication of the surroundings. Little touches such as the cat sitting on a pile of rubbish add interest to an otherwise bleak scene.

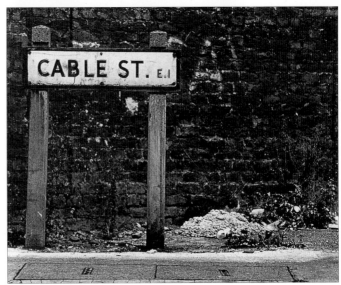

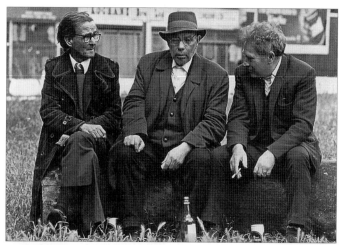

RIGHT Alcohol can be a refuge for many people, mainly men drinking openly on the streets, in doorways and in the few open spaces. Confronting such people may seem daunting, but sharing the time of day and a cigarette is less likely to arouse suspicion and ill-feeling than lurking behind a wall.

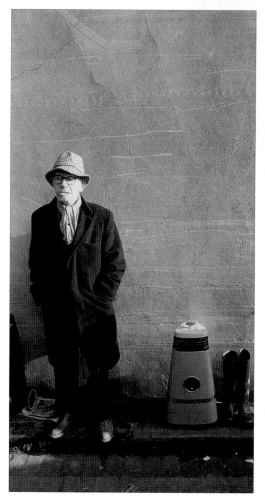

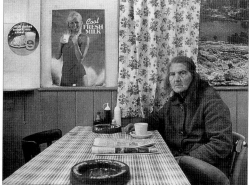

ABOVE Nobody knew where this woman lived. She would appear nearly every morning at six when the café opened. She always had two cups of tea and a sandwich. She never said a word, but indicated that she did not mind having her picture taken. The viewpoint from one end of the table gives a strong sense of perspective. Many social statements could be read into the surroundings.

LEFT This shot was taken near a street market. In one section people sell what others have long since discarded. This trader selling just a handful of items stands against a crumbling backdrop. It is a cold day and although he is well wrapped up, he still seems to be clutching himself to keep warm.

Shooting a Still Life

Still life photography can be rewarding to do, as well as resulting in a pleasing image. Taking such pictures calls for patience and an eye for a good composition and theme. Still lifes are among the best of visual exercises. Innumerable famous painters, past and present, have turned to the still life at some time. Much of their work has in turn inspired photographers.

Almost any object can form part of a still life. There may be a collection of things with a particular link – for example, objects brought back from visits to a particular country. Such a collection could be interesting simply because everything came from that place. But everyday objects found around the home can be made into an equally satisfactory assemblage. When positioning the items, always check the view through the camera. When photographing flowers, which can wilt, or other fragile objects, add them to the arrangement last.

It is vital to pay attention to lighting, which conveys mood. A still life can be photographed in daylight, but shooting indoors gives far more control. There is no need for an elaborate studio or lots of lights; many pictures can be taken with a single light and a few reflectors and diffusers. A tiny adjustment of one of these, or repositioning an object, can make a great difference to the way a shadow falls and change the whole effect.

The shot will be taken from quite close in, probably using a standard lens or a medium telephoto. Every little detail will show up – a crease in a tablecloth, dust on a plate.

Working in film, the best camera to use for such work is a medium or large format one such as 5 × 4; but adequate results can be obtained on 35mm if the composition is strong.

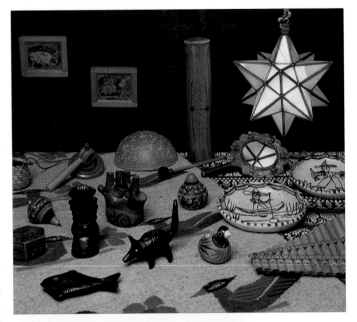

ABOVE For this collection of Mexican handicrafts a small light bulb was put in the lamp to create a realistic glow. The exposure time was 1 sec to pick up this light; the rest of the picture was briefly lit by flash during this exposure.

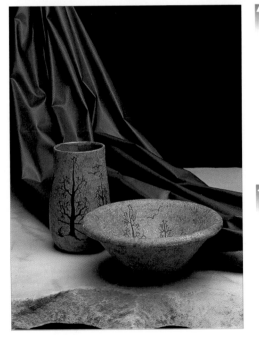

LEFT Some of the best still life arrangements are the simplest. This one was constructed with a piece of rough marble. The two ceramic pieces are by the same potter. A drape of shiny cotton material completes the ensemble.

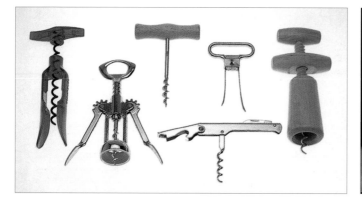

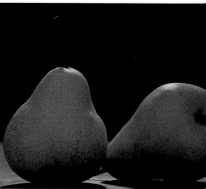

▲ **ABOVE** Backlighting still life collections gives a very clean effect and can make the objects – in this case a collection of corkscrews – seem to float in space. They were laid on a piece of acrylic sheet lit from underneath, with another light directed down on them from above.

▼ **BELOW** The seashells and rocks were collected over some time, and photographed at home. They were laid on a slab of rough stone and the composition was arranged while constantly checking through the viewfinder. One light with a diffuser and two reflectors was used, and just before the shot was taken the whole area was misted with water, using a houseplant spray.

▲ **ABOVE** This shot uses a black backdrop. A single light was placed above the pears, shining down on them from slightly behind. A large white reflector was placed in front of the camera, with a hole cut in it for the lens. A lens hood was used to keep stray light from falling on the lens itself. The reflector throws back a little light on to the pears so that they are softly illuminated.

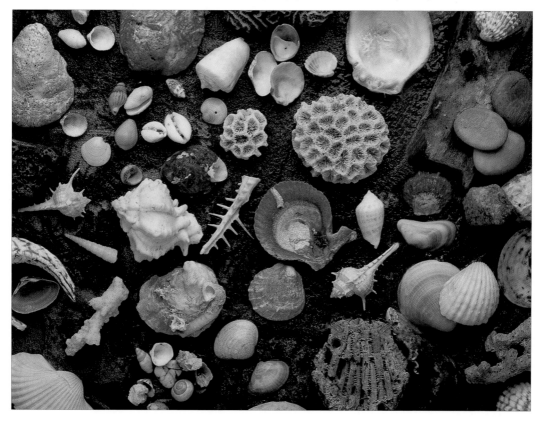

Shooting for Manipulation

Most amateur digital photographers (and all professionals) use computers and image-editing software as part of their photographic workflow today. Often this will be for the purpose of standard editing, such as sharpening, cropping or adjusting white balance or contrast, particularly if the images have been shot RAW, in which case no in-camera processing will have occurred and the images will need to undergo such basic editing processes before they can be printed.

There are a number of occasions when photographers will shoot images in the knowledge that they will be manipulated on a computer at a later date – during the process often referred to as post-production.

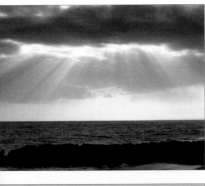

High-dynamic range

One of the most common occasions when photographers will deliberately shoot for post-production is when the dynamic range in the scene exceeds the camera sensor's ability to capture it. If, for example, due to a bright sky and dark land, the sensor is unable to record both highlights and shadow regions without either the former 'blowing out' or the latter 'filling in' and losing all shadow detail, then often the best course of action is to take two shots – one exposed for the sky and one exposed for the land – and compose them on computer as one image that successfully renders the entire tonal range of the scene.

RAW

Shooting in RAW allows you to adjust the exposure on a computer later and thus create two images (one each for the sky and land) that can be merged as one file. In many ways it increases the dynamic range of the sensor, but the difference between the highlights and shadows is often so great that the extra exposure compensation added in post-production is such that you run the risk of introducing noise into the darkest areas of the image – those most prone to noise.

Panoramas

Photographers will often deliberately shoot for post-production when they want to create panoramas. In such instances, the photographer will take two, three or even more slightly overlapping shots of a panoramic scene, often with the aid of a tripod to ensure the images are aligned accurately. Later the images can then be downloaded and 'stitched' together to form one long panorama.

LEFT AND BELOW A very good reason to keep a small library of different types of sky – stormy, cloudy or sunny – is that you never know when you'll want to superimpose a more interesting sky over a good shot with a dull sky; but be aware of the ethical compromise.

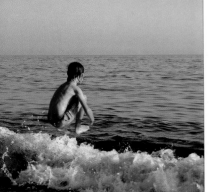

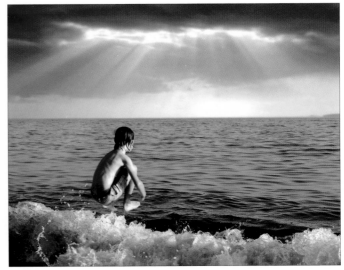

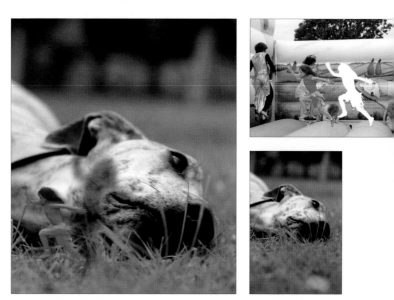

Most examples of image-editing software feature commands that partially automate the process of merging the images together by looking for repeated 'patterns' of a scene from each shot and laying them on top of the other.

Photomontage

The third common reason for shooting for post-production is to create photomontages. This fairly old technique has been around more or less since the advent of photography and involves merging two or more, often incongruent, images together to make one image. In conventional film photography, this was usually only achieved by carefully cutting out the various components with a craft knife and assembling them on the main background image – with mixed results. With today's powerful image-editing software, featuring sophisticated cut-out tools, Layers and Blending Modes, it's now much easier to merge images together seamlessly to create all too credible scenes.

Image libraries

Now that photographers are able to potentially merge two images together seamlessly, many have 'libraries' of image elements, such as sunsets, blue cloudy skies, deserted beaches and so

on, which they add when they have the option of photographing a potentially useful element. In this way, they can replace, for example, a slightly dull-looking sky in a particular shot with a much more photogenic one, to give the whole image a makeover.

Ethics

Inevitably, there are certain ethical issues affecting image manipulation. One professional photographer was struck off a well-known news service for slightly increasing the density of palls of smoke following an explosion to give the image an added sense of drama. A similar effect could have been achieved using traditional techniques in a darkroom, but the fear of digital image manipulation in

professional circles is so great that draconian punishments are often meted out. Naturally, for amateur photographers who are displaying their photographs for family and friends, there's not an issue, but it may become one if images are entered into competitions and the rules strictly state that only minor enhancements to images are allowed.

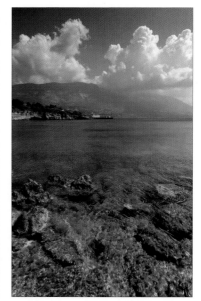

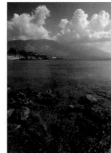

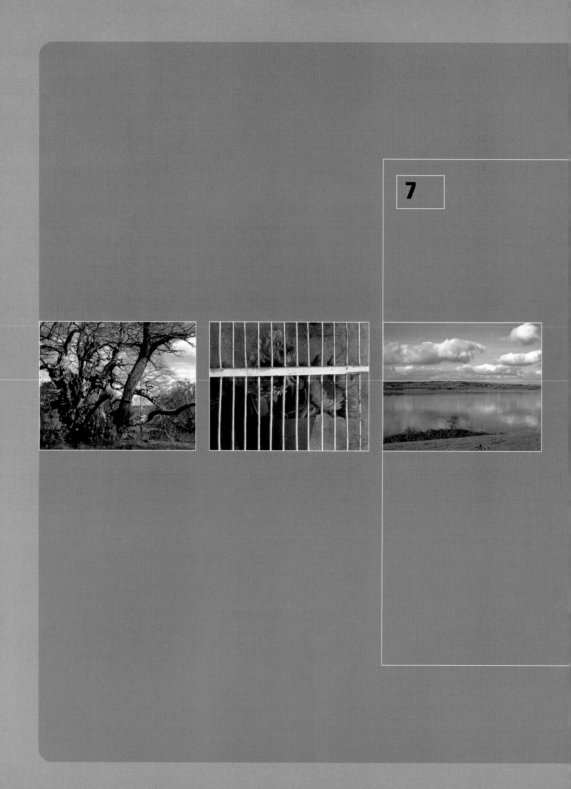

7

Practical Photography – The World around You

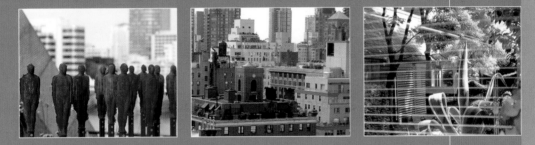

Photographers often see things in a slightly different way to other people, and this is the secret to successful pictures. Becoming good at finding such shots that show this 'other viewpoint' involves really looking, everywhere as you go. You need control over your equipment and to make an extra effort to get up half an hour earlier, walk a little farther, stay on location longer, or simply try to look at the world around you with fresh eyes. This will set your pictures apart from the average. This chapter looks at choosing locations and subjects, finding the best viewpoint and light, putting people in the shots and ideas about composition.

Landscapes: General Composition

The main subject matter of photographs taken when you are travelling will probably be landscapes. In landscape photography it is very important to take care with composition, in order to avoid producing dull shots that mean little to people looking at your photos – for example, of a lot of sky with only a thin strip of land. A commonplace image can be transformed very simply by paying attention to shadow, colour and detail, all of which are paramount in producing good landscape shots. As well as providing you with a great visual record of your studies, meaningful and striking landscape shots are very much sought after by various potential buyers.

Varying a landscape shot

• Rotate the camera slightly to one side; this may cut out unwanted scenery or bring in an added point of interest.
• Move the camera from a horizontal to a vertical position; sometimes the smallest of movements which does not even involve moving your feet can have a dramatic effect and allow you to see different points of interest.
• Try isolating a portion of the landscape against a backdrop from a different part of the image; this can emphasize scale or make a coloured field, for example, stand out from surrounding pastures.
• Notice the position of any trees; a single isolated tree or a group of trees apart from a wood or forest can be used as a device for leading the eye into the scene. Tractor furrows, pathways and rabbit tracks or a meandering stream or river also have a similar effect.
• An object in one corner of the picture adds to the composition; be careful that there is enough variety in a sequence of shots – do not always place an object in the same corner or the series begins to look dull.

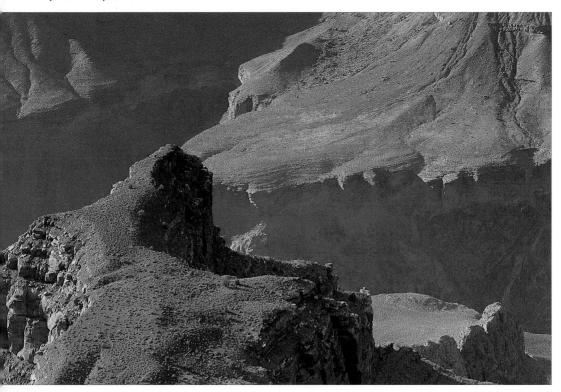

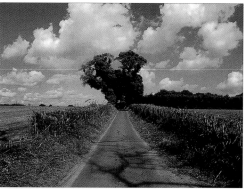

RIGHT Although the two shots to the right were taken very close to each other, one is a far better composition than the other. In the vertical picture the road and tree balance one another, drawing the eye to the centre. The tree is a bold dominant feature; the way the narrow road converges adds a sense of curiosity – what lies beyond? In the horizontal picture the tree appears to lose its dominance and the expanse of fields on either side diminishes the power of the converging sides of the road. It is clear that the smallest adjustment can make a considerable difference to the overall composition.

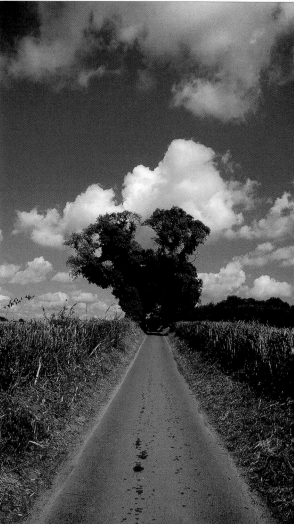

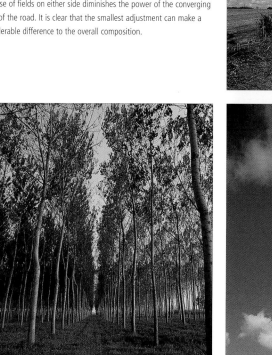

ABOVE This grouping of trees is common around the River Po in northern Italy. The planting arrangement is exaggerated by going in close using a wide-angle lens so that the long lines between the rows form a focal point for the composition. The evening light helps to create a pleasant atmosphere.

LEFT Give some thought to which lens to use when composing a landscape shot: it is one of the most important factors in a successful composition. By using a 200mm telephoto lens this picture has been framed without any sky. The eye is drawn to the slightly pink terrain of the foreground while the grey rock of the canyon forms the background. The long lens has compressed the shot, further emphasizing the foreground. The trees in the foreground look like tiny bushes and this gives an indication of the scale of the canyon.

Landscapes: Choosing a Viewpoint

Often the view that looks most spectacular to your eyes does not come out nearly so well in your shots. This is not necessarily because of any technical fault: it may be just that the wrong viewpoint was chosen when pressing the shutter. All the time you look at anything, your eyes are editing the scene and suppressing uninteresting details. In contrast, the camera records just what is in front of it, and unless you have taken care to exclude things you do not want, they will appear on the print.

In many cases the picture could be improved beyond recognition by moving a short distance. The basic viewpoint may be fine, but perhaps a higher or lower viewpoint is needed; try standing on a step, or crouching down. It is worth taking time to explore a variety of viewpoints. Even when you have taken your shot and are walking away you may suddenly see a better shot. If you do, take it. After all, even if you are shooting with film, that is the least expensive component in photography. Of course if you are shooting with a digital camera you merely need a spare memory stick to use. Take lots of shots, as you may never return to that place, or the light may never be the same again – so do not worry about using up another couple of frames or trawling through lots of similar images on your computer when you get home. The chances are that later, on closer scrutiny, one of the shots will stand out as far better than the others.

Parallax error

One common reason for not getting the picture you want is parallax error. A camera with a separate viewfinder for the lens – that is cameras that are not single lens reflex cameras – gives a slight difference in framing between what you see and the picture you take. This makes no noticeable difference when photographing a distant object or a landscape, but the closer you go in, the greater the error. If the landscape shot has a foreground you will certainly have to allow for parallax. If you do not, a detail you expect to be in your photograph may simply not appear, and vice versa. With a digital camera, your screen view will show you exactly what the camera sees, thus avoiding parallax error.

▼ **BELOW AND BELOW LEFT** From looking at the background of the buildings and cliffs it is clear that both these pictures were taken from almost the same place. But the foregrounds are quite different. This shows the effect that altering the viewpoint slightly can have on the finished picture. Although both compositions work well, the one on the left is taken from a better viewpoint in relation to the sun.

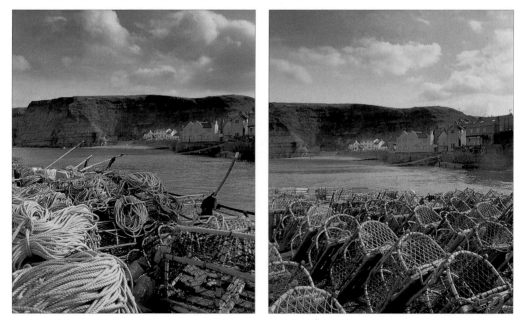

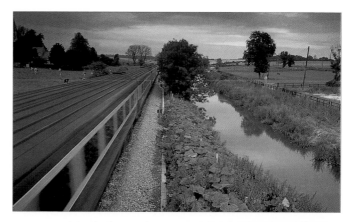

RIGHT A central viewpoint from a bridge over both the railway track and the canal has created an interesting juxtaposition. A fairly slow shutter speed of 1/60 of a sec was used. This has made the express train slightly blurred, which adds an air of speed. In contrast the canal looks calm and tranquil, a bygone and slower mode of transport.

BELOW Taking this shot from a viewpoint some way up the bank of the lake has brought the pavilion on the far side into clear view. In a view from the water's edge, the bridge in the middle distance cut into the pavilion, spoiling the composition.

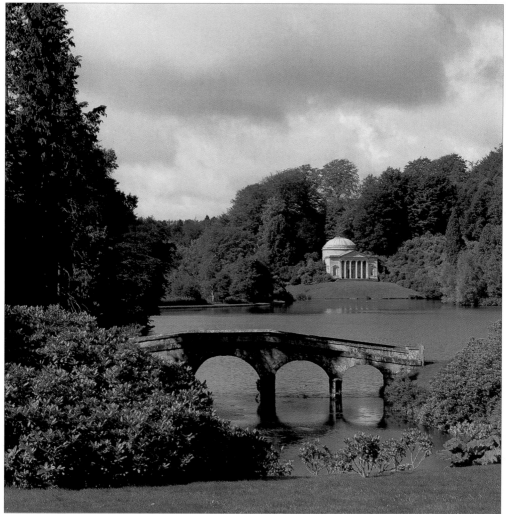

Perspective

In photography, perspective means creating a feeling of depth on what is actually a flat picture surface. There are several ways to get this effect and all of them are quite simple. It is strange, then, that so many photographs lack this element which can make all the difference to a shot.

In landscape photography a simple way of gaining a sense of perspective is to use a foreground. Often you can add a tree at one side of the frame, or with its foliage filling the top of the picture. This simple addition creates an illusion, the impression that there is space between the viewpoint, the foreground and the background. Compare this to a picture with no foreground features – it will look flat and dull.

Strong, naturally formed lines can create a powerful sense of 'linear' perspective. Try standing at the end of a recently ploughed field. Look at the lines of the furrows running away from you. They will converge towards a central point in the distance – what in the formal study of perspective is called a vanishing point. Taken from a low viewpoint these lines will create a strong feeling of depth.

When photographing buildings it is not difficult to exaggerate perspective. A shot of the front of a building taken straight on may lack impact whereas a more dramatic effect may be achieved by moving in close and looking up so the verticals converge and seem to tower over you.

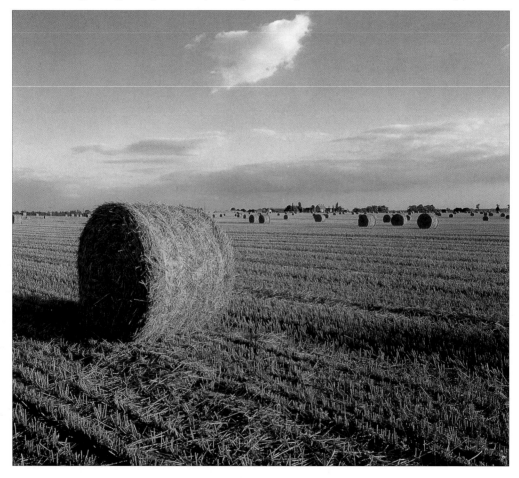

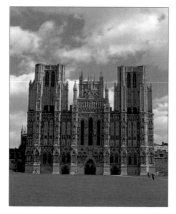

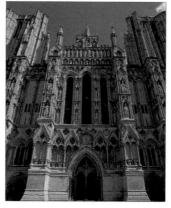

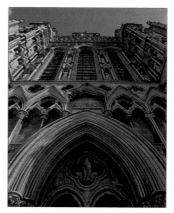

ABOVE In this picture of Wells Cathedral in the UK, the viewpoint was directly in front. Although it shows all the façade it lacks depth. There is no sense of perspective at all.

ABOVE Here the viewpoint is closer. The camera is tilted upwards and the two towers converge towards the top centre of the frame. This creates a more powerful image.

ABOVE The viewpoint is nearer still and the verticals converge even more sharply. This slight change of viewpoint and camera angle greatly increases the perspective effect.

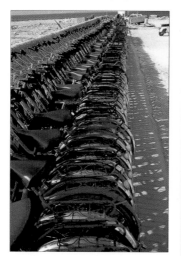

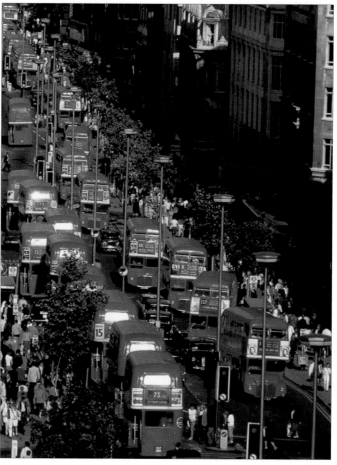

ABOVE Another example of linear perspective: the bicycles create a seemingly endless line converging at an infinite distance. Lines of objects are one of the most effective ways of conveying perspective.

RIGHT These red buses snaking down London's Oxford Street give a good sense of linear perspective. The uniformity of their colour adds to the feeling of depth.

LEFT Going close to a foreground bale with a 21mm wide-angle lens makes it seem far from the other bales. This technique helps you add perspective to your photographs.

Landscapes: The Weather

There is no such thing as perfect weather for photography. Of course, photographing people on a beach holiday in the pouring rain may present a few difficulties, but many inclement weather situations are in fact the basis for original and dramatic photographs. Overcast skies can be used to advantage and reveal more about the immediate environment than if the sun were shining on a clear day. Rain can be evocative, portraying isolation and stormy conditions. Wintry, and especially snow-covered views provide good, clear images; these are best shot in sunshine to obtain the best view of the shadows cast on crisp snow – an effect which is lost if the sky is heavy.

Predicting where light will fall is important; try to look at a map to gauge where the sun will shine strongly, and rise and set. Make sure the camera is in position at the right time to get the full effect of the quality of light required, particularly if unusual weather conditions produce dramatic cloud formations.

▼ **BELOW** Knowing where the sun is going to set means that full advantage can be taken of warm evening light. The same shot taken earlier would have lacked atmosphere.

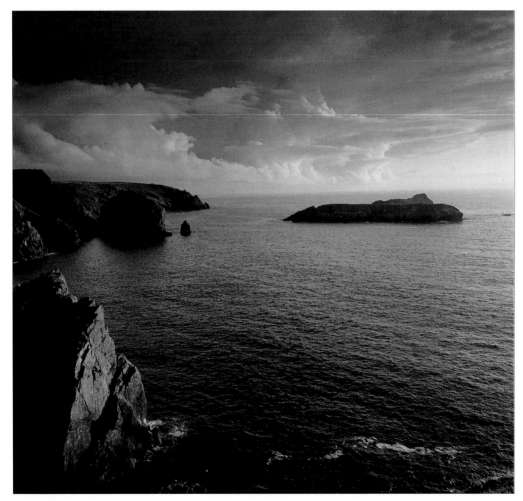

Extreme weather kit care

If the weather is very cold the shutter on the camera may freeze and valuable picture opportunities may be lost. Extreme heat can ruin film, so keep it wrapped in foil as this will keep it a little cooler. As big a lens hood as possible may help to shield the lens from the rain; beware of cutting off the corners, or 'vignetting' the picture. Do not let weather conditions prevent photography – be prepared to have a go: the results could be surprising!

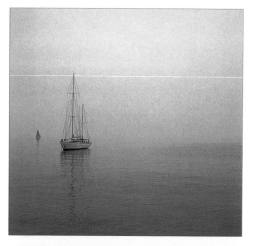

LEFT Mist and fog should not be a deterrent to photographers. This almost monochromatic picture has a strange eerie quality to it. Is the boat perhaps drifting and abandoned? Hazy air can add an enigmatic quality to shots.

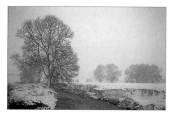

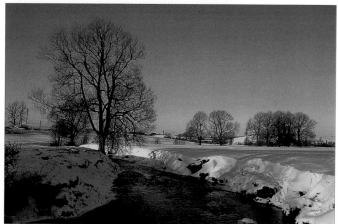

ABOVE AND RIGHT Snow creates wonderful picture possibilities. Take care not to underexpose: there is so much reflected light that exposure meters may read the conditions as being brighter than they are. Wait for different light on snow scenes. Here the picture with the sun shining brightly, right, certainly enhances the overall effect.

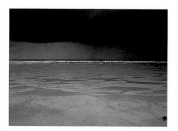

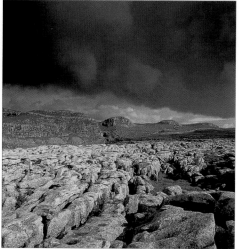

ABOVE Even in the rain dramatic pictures can be taken. This storm over the Atlantic illustrates the qualities of cold and isolation. A slow shutter speed can help to emphasize the driving rain.

LEFT The heavy rain cloud hanging over the limestone pavement illustrates perfectly the visual effect overcast weather can produce. Here it is particularly apt as the cloud hangs over rock which has been eroded by rainfall over the centuries, so the image has a double purpose, it is visually pleasing as well as instructive.

Landscapes: Time of Day

Throughout the day the sun constantly changes position. In photographic terms this movement is more than one from east to west: any change in the sun will produce a different effect on any landscape. In the early morning and evening the sun will be quite low; the shadows it casts will be long and dramatic. In winter the sun will be lower still and these shadows will be even more exaggerated. At mid-day the sun will be high and the shadows cast will be shorter. In some cases this can lead to flat and featureless shots, so take care at this time of day.

The other factor to consider is that the light cast by the sun in the early morning and late afternoon will have a warmer tone than that of midday light, so pictures taken at these times will appear redder or more orange than those taken in the middle of the day. It is well worth making the effort to get up early, before the sun rises, to be in position to capture the quality of light as dawn breaks. A little research beforehand will show where the sun will be and what it will fall on, depending on the time of year. Early and late rays of sunlight can illuminate an isolated area of a landscape in much the same way as a giant spotlight trained on the scene.

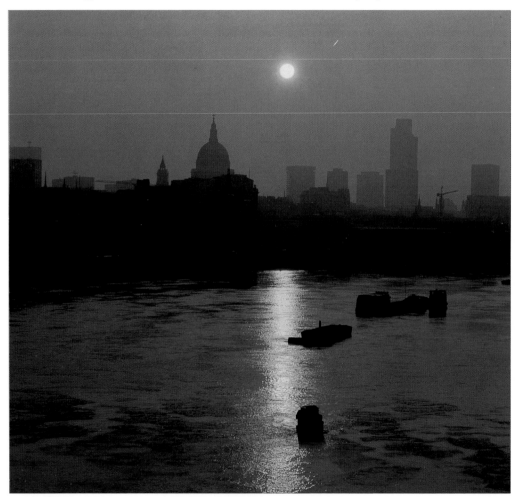

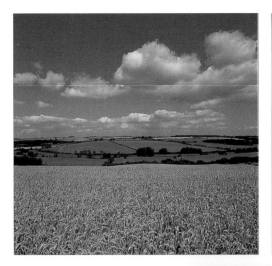

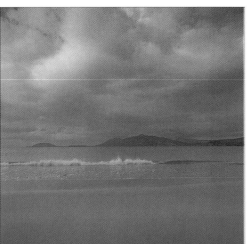

ABOVE This shot was taken at mid-morning, yet there is enough of an angle in the light from the sun to create shadow detail. The well-defined clouds have broken up what could have been a bland sky so that the general result has equal focus and visual impact in all areas.

ABOVE RIGHT The early evening sun was very low on the horizon when this picture was taken. It has just started to tinge the clouds with red and darken the golden sand. By using a wide aperture, a fast enough shutter speed could be used to capture the gently breaking waves.

LEFT This picture was taken just after the sun has risen and the quality of light is very warm, casting a golden reflection on the River Thames. The early morning mist has diffused the sun and gently bathed the scene with a sense of calm. A little prior research meant that the picture was taken at exactly the time the sun appeared between the dome of St Paul's Cathedral and the National Westminster Bank Tower. If the shot had been taken two months earlier, the sun would have appeared to the right of the tower; four months later it would have been to the left of the cathedral dome.

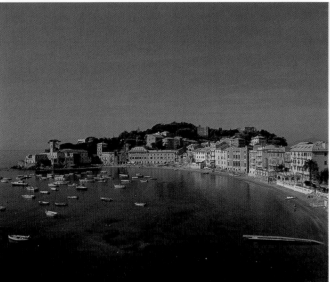

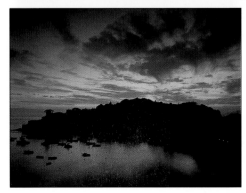

ABOVE AND LEFT These pictures were taken from the same viewpoint. The evening sky is a dramatic orange. In the morning, above, the sun is behind the camera and the light quality is much cooler. A polarizing filter was used to enhance the colour of the sea.

People in Landscapes

Landscape photography is often enhanced by the inclusion of a human figure. This technique of combining people with landscapes can be used to illustrate a particular activity in a certain area, or to show the type of landscape a person may work or live in. Human figures add scale to a particular feature of a landscape, such as a large rock or the height of a tree. Showing a person isolated within a landscape is an effective way of showing the desolate or lonely aspect of a region. On overcast days a person can help to enliven an otherwise dull situation. If the person is working try to let them continue with the task already started. Reassure the subject that he or she is a welcome part of the shot – many people assume that they are in the way and try to move out of the picture.

On a walking holiday, for instance, it might be better if your companions were seen coming through a gate or along a path while the camera is positioned on higher ground than the people to be included; but also remember not to let your shadow creep into the picture. In the early morning or late afternoon shadows will be well defined and long. If people are to feature in the foreground of a picture make sure that they do not block out an important point of interest in the middle or background. On the other hand, if there is something unsightly in the background the inclusion of a person can help conceal the object.

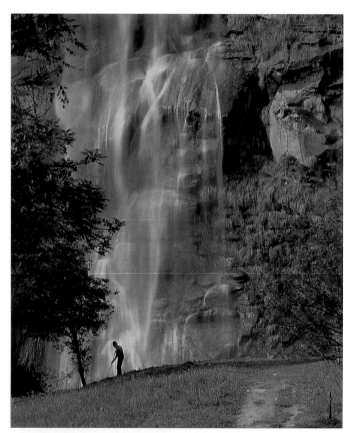

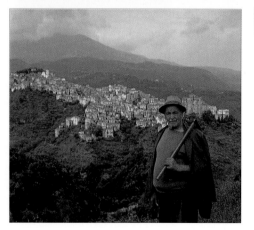

▶ **RIGHT** The shepherd in the foreground helps to create a sense of space between himself and his village. He also diverts the eye away from the overcast weather. Local people are often very pleased to be in photographs; do not be afraid to ask them to pose.

▲ **ABOVE** The man has been included in this picture to give a sense of scale; without him it would be almost impossible to tell accurately how high the waterfall is. Consider the picture without the man: the composition would be very different because the added point of interest makes a great juxtaposition to the waterfall.

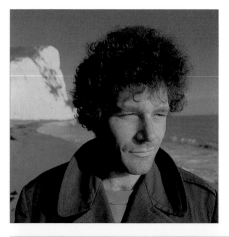

LEFT This shot was taken in the early morning light. The warm tones of the sun highlight every feature of the man's face while the cliffs behind provide both an interesting backdrop and a sense of location. This type of light would be too harsh for some people, and it may be better to wait for the position of the sun to move or to move the person into a shaded area.

BELOW This shot was taken in winter; the people standing by the seashore add a clear sense of the desolation of the beach at this time of year, yet in contrast the setting sun bathes the sky and surrounding landscape with a warm glow.

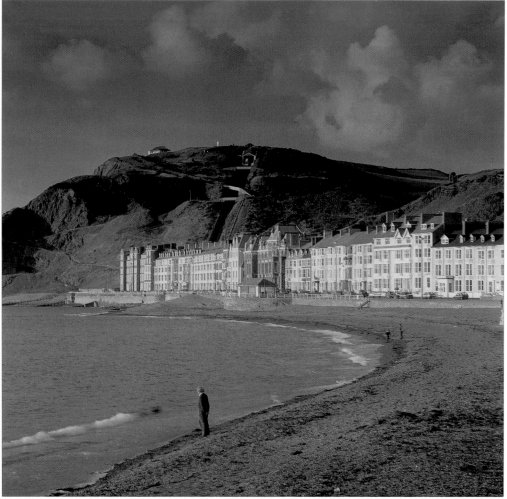

Landscapes in Black and White Film

Often a black and white photograph of a landscape can be far more evocative and dramatic than one taken in colour. However, some detail, for instance in a cloudy sky, can become flat and grey if a filter is not used. To make white puffy clouds stand out against the sky use a yellow filter. For even greater drama use a red one, which will turn the sky very dark.

A graduated neutral density filter will give a greater exposure to the sky area, thus darkening and dramatizing it compared to the land or sea below. Or, provided there is detail on the negative, the sky can be 'burnt in' at printing stage. This means giving certain areas of a print more exposure ('printing them up') or less exposure ('holding them back') than the rest of the picture by partly masking the print under the darkroom enlarger.

Another advantage of black and white for print making is that there is a range of paper grades to choose from. A print made on grade 1 paper will be soft, and one made on grade 3

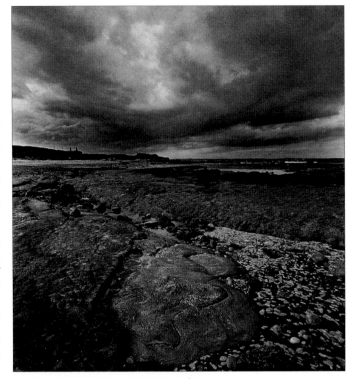

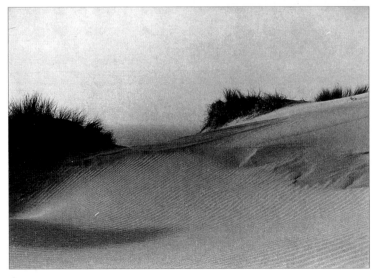

ABOVE This picture shows a good tonal range. The wide-angle lens was pointed downward to emphasize the texture of the rock in the foreground. A neutral density graduated filter was used to retain detail in the sky, and this was further emphasized when the print was made.

LEFT This high-key picture of sand dunes has an almost tactile quality. Keeping the tones to the lighter end of the range has enhanced the softness of the windswept sand and given the picture a feeling of peace. When working in conditions like these be careful that sand does not get into equipment.

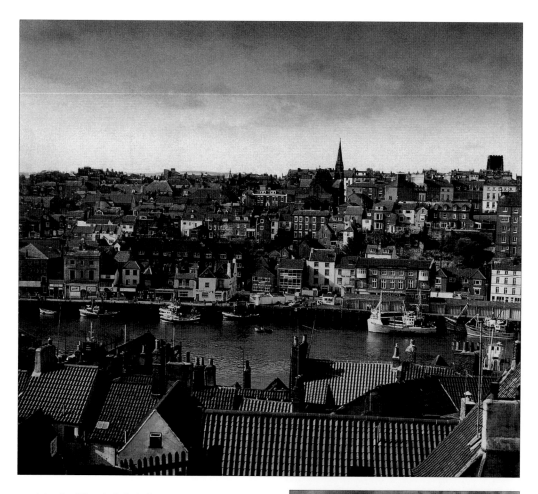

much harder. The whole feel of a picture can be altered by choice of paper.

The essence of a good black and white picture is its tonal range – not necessarily extremes of black and white. That would be a high contrast print, and it might be interesting, but subtle gradations of tone are what make a rich print.

Fine-grained film, 100 ISO or less, will give better shadow detail than faster film, and will allow far bigger enlargements to be made while retaining the quality of fine grain. Many top landscape photographers use a medium or large format camera, with the larger film size allowing them to make large prints yet retain all the subtle tones and details.

ABOVE The rooftops in the foreground add to the feeling of depth in this picture. A 150mm telephoto lens has slightly compressed the scene, bringing the town on the other side of the river closer in.

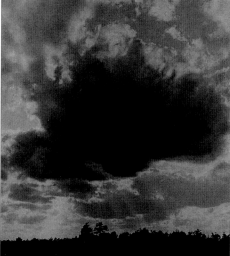

RIGHT Filters can make a dramatic difference, as this shot shows. A red filter has made the sky very dark. For a less extreme effect, a yellow filter will help to retain detail of white clouds.

Seascapes

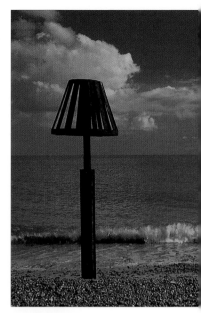

Special care must be taken when photographing seascapes, as in an environment with so many reflective surfaces the meter can be fooled into measuring the scene as brighter than it is. This can lead to underexposure and disappointing end results. To overcome this problem take a meter reading close up of the mid-tone detail.

If the camera is one with built-in autoexposure but no manual override, first decide on the composition. Then point the camera to an area of mid-tone detail such as grey rock. Depress the shutter release button half-way; this will activate the meter and the camera will record the reading. Keeping the shutter depressed in this position, move the camera back to the scene of the original composition. Now gently depress the shutter release button fully and take the picture. To take a similar picture from a different viewpoint, you will have to repeat the process for each shot.

Some cameras with a built-in autoexposure meter have a special mark on the shutter ring labelled AEL, or autoexposure lock, for taking readings like this. Its action is similar to semi-depressing the shutter release button.

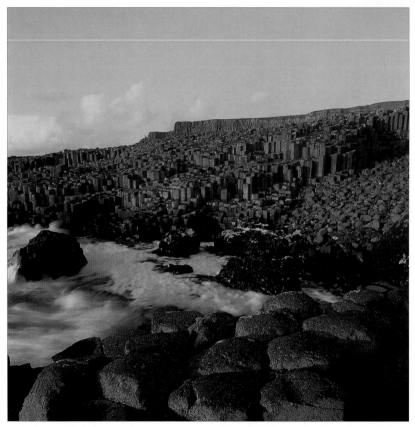

LEFT Movement in the sea at the Giants' Causeway in Northern Ireland is captured and emphasized by a slow shutter speed, to make it look as if the sea is really pounding at the unusual hexagonal rocks that are a famous landmark in this area. The rocks are lit by warm light as sunset approaches, and the strong shadows bring out these strange forms.

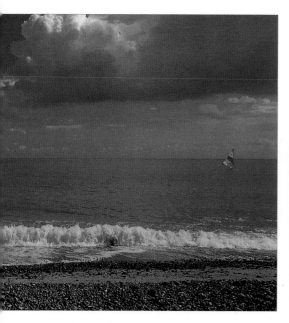

BELOW This picture was taken as a hurricane approached; in high winds it is important to hold the camera steady, perhaps bracing it on a firm surface such as a rock or low wall if you do not have a tripod. Even at relatively fast shutter speeds, such as ¹/₁₂₅ sec, camera shake will lead to blurred pictures.

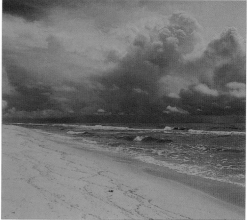

ABOVE Always look for points of interest when shooting a seascape. This unusual high tide marker creates a focal point in the foreground while the bright colours of the windsurfer's sail create a balance in the overall composition without dominating the scene. Imagine the same picture without these two elements. Would it have been as interesting?

BELOW The addition of a polarizing filter for this atmospheric shot gives the sea a translucent quality. In order to check the effect of a polarizing filter when using an SLR camera, rotate the filter while looking through the viewfinder. Turn it until the desired effect has been achieved, then take your shot.

Special kit for seascapes

1 A lens hood – this should be fitted to your camera at all times, whether or not beside the sea, but is particularly important in cutting down any unwanted reflections which may flare on the lens.

2 A polarizing filter – this makes the blue colours of the sky much richer and enhances the clarity of any small white clouds. The filter will also change the reflective nature of the surface of the sea.

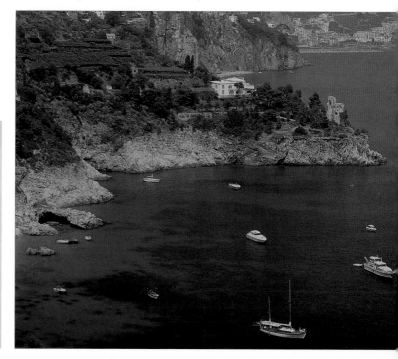

Waterways

Lakes, rivers, streams or canals offer an entirely different variety of photographic opportunities from those found by the sea and in coastal regions. The surrounding areas are often reflected in the surface of the water, adding an extra dimension to the photo and duplicating what is often the most spectacular scenery.

The same problems of measuring exposure encountered when taking seascapes also apply to pictures of large stretches of fresh or inland water; the exposure metering system may judge light as being brighter than it is because of the light coming from the expanse of reflective water. As with sea shots, compensation must be made for this in order to avoid underexposure and ruined pictures.

Take care when choosing a viewpoint for water photography. Make sure the surface, especially of rivers or canals, is free of factory effluent, waste products and debris, unless this is the detail to be highlighted.

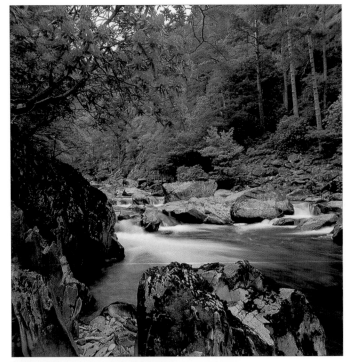

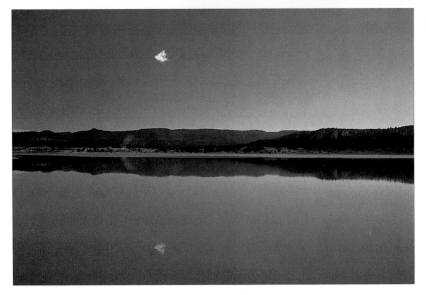

LEFT If a shot is taken very early in the morning the water surface is often quite still. This creates a perfect mirroring medium. The inclusion of the single cloud adds depth to the image as well as providing an extra point of interest, drawing the eye upwards as well as to the reflection in the water.

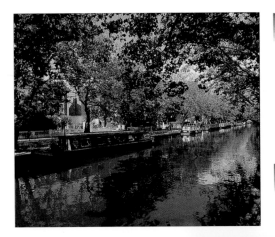

LEFT Colour and detail are not always easy to find in the composition of a water shot. Here the canal boats add bright spots of colour in what would otherwise be a rather dull stretch of water. The trees help block out unwanted buildings and provide a neat frame for the picture.

BELOW Choice of viewpoint is always of paramount importance when photographing water, especially where reflection is included. Here the dramatic picture of the reflected snow-capped mountain is altered by the plants growing beneath the water. Make sure there are no unwanted intrusions in the final shot.

LEFT This shot was taken from a rock set slightly out from the bank. The exposure used here was calculated to give maximum depth of field and the slowest possible shutter speed. This means that the rock in the foreground is very sharp while the water is blurred, emphasizing the speed at which the river is flowing.

Shooting still water

Water is usually at its stillest very early in the morning before the wind, if there is any, has begun to blow. If the surface of the water is completely still, the surrounding scenery reflected in it can produce a striking mirror image. If you are printing off your shots, try mounting the final prints vertically instead of in the conventional horizontal fashion. At first glance the picture will be a striking abstract image and many unusual and often amusing effects can be produced by a little experimentation with different presentation angles.

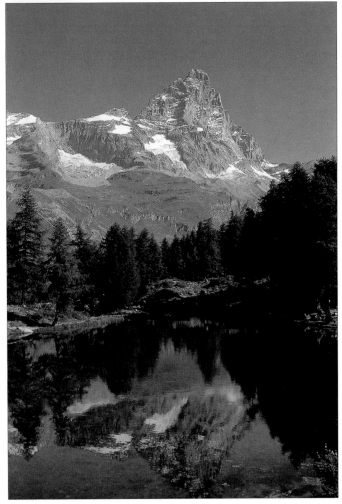

Skies

According to the time of year, the ever-changing light, weather conditions, cloud formations and seasonal changes provide an endless range of photographic opportunities when taking pictures of the sky. Although sunsets are a favourite subject for many photographers, not all sky shots need be taken at dusk, and in fact many of the most effective shots are captured at different times of the day.

The essential point to remember when photographing skies is to judge the exposure so that the important details, such as clouds, are recorded. A polarizing filter will help to darken the sky while retaining the detail if the shot is of a blue sky with puffy white clouds. A neutral density graduated filter could be used to similar effect or, for real drama, combined with the polarizing filter. As well as the neutral density graduated filter, a graduated colour filter such as a tobacco graduated filter can be added. This will turn the sky a sepia colour while retaining the natural colour of the land.

When photographing an area you know well, try to be in position early to take advantage of the changing light patterns and the different effects this has on the sky, as well as on the land or water below.

When shooting at sunset or sunrise be prepared to work rapidly as the sun moves surprisingly quickly. Also be on the lookout for the changing colour of the sky. A broad swathe of pink can quickly become a vibrant red. At sunset watch for light playing on clouds; an aura of light from these will look far more dramatic than a clear sky. As exposures will be quite long at this time of day a tripod is essential, and a cable release will also help reduce camera shake.

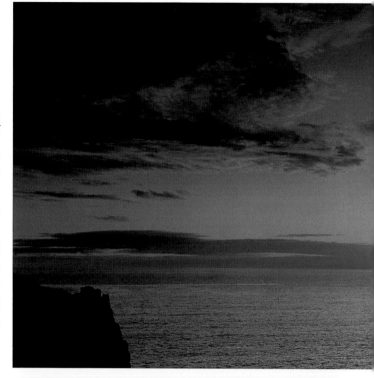

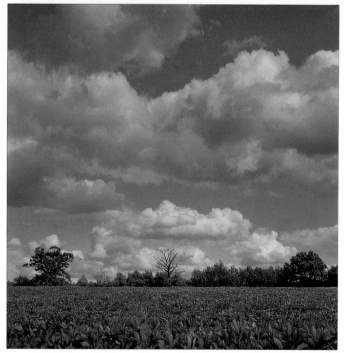

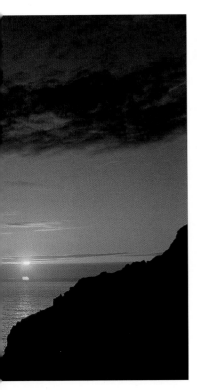

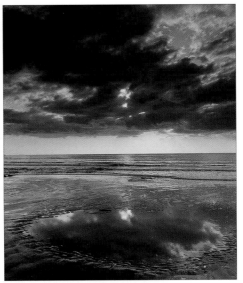

LEFT This shot was taken just before sunset. By using the small amount of water in the foreground interest is focused on the sky and the composition greatly enhanced. The backlighting on the ripples of the wet sand has added texture. In a situation like this carefully consider the reflective surface from various positions to obtain the best viewpoint.

BELOW Here there is an almost perfect mirror image of the sky captured in the surface of the sea. It is best to take this kind of picture when the water is very calm, for obvious reasons. Watch out for unsightly objects or rubbish floating in the foreground. Sometimes rubbish can float just beneath the surface and you might not notice it immediately.

ABOVE This picture was taken just before the sun set, and its light bathes the few clouds that remain in a golden aura. At this time of day a tripod is essential as the exposure required will be quite long.

LEFT By using a medium neutral density graduated filter all the detail of the clouds has been retained. A wide-angle lens combined with a low viewpoint has emphasized the sky and it dominates the picture.

Reflected skies

Skies that reflect into water, for example, make very good subjects. Either try to photograph the water when the air is completely still so that a perfect mirror image is achieved, or isolate a small area of water such as a puddle or pond to create foreground interest.

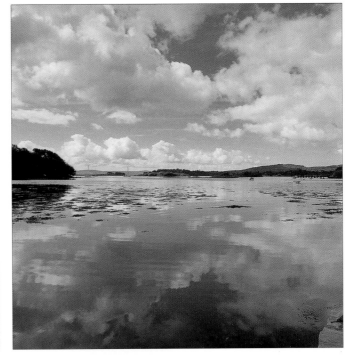

Reflections

Reflected images, whether in buildings, water or glass, can make very intriguing pictures. The majority of these can be made to look abstract and as such can be very rewarding photographs. Shop windows, car body work, modern buildings: a close look at any of these will yield a surprising number of opportunities. Examine the materials that buildings are constructed from; different types of glass will reflect in a variety of ways, for example. The many panes in an older window, for instance, will provide a multiple-image reflection. The many angles of a modern glass building mean that the image can be photographed reflected into itself. As well as creating fascinating shots of modern architecture the eye is led into a visual conundrum. Try having several prints made of such images and have half of them reversed. When they are mounted together the effect can be quite startling and a whole new range of creative possibilities opens up. This effect works equally well in black and white as well as colour.

Rain, or rather the puddles it creates, also offers many opportunities for interesting reflections. A wet road, too, can provide a strong reflective surface, but beware of flare. A reflection is a trick or effect that arches your eye. As a photographer it is up to you capture and interpret the image so that others can share your vision.

▶ **RIGHT** Well-known landmarks can look refreshingly different when photographed reflected in another surface. Always be on the look-out for modern buildings with mirror glass which, depending on the angles, will reflect itself or typical aspects of a city in a new way. Here the familiar London bus is blurred but quite recognizable although it has taken on an abstract quality.

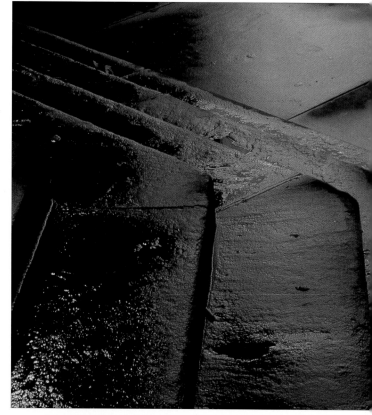

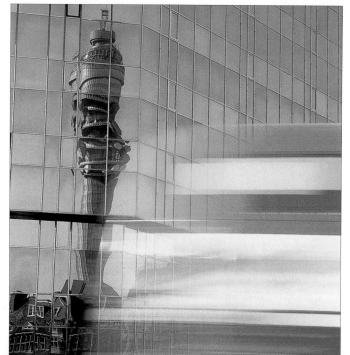

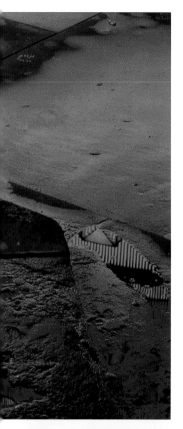

LEFT A multiplicity of reflections and neon light make this picture into a strong graphic image. This shot was taken at dusk; the same scene in daylight lacked impact. Always think about the surrounding lighting: the bright colours of neon lights, especially those in signs which are constantly changing, can give extraordinary results reflected in wet surfaces.

RIGHT This shot is a combination of reflected neon light, glass and steel which has several visual layers to it. By choosing the viewpoint with care, a strong geometrical composition is created.

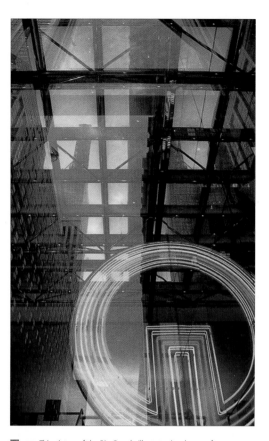

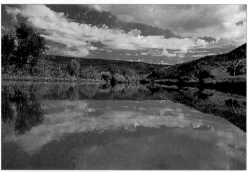

LEFT This picture of the Rio Grande illustrates just how perfect some mirror images can be. If viewed on its side the image takes on a completely different dimension. Many images lend themselves to this treatment and it is worth experimenting with aspects of presentation for a varied effect.

BELOW LEFT This shot was taken in a store window in Chinatown, Los Angeles. At first the images are confusing as it is not immediately obvious what is reflected in which surface. The green flag with the strong Chinese lettering is the backdrop to the store window, and the street scene is reflected in the window. Optical illusions of this type arouse curiosity as well as providing unique photographic images.

Travel prepared

If you make a habit of always carrying a camera, you will be ready to capture fleeting reflections. Often, changing your angle or viewpoint can lead to a more interesting reflection that other passersby might miss. Always keep your eyes, and mind, open to unusual possibilities.

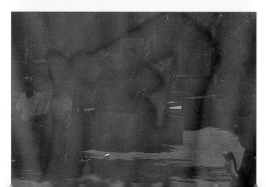

Autumn

Each season has its own unique characteristics but autumn provides the photographer with a spectacular range of rich, strong colours that lend themselves immediately to composition. Of all the seasons it is the one that lasts the shortest. Just when a tree is at its peak a strong gust of wind can blow off most of its leaves leaving it bare. Even without wind a tree will take a little over two weeks to shed its leaves so it is important to seize the opportunity quickly for photographing these tremendous colours.

As well as photographing large swathes of broad-leafed trees try to look for spots of isolated colour to provide contrast. These might be provided by a lone tree set in a landscape or a single leaf blown onto the ground.

Experiment by being aware of situations from different positions and angles. Looking up towards a blue sky can make a wonderful backdrop to golden leaves, while the use of a wide angle lens in a forest can, from a low viewpoint, make trees appear to soar skyward.

With autumn in mind, you can prepare your composition earlier in the summer, ready to shoot the new autumn colours.

BELOW Autumn is a rapidly changing season and the photographer needs to be aware of this to take full advantage of the range of shots available. A few days before this shot was taken these ferns were green. Now, the early morning light has intensified their deep rust colour. The tree in the foreground leads the eye into the picture and helps break up an almost entirely blue sky.

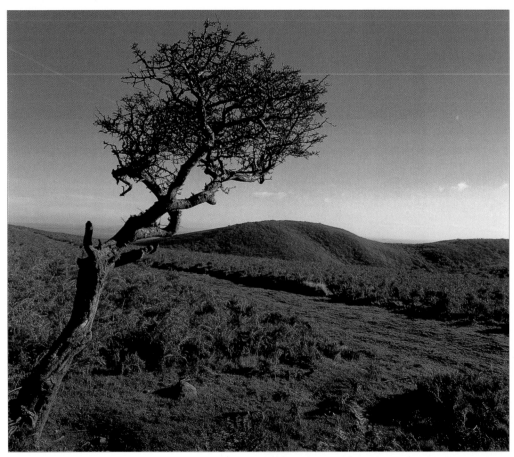

RIGHT It is not only trees and leaves that present an image of autumn: these windfall apples show what can be found by the alert photographer. Always be on the lookout for the unexpected.

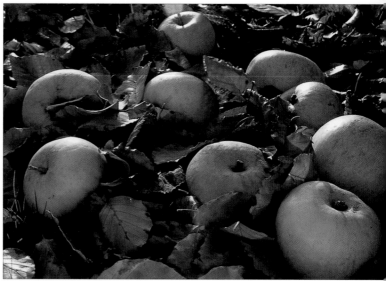

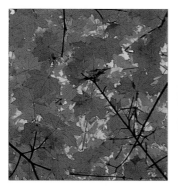

ABOVE Autumn leaves provide very good detail for close-up shots. These were photographed against the sky. If a slow shutter speed is used wind may be a problem unless the subject is shielded.

BELOW A low viewpoint is used to its full advantage here. The slender tree trunks soar skyward and their golden leaves form a colourful canopy. There is just enough light filtering through on to the foliage below to form some interesting patterns and keep the exposure even.

Photographing leaves

• Try to place leaves together and examine the contrasts in their colours, shapes and sizes.
• Consider what the leaves might look like backlit.
• When photographing leaves in close-up, so that the detail of the veins as well as the colour becomes a vital part of the image, extension rings or bellows may be necessary.
• When backlighting leaves or photographing from very close up, the leaf must be kept still. Some sort of windbreak may be needed; alternatively a modest lighting set-up can be erected indoors and the leaves arranged there. Whichever method is used, always watch out for large uninteresting shadows; these may not be very noticeable at first, but once photographed in close-up a small area may look ugly if one leaf casts a long shadow on to another.

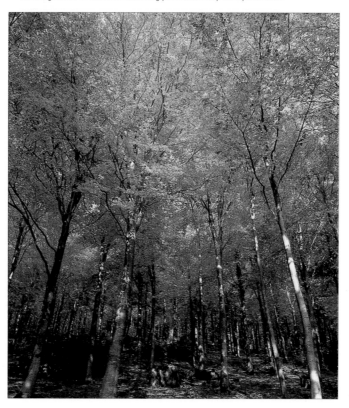

People

If you study travel photographs you will be surprised at how often you can recognize the country, even a particular city, by looking at the people in the shots. This may be something as obvious as a shot of a guard outside Buckingham Palace or a portrait of someone in front of the Eiffel Tower. But other, more ordinary forms of dress can also convey the location – especially when it is combined with local architecture.

Thanks not only to our own travels but also to television, newspapers and magazines, many places around the world are now much more familiar. Photographs which in the past would have been fascinating glimpses of exotic places are in danger of becoming mere clichés, but adding people to these views can lift them out of the ordinary.

Most local people do not mind having their photographs taken and some, such as uniformed guards, positively expect it. In all these pictures the people were unknown to the photographer, but in three of them it is clear that they were well aware of being the main focus of interest. Be aware that if you are planning to sell your shots you will need to think about model release forms, where identifiable people in your shots give their permission for their image to be used and published or sold. If you do not have signed model releases you will have to declare this when selling the image. Release forms are not always demanded by newspapers or for editorial work but usually are needed for commericial or advertising work. It is a good idea to carry release forms with you just in case, as a picture with a signed release is worth more than without.

▼ **BELOW** These people in Orvieto in Italy made a diverse group. Shots like this one can be used in a series of pictures of an area to lend it human interest.

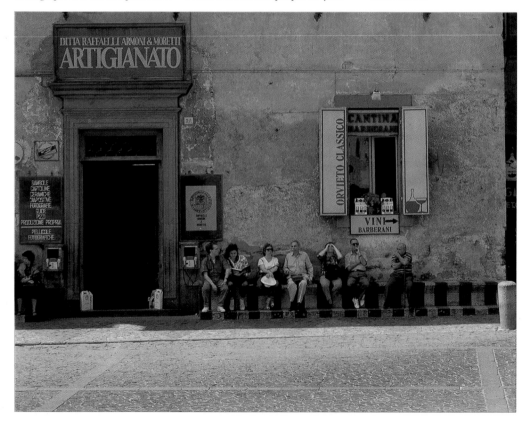

Always look out for the unexpected detail that gives the key to the location. It could be a sign on a door or a detail of a building, even something as mundane as an advertising hoarding. Clothing, as well as the overall lighting of the picture, gives a good idea of the climate of a place.

Think about viewpoint when taking pictures like these. It may be worthwhile to crouch down and take the shot from below. It will make people look more dominant than if you are looking down on them. Consider also whether it is best to have them in the centre of the frame or to one side. In the latter case, if you are using autofocus and your camera has an autoexposure lock, first point the camera at the people, semi-depress the shutter release and hold it down to lock the setting, then move the camera to the desired position and take your shot.

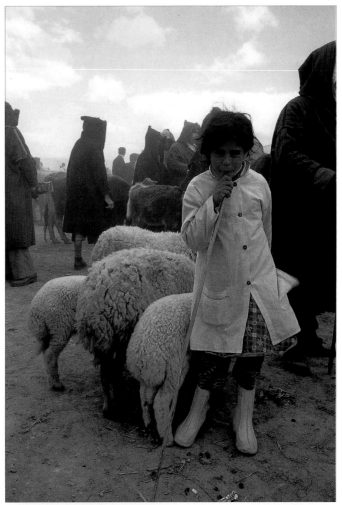

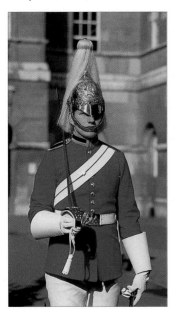

ABOVE By restricting the depth of field, the buildings in the background have been put out of focus very slightly. This has helped emphasize the guard's vivid red uniform and the fine detail on his helmet so that he becomes the focal point.

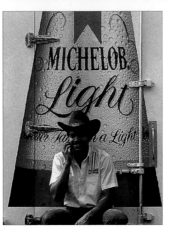

ABOVE The girl is small, but a low viewpoint has made her the centre of interest. Always think carefully about the angle from which you take your portraits. The slightest change can alter the emphasis.

LEFT The beer truck made an interesting background. Always be aware of unusual possibilities. The man was a complete stranger, but he was perfectly happy to be photographed. His clothing and the background positively shout 'America!'

People at Work

When travelling, good shots of people at work can complement scenic pictures and add an extra dimension to a record of a journey. These people pictures will often provide a more intimate insight into places visited and show what is special about a particular area, and what it is like to work there. Often, there is an interesting reaction from people to seeing a camera or being photographed, and this shows a relationship between you as the photographer, them as the workers, and the place itself. These pictures can be displayed in an album or online gallery beside pictures of landscapes, buildings and family. Shots of factories or farms which offer tours, waiters serving in a restaurant, or a craft centre with unusual items may all capture the essence of the holiday or trip and serve as a useful reference later on.

BELOW This man was one of the few professional lute makers in the world. The work is very delicate and slow; one slip of a chisel and the whole instrument could be ruined. This shot was taken by a window using the available daylight that is filtering through. The intensity of the work is reflected in his expression. A 100mm lens was used to afford a clear view of what he was doing while still keeping some distance from him so as not to disturb his concentration.

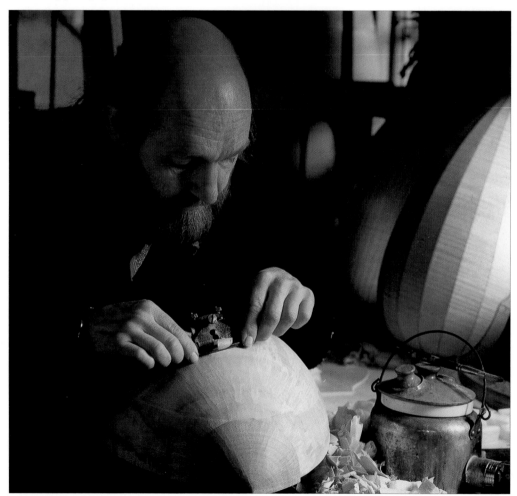

If the work that people are engaged in is very detailed, try to get in close. Remember not to get in their way and so become a nuisance.

If you are indoors and the light is low flash may be needed. Try to bounce it off the ceiling or diffuse it. Nothing is worse than a harsh blast of strong flashlight that burns out the foreground but leaves the background dark and murky. Pay attention to the background, too; does it add something to the shot? Does it provide any information about the work being done, or is it a useful plain backdrop?

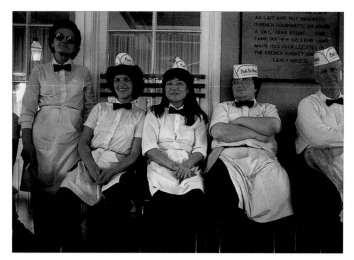

ABOVE The waiters and waitresses in this café in New Orleans are relaxing while off duty. This type of shot not only shows people in their work environment but also helps to build up an overall picture of life in a particular town or city. Try to think ahead and decide which aspects of a trip will be the most memorable and descriptive.

BELOW Always look around to examine what props are available; these are usually part of the person's work and add extra visual interest to the picture as well as providing information about the job itself. If the people to be featured in the shot seem shy, start by taking pictures of the surroundings so that they become used to a photographer's presence. Talk to them about their work. If they sense genuine interest they will soon gain confidence and appear naturally relaxed in the picture.

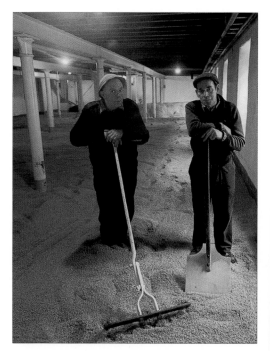

ABOVE These men work in the malting room of a whisky distillery on the Orkney Islands of Scotland. By including their work implements in the picture a clear image of their job is captured as well as adding an air of spontaneous activity. The same implements also served as convenient resting posts while the men steadied themselves during the long exposure.

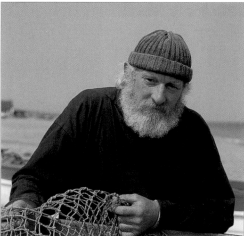

Local People

People will add colour to travel pictures, especially when featured in shots presented alongside others concentrating on landscape, architecture or the sea. A series of pictures of the people of a locality can form a portrait of life in that region. To catch the spirit of local life and activities, go in close so that people are related to their work or environment.

When photographing strangers politeness is the key. If people are approached in a friendly and reassuring way only the most recalcitrant will object to being photographed. Remember, though, that in some

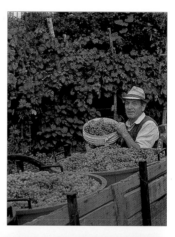

▶ **RIGHT** Being quick to spot a good shot and seize the moment is the essence of a good travel shot. This grape grower was seen driving his tractor laden with grapes down a country lane. He agreed to be photographed, and a series of portraits was taken in the late afternoon sun.

▼ **BELOW** Close cropping of these soldiers emphasizes their rich uniforms, and the gold of the gates behind them forms an effective backdrop. As events like this happen on a daily basis in most capital cities, you will have many opportunities to shoot opulent-looking local ceremonies.

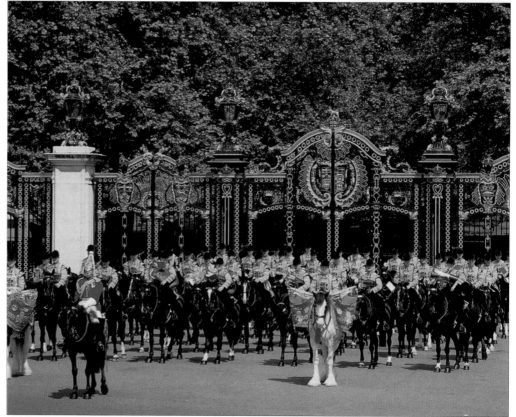

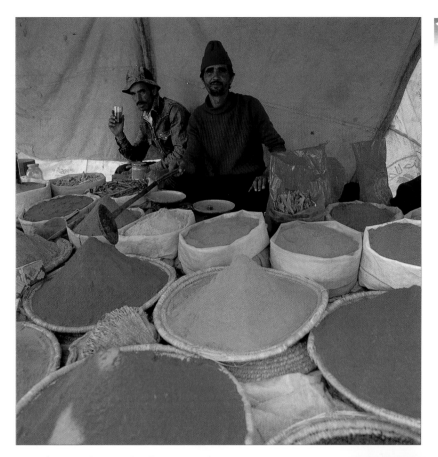

parts of the world it is inadvisable to photograph people – or even to make drawings of them. In some cultures there is a belief that if people are photographed their soul is removed. However strange such an opinion may seem it is important to respect it. Remonstrating with people will only make matters worse. It would be far more productive to find someone in authority and use your best diplomatic skills to get them to reassure and persuade your subjects to give their assent. In most cases such an approach, aided perhaps by a small gift, will win the day. A very effective method is to offer them a Polaroid portrait. If you are using a digital camera you can at least show them the images you have taken on the screen, which is enough for most people.

RIGHT Careful selection of colour will say much about the climate of a locality. It does not always have to be vivid; here the colours are muted but give a feeling of warmth. This shepherd was spotted by chance on a drive through a remote part of Sicily. Although his sheep were giving him and his dog problems he readily agreed to be photographed. His clothes convey the feeling of someone who works out of doors, and his hat indicates that the climate is hot, protecting him from the strong sunlight. Such ingredients in photographs put across a sense of place.

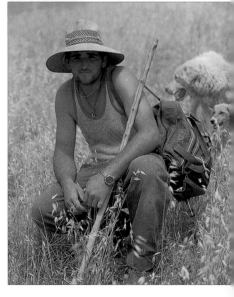

Flora

Plants provide good material for the photographer. It is worth considering not only exotic plants but also more commonplace varieties. Apart from colour, texture plays an important part in a striking image. All plants look their best at a certain time of year. If any plant is of particular interest, check when it is in season, especially if you have to travel any distance to photograph it.

Original effects can be created by isolating one plant in a mass of others, perhaps using the shallow depth of field afforded by a telephoto lens. There are other opportunities for unusual viewpoints; for instance a plant or group of flowers, or even trees in the foreground of a scene adds interest in its own right and can also mask an unwanted object that would otherwise spoil the picture.

Close-ups

- If you are taking close-ups of flowers, depth of field will be very small, especially if you are using extension rings or bellows. You will therefore need to stop down as much as possible, and to use a long exposure. If there is even the slightest breeze the plant will have to be sheltered from it, or it will sway and blur the picture.
- Lighting can also be a problem when working so close. If you are using available daylight you must take care not to cast a shadow from yourself or your equipment. A ring flash could be a useful accessory. This gives powerful but almost shadowless illumination. The flash tube forms a complete ring around the lens. Units for 35mm cameras are quite compact and do not weigh very much.
- A tripod is essential because of the length of exposures.
- Details of trees and other plants are also excellent subjects for close-up shots. The texture of bark can be fascinating, and different shots can be mounted together to make a striking collage.

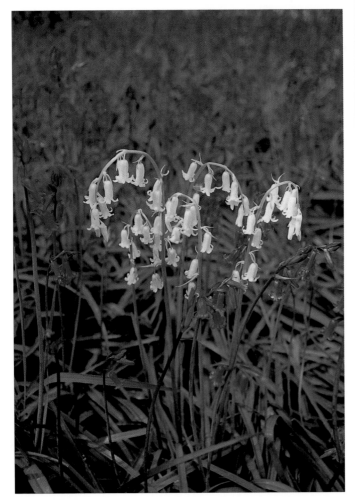

LEFT Look for the unusual. There will always be something of interest on a country walk. This whitebell was growing alone in a sea of ordinary bluebells. Careful use of depth of field has put the background out of focus, making the flower even more prominent in the picture.

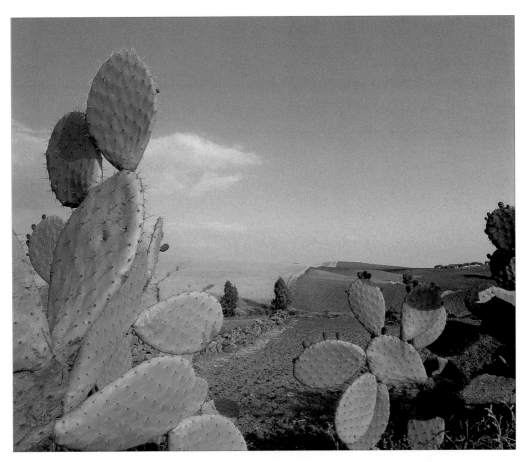

ABOVE These cacti in the foreground frame the view. Not only do plants in the foreground add to the composition, they can also be used to hide unsightly objects.

BELOW The texture of tree bark can be very satisfying to photograph, especially when several varieties are mounted together. A whole series of pictures can be built up over the years. This applies equally to many other natural forms. If you can, keep a record of the type of tree you have photographed and label the images.

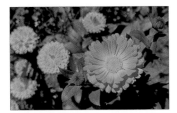

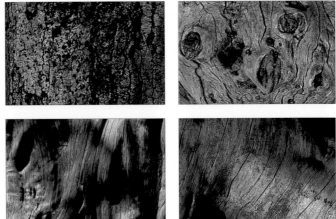

ABOVE By using extension rings it was possible to get very close to this marigold. Depth of field was very limited and a long exposure was needed. This meant that the camera had to be mounted on a tripod and a shield used to protect the plant from wind, so that it did not move and blur the picture.

Wild Animals and Birds

One of the most demanding areas of photography is that of wild or semi-wild animals. Patience is required, and a certain amount of forward planning is useful if not essential. Despite the arduous nature of this type of work, the rewards can certainly make it worthwhile.

While most people do not have the opportunity to travel to the regions best suited to photography of big game, rare birds or endangered species, many live within reach of a farm, safari or wildlife park. Also don't discount your back garden, local park or even city streets and skies. A robin feeding from a bird table in your back garden can, if photographed with care, be a really great image, and a flock of birds in a dusk

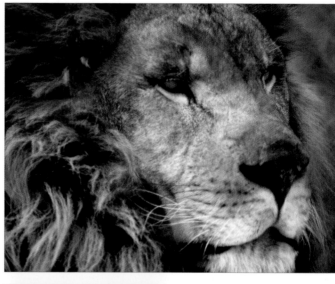

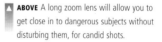
ABOVE A long zoom lens will allow you to get close in to dangerous subjects without disturbing them, for candid shots.

sky interspersed with the static silhouettes of an urban skyline can be truly evocative.

Of course, the chance to shoot wildlife in its natural habitat, such as a tropical forest or African savannah, is even more rewarding, and certainly an experience not to be missed if you are given the opportunity.

When you do leave the comfort of your back garden or local park, some shots will require going to a hide where you can sit and wait for animals to appear. Other subjects can be shot directly from your car – but remember whether by foot or car, any time you approach wildlife do so with great care and respect for the animals. You risk losing a good shot if you scare an animal, but more importantly you may endanger a habitat, a brood of young or even yourself.

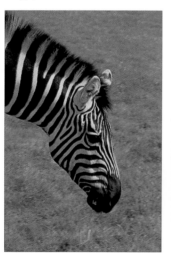
ABOVE If taking a photograph in a safari or wildlife park or zoo, a natural image is perfectly possible as long as the background includes relevant vegetation rather than an unsightly man-made intrusion. A close-up shot can be obtained without frightening the animal by using a 100mm lens.

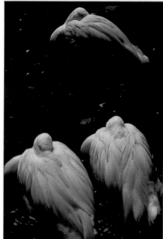
ABOVE Small details are always most effective, especially when photographing fauna. These flamingoes look as if they are asleep yet a careful look at the far bird shows that its eye is open. This shot was taken with a 250mm lens since if the camera had been positioned any closer the birds would have moved away.

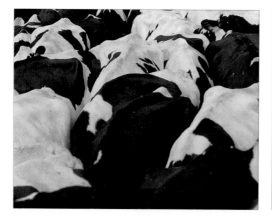

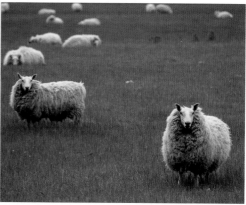

ABOVE This shot of cattle was taken in close from a higher viewpoint. All detail has been cropped out leaving only the black and white hides visible. This technique produces some effective graphic images that usually need a second look before the viewer realizes what the apparently abstract image is.

ABOVE Look for form and patterns in everyday scenes. You will be surprised at the opportunities that the wildlife and domestic animals around you present. Although it would be exciting to be on an African safari, the sheep on the local farm still have something to offer the keen photographer.

RIGHT This shot was taken from a low viewpoint with a wide-angle lens. This produces a dramatic image of the sky. By getting into position and being patient it is relatively easy to obtain effective and at times amusing shots of certain animals, whose natural curiosity means that they eventually come close to the camera for a better look. In this shot, the shutter was fired when the cow was about 1m (3ft) from the camera.

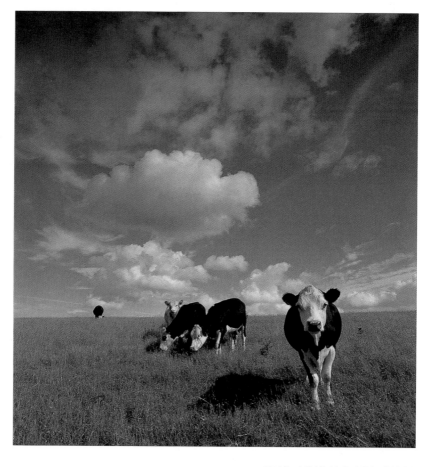

Photographing either birds or land-based wildlife often requires great patience, but waiting for the right shot means spending time in the outdoors which can be rewarding in itself. Of course, when you do manage to capture an animal on your camera, you may be lucky enough to get powerful images of animals in their natural settings that many people will not have seen before.

When photographing wild animals there are some general points that will help you.
• Spend some time observing the behaviour of the animal; watch to see whether it is easily startled, or whether it appears to move in a constant direction.
• Try to select a viewpoint with an interesting background without unsightly fences or buildings.
• Be patient. Calling or gesturing to

an animal will probably cause it to run in the opposite direction. Upsetting wild animals can also be dangerous: however docile they may seem it is important to remember that they are wild. It is best to avoid annoying both the animal and the farmer or gamekeeper.

Your camera
Choose a camera that will give you high quality images even when you crop the final picture, and has a fast frame per second rate as this will allow you to shoot a burst of images quickly to capture the animals as they move. In terms of equipment, although you can photograph wild animals with your compact camera, to capture very powerful photographs, it can help to have certain accessories.

Lenses
It is going to be difficult to get close to the animals you wish to shoot, so you will need a telephoto lens. The best solution is to have a zoom telephoto lens as this will allow you to

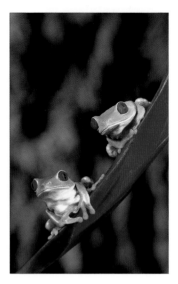

▲ **ABOVE** Patience and a camera set up ready can lead to wonderful shots with a very shallow depth of field to set a subject away from an otherwise distracting background.

capture the animal without too much surrounding detail and will avoid you having to move backward or forwards

▼ **BELOW** For some shots you need a very long lens to get your picture safely. Here the tiger has seen the photographer, but is too far off to be interested.

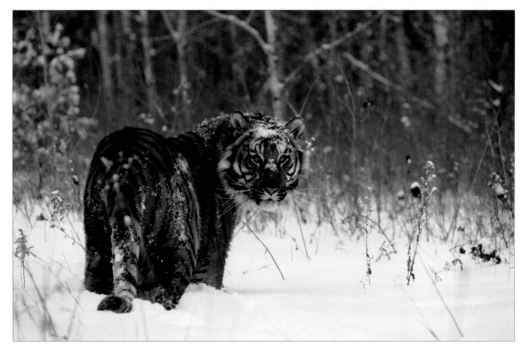

to frame the shot, as you would have to with a fixed focal length. A zoom lens with an equivalent focal length of 70 to 200mm is ideal.

Tripods or supports

Support for your camera and lens is essential for wildlife photography. Depending on where you are shooting from this may be a traditional tripod, a monopod, a beanbag support or a window clamp.

As some of the lenses you will use are fairly long and heavy you may find that you prefer to have the lens supported, not the camera and there are various options for this from lens and camera support manufacturers.

If you are using any form of support the head you use is very important. You need to choose a head that, while providing all the support you need, allows you to move the camera freely and quickly. For this a ball head is a good option, but if you use very long lenses of over approximately 300mm a gimbal style head is the best type. It gives great support for your long lenses and allows speed of movement

▶ **RIGHT** Interaction between groups of animals is fascinating, and gives a truthful insight into their behaviours.

▼ **BELOW** If you know where a photogenic animal lives, you can set up your own camera and wait for the perfect picture.

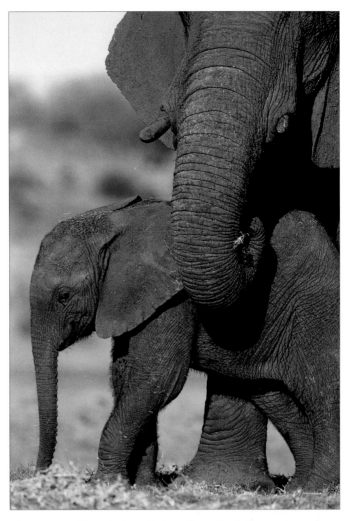

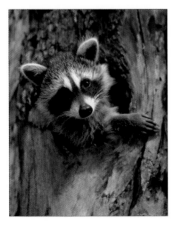

where necessary. The only downside is that these very specialist supports can be expensive.

Bags and protection

Often you may find yourself waiting, or taking pictures in the wind and rain and in these cases you need to protect your precious camera gear. Some cameras and lenses are more waterproof than others but you can take this protection much further, with products such as camera armour that protect your gear from knocks and bumps, and waterproof covering for body and lens alike that still allows for full control over your equipment. Don't forget about yourself – a dry photographer is a much happier photographer.

It's also a good idea to have a strong camera bag that will protect you gear from both wet conditions and any hard knocks. Many rucksacks come with waterproof covers that either are attached to the base or come as a separate package. Some bags are made out of more waterproof materials than others, with better zip systems. Some bags can actually be completely immersed in water and still keep the contents dry.

Make sure that you use a bag you are confident about putting your expensive camera gear into. Your bag also needs to be big enough to hold all of your accessories, so if possible visit your camera store, with the equipment you have and check if it fits before you make a purchase. If you know you'll be on location with your bag, can it hold a water bottle and is there room for food and a jacket? Don't forget to check whether you can comfortably attach your tripod to your bag as this frees up your hands.

Extras

Although wildlife photography involves much waiting, when the photo opportunity does arise you want to be able to shoot lots of frames without worrying about running out of film or memory, so have as much as you can to hand – film or memory are often the least expensive part of any camera bag. Also remember to have spare camera batteries and a lens cleaning kit.

If you shoot digitally, and you are on location all day, shooting lots of pictures, you may also find it useful to

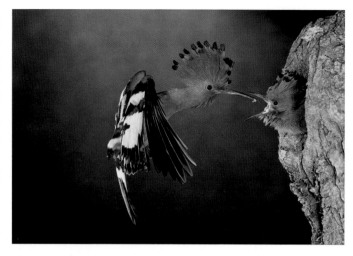

ABOVE A very fast shutter speed and a quick eye can lead to stunning shots. Waiting for a perfect shot like this takes patience.

have a portable storage device where you can upload pictures from your full memory cards. This way you will not run out of memory space and you'll know the pictures you've taken are safely stored. Some of the more expensive versions of these memory drives have colour screens that allow you to preview your shots.

Hides

As the name suggests, hides are little structures where you wait under camouflage in order to get better shots of local wildlife. Some locations will

have permanent hides installed, especially where wild birds are known to congregate, but you can also buy your own domed hides that are easy to erect and travel around with.

If you are shooting from your car some sort of camouflage material to cover the window is a great bonus, as this will allow you to see out but keep you and your shiny camera hidden from your target wildlife.

Getting great shots

So once you have all of your gear, and you are on location how do you get the best shots? Once again, it is about planning and patience. You need to decide where you want to shoot from and in some cases exactly what it is you are going to shoot, then get in position and wait for that perfect opportunity. Sometimes it can take hours, or even days!

Watch the behaviour of the animals to see where may be your best place to work from. In the case of birds, look to see if there is a pattern to the direction they fly in and where they land and perhaps try to get into a position that will allow you a front-on shot of the landing.

BELOW Capturing the bird from a lower angle can let the viewer see a rare angle.

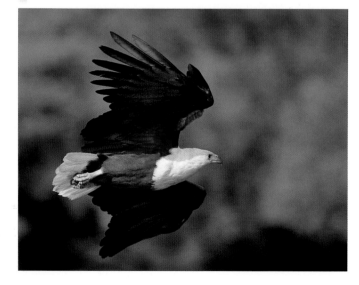

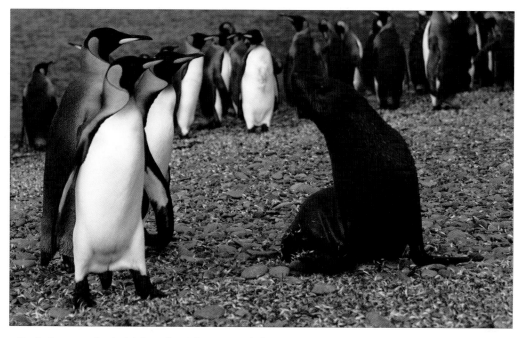

Don't shoot an animal with lots of distracting background, use a shallow depth of field to separate it from its surroundings, take interesting angles and crops, shoot lots but don't shoot wildly. In other words, wait for the right moment before you press the shutter. Shoot both wide and close up shots, as the wider shots can tell the story which you can then unfold with the close-in pictures. Don't always shoot animals in isolation – just as

with people, sometimes groups of animals and their interaction with each other can be very interesting. At times, the interaction between the animal and the people watching it can be fascinating too.

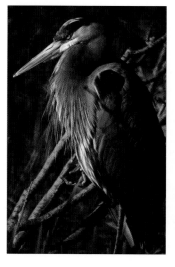

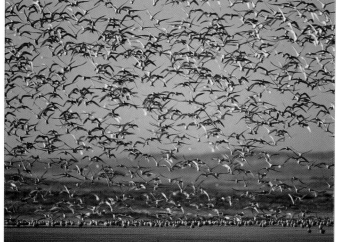

Pets

Pets are always a favourite subject. Before you start to photograph them, it is most important to realize that although pets cannot speak they do have ways of communicating. If you endlessly try to get a dog to do something it does not want to do, it is never going to look happy and the shot will betray its mood. Eventually it will snap at you or even bite. You do have to take this seriously, especially if you are using pets and children together. Both get bored quickly, and when the session is no longer a game for them, stop.

So you will need to work quickly. An autofocus lens and TTL exposure control will be an asset. Very often it is the fleeting expression that makes the shot. Going in close helps to capture this. A medium telephoto lens, say 100mm, would be a good choice. This will help to fill the frame without getting too close to your subjects and disturbing them.

Try to avoid dressing animals up. The best shots are natural ones, not dogs wearing dresses.

As well as shots for the album or framing, pictures of pets are ideal for Christmas and birthday cards.

Most animals grow faster than we do. Keep photographing them: taking a shot every month of your puppy or kitten will form an interesting record of its development.

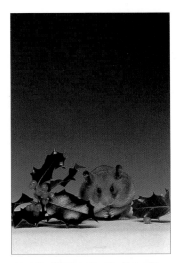

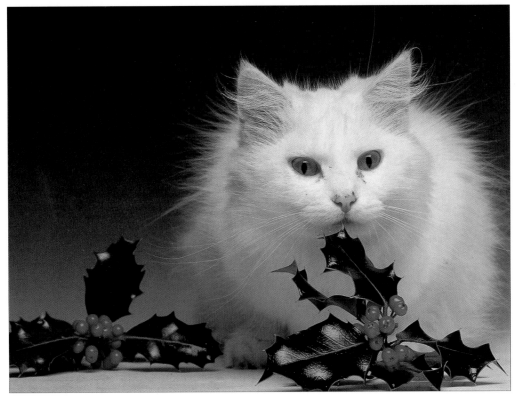

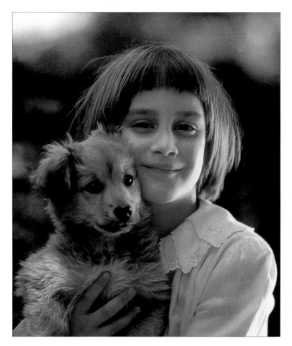

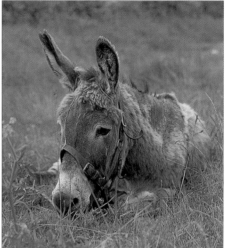

BELOW Some pets are more docile than others. This donkey in Ireland allowed plenty of time to move around and choose the best viewpoint. The background is blurred by using a wide aperture and fast shutter speed. The donkey's face is sharp and crisp, and the shot was taken just as it pricked up its ears.

ABOVE Children with pets usually make very good subjects for photographs. But in both of the subjects' cases their attention soon wanders. When you see either tiring or becoming agitated it is time to stop.

RIGHT The dog looks alert and the fishing net makes an interesting prop. Autofocus and TTL exposure metering help you to work quickly when photographing pets.

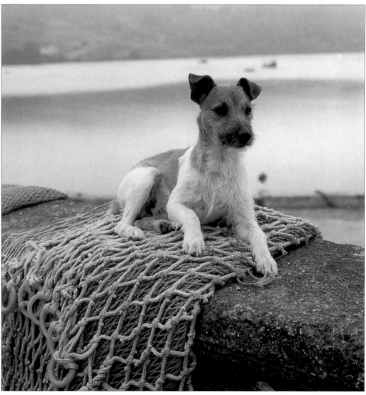

LEFT AND ABOVE LEFT These are ideal shots for a homemade Christmas card. A simple prop such as the holly used here is all that was needed to set the scene. The backdrop is a graduated one shading from white to black, and the scene is lit by flash.

Buildings: General Composition

Buildings present the photographer with an inexhaustible supply of imagery. The most important part of photographing any building is the general composition. The weather can be perfect, the exposure correct and the time of day just right, but a badly framed picture will ruin everything. Here, equipment can be a great help. A telephoto lens can bring closer a distant building and also, depending on the power of the lens, compress the view and so reduce the illusion of space between the main building in the shot and those surrounding it.

A wide-angle lens allows a broader view of an area, and even when the main subject matter is just one small building, it is often interesting and can be important to show the area around it as well. A wide angle can also allow a close-up shot with an exaggerated perspective.

A tall building can appear even taller if the camera is pointed upwards because the verticals will converge, although often these converging verticals are important to avoid.

Wide-angle lenses often display more distortion than standard and longer ones, so if choosing a wide lens make sure you choose one with the least distortion possible.

A shift lens allows the photographer to avoid converging verticals in situations where these are not wanted in the shot. A shift lens alters the axis of view without the need to move the camera, yet allows movement of the lens in relationship to the film plane.

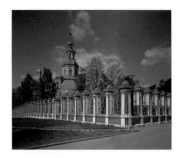

ABOVE The railings around the church form a frame for this picture and produce a pleasing composition. Although a wide angle lens was used the viewpoint was close enough to prevent the church receding too far into the distance. The puffy white clouds help to break up the blue sky and enhance the composition, adding another visual element.

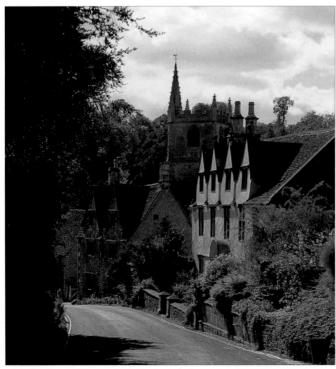

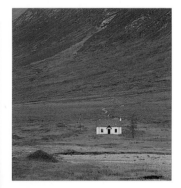

ABOVE A telephoto lens was used for this shot of an isolated Scottish house; the top of the mountains that form the backdrop was deliberately cropped out. By composing a picture in this way the isolation is emphasized and becomes a particular point of interest.

LEFT A small telephoto lens of 100mm was used for this shot. This slightly compresses the buildings making the composition very tight. Ensure that any unwanted intrusions have been moved before taking the shot, or try to stand in a position where they would be cropped out of the frame.

RIGHT By waiting until dusk a certain quality of light is captured; here the tower is bathed in a warm glow. The reflection of the building in the water helps to give a greater illusion of height. The use of a shift lens means that there are no converging verticals, yet the whole building still fits the frame. Remember to ensure when photographing modern buildings that light is not reflected off their exterior surfaces and into the camera lens.

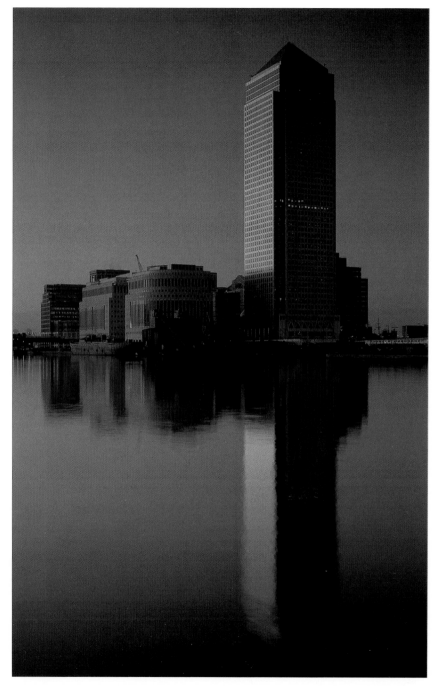

Buildings: Exteriors

Sometimes it seems enough to simply stand in front of a great building, point the camera and press the shutter, especially if the building is so famous that there does not seem to be anything to add. In many cases this may be true, but if everyone followed this path the results would be repetitive and tedious. There are always new ways of representing a familiar object: unusual angles, different lighting conditions, a section of an exterior. All these elements can enhance a photograph of a building.

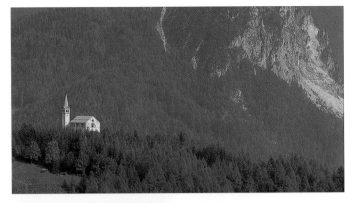

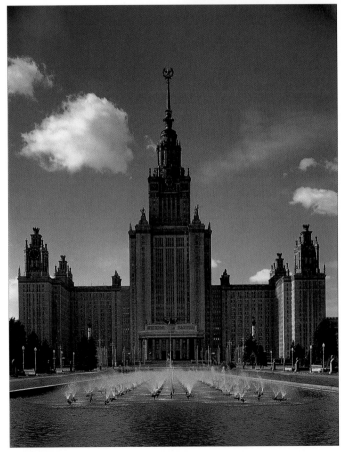

Atmospheric details

• Time of day is an important consideration when photographing buildings. If, from a chosen viewpoint, the sun rises behind the building, this could result in a hazy image making the building look rather flat. If there is time, wait until the sun moves round, perhaps bathing the building in a warm afternoon light and creating strong shadow detail.
• Clouds can provide an added dimension. Sometimes even a radiantly blue sky will benefit from a few puffy white clouds above a building. Also, billowing storm clouds will add drama and perhaps a somewhat theatrical appearance to the shot.

LEFT The New University in Moscow was photographed when the sun was at its highest and therefore illuminating the exterior evenly. A shift lens was used so that the full height of the tower could be included in the shot without needing to tilt the camera upwards. This would have caused converging verticals.

LEFT Isolated in a mountain range, this white church stands out in a shaft of sunlight. This shot was taken after waiting for half an hour while a cloud obscured the sun; without the sunlight the scene was flat and uninteresting. It is always worth waiting patiently for changes in the light to obtain a better photograph.

BELOW By standing to one side of this street a rather ugly wall was cropped out. A medium telephoto lens, 135mm, was used and has slightly compressed the buildings and brought closer the fields in the background. This has produced a tight composition with the emphasis on the row of housing without any unsightly distractions.

BELOW This shot was taken using a medium telephoto lens. The buildings in the foreground enhance the cathedral of Siena as it stands majestically over them, dominating the skyline. The whole city is bathed in late afternoon light which adds warmth and enhances the predominantly terracotta hues of the buildings.

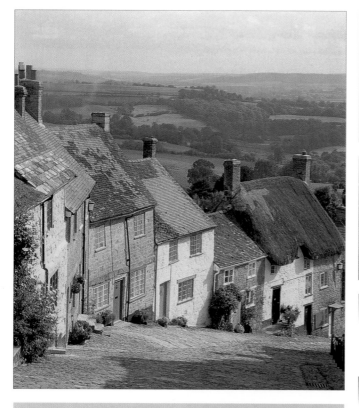

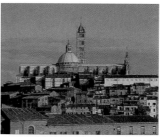

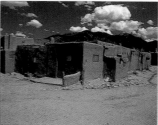

ABOVE The white puffy clouds, enhanced by a polarizing filter, hang gently over these adobe buildings at Taos, New Mexico, and help to provide extra detail. They also break up the rather monochromatic shot.

Shooting verticals

• Different lenses can completely alter the perspective of a building. Pointing the camera upwards, at a skyscraper for instance, will make the verticals converge. This can add greatly to the dynamic qualities of the image.
• On the other hand, another building could be shown with converging verticals and might look distorted, seeming to be in danger of toppling over. Every building composition should be assessed individually.
• A telephoto lens can be used to photograph a building from a distance. The building can be brought closer and the foreground compressed. This will give the impression of increased grandeur to the main building in the shot.
• For more specialist photography of very tall buildings a shift lens can be used. This allows a building to be photographed so that its vertical lines remain upright without needing to tilt the camera upwards. This would create converging verticals.

BELOW This picture of a skyscraper shows the extreme effect of converging verticals. By pointing the camera upwards the height of the building has been exaggerated and its sides appear to meet at a point in the sky. A wide-angle lens has helped emphasize this.

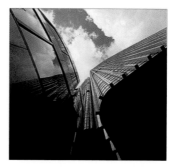

Buildings: Interiors

One of the main points to consider before photographing the interior of a building is the amount of light available. In the majority of cases this is very little compared to outdoors. Our eyes are adept at adjusting to different light conditions, so we soon cease to notice that certain conditions are rather dull. The only way to record a usable image is to increase the exposure or to light the interior artificially by using flash. Many cameras have built-in flash or a flash attachment connected to the hot shoe of the camera or to a bracket on one side of the camera body. However, even with the most powerful of these flash units there still may not be enough light to illuminate the interiors of very large buildings. When you do want to light the interior of such a building, more powerful studio-style flash heads that are either plugged into the mains or powered by large batteries are used.

With film, even where a fast film is used with available light the result is very grainy and much of the shadow detail will be lost. A far better solution is to mount the camera on a tripod and use a long exposure. Of the pictures shown on this page none was shot on film faster than 64 ISO, and in only one picture was flash also used.

If you do use the natural light only, care needs to be taken when windows or the outside are shown in the shot as you may find that by getting the right exposure for the interior, the windows are blown out. To show detail in both the interior and the windows you will need to use artificial light for balance.

Inside monuments crowded with visitors some extra thought should be given to viewpoint if you don't want people in your shot, although when shooting on a tripod with a long exposure some of the moving people will be so blurred as to disappear from your image. In some monuments tripods are not permitted; so use a monopod or find a firm surface, such as a pew, floor, table or window sill.

Where possible, when photographing buildings, inside or out, use a tripod. It will help to frame your picture perfectly and help ensure that your picture is pin sharp and still allows for a good depth of field by using a smaller aperture. It also helps make sure that all the lines in your image are straight. To help even further, if your camera allows it, you can replace the focusing screen with one that has grid lines on it. Details like these will help take your photography to the next level.

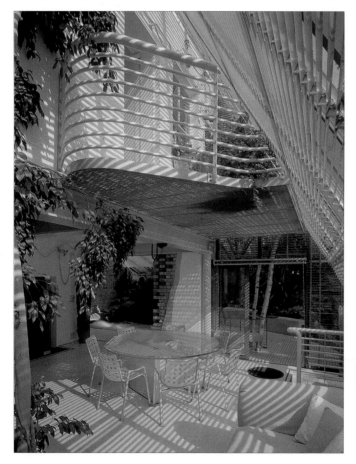

LEFT This interior was shot entirely in natural light. The blinds were angled to let in as much sun as possible while at the same time using them as a creative tool to cast very effective constrasting stripes of shadow. The result is a an architectural, man-made interior bathed in bright natural sunlight.

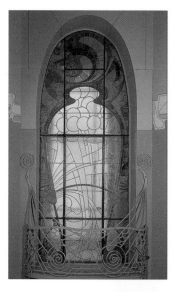

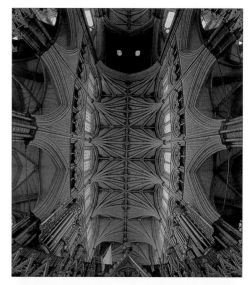

RIGHT By using a fisheye lens, an unusual angle of the ceiling of Westminster Abbey has been achieved. Even though the Abbey was opened to the public, tilting the camera upwards means that people have been cropped out. The day was overcast so there are no strong shadows on the sides of the buildings. This made the exposure relatively even, although long, and no other lighting was required.

ABOVE In this shot the window is illuminated by the light outside. This was not powerful enough to illuminate the walls inside without losing the detail of the stained glass. By balancing the exposure of the flash on the walls with the light coming in, an even exposure was achieved.

RIGHT Flash is forbidden in the Long Room in the Old Library of Trinity College, Dublin, so available light was used. The shot was taken from the balcony to add a feeling of depth. If the shot had been taken from ground level the camera would have to have been tilted upwards and this would have led to converging verticals.

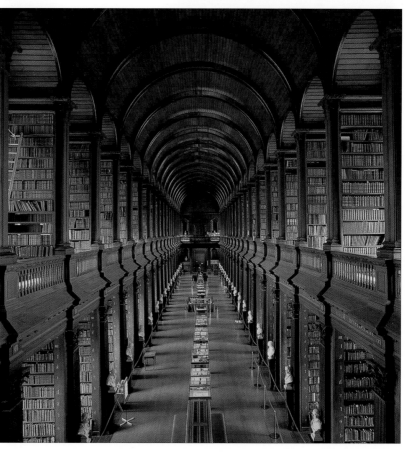

Buildings: Details

Buildings provide many opportunities for the photographer to create exciting and, in many ways, unusual images of scenes that are always present but which the majority of people pass by without noticing. Sometimes it is not always possible or beneficial to include a building in its entirety in a single photograph. In some cases the building may be quite dull to look at, and it is only by isolating a small section of carving or ceramics, for instance, that a strong and worthwhile shot will be obtained.

The time of day can play an important part in photographing details. When the sun is low or at an acute angle to the subject strong shadows will be created. This can enhance the graphic qualities and result in unusual, if not abstract, images.

It will be rare that an interesting angle cannot be found for even the most plain and mundane building, and in the majority of cases what makes a photograph 'good' is the amount of time the photographer has spent looking for an unusual point of view, often going in close on detail and framing the picture to hide or crop unwanted intrusions. In certain cases close-up shots of architectural detail may, over a period of time, provide a series of pictures that could be used together or to form a collection of individual themes or styles. With interior details precise framing can be important and it would be beneficial to use a tripod. This is not just in instances where there may be less light and so longer exposures will be necessary, but also in situations where

symmetry is a key element, for example with a vaulted ceiling. Nothing is worse than seeing a final image where care has been taken with exposure and general composition but where one of four pillars, for example, is not quite square. With a tripod this 'squaring up' can be achieved with a greater degree of precision than can be expected with a hand-held camera.

RIGHT Churches in particular provide many photographic opportunities. Details of figures, columns, masks and stone work could over a period of time form the basis of a historical collection. A photograph like this says more about the spirituality and beliefs behind the building, as well as commenting on its age and ultimate deterioration, than a shot of the whole building from a distance could do.

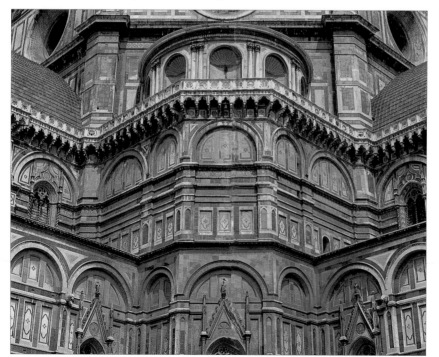

LEFT It was impossible to fit the whole of Florence cathedral into a single shot. Also the unsightly aspects of mass tourism seemed at odds with this majestic building. By concentrating on one section and pointing the camera up, the shot shows the uninterrupted beauty of the stone work.

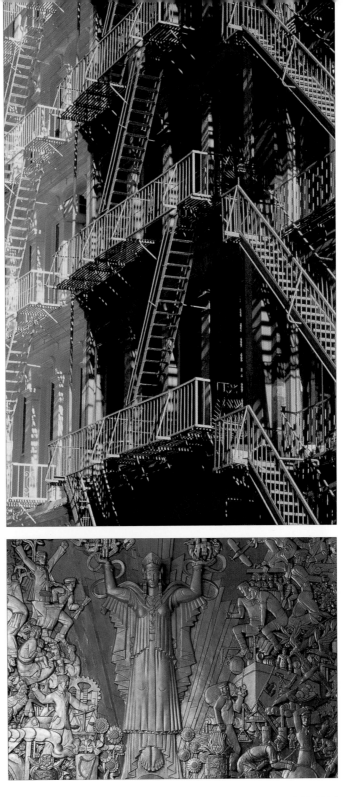

RIGHT By going in close on these New York fire escapes and taking advantage of the low afternoon winter sun, a strong graphic image has been created. If the lower part of the building had been included the result would have been less abstract and less dramatic.

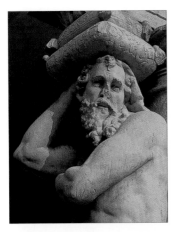

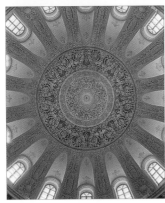

ABOVE This building had been converted into mundane offices with uninspiring furniture. The ceiling, in contrast, had been preserved and by choosing the viewpoint with precision and mounting the camera on a tripod, a perfectly symmetrical image was achieved.

RIGHT The hallway of the old *Daily Express* newspaper building in London's Fleet Street is one of the capital's greatest Art Deco interiors. To show the detail of this metallic mural it was lit from one side. If the light had been directly in front the picture would have looked flat and 'hot spots' would inevitably have appeared.

Buildings at Night

Urban buildings seen at night can often be far more evocative of a cityscape than they appear to be in daylight hours. Some cities, such as New York, seem to literally throb at night and are lit for the great part by garish neon light which looks strangely fitting.

The best time to take modern cityscape shots is about half an hour after sunset when the sky takes on a deep blue hue, which is far more attractive as a backdrop than a completely black sky. This quality of light lasts for a very short time, usually only 10–15 minutes. If you are prepared, such a length of time will be adequate, except of course that it will only provide perhaps one or two shots in any one evening. Because the light is low, exposures will be long and a tripod will be essential in most cases. Decide on the shot you want, whether you want to include 'city life' such as people or cars, or look up at the sky, and set up your shot accordingly.

Additional lights

• If the composition of the building includes a street the head- and tail lights of passing cars can be an added ingredient. By using a slow shutter speed the lights will appear as trails of light snaking through the man-made canyons of the city.
• Be careful to avoid flare from external lighting such as street lamps. Sometimes a standard lens hood will be inadequate and a shield may need to be improvised from a piece of card, a book or a map, for instance; alternatively, shift position to stand between the camera and the light.

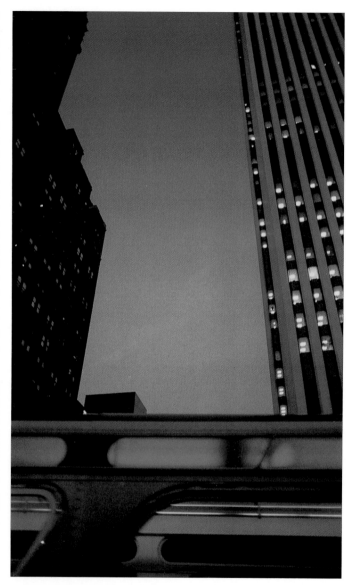

ABOVE This shot was taken at the premium twilight hour. The camera viewpoint looks upwards. This has caused the two skyscrapers to converge but this has the effect of exaggerating their height and adding an impression of enclosure within the city. The bus fills the bottom of the frame horizontally and reinforces the sense of movement. The side windows of the bus, turned green as they are lit by fluorescent tubes, add to the theme of night-time and its lighting in the city.

BELOW The lower shot of the Colosseum in Rome strikes a perfect balance between the illumination of the stone of the building and the colour of the twilight sky. The trails of the head- and tail lights of the traffic help to fill the void created by the road, and give a sense of Rome as a busy living city as well as an ancient monument. The upper shot, taken from the same viewpoint, shows the effect of inadequate lens shading as the flare from a street light has flawed the picture.

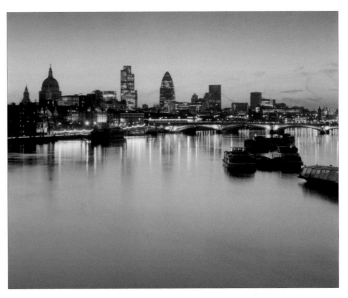

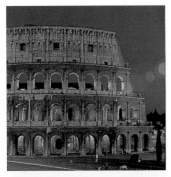

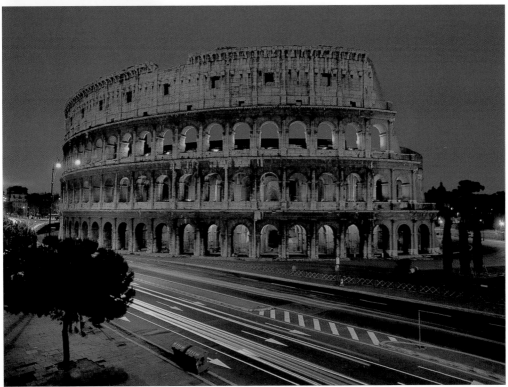

ABOVE Allowing such a large expanse of water, with the skyline in the top third, focuses on the still water and reflections. The calm juxtaposes well with the busy city – this image has a feeling of tranquility after the working day and before the nightlife begins.

Still Life

Travel often has the effect of making us more visually alert. Many things in our day-to-day lives may pass us by without us giving them a second glance. However, a new environment provides visual stimuli; to the photographer these stimuli provide a new awareness of photographic possibilities. Many items around us may not be very interesting in themselves, but gathered together in a collection, perhaps as a grouping of souvenirs from a particular place and photographed in an attractive way, a still life picture is created.

Still life arrangements have inspired painters throughout time and the same inspiration provides photographers with many creative opportunities. It is a useful discipline to look closely at, and arrange and light a group of inanimate objects. Sometimes these arrangements already exist and all that is required is to see the potential for a good shot.

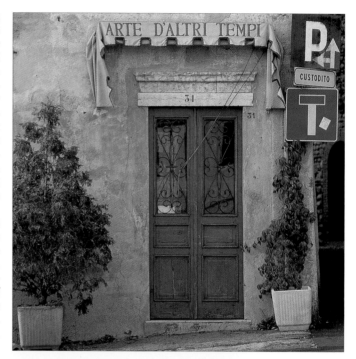

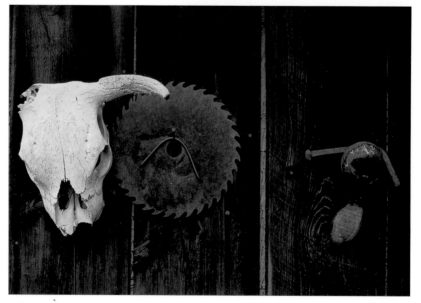

LEFT This is a good example of a ready-made still life. All the objects were fixed to the side of a barn on a ranch in Arizona. This shot frames them to their best advantage; no other preparation was needed. To the ranch owners this was just an assortment of objects rather than a creative arrangement. It is often worth looking around at familiar objects to view them with a fresh eye.

RIGHT Some still life arrangements present themselves; this collection of African craft objects and furniture was lying in the corner of a room, lit by weak sunlight coming through an open window. A white reflector to the right helped throw back just enough light to illuminate the shadow areas.

LEFT By cropping the picture tightly – a medium telephoto lens was used – any extraneous details can be excluded. The texture of the wall provides a perfect canvas for setting off the doorway, the shrub and the traffic sign.

BELOW RIGHT A large aperture was used to emphasize the colour of these flowers by minimizing depth of field and throwing the background out of focus. The lines of the steps beyond are still just discernible and lift the background so that it remains a composite part of the picture without being too bland.

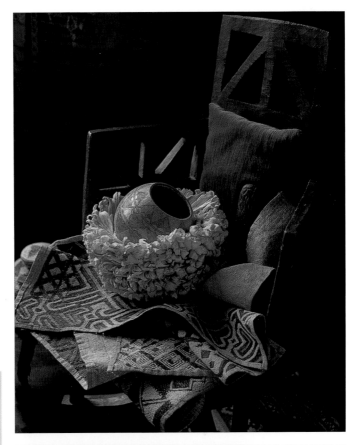

Still life checklist

• Should the arrangement be lit with flash or is there enough available light?

• Examine the available light for any creative elements: does a shaft of light fall at just the right angle?

• Which angle would look best for the shot? Imagine the arrangement in the centre of a circle. Stand a certain distance from the objects and walk around them slowly, stopping at regular intervals. Every pause provides a new visual angle and a different shot.

• Which viewpoint? Consider the arrangement from eye level, as well as from above and from below.

• Every visual angle provides a different background: which one is most suitable and complements the objects most effectively?

• Consider the depth of field: should the background be sharp or blurred?

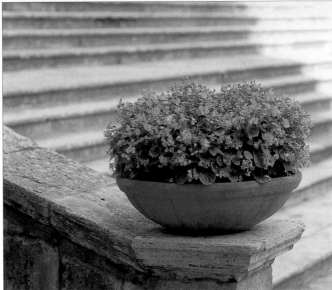

Patterns

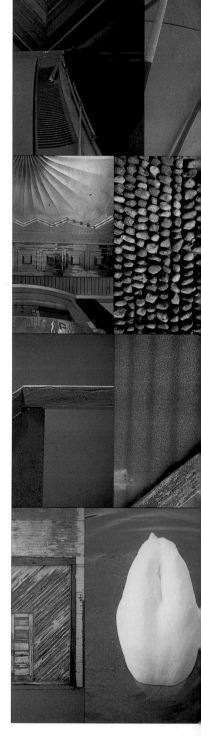

Now that you are getting used to the idea of the way a photographer needs to look at the world with a rather different perspective to most people, exciting possibilities are opening up. Scenes that once seemed 'unphotogenic' and dull now, hopefully, have taken on a new dimension. There are always interesting details, colours, angles or textures, and there is always a new way to look at things. Your photography can reinterpret even the most mundane scene to become a fascinating image or montage.

One of the most thrilling aspects of photography is, therefore, travelling to new places. Take every opportunity you can, even if it is only a day trip, and take your camera bag with you. The refreshingly new viewpoints that travelling to new places often provides may foreground scenes or details that appear isolated from their immediate surroundings. This might be due to the way the light falls or may be because of an object's texture, or a combination of both these elements. Such images need not be confined to a documentary record of a place but can be used to startling creative effect.

What is your angle?

Examine the patterns created by an object or group of objects; often when such objects or scenes are carefully framed they form an interesting composition. Sometimes the pictures have a very abstract appearance, and they may need careful viewing to see exactly what the subject is. You may become very interested in this abstract quality and capitalize on it to produce a montage of mysterious images that need to be carefully examined to discover what they are.

Alternatively, you may want to focus on the pure aesthetics of patterns. For example, you may find the look of the vertical stripes and sheen on corregated plastic next to a tangle of fishing nets and ropes something that simply 'pleases your eye'. It is effective to combine the aesthetic and abstract too, but try not to muddle up too many places in one presentation – ideally you should be telling the story of one trip or one place.

It has become quite popular to frame photographs of details, textural images or abstract patterns for display in homes, restaurants and may other interiors. Producing your own collection for display around your home is of course very rewarding. The prints also make good gifts and, with practice, you may find you have work that is good enough to sell.

Considerations for each shot

• Would it look best if framed symmetrically?
• Do the lines of perspective increase or decrease with the chosen viewpoint? If so, which is best?
• Is texture an important part of the picture? If so, does the light need to come from the back or the side to emphasize the texture?
• Would going in close help to achieve the effect better than being positioned farther back?
• Would using a wide-angle or a fisheye lens create a more interesting or subtle effect? This can be especially striking when looking up at a ceiling of a building, for instance, particularly if all the horizontal and vertical lines have been carefully aligned.

▶ **RIGHT** Consider using prints or transparencies in a collage of different patterns. Try reversing one of the pictures and butting it up to one that is the correct way round.

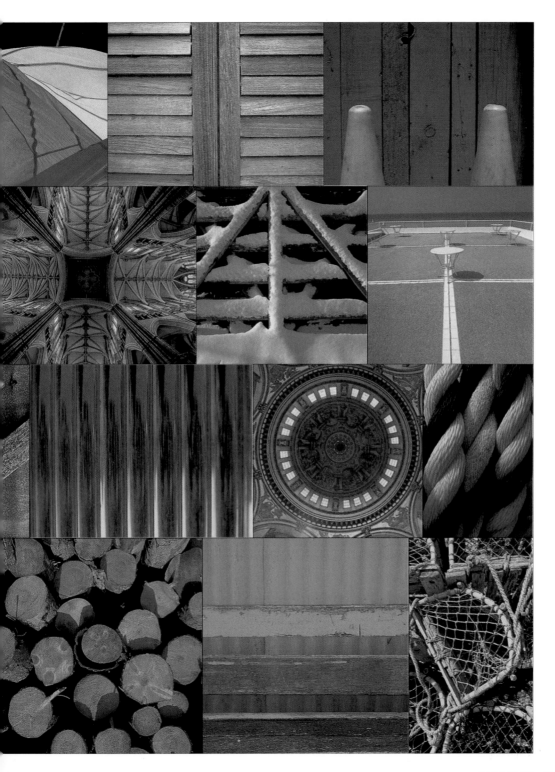

Events

All over the world events take place that are worth a special journey. One such is London's Notting Hill Carnival, the largest street festival in Europe. People flock from far afield to see the parade, dance and share the street parties. Some come for that reason alone, others as part of a wider tour of the city or the country. If the weather is good it makes the perfect opportunity for a photographer to produce an enduring and fascinating record of a vibrant weekend.

Timing it right

If you decide to make an event such as a carnival the high point of your trip, a little planning will avoid disappointment. Make sure you arrive at the right time: this may sound obvious, but some events do not always happen on the same date each year, especially if they are associated with a movable festival such as Easter (which also happens on a later date for the Orthodox Church).

Be prepared

If you are working with a film-back camera, take plenty of film. This will help to keep your pictures consistent, as they will all be from the same emulsion batch. With film bought locally you can never be sure how long it has been lying around in the store, perhaps exposed to damaging heat. You often see film being hawked around tourist sites unshielded from the blazing sun. Professionals keep their film refrigerated. You cannot take a refrigerator with you, but at least you can keep your film as cool as possible. If you are shooting with a digital camera remember to carry plenty of spare memory cards. Events always provide many more photograph opportunities than you expect.

Choosing a theme

At huge and varied events it is difficult to get just one picture that says everything. That is not to say that you should not look out for such a shot. A better approach might be to shoot as much as you possibly can, and to assemble these pictures as a montage on a particular theme, or a diary of events. Themes could be faces, floats, costumes, food, or the onlookers themselves. Many events last for several days, so you will have plenty of time to get all your shots. Unlike with more tranquil travel photography, where you will be looking for architectural details, at a carnival you need to get a sense of crowds, noise and colour. Lots of photographs of laughing faces, signs, flags, dancers and food and drink stalls will capture the event perfectly.

Security

Events such as the Carnival are unfortunately a magnet for pickpockets. Try not to advertise any expensive kit you have. If you are carrying a case for accessories keep it properly secured. Be alert for children who beg you to take their picture. It sometimes happens that, while you are concentrating on the shot, one of their colleagues is lifting your valuables. A backpack, kept securely zipped up, may be a far easier option than a standard holdall, and it will keep your hands free for impromptu shots and, of course, holding the occasional snack and drink as you enjoy the event.

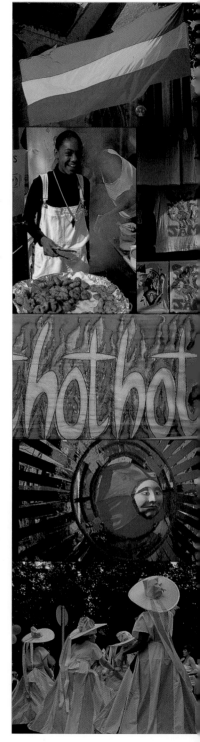

▷ **RIGHT** A collection of images placed together effectively captures the atmosphere of London's Notting Hill Carnival. Small details can be placed next to wider shots of dancers and street scenes to convey the sense of colour and exuberance.

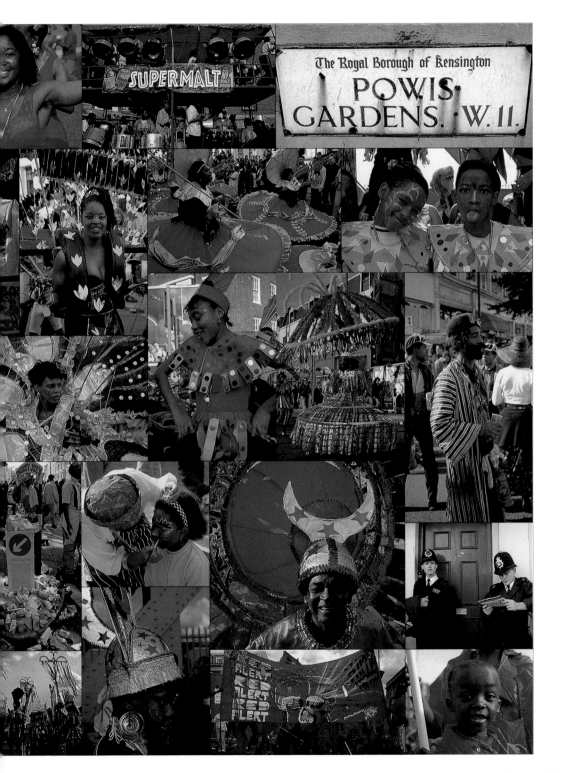

Fireworks

Photographs of fireworks are fun to take and good to look at. They can be absolutely stunning when blown up to very large prints. Displays over water or over impressive landmark buildings tend to be particularly photogenic. As with so many successful photographs, a little advance planning is necessary to ensure success. If photographing at a public display, get there early. It makes no difference what the weather is like: even in pouring rain people will flock to see a first-class display Only very heavy fog will mar the event. Once in position, try to find out where the fireworks will be set off from.

Multiple exposures

Many of the most successful shots of fireworks, especially of rockets or other aerial displays, are in fact multiple exposures. There are two ways to achieve these shots. In either case the camera should be set on a tripod and a cable release fitted. Try to ensure that no one will jostle the camera —

this can be difficult in a crowd. Point the camera at the place where the rockets are expected to explode.

If the camera has a multiple exposure device, take two or three shots of the rockets. For 100 ISO film the correct exposure is in the region of 2 sec at f/5.6.

If the camera will not take multiple exposures, set the aperture to the same size but turn the shutter ring to the B or T setting. Have a lens cap or some other device ready for covering the lens. Before the rockets go off, cover the lens and fire the shutter. If using the B setting, keep the cable release depressed. When the rockets explode, take off the cap for about 2 sec, then replace it. Repeat two or three times, then close the shutter by letting go of the cable release (for B) or pressing it again (for T).

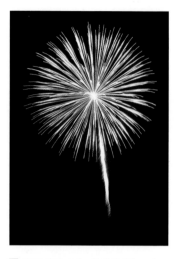

ABOVE Photographs of individual fireworks can be quite effective. Depending on the brightness of the firework, an exposure of 2 to 4 seconds at f/5.6 will probably be right.

BELOW The exposure for this picture was 5 sec at f/8 and recorded the trail of the sparkler. Flash could have been used to light the person holding the sparkler.

BELOW AND RIGHT These pictures were taken with multiple exposures. The film was 100 ISO, and the aperture was f/5.6. Each of the exposures was 2 sec.

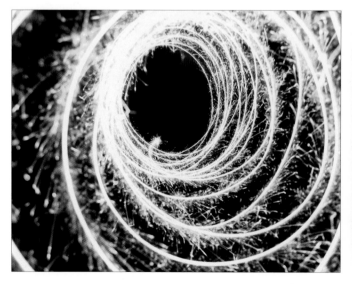

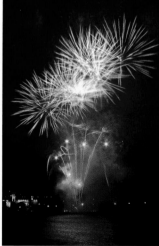

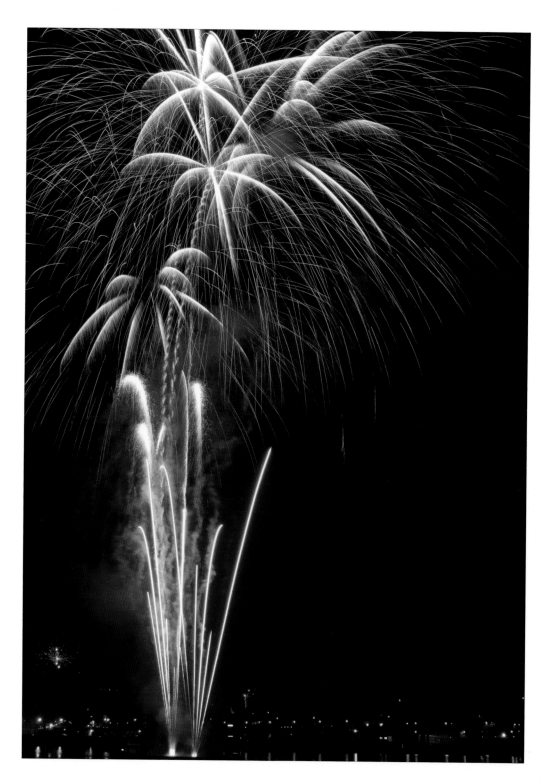

Making a Picture Series

When you are photographing an event you need to consider how many different things will be happening. Sometimes you'll find that there is so much diversity that you are spoilt for choice. In other instances the focus of interest may be narrow, and you will need to shoot from as many viewpoints as possible to give an informative account of the occasion.

Planning in advance

It is always helpful to try to reconnoitre the place beforehand. Once the event begins you may not be able to move about easily, especially if you are burdened with a camera case and a tripod. In such a situation, try to pick a spot that will give you a good view of the main action. Also find out when the event is to begin, so that you

can be there in plenty of time to get a good position at the front of the crowd. For example, it is surprising how early people start to congregate for popular acts at Glastonbury festival, shown here.

If you cannot get a good view, try to take a small, lightweight set of steps. You will be able to see over people's heads, and you may get an unusual angle on the proceedings.

Also try to work out beforehand which will be the key shots that you simply must have. You could make a list just in case, in the heat of the moment, you forget what you meant to do. This may seem obsessive, but hardly anyone makes a movie without a script. For example, at Glastonbury festival you might plan to capture:

- a major performer
- a range of shots of the crowds – individuals in fancy dress, and large groups moving around the site
- the campsite itself

This does not sound like a lot, but it is amazing how quickly an event can pass by and suddenly be over; it can seem like seconds if you have got caught up in it.

▼ BELOW At an event such as Glastonbury look for backgrounds that add meaning. The surreal leaf sculpture and colourful clothing say something about the ethos of the event and the people that congregate there. The shot also says a lot about the hugely sociable, easy-going atmosphere. Some eye contact and connection with the girl rubbing her aching feet works well.

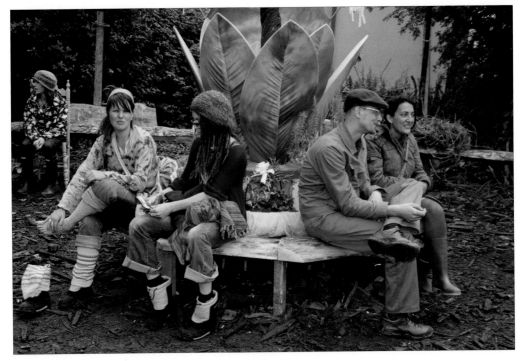

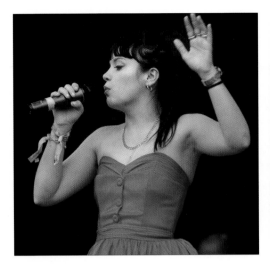

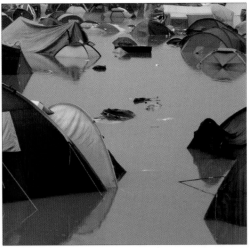

Equipment

Have a range of lenses, or if possible two camera bodies with zoom lenses – one could be 28–80mm, the other 100–300mm. In this way you will be able to work quickly with the minimum of weight. A monopod will help you to brace the camera. This is really important if the weather is dull and a long exposure is needed.

RIGHT As well as the performers and campsite shots, images of the festival goers help to give the series atmosphere. Choosing this image shows that fun was had despite the weather, but other images of less amused 'revellers' could have told a different story entirely.

BELOW Move in for a portrait of a child that sums up the event's appeal to all ages.

ABOVE An essential shot at a festival is of a well-known artist such as Lily Allen performing on the main stage. Of course if you can get backstage it will be a fantastic bonus. Otherwise, use your zoom lens.

ABOVE 2007 was a particularly wet year at Glastonbury festival, as this shot of the campsite shows. Like the performer, this photograph helps document the exact date of your picture series.

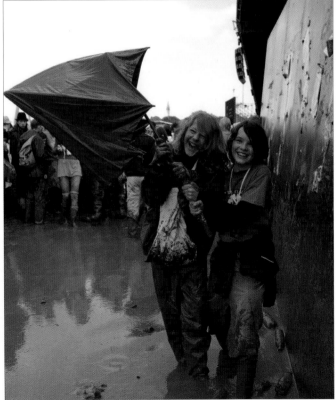

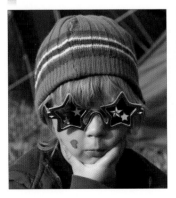

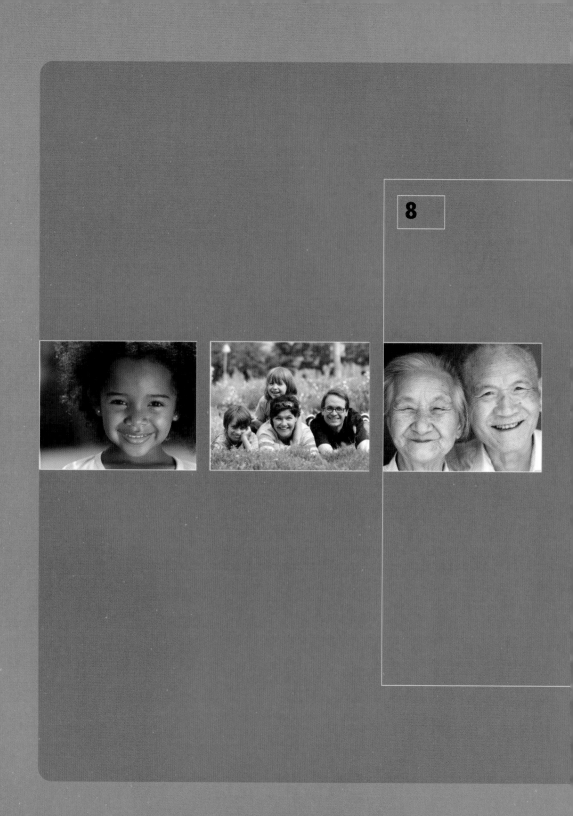

8

Portraiture

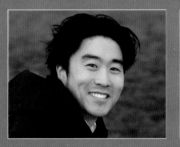 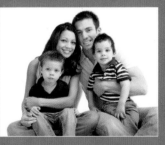 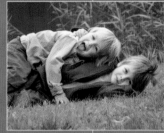

Portraits can be some of the most emotive of photographs, whether prompting a happy memory with a light-hearted family group on holiday, a stylish commissioned shot of a sports star, or a more demanding series of images of a community affected by a natural disaster. Whatever the subject matter, the choice of location and background, the style of lighting both in and outside of the studio, the type of camera and lens used, film stock and viewpoint all affect how your photograph will look. As the photographer you can take complete control over your subject matter and this chapter will show you how.

Portraits: Backgrounds

A key element in shooting a portrait is the care given to the background. Yet so often it is given very little thought and the finished photograph is spoilt by unwanted distractions. In some situations, such as in a studio, the background can be altered at will and could range from a simple plain white or black backdrop to a more elaborate purpose-built set, or even a back screen projection.

When photographing people in their homes, at the workplace or outdoors, it is important to use the existing environment to the best advantage. This may mean including

RIGHT Here the glass panels of the door make an interesting background without becoming an intrusion. They are slightly out of focus but they are still identifiable. This makes the child's face appear to spring out from the doorway as if one has captured her in a game of hide and seek.

BELOW In this shot of a woman on a fairground stall the exception proves the rule. The background dominates the picture and the stall-holder looks completely lost. However, the woman appears about to be buried in an avalanche of her own wares – adding a touch of humour to an otherwise rather mundane scene.

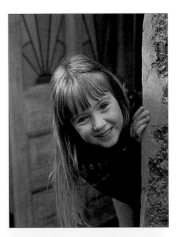

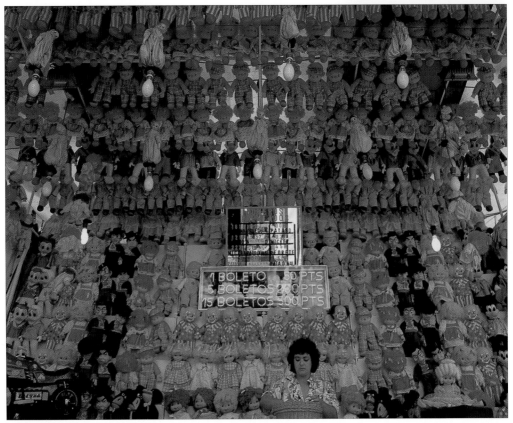

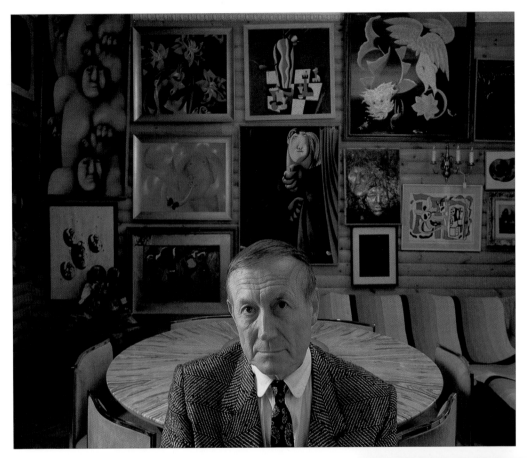

the work the person does – or even a relevant hobby or collection – without letting the subject become a secondary element within the picture. Of course, your subject may have their own ideas about where they want the shot to be taken. The choice may be interesting and work, but you might need to persuade them otherwise.

Thought should be given to where the subject of the portrait is to sit or stand, as well as the distance and angle of the camera in relation to both the person and the background.

Choice of aperture is another consideration to be taken into account; a small aperture will produce a greater depth of field than a large one, and so more of the background will be in focus – which may well prove distracting.

ABOVE The Russian poet Yevgeny Yevtushenko in his Moscow apartment. Although the background is very busy his collection of paintings is highlighted as well as him. By placing the poet in the centre of the frame with the relative neutrality of his dining table directly behind, he stands out and the eye is immediately drawn to him.

RIGHT This picture of a model was achieved by placing her on a background of shiny plastic. The lighter blue stripes were placed diagonally on the darker stripes and the colours were chosen to complement her make up. This hardly elaborate but highly effective background shows what can be done to obtain an eye-catching shot without spending a great deal of money.

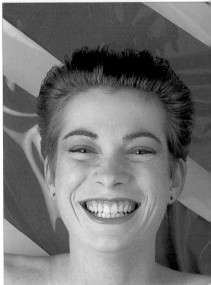

Portraits: Props

Props are items introduced into photographs that can either add something to the composition or tell us more about the person featured, perhaps providing information about a job or a hobby. Used successfully, props should enhance the picture without over-powering the person. In their simplest form props might be an addition to the clothes someone is wearing – a hat or a flower for instance. Sometimes a bunch of flowers placed in a vase near the subject will give a certain 'lift' to the shot. It could be that by placing people against a backdrop of their work the item they produce or create becomes a prop in itself.

In a working environment there are endless possibilities for adding available props to a shot. These may take the form of a background or may completely surround the subject. If the people featured are in an active position, do not pull back so far that they become insignificant. In situations like this it is possible that the prop can subtly convey the atmosphere rather than becoming a visually dominating part of the picture. For instance, if a man is involved in working with molten metal, heated in a furnace, it would be the sensation of the intense heat rather than a prominent shot of the furnace that would say far more about the atmosphere. Going in close to the man and showing the heat reflected on his brow while keeping the furnace in the background, you could create an evocative composition.

As a photographer, always look for props in the immediate situation and employ them in the same way as an imported accessory.

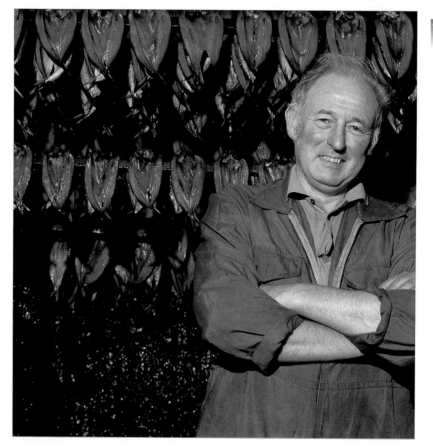

LEFT This shot was taken in a 'smoker', the room in which kippers are cured. The room had jet black walls and was quite small. By placing the owner in front of several rows of newly smoked kippers, the fish themselves provided the props to illustrate his work.

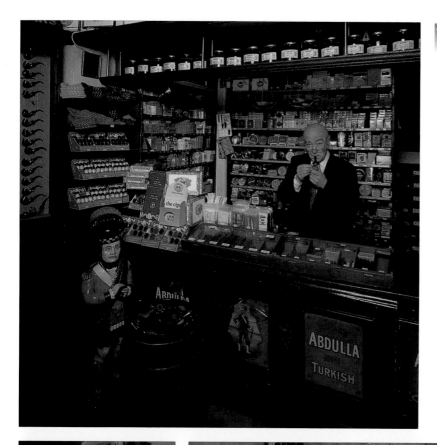

◄ **LEFT** Upon entering this tobacconist's shop it seemed that the entire place was full of props. Positioning the owner, lighting his pipe, among his wares added an extra visual dimension to the shot as well as conveying his character.

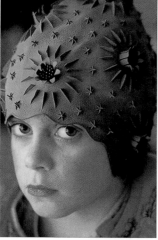

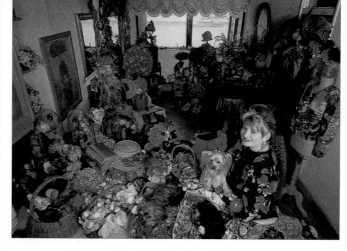

▲ **ABOVE** Costume can provide effective props in portraits; here the simple inclusion of an unusual hat changes the character of the shot and its subject.

▲ **ABOVE** This woman lived in a small apartment. She made exotic and expensive clothes and the purpose of the shot is to show her and her work together. Since her work is so colourful, it was decided to use it to fill the room and to cover the kitchen worktop in the foreground. The room takes on a swirl of colour but the woman remains a prominent part of the shot.

Portraits: Selecting a Viewpoint

Taking good shots of people depends on many factors. One of the most important is where you take the picture from. It is difficult to set down hard and fast rules about this, and obviously it depends on the situation. But one or two general points are always worth bearing in mind.

If you choose a high viewpoint to photograph a person full length this will have the effect of shortening them. But if you kneel down you will exaggerate their height. A quick look in any fashion magazine shows many examples of this stance, with models who appear to have legs that go on and on, thanks to the point of view. With young children and babies it may be necessary to get down on the ground and choose an extremely low viewpoint for an effective shot.

When photographing groups or crowds of people it is generally best if you can remove yourself from the throng and view them from a distance, or perhaps from above.

At a special event you may be able to emphasize the detail of a uniform or costume to make an individual or small group stand out from the rest.

When you go in close the viewpoint you take can emphasize or exaggerate a person's expression. But remember that if you go too close with a wide-angle lens it is very easy to get distortion, which may look unflattering or give a comic effect.

Your next consideration is exposure. If people are moving about rapidly TTL metering may be an asset, but when taking shots by this method beware: the meter is reading for the general scene and not for a predominantly dark or light area which may be the centre of interest of the picture. You may need to compensate for this to get a correct exposure.

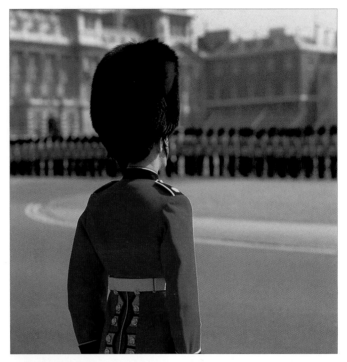

ABOVE At formal events like the Trooping of the Colour in London it sometimes pays to look for a different angle as well as the more obvious shots. A viewpoint behind this guardsman emphasizes the colour and detail of his uniform. The line of soldiers can be seen out of focus in the background, which helps to concentrate attention on him.

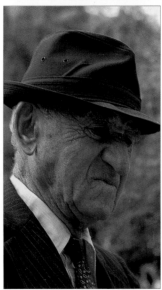

LEFT Going low and looking up at this man's face has helped to highlight his features and expression. He is playing chess and I wanted to capture his expression. If people are wearing hats be careful that the brim does not cast an unwanted shadow across their face.

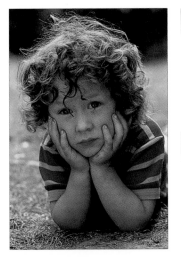

LEFT This shot was taken from ground level, lying in a similar position to that of the boy. The emphasis is on his face and this has been exaggerated by going in close. Using an 85mm lens at this distance has helped to reduce distortion and has put the background slightly out of focus so that nothing distracts us from his gaze.

BELOW It is very difficult to get a general shot of people from ground level in a crowded place, such as a bustling market scene. This shot shows as many people as possible, with the stalls and some of the goods they sold and was taken from a communal balcony. The angle the shot was taken from makes a strong diagonal of the crowd that enhances the composition.

Improving

As with all art forms, practice really does make perfect. Always review your shots and try to learn what has worked and what has not. You will find that you mentally refer back to these shots when you are taking new ones. Gradually your photography will improve, as you eliminate errors and capitalize on successes. Keep your eye on what other photographers are doing, changing fashions, new photo sharing sites and of course, new kit that can help you improve.

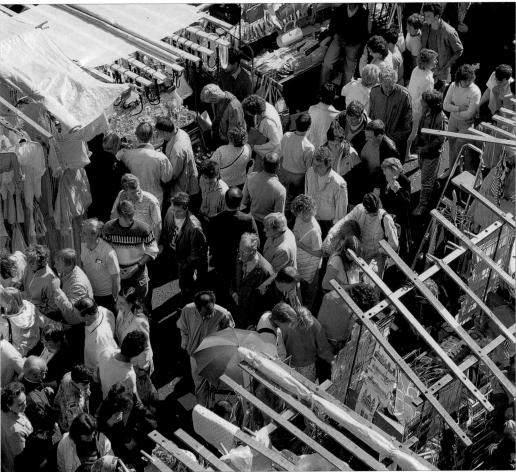

Lighting in the Studio

Many people are daunted by the idea of taking photographs in the studio. But generally speaking, the majority of photographers find that handling studio lights is an easy skill to pick up and become competent in.

Look through various magazines which feature pictures taken in a studio. The lighting techniques are as varied as the subjects they light. In some only one light is used, in others five or more.

The least expensive light available is a photoflood with a reflector and stand. But many people find the glare and heat from such lights uncomfortable when they are sitting for a portrait, which will, of course, lead to bad results. An alternative is studio flash. The units work from the mains and are much more powerful than a camera's built-in flash unit or one that fits onto a camera hot shoe. Each unit has its own power supply; some of the most powerful have attachments for additional flash heads.

Flash attachments

As well as the standard reflector there is a whole variety of different attachments that can alter the character of the light. These include large umbrella-type reflectors in white, silver or gold, which bounce diffused light on to the subject, giving a softer light than a standard flat reflector.

An even softer light can be obtained by using a 'softbox'. These come in various sizes, but all work on the same principle. The box fits over the flash head. It has a highly reflective silver lining, and a diffusing material stretched over the front. Other diffusers can be stretched over the first one to diffuse the light even further.

Another lighting attachment is called a 'snoot'. This directs a thin beam of light on to the subject. It is not the same as a conventional spotlight, which has a broader beam which can be focused. Spotlights can also have inserts placed between the lamp and the lens, which throw patterns onto the lit area.

As with all accessories, special lights have to be used carefully and creatively. Used by themselves they will not produce miracles.

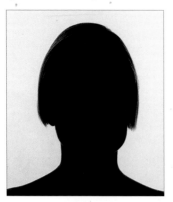

ABOVE Here only the background is lit, to make it white and silhouette the subject. This technique has to be used with care, as an overlit background can cause flare. When framing the subject take care that the lighting equipment does not appear in shot.

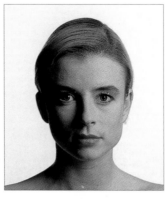

ABOVE Using just one light has lit one side of the model's face. This has left the other side of her face with dark, unattractive shadows, especially by the nose and eyes.

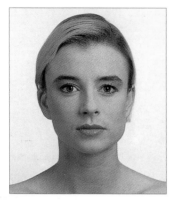

ABOVE A 'fill-in' light has been introduced on the left side. This is less powerful than the main light. It has softened the shadows without making the face look flat. A reflector would have a similar effect.

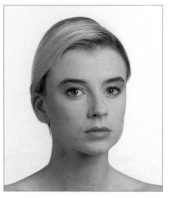

ABOVE Another light has been used over the model's head to give more body to the hair. It was attached to a stand with a boom, an arm extending sideways. A boom allows a light to be brought close to a model.

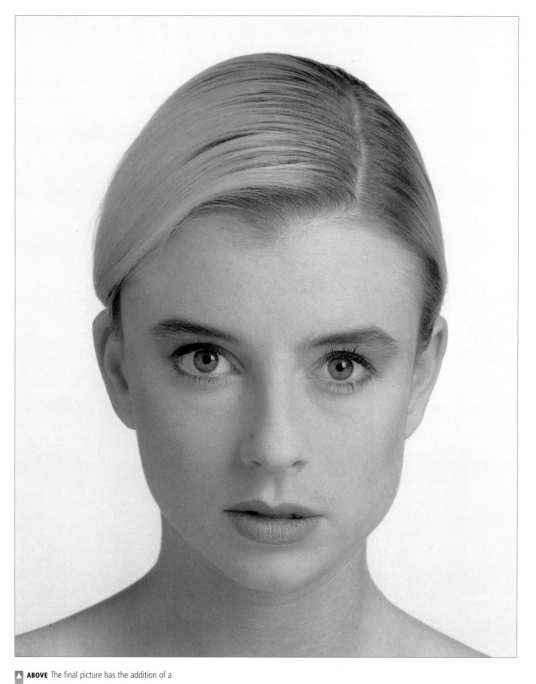

Portraits in the Studio

There are many advantages to taking portraits in a studio. For a start, the photographer has complete control of the lighting, and the choice of backgrounds and props. Also, depending on the type of photograph, clothes and make-up can be specified or chosen and altered.

Some photographers, and even more so their models, can feel inhibited by the studio environment, however. A bare room with only a few lights and rolls of background paper can seem an impossible setting for the creation of an interesting picture. But it only takes a little know-how and a measure of confidence to achieve a whole new dimension in photography.

Studios do not have to be elaborate, lofty or spacious. In fact, a reasonable-sized room in an ordinary house can work just as well as a studio, as the shot of the girl against a white background demonstrates.

To improvise a studio at home, hire lights from a professional photographic dealer, or perhaps buy one or two modest units as a start. However, good flash equipment would be a better investment than floodlights. It is generally more powerful, which allows shorter exposures than are possible with photofloods. It is also more comfortable to work with. Photofloods get very hot, and after a while this can make conditions uncomfortable. People also find the constant glare irritating.

An alternative is to hire a purpose-built studio. There are a number of these and they are always being advertised in photographic magazines. It is often a good idea to join a local photographic society, which can probably provide access to such facilities as well as equipment, assistance and even models.

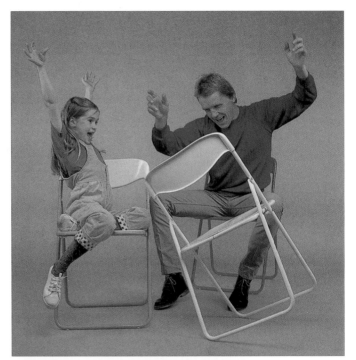

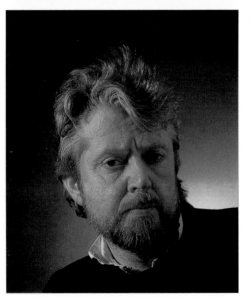

ABOVE One of the advantages of taking pictures in a studio is that seamless backgrounds can be made with long rolls of paper. These can be hung from the wall or ceiling, and extended along the ground to conceal visible corners. A hired studio should normally provide such backgrounds, though all the paper that is used usually has to be paid for.

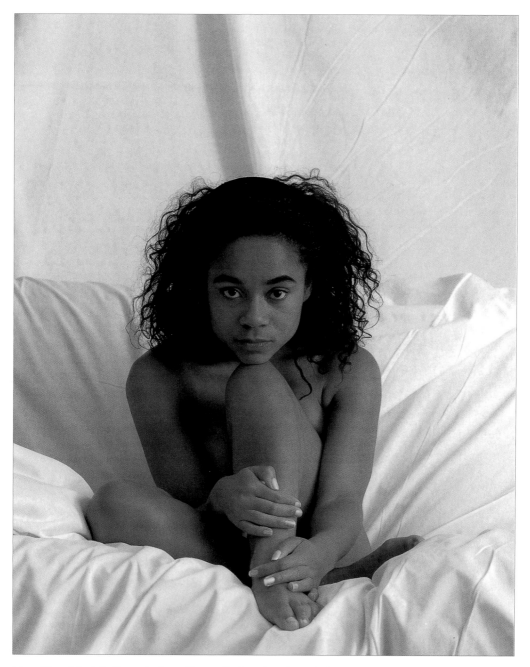

LEFT This man's face is lit with a very low-key light. This has heightened his features and given him an enigmatic expression. Another light with a snoot (this gives a directional beam) was projected on to the background to give a graduated appearance.

ABOVE This picture shows what can be done in the home. A length of white cotton material was pinned to the wall and draped over a sofa. One flash was used, fitted with a large diffuser called a softbox. This was powerful enough to illuminate both the girl and the background. Some people – both photographers and models – find it less intimidating to work in an ordinary home than in a proper photographic studio. But as confidence and adventurousness increase, an improvised home studio can become a restriction, unless of course the room is very large.

Formal Portraits

Formal portraits do not mean that subjects have to sit or stand to attention, otherwise the picture will look stiff and uncomfortable. In the early days of photography when exposure times were measured in minutes people did have to sit very still to avoid blurring the picture. Photo-graphers even used special clamps at the back of their sitter's neck and waist to brace them in position. Fortunately these days are long past.

The most important thing in any portrait, formal or otherwise, is to capture the expression that best illustrates a person's character or status, or both. However formal the portrait might be, try to enter into a dialogue with the sitter. Discover a common interest, and the conversation will become easy and relaxed.

Even if the sitter is a complete stranger, try to plan the general nature

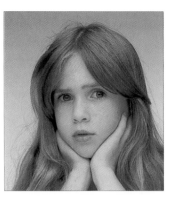

ABOVE Although this portrait of a young girl was taken in a studio, it is full of flair and vitality. An immediate rapport was struck up with her so that she felt relaxed. Atmosphere is very important in any situation where there is close communication between photographer and model. It would be disastrous to start a session in an atmosphere of tension on any shoot.

of the shot in advance. It makes a bad impression if the first thing the photographer does after meeting the sitter is to stare hard at him, as if undecided what to do. But it is also important to plan wisely; it produces an even worse impression if, after a few shots, it becomes clear that the setting does not work, so that all the equipment has to be altered.

Often, time is of the essence. Some people, such as public figures, are very busy, and they may be under the impression that photographs can be taken as quickly as if they had walked into an automatic photo booth. Knowing what is wanted, and directing sitters with flair and firmness, can yield strong portraits in a relatively short time. The results will please them and enhance the photographer's reputation and the clients are more likely to return.

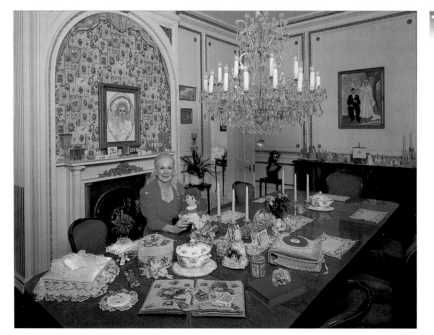

LEFT This room looks formal, yet the woman's expression gives the portrait warmth and there is the impression that it was a relaxed shoot. Both the room and the hallway which is visible through the far doorway had to be lit. If the door had been shut the atmosphere might have seemed a little claustrophobic. Being able to see beyond the room adds space and light. Although the picture takes a wide view, there is no doubt that the woman is the centre of attention.

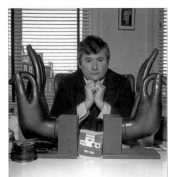

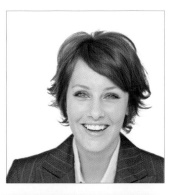

LEFT Formality need not mean rigidity. In this portrait of the photographer Terence Donovan the composition's formality and symmetry give him an enigmatic quality. For those who do not know his reputation as a photographer there are a few props to give a clue to his profession. Terence Donovan also runs a film production company, and there is just a hint of the entrepreneur here.

RIGHT Even with formal shots for company literature, it is still important to engage the subject and produce an attractive portrait.

RIGHT The portrait of the former Speaker of the House of Commons in London had to be taken in a 10-minute session. His gown and wig might have made him look intimidating and rigid; instead they signify the status of his position and are in keeping with a portrait that is both formal and interesting. Although the Speaker appears small this is in effective contrast to the grandeur of the room.

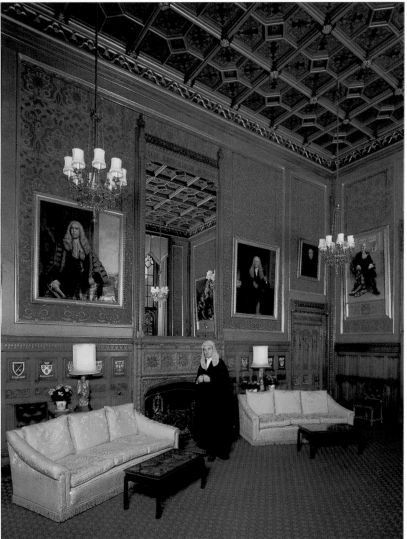

Informal Portraits

Many portraits work because they have an informal look that most people would call 'natural'. But pictures like these need thought to make them successful. For instance, it is pointless to take lots of shots in a casual manner if the exposure or focus are incorrect or the shot is badly composed. With a little forethought all these problems can be avoided, but at the same time there is no need to be so preoccupied with the mechanics of photography that it causes inhibition and the pictures are unspontaneous.

As with all aspects of photography, the most important thing is being so familiar with the equipment that all

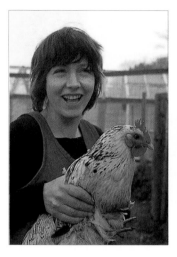

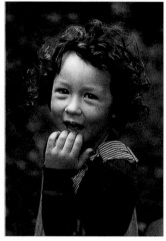

▼ **BELOW** Pictures like these come readily to the alert photographer. Always have the camera charged up and loaded with film or a memory stick to avoid wasting time. The person might move away – or in this case merely put on his socks and shoes.

▲ **ABOVE** This picture radiates spontaneity, warmth and humour. It is a good example of capturing the moment, which swiftly passes when dealing with animals. Going in close helps the general composition and focuses attention on the woman and the chicken.

▲ **ABOVE** An ultra-fast film, 1600 ISO, has perfectly caught this young boy's cheeky expression. The grainy quality of the film, far from being a drawback, adds to the picture. The day was dull and the area surrounded by trees, so it is unlikely that a slow film would have given an adequate picture. Especially with informal portraits, be ready to try something different and do not be afraid to push film to its limits.

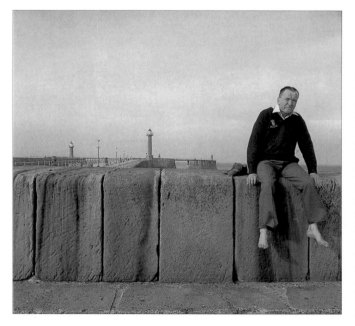

the controls become second nature. Once these are mastered it is possible to concentrate on technique and become more adventurous.

If you are using film, this might mean experimenting with a different type. Try a high-speed one such as 1600 ISO. This will give very grainy results, but that is by no means an unattractive effect, as one of the pictures here shows. Also, using such a fast film allows pictures to be taken in almost any conditions. The film can even be uprated to 3200 ISO. (Remember that if this is done the whole film has to be shot at this rating, and when giving the film to the processing laboratory the technicians will need to be told that it has been uprated so that they can increase development time.)

A zoom lens, especially when combined with an autofocus mechanism, makes for faster work since focal length can be changed without the need to swap lenses.

Ultimately, of course, it is the photographer's eye that seizes upon that good shot, however much advanced equipment may be available. You may well have an instinct for a good shot, but it is equally something that can be learned.

▶ **RIGHT** This couple was photographed informally at a barbecue. Using a 100mm lens makes them fill the frame without the need to go so close as to make them feel uncomfortable. Her vivacious smile contrasts attractively with his whimsical expression. The result is relaxed and charming.

▼ **BELOW** Even when going in close, it is still possible to achieve a relaxed portrait. The old man's weathered face is set against a plain background which isolates and emphasizes his face. The ladder acts as a prop and introduces an informal element into the composition.

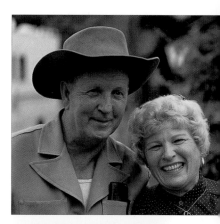

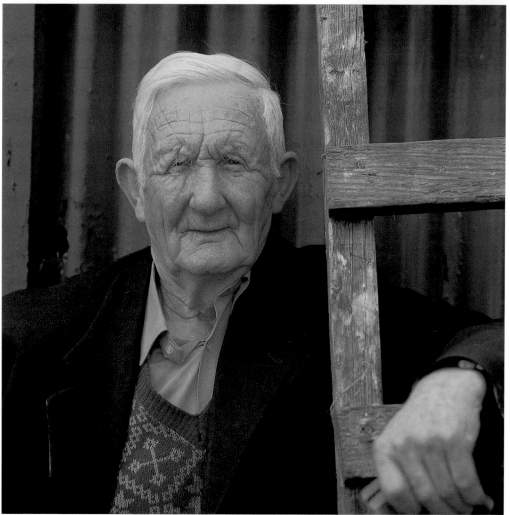

Full-length Portraits

Not all portraits of people need to be head and shoulders or full face. Sometimes the only way of achieving a good portrait is to photograph a person full length, and to include some of their environment.

When choosing a viewpoint for full-length portraits it is important to remember that photographing a standing person from low down will accentuate their height and make their legs look longer. Conversely, photographing the same person from a high viewpoint, looking down on them, will foreshorten them and make their legs look shorter.

BELOW This picture of distillery workers was lit by flash. The warehouse was large, so they were grouped tightly in a confined space to give more or less even lighting. Also, they are placed quite close to the background so that the light does not fall off sharply behind them. In such situations, look carefully and try to get the best out of the environment.

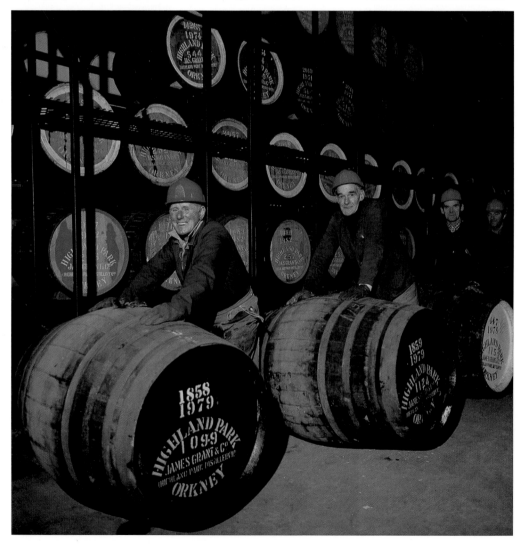

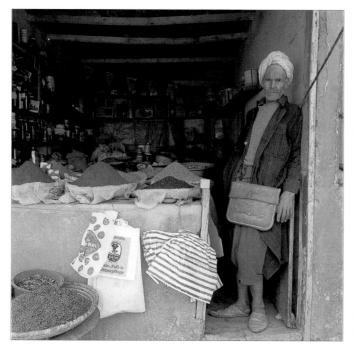

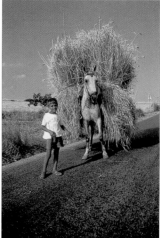

When using a wide-angle lens, care must be taken if the person is placed at the side of the frame. Some wide-angle lenses distort the extreme edges so that, for instance, a face can look 'stretched'.

When photographing a group of people full length, make sure that all their faces can be seen. This is not just a case of careful positioning, but also of making sure that the shadow cast by one person does not fall across the face of another.

If the portrait is lit by flash make sure that this is spread evenly. Many built-in flash systems do not produce a very powerful light. A person standing in a large room may be well lit but the background will be dark and murky, because the flash was not powerful enough to light the whole room.

When photographing people full length outdoors in bright sunshine, be careful if anyone is wearing a hat. The brim can cast a dark shadow on the face. If necessary use fill-in flash to soften this shadow and prevent obscuring the facial expression.

ABOVE In bright sunlight, be careful that ugly shadows do not fall across the faces of the subjects. In this picture the man was positioned in the doorway to keep the light evenly spread. Just moving someone back or forward could make all the difference. Do not be afraid to tell people what to do.

BELOW This full-length portrait was taken from a high viewpoint. By sitting the woman in a chair the problem of foreshortening has been avoided. The camera was on a tripod in a fixed position, so that items could be moved around the room till they looked right in the viewfinder – even the dog.

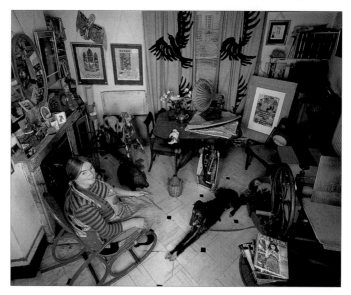

People in the Home

Many people do not take pictures at home except on special occasions such as a birthday or Christmas. But there are many other times when good opportunities for photographs present themselves, and often these can lead to excellent portraits.

One advantage of taking pictures at home is that people feel relaxed because they are in their normal environment. Another is that they are surrounded by objects that reflect their personality, which can be brought into pictures as interesting props or backgrounds; these will reveal the varied aspects of their way of life, and their interests.

RIGHT Children like helping around the house and such occasions can provide good opportunities for pictures, especially if there is a camera loaded and ready. Even better, this should be a simple model that anyone can use. If it is loaded with medium to fast film such as 200 ISO, it should cope with most situations without flash.

BELOW These friends photographed in their conservatory is a good example of balancing flash with daylight. The picture looks as if everything is lit by daylight, but in fact if flash had not been added to the foreground, the women's faces would have been in deep shadow. The shot shows an informal, friendly moment during a formal shoot.

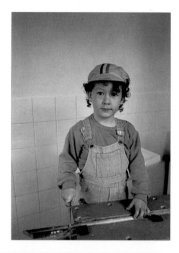

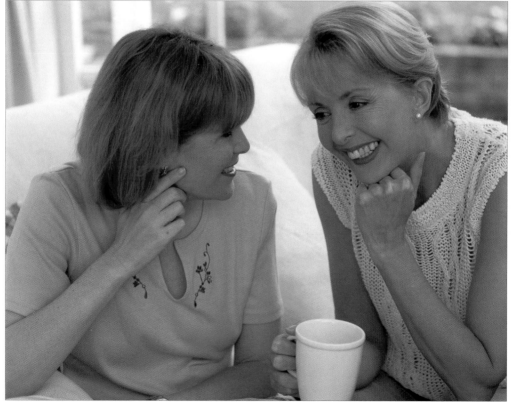

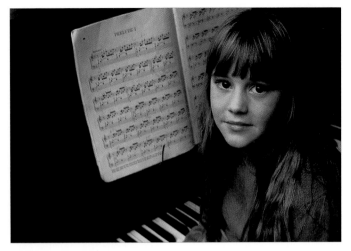

There is plenty of opportunity for spontaneous pictures in the home, especially of children. They may be doing the most ordinary, everyday things but even these, when viewed through the camera, can be seen in a new light. This is one reason why it is so important to have your camera ready. Buy an inexpensive compact camera for use around the house. This can always be kept loaded or charged and ready to hand. It should have a built-in flash for quick shots in all conditions. In this way there will never be a reason to miss a picture – and many pictures will be well worth the effort.

BELOW Although this portrait is posed it has a relaxed, on-the-moment feel to it. The subject is a relaxed, informal person, hence the pose. The musical scores in the foreground hint that the subject is a composer, or at least that music is important to him. Two flash units were used. One was directed at the man and the foreground, the other to light the area behind. These were balanced so that the scene outside the window was correctly exposed as well.

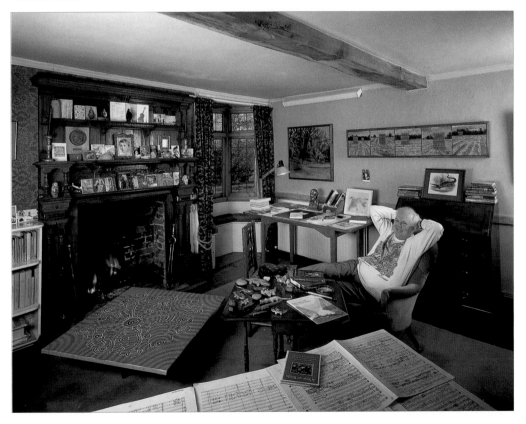

Outdoor Portraits

Bright, sunny days offer good opportunities for taking portraits outdoors. But they can cause problems too. Bright sunlight can create harsh shadows, and make people screw up their eyes and squint, which looks most unattractive. To get round this problem, try to move the person being photographed into an area of shade. Alternatively, turn them away from direct sunlight and use a reflector to throw light back into their face. If the person is wearing a hat and the brim is casting a shadow across their face, use fill-in flash to soften the shadow.

Another problem with portraits outdoors is that the wind blows people's hair about and leaves it looking messy. If possible, look for an area sheltered from the wind.

Be on the look-out for good backgrounds. You might see interesting textures, such as a stone wall, or a good view. If the background is not photogenic, consider ways of cutting it out after. This can be done by going in close and framing the picture tightly, or by using a large aperture to throw the background out of focus.

When photographing groups of people make sure that one does not cast an ugly shadow on another.

Bright but hazy days give an even, shadowless light, but in certain conditions and with some colour films the results may be too cool. To solve this try using an 81A filter. This will warm up the tones.

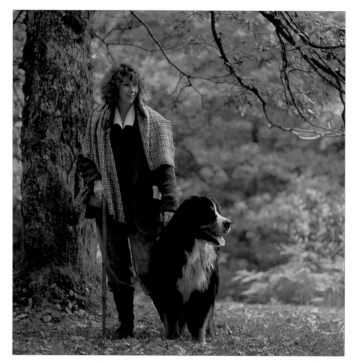

▲ **ABOVE** Even on a dull overcast day good pictures can be taken. Photographing this person out walking her dog against a wooded background has cut out the dull sky. A 250mm lens has reduced the depth of field, so that the focus is firmly on the subject.

▶ **RIGHT** A low viewpoint and going in quite close lets this boy dominate the picture. The surrounding landscape gives a feeling of spring, and the boy's expression is one of playfulness. When taking portraits out of doors experiment with different viewpoints, otherwise pictures will have an air of sameness.

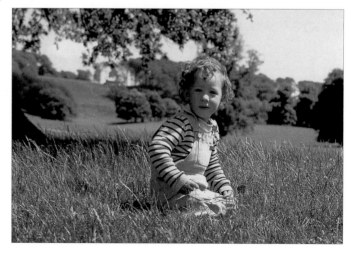

RIGHT These young girls form a well-proportioned group. They were photographed with the sun to one side and slightly behind them. This has avoided ugly shadows under their eyes, and stopped any one of them from shading another. The background is dominated by the pool; the wall is unobtrusive and does not spoil the composition.

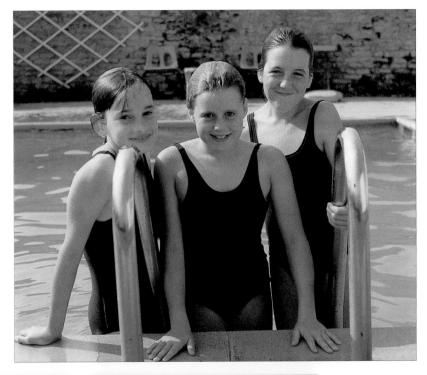

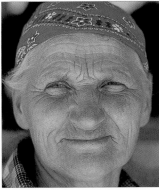

LEFT Focusing directly on this man's eyes shows the full character of his face. Every detail of his beard is sharp. He was photographed under a white blind that acted as a diffuser so that the light, although bright, does not cast any shadows on his face.

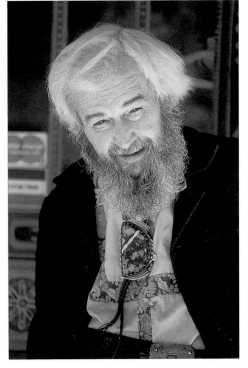

ABOVE In this picture of an elderly woman, a 100mm medium telephoto lens combined with a wide aperture has put the background out of focus. It has made the splash of green behind the subject unobtrusive, but the colour complements that of her headscarf. She is in a relatively shaded area, so that her face glows with an even, natural light.

People in their Environment

Photographing people in their own environment can be very rewarding, especially when you are on holiday and trying to get shots that capture the essence of a place. Generally strangers are only too willing to be in your shots – particularly if they are in an area where tourists are commonplace. However, if you want to photograph someone close-in, you should always ask their permission first. There are several reasons for this:

• It is polite. If you are friendly they will not feel threatened. However, if someone suddenly started taking pictures of you without asking, you would probably be annoyed.

• Once they know they are the centre of interest in your photograph, people are more likely to do what you ask. This is important because, although they may be attractive and their environment interesting, they may be standing in a less than ideal place and would be much better framed if you asked them to move slightly to one side, or perhaps onto a step. You might be able to get a better background by moving yourself, but if you creep about you are likely to upset them and make them uncooperative if you do finally decide to ask them to move. In this case you will have lost the chance of a good photograph.

• Once you have gained their confidence, they may show you another area or aspect of their lives which you would otherwise overlook. This may well prove more interesting than the original scene.

• Having gained their cooperation and moved them into the position you want, look carefully at the light falling on their faces. Are they in bright sun which creates ugly shadows under their eyes and noses? Or is the sun behind them and shining into the lens? In either case do not be afraid to move them again until you are happy with the frame. You may never get another chance.

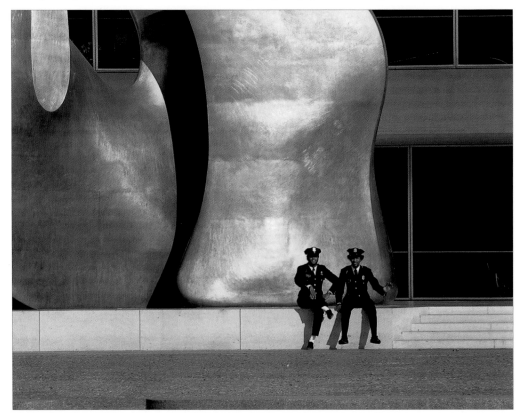

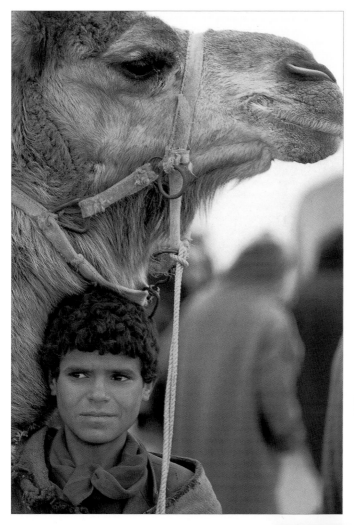

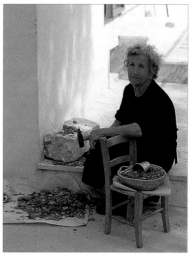

ABOVE This woman was cracking almonds outside her house. Her position was fine, but she was in strong shadow. By placing a small portable reflector to the right of the camera, just enough light was bounced back on to her. This is an example of a situation where a very bright background can give a misleading exposure reading.

BELOW This shop was a good photographic setting but inside, where this couple was, it was too dark. The couple agreed to move into the doorway where the light was better than within the shop, but the shot still needed something more, so they also agreed to hang sausages around the doorway. As a final touch, they are holding one of their whole hams. A good shot was created.

ABOVE Markets, like this souk in Agadir, Morocco, provide a wealth of opportunities for the alert photographer. This young boy was leading his camel through the throng of people gathered around the vendors. He is dwarfed by his camel, which has a typically arrogant expression. In situations like this feel free to move around the person until he is in the best position with the light. The other people in the souk fill the background, but are out of focus so they do not intrude.

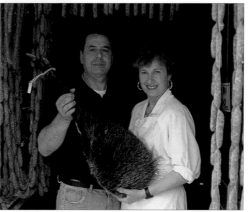

LEFT Although the picture was taken from some distance, these security guards at the Museum of Art in Washington DC were well aware that they were being photographed, and they played to the camera. Their presence emphasized the monumentality of the bronze sculpture that serves as a backdrop. Always be on the look-out for such a juxtaposition.

In Poor Weather

Poor weather does not have to deter you from photographing people. Sometimes it can actually add to and animate a photograph. But before taking your camera out in pouring rain, remember that cameras should not get wet. A camera that gets thoroughly soaked – or worse still, dropped in the sea – will probably be irreparably damaged.

If the skies are full of fast-moving clouds with quick bursts of intermittent sunshine, extra care will have to be taken with exposure. If the sun is out when you take your reading but behind cloud when you take your shot, the photograph will be underexposed. The reverse will be true if the sun is obscured when you take your reading but then comes out before you take your shot.

Look for something that will lift your shots in poor weather, and give them a point of interest. An isolated colour, or a figure in a landscape, will dispel the grey look. Do not be deterred by bad weather conditions.

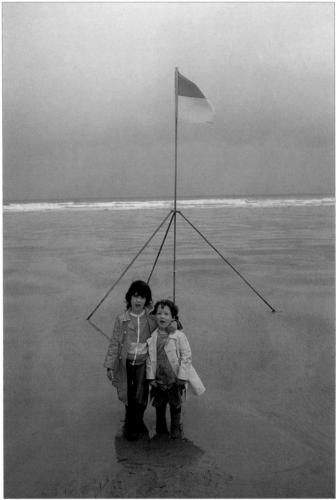

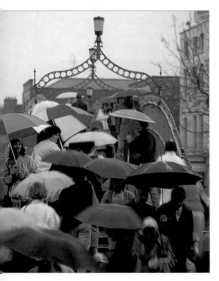

LEFT Here is a good example of making the best of a picture in poor weather, as people cross Dublin's Halfpenny Bridge in the pouring rain, their umbrellas jostling for space. The two large coloured umbrellas stand out in an otherwise monochromatic scene. The picture was taken inside a doorway which helped protect the camera from the rain.

ABOVE As you go for a walk on a dull, overcast day, you are all the more likely to notice a splash of colour that can make all the difference to a photograph. The flag on the beach marked the area of safe bathing. It was pure coincidence that the red and yellow of the flag matched the colours of the children's coats. Even something as simple as a patch of colour can enliven a dull scene. Be prepared at all times for a spontaneous shot.

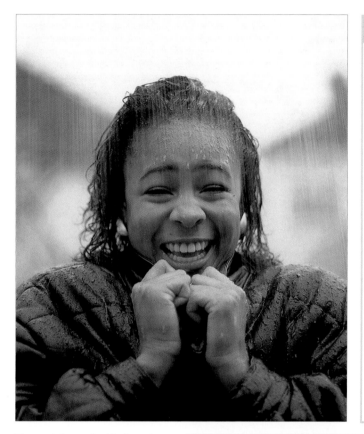

Keeping your camera dry

• If you are with other people, have them hold an umbrella over you. If not, try to stand beneath some shelter.

• A lens hood will protect your lens from rain. If the lens does get splashed, wipe the drops off immediately with a soft cloth or lens tissue. If you do not do this, they will show up on your photographs as unsightly out-of-focus blobs.

• A plastic bag put over the camera when you are not using it provides quite good protection from the wet. A more robust option for any watery adventures such as canoe trips is a plastic, fully sealed waterproof camera box.

• You can purchase a rain cover made of a very thin urethane-coated nylon that you attach to the lens hood and the camera base. You can operate the controls and even change the film, if using it, through the waterproof fabric.

ABOVE A close-up of a girl in the pouring rain shows just how animated a poor-weather shot can be. Her brilliant smile and bright eyes express fun and cheerfulness, even though she is getting soaked. Going in close puts the emphasis on her rather than the dreary background. A lens hood protected the lens from splashes.

RIGHT Although this shot was taken in the summer a dull sea mist was drifting inland from the coast. The isolation of the child looking for shells on the beach is emphasized by the mist. The Victorian railway viaduct in the background helps to relieve the gloom. If there had been more people in this shot they would have distracted from the image of the private world the child inhabits.

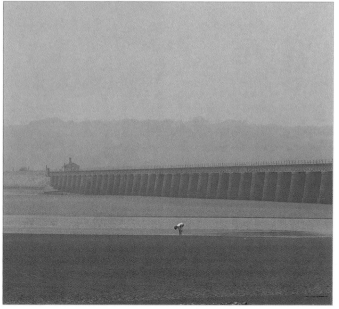

Holidays

More photographs are taken on holiday than at any other time. Being in a new environment is a good incentive to get good shots of family or friends, not to mention new and interesting buildings and scenes.

There are a few points to remember before setting off: take plenty of film or digital memory cards; make sure that all equipment is in working order and that any batteries are fresh. For a beach holiday, take a plastic bag to protect the camera from sand as it can ruin lenses. If any gets on the front element, blow it off – cleaning the lens with a cloth would have the same effect as sandpapering it.

Bright sunlight can cast deep and unattractive shadows under people's eyes so it is important to think about portable lighting equipment. Flash can be used to fill in these shadows. Another solution is to use a reflector to throw light back on to the subject's face. At the seaside there are vast areas that reflect light, and it is easy to be misled by the reading given by a light meter. If possible take a meter reading from a neutral area.

Look out for spontaneous shots. Candid shots, even of total strangers, can make a good picture – competitions have been won by such pictures so be prepared for that instant shot.

Wherever the scene of the holiday, it is likely that there will be some event such as a fair or festival. These provide local colour, and should be used to advantage. They can include information about customs and traditions which adds an air of authenticity and situation to the shot.

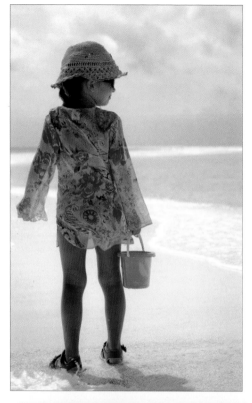

LEFT Young children make delightful subjects, none more so than this girl with her bucket. Be careful with exposure in seaside shots, since the glare from the sea and beach can fool the meter into underexposing the subject.

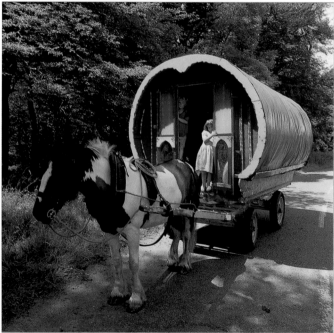

RIGHT These children were on a Romany caravan holiday in Ireland. They agreed to be photographed as long as the horse and caravan were included in the shot.

BELOW Although slightly posed, this picture of a young girl at a swimming pool is an attractive holiday portrait. The line of the white wall adds to the composition and makes an effective contrast with the blue of the pool. Shots like this can be fun, but it is important to work quickly so that being photographed does not become a chore for the child – boredom cannot be disguised.

BELOW In the holiday season most countries provide good set-piece events. Events can happen spontaneously, so be prepared. It is important to get the best viewpoint for a shot, as far as this can be done without being rude or pushy. Failing this, hold the camera above the heads of the crowd and point it at the action – it may be an outside chance, but it could work!

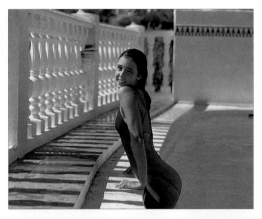

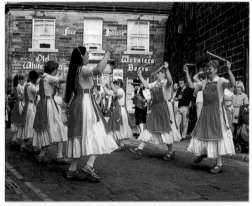

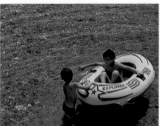

ABOVE This picture, taken from a high viewpoint, shows what can be achieved by looking for a new and striking angle. Seen from above, the water is translucent. The dinghy adds a splash of colour. The two boys did not know they were being photographed, and the spontaneity of this simple shot adds to its effect.

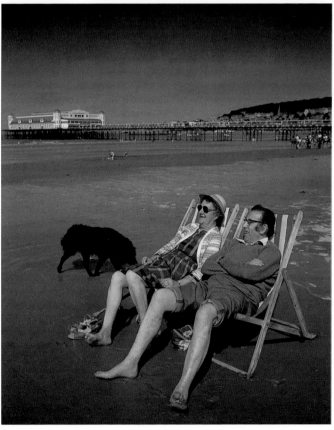

RIGHT This couple fits in well with most people's idea of the British on holiday. The photographer did not know the people, but they happily agreed to be photographed. The picture is full of good-natured humour. Only a camera ready for instant use will capture the mood in this way.

Mother and Child

When photographing children it is often a good idea to include their mother. She is usually the closest person to the child and the best suited to allay their fears and help them to adopt the best position.

Use a photographer's eye to look for the best viewpoint and lighting to show the natural bond between mother and child. As in any situation when photographing more than one person, be careful that the mother's head does not cast a shadow on the child's face.

If working indoors try to use available light. This will be less distracting to the child, which may be alarmed if a flash is used. If flash is necessary, soften the light as much as possible. This can be done by bouncing the light off a suitable surface such as a white ceiling or white board.

Alternatively put a diffuser over the light. This can be tracing paper or even a handkerchief. Take care here not to underexpose the photograph. The best way to avoid this is to use a flash meter, which shows exactly how much light is falling on the subject. If the mother and child are by a window, a reflector can be used to throw some natural light back on them.

When working out of doors make sure that neither the mother or child gets cold. Not only is it uncomfortable for them, but they might be shown with red noses.

Above all, be aware that most children can only concentrate for a short time. This will mean working very quickly. Conversely, a good deal of patience may be required to catch the child at the best moment.

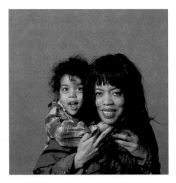

ABOVE This photograph was taken in a studio. Care was needed to keep the light from casting the mother's shadow over the child. Placing the child behind the mother has created an informal mood and it looks as if a game is in progress. Try to make pictures look fun, especially in the artificial conditions of the studio.

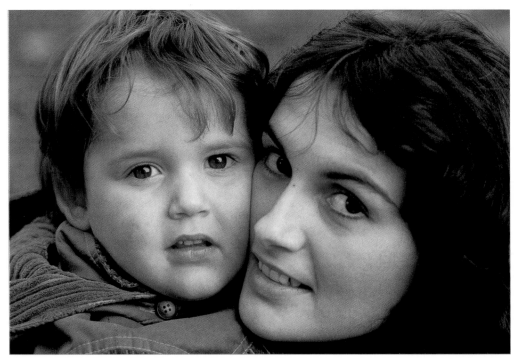

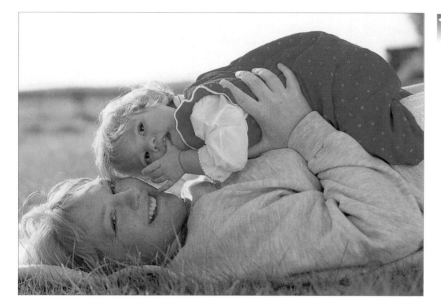

LEFT This picture was taken against the light and a reflector was used to bounce light back on to the mother and child. This has given a soft halo effect to their hair and made the picture look warm and summery. Asking them to lie down on the grass has further increased the air of a natural bond between mother and child. The low viewpoint makes the viewer feel part of the picture.

RIGHT Draping a white sheet over the window has created a very soft background. The mother and child were lit by flash softened by a diffuser. This has softened the overall effect even more, perfectly fitting the mood. In this case the baby was fascinated by the flash light, and it proved a useful diversion for him. Using a 100mm lens allowed a comfortable distance between the camera and the subject.

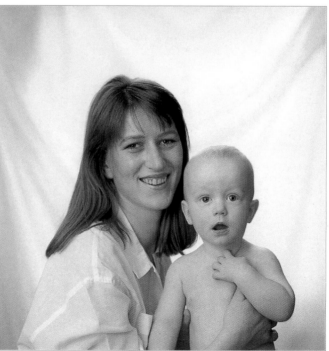

LEFT Going in very close has achieved an intimate picture of a mother and her son. It was taken on a chilly autumn day, and they are huddled together to give a snug effect. In such situations take care that the child does not get too cold and become distressed.

Babies and Young Children

Photographs of young children can bring pleasure to many people, not only their parents and close relatives.

The important thing to remember is that young children tire easily. Patience will be needed to get the best out of what might be a very brief photographic session. If the child seems to be becoming unhappy it is best to take a break and restart at a later time. Try to avoid dressing young children up in strange costumes, as these can humiliate them. The child should be having fun, and not be made fun of.

Natural light is probably the best, as it will not distract or distress the child. Very young babies are often upset by flashlight.

Try to think ahead about backgrounds. An ugly intrusion can ruin what would otherwise be a great shot, and there may not be a chance to move the subject. As well as more formal portraits, try to photograph the young child engaged in some activity – playing, or perhaps at bathtime.

When photographing small children in a studio or away from home, have a few toys around for them to play with. They may well not be able to understand a request to go to a particular place or do something specific. Often the only way of getting the right expression from a child is to play the fool.

With children who are two years old or more, Polaroid pictures can be a great help at the photography session. They will be fascinated by seeing the results instantly, and the pictures are also useful for checking exposure, lighting and general composition.

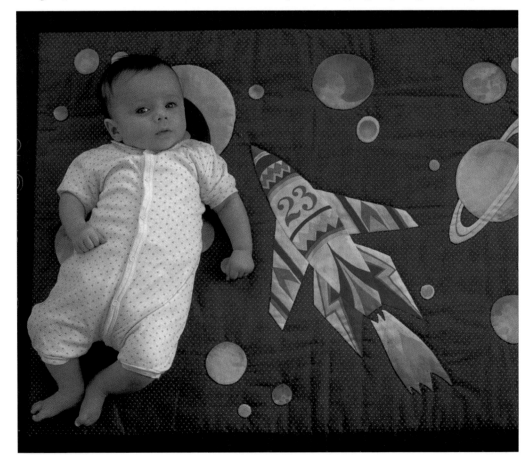

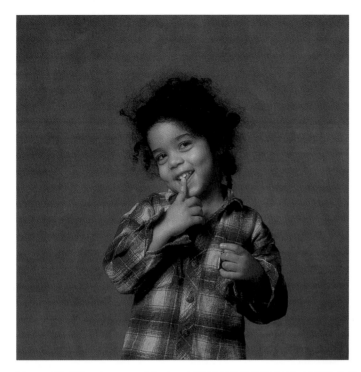

BELOW **BELOW** Bath time can be fun for young children and provide plenty of opportunity for natural-looking portraits. This one was taken with a flash and natural light coming in to the bathroom and it has a shallow depth of field. By working quickly, several good shots could be taken.

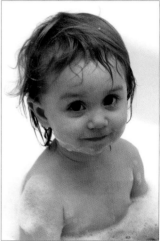

ABOVE This child acted spontaneously for the camera in a studio which other children would have found daunting. Several shots were taken, each one with a different expression. They were lit by a flash unit which had a fast recycling time so that shots could be taken in close succession. Editing the pictures was difficult as each one had its own character, but this one was finally declared the winner.

RIGHT Going in close on this baby's face has given full emphasis to his expression. Soft lighting has given a feeling of gentleness. A good deal of gesticulation, face pulling and cooing by the photographer and the child's parents were needed to maintain his interest. Never prolong a session with a young child to the point where it becomes upset. At the first sign of unhappiness, it is best to stop and try again later.

LEFT Always look out for unusual backgrounds, so that your shots have variety. This picture was taken by natural light from a window, with a reflector used to throw light back and give a fairly even illumination.

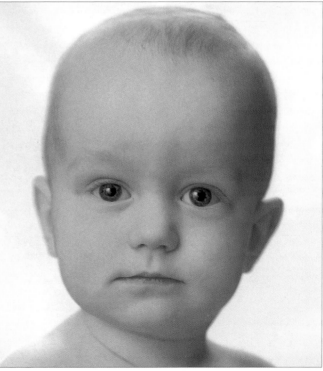

Children

Children are ideal subjects for photographs, for many reasons. From the moment they are born there is a visual record of their development which will not only be a pleasure to their parents and grandparents but will also be fun for them to look back on. Even with home video cameras, it is hard to beat a still picture that captures a fleeting moment in a child's life. And last but not least, even with film, an unlimited number of copies can easily be made and sent to friends or relatives anywhere in the world.

There is no need to photograph every breath children take, but at least try to make a record of important events such as birthday parties. These in themselves will make a fascinating series of pictures that show the child growing and changing. It will also provide the children with pictures of their friends.

Often the best way to photograph children is to take a candid approach, especially when they are absorbed in some activity. A medium telephoto or zoom lens – 80 to 200mm – will be useful in such cases, making it possible to keep at a certain distance but still fill the frame. A film with a speed of about 200 ISO should allow work in moderate lighting conditions without a tripod or flash, either of which could distract the child and destroy the spontaneity.

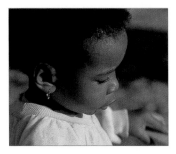

ABOVE This portrait of a small girl captures a spontaneous expression that is at once both intimate and charming. The warm light and her yellow jumper make a pleasing contrast with her dark skin and hair colouring. Always be on the look-out for quick shots like this when it comes to photographing children.

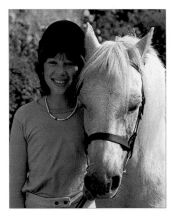

ABOVE Children's hobbies and pastimes provide many opportunities for pictures. Although this picture was taken in close, the girl was not inhibited as she was happy to be photographed with her pony.

RIGHT Children can become totally absorbed in what they are doing. Standing back so as not to inhibit the subject usually makes for a better picture. A telephoto lens is useful in such situations, as it allows a frame-filling shot, perhaps without the child even being aware of the photographer.

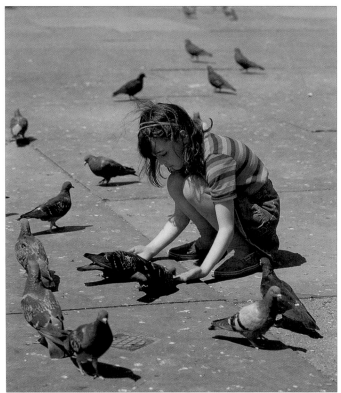

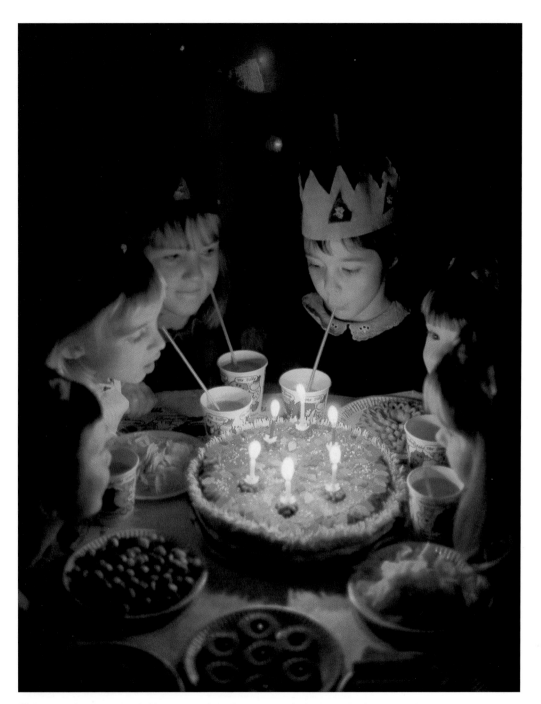

▲ **ABOVE** Special occasions such as birthday parties provide excellent opportunities for the photographer. This picture was lit entirely by the candles on the birthday cake. A 400 ISO film allowed an exposure just short enough for the camera to be hand-held. If flash had been used the atmosphere would have been killed, and the candles would have faded into insignificance. The picture also captures the birthday cake, over which a good deal of trouble has been taken.

Children at Play

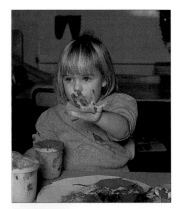

Children play naturally, so play gives good opportunities for natural pictures. Even in a favourite pastime children may lose interest in a few minutes, so quick work is needed to capture a good expression or gesture.

When working indoors, in the interests of speed it is probably best to use flash. This may upset a few children, but if they are busy they will probably take it in their stride. They may even be fascinated by it.

An alternative is to use a fast film and available light. If this is from an ordinary tungsten light bulb it will be necessary to balance daylight film with an 80A filter; otherwise the photograph will come out with an excessively warm, orange cast. There are now a few fast tungsten-balanced colour negative films, and a better selection of colour reversal ones. However, with these, if any other shots on the film are taken out of doors it will be necessary to use an 85B colour balancing filter to avoid a blue cast.

Try to think of different angles when photographing children at play. Consider a high viewpoint, looking down on them. This will make them look diminutive, but that may be an attractive effect. If the background is unsuitable, go in close to eliminate it, or use a large aperture so that it is out of focus. If the child is absorbed in painting or reading, try to get a shot that shows that concentration.

If the child gets bored, give up straightaway. Persistence will only produce tears of frustration and tantrums, and may put the child off further photographic sessions. A few Polaroid pictures taken to begin with will usually interest children and make them more patient when shots are taken with normal film.

RIGHT, BELOW AND BELOW LEFT These pictures were taken in a nursery school. The children liked being photographed; it was a new experience for them. However, young subjects can lose interest quickly. Patience on the photographer's part is paramount in such situations, and if you are good at interacting with children, all the better.

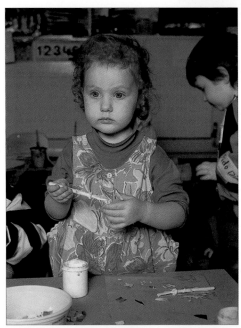

BELOW Although the ball is slightly blurred, this adds to the feeling of movement. The shot was taken at $1/125$ sec. A faster speed might have frozen the ball and the feeling of action would have been lost.

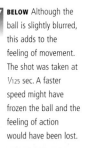

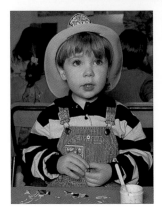

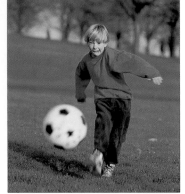

BELOW Sometimes the simplest shots are the best. This one of a girl surrounded by soft toys was taken using natural light streaming in from a window, diffused by a net curtain.

RIGHT Colour plays an important part in giving this shot a feeling of fun. The primary colours here convey excitement, aided by the boy's red sweater.

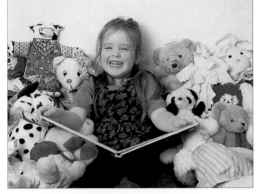

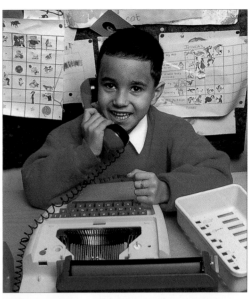

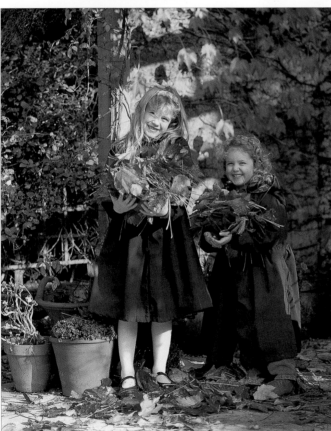

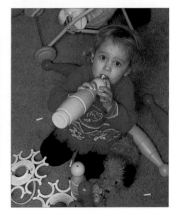

ABOVE Look for different angles when photographing children. Looking down on this small girl has increased the sense of her diminutive size. The picture was lit with a flash attachment on the camera's hot shoe.

LEFT When photographing children (or anyone) out of doors in bright sunlight look out for harsh shadows. Make sure the background does not dominate the picture, and is not ugly or uninteresting.

Older Children

Younger children can soon get bored and restless when being photographed, but older children also can be awkward in front of the camera. They have often reached a stage in life where they are worried about how they look, or do not interact willingly with adults – including photographers. The best approach is to put children of this age group in an environment where they are at ease. If they feel comfortable in their surroundings they will be more likely to respond to you as a photographer, and this will lead to a much more successful and rewarding portrait. Discuss with them what you are doing and where

possible let them have some input into the shoot, and give their ideas, but always remember you are in charge and don't let them take over as you could waste shoot time.

Think hard about the location and background, and try to make the poses as natural as possible. Use natural light wherever you can, perhaps using a hand held reflector to throw light back on to faces.

Build props into your shots that the children actually use, perhaps a musical instrument, a pair of football boots or a favourite book or game – something that comments on the child as an individual.

With groups of older children it is often difficult to get them all to do the right thing at once. Try to position them to ensure that no one obscures anyone else, but encourage them to relax, talk and move a little rather than sit rigidly, as this way you will get a sense of their relationships or group dynamic.

Experiment with different angles and lenses, and do not be afraid to bend a few rules. The result can repay all the effort. Perhaps because they are more reluctant subjects, older children tend to be overlooked in portraits. However, they are at a vibrant and interesting age.

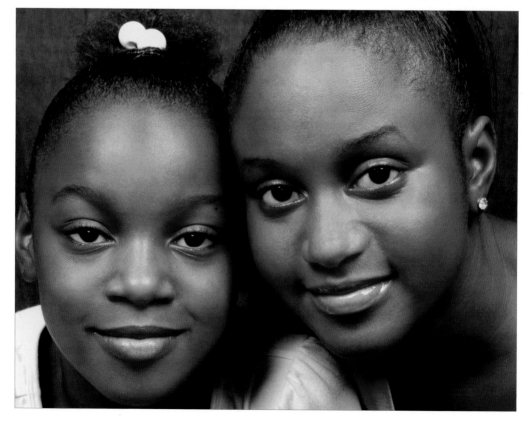

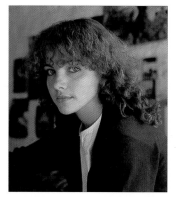

ABOVE This picture of a teenage girl was taken using available light coming through her bedroom window. Photographing her in familiar surroundings made her feel relaxed and at ease from the start. The posters on the wall behind her were put out of focus so as not to distract from her, and the camera was focused on her eyes.

LEFT If you can, photograph older children with their siblings or friends. They will relax and enjoy the photographic session more, and your shot will have the added advantage of showing family resemblance or a close relationship.

RIGHT This picture accentuates the subject's sense of humour. Although it does not show her whole face it is a flattering shot, particularly because the fresh green of the grass is picked up in the girl's shirt and the book cover. Choosing props, clothing and colours carefully can make all the difference – here, lots of different colours would have detracted from the shot. The white pages of the book have also acted as a reflector, which has a brightening effect on the skin and reduces any shadows under the eyes.

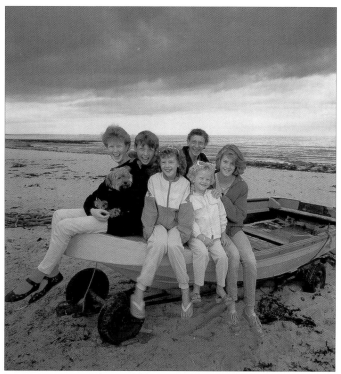

ABOVE These children were on holiday. The older ones kept teasing one another, but eventually they got themselves together and formed this group. Care was taken to make sure that no one covered anyone else.

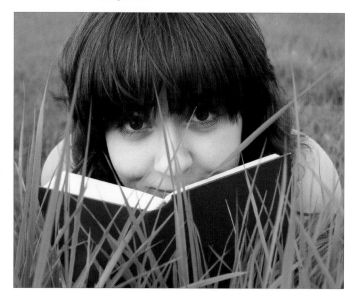

Groups

Very often when photographing groups of people there is always someone looking the wrong way, keeping their eyes shut or making a silly gesture or face. As a photographer it will take all your expertise as a director to get everyone to do what you want them to do when you want them to do it. The knack is to strike a happy medium between a jovial atmosphere and firmness. Of course, not all groups of people that you photograph are going to be under your control. They may not even be aware of your presence. If this is the case it is then up to you to find the right angle and be ready for the right moment. You will need to get yourself into a position where the light is at its best.

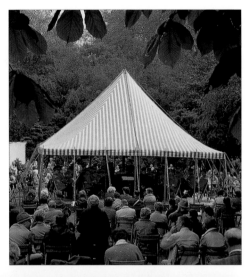

LEFT By including the overhanging foliage from the tree in the foreground a natural frame to the picture has been achieved. The people listening to the band have also added foreground interest. These details help to draw the eye to the main centre of interest, the group of bandsmen playing under the canopy of the bandstand.

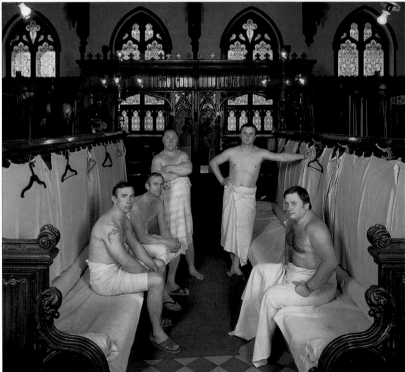

LEFT This shot was taken in a steam bath in Moscow. The attendants were only too willing to pose for the photograph and directing them to the required positions was quite easy. The lighting was a combination of flash and available light. The camera was mounted on a tripod and the shutter fired with a cable release. This meant that it was easier to keep an eye on the attendants' gestures and expressions and to direct their poses as required. Because of the building looks more like a gothic church than a steam bath, an incongruity has been achieved.

It might be advantageous in certain circumstances to photograph people while unaware, but then if they discover what you are up to they may get annoyed or move away. Often if a group of people know they are being photographed they will play for the camera and probably agree to your requests. If you are shooting indoors the chances are you will be able to direct people to adopt the positions you want. Take a good look at their characteristics. Decide who is the most interesting so that they can be in the foreground or in some other prominent position.

If there are many people to fit into the group, position them or take a viewpoint so that no one is obscured by anyone else. Consider whether some would be better sitting while others stand. It would be an advantage to work with the camera on a tripod and use a cable release. In this case you can position everyone to your liking. Also, when it comes to taking the actual shot, you can keep an eye on the group better from the camera viewpoint than looking through the viewfinder all the time. If you do use this method and your camera is set to auto exposure you will have to cover the viewfinder. On nearly all cameras there is a small button that brings a shield over the viewfinder. This cuts out light from entering the eyepiece – if this happens it will affect the camera metering mechanism and result in underexposure.

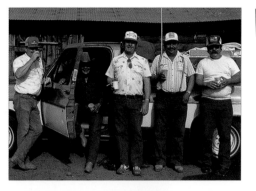

LEFT Either because they were drinking or because they were naturally confident, these men had no inhibitions about having their picture taken. Always look out for spontaneous situations but ensure that unwanted details are cropped out of your shots.

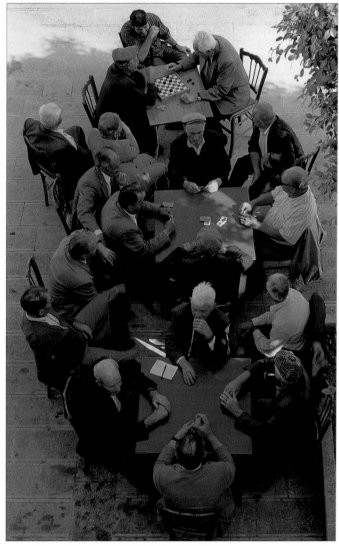

▶ **RIGHT** These men were playing cards on a terrace that was overlooked by a car park. It was a matter of chance that they were seen from this angle but full advantage has been taken of the viewpoint. Although the players became aware that they were being photographed they were too absorbed in their game to care. With a large group like this invariably someone will be looking the wrong way or making an unwanted gesture. Since it was not possible to direct them, several shots were taken so that a selection could be made.

Older People

Taking pictures of older people can be very rewarding for the creative photographer. Often they will have aged in a way which reflects their working life. For instance, a person with an outdoor occupation is likely to have a tanned, lined face – unlike an office worker. It is these physical characteristics that make such photographs so interesting.

At the same time, the photographer should show some sensitivity toward someone who is no longer young, not just in the way they are portrayed but also in the effect that a long photographic session, or even the use of flash, might have on them. If someone is a real character but frail, try working over several short sessions, and if possible use available light.

Older people are not only interesting in their own right but may well be surrounded by items collected over a lifetime, or they may be dressed in a way that reflects their life, as in the case of the Chelsea Pensioner shown on the opposite page.

A serious approach may be required to illustrate inadequate living conditions or illness. But if it is not, look for humour in pictures. This is not the same as being humiliating or patronizing. An easy way to photograph an older person might be to strike up a conversation with them. If so, be patient and do not give the impression that they are repetitive or long winded.

Look for different viewpoints, or go in close and concentrate on a particular area such as hands or shoulders. Black and white photography may be better suited than colour, since it allows greater expression and more evocative images.

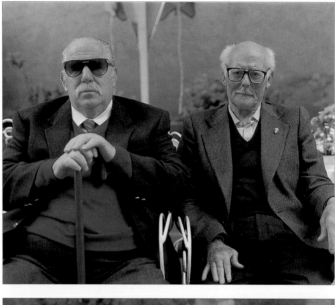

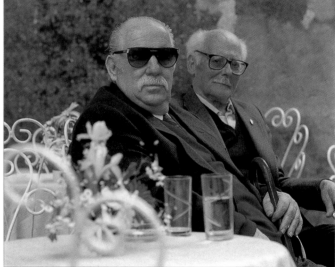

ABOVE These two men were photographed outside a café in Italy. They had no inhibitions about having their pictures taken, which meant that several angles could be explored. They were delighted with an instant Polaroid picture, which made them more receptive to being photographed. A medium telephoto lens, 100 mm, put the background slightly out of focus, drawing attention to their faces.

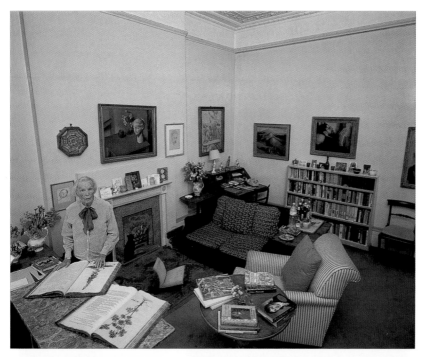

LEFT The picture was taken from a high viewpoint, as the room was rather small and as much of it as possible was required for the photograph. The woman is Frances Partridge, who was the oldest surviving member of the Bloomsbury Group when the shot was taken. She is surrounded by reminders of the group, including a portrait of Lytton Strachey.

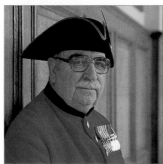

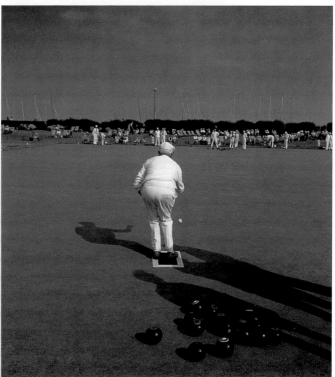

ABOVE Many older people wear clothes that symbolize their way of life, such as this Chelsea Pensioner. His hat and red coat add picturesque colour. His face is full of character and is lit by hazy sunlight. If the subject of the shot wears glasses, care should be taken with reflections, especially when using flash.

RIGHT Always be on the look-out for a humorous shot, but do not try to make fun of older people in a humiliating way. Most people have a sense of humour and will see the amusing side of a picture that tells a good story.

Candid Shots

Candid photography is when people are photographed in a natural or unposed way and may be unaware of the camera. Being prepared is essential – carry a camera at all times and have it ready for use. Since the opportunity for shots may occur when the light is low and there is no time for flash, or when flash might be intrusive, if you are using film go for a medium-fast film 200 or 400 ISO.

If you do take a photograph quickly and the subject is still in position, see if you can shoot from a different viewpoint that may be better. Even if the person moves away altogether you will still have that important first shot, but chances for improvement are usually available. Perhaps the best lens to use would be a 80–300mm zoom lens. This means that the pic-ture can be framed in such a way as to crop out any unwanted detail. It also means that you can get in close to the subject from some distance away. In this way you can work unnoticed without inhibiting the person and ruining the spontaneity of the shot. In candid photography it is often the look, gesture or position of a person that makes the picture.

It is an advantage to have through the lense (TTL) metering, preferably with spot metering facilities. This means a reading can be taken from the subject's face and you can expose for the skin tone. If the person is against a bright reflective background then there is the risk of underexposure if the meter takes an average reading; this is because the background would give off the most light.

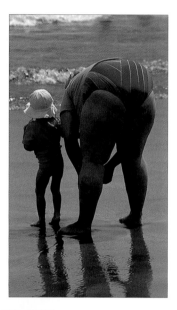

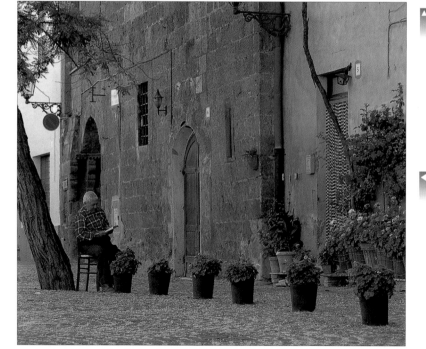

ABOVE This is an example of being prepared for a spontaneous shot. The woman bending over the child makes the obvious comment on 'little and large'. The shot was taken using a 300 mm lens that kept a good distance between the woman and the camera.

LEFT This man was quietly reading his book. After the initial photograph was taken another viewpoint was found. This made a better composition with the row of flower pots and added interest to his surroundings. Never think you have captured the perfect shot until you have exhausted all the possibilities.

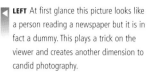

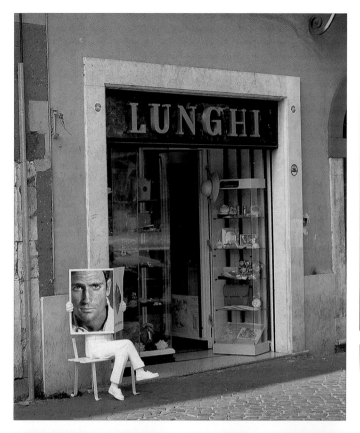

LEFT At first glance this picture looks like a person reading a newspaper but it is in fact a dummy. This plays a trick on the viewer and creates another dimension to candid photography.

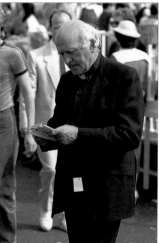

ABOVE Is it the surprise of seeing a priest gambling that makes this candid picture a success? He was absorbed in selecting the winner in the next race and was oblivious to having his picture taken even though he was quite close to the camera.

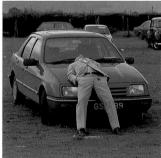

ABOVE Having had a little too much to drink, this man fell asleep on his car. Shots like this abound for the alert photographer.

RIGHT Even when people appear to be unaware of having their photograph taken, a second glance may contradict this. This boy in a Tunisian market appears to be asleep but a careful look shows that he is in fact watching from the corner of half-closed eyes.

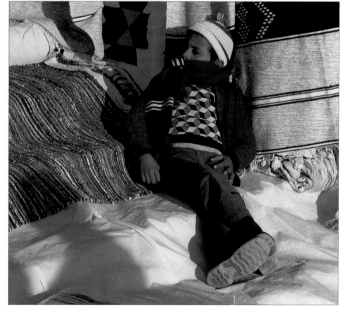

Going in Close

Sections of the face and other features of the body that can lend themselves to being photographed. Some of these pictures can be evocative and sensual. Others can be character studies, such as shots of wrinkled skin, and you can bring in the story behind the subject matter, showing perhaps a pair of hands at work.

Remember that the longer the focal length of lens you use, the shallower the depth of field will be at any given aperture so use your longer telephoto lens where possible. You can also use a tilt lens to create very shallow depths of field at a chosen angle.

Most standard lenses will not focus close enough, and a close-up attachment of some kind will be needed: extension rings, bellows or a macro lens. Close-up lenses that fit on to the front of an existing lens are available, but the quality of the image is not great. Some telephoto lenses can also be focused to quite short distances and will give excellent close-up shots.

For close-up work it is advisable to use a tripod. Extension tubes and bellows will reduce the amount of light passing through the lens, so exposures have to be long. They are made even longer by using a small aperture to make the most of the available depth of field. When using natural light, and with the lens stopped down to f/22 or even f/32, an exposure of a second or more may be needed. The subject also has to be kept still.

If lighting a close-up picture with flash, be careful of shadows. As the camera will be only a short way from the subject, ensure that it does not cast its own shadow onto the area.

Once the photographs have been taken, consider enlargements. Larger-than-life body details can take on a strikingly abstract quality.

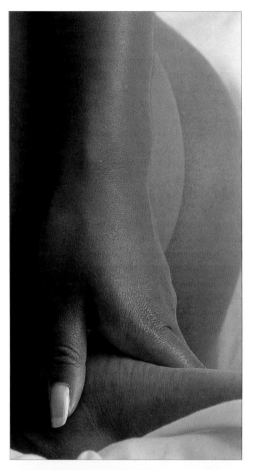

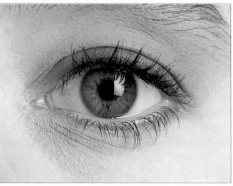

LEFT Going in close on this girl's hand, with her own body as the background, has created a sensual picture. A 100mm lens focused at its nearest distance was used – this shows that close-ups are possible without special lenses or accessories.

RIGHT This picture was taken with a macro lens. The subject's feet were surrounded with a white sheet so that they became isolated and took up the whole focus of the picture. They were lit with flash, using a 'softbox' to diffuse the light and soften her skin. The angle of view gives a sculptural effect.

LEFT This shot used a combination of extension rings and macro lens. The eye was 5 cm (2 in) from the front of the lens. A tripod and support for the girl's head were essential. The picture was lit by flash and the depth of field, even at f22, was virtually non-existent.

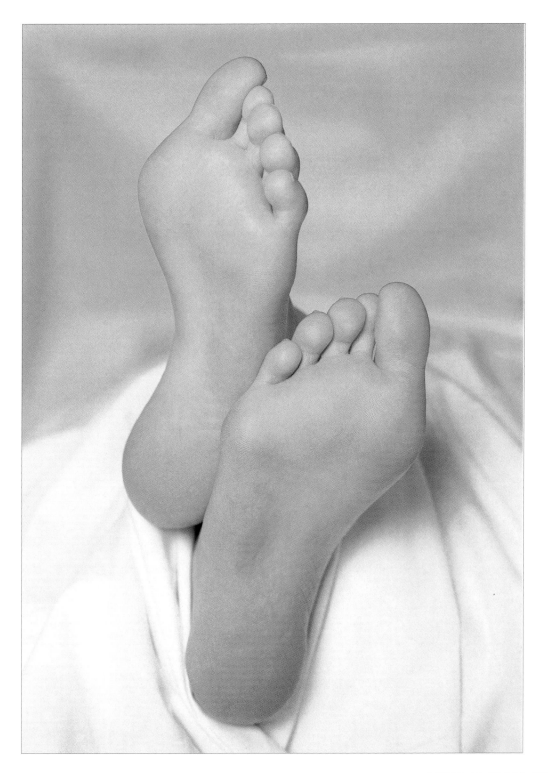

High-key and Low-key Portraits

High-key pictures are those where the tonal range is predominantly light. These are not to be confused with high-contrast pictures, which are images that have extremes of tone with few if any mid-tones. In contrast, low-key pictures have a tonal range mainly from the dark end of the scale.

Again, these are not the same as low-contrast pictures, which are images which have a narrow range of tone — this is probably due to underexposure, and the prints will have a muddy look.

When a full tonal range is easy to achieve, why, then, take high- or low-key pictures?

High-key pictures can look very romantic, and sometimes achieve an ethereal quality. If the background to a picture is uninteresting or intrusive it may be possible to fade it out by overexposing it. This may cause flare around the subject but, handled carefully, even this can be used to

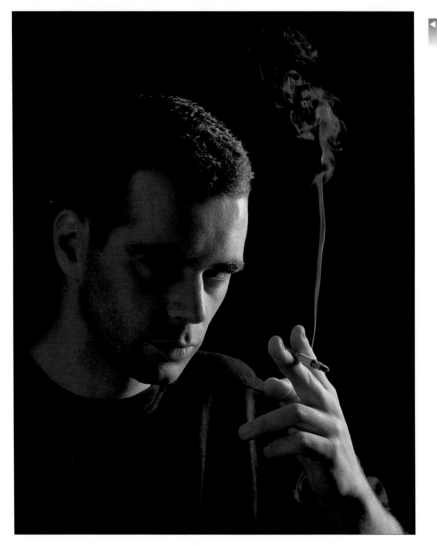

LEFT This low-key picture was taken in a studio, using just one light. This was placed to the side of, and slightly behind, the model. A reflector to the left and just in front of him bounced back just enough light to give detail in his face. The smoke from the cigarette shows up because it is backlit. If the light had been at the front the smoke would not have been visible.

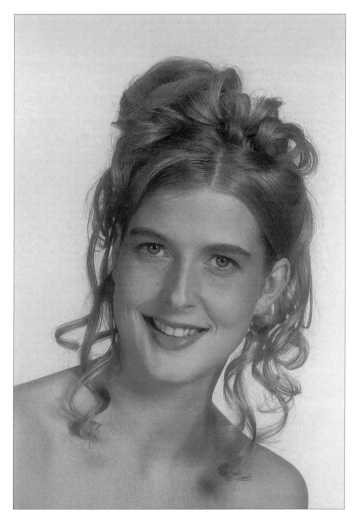

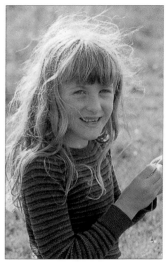

creative advantage. High-key pictures can portray freshness, a virginal quality, or the innocence of the baby.

Conversely, low-key pictures can convey isolation or loneliness. They can be very atmospheric. The easiest way to create low-key effects in the studio is with what is known as a 'rim light'. The light is positioned behind the subject. This creates a slight halo effect on the side the light is coming from. Using a reflector or a fill-in light can give the shaded side of the face just enough tone. The result is an image with dark tones, but one in which the subject is easily discernible.

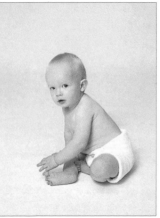

LEFT This baby was photographed on a continuous roll of white background paper in the studio, so that there is no line at the junction of the floor and wall. A large 'softbox' light was used, and this has created a very high-key picture.

Black and White Portraits on Location

Photographing people out of doors or in their homes in black and white can give strong and incisive images. Unlike photographing in a studio, however, you do not have full control of the lighting.

When using available light, some thought is needed to make the lighting work. When a flashgun or a portable flash unit is used, the light can be put where it is needed. If bright sunlight is causing shadows on

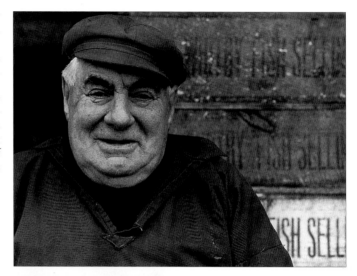

▶ **RIGHT** Background can say a lot about the person in a portrait. Here it gives just enough of a clue to show that he is a fisherman. Black and white has worked well here to give a 'gritty' appearance to the picture.

the person's face, there are several choices. One is to move the person to an area of shadow where the light is more even. Another is to use fill-in flash to soften the shadows.

If shooting against the light, a reflector can be used to bounce light back on to the subject's face. If, on the other hand, it seems that a silhouette would make an evocative image, take the exposure reading from the light behind the subject.

When working out of doors, even if the light is bright, it can be interesting to use a film faster than would normally be chosen. This will give increased contrast and grain, even a 'gritty' look, as the picture of the youths shows.

◀ **LEFT** When out and about, always be on the look-out for an unusual or spontaneous portrait, such as this one of a boy hiding behind his balloon. Having a camera loaded and at the ready allows the alert photographer to seize such moments.

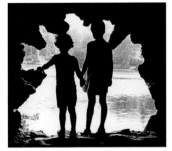

Always look for a new angle, especially when photographing groups of people. There is nothing duller than a straight line of people rigidly sitting or standing. Keep watch for an unexpected chance, and always have the camera loaded and ready.

Remember that, unlike colour film, black and white is not affected by differences in light sources. Whether shooting in tungsten or fluorescent light or daylight, only the intensity of the light need be considered.

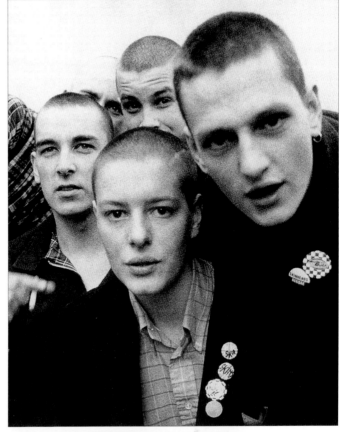

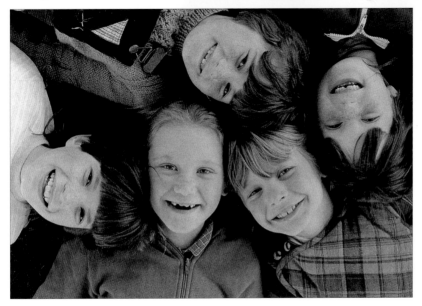

▲ **ABOVE** These youths were allowed to position themselves as they wanted. A fast film, 1600 ISO, has given a grainy effect which suits their rather menacing air.

◀ **LEFT** Asking these five youngsters to lie on the ground and look up at the camera has given the picture an unusual viewpoint. This shot might have worked equally well if the photographer had lain on the ground and looked up at the subjects.

Black and White Portraits Indoors

With black and white as with colour, photographing people in a studio gives total control over the lighting. For black and white shots, look for lighting that gives a good tonal range, or an unusual directional light that will give a striking effect.

Getting the right exposure is just as important with black and white as it is with colour, but when making prints in the darkroom there is far more latitude for altering the final image. 'Shading' and 'dodging' – that is, holding back shadows or the underexposed areas of the negative, and selectively printing up highlighted or overexposed areas of the negative – can be done when making a print with an enlarger.

Before taking any pictures in a studio try to work out the effect that is wanted. The sitter will be put at ease if they see the lights and equipment being handled in a confident manner.

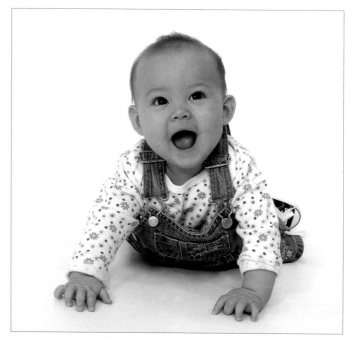

ABOVE Rolls of studio background paper are available from professional photographic stores. These are a standard 3m wide × 11m long (10ft × 36ft), and come in many colours. When suspended from a wall or ceiling they can be extended along the floor. This creates a seamless backdrop on which to position the subject.

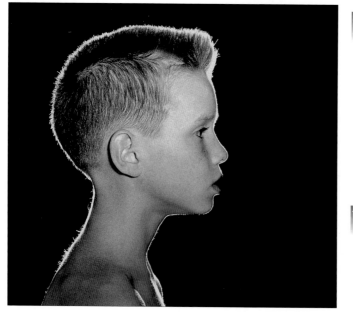

LEFT A light was placed directly behind the young boy and pointing straight at him. The light was fitted with a 'snoot', which has narrowed the beam down to create the bright outline around his head. A weak directional light was used to illuminate his face. The picture was taken against a black backdrop.

RIGHT Taking portraits in the studio allows complete control over lighting and composition. The possibilities are endless, as these three pictures show. Here the group is arranged to give prominence to the leader. The main light is coming from the right, but a weaker fill-in light has been put at the left. This arrangement shows some modelling in their faces. If the two lights had been of the same strength, ugly cross shadows would have occurred and their features would have looked flat.

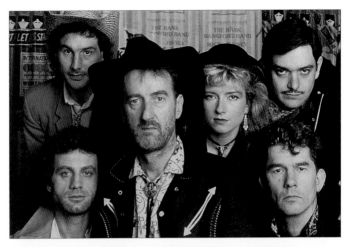

RIGHT Placing the main light directly in front of and below the group, shining upwards, gives an eerie effect. When positioning lights in a studio always return to the camera viewpoint to check the result.

BELOW RIGHT Standing on some steps and looking down on the group gives another angle. Whether photographing groups or individuals, always look for new viewpoints and lighting effects. The possibilities are limitless.

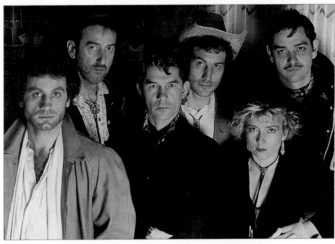

Learning to use lights

Explore the effect that one light can have on someone's face. If it is placed at an angle of 45 degrees to their face, set medium-high so that the shadow falls between the nose and half-way down the upper lip: the effect will be reasonably natural. If the light is straight in front and higher, there will be heavy shadows under the eyes, nose and chin. A light set below the face pointing upward will give a ghostly look. Practice, and a keen eye for where shadows fall, will soon make it easy to achieve a desired style. Once the basics have been mastered, all that is needed is a little imagination.

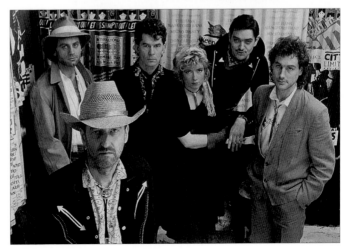

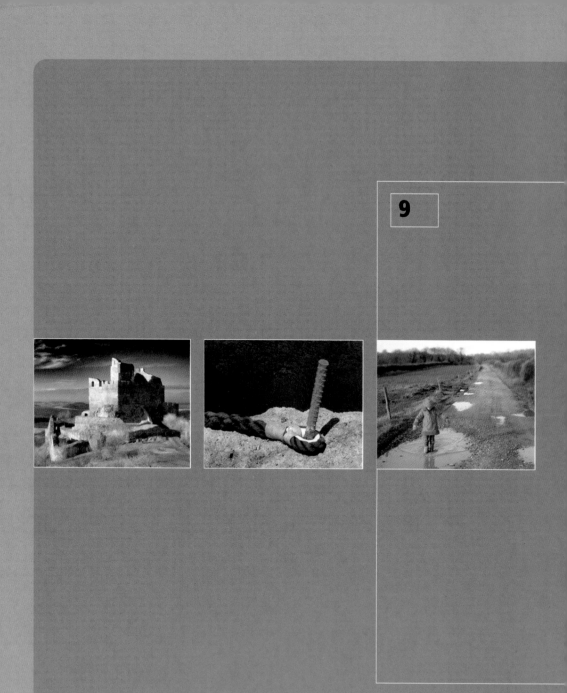

9

Basic Image Editing

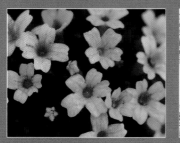 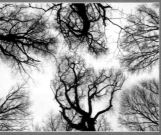 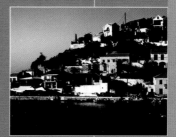

For those of us shooting digitally, most holiday snaps and family photographs can be printed directly from the memory card or camera. But for images you've really worked on, and shot in RAW to maximize quality, you may want control over the image's brightness levels, sharpness and so on. This chapter looks at the basic image-editing tasks that help to enhance your digital images. The projects are based either on Photoshop CS (the industry-standard editing application) or Photoshop Elements (the best-selling image-editing software). If you are a film user, you can still take advantage of image-editing by simply scanning your transparencies or prints.

Computers and Monitors

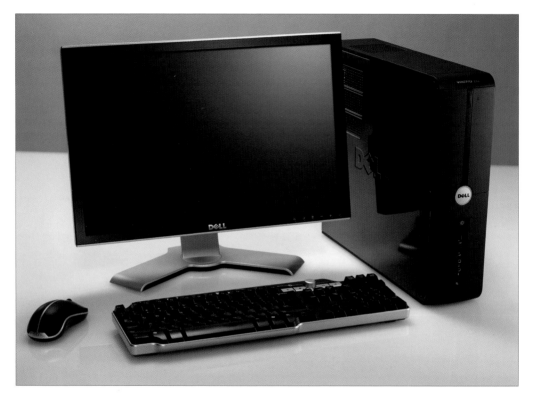

With computers now being such a principal component of the modern digital photographer's workflow, it's worth spending a little time looking at the specifications and peripheral devices you'll find either necessary or useful for image editing and storing your digital photographs.

Processing specifications

Computer technology, along with digital camera technology, has come an extremely long way in recent years, and will continue to do so. It is safe to say that just about any modern computer is likely to have sufficient processing power to run most of the image-editing software available, but here are some specific details:

• If you work on a PC running Windows®7, the minimum processing power you need is a 1GHz processor, 1GB RAM (32-bit) or 2GB RAM (64-bit), and 16GB available hard disk space (32-bit) or 20GB (64-bit). To run Windows®8 you need the same specification as above, but additionally a Microsoft DirectX 9 or higher graphics system.

• If you work on a Mac running the more recent OS operating system (OS X 10 and after), you will need at least 2GB of RAM, and 8GB of hard disk. Remember that for either operation system these are the minimum requirements – the higher the specification of your computer, the faster your software will run.

ABOVE Choosing the right computer is important for image editing, as the software you need to run will place huge demands on its processor, memory, monitor and operating system.

For either operating system, the monitor should have a resolution of at least 1,024 x 768 pixels, with a 24-bit colour video card.

Your system should also have a CD/DVD reader/writer so that you can load software and burn discs as a way of storing, sharing and backing up your images. You will also need a good internet connection – the faster, the better – as much of today's software is updated remotely. Additionally, you'll be able to download software on trial.

Finally, ensure that your computer system has appropriate connection ports; either USB, USB 2.0 or FireWire. These will enable you to download images directly from your camera or via a card reader, as well as provide connectivity for other peripherals, such as printers, scanners or external CD/DVD readers/writers and backup hard drives.

With the computer specification detailed above, you should be able to run most image-editing software, but remember that these are the minimum specifications and if you can afford to buy a computer with a higher spec, then do so.

Upgrading

If you find that your computer runs slowly, or that you can't use all the programs you'd like to use at one time, it may not be necessary to buy an entirely new system. There are numerous companies that produce memory upgrades that will be compatible with your computer and are relatively straightforward to install. A quick search on the internet will usually provide a whole host of companies.

If you think your computer is running unreasonably slowly, you should check to ensure that you don't have any viruses, as these will affect your computer's performance and may cause more extensive damage. There are many examples of virus software available that can identify and remove most common viruses.

External hard drives

No matter how long you think the hard disk space on your new computer will last, sooner or later it will be filled with your digital pictures. Before you get to that stage, you may want to consider purchasing an external hard drive for extra space. External hard drives can also act as a backup for your images if, in the worst-case scenario, you experience a complete hard-drive failure.

Monitors

Your computer monitor is very important, as you'll be making adjustments to your images based on how accurately and consistently it displays tone and colour. Most modern monitors are more than adequate for image editing. All are capable of displaying the maximum 16.7 million colours, which is about the same number of colours distinguishable by the human eye. In addition, they also have a resolution of at least 1,024 x 768 pixels, which is perfectly adequate for just about all image-editing needs.

In terms of size, buy the biggest monitor you can afford, as the larger the screen, the easier it is to display images at a good size, along with the various image-editing dialog and tool boxes. Aim for at least a 22- to 24-inch monitor, but again, bigger is defintely better. The drawback to a large monitor is the amount of room it takes up. But at least today's flat LCD screens take up less space than the old CRT monitors.

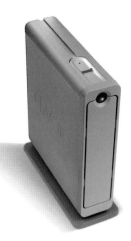

ABOVE When you start loading up your computer with digital photographs, the space on your hard drive will quickly fill up, irrespective of its size. An external hard drive that connects to your computer using FireWire or USB is the perfect answer.

BELOW FireWire and USB are the two most common ways of connecting peripheral devices to your computer. Some are very useful, such as printers and scanners, while others, such as a USB fan or torch, can be a bit more fun.

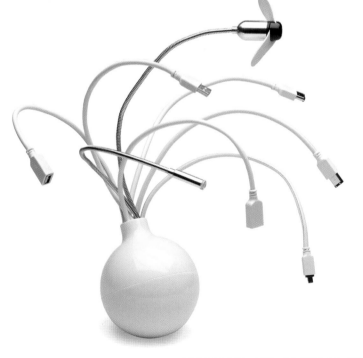

Image-editing Software

With digital photography now the principal method that most people use to capture and share their images, it's hardly surprising that there is a wide range of image-editing software available. The sophistication of image-editing software varies enormously, and this is reflected in the prices of the various packages – the most powerful, Photoshop, costs as much as a semi-profesional dSLR. At the other end of the scale, there is software that you can download for free. Here's a quick rundown of the most popular examples.

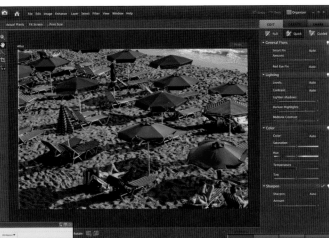

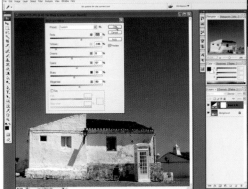

ABOVE Photoshop Elements offers many of the features of the 'full' version of Photoshop, but at a fraction of the price, which is why it is one of the leading image-editing programs among digital photography enthusiasts.

ABOVE The latest version of Adobe's powerful image-editing software, Photoshop, has a staggering array of editing commands and tools. One of the latest additions is the easy-to-use black and white conversion command.

Adobe Photoshop

Photoshop has been the industry-leading image-editing software for many years, and looks set to remain so. Adobe offer all their software on a monthly subscription basis. This not only makes the software more affordable for non-professionals but also ensures that updates are available instantly via an internet connection.

The full version of Photoshop provides photographers with a phenomenally powerful editing tool, capable of performing every conceivable image-editing task. It does, however, require a long learning curve, and for most amateur photographers the software is likely to offer more than they really need.

Adobe Photoshop Elements

Despite costing a fraction of the price of Photoshop, Photoshop Elements draws on its bigger brother for many of its features, including Layers and Blending Modes, as well as many of the more familiar commands, such as Levels, Sharpening, Hue/Saturation and so on. Few photographers would actually miss the features available in Photoshop that don't appear in Elements. In fact, in many ways Elements is more geared to the photographer than Photoshop, and features Quick Fix editing tools specifically for photographs. Despite offering very powerful editing, viewing and sharing tools, Elements is an intuitive program and relatively easy to learn thanks to the layout, the program's structure and the various 'wizard', or help, functions.

Elements has also evolved to become an extremely capable image organizer. Images are automatically downloaded from the camera or card reader, then organized by date, and can then be renamed by batch. Digital 'albums' can be created and filled by dragging and dropping images, after which you can add key words, making images easier to find later on.

Corel Paint Shop Pro

Similarly priced to Elements, Paint Shop Pro offers a high degree of image-editing sophistication, with some features on a par with the full version of Photoshop. Early versions of Paint Shop Pro were difficult to navigate and the program was quite cumbersome, but thanks to a newly designed user interface and the inclusion of a number intructional videos and tutorials, the later versions of the software are much more user-friendly. Perhaps the one signficant drawback to Paint Shop Pro is that it is only availabe on the Windows platform.

Adobe Photoshop Lightroom

Lightroom is an example of what is often described as a RAW-processing program. It is designed for editing and organizing large numbers of RAW images. Unlike older, more conventional image-editing software, which works by altering the colours and tones of the individual pixels that make up an image, RAW processors make adjustments through a series of instructions (known as parameters), which overlay the original image data. As the original data are left untouched, this form of editing is known as 'non-destructive'. While non-destructive editing does not allow levels of editing down to pixel level, it is sophisicated enough to perform the vast majority of editing tasks that most photographers require, such as colour and tonal adustments, spot removal, sharpening and noise reduction. And because you're editing the uncompressed RAW data, the level of control is excellent.

Although it's possible to edit RAW images using Photoshop and Elements via the Adobe Camera Raw (ACR) plug-in, with Lightroom the opreation is seamless. The program provides an intuitive user interface, is easy to master, and excels at organizing and sharing images. If you shoot RAW for optimum image quality, Lightroom has a great deal to offer.

Picasa and iPhoto

Available as a free download for Windows and Mac OS, Picasa is a very easy-to-use, basic photo editor. Although you don't get the sophisticated tool set and commands found in the editors discussed earlier, it may provide you with everything you need to brighten up and crop your holiday shots.

Similarly, iPhoto, bundled free on every new iOS device, is a basic, no-frills photo editor that performs all the basic editing tasks. Again, it may not offer the level of control of dedicated image editors, but it does have all the tools you need for simple image enhancement.

Free trials

Most software is available free for trial periods. Research online the software you like the look of and give it a go.

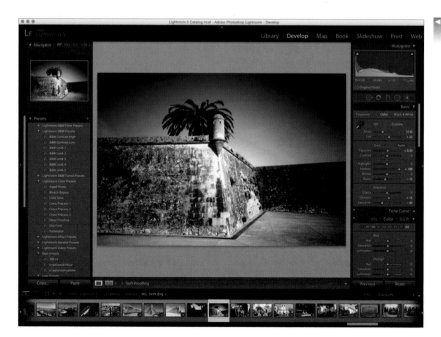

LEFT Lightroom is a powerful RAW processing tool that allows you to edit and organize large numbers of images effectively and with ease. Its sophisticated, non-destructive way of working means that you can make as many adjustments as you like without affecting the original RAW image data. So if you don't like what you've done, you can always go back – to the very start if necessary. As a RAW processor it works in 16-bit mode so that colour and tone are rendered smoothly.

Cropping and Rotating

As you take more photographs, framing your shots will become an instinctive part of the picture-taking process. As well as beginning to identify attractive compositions, you'll also find yourself starting to watch for vertical (or horizontal) edges to confirm that the camera is held level and that your images will turn out straight.

Sometimes, however, there just isn't time to worry about making sure everything's perfect, and it's all you can do to grab a shot at all before someone gets in the way. When a photograph comes out looking incorrectly aligned on your computer screen, the answer is to 'reframe' using image-editing software.

RE-FRAMING A PHOTO

This shot has a number of problems that could be tackled, but the key issues are cropping and rotation.

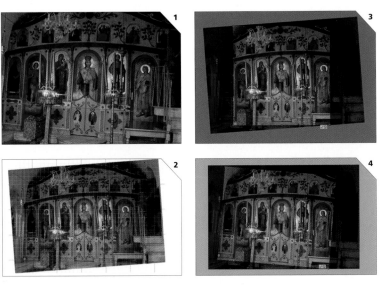

1 In Photoshop Elements, it's easy to straighten a shot using the Straighten tool, which you can find halfway down the main toolbox.

If you're using the full version of Photoshop this tool isn't provided, so skip to step 4 which will explain how you can rotate the image manually.

In the Options bar at the top, ensure the Canvas Options drop-down menu is set to 'Grow' or 'Shrink Canvas to Fit'. This means that your image will be left intact after it's straightened. To straighten the picture, click and drag along any line in the image that should be horizontal, such as the tops of the light grey front panels in the example shown here.

2 This seems to produce the correct result. If you want to check, go to View > Grid. Compare both the horizontal as well as the vertical features against the nearest gridlines. Unless the subject is shot

straight-on, you may not be able to get everything perfectly straight, in which case it may be easier if you rotate the image manually, as explained in Step 4.

3 Once straightened, it is likely that you'll need to crop the photograph. You can crop any image that isn't composed as tightly as you'd like by selecting the Crop tool.

In the Options bar at the top, set Aspect Ratio to 'No Restriction', to crop freely.

Click at one corner of the area you want to retain and drag diagonally to the other. The area outside is dimmed to indicate what will be cropped out of the picture. Drag any side or corner handle of the crop box to adjust it, then either click the green check symbol or press Enter to apply the crop.

This photograph has been cropped square to eliminate the blurred figures on the right. The midpoint of the altarpiece is aligned with the centre of the crop.

4 You can also use the Crop tool to rotate an image manually. First, display the grid (as in Step 2) before you activate and configure the Crop tool as in Step 3.

Drag around the rough area you want to crop to, then move the cursor just off any side or corner handle to show the rotation symbol. Click and drag to rotate the cropped area. Unfortunately, there's no option to display a grid that follows the rotated area, so you'll have to judge by eye.

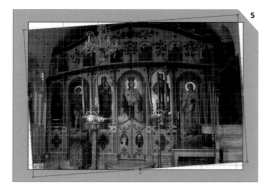

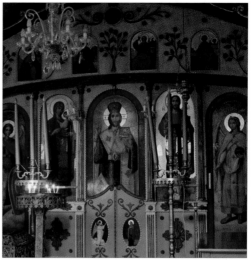

5 Alternatively, you can select the entire image by choosing Select > All, from the menu then Edit > Transform to reveal the Transform commands.

When you rotate the bounding box, the image rotates in real time, allowing you to check it against a grid.

However, the canvas isn't enlarged to accommodate the rotated image, so you may want to create some extra space. Use Image > Resize > Canvas Size and enter values that you think will be enough to encompass the rotated image. Unless you're rotating by a multiple of 90°,

rotating is a fairly destructive process, so if you're at all unhappy with your first try, go to Edit > Undo to retrace

your steps before rotating again. That way you'll retain as much of the image information as possible.

CROPPING TO A SPECIFIC SIZE

You can also crop an image by inputting the dimensions and resolution value in the Tool Options bar.

1 Here, we want to crop the image to 4in (10cm) square with a resolution of 300ppi.

2 Now you simply drag the Crop tool over the image. You can reposition the selection, if necessary, to ensure the best possible crop and click OK. The image will now automatically be 4in (10cm) square at 300ppi.

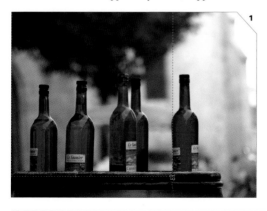

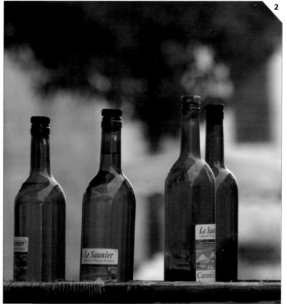

| 🔲 ▾ | Width: 10cm | ⇄ | Height: 10cm | Resolution: 300 | pixels/inch ▾ |

Brightness

Getting the exposure right every time isn't easy, no matter whether it's the photographer setting the controls or the camera's automatic function. Sometimes it just comes out wrong, and at other times there's a good excuse in the form of tricky lighting. The classic example is the situation where you have bright sunlight in the scene, but not on what you're shooting. Almost inevitably, while the shot's overall brightness may or may not be correct, your subject will look dull. When starting out with image-editing software, you may be tempted to reach for the Brightness command. Don't! It's rarely effective, and invariably destructive, discarding tonal information that can't be retrieved with further edits. Instead, turn to Levels, (here using Photoshop Elements) as explained in this project.

ADJUSTING BRIGHTNESS WITH LEVELS

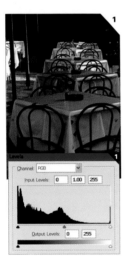

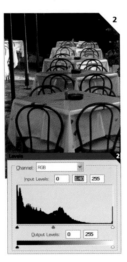

In this example, the image is slightly too dark.

1 Bring up the Levels dialog box by going to Image > Adjustment > Levels, where a histogram will show dark values at the chart's left, and light values at the right.

Here, pixel values are bunched at the dark end (left side) of the scale, with almost nothing brighter than a midtone except for a spike at the white end (right side), which represents the very few highlights in the image.

2 Two factors can make an image look dark; an absence of lighter values and the gamma (or grey) value. This is the location of the midpoint between white and black. To increase the gamma, click on the grey triangle below the histogram and drag it to the left.

If Preview is checked in the dialog box, the image will lighten. If pushed too far, increased gamma can make an image appear washed out so, in most instances, stop at about 1.4.

3 Now, to stretch the tonal range up into the lighter values, grab the white triangle at the right of the histogram and drag it to the left. Although it looks as if you're compressing the scale, you're actually expanding it. All those pixels represented by the black column above your marker become white, while the rest spread out across the scale, preserving the same relationships. The result is a brighter picture with more obvious light tones.

Bear in mind that any values to the right of your white marker will be 'burned out', which means they'll end up completely white, with highlight detail getting totally lost. Go too far and the image quality will suffer.

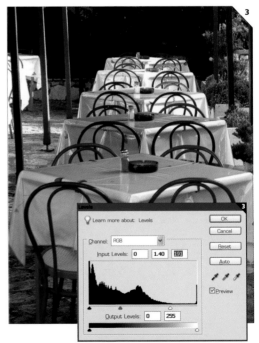

4 To see the effect you've had on the histogram, click OK when you're happy with how the picture now appears, then open the Levels dialog again via Image > Adjustment > Levels. The histogram shows a 'comb' pattern. Where tonal values are forced to spread out across the scale, gaps are left between them. This isn't a problem, but it represents a lack of tonal variation in the image and illustrates why an image that's shot right to start with will generally look richer than one you've had to correct using image-editing software.

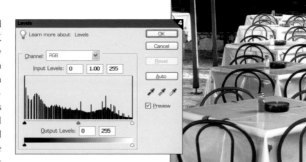

5 There is another way to correct brightness by using the Levels dialog box. Making the assumption that your image is slightly too dark, click the white Eyedropper icon, situated at the right of the Levels dialog box. This gives you an Eyedropper cursor.

Move it onto the image and click on a point that's bright, but not the very brightest value in the image. The effect is similar to dragging the white marker on the histogram back to this value, with pixels of this brightness becoming white. Setting the white point also affects colour balance, so by clicking on a point that should be neutral or white you can correct a colour cast at the same time.

If a shot is too light, you can correct it by reversing the advice here – that is, by selecting the black Eyedropper icon and this time clicking on an almost black element of the image.

DARKENING AN IMAGE

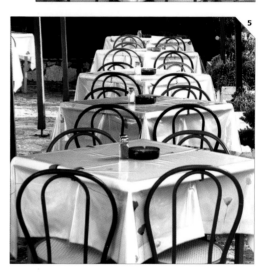

In this example, the image is slightly overexposed.

1 By moving the gamma point in the Levels dialog slightly to the right, you can darken the image.

Adjusting Contrast

There will be occasions when you've got the exposure right, but the picture still looks a little dull, and nine times out of ten the reason for this is a lack of contrast. While a lack of contrast can be a symptom of narrow tonal range, there's no hard-and-fast rule about how 'contrasty' a picture should be. It's really a matter of taste and what's appropriate for the specific image. For example, many classic monochrome landscape pictures have low contrast and rely on a subtle gradation of tone to maintain the viewer's attention. Most often though, you'll be looking to increase contrast to add impact to your pictures. Here's how to do it using Photoshop Elements.

INCREASING CONTRAST FOR IMPACT

Shot in hazy conditions, which hasn't been helped by the use of a telephoto lens, this image of cliffs has low-to-medium contrast.

1 To boost this contrast, go to Brightness/Contrast, which is found under Enhance > Adjust Lighting (in Photoshop Elements), or Image > Adjustments (in Photoshop). Increasing the Contrast setting to +40 gives a promising boost.

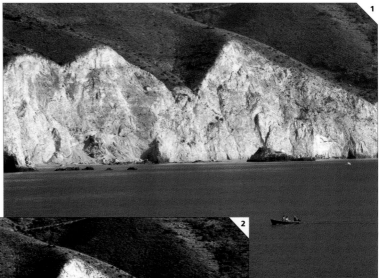

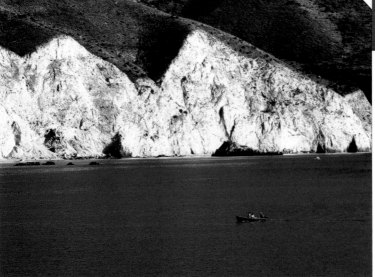

2 The Contrast command is a blunt instrument, however, and increasing the amount just a little too far can result in the lightest areas burning out completely, as can be seen here.

If you bring up the Info palette and move the mouse pointer over these areas, you'll see values of R=255, G=255, B=255 throughout, meaning that all the highlight detail is lost. This can happen even with modest adjustments.

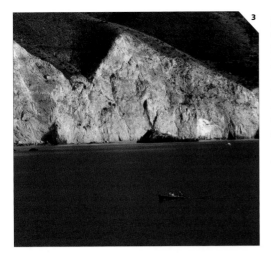

3 A far better option is to turn to the more powerful Levels command found under Image > Adjustments. In a low-contrast image, you will probably find that the histogram will show a lack of tonal values at the right and left ends of the scale – that is, the lightest and darkest values. Values cluster around the middle, falling off rapidly.

To correct this, grab the black and white markers in turn and drag them from the ends of the scale toward the middle. Leave each one at the point on the scale where the values start to rise. This gives a more subtle correction that leaves detail intact, allowing you then to control the result more precisely.

With some photographs, the histogram may appear to be all right, but the impression is still of low contrast. Moving the black and white points inward will still be effective, but make sure you watch out for lost detail in the shadows and the highlights.

4 Don't forget the gamma setting, represented by the grey marker in the middle of the histogram. Moving this to the left will emphasize the darker tones more, giving a bolder image. Moving it to the right will make the scene more pale and washed out.

Adjusting this setting along with the black and white points allows you to control the image's contrast and both the lightness and darkness independently. For example, here we've left the white marker alone, but have moved the black marker

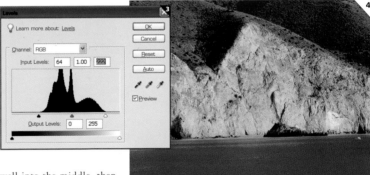

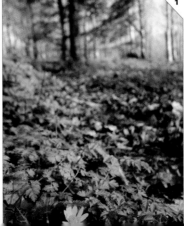

well into the middle, then increased the gamma by dragging the grey marker toward it (that is, to the left). This gives the sea higher contrast and detail.

USING AUTO-CONTRAST

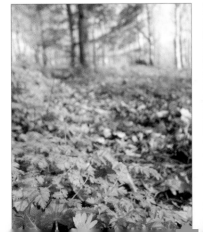

Here is another alternative to adjusting the black and white points manually in the Levels command.

1 Try Auto Contrast (found under Image > Adjustments > Auto Contrast). The effect is similar to performing Step 3 manually but this method has the added advantage of not affecting the colour balance as you can see here.

Correcting Colour Cast

Most digital cameras come with good Auto white balance (AWB) correction built in. This element of the camera's internal processing software analyses the scene you are shooting and attempts to correct any colour cast caused by strongly tinted light, such as that created by tungsten or fluorescent lighting. You can usually override the AWB correction and select the specific white balance mode that you want to use.

For example, if you are taking pictures indoors with incandescent lights or fluorescent striplights, you can select either of these options from the white balance menu and your camera will adjust the tone to be more natural, despite the ambient lighting conditions. However, these settings are seldom perfect and the camera can be tricked into making the wrong correction, which will result in a colour cast across the entire image.

USING LEVELS TO CORRECT COLOUR CAST

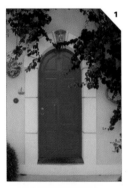

In the example shown here, the camera's Auto white balance was set to tungsten by accident, which has caused all sorts of colour issues.

1 A cold blue colour cast has affected the entire image, most obvious in the stone door frame, which should be brilliant white.

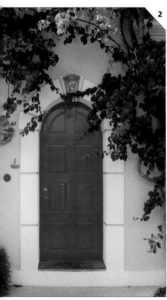

2 There are many methods you can use to correct colour cast problems in image-editing software, but by far the most powerful is the Levels command. Let's first try Auto Levels (Image > Adjustments > Auto Levels). When you are using Auto Levels, Elements finds the lightest and darkest pixels in each of the three colour channels (red, green and blue) and changes them to white and black respectively.

In this specific example, Elements hasn't done a very good job, and the resulting image has become too yellow and looks a little washed out. Use the Undo function (Edit > Undo) to revert to the previous image.

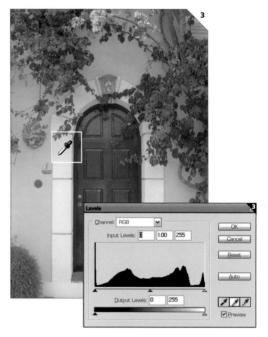

3 This time, let's see what happens when you take more control over the adjustment. Bring up the Levels dialog window, then click on the grey Eyedropper tool, which is the middle icon of the three found at the bottom right of the Levels dialog. Click on any grey part of the image with the tool, to tell Elements what the neutral tones are. Elements will rebalance the colours so that the area you clicked on becomes a neutral grey.

Don't be tempted to click on an area that is too bright or too white (such as the stone door frame), as this will give an entirely incorrect result, as shown in this example.

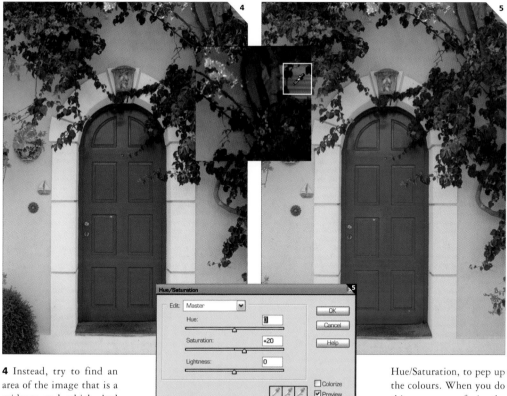

4 Instead, try to find an area of the image that is a midtone and which, had the image been correctly balanced to begin with, would have been close to a neutral grey. Here, a piece of stone cornice at the top right of the image has been selected. Clicking on the shaded areas in the grooves provides a much more accurate result.

5 Now the colour cast has been removed, it's often a good idea to increase the saturation using Enhance > Hue/Saturation, to pep up the colours. When you do this, you are safe in the knowledge that you won't be making the colour cast worse. Here, the saturation level has been increased by +20 to add more intensity to the colour.

USING AUTO COLOUR

Alternatively, you can try an automatic command to correct the orangey-yellow colour cast that is evident in this example.

1 The Auto Color command (which is found under Image > Adjustments > Auto Color) can sometimes be a bit hit and miss, but here it has successfully removed the colour cast of the street lamps in this outdoor café.

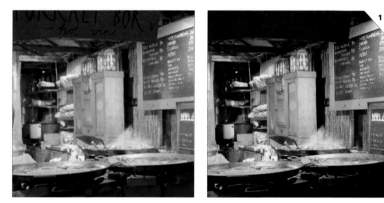

Curves

The Curves function is one of the tonal adjustments that is most often used by professional retouchers. The progression from dark to light in the image is depicted as a diagonal line, which you can reshape into a curve – or whatever shape you wish – to render the picture's tone exactly as you want it. Curves is a long-standing key feature of Photoshop, enhanced in recent versions to offer more information and control over individual colour channels. It has also been recently introduced into Photoshop Elements.

ADJUSTING TONE WITH THE CURVES TOOL

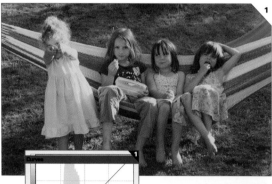

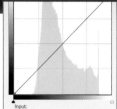

1 An extremely powerful and versatile tool, Curves can be used to adjust the tone of any photograph, but it's also a useful alternative to Levels for boosting a shot that looks a little flat and dull, such as this one.

Start by going to Image > Adjustments > Curves to open the Curves dialog box. As with Levels, you're shown a histogram in which each vertical bar represents the number of pixels of a certain value, from dark at the left of the scale to light on the far right. Overlaid on this histogram is a diagonal line that shows the relationship between the original image (or 'input') on the horizontal axis, and the result of the Curves function (or the 'output') on the vertical axis.

2 With this particular image, the grey histogram in the background fades off at both ends of the scale, indicating there is a lack of shadows and highlights.

As with Levels, you can shift the black and white points to fix this by dragging the markers at the left and right of the horizontal axis toward the middle. Move them to where the values start to climb and you'll see the end points of the diagonal line will then move along with them.

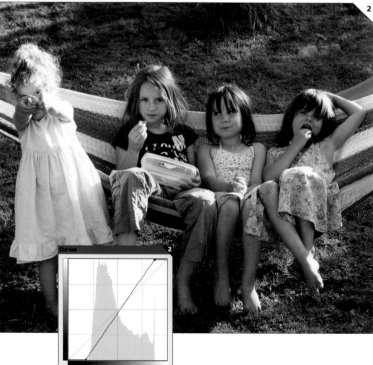

3 In the Levels dialog, you could then adjust the overall tone by moving the central grey or gamma slider to the left or right. Curves gives you greater control of the progression from dark to light. Click on the middle of the diagonal line and drag downward. The picture will look darker overall as shadows become deeper, but it still retains the brightness and detail of the highlights.

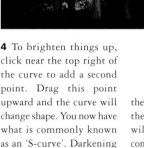

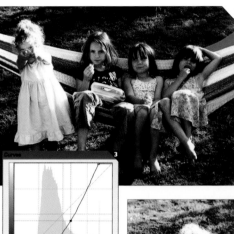

4 To brighten things up, click near the top right of the curve to add a second point. Drag this point upward and the curve will change shape. You now have what is commonly known as an 'S-curve'. Darkening the shadows and lightening the highlights in this way will create a bold, high-contrast image.

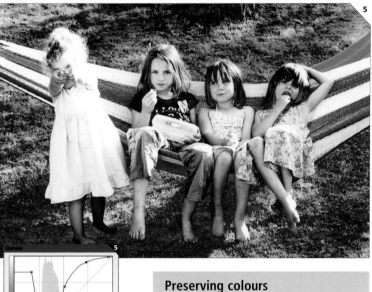

5 Curves can be used creatively in addition to correctively. The curve shown here produces a high-key image with false-colour shadows for a psychedelic effect. On monochrome images, a curve that has several peaks and troughs will give a metallic look. Experiment for yourself to see what effects are possible.

In general, when you're not aiming for special effects, your curve should remain smooth and, from left to right, each point should be higher than the last. Otherwise you'll create areas of flat, featureless colour within the image.

Unless you need to bring in the white and black points, make the curve continue smoothly to each end of the scale, without flattening out. This avoids the problem of clipping shadows or highlights.

Preserving colours

Notice how colour, as well as lightness, is affected as you adjust the curve. As the image gains contrast, colours also become more saturated. If you want to adjust contrast while preserving colours, switch your image from RGB to Lab mode (Image > Mode > Lab color) before using the Curves command. You can then adjust the curve for the Lightness channel only, which affects contrast and not colour.

Dodging and Burning

The slightly strange-sounding terms of 'dodging' and 'burning' goes back to the days of the traditional dark-room. Both terms refer to localized print-exposure control as the photosensitive photographic paper is exposed to the light from the film enlarger.

For example, a common use of burning is to ensure a bright sky is sufficiently exposed to bring out detail in the clouds. The photographer will make a rough mask of the foreground, and, after a set time, use the mask to cover the foreground so that the sky receives a few more seconds of exposure to the light, therefore making it darker. Dodging works in the opposite way. If parts of the image are in deep shadow, the photographer will make a mask to cover those areas part way through the print-exposure time. By doing this, he or she reduces the light striking the shadow areas, making them lighter than the rest of the image so that they hold fine shadow detail.

The digital versions of dodging and burning tools are intended to replicate these effects. In other words, they allow specific parts of an image to be made either lighter or darker, primarily to bring out detail in those regions that might otherwise be lost.

ADJUSTING LIGHT AND SHADOW

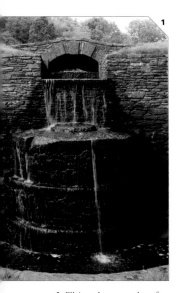

1

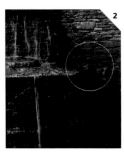

2

1 This photograph of a water feature was taken on an overcast day. Detail has filled in the darkest (under-exposed) regions of the photograph, while the top of the feature and the trees beyond are overexposed and have taken on a faded look. With careful dodging and burning, we should be able to balance the two regions.

2 To extract the detail from the darkest shadows, select the Dodge tool from the Toolbox. Make sure that the Exposure is set to between 5% and 10% in the Tool Options bar, and then set the Dodge tool to Shadows, using the drop-down menu in the Tool Options bar. Now adjust the tool to an appropriate size and then 'paint' over the worst offending areas.

You might discover that the results are sometimes a bit slow to appear, and rather than lightening the area, the Dodge tool can sometimes make the area appear a little cloudy.

3 To darken any over-exposed areas, select the Burn tool (it's in the same location as the Dodge tool), but this time use an Exposure setting of around 50% and select Midtones from the Tool Options bar. Brush the Burn tool over any overexposed areas. The Burn tool does a better job of darkening highlights than the Dodge tool does of lightening shadows, but control is still quite tricky.

4 Because the Dodge and Burn tools are tricky to control, the most effective way to dodge and burn areas of an image does not involve using these tools.

Instead, begin by creating a new blank layer by clicking on the 'Create a new layer' icon at the top of the Layers palette. In the Blending Modes menu at the top of the Layers palette, change the Blending Mode to Overlay.

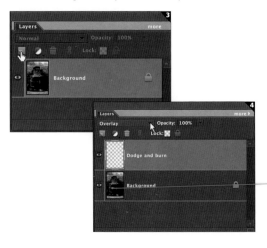

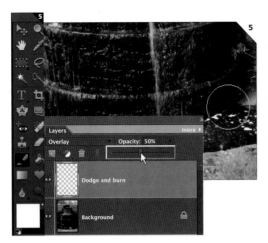

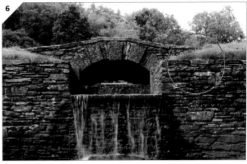

5 Select the Brush tool in the Toolbox, and click on the default Background/ Foreground icon at the bottom of the Toolbar to ensure that the Foreground and Background colours are black and white.

Next, click on the small right-angle arrow icon next to the default colour icon to exchange them, so that white is now the foreground colour. Use the square bracket keys to set an appropriate brush size, and in the Tool Options

bar set the Opacity to a value between 30% and 50%. As before, paint over the shadow areas. You should notice that the adjustment is much quicker than before and that the lightening effect is much more successful than using the Dodge tool.

You can also increase or decrease the Opacity if you want to increase or decrease the dodging effect. Another option is to increase or decrease the layer's Opacity in the Layers palette.

6 To replicate the Burn tool, you simply select black as the foreground colour. As previously, paint over the overexposed highlights to darken them and add some colour. Notice how the trees

and foreground grass now look much more vibrant. Again, you can use the Opacity slider in the Tool Options bar if you want to adjust the strength of the burning effect.

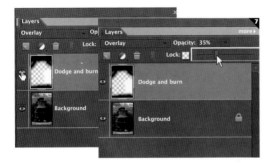

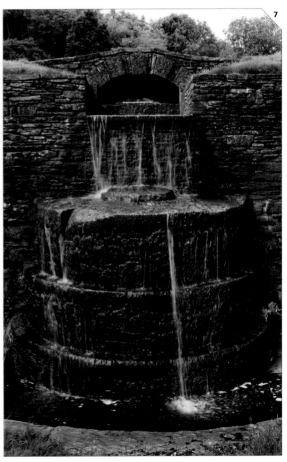

7 When you're happy with the overall adjustment, try clicking on the Dodge and Burn layer's visibility eye to turn it off and on.

This shows an instant 'before and after' of the effect that the layer is having.

If you wish, you can go back and paint black on any over-dodged areas and vice versa. Alternatively, you have the option of reducing the overall Opacity of the Dodge and Burn layer as well, to reduce the intensity.

Sharpening

Sharpening is one of the most important functions of image-editing software. Although used primarily when images have been shot using the RAW files format, (which therefore require some post-production editing), sharpening can also help when you find a shot isn't perfectly focused, just as long as the problem isn't too severe. Even on pictures that already look crisp, an additional amount of sharpening can ensure detail really pops out, especially if you are going to make a print. Sharpening also has an important technical function in countering the softening caused by scaling an image to make it larger or smaller.

APPLYING UNSHARP MASK

1 Before you think about sharpening any image, it is best to view it at 100% magnification first – that is, with one pixel on the screen representing one pixel in the image. For corrections such as tone and colour adjustments, you'd want to zoom out so that you can see the whole image, but sharpening can only be judged at 100%.

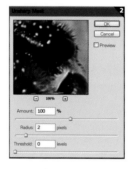

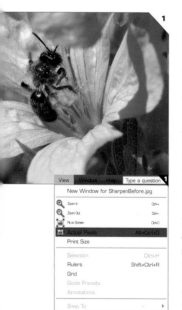

2 The best command to use for almost all sharpening purposes is Unsharp Mask. The name reflects the fact that this filter works by subtracting a blurred copy of the image. It's a digital version of a technique which is used in traditional image processing. In all versions of Photoshop, the command is found in Filter > Sharpen. However, in Photoshop Elements 5, it was moved to the Enhance menu.

Choosing Unsharp Mask brings up a dialog box that contains three sliders and a small preview window. Tick the Preview box to see the result on the main image, or untick it to compare the preview against the original. Your task is to find the right slider settings for your picture. Start by trying Amount: 100%, Radius: 2, Threshold: 0. With low-resolution images, use a Radius of 1 for greater sharpening.

3 See what effect this has on the image. Most images will have limited depth of field, so concentrate on the areas that are meant to be in focus. It's these that you're aiming to sharpen.

The bee in this high-resolution picture needs to be sharp, to draw the eye and create contrast with the softer petals, giving us an impression of the world at the insect's scale. To do this, increase the Radius setting until the detail becomes noticeably harder-edged. Here, 3.5 pixels is enough.

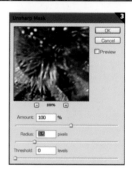

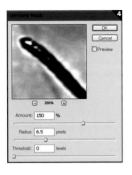

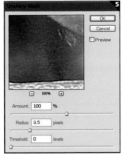

4 You can also increase the Amount if you need to create a stronger effect. It's important not to increase these settings too far though, so watch out for 'halos' around edges and a loss of subtle detail.

In this case, slightly over-zealous sharpening has created a marked glow around the bee's antenna, whereas the highlight detail has filled in.

5 Having set the first two sliders for the best result on key areas of detail, use the third, the Threshold slider, to mitigate any unwanted side effects.

Here, the low-contrast background areas, such as the distant foliage behind the petals, originally looked smooth, but the Unsharp Mask brings out noise (digital grain) in smooth areas of the image.

Sharpening down

When you print an image using a four-colour process (which is the method used to produce this book), the pixels are converted into dots of ink using half-toning. This has a softening effect, so to keep the picture looking crisp, you should sharpen a little more than normal. The dithering, or stochastic screening, method used in modern inkjet printing has less effect on sharpness.

It's often said that a digital image cannot be enlarged beyond its proper size without loss of quality, but it can safely be reduced. That's not strictly true, because when an image is reduced in size, it won't appear nearly as sharp. Before printing a high-resolution photograph at a small size, resample it using Image > Resize > Image Size. At the bottom of the dialog box, tick Resample Image and set the resampling method to Bicubic Sharper. Then enter the required physical dimensions under Document Size and click OK.

For even better results, especially with very small printed images, try resampling in stages, reducing by no more than 70% each time, using Bicubic Sharper. Apply Unsharp Mask at 100% with a 0.5 pixel Radius to the final, reduced image.

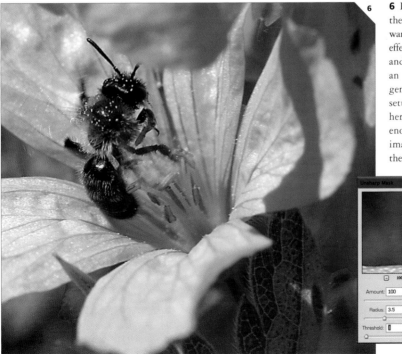

6 It is a good idea to use the Threshold setting if you want to limit the sharpening effect to high-contrast edges, and leave softer areas in an image untouched. In general, a small Threshold setting will be sufficient – here, a setting of 4 was enough. Pan around the image before applying the Unsharp Mask filter.

Advanced Sharpening

Some photographs present a challenge because they're substantially out of focus. This may be due to slightly inaccurate manual focusing, a subject being in motion at the time the picture was taken, the camera's autofocus picking out the wrong part of the scene or autofocus being compromised by low light.

Software sharpening can never completely correct poor focus, but it can help to restore a reasonable impression of sharpness. However, it is very difficult to achieve this without serious unwanted effects. Limiting unwanted effects requires more advanced techniques than simply applying the Unsharp Mask, as shown here.

MANUALLY IMPROVING FOCUS WITH UNSHARP MASK

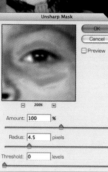

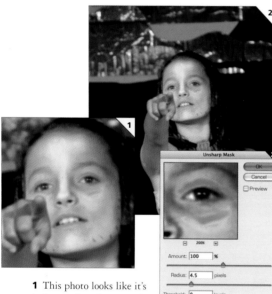

1 This photo looks like it's in focus at first glance, partly because the red and gold decoration in the background is unfocused, which makes the foreground subject look sharp by comparison.

At 100%, however, you can see that the face is very soft, with the eyes in particular lacking the hard detail that would give the shot real impact.

On your own photograph, identify an area such as this where you feel you need to concentrate your efforts.

2 It may be helpful to zoom to 200% in order to get a really clear view, then go to Filter > Sharpen > Unsharp Mask and set the sliders to a base level, as discussed earlier. On such a soft image, there'll be little or no visible improvement, so increase the Radius until you start to get an actual result. In the image shown here, there's a noticeable boost at 4.5 pixels.

3 Such strong sharpening produces side-effects you don't really want, such as distinct halos around edges and an increase in noise. Part of the reason for this is that you're working on a colour image, and increasing the contrast at the edges also has an impact on the appearance of the colours. To avoid this, you just need to separate the light and dark tone information from the colour information. This can be easily done by simply switching your image from the normal RGB colour mode, where three channels store the red, green and blue values for each pixel, to Lab Colour.

To change to Lab Colour, cancel the Unsharp Mask dialog box and select Image > Mode > Lab Color.

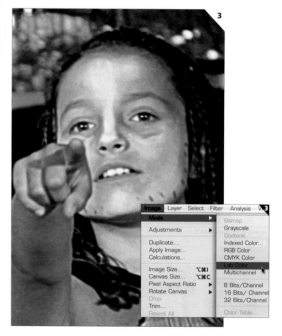

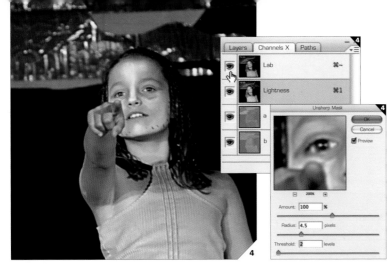

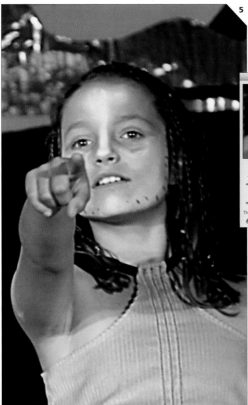

4 If you look at the Channels palette, you will see the image is stored as 'a' and 'b' channels (which contain colour information), plus Lightness.

Click the Lightness channel and the image then appears in monochrome, showing only the lightness of each pixel, rather than its colour. Click the box to the left of the composite Lab channel at the top to re-display the 'Eye' icon. Although you're viewing the full colour image, you will only be working on the Lightness channel when you apply the sharpening.

Open the Unsharp Mask filter and you'll see the preview within the dialog box reflects the monochrome Lightness channel. You should now find it easier to set a Radius that gives a clear improvement, but without excessive halos.

Watch for excessive noise in the low-contrast areas, but a small Threshold, such as 2 pixels, should be more than sufficient to fix this in most cases.

5 Using higher settings isn't the only way in which you can increase the effect of sharpening. It can be more effective to sharpen twice, so go back to Unsharp Mask and try a smaller Radius, and, if necessary, use a higher Threshold to avoid noise.

Smart sharpen

Adobe offers another sharpening command that has the option of using a method similar to Lab conversion to minimize unwanted effects, while keeping your image in RGB. If in Photoshop, go to Filter > Sharpen > Smart Sharpen. If you're using Photoshop Elements 5 or above, then go to Enhance > Adjust Sharpness.

The Remove drop-down menu provides a selection of methods. It's possible to minimize halos by selecting Lens Blur, but you'll probably discover that you need stronger settings to get a visible improvement. There's no Threshold control here, so you don't have direct control over any resulting noise.

In Photoshop, you can click Advanced for extra controls that limit the sharpening effect to shadow or highlight areas. This is useful feature if the sharpening settings that give the best result in the area of interest cause halos or noise in other areas.

One way to think of it is that the first Unsharp Mask brings out edges from the background, and the second Unsharp Mask sharpens those edges. When you've got the best result, convert the image back to RGB using Image > Mode > RGB Color.

Cloning Tools

Cloning tools are an important feature of most image-editing programs. They are powerful editing tools that in simple terms copy, or 'clone', the pixels from one area of an image and place them over another part of the image. This is usually done in order to remove unwanted marks, blemishes or even entire objects. Because there is a number of different types of elements that you might occasionally want to remove, most image-editing software packages offer a range of cloning tools. These make it easier to ensure any corrections that you make are all but invisible to see, and they speed up the image-editing process. Here we'll look at the main Cloning tools offered by Photoshop, but other applications offer a range of very similar tools.

REMOVING UNWANTED MARKS AND OBJECTS

Spot Healing Brush

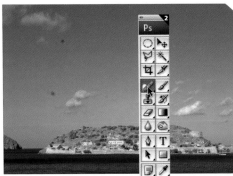

2 Both Photoshop and Photoshop Elements have the perfect tool for deleting dust spots from images; the Spot Healing Brush.

Simply select the tool from the Toolbox and adjust the brush size using the '[' and ']' keys until the brush cursor fits neatly over the offending spot. Then all you need to do is click the mouse button.

3 The same tool works equally well on any skin blemishes, such as spots, freckles and moles.

The Spot Healing Brush has two options available in the Tool Options bar. Proximity Match samples pixels from around the edge of the selection to replace the blemish, while Create Texture samples all the pixels in the selection.

1 Before cameras had built-in dust removal systems, dSLR users would suffer from dust entering the camera body and attaching itself to the image sensor.

Even with these new dust removal systems, dust can still find its way onto the sensor. It manifests itself as dark spots that are most noticeable in uniformly coloured areas of an image, such as a very clear blue sky. They also become far more obvious when a small aperture is used.

The spots will continue to appear in the same place, frame after frame, until the sensor is cleaned.

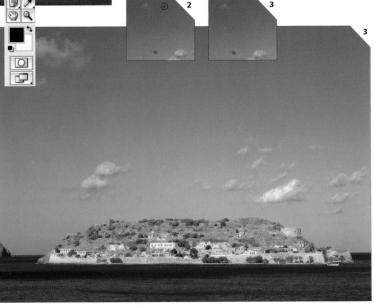

Healing Brush

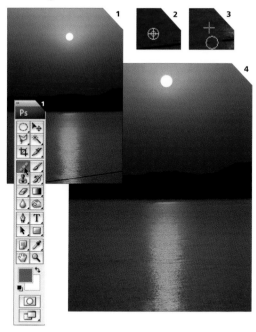

1 The Healing Brush tool is twinned with the Spot Healing Brush and works in a similar way. The sunset image shown here suffers from having a telegraph cable running along the bottom edge, which was unavoidable.

2 Select the Healing Brush from the Toolbox and use the '[' and ']' keys to adjust the brush size. The tool works more effectively if you use a soft brush.

To begin sampling, hold down the Alt key as close as you can to the start of the area that you want to replace. The Round Brush icon will then turn into a target to indicate that the tool is now in 'sample' mode. This signals that you can now begin to fix the problem area, in this case, the telegraph cable.

3 Sample the area and then paint over the offending cable. You'll notice a cross near to the brush symbol, which moves along as you paint. This indicates the area that the tool is sampling. Here, for example, the tool is automatically sampling from the golden coloured water as it moves along the cable.

4 Removing the cable from this photograph took a matter of seconds using the Healing tool.

Clone Stamp

1 If the area that you want to replace is comparatively large and the region from which you are sampling is not a uniform pattern, the best tool to use is the Clone Stamp tool. In this image, for example, it would look better if the large sign on the rocks could be removed.

2 As with the Healing Brush, start by selecting an appropriately sized soft brush and then hold down the Alt key to sample the part of the rock that you want to copy.

3 When you've done this, release the Alt key and then click with the brush on the area that you want to replace. You may find that clicking the brush more than once helps to delete the area.

4 Continue to sample from different regions to avoid creating regular patterns of tell-tale signs of cloning. You may find that you need to go over parts of the image that have already been sampled. By adjusting the brush size and sampling from various parts of the image, you should soon be able to create a realistic-looking replacement area of rock face.

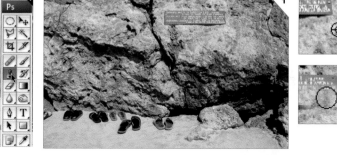

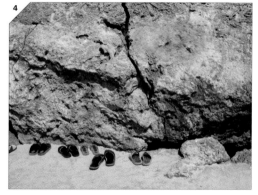

Advanced Cloning

The Clone tool is an indispensable item in Photoshop's and Photoshop Elements' tool chests. If you have unwanted objects or artefacts in your image that spoil an otherwise perfect shot, the Clone tool is probably the first tool to reach for. By allowing you to sample and paint using nearby pixels, you can use this tool to effectively eradicate, extend or duplicate elements in your scene – usually with a few strokes of the mouse.

DISCARDING UNWANTED ELEMENTS

1 In this photograph, modernity is encroaching on an otherwise picturesque, rooftop townscape. You could probably get away with leaving in the aerials, but the satellite dishes have to go. Here, the Clone tool comes to the rescue.

2 Start with the removal of the satellite dish on the right. First, begin by sampling an area of stone wall from anywhere around the dish by holding Alt and clicking on the image. Don't click too close, but not too far either, from the area you want to remove from the picture.

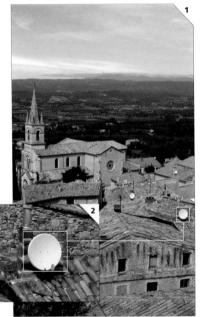

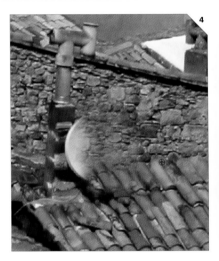

4 To replicate the top edge of the roof tiles, place the Clone tool over an existing edge section, and clone out the appropriate part of the dish. You may find using a harder brush provides a cleaner, more distinct line.

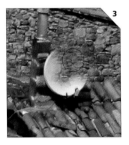

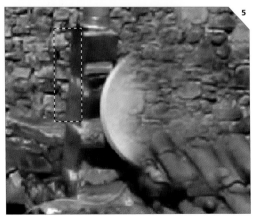

3 Set the Clone tool's brush to a smallish size, sample the wall and, using single clicks, cut out the part of the dish that's in front of the wall.

5 For areas that contain straight lines and in which there is a great deal of contrast between one region and the neighbouring one, such as the edge of the chimney stack 'overlapping' the stone wall in the background, the best method is to draw a selection around the existing side and copy it. Now we'll paste the copied selection over the remaining part of the satellite dish.

6 After roughly positioning the copied selection, use the transform commands to flip the section and rotate it into the right position. Flatten the layers and tidy up the new section using the Clone tool as before.

7 You can do the same with the remaining smaller dishes, cloning them out carefully, but always paying close attention to what patterns of pixels are immediately around them. If you choose your sample areas carefully, the final result should be a seamless image free from any unsightly satellite dishes.

When undertaking detailed cloning work such as that shown here, it pays to zoom right in when doing the cloning and then zoom out to normal size to see the correction in context.

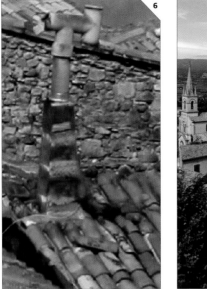

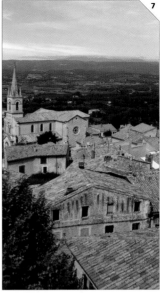

REMOVING AN IMAGE WITH THE PATCH TOOL

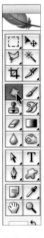

Photoshop also has a powerful, quick and easy tool for removing just about any item, from small facial blemishes to entire objects. It's called the Patch tool.

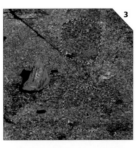

3 Once you have made the selection, click and drag it to an area on the image that most closely resembles the background of the object that you are trying to remove, and then release the mouse.

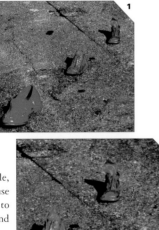

1 In this example, we are going to use the Patch tool to remove the last and smallest of these three red shoes in the image.

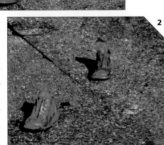

2 With the Patch tool selected, draw around the object you want to remove. Once you've done this, the selection will change to the familiar dotted line, or 'marching ants'.

4 Photoshop will sample the new area onto which you dragged the selection and use it to replace the initial area.

How effective the result is depends on the complexity of both the selected area and the sample area. Here, the random pattern of the road has resulted in a pretty convincing fix.

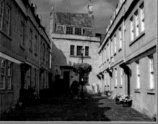
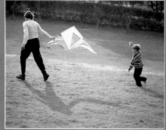
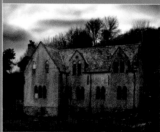

10

Advanced Image Editing

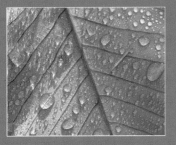 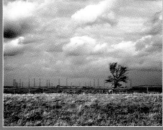 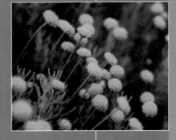

Image-editing applications have much to offer in terms of image enhancement. Here we're going to concentrate on pixel-based software, such as Photoshop, Elements and Paint Shop Pro. This type of software works on a layer-based system, allowing you to make localized or wholesale adjustments to an image without affecting the original. Using layers and controlling how they interact with each other by applying a variety of blending options, along with a vast array of editing tools and creative filters, opens up endless possibilities for your images. We'll also take a brief look at how Lightroom, a popular RAW processor, allows you to edit images.

Introducing Layers

Layers were first introduced with the third version of Photoshop, Photoshop 3. Their introduction turned image-editing software on its head. Layers make editing images much easier than if you have to work on a traditional single-layered canvas. They allow you to do things that would be impossible with a traditional 'one-layer' canvas.

The concept often employed to explain how layers work is that of a stack of transparent sheets, such as those you use on an overhead projector. Although you begin with a single layer (often called the Background layer) you can create a new, empty, transparent layer above it, as if slipping a new transparency on top of the original stack on the projector. This enables you to draw on the new layer, on top of the background layer, without actually altering the background itself. You can slide the sheet around to move the new elements relative to whatever is on the background, which will remain unaltered. You can keep adding new layers whenever you want. Most image-editing software now supports layers; here, Photoshop was used to illustrate the concept.

BASIC LAYER CONSTRUCTION

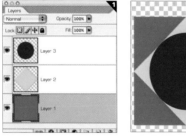

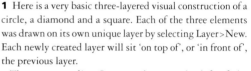

1 Here is a very basic three-layered visual construction of a circle, a diamond and a square. Each of the three elements was drawn on its own unique layer by selecting Layer>New. Each newly created layer will sit 'on top of', or 'in front of', the previous layer.

The corresponding Layers palette to the left of the illustration shows how one layer actually 'sits' on top of (or in front of) another. The Layers palette shows that the red 'background' square sits below a yellow diamond on which is placed a blue circle.

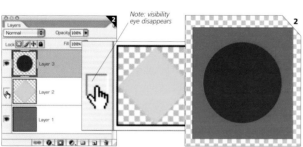

Note: visibility eye disappears

2 By clicking the 'Visibility eye' next to the Layer thumbnail in the Layers palette, it is possible to turn specific layers 'on' and 'off', making them visible or invisible. Here, clicking the Visibility eye next to the yellow diamond Layer thumbnail has rendered that layer invisible, leaving only the red square and the blue circle. Being able to turn layers 'on' and 'off' can help you to appraise images before and after an adjustment has been made.

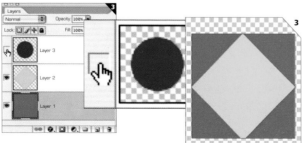

3 Here, the blue circle layer (Layer 3) has been turned off by again clicking on the Visibility eye, leaving only the red square and the yellow diamond visible. Not only do layers behave independently of one another, allowing you to apply adjustments to individual layers as opposed to the entire image, but you can also change their order simply by clicking and dragging the layers around in the Layers palette. This is shown in the next step, Step 4.

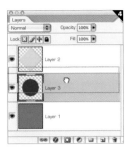

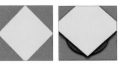

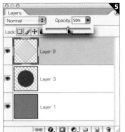

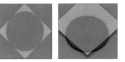

4 In the image above right, the blue circle layer has been dragged underneath (or behind) the yellow diamond layer. As you can see, the diamond totally covers up the blue circle. However, as an illustrative exercise, the three-dimensional image shows how the blue circle is actually hiding underneath the diamond.

Unlike transparent sheets on a projector, digital layers are genuinely transparent, so no matter how many layers you add, the layers beneath will always remain sharp and clear. Digital layers differ in other ways, too: for example, it is possible to adjust the transparency – or 'Opacity' – of the elements. This allows elements on a 'lower' layer to start to appear through the upper layer. How visible they become depends on how transparent you make the layer above.

5 Using the Opacity slider to reduce the transparency of the yellow diamond layer allows the blue circle to start showing through the layer. Notice, however, that in reducing the opacity of the diamond layer, the saturation has also been 'weakened', draining it of its yellow colour. Wherever it interacts with another

colour, such as the red and the blue, a fourth and fifth colour are created.

The way that the hue, saturation and brightness values of individual pixels on one layer react with the corresponding pixels on another layer is governed by Blending Modes, another powerful feature of many software-editing programs, and usually found in the Layers palette. For more information on Blending Modes and how they work, turn to pages 430–431.

LAYERS IN PRACTICE

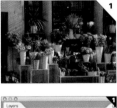

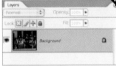

1 When you open an image in Photoshop, it's just like a normal photograph or artist's canvas. There's a single layer (called the Background layer), onto which you can draw or paint directly, or otherwise alter, using any of the editing tools. The heart of layers in most image-editing software is the Layers palette, which shows you all the layers that you have in your document.

2 Duplicate the background layer by creating a copy. You can do this in several ways, but the easiest is to drag the Background layer onto the 'Create a new layer' icon, which is at top of the Layers palette.

Alternatively, go to Layer > Duplicate Layer. You can now safely edit a copy of the image, while keeping the original background layer

intact. In this example, desaturate the duplicate layer by going to Image > Adjustments > Desaturate.

It's good to get into the habit of giving your layers names, as this will help you track your editing. Simply right-click/double-click in order to highlight the relevant layer text in the Layers palette and type in the new name.

3 A simple way to exploit layers is to remove parts of upper layers to allow layers below to show through. Select the Eraser tool and delete around half of the black and white layer to let the original colour layer show through. When happy with the result, go to Layer > Flatten Image. All the layers will be combined onto one layer to keep file sizes down.

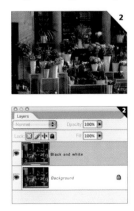

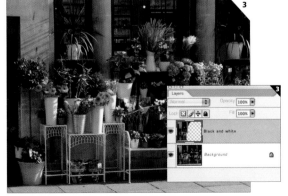

Using Layers

Having learned the basic concept of layers, and seen how by duplicating and altering the background layer you can create some interesting effects, let's see what happens when you combine two or more images to create one composite image. This could be the familiar photomontage type of composite, where images blend into one another to create a surreal piece of art, or when two or more images are combined to create an entirely believable scene. Here, using Photoshop Elements (but again other software will work in much the same way), we're going to replace the sky in one image with that from another, resulting in the creation of a new atmospheric shot. Replacing an uninteresting sky from a picture taken during an overcast day with a clear blue sky from another image is a common advertising trick.

COMBINING IMAGES USING LAYERS

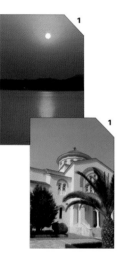

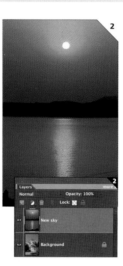

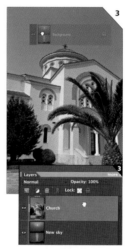

4 Use the Magic Wand tool to select the blue sky above the church. If it doesn't select all of the sky, hold down the Shift key and click on those regions that were missed. This will add them to the selection. Now, once you've selected the sky, go to Select > Feather and enter a value of 1 to soften the edges of the church so that they will blend more realistically with the sky. Press the Backspace key to delete the blue sky.

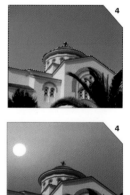

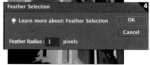

1 Here are the two source images – one of a Greek Orthodox church under a clear blue sky, and the other of a late afternoon sun. The images are very different in mood, colour and camera angle, but combining them using layers is a relatively quick and easy exercise. The more uniform the sky you want to replace is in tone and colour, the easier it is to cut out of the image using the Magic Wand tool. You should bear this in mind when selecting potential images for sky replacement.

2 Start by combining the two images into a single document. In the Layers palette, click and drag the background thumbnail image of one photograph and drop it into the canvas of the other image. A border appears around the image to indicate you can drop it, and holding down the Shift key will ensure the image is centred. Here, the sunset has been dragged onto the church image, covering it entirely. However, the Layers palette indicates there are two images.

3 Right-clicking/double-clicking on the Background layer of the church file allows you to convert it into a normal floating layer so that you can change the layer order. Unless you do this, you won't be able to move the Background layer, as it is locked.

Photoshop Elements will ask you if you want to give the new layer a name. Call it 'Church'. Drag the church layer above the sky so that it is now the uppermost layer in the Layers palette and covers the sky image.

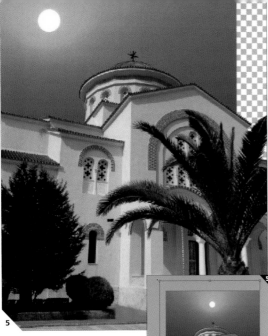

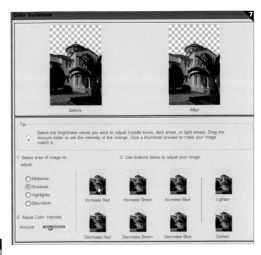

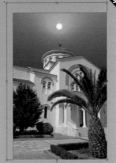

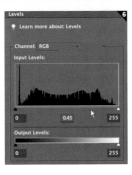

5 Now you need to move the sun a little to the left, so it's in line with the shadows on the church. To do this, you have to make the New sky layer a bit bigger, or there won't be enough sky on the right-hand side. Go to the Layers palette and select the New sky layer. In the Tool Options bar at the top of the screen, ensure Show Transform Controls is checked. This puts a box around the layer with eight rescale boxes – four at each corner, and four in the middle of each side. You'll have to zoom out to see these more clearly, which you can do by going to View > Zoom Out. Repeat the command until you can view the entire area, then resize the viewing window. Making sure 'Constrain Proportions' is checked in the Tool Options bar, grab one of the corners and rescale the sunset sky so that it is large enough to move to the left. Use the Move tool to reposition it.

6 You need to make the building and sky blend more closely in terms of tone and coloration. With the church layer selected, go to Image > Adjustments > Levels to open the Levels dialog window. Move the centre gamma (or grey) point to the right to darken the image of the church.

7 To adjust the colour of the church so that it matches the sunset sky, go to Image > Adjustments > Variations and click on Increase Red to warm the image.

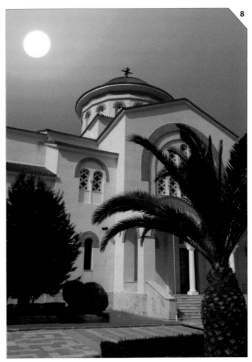

8 Here, you can see the successful final result. Simply by slightly repositioning the sun to the left, and getting the church to match the colour and brightness of the sky, it has been possible to create a believable and atmospheric image, using only two layers.

Adjustment Layers

Image-editing adjustments can enhance dull pictures and give you the creative control to overcome problems with lighting, colour casts or even exposure. Unfortunately, there is a catch. Once you've applied such adjustments, they can be difficult or even impossible to reverse, and if you apply several adjustments one after another, you may degrade image quality. However, many editing applications offer a way of applying adjustments that, while affecting how the image looks, actually reside on a separate layer. Using these 'adjustment' layers allows you to apply the entire range of editing tools and commands without affecting the background image. In this way, you can work on an image, applying brightness, colour and tonal corrections, which you can later go back and adjust or delete entirely, if you like. Here, we're using Photoshop Elements to show how versatile adjustment layers are.

CONTROLLING THE IMAGE ENVIRONMENT

1 Open the image you want to edit. Here, we're going to turn this daytime shot into a brightly lit night shot. Go to Layer > New Adjustment Layer to see a submenu of layer adjustments that can be applied in this way. Choosing an adjustment brings up a dialog box that allows you to give your adjustment layer a name. If you're making a lot of changes to a photograph, or want to create a multi-layer composition, it pays to remind yourself of the purpose of each layer by giving it a name.

Like other layers, an adjustment layer has its own Blending Mode and Opacity. You can leave these at the default settings for now, as you can always go back and adjust them at a later stage.

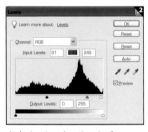

2 Click OK. You now get a dialog box for the selected adjustment, in this case Levels, which you can use in the same way as normal. Tick Preview to see the result on the main image. Here both the left-hand (black) point and the central gamma (grey) point have been moved to the right to darken the image, turning day into night.

3 When you click OK, the adjustment is applied to your image, but it isn't applied directly. If you look in the Layers palette, you will see that you've created a separate layer containing the adjustment, with the name you applied in Step 1. Hide this by clicking on the Eye icon to the left of its name. The original image is then revealed, unaltered.

While the adjustment layer is selected, you can click the Opacity drop-down menu at the top of the Layers palette to reduce the strength of the adjustment. Do this by dragging the slider. If you change your mind about the adjustment made, double-click the thumbnail at the far left of the layer name, which depicts the adjustment. In this case, a histogram for Levels is shown. The Levels dialog is reopened, allowing you to fine-tune the settings. To remove the adjustment altogether, delete the layer.

Because the adjustment is applied to the image 'live', you can add as many adjustment layers as you like, and change them as often as necessary, without any cumulative degradation in image quality.

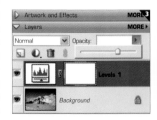

4 The thumbnail to the right of the Adjustment layer thumbnail represents a layer mask. By default this is white, which indicates that the adjustment applies to the whole image.

To apply an adjustment layer to a limited area of an image, first create a selection. Here, the sky has been isolated using the Magic Wand tool. If you've already added an adjustment layer,

remember to select the Background (or whichever layer contains your image) in the Layers palette before creating the selection, then switch back to the top layer so that your new adjustment will appear above this.

Now, go to Layer > New Adjustment Layer and select the required adjustment. A Hue/Saturation layer is used here to knock back the sky. The Hue is shifted to the left to make the blue of the sky colder, while the Saturation is reduced to make the blue less vivid, and Lightness is increased to match the tone with the snow in the lower part of the image, balancing the composition better.

5 Click OK to create your masked adjustment layer. In the Layers palette, the Mask thumbnail shows the area the adjustment is applied to in white, and the rest in black. For more information on how to use layer masks, go to pages 440–441.

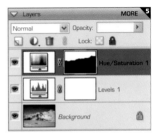

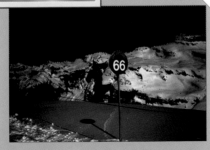

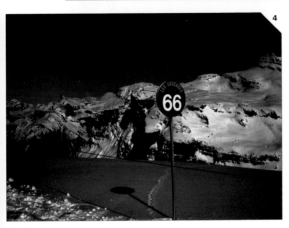

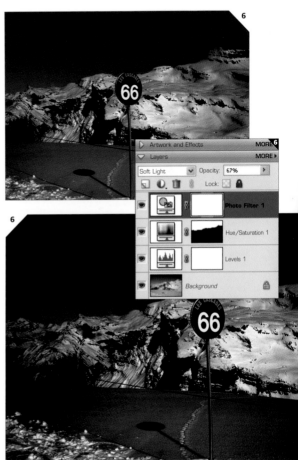

6 You can also use an adjustment layer's Blending Mode to alter its effect. Here, a blue tint has been added to the whole image using Layer > New Adjustment Layer > Photo Tint. The resulting artificial monochrome look isn't entirely satisfactory. In the Layers palette, changing the Photo Tint adjustment layer's Blending Mode from Normal to Soft Light helps to increase the contrast while preserving more of the underlying colour. Reducing the Opacity also helps to control the effect.

Blending Modes

In the last project we saw how altering the Blending Mode of an adjustment layer changes its effect on an image, but Blending Modes can be used for lots of other purposes, too. Every layer has a Blending Mode, which by default is Normal, meaning that anything in the layer covers up what's on the layer beneath. Again, most editing programs offer Blending Modes; here, we're going to use Photoshop to walk through some practical examples.

ADJUSTING TONAL AND COLOUR VALUES

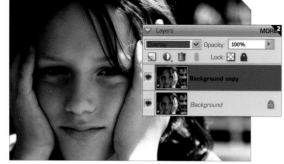

1 To use Blending Modes, you'll need an image with more than one layer. In photography, a useful way to exploit Blending Modes is to copy a single image onto itself and adjust the uppermost image.

Open your photograph and go to the Layers palette. Right-click/double-click on the Background layer and choose Duplicate Layer from the menu. In the dialog box, rename the new layer, or just click OK.

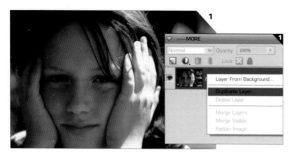

2 The blending mode of the current layer is shown in the drop-down menu at the top left of the Layers palette. Try changing it from Normal to Overlay. This serves to intensify the image, making the shadows darker, highlights lighter, and colours more saturated. This also gives the image a 'contrasty' fashion-photography look.

3 For an even 'hotter' look, try choosing Color Dodge. This brightens the image by increasing contrast and giving it greater colour saturation. With portrait photographs, which typically contain red and yellow tones, the result is reminiscent of a shot taken under intense sunlight. You can also still use the Opacity slider to reduce the effect of the blending mode layer.

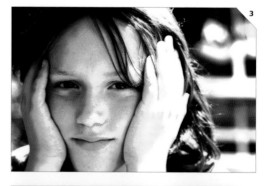

4 For a quick soft-focus effect, use Gaussian Blur (Filter > Blur > Gaussian Blur) with a large Radius – in the case of this high-resolution close-up shot, it is 24 pixels – which will soften the layer. With Blending Modes such as those mentioned above, underlying detail still shows through, while low-contrast areas, such as skin texture, are smoothed out.

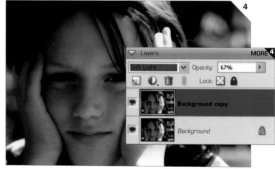

5 Blending Modes can also be used to help you combine images. In this example, a thought bubble has been added to a new layer using the Custom Shape tool and its Opacity has been reduced to allow the image below to show through. We now want to add an image scanned from a child's drawing.

6 In the Normal blending mode, the white paper covers the image and the bubble. Switching to Multiply superimposes the drawing on the bubble, as intended.

Blending modes explained

Understanding Blending Modes will help you to choose the correct ones when it comes to editing your images. A standard colour image stores red, green and blue (RGB) numbers for each pixel, giving each one a value from 0 to 255. This set of numbers is the pixel's colour value. In a layer blend, the colour value of the pixel in the layer is the 'blend colour'. The value of the pixel in the image as it was before the layer was added is the 'base colour'. A mathematical operation is applied to these values, producing a 'result colour'.

Two of the basic blend modes are Multiply and Screen. Adding a layer in Multiply mode simulates placing two slides in front of a projector's lamp at the same time. Both block some light, so the combined image is darker. Multiply works by multiplying the base and blend colours, then dividing by the maximum value of 255. For example, if you're layering an image on itself, and the R (red) value of a pixel is 100, the result will be (100x100)/255 = 39.

Screen mode does the inverse of this, resulting in a lighter image. Overlay mode combines Multiply and Screen. Where the base colour is dark, Multiply is applied, and where the base is light, Screen is applied. The result is a marked increase in contrast.

Blending modes are grouped by those that lighten an image, those that darken an image and those that do both. These groupings also tell you the neutral colour for each mode. When darkening, any pure white in the layer will leave the underlying image unchanged. When lightening, the same is true of black. And with balanced modes, 50% grey is normally neutral.

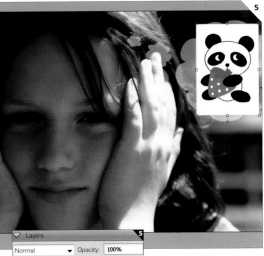

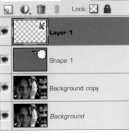

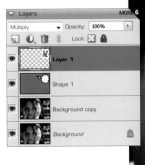

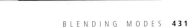

Merge for High Dynamic Range (HDR)

For many people new to digital photography, the phrase 'Merge for HDR' may sound completely baffling, but in fact it's an easy concept to grasp.

Merge for HDR (High Dynamic Range) is simply a way of merging together a number of differently exposed images of the same scene in order to increase the dynamic range in a photograph. Digital cameras are only capable of capturing a set range of tones in a single frame, and any tones outside of that range became either pure black or pure white, with no detail visible. However, a number of editing applications now allow you to merge several images that have been taken using different exposures, to capture a much greater range of tones. These all work in more or less the same way, but here we're going to use Photomatix Pro. This works either as a stand-alone program or a plug-in.

CAPTURING A FULL RANGE OF TONES

1 In high-contrasting lighting conditions, such as occurs when photographing a bright sky and a relatively dark land area, it's unlikely that your camera will be able to capture the complete range of tones from bright highlights to dark shadows. The rule of thumb is to set your exposure to capture the highlights, letting the shadows underexpose to pure black. The rationale is that areas of black shadow are visually less offensive than areas of 'blown-out', pure white highlights. With digital photography, however, it's a relatively easy job to overcome the issue by taking a sufficient number of images that capture the full range of tones in the scene you're photographing. To help you do this, most cameras have a bracketing mode that will automatically adjust the exposure setting so that you can easily capture different exposures, as shown here in this scene of the famous gardens at Stourhead. Using auto exposure bracketing (AEB) and the camera set to continuous shooting mode, three images were taken in quick succession, one capturing the bright sky, another the midtones and the third the darker tones in the foreground. Now we can combine the three frames to make one HDR image.

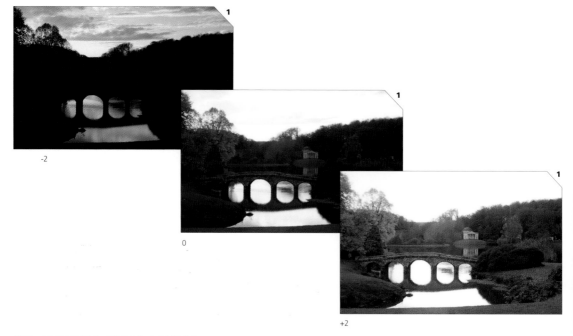

2 The next step is to open the images in the HDR software. There are a number of HDR programs available, and most offer a good level of control, along with some preset settings to choose from.

After selecting your source images, you will be presented with a dialog box that allows you to determine the settings that the software will apply to the images.

Ensure that you check the images will be aligned. Decide on the level of noise reduction you wish to apply and whether or not you want the software to fix chromatic aberrations. How good the software is at these tasks will vary. You may wish to use your standard software to correct such issues after the HDR program has combined the images.

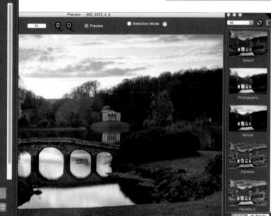

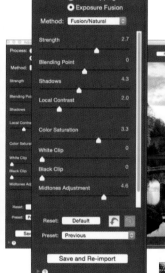

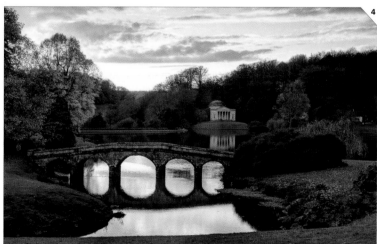

3 Photomatix Pro's comprehensive control panel and powerful tone mapping algorithms let you determine the look of the merged photos – from naturalistic to hyper-realistic to surrealistic, and all stages in between. The choice is yours. The software also features a good number of presets which give you a good starting point from which to work.

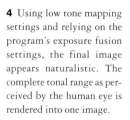

4 Using low tone mapping settings and relying on the program's exposure fusion settings, the final image appears naturalistic. The complete tonal range as perceived by the human eye is rendered into one image.

Using the Selection Tools

Selections are crucial to precise image editing, no matter what application you're using. There are literally scores of ways to make selections, and which one you choose to use will depend on the nature of the area you want to select and the specific software you're using; here, we're using Photoshop Elements. Although each of the tools can be used independently, the real power comes when you combine a number of Selection tools to isolate the area you want. For example, the Magic Wand is great for selecting ranges of similar colours, while the Marquee tools are very effective for selecting discrete islands of pixels, regardless of what colour they are. Using the Add or Subtract options, you can use the Marquee or Lasso tool to clean up a selection made using the Magic Wand, or vice versa.

SELECTING TO ALTER ELEMENTS OF AN IMAGE

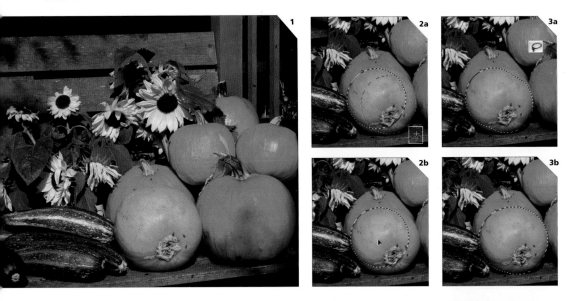

1 If you want to make a selection in an image such as this, there are a number of options. Let's run through a few simple ways of adding to selections that will help speed up the process.

2 One of the pumpkins at the bottom left is a slightly different colour to the rest, so let's start by making this pumpkin even more off-colour. A simple option is to use the Elliptical Marquee tool – clicking and dragging from the middle of the pumpkin while holding down the Shift key to drag out from the centre will automatically create a perfectly round selection. You can move the selection by dragging inside it, and using Shift (to add) and Alt (to subtract) to fine-tune the selection, dragging out additional areas to add to or cut away from the current selection.

3 With the outline shape of the pumpkin selected, holding down the Alt key while using the Lasso tool (a small '-' minus sign will appear next to the tool's cursor) allows you to draw around the woody, fibrous base of the pumpkin to deselect it.

Once the pumpkin has been accurately selected, we can use the Hue/Saturation command to radically alter the colour of the pumpkin.

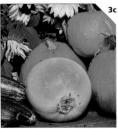

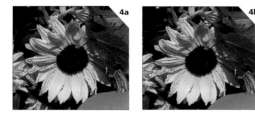

4a **4b**

4 Next, let's turn to the Magic Wand tool to select a sunflower. Begin by moving the tool around and adding to the selection by holding down the Alt key. Note that if you inadvertently select a large unwanted area, switch to the Lasso tool and, with the Alt key held down, draw around the unwanted selection to deselect it.

5 Once the flower-head has been accurately selected, the Hue/Saturation command can again be used to change its colour.

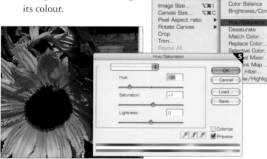

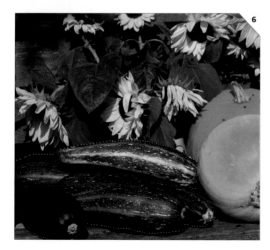

6

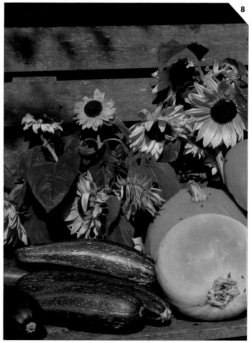

7

7 Having made the initial selection with the Magic Brush tool, the Lasso and Magnetic Lasso tools can be used to add to (by holding down Shift) or take away from (by holding down Alt) the selection. With the selection completed, that region of the picture can be recoloured.

8

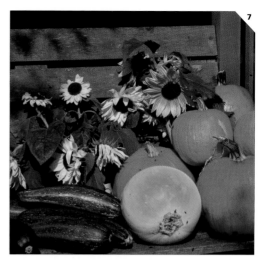

6 Next, try using the Magic Brush tool to make a rough selection around the courgettes (zucchini). If you don't have a version of the software that features the Magic Brush, then you can use one of the equivalent selection tools.

8 By using a variety of tools, and by adding to and subtracting from selections, it's surprisingly easy to make even the most difficult selections and arrive at a positively multicoloured collection of fruit and veg.

Making Cut-outs

One procedure that you may find you need to carry out from time to time – particularly if you're keen on creating photomontages, making composite images of family members or friends, or placing objects in front of different backgrounds – is to make accurate cut-outs. All editing software will have the necessary tools to create accurate, natural-looking cut-outs.

As always, there are a number of ways of performing cut-outs, some of which might involve the use of the Selection tools discussed on the previous pages. In this example, however, Photoshop Elements is used to create a 'mask' around the image to be cut out, as this offers the greatest control and allows the cut-out to be constantly revised until you're happy with it.

USING THE MASK TOOL FOR CUT-OUTS

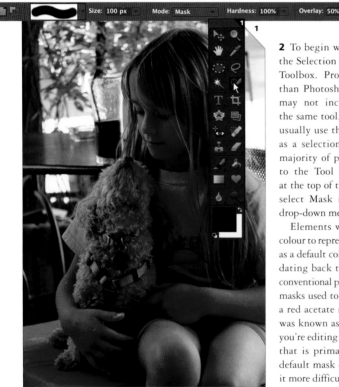

2 To begin with, click on the Selection Brush in the Toolbox. Programs other than Photoshop Elements may not include exactly the same tool, but you can usually use the Brush tool as a selection tool in the majority of programs. Go to the Tool Options bar at the top of the screen and select Mask in the Mode drop-down menu.

Elements will use a red colour to represent the mask as a default colour, a feature dating back to the days of conventional printing, when masks used to be cut out of a red acetate material that was known as Rubylith. If you're editing a photograph that is primarily red, the default mask colour makes it more difficult to see what you're doing, so simply click in the colour square and select a different colour for the mask.

It's also possible to change the Opacity of the mask, but for most editing jobs, leave it set to 100%.

3 Set Hardness to 100% initially, to ensure that there is a crisp edge. Adjust the size of the brush using the '[' and ']' keys, and begin painting the mask over the area you want to cut out. For large areas, where there's little risk of painting over the background, use a large brush, as this will speed up the job.

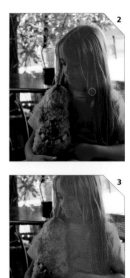

1 This image of a little girl and a dog presents an interesting array of problems in terms of creating an accurate cut-out. First, you will have to cut out around the hair of both the girl and the dog, which is notoriously difficult to deal with, and, second, the background is far from being uniform in colour, which makes it impossible to select using the Magic Wand tool.

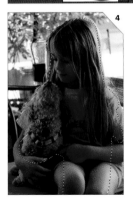

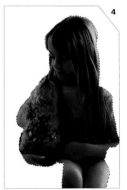

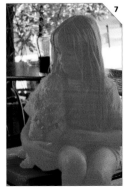

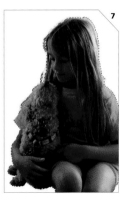

4 Although you're painting a mask, you are in effect making a selection at the same time.

To view the selection, go to the Tool Options bar and change the Mode from Mask to Selection. The familiar

marching ants selection will appear. For this exercise, the Backspace/Delete key has been pressed to show how the mask is progressing. Click Edit > Undo to go back a step and bring back the background.

7 Once you're happy with the mask, go to Filter > Gaussian Blur and blur the mask with a Radius of 0.5, just to soften the edges of it slightly.

Next, convert the mask back into a selection in the Tool Options bar. Here, the background has been deleted to leave the cut-out on a white layer.

5 When you get to the more detailed areas, such as around the dog's coat, reduce the size of the brush so that you can trace the edges far more accurately.

You can also reduce the brush's Hardness value in the Tool Options bar. This creates a softer-edged brush, which means you will be able to soften the edges of the selection.

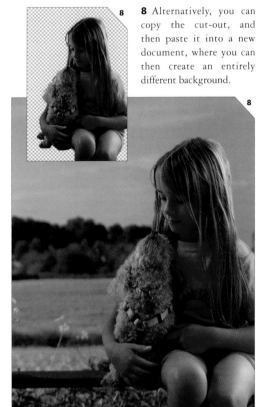

8 Alternatively, you can copy the cut-out, and then paste it into a new document, where you can then create an entirely different background.

6 If you inadvertently paint over the background, simply hold down the Alt key and brush out the mask.

Zoom into the image as you go to refine the mask, using a very small brush to get into difficult areas.

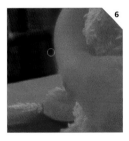

Creating Montages

Having learned how to make selections and accurate cut-outs of individual elements within an image, it's time to put all these skills together to make a photomontage. Using image-editing software to create a photomontage is much quicker and easier than using old photographs and a pair of scissors and, because you can blend images, the results are much more satisfactory. Before you start to create your montage, it's a good idea to place all the images that you're considering using in one readily identifiable folder so that you can access them quickly and easily. All editing software is capable of creating photomontages; here, we're using Photoshop.

COLLATING PHOTOMONTAGE ELEMENTS

1 The first image you select for your photomontage is the most important, as it will form the central point of your image, and set the scene in terms of subject and tone. This particular image has been chosen because it has plenty of space around the main subject into which new images can be added.

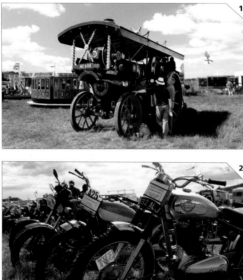

2 Open the second image and make any editing adjustments you need. You may have to adjust the crop, the sharpness, or adjust the brightness levels to try and ensure that it matches the first image as closely as possible. This is best done with both images on screen at the same time so you can get the best possible match.

3 Use the Move tool to drag the second image onto the first. In the Layers palette, you will see that the second image has been automatically created on a new layer. Give the layer an appropriate name so you can keep track of the various elements of the montage. In this example, we've labelled our layer 'Bikes'.

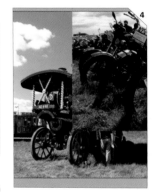

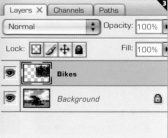

4 Ensuring that the 'Show Transform Controls' box is checked in the Tool Options bar, click on one of the corner boxes and, while holding down the Shift key to retain the image's proportions, rescale it to the size you want. When you're happy with the size and position of the second image, click OK.

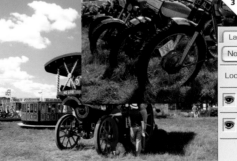

5 Go to the Toolbox and select the Eraser tool. In the Tool Options bar, set the Opacity to around 30% and use the '[' and ']' keys to select a suitable brush size. Carefully begin to rub out parts of the second image that you don't want to appear in the montage. Concentrate first on the edges, and remember that if you make a mistake you can always click Undo to undo the step.

6 Repeat the exercise with as many additional images as you like, remembering to give each new layer its own name in the Layers palette so you can keep track of the elements in your image.

7 When you have all your elements in place and you're happy with the composition, try experimenting with various Blending Modes and reducing the Opacity of some of the layers. This can add greater depth to the montage. Once you are satisfied with the way the piece is looking, go to Layers > Flatten Image before choosing Save to save the file on your hard drive.

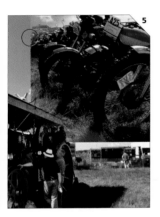

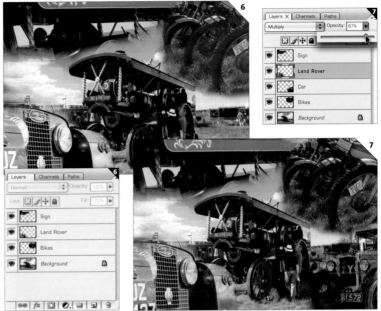

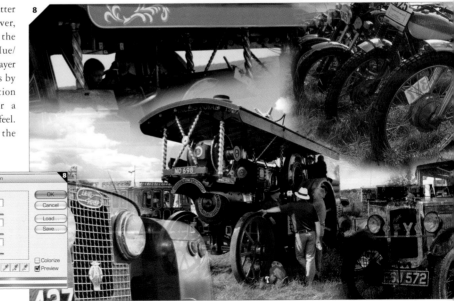

8 Given the subject matter of this montage, however, before we flattened the image, we used a Hue/Saturation adjustment layer to desaturate the colours by moving the Saturation slider to the left for a faded, slightly nostalgic feel. It also helps to unify the montage visually.

Layer Masks

A number of the more advanced image-editing programs have a powerful editing tool at their disposal, known as 'layer masks'. Creating a 'mask' was described previously, and the project here is a continuation of that in some ways. As we know, the term 'mask' derives from conventional printing where, in order for part of an image to remain unaffected by additional processes, a mask cut out of acetate was made to protect it. Digital layer masks work in much the same way, but are far more flexible. Here, we look at how layer masks can be used in Photoshop, or Photoshop Elements, although similar principles apply to most editing software.

USING LAYER MASKS TO ALTER IMAGES

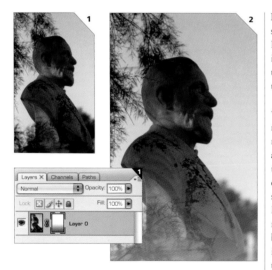

The aim here is to apply a simple mask to this image of a bust.

1 Go to the Layers palette and then begin by double-clicking the Background layer. It will ask if you'd like to rename the layer – click 'yes' to Layer 0. The reason why you have to do this is because a layer mask cannot be applied to the Background layer.

Click on 'Add layer mask' in the Layers palette. A white box will appear next to the image thumbnail.

2 Ensuring that the layer mask is active (it will have a double outline), return to the main image and draw a simple black gradient over the image. Part of the image will fade out. Looking at the Layers palette you'll see the part of the image that has faded out is represented by a fading black gradient in the Layer mask thumbnail.

Wherever black appears on the layer mask, the corresponding part of the image will be shown deleted (but it's still there until you flatten the image).

Let's apply this in a very simple 'real world' project. Here, the aim of the exercise is to mask the opening to this castle wall and replace the background.

1 Click on the 'Add layer mask' icon to create the mask. Return to the image and, with the Brush tool set to paint black, start to paint out the opening. Use a small, soft brush to paint the outline, and then fill the remainder with a larger brush, making sure Opacity is set to 100%. Looking at the Layer mask thumbnail in the Layers palette reflects where you've been painting.

2 Once the layer mask is complete, open the image for the replacement view and use the Move tool to drag it onto the main castle wall image.

In the Tool Options bar, ensure 'Show Transform Controls' is checked and then resize the new layer.

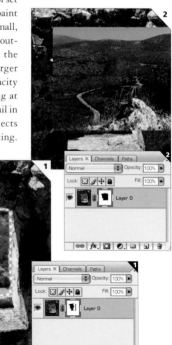

3 To get the new view to sit under the window, go to the Layers palette and move the new layer below Layer 0. You can independently edit the layers so they match in terms of tone and lighting. With the mask in place, it's easy to use any view you want.

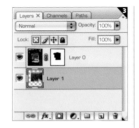

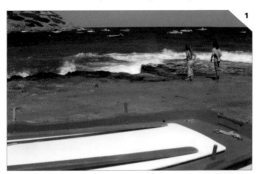

CREATING COMPOSITE LAYERS

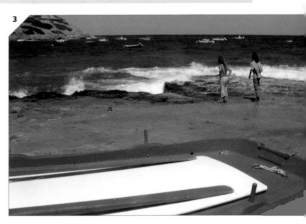

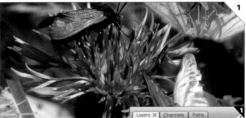

Layer masks are a great way to create composite images, as shown in this insect image.

1 Drag your new image onto the Background image, rescale it and then add a layer mask to each new layer. With the layer mask in place, paint with a black brush to reveal the layer underneath. Painting with a white brush reinstates any of the new layer that may have been removed.

ADJUSTMENT LAYERS AS LAYER MASKS

Photoshop Elements doesn't support layer masks in quite the same way. However, any new adjustment layer is automatically presented with its own layer mask, which can then be used in the way described previously.

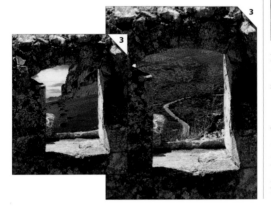

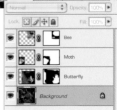

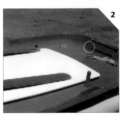

1 In this example, we're going to use the layer mask that comes with a Hue/Saturation adjustment layer to create an image in which parts are coloured a sepia tone while other parts remain in full colour.

2 Having created a Hue/Saturation adjustment layer, clicked Colorize in the Hue/Saturation dialog window, and adjusted the sliders to create a sepia effect, the layer mask can now be selectively painted out using a white brush to reveal the colour underneath.

3 In a matter of moments, painting with white on the adjustment layer's layer mask has returned the foreground boat and distant figures to the original colour.

Meanwhile, the rest of the image has the sepia tone created by the Hue/Saturation adjustment layer.

Photoshop Filters

Photoshop and Photoshop Elements provide a huge variety of filters. These can alter an image in all manner of ways, from manipulating colours, adding textures, exaggerating or removing detail, picking out edges, simulating a painting or drawing, pinching or twisting the canvas, and more besides. You may not use them every day, but you can have endless fun exploring the creative possibilities.

One thing to remember with Filters is that the lower the resolution of the image, the greater the effect of the filter. The Filter Gallery provides a special user interface for many of the filters, with a large preview panel that you can enlarge further by expanding the window. The round button with two chevrons, to the left of the OK button, shows or hides the filters list, which also provides thumbnails to illustrate each effect. Using the Gallery is the best way to familiarize yourself with the filter names and their corresponding effects. Here is a small selection of available filters.

Posterize

The filters in the first group, Adjustments, are the simplest. Posterize, for example, simply reduces the number of colours in the image. Adjust the number of Levels for the desired effect, which is typically reminiscent of garish low-quality reproduction, as in Pop Art.

Cut-out

The Artistic filter set is slightly more sophisticated, with multiple sliders that give greater control over the results. The default settings often work well enough, however.

The Cut-out filter divides an image into areas of flat colour. Here settings of 5 Levels, Edge Simplicity 4 and Edge Fidelity 2 were used.

Film grain

Filters don't only (or always) do what they claim to do. Film Grain, for example, is at its most effective when used to simulate bad printing rather than grainy film.

Set the Intensity and Grain to high values, then increase the Highlight Area to restore image brightness at the expense of detail.

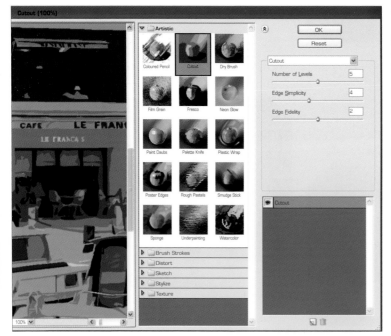

Gallery page

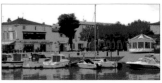

Posterize

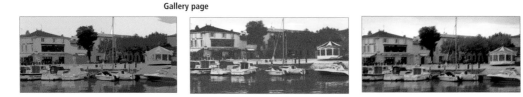

Cut-out

Film grain

Rough pastels

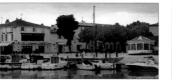

Accented edges

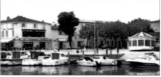

Diffuse glow

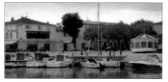

Glass

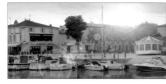

Spherize

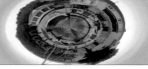

Polar coordinates

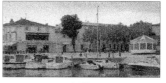

Pointillize

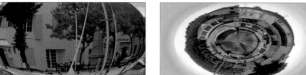

Lens flare

Glowing edges

Stained glass

Rough pastels

Look out for Size, Length or Scaling settings, as these will need to be adjusted according to the resolution of your image. Here, the filter has been used with Stroke Length 17 and Canvas Texture 166%.

Accented edges

Several filters emphasize edges. Accented Edges (under Brush Strokes) is one of the more versatile, and demands more slider fiddling. At its best, it will mimic a pen and water-colour sketch.

Diffuse glow

The Distort filters serve disparate purposes. Diffuse Glow is a distortion filter because it shifts pixels, but its purpose is to create a soft-focus effect. Increase Glow Amount for a stronger effect, and increase Clear Amount to restore detail.

Glass

At low settings, with the Frosted Texture selected, the Glass filter puts your image behind sandblasted glass.

Adjust the Scaling to suit the image size, or switch the texture to Tiny Lens and increase the settings.

Spherize

The distortion filters can be great fun to use. Apply the spherize filter with a positive value to create a fishbowl effect. The maximum 100% setting isn't all that strong, so try applying it more than once. A small negative setting can be useful for countering wide-angle lens distortion.

Polar coordinates

The most extreme of the distortion filters is proabably Polar Coordinates. A good tip is to rotate a landscape image 180% (that is, turn it upside down) before applying Rectangular to Polar. Try this on a panoramic landscape with a dark sky, then layer a picture of the Earth in the middle.

Pointillize

The Pixelate filters break images into colour cells. Pointillize mimics the 'pointillism' technique of the Impressionist painter Georges Seurat.

Lens flare

The Render filters are among the most sophisticated. Lens Flare simulates the rings that are produced by shooting toward the sun or a strong light source. Click to align the centre of the flare with the source, and choose a lens type to set the size and appearance of the flare.

Glowing edges

The Sketch filters are intended to work with hard-edged images, and often draw a blank with detailed images. More rewarding are the Stylize filters, which include Extrude, and are worth trying. Glowing Edges turns any image into neon, but keep the Smoothness setting high.

Stained glass

Texture is an intriguing set of filters. The Stained Glass option creates white leading instead of black. To fix this, invert your image, then go to Filter > Texture > Stained Glass, set the Light Intensity to 0, adjust the other sliders as you like, click OK, then invert again.

Dramatic Skies

One of the key elements of many successful landscape photographs is a sky that, without detracting from the remainder of the image, can grab and hold the viewer's attention and add to the overall atmosphere of the image – whether it comprises forbidding, stormy rain clouds or a clear, unadulterated, azure blue.

However, setting the correct exposure for both sky and land is sometimes impossible, especially if your camera cannot be fitted with a grey graduated filter, commonly known as a grey grad filter. These filters are tinted at the top and gradually fade to clear at the bottom, and are designed to prevent a sky being overexposed when the photographer has set the correct exposure for the land. However, it is mainly only dSLRs and some hybrid cameras that accept such filters, and not every dSLR owner carries them around at all times.

However, as long as you can manage to stop the sky from 'blowing out' altogether, and retain most of the detail, you can enhance the sky in your image-editing software and recreate the effect of a grey grad filter.

ENHANCE LIGHTING WITH GRAD FILTERS

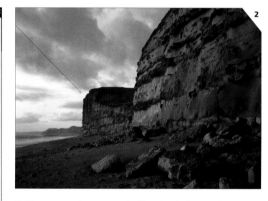

1 Although there isn't a dramatic difference in light levels between the sky and the land in this image, a grey grad filter would have brought out more depth in the clouds and given them a little more body.

2 To recreate the grey grad effect, begin by creating a new blank layer (Layer > New > Layer) and call it Gradient. Ensure the Foreground/ Background colours in the Toolbar are set to the default of black as the foreground colour and white as the background colour. Now, select the Gradient tool in the Toolbar and in the Tool Options bar select the 'Foreground to Transparent' gradient option.

Next, draw a line across the sky. You will see that the line runs diagonally from the top left of the image to the start of the cliffs.

3 After releasing the mouse, the area along the gradient line will darken. This is the result of creating a black-to-transparent gradient over the original image. Experiment with the length of the gradient line to see how it influences how much of the image is affected.

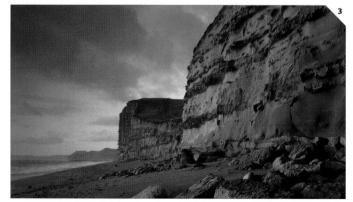

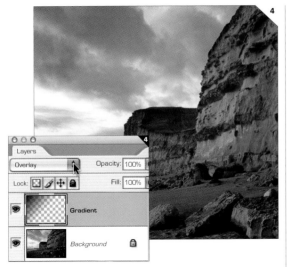

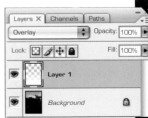

4 To complete the grey grad effect, go to the Layers palette. Ensure the Gradient layer is selected and change the Blending Mode to Overlay. The background clouds will now blend into the dark grey gradient and become darker.

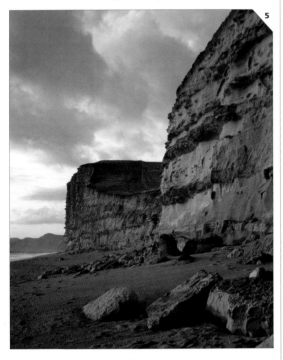

5 You can temper the effect of the gradient by reducing the Opacity of the Gradient layer. With this image, however, the sky could be enhanced further, so the Gradient layer has been duplicated, doubling the effect it has on the image.

BRIGHTEN DARKENED AREAS

It is possible to use a similar technique to brighten areas of an image. In this example, the lower half of the image is very dark.

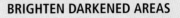

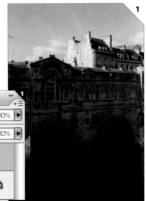

1 As before, create a new blank layer, but this time choose white as the foreground colour instead of black before you draw the gradient rule. To do this, simply click on the right-angled arrow icon to switch between the two colours. If the foreground and background colours are anything but black and white, simply press the 'D' key (for 'default'). As before, change the gradient layer's Blending Mode to Overlay.

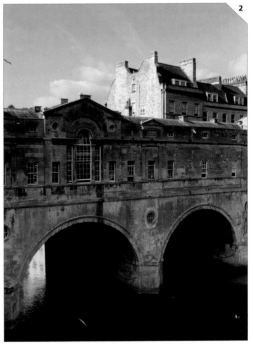

2 With the white gradient layer set to Overlay, the water and lower part of the building are dramatically brightened.

Black and White Conversion

Creating good black and white images from your colour originals is not as easy as it sounds. You might think that all you have to do is remove the colour information in the digital image, and technically that is precisely what you do to get an essentially greyscale image.

Artistically, however, the results of such a simple process are rarely as good as you'd expect without some digital tweaking along the way. Part of the reason for this is that photographers have long used coloured filters to alter the image before it's captured on black and white film. Different coloured filters cause different objects or areas to be brighter or darker when photographed, depending on their colour.

This is important, because although certain objects, such as grass and sky, are different colours, their brightness may actually be very similar. This can result in a 'flat' black and white image, where similar areas merge together unless a filter is used on the lens. But rather than spend money on filters, you can replicate the effect in Photoshop.

REPLICATING FILTERS IN PHOTOSHOP

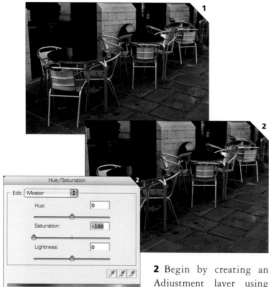

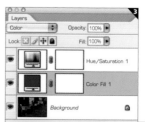

3 Just as a photographer uses coloured lens filters to adjust the brightness of the objects in the scene in relation to one another, you can prefilter the image before it is desaturated. To do this, simply create a new layer above the background layer and then fill it with a solid colour. With the background layer selected in the Layers palette go to Layer > New Fill Layer > Solid Color and click OK. In the subsequent Colour Picker box, choose an appropriate colour. Here, an electric blue has been selected. Set the Layer Blending mode of the Color Fill layer to Color. The image becomes washed out, but the pavement is now much lighter.

2 Begin by creating an Adjustment layer using Hue/Saturation to remove the colour information from the image. Set the Saturation slider to -100 to do this.

While the colour has gone, the image now looks dull and lacks contrast – this is often described as 'flat'. Now, the dark pavement dominates the picture, and the chairs and tables appear a little lost against it.

1 Here's the original colour image that we want to try and convert into a black and white photograph. There's not a lot of strong colour in the shot to start with, as the pavement, tables and doors are all neutral colours. This makes it more of a challenge to convert it successfully into a black and white image.

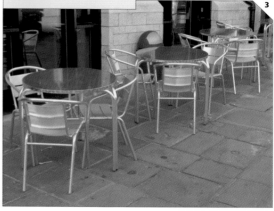

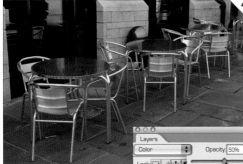

4

5 By adding a Brightness/ Contrast Adjustment layer above the Hue/Saturation layer, you can add some contrast to the image.

Move the Contrast slider to the right until you get the appearance that you want. The resulting image is a much snappier conversion and the tables really stand out from the pavement.

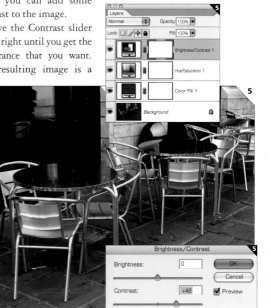

4 You can adjust different colours in the image by changing the Hue of the Color Fill layer. This is like changing the filter on a lens.

In the Layers palette, Right-click/Double-click the Layer thumbnail on the Color Fill layer.

Make sure that H is selected in the HSB section of the Color Picker and drag the slider to adjust the

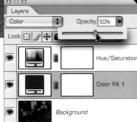

hue of the colour filter. This will change the relationship between the various tones.

Here, the Color Layer Opacity has been reduced to 50%, so the effect does not appear as strong.

6

6

6 The advantage of working with adjustment layers is that you can go back and edit each adjustment at a later stage. In fact, you can even save documents as Photoshop (.psd) or TIFF (.tif) files with the adjustment layers in place.

The only instance when you can't go back and alter an adjustment layer is once you've flattened an image. This is usually used as a way of keeping

the file size down and is done by selecting Layer > Flatten Image.

In the two images shown here, the Hue/Saturation dialog window was activated by Right-clicking/Double-clicking the Hue/Saturation Adjustment layer in the Layers palette. Checking the Colorize button and also altering the Hue and Saturation sliders will adjust the colour as well as the intensity of the image.

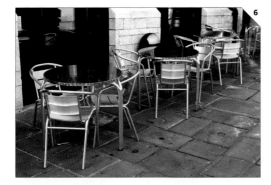

Converging Verticals

One of the most common problems with photographs of buildings – particularly extremely tall ones – is that in order to fit the entire building into the frame it's usually necessary to point the camera upward. When you do this, the side walls of the building appear to get closer together the higher up you look. The effect is similar to looking at a long, straight road, where the edges will appear to converge the farther you look down the road. With these long distances, the road often appears to meet at a 'vanishing point', and this is the same with buildings. To achieve really accurate shots of straight buildings, professional photographers use specialist equipment, but you can go some way to improving converging verticals using your image-editing software.

CORRECTING PERSPECTIVE ISSUES

Taken several years ago using a conventional 35mm film camera, this image was then scanned into the computer.

1 This well-exposed picture managed to capture the remarkable detail of the building, so it's worth spending a few minutes on it to adjust the problem of the converging verticals.

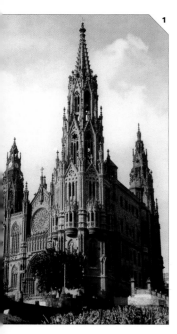

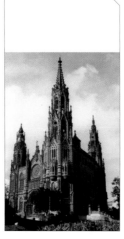

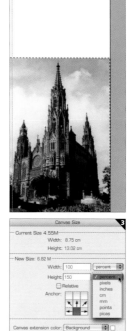

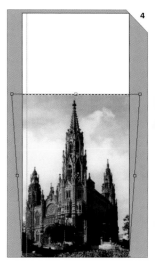

2 Begin by increasing the height of the canvas that you are working on, by going to Image > Canvas Size.

In the dialog window, you should then click the lower middle square next to the Anchor. This indicates that the canvas only needs to be extended upward from the 'ground'.

Click on the pull-down menu next to the height box and select 'percent'. Enter 150 into the height box to increase the height of the canvas by 50%.

3 Using the Rectangular Marquee tool, make a selection of the original image. Next, go to View > Rulers and drag a vertical line from the edge of the frame onto the image area to use as reference to ensure you get the walls vertical.

4 Go to Edit > Transform > Perspective and you will see that corner points appear at the corners as well as at the central points of the sides of the image.

Drag out one corner of the selection and you will notice that the corner point on the opposite side will begin to move out at the same time. Keep dragging until the side walls appear vertical. Compare it with the ruler guide you placed earlier. When it looks as if the vertical walls are straight, make a note of how much wider the top part of the picture has become by checking the measurements in the Tool Options bar.

Here, the width has been increased by about 120%. Once you're happy with the adjustment, you should confirm by clicking the check box.

5 With the selection still active, go to Image > Transform > Distort. Grab the top middle handle with the cursor and stretch the building upward. The image will stretch in real time, which means you can see the effect of the adjustment as you go.

For guidance, you should keep on stretching the image until the height has reached 120% in order to counter the effect of the perspective adjustment.

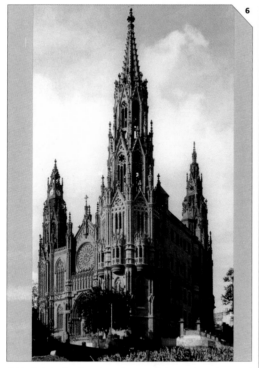

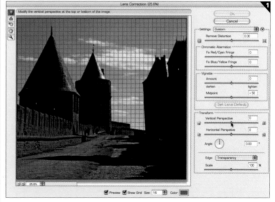

6 To finish, deselect the selection (Select > Deselect) and use the Crop tool to crop out the unused canvas.

USING DISTORTION FILTERS

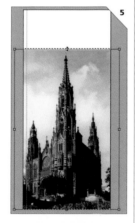

More recent versions of Photoshop and Photoshop Elements have a distortion filter that allows you to correct issues such as converging verticals, as shown here.

1 Go to the Filter menu. In Photoshop it is called Lens Distortion, while in Elements it's known as Correct Camera Distortion; both work in the same way.

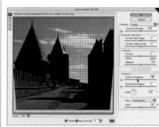
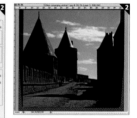

2 By moving the Vertical Perspective slider to the right, the buildings can be set to align with the grid. With the correction made, click OK.

3 Now simply crop away the newly created transparent elements of the image at the bottom of the frame.

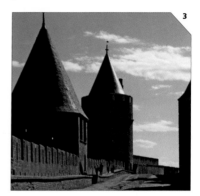

Soft-focus Effect: Landscape

In the days of traditional film cameras, photographers would experiment with numerous materials and techniques to achieve a soft-focus effect, ranging from smearing petroleum jelly on a clear filter fitted to the camera's lens to taking photographs through a pair of old stockings, or simply using a dedicated soft-focus filter.

All of these methods are perfectly valid today, but it's no surprise that it's possible to recreate a soft-focus effect during post-production in almost every image-editing program. Again, this has the benefit that the photographer has greater control over the effect and will also have a straight, unfiltered image.

SOFT FOCUS WITH LAYERS AND FILTERS

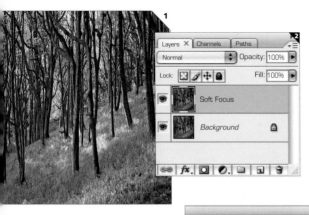

3 Most of the image-editing software packages have a soft-focus filter effect, and Photoshop Elements and the full version of Photoshop are no exception.

In these Adobe programs, the effect is known as Diffuse Glow, and the filter is found under Filter > Distort > Diffuse Glow. There are three sliders that control the overall effect of the filter, and it's well worth spending a little bit of time experimenting with these to see what effect they have on the image in the preview window.

If the image you have is too large for the preview window, you will find that there is a menu at the bottom left-hand corner of the dialog window allowing you to set 'Fit in View'.

1 This striking image of a field of spring bluebells in a wood is exactly the sort of photograph that might be successfully enhanced by incorporating filters and layers for a soft-focus effect.

2 Start by duplicating the Background layer (Layer > Duplicate layer), so you can delete any effects that you don't want, while retaining the original.

An alternative method of duplicating the layer is to go to the Layers palette and then drag the Background image thumbnail onto the 'Create a new layer' icon. It's helpful to rename the new layer 'Soft focus'.

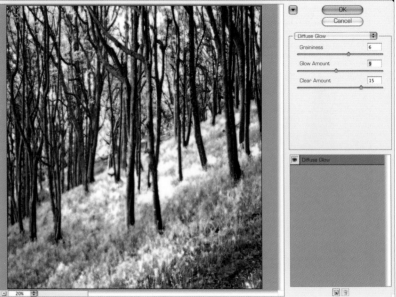

4 Once you feel happy with the filter effect in the preview window, click OK, and the filter will then be applied to the copy of the original image. The Diffuse Glow filter in Photoshop has created a pleasing effect, but you may decide that you want to reintroduce some of the original colour of the bluebells by reducing the Opacity of the Soft-focus layer in the Layers palette.

5 If your software doesn't have a soft-focus filter, or if you're not pleased with the result the filter provides, the alternative is to use Gaussian blur instead.

On the Soft-focus layer apply a fairly liberal amount of Gaussian blur. Here, the Radius has been set to 30 to give an obvious soft-focus feel to the image.

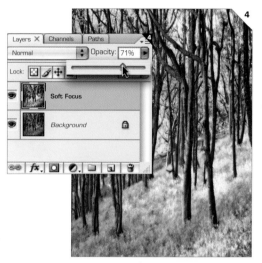

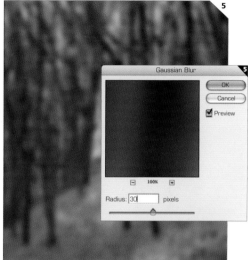

6 As well as blurring the duplicate layer, it's worth brightening it using Levels (Image > Adjustments > Levels). Here, the white and central gamma points have both been moved to the left.

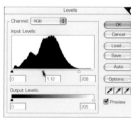

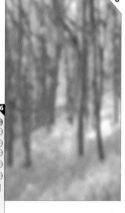

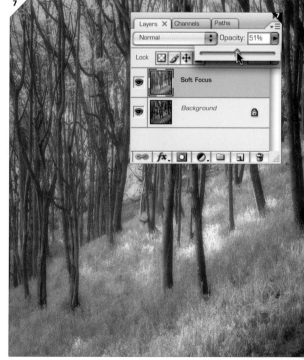

7 Return to the Layers palette and reduce the Soft-focus layer's Opacity so that the original image begins to show through, as before.

At this point, you should try experimenting with the Opacity slider until you've reached the right amount of softening, then go to Layer > Flatten Image to combine the layers. It's worth remembering that once the layers have been flattened, you'll need to give the file a separate name or you'll overwrite the original. To do this, go to Save As and then key in an appropriate name.

Soft-focus Effect: Portrait

It's not just landscapes that can benefit from a soft-focus treatment. For many years, portrait photographers who shot on film also used soft-focus techniques and effects in their work. Often, soft-focus filters were used to flatter the sitter, as the softening effect hides blemishes and can make skin appear smoother. Alternatively, the effect could be used to provide a more dreamy, other-worldly result, which particularly suits portraits of children. The digital technique for a soft-focus portrait is quite similar to that of the soft-focus landscape, but it involves the use of Blending Modes, and introduces one or two further steps to fine-tune the result.

SOFT FOCUS USING BLENDING MODES

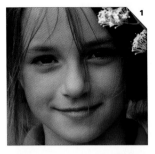

1 Here, we're going to apply a digital soft-focus effect to this portrait using Photoshop. Of course, the same technique can be used in other editing software. Although the girl is young enough to show no signs of ageing, the effect will give the shot additional charm.

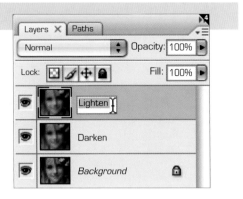

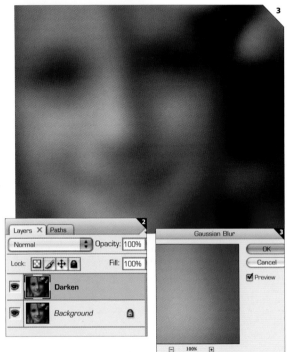

2 Begin by duplicating the Background layer. You can do this either in the Layers palette by dragging the Background thumbnail onto the 'Create a new layer' icon or by going to Layer > Duplicate layer.

As before, it is a good idea to rename the new layer, in this case 'Darken', as this helps you to keep track of the various layers as you work through the project.

3 As with the soft-focus landscape effect, go to the Filter menu and select Blur > Gaussian Blur.

Set a large Radius of around 30 pixels. As you have seen with the landscape project, the image will become instantly indistinct and unrecognizable.

4 Duplicate the Darken layer using the same method as duplicating the Background layer described in Step 2. Rename this third layer 'Lighten'.

Click on the Darken layer and, using the drop-down menu at the top of the Layers palette, select Darken blending mode. Next, reduce the Opacity to around 40% but note that this will have no visible effect on the image at this stage.

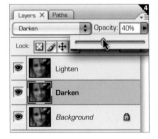

5 Next, click on the Lighten layer and set the Blending Mode to Lighten. Reduce the Opacity to around 60%.

At this stage, the soft-focus effect should have become apparent. However, by applying it to the entire portrait, the sparkle in the eyes, which is one of the most important elements of a portrait, has been lost.

6 To bring back some of the missing spark, we need to reduce the effect of the soft-focus 'filter'.

To do this, select the Darken layer and click on the 'Add Layer mask' icon at the bottom of the Layers palette. This will introduce a new blank Layer mask thumbnail next to the Darken layer thumbnail.

7 First, ensure that the Layer mask is active (it will be framed by a thin black border if it is) before going to the Toolbox to choose the Brush tool. With black as the foreground colour, start painting over the eyes.

Remember that you can easily adjust the size of the brush using the '[' and ']' keys. As you paint over the portrait, the eyes should come back into focus and regain their sparkle. Notice how the Layer mask in the Layers palette will also indicate which areas you have been painting.

If you want to return to a more soft-focus effect, just press 'X' to change the foreground colour to white and paint the mask back in.

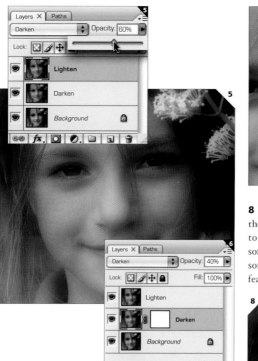

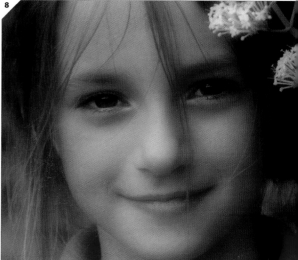

8 When you have finished, the final photograph ought to appear as a pleasing soft-focus portrait that has softened the main facial features and the skin, but which still enables the eyes to show clearly through. Once you're fully satisfied with the final result, you need to go to Layer > Flatten Image and save.

Soft-focus alternative

The technique described here uses Layer masks, which are not available in some image-editing packages, such as Photoshop Elements.

However, a very similar effect can be achieved by simply duplicating the Background layer and applying the Gaussian Blur filter to the new layer. You need to reduce the Opacity of the blurred layer in the Layers palette and then use the Eraser tool to reveal the sharper background layer.

Recreating Depth of Field

Depth of field is one of the indispensable tools of the creative photographer. For stunning landscapes, setting a narrow aperture, compensated for by a long exposure, can help achieve pin-sharp focus on everything from the closest foreground detail to the horizon.

But when shooting portraits, sports, children or food, using a wide aperture to reduce the depth of field can add impact and drama. Because limiting the depth of field

in this way demands a reasonably fast (and expensive) lens, it's also one of the factors that differentiates professional shots from the average holiday snap. If it proves impracticable to shoot with a wide aperture to get a shallow depth of field, or you just don't think of it until you're looking at the finished image, the effect can be recreated using software, with the careful application of selective blurring. The challenge is to make it look real.

APPLYING A SHALLOW DEPTH OF FIELD

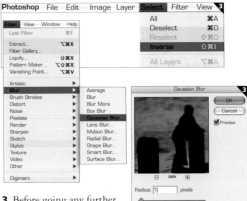

1

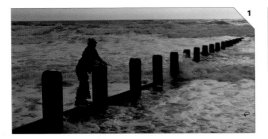

3

1 First, decide where you want the point of focus of the image to be. Usually, your intention will be to bring out a particular object or figure. In this photograph, it's the boy standing on the groyne.

You'll need to make a selection to separate this from the rest of the scene, using one of the methods shown earlier. The selection doesn't need to be absolutely precise for this technique, so you can work quickly.

2 Creating a depth of field effect that's realistic isn't as simple as keeping your intended subject sharp and blurring the rest of the scene. Everything of equal distance from the lens should seem equally sharp, so you need to add anything that lies on the same focal plane as your initial subject.

In this picture, nothing is directly in line with the figure except the groyne, so the Rectangular Marquee tool can be used to select the strip of groyne around the boy.

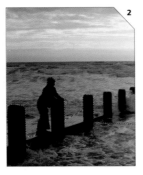

2

3 Before going any further, you should save your selection by choosing Select > Save Selection. Remember to select 'New' at the top, give your selection a name, and then click OK so that it is saved for future reference.

What you actually want to select now is the area that you're going to blur, which means everything outside your subject. Choose Select >Inverse to invert the selection. You may also want to hide the 'marching ants' border temporarily by pressing Ctrl + H (on a PC) or Command + H (on a Mac). Then, once you have done this, go to Filter >

Blur > Gaussian Blur. In the Gaussian Blur dialog box, the Radius setting governs the strength of the blurring. To create the impression of depth of field, you will require a Radius of several pixels.

If you attempt this in one go, you'll find that it will create an unnatural halo effect around the subject, which will even be visible in the preview.

Here, for instance, you can see that the colours within the subject appear to be 'leaking out' into the background.

4 To avoid this, start with just a 1 pixel blur Radius. Click OK, then go to Select > Modify > Contract.

In the dialog box, set a size of 3 pixels and click OK. This will make the selection shrink away from the subject. However, since the selection no longer follows the outline of an object, you'll need to feather it to avoid the problem of creating a hard edge, so go to Select > Feather. Set a Radius of 3 pixels and click OK. Having done this, reopen Gaussian Blur and this time set Radius to 1.5 pixels. Click OK.

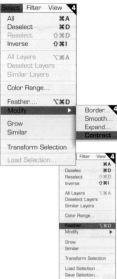

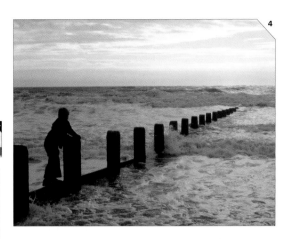

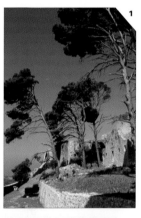

QUICK FIX USING LAYER MASK

Using layer masks, you can emulate depth of field.

1 Duplicating the background layer, click Add layer mask. Next, draw a Black to Transparent gradient over the image once the mask is active. The areas painted black will stay in focus.

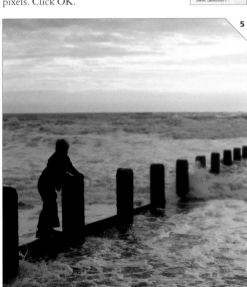

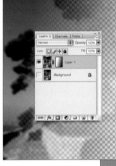

5 To complete the depth of field effect, you just need to repeat the same sequence of three filters with slightly larger sizes each time: for example, 10 pixels for Contract and Feather, and 10 pixels for Gaussian Blur, then going to 40 pixels and so on. In most scenes, these steps will give a realistic result without forcing you to think about where the focus should fall off. Here the sea in the background ends up looking heavily blurred. It is also the area that would be most out of focus if you took the shot using a wide aperture.

The resulting image is a believable narrow depth of field shot, with the emphasis on the figure.

2 On the duplicate layer, click on the thumbnail and apply Gaussian Blur. The gradually un-masked area will become blurred leaving the masked area sharp.

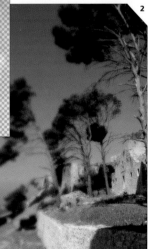

Creating Panoramas

The concept of taking a number of consecutive images along the length of the same scene in order to stitch them together to create one long panorama has been around for a long while now. Today, increasing numbers of digital camera manufacturers are going to great lengths to develop dedicated 'Panorama' settings for their cameras, which allow photographers to align the individual shots more accurately.

Image-editing software manufacturers have constantly refined their applications to improve the stitching capabilities of the programs. Adobe's latest version of Photoshop, for example, is now so sophisticated that it's no longer necessary to use a tripod and manual exposure to ensure an accurate end result – the software will deal with this for you. But if you don't have such advanced software, here's the best way to achieve great results.

STITCHING TOGETHER A SET OF IMAGES

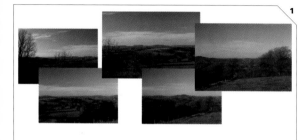

1

3 In this specific case, you can see that even the mighty Photoshop CS2 hasn't done a particularly good job of aligning the images. So, you will need to make changes to the image manually.

4 By clicking on parts of the image, the pictures can be rearranged into the correct order. Photoshop will then automatically align the images by matching the pixels together.

1 These five images were taken using a tripod and, having determined an acceptable exposure for the entire scene, they were all shot in manual mode. The tripod helps you to align the various images accurately, while shooting in manual ensures there's no variation in the brightness values of the individual shots.

Once the shots have been taken, download them, and place them in a folder on your computer's hard drive for safety.

2 To start, bring up the Photomerge dialog box in Photoshop, and go to File > Automate > Photomerge.

Navigate to the files that you have decided to include in the panorama and then click OK.

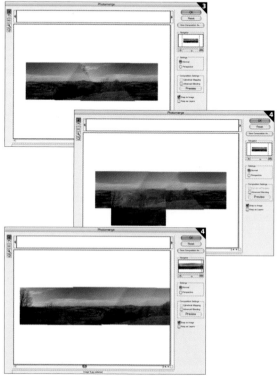

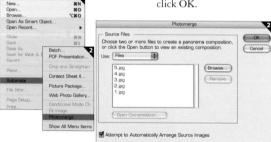

5 With the shots now in the correct order, selecting Advanced Blending will greatly improve the 'joins' between the images, as shown in the Preview.

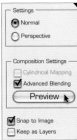

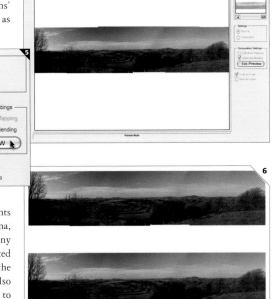

6 Before any improvements are made to this panorama, you need to cut away any of the landscape's unwanted background area using the Crop tool. This will also help to keep the file size to a minimum.

7 With the background cut away, perform any global changes you'd like to make to the panorama. Here, for example, the brightness has been increased using the Levels command.

Now zoom in to fix any specific areas in the image that don't match exactly. With so much sky in this image, some of the tones aren't equal. Use the Clone Stamp tool to correct these, along with any areas where the join is visible.

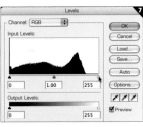

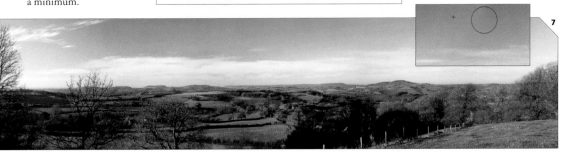

8 Both Photoshop CS3 and Elements 6 have a more powerful picture-stitching tool, which works in much the same way as in previous versions, but when you open Photomerge you have various options for stitching the images together. The 'Panorama' setting offers a true panorama representation, while the 'Cylindrical' setting will provide the view that we're more accustomed to, as does 'Reposition Only'.

It does pay to experiment with these various options. However, note how CS3 and Elements have both merged the images so successfully that, in fact, no remedial work (other than tone and colour) has been required to get to the finished image.

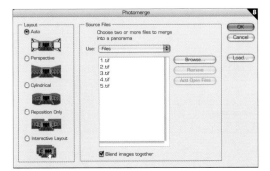

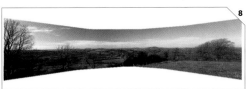

Hand-tinted Photographs

Before the advent of colour photography, the only way to add colour to a photograph was to use coloured oil paints and physically paint the image.

Although the results were never intended to be realistic in the way we view colour pictures today, hand-tinted photographs were immensely popular and they achieved a unique visual quality that couldn't be replicated with the arrival of colour film.

With image-editing software, it's now possible to recreate the effect of 'vintage' hand-tinted photographs, but without the mess – or irreversible nature – of paint. The exercise is easy and fun, and an ideal project for children. The colours can be as muted or as garish as you like, and can either emulate the look of old, Victorian, hand-tinted photographs or can create vibrant works that appear to be influenced by modern artists.

ADDING COLOUR TO A COLOUR IMAGE

In this first example, the starting point for adding colour is a colour image.

1 In the Layers palette, duplicate the Background layer by dragging the thumbnail onto the 'Create a new layer' icon, or by going to Layer > Duplicate Layer.

2 Select the duplicate layer, go to Image > Adjustments > Desaturate and create a black and white image.

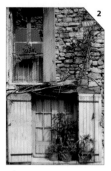

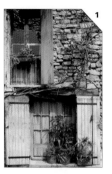

3 All you need to do now is select the Eraser tool from the Toolbox and then set the Opacity in the Tool Options bar to between 30% and 40%.

Next, simply erase the black and white image to reveal the colour layer that is underneath.

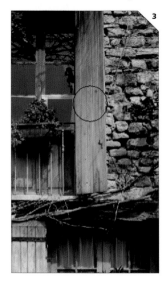

4 An optional step is to blur the black and white layer by using the Gaussian Blur filter. Experiment with the amount of blur to achieve the effect you want.

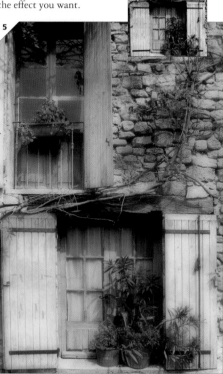

5 As always, you can adjust the Opacity of the top layer to increase or reduce the intensity of the colour.

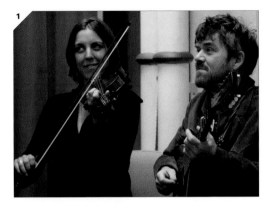

Here, the black and white image could have been scanned into the computer, shot in black and white mode on a digital camera, or converted to black and white.

1 Begin the exercise for this image by going to Image > Mode > RGB Color, so that you can add colour to the image.

2 Next, we need to duplicate the Background layer (Layer > Duplicate layer). In the Layers palette, change the duplicate layer's Blending Mode to Color using the drop-down menu. Then, make sure that you rename the layer 'Colour'.

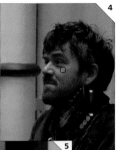

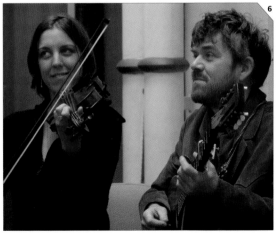

3 The first tone you need to add is a flesh tone to all the exposed areas of skin. One option for doing this is to open a colour image that features a flesh tone (such as a portrait), and then use the Eyedropper tool to sample an appropriate area. Click on the skin to change the foreground colour to the chosen tone. This will be visible in the Foreground Color box at the bottom of the Toolbox.

Alternatively, you can click on the Foreground Color box to bring up the Color Picker. Navigate your way to an appropriate colour by using the slider and the cursor.

4 Choose a small, soft brush (adjustable with the '[' and ']' keys) and set an Opacity of around 30% in the Tool Options bar.

Start to paint over areas of skin on the Colour layer with the flesh tone you selected in Step 3.

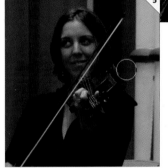

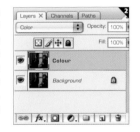

5 Once you've coloured the skin, return to the Color Picker and choose colours for other areas of the image. Don't worry too much about painstakingly painting in the exact areas, as the intention is to create only the suggestion of colour for each major element of the image, rather than to create a full-colour photograph.

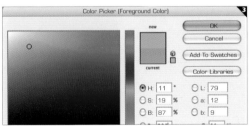

6 For this image, a total of six colours were used to colour the entire photograph. The Colour layer was then blurred slightly using the Gaussian Blur filter.

Restoring Old Photographs

The various cloning options and healing brushes covered earlier in this book are extremely powerful and versatile tools, and are ideal for fixing and restoring old or damaged photographs. These are a significant advance on the conventional restoration methods using inks and tiny paintbrushes that were all that was available several years ago. Nowadays, armed just with a desktop scanner, a computer and some fairly inexpensive image-editing software, it's possible to repair photographs to a much higher standard.

USING SOFTWARE TO RESTORE IMAGES

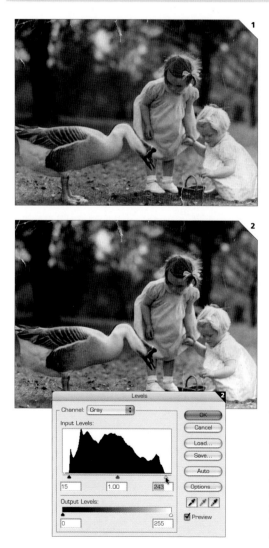

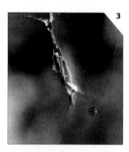

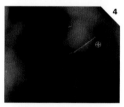

1 This delightful picture of two sisters feeding a Chinese goose was taken in 1938. The last 70 years haven't been kind to the original print and there are tears, creases and numerous dust and scratch marks.

2 After scanning the print, the first step is to check the tonal levels. Opening the Levels dialog (Image > Adjustments > Levels) shows that both the black and white points aren't at their optimum. Both points have been brought in a little so they sit under the ends of the histogram, giving the image a little more contrast.

3 The next step is to systematically fix and restore the numerous tears, creases and scratches. For large damaged areas, the best tool is likely to be the Clone Stamp tool. Clone a point that matches as closely as possible the area you're trying to repair, and remember to keep taking samples from other areas to avoid creating repeating patterns. Remember to use the '[' and ']' keys to choose a brush of the appropriate size. Use Edit > Undo to reverse any corrections that go slightly wrong.

4 For much smaller scratches, try using the Healing Brush tool. Sample as closely as you can to the area to be repaired and move slowly along the scratch.

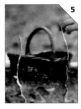

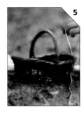

5 All images will have slightly more complex areas to repair. For these, you should revert to the Clone Stamp tool and then sample those areas that share the same pattern as those you are attempting to repair. It's possible that you may find suitable sampling points in entirely different parts of the scene.

6 If you have the option of using a Patch tool, try using this on those areas where there is no obvious pattern, such as here, where the emulsion has become rather sticky, leaving a drying mark. Now draw around the offending area and drag it to an area that closely resembles the part that you are trying to correct.

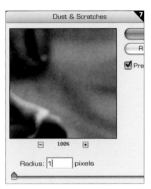

7 This particular image was also suffering from a fair amount of dust damage.

To remedy this, apply the Dust & Scratches filter (Filter > Noise > Dust & Scratches), with a very small Radius. Too high a Radius will often soften an image to an unacceptable level.

8 Having made the repairs, the image should almost be as good as the original.

9 With the image stored in your computer, you can make any number of changes to it. Here, Hue/Saturation was used, clicking the Colorize option to apply a light sepia tone. With a Levels adjustment layer, the contrast was then increased to give the picture a vintage feel.

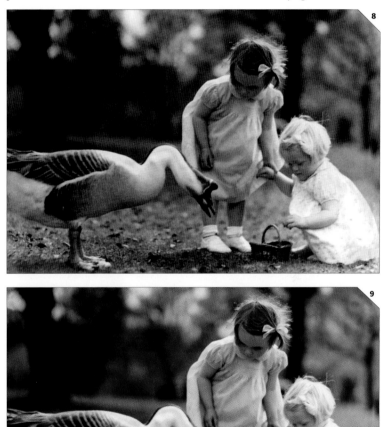

Retouching Portaits

The great thing about digital images is that they can be easily altered, right down to the pixel level if necessary. This means that it's not only really easy to fix old and damaged photographs once they've been scanned, but it is also easy to edit and fix less-than-perfect digital shots.

One of the most common retouching techniques is to remove skin blemishes and the subtle signs of age in portrait pictures. Practically every image you see in advertising (particularly in the fashion and beauty industry) has been 'fixed' digitally to make the models appear as perfect as possible.

However, it's quite straightforward to do similar work yourself using image-editing software. Without going to quite the extremes that the fashion industry does, impressive results can be achieved relatively quickly and easily using a few simple commands and common tools.

DIGITALLY RETOUCHING SKIN

1 The subject in this shot has a few wrinkles, crow's feet around the eyes, and the odd blemish here and there – a bit like most of us. Using almost any editing software, the age lines can be reduced and the skin generally cleaned up to make the subject appear younger.

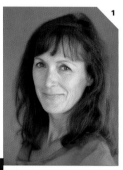

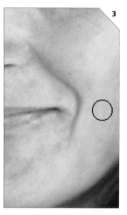

3 The laughter lines around the subject's mouth can also be removed or at least smoothed out slightly, but for this adjustment it's far better to use a larger brush because the skin tone changes quite a bit.

The larger radius and soft edge of the brush will help even out the variation in tone and therefore ensure that the image retains a realistic appearance.

2 Close inspection shows the task at hand in more detail. The first step is to remove (or reduce) the crow's feet around the left eye.

First, make a duplicate copy of the Background layer before you start working. By doing this, you can easily rectify any mistakes, or reduce slightly over-zealous retouching. Preserving the original also makes it quick and easy to make before-and-after comparisons.

Using the Clone Stamp tool and a small, soft brush set to an Opacity of around 40% in the Tool Options bar, sample an area close to the uppermost line of the left eye's crow's feet and simply clone it out in one smooth stroke. As you work down you'll have more clean skin to sample.

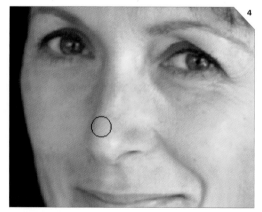

4 Once all the major lines have been removed on both sides of the face and on the forehead, you can start fixing the blemishes on the nose. Sample areas of similarly coloured skin with the Clone Stamp tool and dab out the marks.

5 Finally, create a new layer by clicking on the 'Create a new layer' icon in the Layers palette.

Using the Eyedropper tool to take samples, paint over the duplicated original with the Brush tool, making sure you concentrate on areas where you want to even up the skin colour. Applied carefully, and with a low Opacity set in the Tool options bar, this will add the final gloss to the end result.

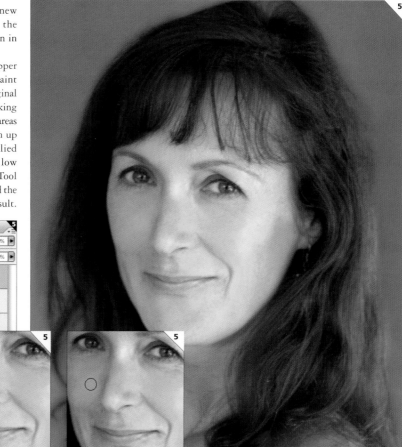

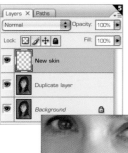

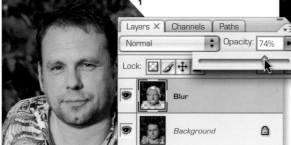

QUICK RETOUCHING WITH GAUSSIAN BLUR

For a very quick fix, you can use the same technique for soft-focus portrait effect, but to a lesser degree.

1 Duplicate the background image, then apply a small amount of Gaussian Blur (you can experiment with quantity).

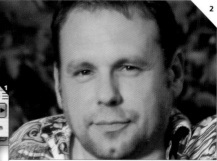

2 Next, use the Eraser tool to erase the blurred layer around the eyes, mouth, hair and any other areas you would like to remain sharp.

Adding Type

Having the ability to create type for use on its own or to add to images allows the amateur photographer to turn into an amateur graphic designer, albeit for a short period of time. Adding type to images opens up a whole new world of possibilities, ranging from greeting cards and invitations, through to postcards and CD cover designs. The possibilities are literally endless.

Just about all image-editing applications have some form of type capability, but some are more sophisticated than others. Photoshop and Photoshop Elements have plenty to offer, and adding type to an image using either package is easy and intuitive. The range of type fonts, styles and effects is breathtaking – and it's possible to download even more fonts from the Internet.

INTRODUCING TEXT TO IMAGES

1 To begin adding text to an image, select the Text tool from the Toolbox. Photoshop, Elements and many other image-editing programs feature both Horizontal and Vertical Text tools. Here, the Horizontal type tool has been chosen.

With the Text tool now selected, place the cursor in the approximate position that you want the text to appear. Don't worry too much at this stage about getting it in exactly the right place, as you can move the text at any time until you flatten the image's layers.

2 Type the text you want to appear. The type will appear in the style of the last font that you used.

Once you've finished typing, click OK in the Tool Options bar. When you press OK, a new layer with your text is automatically created in the Layers palette.

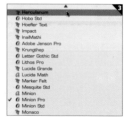

3 Once you've placed the text on the image, you can then style it in any number of ways. Going to the Tool Options bar presents you with the opportunity to select or change the type font, size and colour. There are a huge number of fonts to choose from, and usually one that will serve your purpose.

4 Clicking on the 'Create warped text' icon brings up the Warp Text dialog. This features numerous weird and wacky custom shapes and patterns that allow you to shape your words. Clicking on a specific shape, such as 'Fisheye', brings up a further dialog box where you can control the specific size and shape of the effect.

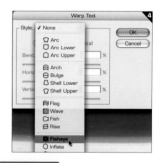

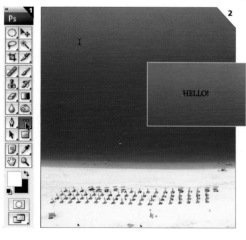

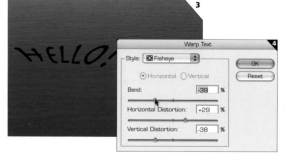

5 Once you've selected the Warp Text style, go to the Layers palette and click on the 'Create layer style' icon. This will bring up a whole host of additional styles that can be applied to your type.

Here, 'Drop Shadow' has been selected. 'Outer Glow' was then selected in the Layer Style dialog box and some adjustments to the 'Drop Shadow' settings were made to achieve the effect shown here.

6 The black type looks a little dull, but clicking on the coloured box in the Tool Options bar brings up the Color Picker, where you can quickly and easily select a different colour.

Having chosen a colour and applied Layer styles to the text layer, return to the Layers palette and then you can see precisely which styles have been applied.

Clicking on any of the style icons will bring up the relevant dialog box where further adjustments can then be made.

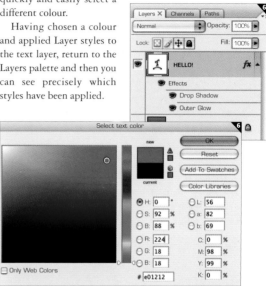

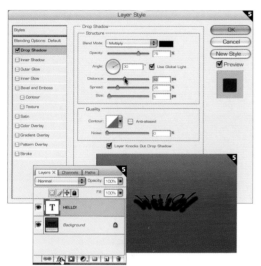

7 Finally, before 'fixing' the type, click on the Move tool and, with 'Show Bounding Box' checked in the Tool Options bar, you can now reposition, rotate and stretch your text.

8 Clicking on the Type tool to add additional text will keep on creating new layers that you can refine, style and re-edit until you eventually decide to go to Layer > Flatten Layers.

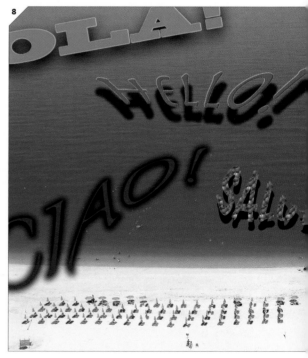

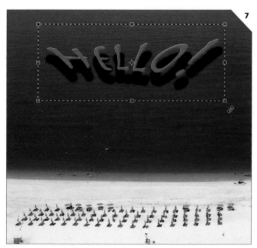

Adding Borders

Having created your own photographic masterpiece, why not try adding a border as a final creative touch? As with just about anything related to image-editing, there are countless ways of adding a border to an image, but the method described here allows you to experiment freely and easily with Adobe's extensive and powerful set of Filters, available in both Elements and Photoshop. Other programs have similar filter sets that can be applied in the same way, and if you don't like the one you initially select you can go back and try another until you find one you do like. Sooner or later you'll find a border effect that adds a touch of professionalism to your image.

USING A FILTER TO ADD A BORDER

1 Open the image to which you want to add a border, then select the Rectangular Marquee tool and draw a border around the inside edge of the image. You could just as easily use the Elliptical Marquee tool to create an oval border around the image, or you could even draw a freehand border with the Lasso tool.

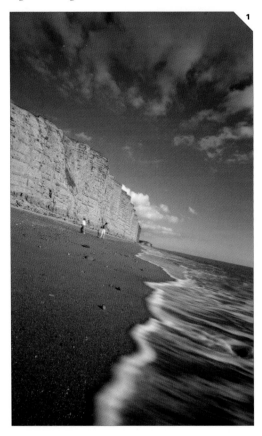

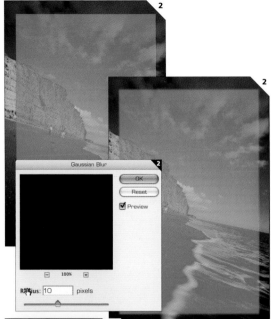

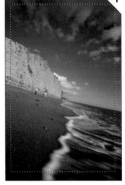

2 With the border in place, go to Select > Inverse and then click the 'Edit in quick mask mode' icon at the bottom of the Toolbox. Blur the mask slightly using Gaussian Blur (Filter > Blur > Gaussian Blur). The more blur you add at this stage, the more noticeable the blur will become when you get to the end.

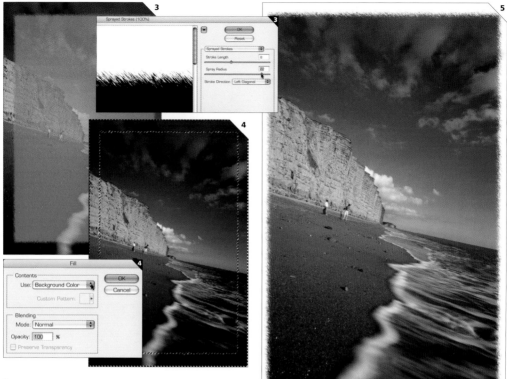

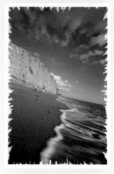

3 Go to Filter > Brushed Strokes > Sprayed Strokes, and experiment with the settings until you see a result you like in the preview window. You should remember that you are applying this filter to the mask, rather than the image itself, and bear in mind that the higher the resolution of the image, the less the effect of the filter. When you're happy with the settings, click OK.

4 To return to the main image, click the Quick Mask mode icon to turn the mask into a 'marching ants' selection. Then go to Edit > Fill and fill the border with a colour you feel is appropriate. In this example, white was chosen as the border colour.

5 The finished, bordered image is shown here.

ALTERNATIVE BORDERS

In the additional examples shown here, the same technique has been used to apply borders using the Extrude Edges, Glass (Tiny Lens), and Spatter filters. Experiment using any filter you like; some, however, are more appropriate for this task than others. You can use the History palette to go back each time to try another option – just delete the Filter Gallery line and start again with another filter. If you don't find a filter that works for your image, numerous websites allow you to view and download other border effects – some you have to pay for, but others are free.

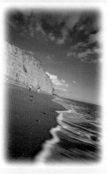

Spatter

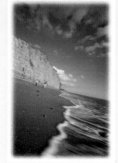

Glass (Tiny Lens)

Extrude Edges

Processing RAW Images

As digital camera technology has improved, combined with advances made in digital imaging software, an increasing number of enthusiast photographers are shooting and editing in the RAW format. As we discussed earlier, capturing images using your camera's native RAW format provides you with far more digital information compared with shooting using the JPEG format. The data are uncompressed and saved as a 12-bit or 14-bit file compared with JPEG's 8-bit information. The drawback to shooting in RAW is that images cannot be printed or shared until you have processed them.

The earliest popular RAW processor was a plug-in application available with both Photoshop and Photoshop Elements. Called Adobe Camera Raw (ACR), this plug-in allowed you to make basic corrections to uncompressed RAW files before opening them as 16-bit TIFF files in the host program. The image-quality benefits of being able to edit the RAW data before completing other editing tasks soon won favour across the photo community. This saw Adobe develop a dedicated RAW processor and image organizer in the shape of Adobe Photoshop Lightroom. Here we take a quick look at how Lightroom works.

RAW PROCESSING WITH LIGHTROOM

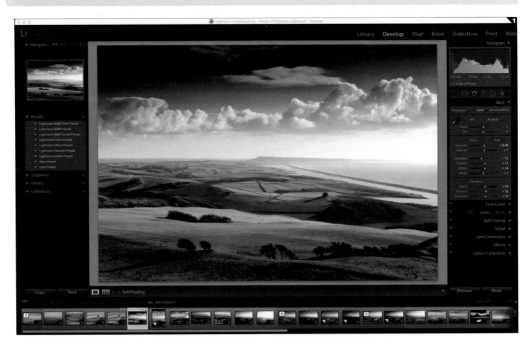

1 For such a powerful image-editing tool, Lightroom is a surprisingly easy program to learn. The user interface is attractively designed, and the entire workspace can be rescaled to fit the aspect ratio of your screen. Lightroom comprises seven discrete modules or workspaces accessible at the top right of the screen. These are: Library, Develop, Map, Book, Slideshow, Print and Web. These modules are intended to reflect a photographer's typical workflow. Images are imported from the camera into the Library. They are then optimized and edited in the Develop module before being shared in either Book form, as a Slideshow, Print or via the Web. The Map module allows you to pin where your images were taken on a detailed map and provides you with GPS coordinates. With a GPS-enabled camera, images can be plotted automatically – ideal for travel.

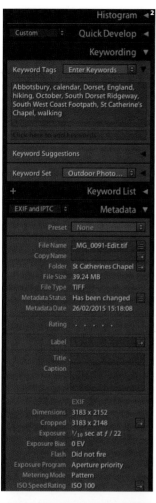

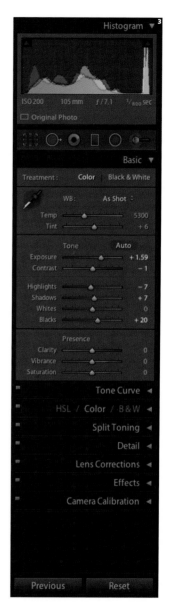

2 When importing images from the camera into Lightroom's Library module, you can create folders with unique names, and include key words to make searching for specific images easier at a later date. Lightroom will also automatically import all the EXIF data associated with the individual images. This includes the camera settings, image type, image size, and so on. This powerful feature set means you can easily keep track of your digital assets.

3 The Develop module is Lightroom's principal workspace used for editing images. Grouped together in logical palettes that can be expanded or collapsed by clicking the white arrows, the tools in the Develop module allow you to straighten and crop photos, adjust tone, colours, brighten or darken highlight and shadow regions, apply sharpening, lens corrections, such as chromatic aberration, convert images to black and white, and much more. The program is sophisticated enough to allow you to apply all these corrections to the image as a whole or to specific areas. Most corrections are made using sliders that work in real time, so that you can see the changes being made as you make them.

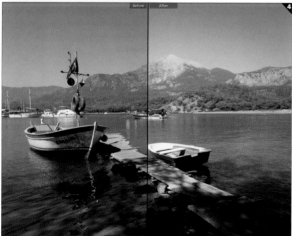

4 Another useful feature in Lightroom is that when in the Develop module you can set the main image to reveal how your image appears before and after your adjustments.

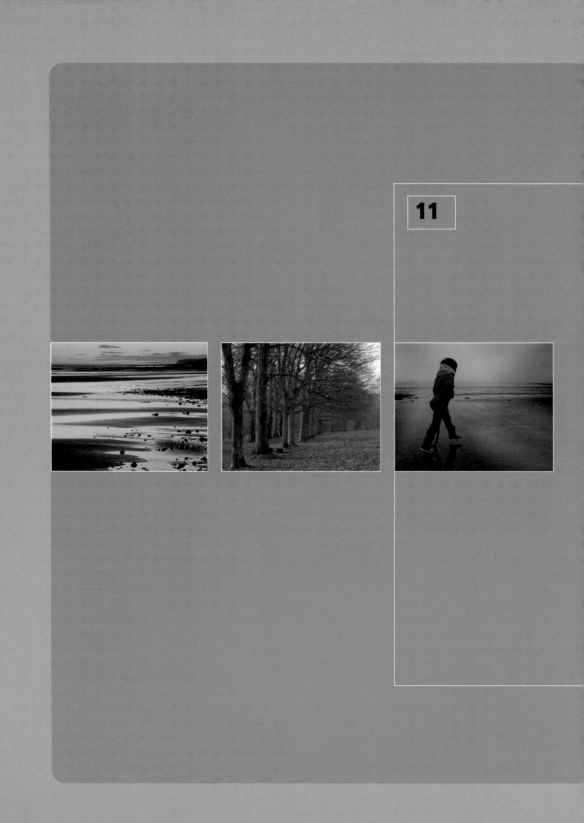

11

Viewing and Sharing

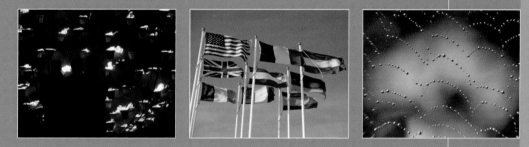

Whether it's simple family snaps or potential competition-winning
art photographs, sooner or later you'll either want to make prints
or create an electronic version that can be sent via e-mail, or create
a slideshow on disk. Chapter 11 provides you with all the information
you need to produce professional-looking prints, or to choose a series
of images that you can then transform into a picture gallery or
slideshow, complete with captions and background soundtrack.
The chapter concludes with all the essential information you'll
need to keep your invaluable images safe for many years to come.

Scanners and Scanning

While most amateur photographers and more and more professionals now shoot exclusively with digital cameras, many people still find a scanner a useful addition to their digital photography workflow. You may have a number of old prints, negatives or slides you would like to work on digitally, which can be edited and enhanced in some way, or you might still prefer shooting using high-resolution, medium-format film that then needs to be scanned before printing. There could be any number of reasons for wanting the ability to scan images into the computer.

Flatbed or film

There are two types of desktop scanner – flatbed and film. The former is the most common, featuring a hinged lid that closes down over a glass surface, or 'platen'. The size of the platen determines the size of the prints that can be scanned. Most flatbed scanners are A4 paper size, capable of scanning prints up to around 10 × 8in (25 × 20cm), which is more than enough for most needs. Most recent flatbed models also feature some form of film

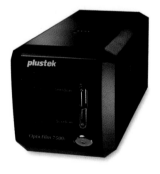

ABOVE If you still shoot a lot of film or have a large library of film images, a film scanner will provide you with the necessary resolution to capture all the detail from the film.

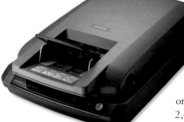

ABOVE Most flatbed scanners have a built-in transparency hood, which means you can scan your slides and negatives, as well as prints.

or slide carrier in the lid, known as a transparency hood, making it possible to scan individual slides or strips of film. However, flatbed scanners are primarily designed to scan prints, and many do not offer the high resolution needed to make the most of film. For this reason, if most of the material you intend to scan is film, you'll get better results from a dedicated film scanner.

What to look for

Both film and flatbed scanners work in more or less the same way. An imaging sensor, such as a CCD, records the colour and tonal information from the print or film, which is converted and stored as digital data in much the same way as it is in a digital camera. The difference is that the sensor in a scanner scans the information a line at a time, hence the term 'scanner'.

Resolution

There are three factors to bear in mind when looking to buy a scanner: resolution, colour depth and dynamic range. Resolution figures for scanners are often given as two figures, such as 2,400 × 4,800ppi. The first figure represents the actual 'optical' scanning resolution of the sensor, while the second represents how finely the scanner head moves. Rely on the first figure and ensure the figure you're quoted is the actual resolution and not an 'interpolated' one. If you want a flatbed scanner to scan images in order to make prints, a resolution of 2,400ppi will be perfectly adequate for most uses. For film scanners, a higher resolution is required, and around 4,800ppi would be sufficient.

Colour depth

The number of colours a device is capable of recognizing is also key. Even the most basic scanners offer 24-bit colour, meaning they are able to distinguish among 16.7 million colours. If you can afford to, buy a scanner that offers 36-, 42- or even 48-bit colour. The increased colour depth will provide you with greater scope when editing the colour in your images, as well as being able to better render detail in shadow areas.

Dynamic range

Another factor governing a scanner's ability to capture subtle detail in highlights and shadows is its dynamic range. Dynamic range in scanners runs on a scale with a theoretical maximum of 4.8. In reality, professional drum scanners with a resolution of 11,000ppi achieve a figure of around 4. For flatbed scanners, you should look for a model with a dynamic range (DMax) of 3+ if you are scanning colour prints. For scanning film, look for a dynamic range of 3.8+.

Be wary of manufacturers' claims, as there is no standard means of measuring dynamic range, so two scanners with the same quoted DMax figure might not actually have the same dynamic range.

Scanning

All scanners come equipped with their own software that enables them to perform scans. Once this software is loaded onto the computer you can either start scanning by launching the newly loaded software, or you can usually access the software via your image-editing software.

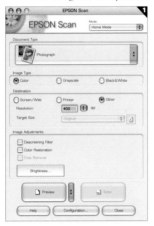

1 If you're in Edit mode in Elements or using Photoshop, begin the scan by going to File > Import > [Your scanner]. In Elements' Organizer mode you can go to File > Get Photos > From Scanner. Other image-editing software will have a similar command. With the software launched, you usually have the option to create a preview of the scan.

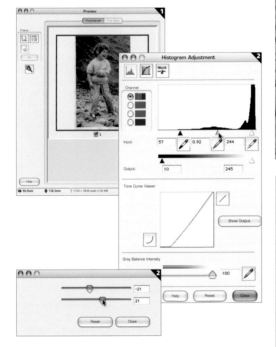

2 Having created a preview of the scan, you will usually have the option of adjusting the image before the final scan is made. In Epson's basic 'Home Mode', for example, you can adjust brightness and contrast levels, whereas if you are using the more sophisticated 'Professional Mode' you will have greater control over the scan.

3 Once you're happy with the preview view, click Scan to complete the scan. Depending on the resolution you've selected for your particular scan, the process will be complete within approximately 1–5 minutes.

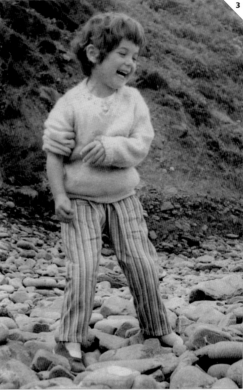

What resolution?

Deciding at what resolution to scan prints, negatives and transparencies can be confusing, as much will depend on how large the final image is intended to be used. Here are some useful guidelines:

Original Source	Use/Size	Scanning resolution
Print	Web	72–100ppi
Print	Same size as original	200–300ppi
Print	Twice size as original	400–600ppi
Print	Four times original	800–1,200ppi
Pint	Half size of original	100–150ppi
35mm neg/slide	6 x 4in (15 x 10cm)	1,200ppi
35mm neg/slide	10 x 8in (25 x 20cm)	2,400ppi
35mm neg/slide	18 x 10in (46 x 25cm)	3,600ppi

Printers

Once you've captured your images, either via a camera or scanner, sooner or later you'll want to start printing your favourite images to show friends and relatives, or even to exhibit. Home printing, either direct from the camera or via a computer, is increasing in popularity and there is now a huge variety of printers available for the job.

Inkjet

The once-lowly inkjet printer was given a new lease of life with the advent of digital photography. At one point it seemed that the laser printer would supersede the inkjet, but it quickly transpired that inkjet technology lent itself perfectly to digital imaging and today, despite there being affordable colour laser and thermal (or dye sub) printers emerging onto the market, inkjet printers still provide the highest-quality images for the price.

Size

Inkjet printers are available in a wide variety of sizes. On the one hand, there are small 'portable' models that print standard 6 × 4in (15 × 10cm) prints, which are ideal for family holiday snaps, while at the other end of the scale, there are professional printers capable of producing poster-sized prints. If you're an enthusiastic amateur, it's certainly worth buying a printer capable of printing A4-size paper. It doesn't mean you can print only A4 – a tray will hold and feed smaller-sized paper for printing snaps – but it does give you the option of producing good-sized prints of your favourite images should you wish to display them framed and hung on a wall. You may even want to consider an A3 printer, bearing in mind that in the longer term the paper and inks will cost a lot more than the printer itself, which may not cost a great deal more than an A4 printer.

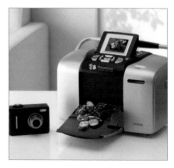

Dots per inch

A printer's ability to resolve fine detail, in other words its resolution, is measured in dots per inch (dpi), which should not to be confused with the image's own resolution, which is measured in pixels per inch (ppi). A dpi figure tells you how many droplets of ink the printer is capable of printing on an inch of paper, so the higher the number the greater the resolution. Most printers today have settings ranging from 360dpi, through to 720dpi, 1,440dpi and up to 2,880dpi. The lowest resolution should be used for basic print jobs such as letters, using standard plain paper, while the higher resolutions should be used in conjunction with higher grades of photographic-quality paper. The paper you buy should tell you what resolution can be used. Printing with a high-resolution setting on standard paper will simply result in too much ink being applied.

Numbers of colours

Another aspect to consider when assessing an inkjet is the number of different colours it uses. All inkjet printers use the basic secondary

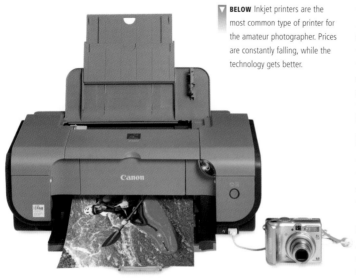

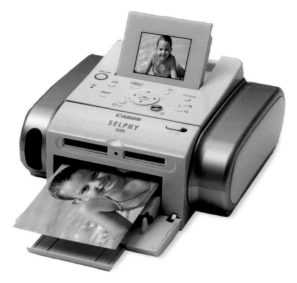

the final, protected image is complete. If you're considering a dye-sub printer, don't be thrown by the advertised resolutions of 300 – 400dpi. Because dye-subs work in a different way to inkjets, these comparatively low resolution figures actually equate to a very high print resolution. In fact, dye-sub prints probably resemble traditional colour prints much more closely than inkjet prints in terms of feel and texture.

When it comes to image quality, many claim dye-sub printers to be as good as inkjets, but print for print they tend to be a little more expensive, particularly the less common A4-sized (letter) printers. However, with more and more people buying these small but sturdy printers, it's possible that the consumables will come down in price.

Laser printers

While affordable laser colour printers are now available, these still tend to be used in offices for producing large numbers of colour reports or similar uses. Laser printers are not yet as close to photographic-quality prints as inkjet and dye-sub printers and are rarely thought of for home use.

colours – cyan, magenta and yellow (CMY) – to replicate the reds, greens and blues (RGB) of the digital image and, in addition, all printers also use a black ink (K) to add depth to darker regions of an image. While in theory, CMYK are the only colours you need to produce all the visible colours of the spectrum, some of the more sophisticated printers have additional colours, such as light cyan and light magenta, to improve subtle colour gradation. Some even include an additional light black or grey for improved neutral tones in black and white prints.

Direct to printer

You don't have to own a computer to enjoy the benefits of photographic-quality home printing. A number of manufacturers, such as Canon and Epson, produce printers that can print directly from a digital camera or a memory card. Such printers are capable of producing excellent results, but be certain to look into how much editing can be undertaken. Some, for example, will only allow simple cropping, while others may have the option of making brightness and tonal corrections and other more sophisticated adjustments. However

comprehensive the 'in-printer' editing capabilities, they will still pale into insignificance compared with what can be achieved using image-editing software.

Dye-sub printers

Although inkjets are the most popular photographic-quality printers for the home, there are alternatives. There is an increasing number of dye-sublimation printers available on the market. Most are small, portable printers producing 6 × 4in (15 × 10cm) prints, and many have been designed to print directly from a camera or memory card.

Dye-sub printers use cassette-like cartridges that are loaded with strips of cyan-, magenta- and yellow-coloured ribbon. An additional clear coating ribbon is used to add a protective coating to the prints. As the paper passes through the printer, the colour ribbon is heated and the dye in the ribbon transferred to the paper. The paper passes through the printer four times before

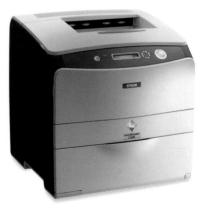

Paper and Ink

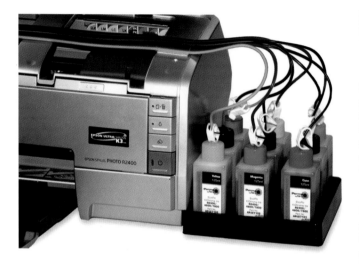

No matter how much you pay for an inkjet printer, there are two further factors that will certainly govern the quality of the prints it produces – paper and ink. Using cheap, inferior consumables is likely to cost you far more in the long run.

Paper

To achieve the best-possible print quality from your printer, consider carefully the paper you're using. As a rule of thumb, the heavier the paper, the better it is likely to be. If you've ever tried printing a colour picture onto plain copy paper you'll know how dismal the results can be, as the inks spread and the colours appear dull and muted. Such paper weighs around 80gsm (grams per square metre). To achieve 'true' photographic-quality prints – be wary of the names manufacturers give to their various papers – you'll need to use a paper weighing between 210 to 250gsm. Unfortunately, compared with lighter papers, such heavyweight paper is quite expensive, particularly in A4 or A3 (letter or tabloid) sizes. With such paper costing a premium, you may want to use a lightweight paper for proofing, and smaller sizes for your holiday and family snaps.

Inks

As well as paper weight and quality, the inks you use will also affect how good your prints look, and how long they last. There are numerous third-party ink manufacturers that on the surface provide much better value for money than the branded inks produced by companies such as Epson and Canon. But, although such inks are less expensive, it may well be the case that they are a false economy. First, third-party inks may not provide you with the quality you want for your prints, and, second, it's likely that they will fade much quicker, particularly if exposed to daylight.

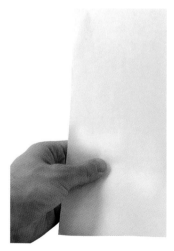

RIGHT The paper you use for your prints will play a big part in print quality. For your best photographs, make prints on the best quality paper.

Of course, these inks have a use for producing short-lived 'fun' projects, such as greetings cards, or proofs, but if you want the best-possible quality and longest-lasting prints, the best solution is to use inks produced by the same manufacturer as the printer.

Ink flow

One alternative that may offer some savings, particularly for medium-to-heavy print usage, is an inkflow system. Offered by companies such as Lyson (www.lyson.com) and Permajet (www.permajet.com), these systems feature large refillable ink containers that are connected to the printer via a series of narrow tubes, which in turn connect to the printer nozzles.

Although initial start-up costs can be quite expensive, when it comes to refilling, the inks are much cheaper to buy separately compared with buying an entire set of colour cartridges.

In addition, the various coloured inks are used and replaced individually, so you only need to replace those colours that have run empty.

With some colour cartridges, you have to replace the whole cartridge as soon as one colour runs out. As well as the financial incentive an inkflow system may offer, there's also an environmental advantage that all of us should consider.

Specialist inks

Lyson and Permajet also manufacture specialist inks that are designed specifically for photographers using inkjet printers. As well as coloured inks, which are designed specifically for use in certain makes of printer, these companies also produce a series of grey and black inks, which are used together to produce high-quality black and white prints. The use of grey inks in addition to black helps to highlight the subtle tones of the black and white image to their very best advantage.

Both these companies make strong claims for the longevity of their pigment-based inks, with some calculated to last over a hundred years before they begin to fade.

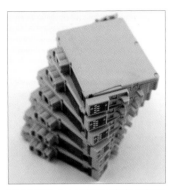

ABOVE The more sophisticated inkjet printers use individual colour cartridges, which means you only need to replace one at a time.

Leave it to the professionals

Although it's possible to achieve great-looking prints relatively easily in the comfort of your own home, it can take time, and many people simply do not get around to it. If this sounds all too familiar, it's worth considering one of the many online printing companies. You'll need a computer and Internet connection for this – and the faster the connection the better. A quick search on the web will throw up a number of companies. It's then simply a case of registering and following the instructions. This will involve uploading the images of which you want prints, making payment, and waiting for them to arrive by post (usually within a day or two). Buying a large number of prints this way is not only very easy, it can work out cheaper than printing them at home, and the results are usually excellent. Most online printing services offer more than just photographs. Photobooks, T-shirts, poster prints, mugs and greetings cards are just some of the more popular ways in which you can get your images into print. Most online companies also double up as online galleries where you can store and share your images.

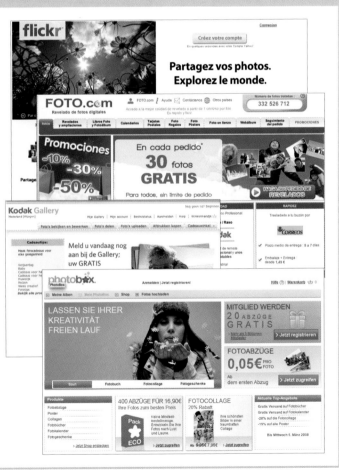

Printing

If you've only just bought a printer, you'll discover that it came with a CD. The disc will contain what's referred to as 'driver' software. This contains all the software needed for your computer to communicate with the printer. Without the driver software, the computer won't recognize the printer and you won't be able to print. To install the software, insert the disc into your computer's CD drive and follow the onscreen instructions. This should be very straightforward and take only a matter of minutes. If you've bought a used or refurbished printer and it doesn't have an accompanying CD, don't worry. Simply go online and search for the printer manufacturer. You'll find all the information you need on the website to download the driver software for your particular printer.

PRINTER OPTIONS AND FUNCTIONS

With the printer set up on your computer and running with good-quality inks and paper, photographic-quality prints are only a few clicks away. Printing is a straightforward process, but there are one or two things to look out for when you first start. Let's run through a typical print job using Photoshop Elements – other software will have very similar commands and dialog boxes.

1 Once you've completed editing an image in Edit mode and you're ready to print, go to File > Print. This will bring up the Print dialog window. Under the Printer's drop-down menu, select the name of your printer.

2 Make sure that your image is going to print in the correct format. In this example, a landscape-format image is incorrectly set up to print in portrait format. To correct this, click on the landscape/portrait format icons in the lower left-hand part of the dialog window.

Before you start printing, it's important to make sure that you have the correct paper size and type set up. Click on Page Setup in the lower right-hand corner of the dialog window.

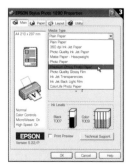

3 In the Page Setup dialog box, choose the paper size from the Size drop-down menu. Here, we've chosen A4.

Click on the Printer tab to bring up the printer's Properties window. There are a number of controls here, but the most important is the Media Type drop-down menu. Click on the type of paper on to which you're going to print. The menu attempts to cover the most common terms used by paper manufacturers.

Once you're happy with the settings, click OK to return to the Page Setup window. Here, click OK again to return to Element's Print dialog window.

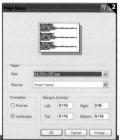

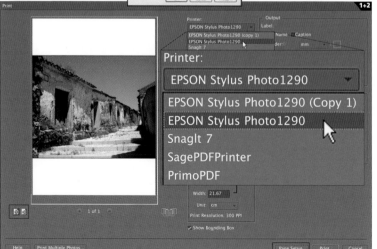

4 With the correct paper size and type selected, it's time to finalize how the image looks on the page before printing. Under the Print Size menu the image will default to Actual Size.

In a way this size is not important, and what's more relevant is checking to see what the Print Resolution figure is toward the bottom of the window, in the Scaled Print Size area. Here, the image is going to print at a healthy 300ppi, which is the optimum print setting. The outer edge of the white border in the preview window represents the size of the paper.

5 But note what happens to the Print Resolution figure if we scale the image down or up. Selecting a smaller print size ($3^1/_2$ x 5in / 8.9 x 12.7cm) from the Print Size drop-down menu has seen the Print Resolution increase to 546ppi, while selecting a larger print size (8 x 10in / 20.3 x 25.4cm) results in the resolution falling to 255ppi. With the 'Show Bounding Box' checked, you can rescale the image by dragging one of the corner boxes.

If, when you first go to print your image, only a small part of it appears in the preview box, and it's entirely covering the preview paper area, check to see what the print resolution is. It may be that your camera saves files at 72ppi, which is not a problem, but it means you will have to rescale the image before printing. Check the Scale to Fit Media box and note the percentage reading. Uncheck the Scale to Fit Media box, input a smaller percentage than you noted, and you should then be able to see the corners of the Bounding Box to help you scale the image. Scale the image to the size you want it to appear on the page. Check the resolution is a satisfactory 200ppi or more, and then click Print.

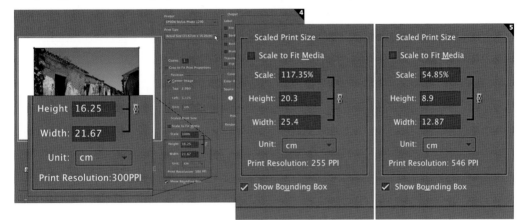

6 To print more than one image on a page, click the Print Multiple Images box in the Print dialog window. This will bring up a Print Photos window. In the Select Type of Print menu, you have various print styles, from Contact Sheet to Picture Package.

7 In the Select Layout menu, you can select how you want your image to appear and whether or not to add a preset border style. The window to the left allows you to add and delete images from the selection.

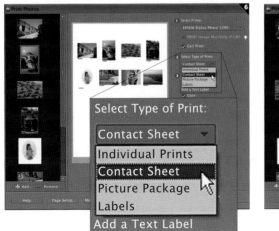

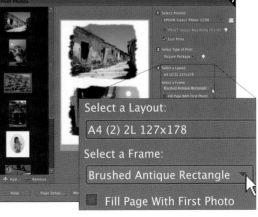

E-mailing Photographs

With so many people now connected to the World Wide Web, more and more of us are staying in touch with friends and family via e-mail. With broadband Internet access becoming increasingly widespread, it is now viable to send images without fear of wasting the recipient's time as they download relatively large files. Even so, unless you know that images are specifically going to be required for printing, it still pays to reduce file sizes for onscreen viewing. The more sophisticated image-editing software packages make it very simple to e-mail images.

SHARING YOUR IMAGES

1 Using Elements to send images via e-mail only takes a few clicks of the mouse. Select Share in the main viewing window and click the E-mail Attachments button to bring up the E-mail dialog window, where you can choose your preferred e-mail application.

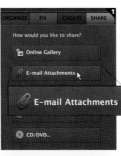

2 If the image you want to send is open in the Edit window, it will automatically be selected and placed in the E-mail Attachments window. In the same window, click the Convert Photos to JPEG box, as this is by far the most efficient format in which to e-mail images. Elements' default Maximum Photo Size settings are fairly standard, and images measuring 800 x 600 pixels will display well on most computers, including laptops. If you have

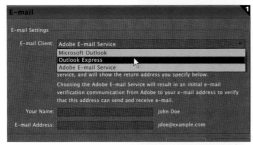

specific needs, then you can select smaller or bigger files. The Quality slider determines how much compression is applied to the image, and the lower the number, the greater the amount of compression that is applied. This will also lower the quality. The higher the number, the less compression is applied and the higher the quality.

Once you've chosen the image size and compression setting, Elements will tell you how large the file is and how long it estimates it will take to download via a slow, dial-up speed connection.

If you think the file is going to take too long to download, simply reduce the file size or increase the compression.

3 If you want to add any images, click the '+' symbol at the top of the E-mail Attachments window to bring up the Add Photos dialog window. From here you can navigate to your image collections and add whichever images you choose. When you've chosen, click Done to return to the E-mail Attachments window. If you're happy with your selection, click Next.

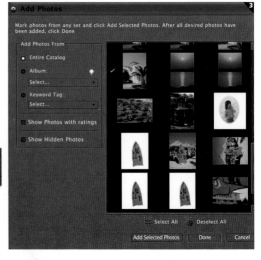

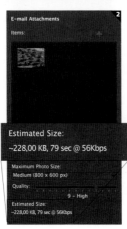

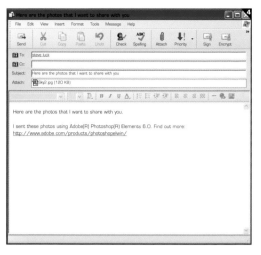

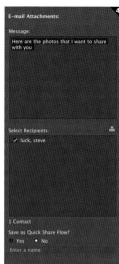

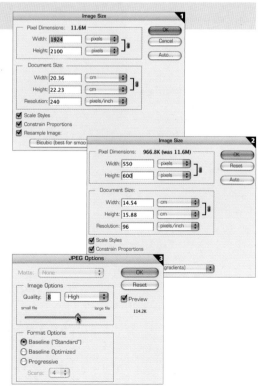

4 In the next screen you'll be given the option of typing your message and selecting the people to whom you want to send the images. After choosing the recipients, click Next and Elements will open up your preferred e-mail application with a pre-formatted new e-mail message to your list of recipients, containing your images and accompanying message. Now all you have to do is send.

ABOVE Sharing images via email has never been so simple. Images can be sent aross the world in a matter of moments.

MANUAL RESIZING

If you don't have Elements, and are unsure of how your software can automatically resize images, here's how to do it manually. All software can resize images in this way.

1 To resize an image for use on a website manually, go to Image > Resize > Image size. This brings up the Image Size dialog box. At nearly 12 MB the notional image is far too big to be used on the Internet.

2 Make sure the Resample Image box is ticked, and use Bicubic Sharper, as this is a specific algorithm for reducing image sizes. Change the image's resolution to 96ppi, which is the resolution for most Windows-based PC screens, and set the Height to 600 pixels, the optimum height for all screen images. This reduces the image's file size to 966K (just under 1MB), but this is still quite big for a web image.

3 Go to File > Save As and rename the file. Use a 'web' suffix so that you don't over-write the original, and select JPEG as the file format. Click OK, and the JPEG Options dialog window will appear. Here, a Quality compression setting of 8 has been chosen, which has reduced the file size to an acceptable 114 K.

You can also save the file as Progressive, which means that when it opens on screen, the image will appear quickly, but blurred, and gradually sharpen with the set number of scans selected.

Online Galleries

Photoshop Elements has a number of extremely useful automated tools to make editing images as easy as possible. One of the most useful is the Online Galleries command. Essentially, this allows you to select any number of your images; Elements will then resize them automatically, and place them in a pre-formatted gallery style. The gallery is then saved, ready for you to upload to the Internet, which is ideal for showing wedding or other special-event photographs to as many or as few people as you like, no matter where they live. If you have Photoshop, you can create similar galleries via the Browser window. Simply select the folder containing the images you want to use and then, still in the Browser window, go to Tools > Photoshop > Web Photo Gallery. There, you'll find a number of preset gallery styles to choose from. Once you've selected a gallery style, Photoshop will automatically resize the images and prepare the gallery for viewing in your web browser.

BUILDING AN ONLINE GALLERY

1 Before you start creating the Online Gallery, you may want to preselect the images you want to include in the Browser window. This will make the process quicker in the long run, but it's by no means essential. Nor do you need to resize any images manually to make them suitable for sending via e-mail – Elements will do this automatically.

To begin creating the gallery itself, click the Share tab to the top right of the Elements' window and then select Online Gallery.

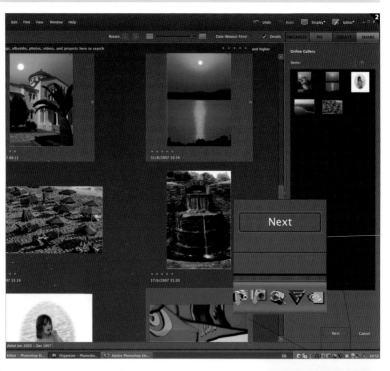

2 Click on the '+' symbol at the top of the first Online Gallery screen to navigate to the collection you made earlier. Drag the folder over to the window, or browse for individual images and drag them across one at a time. You can rearrange the order in which the images appear by dragging and placing the image thumb-nails in the small window. Once you've finalized your selection, click Next at the bottom of the window.

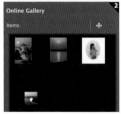

3 Elements will now present you with a variety of gallery templates to choose from. When you select a specific template, Elements provides a brief description of the template you've chosen at the bottom of the window, and also whether or not that template allows you to include captions. With such a diverse variety of gallery styles to choose from, you should easily find a style appropriate for your needs.

You can also choose how you want the images to be displayed in the gallery. 'Interactive' allows viewers to select specific thumbnails to view them at the larger size, while other options, such as 'Standard', will play the gallery from start to finish. Having chosen the gallery template, click Next.

Classic: A classic style to display your photos one by one. Include captions in your photos to tell a story

4 Depending on the chosen template, Elements will present you with a screen where you can customize your gallery. Here you can enter the gallery name and other details about the gallery, such as your name and e-mail address, so that people can easily see who the gallery is from and how to contact you.

In addition, and depending on the type of gallery, you can choose the transition effect (experiment to see which one you like best from the options given, such as Fade, Cut and so on). You can also choose how large you want the images to be saved. There are two standard settings – Broadband and Dial-up, which are self-explanatory. If you know that most of your viewers have a fast Internet connection, then select the first; otherwise it is safer to select the dial-up option.

Online Gallery

Provide a name and location for saving your gallery.

Gallery Name: Summer Holiday

Save To: C:\Documents and...evo\My Documents

Browse...

6 Finally, you have the option to upload and share your gallery using one of the options in the window. How you do this will depend on your Internet Service Provider (ISP). If you have any doubts on how do this, contact your ISP and they'll take you through the steps you need to take.

Elements also gives you the option of burning the gallery onto a CD should you wish to distribute it in this way.

5 After a few minutes, Elements will present you with the complete gallery, which you can run to check that you're happy with it. If you want to change the template style, go back to the Online Gallery window and select Previous, where you can then select another template. Alternatively, if you're happy with the gallery, you will be asked to give it a name and choose a location to save it to on your hard drive. Once you've entered this information, click Next.

Slide Shows

Another excellent way to show off your pictures to friends and family is to create a slide show of your selected photographs – whether they're of a recent family holiday, a wedding or your new home. Most image-editing software packages offer this option, and Photoshop Elements is no exception. In a relatively short space of time you can use Elements' Slide Show option to create a professional-looking slide show featuring all your favourite images, accompanied by music, voiceovers and text, should you wish.

Perhaps somewhat surprisingly, this attractive feature isn't available to Photoshop users, who will have to content themselves with using the Web Photo Gallery feature explained in the last project.

CREATING A SLIDE SHOW

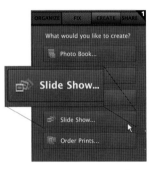

1 Before you start creating the show, you may want to place all the images you intend using in one easily identifiable folder. This will save time, but, as with the Online Gallery, it's not essential. To start, select the Slide Show option in the Create window.

2 The first window provides you with the basic options for the slide show. Most of the options are fairly self-explanatory, such as Static Duration, Transition Duration and Background Color. The Transition box provides a drop-down menu of the various transition styles available to you.

Although you may be tempted to use some of the more exotic-sounding styles, this can sometimes be a distraction, particularly if the Transition Duration is quite lengthy. You're better off keeping the transitions short and simple.

The Pan and Zoom option gives the slide show a professional feel, but it can be a bit too much if applied to all the slides – again, a case of less is more. If you don't click this option in the Slide Show Preferences window, you'll still have the option of applying Pan and Zoom transitions manually to the slides that you think are most suitable for the treatment. Once you've finished selecting your basic preferences, click OK.

3 Elements will now bring up the Slide Show Editor screen. Here, you can select the images you want to include in the slide show by clicking the Add Media button at the top of the screen. This will bring up the familiar Add Photos window, where you can navigate to the images you want to include. Once you've located the images, click Done at the bottom of the screen to return to the Slide Show Editor window.

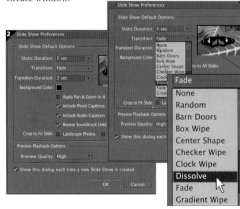

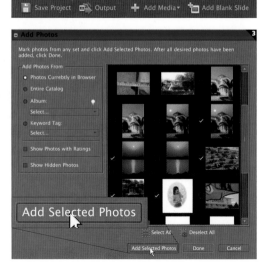

4 The Slide Show Editor is a powerful tool that enables you to customize all sorts of aspects of your show. The images you've selected will appear in a timeline at the bottom of the window. You can select individual images and apply a whole host of effects to them.

Many of the options are geared toward the fun side of slide shows, allowing you to add cartoon animals, different backgrounds, speech bubbles and costumes. If you're using the slide show to make a presentation, you can add text and narrative to make more serious points.

5 One of the most attractive aspects of Elements' slide shows is that it allows you to add sounds or music to your show. Selecting 'Click Here to Add Audio to Your Slide Show' near the bottom of the Editor window will bring up the 'Choose your Audio Files' dialog box.

From here, you can navigate to any music tracks that you might have stored on your computer, such as those you've downloaded for an MP3 player or those that were supplied when you purchased the software. Here, the Sample Music folder has been selected.

6 Once you have chosen your music, you'll see that the music appears as another line underneath your selection of images in the Editor window. You can edit the images to appear at specific points along the music timeline, which is useful if you've selected more than one piece of music. If you've only selected one track, the easiest option is to set the music to repeat and click the Fit Slides to Audio option.

Adding text is just as straightforward. Click the Add Text button and the Text Editor will appear. You can type in the text you want over any specific slide. You have the option of resizing and placing the text where you wish, and you can also change the font and colour of the text.

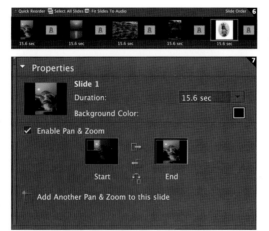

7 In the Properties window you can add a Pan and Zoom effect to individual slides. Click on Start and draw a green square around the area that you want to appear first when the image opens. Click on End and select the area that will complete the slide.

Here, for example, the slide will open with a close-up of the sun and pan out to reveal the entire image. To change the order of any of the images, simply click and drag. To preview the show, click Full Screen Preview at the top of the window.

8 When you're happy with the slide show, click Save Project in the top left corner of the Editor window and Elements will offer several ways to save the show – either as a file on your hard drive, on CD/DVD or straight to your television. Elements provides easy-to-follow instructions and advice to help you make the right choices for your show. A lot depends on how instantly you want to view the show and whether or not your prospective audience lives in the same home as you or on the other side of the world.

Organizing Your Photographs

One of digital photography's greatest benefits is that once you have a camera, a memory card or two, and a computer onto which you can download your images, it costs almost nothing to take photographs. The result is that in a very short space of time you'll discover you have a vast number of images on your computer.

If you're a keen photographer, you'll soon have thousands of images, and keeping tabs on them all will become harder and harder, especially as your computer's hard drive will need clearing out from time to time, in order for your applications to run properly. Once you find yourself adding additional desktop hard drives or burning images to CD or DVD, it's time to consider using some form of image catalogue or database software.

Digital asset management
The buzz term for cataloguing your images is 'digital asset management', which sounds more daunting than it is. As implied earlier, digital asset management is really just an efficient way of keeping track of all your images so that you can find any specific image efficiently. Today, there are numerous cataloguing programs to help you do this.

EXIF
The most effective cataloguing software works by recording all the EXIF data that is embedded by your digital camera every time you take a photograph. Simple examples of EXIF data include the date and time the photograph was taken, the make and model of the camera, and the exposure setting. Some professional cameras will also provide the exact geographical co-ordinates at which the image was shot. This information

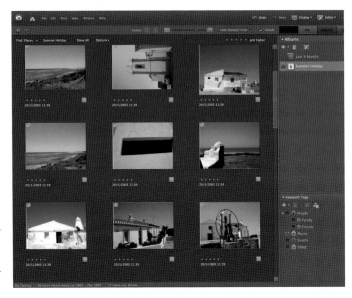

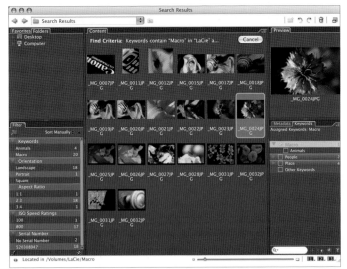

TOP Photoshop Elements' Photo Organizer is an integral part of the image-editing software package. You can switch between browsing and editing and easily create searchable Albums and add Keyword Tags to groups of images or single photographs.

ABOVE Photoshop CS comes with its own sophisticated organizer, known as Bridge. Bridge retains image EXIF data, and will allow you to add and apply keywords to any number of images, making it easy to search for the images at a later date.

is stored along with the image itself and can be viewed by most image-viewing software. In this way, you can use EXIF data to search for specific groups of images.

Keywords

In addition to storing and retrieving searchable EXIF data, most image-cataloguing software can be 'programmed' so that keywords, such as an event, a location or other textual descriptions, can be input and then searched for.

Image-editing software

Many image-editing applications come with built-in cataloguing software, and you may find that this add-on is all you require. Photoshop Elements' Photo Organizer, for example, allows you to import and batch-name photographs, add keywords, rate photographs, rename, move and adjust the dates of your photographs, and perform extensive searches. Even for a relatively large number of images, this may be all you need, and other editing programs feature similar software.

The full version of Photoshop CS also has a sophisticated browser, referred to as Bridge. Bridge is accessed via Photoshop (or any of the

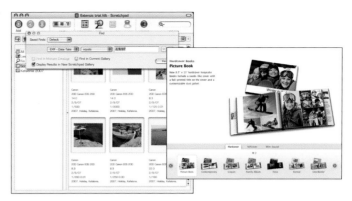

ABOVE Extensis' Portfolio is a dedicated digital asset manager that can hold thumbnails of thousands of images, retaining all the EXIF data and keywords associated with them. New catalogues are easily created and edited, all of which are quick to search.

ABOVE Apple's iPhoto is only available to Mac users as part of the iLife suite of applications. As well as managing photographs, iPhoto features basic editing controls and a link to Apple's electronic and paper-based viewing and sharing packages.

other CS suite of applications) and provides an easy-to-use interface between Photoshop and all the files on your hard disk, or any additional drives. Information on photograph files includes (among other things), the date the file was created, its dimensions, colour mode, EXIF data, and so on. It's simple to assign images a keyword that you can search for later, and once you've located the image you want, simply click on it to open the file in Photoshop.

Cataloguing software

As well as 'built-in' cataloguing software, there are numerous programs dedicated to the same job. Some, such as Extensis Portfolio are ideal for photographers who simply want to catalogue their work. Images can be batch processed with specific searchable data, keywords can be assigned, and folders and subfolders created, edited and moved about.

Just as some editing software provides an organizer to help you keep track of your images, some cataloguing software provides basic editing, viewing and printing tools. For Mac users, iPhoto can be used to enhance images as well as provide a powerful cataloguing application and a sharing and printing interface. Most software developers provide free trials for their products, so have a look at the ones that you think are most appropriate for your needs, and then download a trial version.

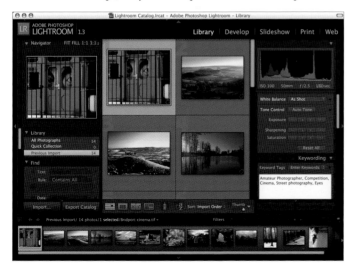

LEFT Adobe's Lightroom is an editing and cataloguing application that does a lot more than just allow you to manage your images. The user-friendly interface also provides access to a number of ways to print and share your images on the web [www.adobe.com].

Storing Your Photographs

Although at first it may feel that your computer's 250 gigabyte (GB) hard drive will last a lifetime, if you're a keen photographer you'll be amazed at how quickly it will begin to fill up with images. Digital bitmap image files are notoriously large when compared with other types of files, particularly when you use uncompressed formats such as TIFF and RAW. If you take a lot of pictures you'll soon be searching for other places to store your images.

However, this is no bad thing, as you should always avoid having all your images stored in one place. There are numerous stories of people losing their entire collection of images and you certainly don't want to be the next. Whether through theft, fire or a hard drive failure, losing an entire collection of unique images doesn't bear thinking about. So what is the best practice for storing images?

BELOW LEFT If you buy a new computer, you should expect a combination DVD and CD burner as standard. If you don't have one built-in, you can buy one to use as an external plug-in accessory.

BELOW MIDDLE There are various grades of CD and DVD. Some, such as these, claim to last for as long as 300 years.

BELOW RIGHT The price of external hard drives is dropping all the time, so by the time the disk on your computer is full, you will find a high-capacity external solution to suit your budget.

External hard drives

Increasingly, many photographers are turning to external hard drives as the preferred storage method. External hard drives are becoming less and less expensive and their capacities are getting ever larger. A 500GB external hard drive is now quite affordable, and getting more so by the week. By the time you've filled that one, you may find that a 750GB hard drive is affordable, and so on.

Whereas most people used to back their images up onto a CD or DVD, these days it may make more sense to store images on an external hard drive and buy a new hard drive every three to five of years or so. Most modern hard drives will work continuously for between 10 and 15 years, and many will last much longer. These periods compare favourably with the lowest-quality CDs and DVDs, which, if not stored in dry conditions, may degrade after only three to five years. However, it is worth noting that some of the more expensive 'gold' CDs and DVDs are claimed to last up to 300 years.

Before investing your money in either storage option, try to find out as much as you can about the life expectancy of the device or media – and remember, don't always rely on manufacturers' claims.

RIGHT If you are archiving your images to CD or DVD, then dedicated disk-burning software such as Roxio Toast can be a good investment. Such software will often let you create a contact sheet to act as a sleeve for the disc.

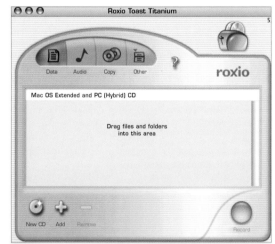

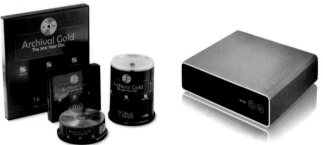

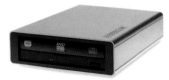

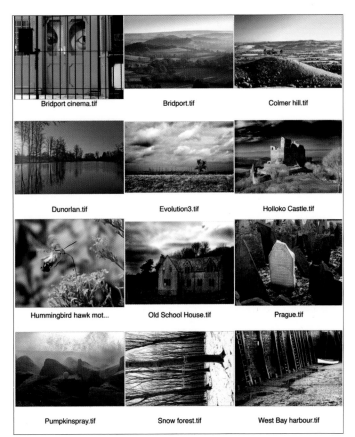

Contact Sheet II

Source Images
Use: Folder

Choose... LaCie:Photos:AP submissions:
☑ Include All Subfolders

Document
Units: Inches
Width: 8
Height: 10
Resolution: 240 pixels/cm
Mode: RGB Color
☑ Flatten All Layers

Thumbnails
Place: across fi...   ☑ Use Auto-Spacing
Columns: 3   Vertical: 0.014 in
Rows: 4   Horizontal: 0.014 in
☑ Rotate For Best Fit

☑ Use Filename As Caption
Font: Helvetica   Font Size: 12 pt

Bridport cinema.tif   Bridport.tif   Colmer hill.tif

Dunorlan.tif   Evolution3.tif   Holloko Castle.tif

Hummingbird hawk mot...   Old School House.tif   Prague.tif

Pumpkinspray.tif   Snow forest.tif   West Bay harbour.tif

Double storage

It pays to have your precious images stored on more than one media. One of the most sensible approaches is to keep your images on both an external hard drive and on CD or DVD, and check that your CDs and DVDs still play every couple of years or so.

For really important images, such as special family events or prize-winning images, it's certainly worth investing in the highest-quality CDs. Additionally, keep your CDs/DVDs in a separate part of the house to the rest of your computer equipment.

Which format?

If you can, try to save your edited images in TIFF format (you'll be given a variety of options in which images can be saved when you go to Image > Save, once you've completed the editing), as this is a 'lossless' file format that won't degrade as the file is opened and saved numerous times, unlike JPEGs. Having said that, however, it can sometimes be very hard to spot image degradation on JPEGs, particularly on postcard-sized prints, so if you haven't got the space to save your images as TIFFs, save them as the highest-quality JPEGs instead. Again, you'll be asked what quality JPEG you want to save your file in once you've selected JPEG as you preferred file format.

RAW

Putting a further strain on your computer's storage capacity is the advice that it's also extremely good practice to save unedited RAW files, as you never know when you'll want to return to these. RAW files can be thought of as 'digital negatives'. As such, they contain all the data captured by your camera at the time the shot was taken, free of any in-camera processing.

RAW format is the ideal format for long-term storage as, in the future, image-editing software is more than likely going to become even better at extracting detail from highlight and shadow regions. Rather than keeping these on your accessible external hard drives, you might want to consider storing these

ABOVE Contact sheets show a number of images on a single printed page. This is a great way to catalogue the images stored on a CD or DVD.

on high-quality CDs or DVDs, but make sure that you keep a simple and comprehensive record of what is stored where.

Contact sheets

A number of people find it useful to print contact sheets of their images. Usually letter-sized prints, contact sheets contain around 12–20 thumbnail images, and they provide an instant visual reminder of what you have stored on CDs. Most image-editing software will have specific commands to help you print out contact sheets.

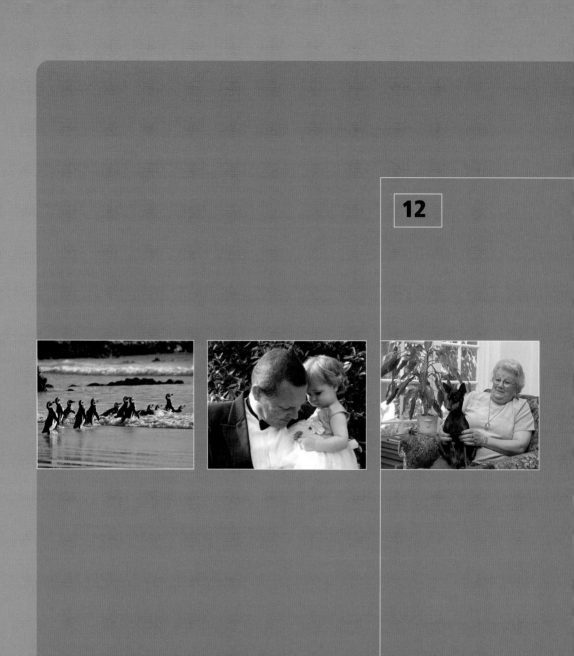

12

Can You Make Money from Your Work?

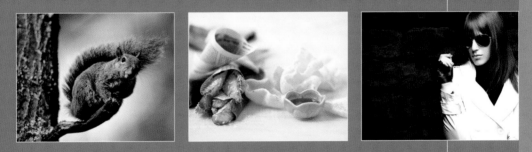

There is money to be made from your art and you do not have to become a full-time professional to do so. Like many things, the more you put in, the more reward you will get. From entering photographic competitions, to having your images held and sold for use by an image library, to taking on jobs such as weddings, events or product photography, making money from your photographs is possible. While digital photography has made some of this more popular, there are still ways you can stay ahead of the competition. In the following chapter advice and guidance will help you approach this stage of your photographic career.

Entering Competitions

With growing skill and more adventurous photography, it may be time to think of entering competitions.

There are many different categories of competition you could enter, but the most common are those featuring portraits, landscapes, or travel photography. You will find competitions through magazines, newspapers, on websites and in galleries, and those organized by photography clubs, village halls, schools or town councils. You should not feel that any thing is beyond you, however prestigious these competitions may seem, or however accomplished previous winners are. If you submit a strong image that fulfils the brief then you stand as good a chance as anyone else.

Within a competition there may be different sections such as individual images, series of images, colour images, black and white images, pictures shot on film and those shot dig-itally and even those shot with a camera phone. There may be sections just for professional photographers, for amateurs, or for students or juniors.

Find out how you should send your entry, and make sure you follow the rules very closely.

• How many images can you submit? What format can your images be (print or digital)? If print, what size?
• Will your print be returned automatically or do you need to collect or arrange for return shipping yourself? If you are sending a print then package your entries carefully. Any print that arrives damaged won't stand a good chance with the judges.
• If digital should it be a tiff or jpg file, what resolution or file size, Adobe RGB or SRGB mode?
• Does the picture have to have been taken after a specific date?
• Should the photograph, or series of photographs be given a title or cap-tion? If so, think hard about this – a relevant and apt title can make the difference if the competition is close. Do not try to be too clever or witty as that can sometimes backfire. Just be relevant.

Stand out from the crowd

Whatever the medium, there will be hundreds of entries – thousands in a national competition – especially when the entries are submitted online. So what will make your picture stand a chance of winning? Well there is no magic formula but there are certain guides you should follow.

In the first place, judges will be looking for an image that exactly fits the theme set for that category. It is amazing how many entrants send in landscapes when the organizers have quite clearly stated that the subject was to be a building or a portrait.

Sloppy photography will not win a competition. Prints must be perfect with no finger prints or rough edges and any borders should be even all the way round, with just a touch more border along the bottom than the top.

Digital images should be exactly the right resolution. They should not be over sharpened or over-processed. Obvious digital fakery passed off as a realistic image will fool no one.

Your image should be sharply focused and of interest. It should be well composed with horizons in the right place and level. The colours should be vibrant, and black and white images should contain a wide

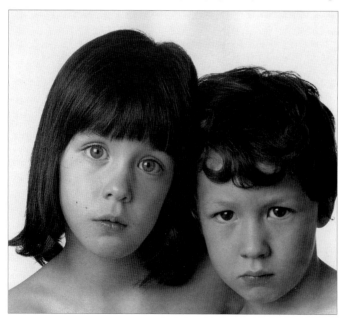

LEFT When entering black and white photographs be sure that the print is of the highest quality. Even the best exposed negatives can be further enhanced in the darkroom. Often a winning shot is a simple beautifully printed and presented.

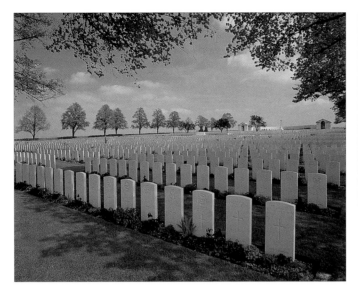

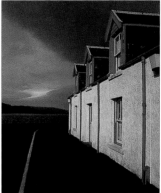

range of tones. Another portrait of the Eiffel Tower in Paris by night, or the pyramids of Egypt, may not get anywhere, as these images have been seen so many times before. Try to be original and execute images that inspire you, not that imitate well-known pictures. As important as the guidelines above are, make images individual. Although there are often rules that you are told you must follow in photography to take a great picture,

sometimes it is the breaking of those very rules that makes a winner because originality can impress.

You must decide how to shoot your pictures in a way that means something to you. Perhaps your portrait that shows the sitter out of focus is done that way for a very good reason. Maybe you decide that your horizon is better off balance or your colour image is better less saturated with bright tones. And perhaps your picture of the pyramids is very unusual and extraordinary enough that and the judges will not have seen that subject shot like that ever before.

Sometimes the landscape you shoot on a perfect sunny day with stormy clouds gathering in the distance, shot at that magic hour just before dusk will win you a prize. Or it may be the

shot taken from your car window on a miserable grey day, with a group of tourists sheltering from the wind and rain under a tree, that does the trick because it captures a moment and a feeling that is often missed.

Photography is a very emotive medium and the viewing, and judging, of it a very subjective thing. So don't feel as though you always have to follow the hard and fast rules as laid down by the camera club or read about in a book or on a technical website about 'how to shoot the perfect landscape'. Always aim to shoot your pictures to the highest technical standard possible and present them in exactly the right way but in terms of subject matter, shoot it the way you see it, so that your individuality shines through.

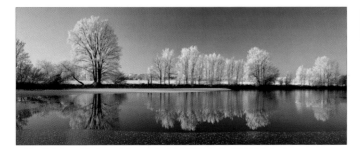

Could You Sell Your Pictures?

If pictures are good enough to enter in competitions then you may well feel you are ready to try to make money from your photography. But what can you do, and do you want a paying hobby, a part time career or to make it your full time job? Of course the more time and effort you invest the more you are likely to get out of it. To start off with, you could sell your work as 'stock' images to a photo library, or you can do portraits, shoot weddings or take pictures at events such as marathons or parties, which sell to attendees and organizers.

A stock, photo, or picture library is a collection of images that are sold for their use by a business. The business can be anything; a book publisher, a design agency, a car manufacturer or a local or national magazine. Any business in fact that uses a photograph will at some point, instead of commissioning an individual photographer to take the pictures they need, buy the licence to use a photograph from a picture library. They do not buy the physical photograph, but the licence to use that photograph for a particular purpose.

The amount of money paid for this 'right to use' will depend on many factors, such as if they want to use the picture exclusively, meaning nobody else can use it, how long they want to use it for, what they want to use it for, where it will be used and so on. Photographs may be licensed in various ways with more exclusive rights-managed images costing large amounts and images that are royalty free with very few constraints on their use costing far less. The cost of licensing a picture, and hence your royalty payment, can range from a few pence to thousands of pounds.

There are lots of picture libraries all over the world, from big players such as Getty and Corbis to newer concerns including Alamy and iStock. Some are very difficult to place your images with and others will let anyone place any image they choose with them. Some may be specialists, for example only stocking travel or aerial photographs, and others may have all types of picture.

The advent of digital photography and the internet has led to a large number of new companies that make it very easy for you to have your photographs for sale on their websites. That said, most libraries hold thousands, if not millions of pictures so making money from stock is not as simple as uploading your picture and watching the money roll in. It is a mixture of good photography, hard work and great luck.

The good photography is fairly obvious, as the right image in the right place and at the right time can do really well to sell an idea or product, or stimulate people's interests, and such a picture can be worth a lot of money.

Although a single sale may bring in only a modest sum, repeated sales of an image over several years can make for a healthy income.

The hard work amounts to more than taking photographs. You will have to annotate, keyword and caption all of your pictures if selling them to an image library. Keywords are incredibly important, as it is these that people search for. You may have taken the perfect picture but if no one can find it, it will make you no money.

The luck element is that hopefully, among the thousands of photographs on a libraries website, yours will be

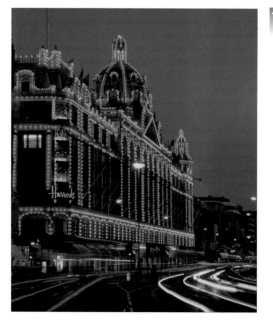

LEFT This picture of London's famous department store, Harrods, has been published in one form or another all over the world, and has been used literally hundreds of times. Its most important ingredient is that it is instantly recognizable. It is also a good composition and correctly exposed.

the one that the picture researcher finds, chooses, and pays for. Look at any large online library and search using any well-known name such as Big Ben, The White House, or the Taj Mahal. See how many pictures come up. Do not be put off by this volume of work, as a good picture should sell. However, be aware of how competitive the industry is and do not expect it to provide you with a huge income for life.

What sells?

There are no rules about what makes a picture sell. Often an original and beautiful shot will be unused forever because it does not fit into any particular subject area. However, one thing is for sure: a picture that is mistakenly under-or overexposed, or out of focus, or simply badly composed, will not sell – no matter how interesting its subject may be.

Sometimes the simplest picture of two people shaking hand against a white background may be just what is needed. On other occasions a stunning or humorous shot of a well known tourist destination fits the bill.

Model permission

Depending on the intended use, a picture with recognizable person, logo or or even building, may need to have a signed model release form. This is a document that each person in the picture has signed to say they give their permission to be featured in the photograph. Some picture uses may not require a model release form but if you can get it, it will open up your picture to many more possible uses.

If you think you would like to start selling to image libraries, then go online and research the companies out there, finding out which ones you think your pictures will fit into well and how professional they are. Always read their terms and contracts very carefully to check up on royalty payments, and get to know how they will use and sell your images.

RIGHT These commuters are blurred but they convey the urgent movement of rush hour in a city. Such pictures have editorial and advertising uses. This one has been published in many newspapers and magazines.

BELOW Landscape shots are always needed by travel agencies, or magazines running features on a region. Good composition, spot-on exposure and a strong point of interest are all vital ingredients for lasting sales.

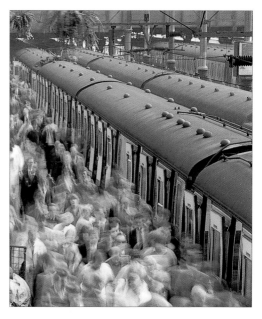

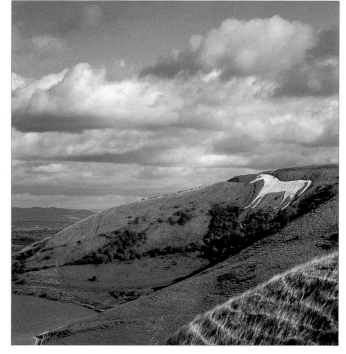

Events Photography

Shooting an event sounds like a glamorous job, but is actually fairly easy to get into. There are quite a few companies throughout the world that organize photography for specific events, and require local photographers to take the photographs. You may find advertisements in camera magazines or online.

Kit for events photography

Taking photographs at an event will require a digital SLR with a fairly fast shutter rate. Your camera will really need to take a minimum of five frames per second. You will need a long lens so a zoom with an equivalent focal length of at least 70–200mm is good.

You may be shooting for many hours and it will be best to switch your viewpoints in this time. so a monopod will be a great help, as it will let you to keep your camera steady but still allow for quick movement to a new site or vantage point.

If shooting for someone else, such as a publisher, they may well provide you with memory cards, usually a very quick compact flash type, but if not, make sure you are well stocked up with as many memory cards as possible. The faster and greater capacity they are, the better.

Protection for your camera is essential. It may start to pour with rain during the event but you will need to keep on shooting, so some specialist camera protection is a must, and this is readily available from most good camera stores. Don't forget a decent rucksack for your gear, plus of course weather protection for yourself, and food and drink. A cold, wet photographer is not a happy one.

At the event

Get to the event early so that you can set up in a good position, where you will be able to see the action clearly. Do a test on all of your equipment thoroughly and get yourself comfortable and ready to shoot.

While you take your shots, remember the brief. Does your employer want all their shots in portrait format? They should have told you what is most important to them, but in general you will need to capture as many people as you can with close-ups

▼ **BELOW** By panning the camera, the focus of the shot is the car, with no distracting background. This shot has been taken at an angle and distance that really shows off the car and allows the driver to be clearly seen – both these factors are important to identify this as a particular, not generic, event.

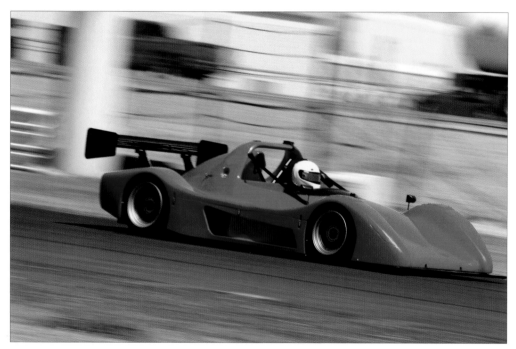

on faces, full length shots and, where relevant, shirt numbers. Shots of the crowd are often also wanted, as they be very atmospheric.

You could end up shooting all sorts of event, including marathons, motor car racing, corporate events and parties. Whatever it is, you will need to plan exactly what equipment is relevant, especially which lenses and flash you will need to use.

Event photography such as this is hard work but it is a very good way to get into paid photographic work as it normally takes place on weekends or evenings and usually only requires a minimum of extra expenditure on camera equipment.

▶ **RIGHT** Timing is, of course, very important. Capturing the tennis player with both feet off the ground in this shot shows the energy and power of her game, and conveys something of the excitement of the event. Static shots of players will not have the same appeal – fans want to see photographs of sportspeople performing at their peak, or pictures that describe a match.

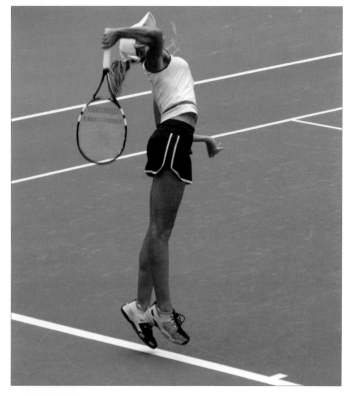

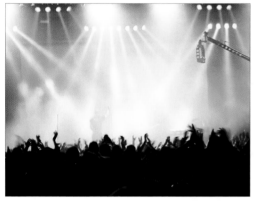

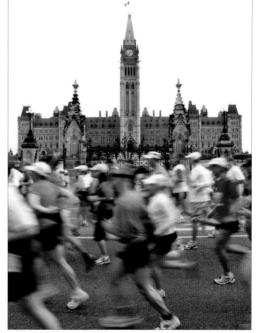

▲ **ABOVE** This a great view of a music event that really captures the spirit and emotion of the performance. You feel as if you are part of the crowd because of the angle of the shot and the way it is lit. The crowd response, as shown by the hands in the air, is really important.

▶ **RIGHT** Among all the shots of individual runners at a marathon or fun run, an interesting overall shot will stand out. This one sets the location brilliantly, and thanks to the motion blur, you can almost feel part of the crowd of runners as they pass this city landmark.

Portraiture

Just as event photography can be used to supplement your current work, so can portrait photography. You can work at weekends or if you choose dedicate more time to it with work during the week also.

You may decide to look for work at one of the many portrait companies throughout the country where training may often be provided, studio locations are already set up and equipment there for you to use.

But if you prefer the idea of going it alone, what can you do? As long as you have some suitable space in which to set up a small studio, this can easily be achieved.

Backgrounds can be bought very easily and they consist of a background support system which can either be a specialized but simple set of two stands with a cross bar from

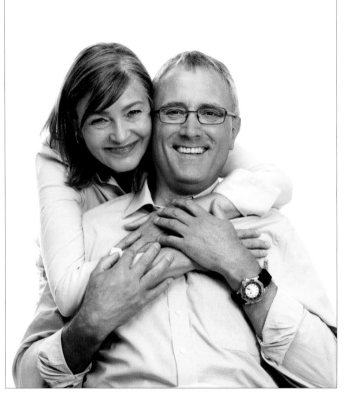

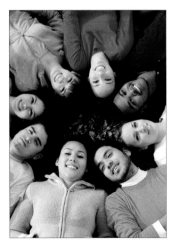

which rolls of paper are supported or, more simply, it could be a paper roll attached to a wall. There are also other more heavy duty support systems available but these are more suited to a permanent, fully-working professional studio.

Any method you choose should allow you to use a variety of backgrounds. These may be paper rolls of different colours such as white, or black, or grey, or a textured paper or rolls and sheets of material of any variety you choose. The more choices you have the more variety you can offer. As well as the background you need to control the lighting. You

▲ **ABOVE** It pays to choose certain aspects, such as clothing, carefully. Items that are neutral and classic work best.

really cannot have adequate control over portraits with either your cameras built-in flash or even a separate flashgun, so you will need some form of studio lighting. Ideally you will need at least two flash heads, with stands to put them on. You will need to 'modify' the light in some way to create the different looks you require for different jobs, so you will need either reflectors, or umbrellas, or softboxes, or a variety of all of these. You also need a way to link the lights to your camera, so you will need a sync lead that is connected at one end to your camera and at the other to one of your lights.

You do not have to have the most expensive camera available but it does need to be of a suitable quality to make enlargements up to the sizes you think your customers will want.

▼ **BELOW** A simple set up in the studio with a white background is great for focusing on the subject. Getting youngsters to play will put them at ease and lead to some great shots. Here, the bubbles add colour and movement.

Remember that the best lens for a flattering portrait is one with an equivalent focal length of between 85 and 135mm. The lens should have a large maximum aperture with a minimum of f/2.8. If you wish to do group portraiture, and your studio space is not huge, you will need a wide lens. Test the space out – a standard lens may be wide enough for you but by testing out your space you will know which lenses you need. But remember that wide lenses are generally not as flattering as standard or long lenses for portraits.

As you are bringing clients into your studio space it must have, either in it or very close, a facility to make drinks and food, and also a bathroom or WC. You may need somewhere for clients to change clothing in privacy and somewhere comfortable for them to sit. Your studio must look professional and be completely clean and tidy at all times.

As soon as you start to charge someone for your services you have to act and work like a professional. Acting as if you are simply taking shots for fun will not inspire confidence.

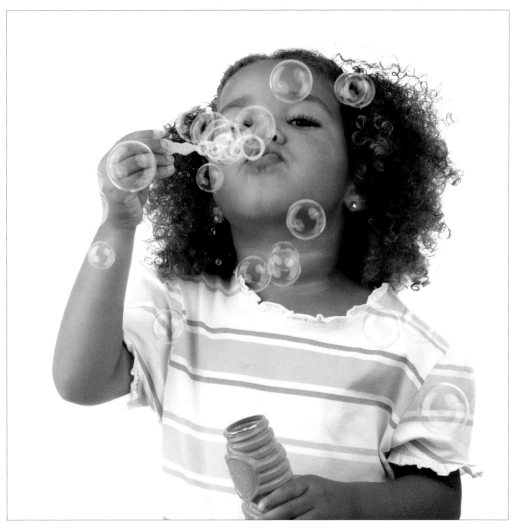

Becoming a Wedding Photographer

Like portrait photography, weddings are a well-trodden avenue to making money out of your photography. You may well have been asked by a friend or family to take the pictures at their wedding, and after taking some shots that have gone down well, perhaps you have decided that you would like to try and get work as a professional wedding photographer.

The traditional way to enter the world of wedding photography is by finding work as an assistant to a photographer, where you will go with them on shoots and help them out with cameras, lenses and organizing the photographs. After this, you can get work as a second photographer at a wedding – this involves you taking photographs as well as the main photographer, getting the shots that they are unable to because they can't be in two places at once. Typically, you may be asked to take candid or detail shots. Once you are comfortable with the general work, you could then start working as the main wedding pho-

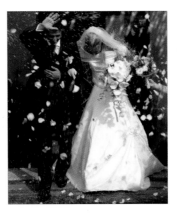

ABOVE This shot isolates the couple from the crowd and captures the sense of fun and excitement on the big day.

tographer, calling all the shots and charging a good fee for the work.

Alternatively, if you are confident or have had practise and good experience of shooting weddings of friends and family, you can try to bypass all the 'apprentice work' and start directly as a wedding photographer.

Although it sounds fairly simple and straightforward, serious wedding photography is a specialized business that requires a lot of commitment and skill. If you get it right, the rewards can be very high.

What you need

You'll need a back up camera in case something goes wrong with your main camera – this is vitally important. You'll also need lots of batteries and memory cards, lenses such as a 24–70mm and 70–200mm zooms, and a wider lens for group shoots. Some wedding photographers work just with prime lenses, some just with zooms, others with a mixture.

You need to be able to light some of your shots, so a flashgun with diffuser is essential. Sometimes two will be needed, and a backup flash is really recommended.

BELOW Make the most of beautiful surroundings – this wil remind the couple of the setting they chose for the celebration.

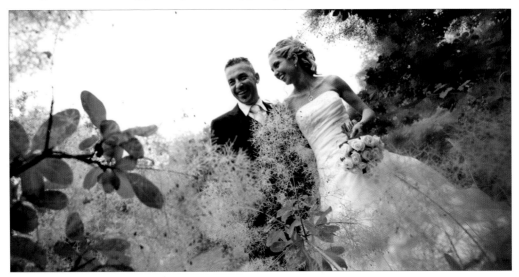

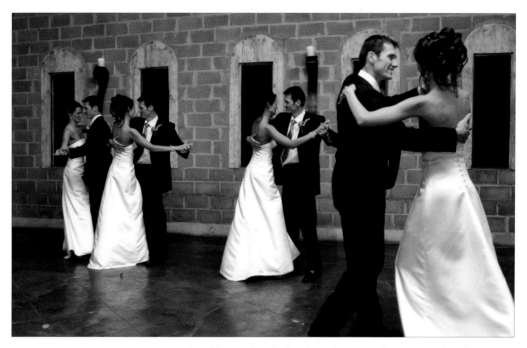

You'll need an excellent, smart and accessible bag to put all this gear in, a pair of really comfortable, but still smart shoes, and lots of ehthusiasm, energy and a really big smile!

To get a good shot at a wedding it is often as much about your own personality and performance as the type of lens you are using.

Preparation and the big day

You will usually secure the job by showing prospective clients your previous work and a few wedding albums, and discussing the package they want. You will meet up with them just prior to the wedding, ideally at the venue itself, to discuss what they want and think about posing the formal shots.

Depending on what you have arranged with the couple, on the day you may be shooting from the brides arrival at the marriage venue, or from much earlier on during the prepara-

tions. You may be asked to shoot the ceremony, the speeches, the cutting of the cake and the first dance. Often photographers are asked to shoot the evening reception too.

During all of this you may also need to shoot both formal and possibly more informal and candid shots, making sure you have photographed the important people and have all the shots that you have discussed with the couple beforehand.

Once you have taken all of your pictures, which may well number over a thousand, you will need to edit, process, and retouch them. Don't forget to calculate the time this takes and factor it in to your fees.

When you are ready, show the pictures to the client, either via an online gallery or in a small book. Once they have chosen which images they want, have them printed to their specifications. It is vitally important to get the size and format right.

All in all, professional wedding photography is by no means easy money, but it can pay well if you are dedicated to it.

Find your own style – if you get the opportunity to shoot a friend's wedding, take it and see what happens. You just may find it's the perfect new career for you.

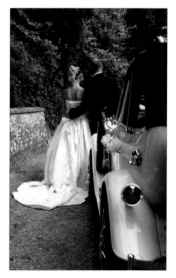

Advertising Yourself

If you want to be successful as a professional photographer, you'll need to get lots of work. You may well get the odd job taking pictures of friends, or get jobs via personal recommendations, but you will never make a really good living as a full time photographer by sitting at home and waiting for work to come to you.

You need to advertise

The internet and e-mail has made advertising your services easier and cheaper than ever before. A good website is the first thing to start with – your business is about pictures, so let people see them. Whether you make a website yourself or pay a website designer to create and build it for you, it needs to be clear and very user-friendly, with your contact details clearly stated and plenty of work

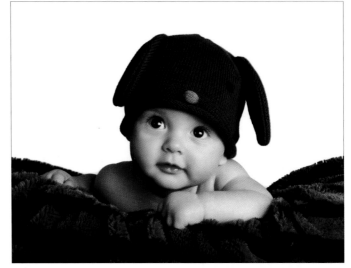

examples for people to look at. Include testimonials from any past clients, if you have some. Finally, make sure that your file sizes are small, so that the site does not take an age to load all your images.

Once the website is up and running, send e-mails to people and local businesses you think may be in need of your services, directing them to your

BELOW Informal but well-posed portraits of couples are likely to sell. Choose a shot that shows you can establish a good rapport with the subjects and that they will enjoy the shoot. Also try to choose attractive subjects and be careful about what is in the background.

ABOVE Baby and family portraits are big business and parents will choose carefully to find a photographer who produces something a little unusual. Do not make the child look ridiculous, but aim for something 'cute' and quirky.

online portfolio. You could also get flyers printed and send these by mail to clients along with a personal covering letter and a business card.

Get listed on free online directories and advertise in free local magazines.

Have a very good portfolio ready so that when you get that phone call, and the prospective client wants to see your work, you have it ready. Your portfolio needs to contain the types of imagery that the client is interested in, so it's no use showing a bride and groom your travel photos, or an events organizer your studio portraits.

Business sense

Many people lose business simply by being unprofessional. Reply to emails and phone calls promptly. Keep your

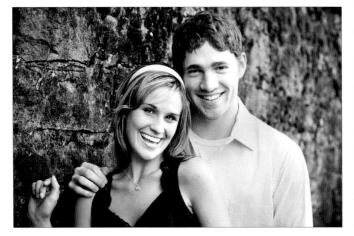

BELOW Informal but well-posed portraits of couples are likely to sell. Choose a shot that shows you can establish a good rapport with the subjects and that they will enjoy the shoot. Also try to choose attractive subjects and be careful about what is in the background.

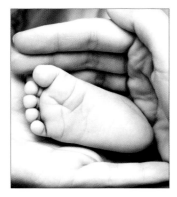

ABOVE Many parents like to take prints of their newborn's feet and a photograph of them holding the baby's foot is another great memento. Using black and white and going in close really accentuates the textures and abstract quality. The hands frame the foot.

RIGHT This shot would sell your services well, as it demonstrates you can pick out details at events and come up with interesting shots. When you are advertising yourself you need to be on the lookout for pictures that show you are a bit 'different' to every other photographer.

BELOW If you want to get into sports photography choose great action, great colour and well framed shots such as this one. Try to choose shots of events you are passionate about – your interest in the subject will shine through in your photography.

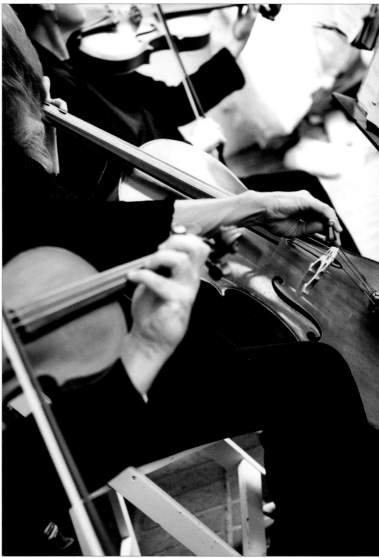

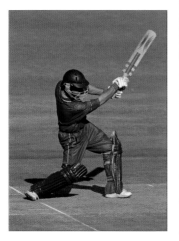

website updated. Have a proper e-mail address, not a free one – preferably link your email address to your website so that you build up a strong identity for your business.

Money matters

Make sure that your valuable equipment is insured in case of theft or damage, and get public liability insurance, as working with other people means you require it.

Evasion of taxes is serious. If you make any money from self-employed work it is your responsibility to let the authorities know.

So in summary, be organized, be professional, be friendly, and provide the very best service that you can, because there are many budding amateurs out there who are trying to turn their hobby into a profession. You need to raise yourself above the competition and build a good reputation.

Glossary

A

AEL (auto exposure lock) A means, usually in the form of a button, of retaining the exposure setting read from one part of a scene. The shot can then be reframed if necessary while ensuring the previously metered element of the scene will be accurately exposed.

Aperture The size of the opening in a lens that governs how much light reaches the sensor (or film).

Aperture priority (A/Av) A semi-automatic exposure setting in which the photographer selects the aperture and the camera determines and sets an appropriate shutter speed to achieve an accurate exposure.

Autofocus (AF) A setting in which the camera's lens is able to focus automatically on a specific part of a scene. All modern cameras have an autofocus function.

B

Bit (binary digit) The basic unit of all digital data; bits are either 'on' or 'off' and represented by the numbers '1' and '0'.

Bracketing A technique in which a variety of exposures, usually three, is made in very quick succession of a particular scene in order to ensure correct exposure.

C

CCD (charge coupled device) One of the two most common types of sensor used today in digital cameras and scanners.

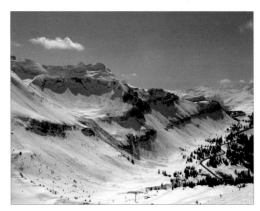

CMOS (complementary metal oxide semiconductor) The second-most commonly used sensor (after CCD) in digital cameras and scanners.

Colour filter array (CFA) A very thin coloured matrix layer that sits above the sensor layer in a digital camera's imaging sensor to enable the sensor to record colour. CFAs feature a matrix of red, green and blue squares.

Compression A method of reducing digital file sizes, such as image files, while retaining as much significant information as possible in order to ensure as high as possible image quality. There are two types of compression: 'lossy' compression, such as that used in JPEG files, discards information that cannot be retrieved – in effect, the higher the compression the lower the image quality. Lossy compression can result in very small files sizes. In 'lossless' compression, such as that used in TIFF files, information is bundled or 'zipped' temporarily while the file is stored, and then unzipped when opened. No information is lost with this compression technique, resulting in high-quality but large image files.

D

Depth of field A term used to described an image's 'zone of sharpness', or how much of the image is in focus. The main way to control depth of field is via the lens aperture.

Digital zoom A function offered by many compact cameras. It works by digitally increasing the size of the pixels being recorded by the sensor, as opposed to an optical zoom, which magnifies the image through a series of lenses before it reaches the sensor. Increasing the size of the pixels can result in poor image quality, and for this reason digital zoom should be used only when there's no alternative.

Dpi (dots per inch) Measurement of the resolution of an output device, such as a printer. See also **Ppi (pixels per inch)**.

Dynamic range The optical range in a scene between the brightest (highlight) and darkest (shadow) areas in which detail is still visible.

E

Equivalent focal length (efl) is the optical focal length of the lens once the size of the sensor is taken into account. The smaller the sensor the longer the effective focal length of the lens.

Exposure The amount of light that reaches a camera's sensor or film. It is governed by the size of the aperture and for how long the shutter remains open (shutter speed).

Exposure compensation (EV) A way of manually overriding the built-in exposure meter of a camera to provide more or less light to the sensor or film.

F

Filter A glass or plastic attachment that fits on the front of the camera's lens. Filters are used for a variety of purposes: polarizing filters are used to reduce glare and reflections, while neutral density filters are used to reduce the light entering the lens.

F number The measure of the aperture of a lens used for a specific shot. A low f number, such as f/2, indicates a large aperture, while a high number, such as f/32, indicates a very small aperture.

Focal length Strictly, the distance in millimetres between a lens's optical centre and the focal point. The focal length is an indication of the magnifying power of a lens.

H

Histogram A visual interpretation in the form of a graph that describes the tonal range of a given image.

I

Interpolation A digital means of artificially increasing the resolution of an image. There are various interpolation algorithms, but generally they all work on assessing adjacent pixels and introducing new pixels with similar tonal and colour values.

ISO (International Standards Organization) Historically, the measurement of the sensitivity of a specific film – the higher the ISO rating, the more sensitive the film. The rating has been adopted by digital camera manufacturers to reflect how sensitive the sensor is to light for any given shot.

J

JPEG (Joint Photographic Experts Group) One of the most commonly used file formats used by digital cameras for storing images.

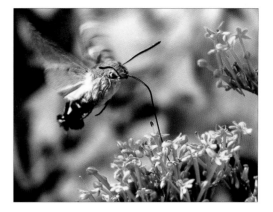

K

Kelvin The unit of measurement used to describe light temperature.

L

LCD screen In digital cameras, the small screen usually found at the back of the camera, used to review (and preview) shots, and to provide information on the camera's settings.

Lens The light-capturing and focusing element of all digital cameras. Lenses usually contain a variety of individual elements that work together to direct and focus the light from the scene onto the sensor.

M

Macro A term used to loosely describe 'close-up' photography or lenses that have the ability to greatly magnify the subject.

Manual A term used to describe any part of the picture-taking process that involves the photographer's direct input. Manual exposure requires the photographer to set the aperture and the shutter speed based on the camera's, or an external light meter's, reading. Manual focus requires the photographer to decide manually on the point of focus. Taking manual control of the camera greatly increases the creative possibilities available.

Metering The system by which all cameras assesses exposure. There are various metering systems from simple spot metering to the more sophisticated evaluative, or matrix, metering.

Megapixel (MP) Literally, 1 million pixels. Megapixels are a measure of resolution most commonly used to describe the resolution of a camera's sensor or a specific image file.

N

Noise Interference of an electronic signal. In digital photography, noise manifests itself as unwanted artefacts in the form of clumps of discoloured pixels or a grain-like pattern in the captured image file.

O

Optical zoom See **Digital zoom.**

P

Pixel (picture element) The basic unit of all digital images; essentially a tiny square with its own hue, saturation and brightness values. Printed or viewed at an appropriate resolution, an image's individual pixels should be invisible to the naked eye. If an image is viewed or printed too large, it may assume a blocky appearance, known as pixelation.

Ppi (pixels per inch) The resolution of a digital image. The greater the ppi value, the higher the resolution.

Program An exposure option in which the camera automatically sets the shutter and aperture setting depending on the light meter reading. It differs from full Auto in that in program shift mode, the photographer can select any of the possible aperture/shutter exposure combinations based on the meter reading.

R

RAW A popular file format available in most digital cameras. RAW files are made up of unprocessed data as captured by the camera's sensor. For this reason, RAW files will usually need to undergo some form of image editing to obtain the optimum image.

Resolution The amount of detail visible in an image determined by the number of pixels. The term can also be applied to describe the resolving power of a lens.

RGB (red, green, blue) Primary colours which, when combined, are used to represent all the colours of the visible spectrum.

Rule of thirds A compositional technique used to promote the placement of the subject elements in key areas of the frame.

S

Shutter delay/lag The time between pressing the shutter release button and the camera taking the photograph. If sufficiently long, shutter delay can result in fast-moving objects moving out of the frame by the time the photograph is taken.

Shutter priority (S/Tv) A semi-automatic exposure setting in which the photographer selects the shutter speed and the camera determines and sets an appropriate aperture setting to achieve an accurate exposure.

Shutter speed The time taken for the camera's shutter to open and close, thereby determining the period the sensor is exposed to the light. Some compacts don't have a shutter; the 'shutter speed' is represented by the sensor being turned on and off.

Stop The term used to describe an exposure value. Increasing an exposure by 1 stop, for example, involves doubling the amount of light reaching the sensor, which can be achieved by either increasing the aperture from f/5.6 to f/8, for example, or reducing the shutter speed from $\frac{1}{500}$ sec to $\frac{1}{250}$ sec.

T

TIFF (Tagged Image File Format) A popular file format available in most image-editing programs, but now used less on digital cameras. TIFF files use 'lossless' compression and therefore retain more image data.

U

USB (Universal Serial Bus) USB sockets and cables are the most common way of connecting printers, scanners and other devices to a computer.

W

White balance A system used in both cameras and image-editing software that helps to eradicate unwanted colour casts; in other words, white will appear white.

Z

Zone of sharpness See **Depth of field.**

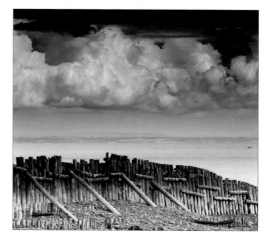

Useful Websites

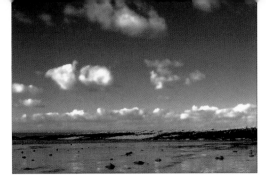

Website addresses can alter, and websites can appear and disappear almost daily, so use a search engine to help you find new arrivals or check addresses.

Adobe (www.adobe.com)
Provides the latest information on products developed by Adobe. Trial software can be downloaded and there are a number of help areas and forums.

Alien Skin (www.alienskin.com)
One of the best-known third-party plug-in software developers. Download trial software and find out about the latest products. Most of the plug-ins are compatible only with Photoshop, Photoshop Elements and Paint Shop Pro.

Apple (www.apple.com)
The Apple website provides the latest information on products, support and free downloads for Mac users.

Canon (www.canon.com)
News of latest products, promotions and a helpful support site from Canon.

Corel (www.corel.com)
Responsible for developing Paint Shop Pro and Ulead PhotoImpact, Corel's website offers free trial downloads along with tutorials, tips and tricks.

DC Views (www.dcviews.com)
Provides reviews on a variety of equipment, as well as acting as a portal to a vast array of associated websites.

Digital Photography Review (www.dpreview.com)
Perhaps the best-known of all the review sites. The website also features a popular forum and helpful glossary.

Epson (www.epson.com)
Epson's website features information on latest products as well as a source for all Epson printer drivers.

ePHOTOzine (www.ephotozine.com)
A popular online photographic magazine featuring reviews of equipment and books, forums and techniques.

Flickr (www.flickr.com)
One of the more popular online picture sites, where you can upload and share your photographs with everyone.

Fujifilm (www.fujifilm.com)
Latest products and support from Fujifilm.

Google Picasa (www.picasa.google.com)
Download Google's free image editor and organizer.

Hewlett-Packard (www.hp.com)
Latest products and support, including printer drivers.

Kodak Gallery (www.kodak.com)
The Kodak website is comprehensive. Navigating to the Consumer Products portal brings up all the information you need for the vast array of digital photography associated products; from here you can also access the online galleries and printing services.

Lynda.com (www.lynda.com)
A comprehensive tutorial resource for shooting and digital post-production.

Luminous Landscape (www.luminous-landscape.com)
A popular digital photography online magazine, packed with reviews, forums, tutorials and so on.

Nazdar Lyson (www.nazdar.com)
Information on all the latest products from this leading supplier of inks and other products for inkjet printers.

Nikon (www.nikon.com)
Vast site providing information on products, forums and support from Nikon.

Nik Software (www.google.com/nikcollection.com)
Latest products and free trial downloads from this popular third-party filter plug-in developer.

Olympus (www.olympus.com)
Comprehensive information on products, support and downloads from Olympus.

Pentax (www.pentax.com)
Vast site providing information on products, support and downloads from Pentax.

Photo-Plugins (www.photo-plugins.com)
Website entirely devoted to free, downloadable plug-ins.

Planet Photoshop (www.planetphotoshop.com)
Provides a wealth of tutorials, reviews, forums and much more specifically geared toward Photoshop users.

Roxio (www.roxio.com)
Latest products and trial downloads from this popular software developer.

Shutterbug (www.shutterbug.com)
Popular online photography magazine and community, featuring reviews, forums and techniques.

Sony (www.sony.com)
Latest information on products and support from Sony.

Steve's Digicams (www.steves-digicams.com)
Latest news, reviews, forums from another popular online digital photography community.

What Digital Camera (www.whatdigitalcamera.com)
A website dedicated to bringing the latest news and reviews on digital photography equipment.

Index

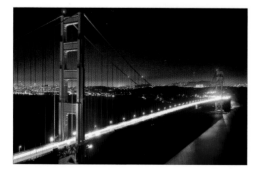

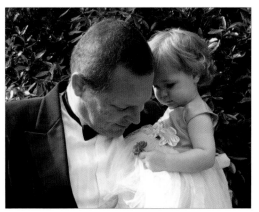

H

hand-tinting 458–9
haze 233
Healing Brush 419
high-key images 198–9
histograms 110–1
Hockney, David, 68
holding a camera 98–9
Holga cameras 17
holidays
  checklist, 26–7
  photography on, 370–1
  preparing for, 370
horizontals 142–3, 155,
  205
hyperfocal focusing 170

I

image editing 11
image stabilization 179
infrared film, 39, 58
ink 476–7
instant cameras, 17
insurance, 23
iPhoto 401
ISO settings 82–3, 158,
  159, 223
  auto ISO 83
  noise 83

J

joiner pictures, 68–9
JPEG format 84, 85, 489

L

landscapes 128, 142, 150,
  243
  black and white, 296–7
  general composition,
    284–5
  people in, 294–5
  perspective, 288
  skies 444–5
  soft-focus 450–1
  time of day for, 292–3
  varying shots, 285
  viewpoint, choosing,
    286–7
  weather, 290–1
layers 400, 424–5
  adjustment layers 428–9
  blending modes 429,
    430–1
  layer masks 429, 440,
    454
  using 426–7
leading lines 148, 155
lenses 90–1
  bridge cameras 88

care of, 28
choice of, 18–19, 92–3
compact cameras 92
dSLRs 89, 92, 99
elements 91
fisheye, 20, 250–1
hood, 22, 299, 369
hybrid cameras 92
macro, 21
mounts, 18
perspective control, 21
prime lenses 93
shift, 21, 324, 248–5
teleconverters 93
telephoto lens 20, 99,
  242–3, 246–7
35mm SLR cameras,
  for, 18
upgrading 93
wide-angle lens 19–20,
  240–1, 244–5
zoom 20, 87, 88, 92,
  93, 252–3
Levels 197, 199
light, shooting against,
  220–1
lighting 39, 208–35
  angle of light 211
  artificial light 112–13
  available light 222–3
  back lighting 218–19
  contrast 192
  direction of light 216–19
  flare 219
  frontal 216–17
  hard 210, 211
  low-light 184, 223,
    226–7
  natural light 112, 223
  quality of light 210–11
  rim lighting 218
  side 217
  snoot, 352
  soft 210, 211
  softbox, 352
  still life, 352
  studio, in, 352–3
  time of day 232–3, 234
  translucency 218
LOMO cameras 17
lomography 32–3
low light 116–17
low-key images 196–7

M

macro lenses, 21
macro photography 167,
  254–7
Magic Wand 344–5

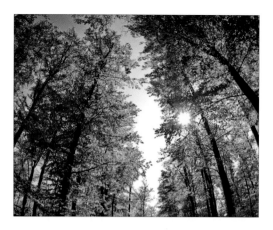

manipulation 280–1
masks 429, 440–1, 454
memory cards 85
Merge for High Dynamic
  Range (HDR) 196,
  432–3
metering
  hand-held meter, using,
    162
  modes 108–9
  spot, 162
  TTL, 350, 386
mirrorless cameras 89
monitors 399
monopods, 23
montages 281, 438–9
  sandwiching
    transparencies, 70–1
mother and child,
  photographing, 372–3
mounts
  SLR cameras, for, 18
moving object,
  photographing, 176,
    266–7
multiple exposures, 54–5
  fireworks,
    photographing, 340

N

negatives
  care of, 52–3
  storage of, 52
neutral density (ND)
  filters 185, 263
Niépce, Nicéphore 8
night photography 226–7
noise
  black and white 203
  compact cameras 86
  ISO setting 83

O

old photographs 460–1
Online Galleries 482–3
outdoor portraits, 364–5
overexposure 198

P

panning 182–3
panoramas 280–1, 456–7
paper 476
parallax error, 286
patch tool 421
pattern 140, 155, 204,
  336
people, photographing,
  babies, 374–5
  candid shots, 386–7
  children, 362, 376–9
  close-ups, 388–9
  finding pictures, 270–1
  general, 308–9
  groups, 382–3
  holiday, on, 370–1
  home, in, 362–3
  local, 312–13
  location, conveying,
    308
  mother and child,
    372–3
  older, 384–5
  older children, 380–1
  own environment, in,
    366–7
  poor weather, in, 368–9
  work, at, 310–11
  young children, 374–5
perspective
  buildings,
    photographing, 288–9
  landscape photography,
    in, 288

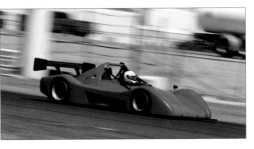

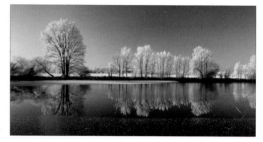

Acknowledgements

The publisher would like to thank the following for kindly supplying photographs for this book: Adam Juniper 228 (bl, bc); Alamy 35, (tr), 252 (t), 342, 343 (tl, bl, br); Cameraclean.co.uk 29 (tr); Canon UK Ltd 18, 19, 80 (t), 90 (tl, tr), 91 (t), 92 (tl, tr), 93 (tr, bl), 94 (bl), 95 (b), 228 (tl, tr), 254 (bc), 474 (b), 475 (t); Colin Barrett 95 (tr); Comstock 154 (tr); Corbis 17 (t), 125 (bl), 127 (t), 146 (t), 182 (br), 194 (bl), 195 (tr), 201 (br), 223 (t), 234, 259 (b), 261 (br), 481 (tr); Dell Inc 398; Delkin devices 488 (bc); Digital Vision 142 (bl), 470 (l); Epson (UK) Ltd 472 (t), 474 (tr), 475 (br), 476 (t); Freecom Technologies 488 (bl, br); Fujifilm UK Ltd 87 (bl, br); Getty Images 68; ImageDJ 107 (b), 126 (br), 155 (tr) 217 (bl), 422 (c); Image Ideas 184 (br); Image 100 128 (br), 147 (br), 172 (t), 173 (t), 258 (t); iStock 1, 2 (l), 3 (c), 4, 5 (tr), 6, (t, bl, br), 7, 8 (bl), 9 (t), 10, 11, 14, 15 (cl), 17 (t), (bl), 20, 21, 25 (b), 29 (b), 34, 35 (b), 39 (tr), 41 (tl, tr), 42, 43 (b), 53 (c, b), 74 (b), 120, (t), 125 (br), 133 (cr, br), 142 (br), 143 (br), 150 (bl), 153 (tl), 155 (cr), 159 (b), 160, 161 (b), 162 (t), 173 (tr), 179 (c), 203 (cr, bl), 213 (b), 214 (b), 228 (br), 236, 237, 242 (bl), 243 (tr), 244 (t), 254 (t), 256 (tl), 265 (tl, bl), 273 (tr), 333 (t), 340, 341, 343 (tr), 357 (tr), 370 (t), 375 (tr), 380 , 381 (b), 476 (br), 477 (tr), 490 (c), 491 (r), 496, 497 498, 499, 500, 501, 502, 503; Jupiter images 202 (bl); LaCie Ltd 399; Marc Wilson 22, 23, 24, 25 (t, c), 28, 29 (tl, tr), 38, 39 (tl, b), 40, 41 (b), 44, 45, 46, 47, 48, 49, 50, 51, 52, 53 (t), 100, 101; Mamiya 16; National Media Museum/SSPL 69 tr, 74 t; Nikon UK Ltd 15 (br), 87 (tl, tr), 88, 89, 90 (b), 93 (tl, br), 241 (b), 243 (b), 254 (bc); Panasonic UK Ltd 94 (t); Photodisk 4 (tl), 5 (bcl, bcr), 133 (t), 144 (b), 145 (tr), 146 (br), 147 (bl), 148 (t), 170 (b), 171 (cl, cr, b), 174, 178 (br), 209 (br), 219 (b), 224 (b), 226 (b), 232 (t, bl, br), 233 (t, c, b), 242 (br), 258 (b), 204 (br), 205 (b), 423 (l), 471 (c, r); Plustek Inc 472 (b); Rubberball 178 (bl), 182 (bl), 184 (t); Samsung 86; Science and Society 69 (tr), 74 (t). All artwork by Jerry Fowler 80, 81, 89, 91, 92, 102, 103, 104, 109, 159, 169, 238. All other images by John Freeman and Steve Luck.

Images are listed in clockwise order from the top (t = top, c = centre, b = bottom, r = right, l = left, tr = top right etc).